DATABASE MANAGEMENT SYSTEMS

D0123778

DATABASE MANAGEMENT SYSTEMS

Raghu Ramakrishnan
University of Wisconsin
Madison, WI, USA

WCB
McGraw-Hill

Boston, Massachusetts ● Burr Ridge, Illinois
Dubuque, Iowa ● Madison, Wisconsin
New York, New York ● San Francisco, California
St. Louis, Missouri

WCB/McGraw-Hill
A Division of the McGraw-Hill Companies

DATABASE MANAGEMENT SYSTEMS

This book is printed on acid-free paper.

2 3 4 5 7 8 9 0 DOC/DOC 9 0 9 8 7

ISBN 0-07-050775-9

Publisher: Tom Casson
Executive editor: Elizabeth A. Jones
Developmental editor: Bradley Kosirog
Editorial assistant: Emily Gray
Marketing manager: John Wannemacher
Project manager: Jim Labeots
Production supervisor: Heather D. Burbridge
Designer: Larry J. Cope
Cover illustration: Mike Wiggins
Typeface: Times-Roman
Printer: R.R. Donnelley & Sons Company

Library of Congress Cataloging-in-Publication Data

Ramakrishnan, Raghu.
    Database management systems / Raghu Ramakrishnan.
        p.   cm.
    Includes bibliographical references and index.
    ISBN 0-07-050775-9
    1. Database management.   I. Title.
QA76.9.D3R237   1997
005.74–dc2d1   97-23748

http://www.mhhe.com

To Apu with love

CONTENTS

Lec2/Ch2 E-R Dgm is missing

PREFACE   xix

1   INTRODUCTION TO DATABASE SYSTEMS   1   *Lecture 1*

1.1   Overview   2

1.2   File Systems versus a DBMS   4

1.3   Describing and Storing Data in a DBMS   5

    1.3.1   The Relational Model   5

    1.3.2   Levels of Abstraction in a DBMS   7

    1.3.3   Data Independence   9

1.4   Queries in a DBMS   10

1.5   Concurrent Access and Crash Recovery   11

    1.5.1   Points to Note   13

1.6   Structure of a DBMS   14

1.7   Advantages of a DBMS   15

1.8   People Who Deal with Databases   16

1.9   Summary   18

2   THE RELATIONAL MODEL   21   *Lec 3 ch3*

2.1   Relations   22

    2.1.1   Creating and Modifying Relations Using SQL-92   24

2.2   Integrity Constraints   25

    2.2.1   Key Constraints   26

    2.2.2   Foreign Key Constraints   28

    2.2.3   General Constraints   30

2.3   Enforcing Integrity Constraints   31

2.4   Query Languages   32

2.5   Summary   34

3   STORING DATA: DISKS AND FILES   38   *Lec 6 ch7*

3.1   The Memory Hierarchy   39

    3.1.1   Disks   40

    3.1.2   Performance Implications of Disk Structure   41

3.2   Disk Space Management   42

	3.2.1	Keeping Track of Free Blocks	43
	3.2.2	Using OS File Systems to Manage Disk Space	43
3.3	Buffer Manager		44
	3.3.1	Buffer Replacement Policies	46
	3.3.2	Buffer Management in DBMS versus OS	48
3.4	Record Formats *		49
	3.4.1	Fixed-Length Records	49
	3.4.2	Variable-Length Records	50
3.5	Page Formats *		51
	3.5.1	Fixed-Length Records	52
	3.5.2	Variable-Length Records	53
3.6	Files and Indexes		55
	3.6.1	Heap Files *	55
	3.6.2	Introduction to Indexes	57
3.7	System Catalogs in a Relational DBMS		59
3.8	Summary		61

4 FILE ORGANIZATIONS AND INDEXES

67

4.1	Cost Model		68
4.2	Comparison of Three File Organizations		69
	4.2.1	Heap Files	69
	4.2.2	Sorted Files	70
	4.2.3	Hashed Files	72
	4.2.4	Choosing a File Organization	73
4.3	Overview of Indexes		74
	4.3.1	Alternatives for Data Entries in an Index	75
4.4	Properties of Indexes		76
	4.4.1	Clustered versus Unclustered Indexes	76
	4.4.2	Dense versus Sparse Indexes	78
	4.4.3	Primary and Secondary Indexes	79
	4.4.4	Indexes Using Composite Search Keys	80
4.5	Index Specification in SQL-92		81
4.6	Summary		81

5 TREE-STRUCTURED INDEXING

84

5.1	Indexed Sequential Access Method (ISAM) *	85
5.2	B+ Trees: A Dynamic Index Structure	90
5.3	Format of a Node	92
5.4	Search	92
5.5	Insert	93
5.6	Delete *	97
5.7	Duplicates *	102
5.8	B+ Trees in Practice *	103

(handwritten margin notes: "Lec 7 ch 8" beside Chapter 4; "Lec 8 ch 9" beside Chapter 5)

	5.8.1	Key Compression	103
	5.8.2	Bulk-Loading a B+ Tree	104
	5.8.3	The Order Concept	107
	5.8.4	The Effect of Inserts and Deletes on Rids	108
5.9	Multidimensional Indexes		108
5.10	Summary		110

6 HASH-BASED INDEXING   116

6.1	Static Hashing		117
	6.1.1	Notation and Conventions	118
6.2	Extendible Hashing *		118
6.3	Linear Hashing *		124
6.4	Extendible Hashing Versus Linear Hashing *		130
6.5	Summary		131

7 EXTERNAL SORTING   137

7.1	A Simple Two-Way Merge Sort		138
7.2	External Merge Sort		139
	7.2.1	Minimizing the Number of Runs *	143
7.3	Minimizing I/O Cost versus Number of I/Os		145
	7.3.1	Blocked I/O *	145
	7.3.2	Double Buffering *	147
7.4	Using B+ Trees for Sorting		148
	7.4.1	Clustered Index	148
	7.4.2	Unclustered Index	149
7.5	Summary		151

8 RELATIONAL ALGEBRA AND CALCULUS   154

8.1	Preliminaries		154
8.2	Relational Algebra		155
	8.2.1	Selection and Projection	156
	8.2.2	Set-Operations	157
	8.2.3	Renaming	159
	8.2.4	Joins	160
	8.2.5	Division	162
	8.2.6	More Examples of Relational Algebra Queries	163
8.3	Relational Calculus		167
	8.3.1	Tuple Relational Calculus	168
	8.3.2	Domain Relational Calculus	172
8.4	Expressive Power of Algebra and Calculus *		175
8.5	Summary		177

9 SQL: THE QUERY LANGUAGE   181

Lec4
ch 4

9.1	The Form of a Basic SQL Query	183
	9.1.1 Examples of Basic SQL Queries	185
	9.1.2 Expressions and Strings in the SELECT Command	187
9.2	UNION, INTERSECT and EXCEPT	188
9.3	Nested Queries	191
	9.3.1 Introduction to Nested Queries	192
	9.3.2 Correlated Nested Queries	193
	9.3.3 Set-Comparison Operators	194
	9.3.4 More Examples of Nested Queries	195
9.4	Aggregate Operators	196
	9.4.1 The GROUP BY and HAVING Clauses	199
	9.4.2 More Examples of Aggregate Queries	202
9.5	Null Values *	205
	9.5.1 Comparisons Using Null Values	205
	9.5.2 Logical Connectives AND, OR and NOT	206
	9.5.3 Impact on SQL Constructs	206
	9.5.4 Outer Joins	207
	9.5.5 Disallowing Null Values	208
9.6	Embedded SQL *	208
	9.6.1 Declaring Variables and Exceptions	209
	9.6.2 Embedding SQL Statements	210
9.7	Cursors *	211
	9.7.1 Basic Cursor Definition and Usage	211
	9.7.2 Properties of Cursors	213
9.8	Dynamic SQL *	215
9.9	Queries in Complex Integrity Constraints *	216
	9.9.1 Constraints over a Single Table	216
	9.9.2 Domain Constraints	216
	9.9.3 Assertions: ICs over Several Tables	217
9.10	Summary	218
10	**SECURITY, VIEWS, AND SQL**	**226**
10.1	Introduction to Database Security	227
10.2	Views	227
	10.2.1 Destroying/Altering Tables and Views	228
	10.2.2 Queries on Views	229
	10.2.3 Updates on Views *	230
10.3	Access Control	232
10.4	Discretionary Access Control *	232
	10.4.1 Grant and Revoke on Views and Integrity Constraints	240
10.5	Mandatory Access Control *	242
	10.5.1 Multilevel Relations and Polyinstantiation	243
	10.5.2 Covert Channels, DOD Security Levels	245
10.6	Additional Issues Related to Security *	246

      10.6.1 Role of the Database Administrator   246

      10.6.2 Security in Statistical Databases   246

      10.6.3 Encryption   248

  10.7 Summary   251

11 QUERY-BY-EXAMPLE (QBE)   **255**

  11.1 Introduction   255

  11.2 Basic QBE Queries   256

      11.2.1 Other Features: Duplicates, Ordering Answers *   257

  11.3 Queries Over Multiple Relations   258

  11.4 Negation in the Relation-name Column   259

  11.5 Aggregates   260

  11.6 The Conditions Box   261

      11.6.1 And/Or Queries *   262

  11.7 Unnamed Columns   263

  11.8 Updates   264

      11.8.1 Restrictions on Update Commands   265

  11.9 Division and Relational Completeness *   266

  11.10 Summary   267

12 EVALUATION OF RELATIONAL OPERATORS   **271**

  12.1 Introduction to Query Processing   272

      12.1.1 Access Paths   272

      12.1.2 Preliminaries: Examples and Cost Calculations   273

  12.2 The Selection Operation   274

      12.2.1 No Index, Unsorted Data   274

      12.2.2 No Index, Sorted Data*   274

      12.2.3 B+ Tree Index   275

      12.2.4 Hash Index, Equality Selection   276

  12.3 General Selection Conditions *   277

      12.3.1 CNF and Index Matching   277

      12.3.2 Selections without Disjunction   279

      12.3.3 Selections with Disjunction   280

  12.4 The Projection Operation *   280

      12.4.1 Projection Based on Sorting   281

      12.4.2 Projection Based on Hashing   282

      12.4.3 Sorting versus Hashing for Projections   284

      12.4.4 Use of Indexes for Projections   285

  12.5 The Join Operation   285

      12.5.1 Nested Loops Join   286

      12.5.2 Sort-Merge Join *   291

      12.5.3 Hash Join *   295

      12.5.4 General Join Conditions *   300

Lec 4.

12.6   The Set Operations *   301
       12.6.1   Sorting for Union and Difference   301
       12.6.2   Hashing for Union and Difference   302
12.7   Aggregate Operations *   302
       12.7.1   Implementing Aggregation by Using an Index   303
12.8   The Impact of Buffering   304
12.9   Summary   305

13   RELATIONAL QUERY OPTIMIZATION   310
13.1   Overview of Relational Query Optimization   312
       13.1.1   Query Evaluation Plans   312
       13.1.2   Pipelined Evaluation   313
       13.1.3   The Iterator Interface for Operators and Access Methods   315
       13.1.4   The System R Optimizer   316
13.2   Translating SQL Queries into Algebra   316
       13.2.1   Decomposition of a Query into Blocks   316
       13.2.2   A Query Block as a Relational Algebra Expression   317
13.3   Alternative Plans: A Motivating Example   319
       13.3.1   Pushing Selections   319
       13.3.2   Using Indexes   321
13.4   Estimating the Cost of a Plan   324
       13.4.1   Statistics Maintained by a DBMS *   325
       13.4.2   Estimating Result Sizes *   326
13.5   Relational Algebra Equivalences *   327
       13.5.1   Selections   328
       13.5.2   Projections   328
       13.5.3   Cross-Products and Joins   329
       13.5.4   Selects, Projects and Joins   330
       13.5.5   Others   331
13.6   Enumeration of Alternative Plans *   332
       13.6.1   Single-Relation Queries   332
       13.6.2   Multiple-Relation Queries   336
13.7   Nested Subqueries *   344
13.8   Other Approaches to Query Optimization *   346
13.9   Summary   347

14   CONCEPTUAL DESIGN AND THE ER MODEL   357
14.1   Overview of Database Design   357
14.2   The Entity-Relationship (ER) Data Model   358
       14.2.1   Entities, Attributes and Entity Sets   359
       14.2.2   Relationships and Relationship Sets   360
14.3   Additional Features of the ER Model   364
       14.3.1   Key Constraints   364

	14.3.2 Participation Constraints	367
	14.3.3 Weak Entities *	370
	14.3.4 Class Hierarchies *	372
	14.3.5 Aggregation *	374
14.4	Conceptual Design Using the ER Model	376
	14.4.1 Entity versus Attribute	377
	14.4.2 Entity versus Relationship	379
	14.4.3 Binary versus Ternary Relationships *	380
	14.4.4 Aggregation versus Ternary Relationships *	384
	14.4.5 Constraints beyond the ER Model *	384
	14.4.6 Need for Further Refinement	386
14.5	Conceptual Design for Large Enterprises	387
14.6	Summary	388

15 SCHEMA REFINEMENT AND NORMAL FORMS 395

15.1	Introduction to Schema Refinement	396
	15.1.1 Problems Caused by Redundancy	396
	15.1.2 Use of Decompositions	398
	15.1.3 Problems Related to Decomposition	399
15.2	Functional Dependencies	400
15.3	Examples Motivating Schema Refinement	401
	15.3.1 Constraints on an Entity Set	401
	15.3.2 Constraints on a Relationship Set	402
	15.3.3 Identifying Attributes of Entities	402
	15.3.4 Identifying Entity Sets	404
15.4	Reasoning About Functional Dependencies	405
	15.4.1 Closure of a Set of FDs	406
	15.4.2 Attribute Closure	407
15.5	Normal Forms	408
	15.5.1 Boyce-Codd Normal Form	409
	15.5.2 Third Normal Form	410
15.6	Decompositions	412
	15.6.1 Lossless-Join Decomposition	413
	15.6.2 Dependency-Preserving Decomposition	415
15.7	Normalization	416
	15.7.1 Decomposition into BCNF	416
	15.7.2 Decomposition into 3NF *	419
15.8	Other Kinds of Dependencies *	423
	15.8.1 Multivalued Dependencies	423
	15.8.2 4NF	426
	15.8.3 Join Dependencies	428
	15.8.4 5NF	428
	15.8.5 Inclusion Dependencies	429
15.9	Summary	429

16   PHYSICAL DATABASE DESIGN AND TUNING   436

16.1   Introduction to Physical Database Design   437

   16.1.1   Database Workloads   437

   16.1.2   Physical Design and Tuning Decisions   438

   16.1.3   Need for Database Tuning   439

16.2   Guidelines for Index Selection   439

16.3   Basic Examples of Index Selection   441

16.4   Clustering and Indexing *   444

   16.4.1   Co-clustering Two Relations   447

16.5   Indexes on Multiple-Attribute Search Keys *   449

16.6   Indexes that Enable Index-Only Plans *   450

16.7   Overview of Database Tuning   453

   16.7.1   Tuning Indexes   453

   16.7.2   Tuning the Conceptual Schema   455

   16.7.3   Tuning Queries and Views   456

16.8   Choices in Tuning the Conceptual Schema *   457

   16.8.1   Settling for a Weaker Normal Form   457

   16.8.2   Denormalization   458

   16.8.3   Choice of Decompositions   458

   16.8.4   Vertical Decomposition   460

   16.8.5   Horizontal Decomposition   460

16.9   Choices in Tuning Queries and Views *   461

16.10 Impact of Concurrency *   463

16.11 DBMS Benchmarking *   465

   16.11.1 Well-Known DBMS Benchmarks   465

   16.11.2 Using a Benchmark   466

16.12 Summary   467

17   CONCURRENCY CONTROL   476

17.1   The Concept of a Transaction   477

   17.1.1   Concurrent Execution and Database Consistency   477

   17.1.2   Incomplete Transactions and Crash Recovery   478

17.2   Transactions and Schedules   479

17.3   Notions of Consistency   480

   17.3.1   Serializability   480

   17.3.2   Some Anomalies Associated with Interleaved Execution * 481

   17.3.3   Schedules Involving Aborted Transactions   484

17.4   Lock-Based Concurrency Control   485

   17.4.1   Strict Two-Phase Locking (Strict 2PL)   485

   17.4.2   2PL, Serializability, and Recoverability   488

   17.4.3   View Serializability *   490

17.5   Lock Management *   491

   17.5.1   Implementing Lock and Unlock Requests   491

   17.5.2   Deadlocks   493

      17.5.3 Performance of Lock-Based Concurrency Control   496

  17.6 Specialized Locking Techniques *   497

      17.6.1 Dynamic Databases and the Phantom Problem   498

      17.6.2 Concurrency Control in Tree Indexes   499

      17.6.3 Multiple-Granularity Locking   502

  17.7 Transaction Support in SQL-92 *   504

      17.7.1 Transaction Characteristics   504

      17.7.2 Transactions and Constraints   506

  17.8 Concurrency Control Without Locking *   507

      17.8.1 Optimistic Concurrency Control   507

      17.8.2 Timestamp-Based Concurrency Control   509

      17.8.3 Multiversion Concurrency Control   512

  17.9 Summary   512

18 CRASH RECOVERY   519

  18.1 Introduction to Crash Recovery   519

      18.1.1 Stealing Frames and Forcing Pages   520

      18.1.2 Recovery-Related Steps during Normal Execution   521

  18.2 Overview of ARIES   522

      18.2.1 The Log   523

      18.2.2 Other Recovery-Related Data Structures   526

      18.2.3 The Write-Ahead Log Protocol   527

      18.2.4 Checkpointing   528

  18.3 Recovering From a System Crash *   529

      18.3.1 Analysis Phase   529

      18.3.2 Redo Phase   531

      18.3.3 Undo Phase   533

  18.4 Media Recovery *   536

  18.5 Other Algorithms and Interaction with Concurrency Control *   537

  18.6 Summary   538

19 PARALLEL AND DISTRIBUTED DATABASES   544

  19.1 Architectures for Parallel Databases   545

  19.2 Parallel Query Evaluation   547

      19.2.1 Data Partitioning   548

      19.2.2 Parallelizing Sequential Operator Evaluation Code   548

  19.3 Parallelizing Individual Operations   549

      19.3.1 Bulk Loading and Scanning   549

      19.3.2 Sorting   549

      19.3.3 Joins   550

  19.4 Parallel Query Optimization   553

  19.5 Introduction to Distributed Databases   554

      19.5.1 Types of Distributed Databases   554

19.6   Distributed DBMS Architectures   555
         19.6.1 Client-Server Systems   555
         19.6.2 Collaborating Server Systems   556
19.7   Storing Data in a Distributed DBMS   556
         19.7.1 Fragmentation   556
         19.7.2 Replication   558
19.8   Distributed Catalog Management   558
         19.8.1 Naming Objects   558
         19.8.2 Catalog Structure   559
         19.8.3 Distributed Data Independence   560
19.9   Distributed Query Processing   561
         19.9.1 Nonjoin Queries in a Distributed DBMS   561
         19.9.2 Joins in a Distributed DBMS   562
         19.9.3 Cost-Based Query Optimization   566
19.10   Updating Distributed Data   567
         19.10.1 Synchronous Replication   567
         19.10.2 Asynchronous Replication   568
19.11   Introduction to Distributed Transaction Management   571
19.12   Distributed Concurrency Control   572
         19.12.1 Distributed Deadlock   573
19.13   Distributed Recovery   575
         19.13.1 Normal Execution and Commit Protocols   575
         19.13.2 Restart after a Failure   576
         19.13.3 Two-Phase Commit Revisited   578
         19.13.4 Three-Phase Commit   579
19.14   Summary   580

20 DEDUCTIVE AND ACTIVE DATABASES   589

20.1   Introduction to Recursive Queries   590
         20.1.1 Datalog   591
         20.1.2 The Fixpoint Operator   594
20.2   Recursive Queries with Negation   595
         20.2.1 Stratification   596
         20.2.2 Aggregate Operations   599
20.3   Efficient Evaluation of Recursive Queries   600
         20.3.1 Fixpoint Evaluation without Repeated Inferences   600
         20.3.2 Pushing Selections to Avoid Irrelevant Inferences   602
20.4   Introduction to Active Databases   604
         20.4.1 Examples of Triggers in SQL   605
20.5   Designing Active Databases   607
         20.5.1 Why Triggers Can Be Hard to Understand   607
         20.5.2 Constraints versus Triggers   607
         20.5.3 Other Uses of Triggers   608
20.6   Summary   609

21 OBJECT-DATABASE SYSTEMS   **614**
  21.1 Motivating Example   616
      21.1.1 New Data Types   616
      21.1.2 Manipulating the New Kinds of Data   617
  21.2 User-Defined Abstract Data Types   619
      21.2.1 Defining Methods of an ADT   620
  21.3 Constructed Types   622
      21.3.1 Manipulating Data of Constructed Types   623
  21.4 Objects, Object Identity, and Reference Types   626
      21.4.1 Notions of Equality   626
      21.4.2 Dereferencing Reference Types   627
  21.5 Inheritance   627
      21.5.1 Defining Types with Inheritance   628
      21.5.2 Binding of Methods   628
      21.5.3 Collection Hierarchies, Type Extents, and Queries 629
  21.6 Database Design for an ORDBMS   630
      21.6.1 Constructed Types and ADTs   630
      21.6.2 Object Identity   633
      21.6.3 Extending the ER Model   634
      21.6.4 Using Nested Collections   636
  21.7 New Challenges in Implementing an ORDBMS   636
      21.7.1 Storage and Access Methods   637
      21.7.2 Query Processing   639
      21.7.3 Query Optimization   640
  21.8 Comparing RDBMS with OODBMS and ORDBMS   642
      21.8.1 OODBMS: ODL and OQL   642
      21.8.2 RDBMS versus ORDBMS   643
      21.8.3 OODBMS versus ORDBMS: Similarities   643
      21.8.4 OODBMS versus ORDBMS: Differences   643
  21.9 Summary   644

22 DECISION SUPPORT SYSTEMS   **650**
  22.1 Introduction to Decision Support   650
  22.2 Data Warehousing   651
      22.2.1 Creating and Maintaining a Warehouse   652
  22.3 OLAP   654
      22.3.1 Multidimensional Data Model   654
      22.3.2 OLAP Queries   657
      22.3.3 Database Design for OLAP   661
  22.4 Implementation Techniques for OLAP   662
      22.4.1 Indexing Methods   662
      22.4.2 File Organizations   664
      22.4.3 Additional OLAP Implementation Issues   664
  22.5 Data Mining   665

22.5.1	Introduction to Mining for Rules	666
22.5.2	The Use of Association Rules for Prediction	668
22.5.3	An Algorithm for Finding Association Rules	669
22.5.4	Generalized Association Rules	671
22.5.5	Sequential Patterns	673
22.5.6	Classification Rules	674
22.5.7	Additional Data Mining Tasks	675
22.6	Summary	677

23 ADDITIONAL TOPICS — **682**

23.1	Advanced Transaction Processing	682
23.1.1	Transaction Processing Monitors	682
23.1.2	New Transaction Models	683
23.1.3	Real-Time DBMSs	684
23.2	Networked Databases	684
23.2.1	World Wide Web	684
23.2.2	Integrated Access to Multiple Data Sources	686
23.2.3	Mobility and Databases	686
23.3	Main Memory Databases	687
23.4	Information Visualization	687
23.5	Domain-Specific DBMS Issues	688
23.5.1	Geographic Information Systems	688
23.5.2	Temporal and Sequence Databases	688
23.5.3	Image and Video Databases	689
23.5.4	Information Retrieval and Text Databases	689
23.6	Summary	690

A THE MINIBASE SOFTWARE — **692**

A.1	What's Available	692
A.2	Overview of Minibase Assignments	693
A.2.1	Overview of Programming Projects	693
A.2.2	Overview of Nonprogramming Assignments	694
A.3	Acknowledgments	695

REFERENCES — **697**

INDEX — **727**

PREFACE

The advantage of doing one's praising for oneself is that one can lay it on so thick and exactly in the right places.

—Samuel Butler

One of the virtues of a relational database system is that it provides a high-level, declarative interface to users. In practice, however, sophisticated users, database administrators and application programmers must have a thorough grasp of what the system does in response to user-level requests. To make the most effective use of a database system, one must have insight into topics such as logical and physical schema design, how a query optimizer chooses an execution plan for a given query, the impact of indexing on performance, and the importance of memory available for buffering. From a performance perspective, all these factors are related, and I believe that they are best understood through a hands-on approach.

This book covers the fundamentals of modern database management systems, in particular relational database systems. It is intended as a text for an introductory database course for undergraduates, and I have attempted to present the material in a clear, simple style. A quantitative approach is used throughout and detailed examples abound. An extensive set of exercises (for which solutions are available online to instructors) accompanies each chapter, and reinforces students' ability to apply the concepts to real problems. The book contains enough material to support a second course, ideally supplemented by selected research papers. It can be used, with the accompanying software, in two distinct kinds of courses:

1. A course that aims to present the principles of database systems, with a practical focus but without any implementation assignments. Optionally, the software can be used to create various exercises and experiments that involve no programming.

2. A course that has a strong systems emphasis and assumes that students have good programming skills in C and C++. In this case the software can be used as the basis for projects in which students are asked to implement various parts of a relational DBMS. Several central modules in the project software (e.g., heap files, buffer manager, B+ trees, hash indexes, various join methods, concurrency control and recovery algorithms) are described in

sufficient detail in the text to enable students to implement them, given the (C++) class interfaces.

Many instructors will no doubt teach a course that falls between these two extremes with a mix of experiment-oriented and implementation assignments.

Note: Exercises using the Minibase software are outlined in several chapters. These exercises should be suitably expanded by instructors, as described in Appendix A. Detailed Minibase exercises and solutions are available online for instructors.

Choice of Topics

The main pedagogical objective of this book is to provide clear and thorough discussions of the topics covered. The choice of material has been influenced by these considerations:

- To concentrate on issues central to the *design, tuning, and implementation of relational database applications*. However, many of the issues discussed (e.g., buffering and access methods) are not specific to relational systems, and additional topics such as decision support and object-database systems are covered in later chapters.

- To provide adequate coverage of implementation topics to support a concurrent laboratory section or course project. For example, implementation of relational operations has been covered in more detail than is necessary in a first course. However, the variety of alternative implementation techniques permits a wide choice of project assignments. An instructor who wishes to assign implementation of sort-merge join might cover that topic in depth, whereas another might choose to emphasize index nested loops join.

- To provide in-depth coverage of the state of the art in currently available commercial systems, rather than a broad coverage of several alternatives. For example, we discuss the relational data model, B+ trees, SQL, System R style query optimization, lock-based concurrency control, the ARIES recovery algorithm, the two-phase commit protocol, asynchronous replication in distributed databases, and object-relational DBMSs in detail, with numerous illustrative examples. This is made possible by omitting or briefly covering some related topics such as the hierarchical and network models, B tree variants, Quel, randomized and semantic query optimization, view serializability, the shadow-page recovery algorithm, and the three-phase commit protocol.

Organization

The material can be divided into roughly seven parts, as indicated in Figure 0.1, which also shows the dependencies between chapters. An arrow from Chapter I to Chapter J means that I depends on material in J. The broken arrows indicate a weak dependency, which can be ignored at the instructor's discretion. The first two chapters cover material that is basic to the rest of the book, and we assume that they are covered first. Chapter 2 presents the relational model and uses SQL-92 constructs to make these concepts concrete. The early introduction of SQL facilitates assignments using a relational DBMS and also offers instructors the choice of covering the ER model early—the discussion of how to translate ER diagrams into tables assumes knowledge of SQL constructs for creating tables, and this prerequisite material is included in Chapter 2.

Each of the remaining six parts is described below, along with its dependence, if any, on the other parts.

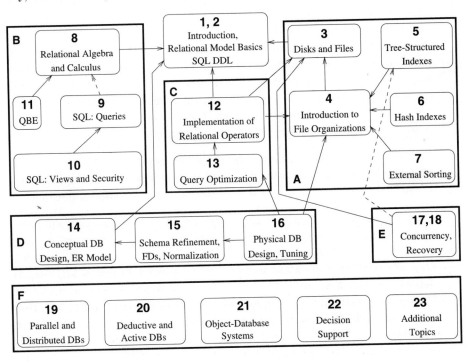

Figure 0.1   Dependencies between Chapters

- **Part A (File Organizations):** Storage media, buffer management, record and page formats, file organizations, various kinds of indexes, and external sorting are discussed in detail.

- **Part B (Query Languages):** Relational algebra and calculus, QBE and SQL. It is worth noting that the coverage of SQL, which follows the SQL-92 standard, is quite extensive. In addition to the data retrieval features of SQL, many important concepts, such as authorization, views and referential integrity, are discussed in the context of SQL.

  Chapter 9 can be taught before Chapter 8. This order may be desirable if an instructor wants students to write SQL queries early. However, an understanding of algebra and calculus will enable students to appreciate the foundations of SQL. Similarly, QBE can be taught without a prior discussion of DRC, but briefly covering DRC first is recommended.

- **Part C (Query Optimization and Evaluation):** Implementation of relational operators and generation of query plans. A basic understanding of indexes is assumed in the discussion of query evaluation. If implementation projects are assigned, covering Chapter 4 before Part C is recommended.

- **Part D (Database Design and Tuning):** Conceptual design, normalization, physical design and performance tuning. The discussion in Chapter 16 assumes a good understanding of query optimization, and in particular, of the use of indexes. In an important sense, Parts A, B and C lead up to the material on database design and tuning. I discuss these topics from a very practical perspective, with several examples. A reader who studies this material carefully will quickly realize that a thorough understanding of several basic issues is essential for good design. The goal is to ensure that the earlier chapters provide the reader with the necessary foundation.

- **Part E (Transaction Processing):** Concurrency control and recovery are covered with an emphasis on locking and logging techniques. The discussion of concurrency control in tree indexes depends on a knowledge of tree indexes.

- **Part F (Advanced Topics):** The discussion of query optimization in parallel and distributed databases assumes an understanding of query optimization in a centralized DBMS. In general, the chapters in Part F should be covered after material from the other parts has been covered. There is little dependence between chapters in Part F, and they can be covered in any order. Chapters on deductive and active databases, object-oriented database extensions, and decision support (data warehousing, data mining and OLAP) are included.

Order of Presentation

The material in the text is presented in the order in which I usually cover it, and is influenced by the order of the accompanying programming assignments, and by my preference for covering all database design topics together *after* covering all optimization related material. Other instructors may want to cover some topics in a different order, based on the needs of their courses. For example, some instructors will want to cover SQL, and perhaps get students to use a relational database, before discussing file organizations or indexing. As another example, in a course that emphasizes database design many of the implementation-oriented chapters might well be skipped altogether, and the ER model may be covered before SQL. The book has therefore been designed to be flexible with respect to the ordering of material, and inter-chapter dependencies have been kept to a minimum. In particular, Parts A through E, regarded as units, can be covered in pretty much any order, although it is best to cover Part A before Part C and before Chapter 16. The remaining inter-part dependencies are minor.

Some additional points to note:

- Several section headings contain an asterisk. This symbol does not necessarily indicate a higher level of difficulty. Rather, omitting all asterisked sections leaves about the right amount of material in Chapters 1 through 18 for a broad introductory one-quarter or one-semester course (depending on the depth at which the remaining material is discussed and the nature of the course assignments).

- It is not necessary to cover all the alternatives for a given operator (e.g., various techniques for joins) in Chapter 12 in order to cover Chapter 13 adequately.

The book contains more material than can be covered in a one-semester course. It can be used in several kinds of introductory or second courses by choosing topics appropriately, or in a two-course sequence by supplementing the material with some advanced readings in the second course. Examples of appropriate introductory courses include courses on file organizations, and introduction to database management systems, especially if the course focuses on relational database design or implementation. Advanced courses can be built around the later chapters, which contain detailed bibliographies with ample pointers for further study.

Supplementary Material

Each chapter contains several exercises designed to test and expand the reader's understanding of the material. Instructors can obtain a set of lecture slides for each chapter through the Web in Postscript and Adobe PDF formats. Slides in Microsoft Powerpoint and a solution manual for the exercises are also freely available online upon request to the author (`raghu@cs.wisc.edu`).

Supplementary project software with sample assignments and solutions is available through the Internet, as described in Appendix A. The text itself does not refer to the project software, however, and can be used independently in a course that presents the principles of database management systems from a practical perspective, but without a project component.

For More Information

The home page for this book is at URL:

```
http://www.cs.wisc.edu/~dbbook
```

This page is frequently updated and contains information about the book, past and current users, and the software. *This page also contains a link to all known errors in the book, the accompanying slides, and the software.* Instructors are advised to visit this site periodically; they can also register at this site to be notified of important changes by email.

Acknowledgments

This book grew out of lecture notes for CS564, the introductory (senior/graduate level) database course at UW-Madison. David DeWitt developed this course and the Minirel course project, in which students wrote several well-chosen parts of a relational DBMS. My thinking about this material was shaped by teaching CS564, and Minirel was the inspiration for Minibase, which is more comprehensive (e.g., it has a query optimizer and includes visualization software) but tries to retain the spirit of Minirel. Mike Carey and I jointly designed much of Minibase. My lecture notes (and in turn many chapters in this book) were influenced by Mike's lecture notes and by Yannis Ioannidis's lecture slides.

Joe Hellerstein used the beta edition of the book at Berkeley, and provided invaluable feedback, assistance on slides, and hilarious quotes. Writing the chapter on object-database systems with Joe was a lot of fun.

C. Mohan provided invaluable assistance, patiently answering a number of questions about implementation techniques used in various commercial systems, in particular indexing, concurrency control and recovery algorithms. Moshe Zloof answered numerous questions about QBE semantics and commercial systems based on QBE. Ron Fagin, Krishna Kulkarni, Len Shapiro, Jim Melton, Dennis Shasha and Dirk Van Gucht reviewed the book and provided detailed feedback, greatly improving the content and presentation. Michael Goldweber at Beloit College, Matthew Haines at Wyoming, Michael Kifer at SUNY StonyBrook, Jeff

Naughton at Wisconsin, Praveen Seshadri at Cornell and Stan Zdonik at Brown also used the beta edition in their database courses and offered feedback and bug reports. In particular, Michael Kifer pointed out an error in the (old) algorithm for computing a minimal cover and suggested covering some SQL features in Chapter 2 to improve modularity. Gio Wiederhold's bibliography, converted to Latex format by S. Sudarshan, and Michael Ley's online bibliography on databases and logic programming were a great help while compiling the chapter bibliographies. Shaun Flisakowski and Uri Shaft helped me frequently in my never-ending battles with Latex.

I owe a special thanks to the many, many students who have contributed to the Minibase software. Emmanuel Ackaouy, Jim Pruyne, Lee Schumacher and Michael Lee worked with me when I developed the first version of Minibase (much of which was subsequently discarded, but which influenced the next version). Emmanuel Ackaouy and Bryan So were my TAs when I taught CS564 using this version and went well beyond the limits of a TAship in their efforts to refine the project. Paul Aoki struggled with a version of Minibase and offered lots of useful comments as a TA at Berkeley. An entire class of CS764 students (our graduate database course) developed much of the current version of Minibase in a large class project that was led and coordinated by Mike Carey and me. Amit Shukla and Michael Lee were my TAs when I first taught CS564 using this version of Minibase, and developed the software further.

Several students worked with me on independent projects, over a long period of time, to develop several Minibase components. These include visualization packages for the buffer manager and B+ trees (Huseyin Bektas, Harry Stavropoulos and Weiqing Huang); a query optimizer and visualizer (Stephen Harris, Michael Lee and Donko Donjerkovic); an ER diagram tool based on the Opossum schema editor (Eben Haber); and a GUI-based tool for normalization (Andrew Prock and Andy Therber). In addition, Bill Kimmel worked to integrate and fix a large body of code (storage manager, buffer manager, files and access methods, relational operators and the query plan executor) produced by the CS764 class project. Ranjani Ramamurty considerably extended Bill's work on cleaning up and integrating the various modules. Luke Blanshard, Uri Shaft and Shaun Flisakowski worked on putting together the release version of the code, and developed test suites and exercises based on the Minibase software. Krishna Kunchithapadam worked on testing the optimizer and developed part of the Minibase GUI front-end.

Clearly, the Minibase software would not exist without the contributions of a great many talented people. With this software available freely in the public domain, I hope that more instructors will be able to teach a systems-oriented database course with a blend of implementation and experimentation to complement the lecture material.

I'd like to thank the many students who helped in developing and checking the solutions to the exercises and provided useful feedback on draft versions of the book. In alphabetical order: X. Bao, S. Biao, M. Chakrabarti, C. Chan, W. Chen, N. Cheung, D. Colwell, C. Fritz, V. Ganti, J. Gehrke, G. Glass, V. Gopalakrishnan, M. Higgins, T. Jasmin, M. Krishnaprasad, Y. Lin, C. Liu, M. Lusignan, H. Modi, S. Narayanan, D. Randolph, A. Ranganathan, J. Reminga, A. Therber, M. Thomas, Q. Wang, R. Wang, Z. Wang and J. Yuan. James Harrington and Martin Reames at Wisconsin and Nina Tang at Berkeley provided especially detailed feedback.

Charlie Fischer, Avi Silberschatz and Jeff Ullman gave me invaluable advice on working with a publisher. My editors at McGraw-Hill, Betsy Jones and Eric Munson, obtained extensive reviews and shepherded this book through two beta editions, greatly improving its form and content. Emily Gray and Brad Kosirog were there whenever problems cropped up. At Wisconsin, Ginny Werner really helped me to stay on top of things.

Finally, this book was a thief of time, and in many ways it was harder on my family than on me. My sons expressed themselves forthrightly. From my (then) five-year-old, Ketan: "Dad, stop working on that silly book. You don't have any time for *me*." Two-year-old Vivek: "You working *boook*? No no no come play basketball me!" All the seasons of their discontent were visited upon my wife, and Apu nonetheless cheerfully kept the family going in its usual chaotic, happy way all the many evenings and weekends I was wrapped up in this book. (Not to mention the days when I was wrapped up in being a faculty member!) As in all things, I can trace my parents' hand in much of this; my father, with his love of learning, and my mother, with her love of us, shaped me. My brother Kartik's contributions to this book consisted chiefly of phone calls in which he kept me from working, but if I don't acknowledge him, he's liable to be annoyed. I'd like to thank my family for being there and giving meaning to everything I do. (There! I knew I'd find a legitimate reason to thank Kartik.)

INTRODUCTION TO
DATABASE SYSTEMS

> Has everyone noticed that all the letters of the word *database* are typed with the left hand? Now the layout of the QWERTY typewriter keyboard was designed, among other things, to facilitate the even use of both hands. It follows, therefore, that writing about databases is not only unnatural, but a lot harder than it appears.
>
> —Anonymous

Today, more than at any previous time, the success of an organization depends on its ability to acquire accurate and timely data about its operations, to manage this data effectively, and to use it to analyze and guide its activities. Phrases such as the *information superhighway* have become ubiquitous, and information processing is a rapidly growing multibillion dollar industry.

The amount of information available to us is literally exploding, and the value of data as an organizational asset is being widely recognized. Yet without the ability to manage this vast store of data, and to quickly find the information that is relevant to a given question, as the amount of information increases, it tends to become a distraction and a liability, rather than an asset. This paradox drives the need for increasingly powerful and flexible data management systems. To get the most out of their large and complex datasets, users must have tools that simplify the tasks of managing the data and extracting useful information in a timely fashion. Otherwise, data can become a liability, with the cost of acquiring it and managing it far exceeding the value that is derived from it.

A **database** is a collection of data, typically describing the activities of one or more related organizations. For example, a university database might contain information about the following:

- *Entities* such as students, faculty, courses and classrooms.

- *Relationships* between entities, such as students' enrollment in courses, faculty teaching courses, and the use of rooms for courses.

A **database management system**, or **DBMS**, is software designed to assist in maintaining and utilizing large collections of data, and the need for such systems, as well as their use, is growing rapidly. The alternative to using a DBMS is to use ad hoc approaches that do not carry over from one application to another; for example, to store the data in files and write application-specific code to manage it. The use of a DBMS has several important advantages, as we will see in Section 1.7.

The area of database management systems is a microcosm of computer science in general. The issues addressed and the techniques used span a wide spectrum, including languages, object-orientation and other programming paradigms, compilation, operating systems, concurrent programming, data structures, algorithms, theory, parallel and distributed systems, user interfaces, expert systems and artificial intelligence, statistical techniques, and dynamic programming. Although we will not be able to go into all these aspects of database management in this book, this is a rich and vibrant discipline.

Database management continues to gain importance as more and more data is brought on-line, and made ever more accessible through computer networking. Today the field is being driven by exciting visions such as multimedia databases, interactive video, digital libraries, a host of scientific projects such as the human genome mapping effort and NASA's Earth Observation System project, and the desire of companies to consolidate their decision-making processes and *mine* their data repositories for useful information about their businesses. Commercially, database management systems represent one of the largest and most vigorous market segments. Thus the study of database systems could prove to be richly rewarding in more ways than one!

1.1 OVERVIEW

The goal of this book is to present an in-depth introduction to database management systems, with an emphasis on how to organize and utilize large databases effectively. The following questions are addressed:

1. How can a user describe a real-world enterprise (e.g., a university) in terms of the data stored in a DBMS? What factors must be considered in deciding how to organize the stored data? (Chapters 2, 10, 14, 15 and 16.)

2. How can a user answer questions about the enterprise by posing queries over the data in the DBMS? (Chapters 8, 9 and 11.)

3. How does a DBMS allow many users to access data concurrently, and how does it protect the data in the event of system failures? (Chapters 17 and 18.)

4. How does a DBMS store large datasets and answer questions against this data efficiently? (Chapters 3, 4, 5, 6, 7, 12 and 13.)

Many kinds of database management systems are in use, but this book concentrates on *relational* systems, which are by far the dominant type of DBMS today. Later chapters cover additional topics such as parallel and distributed database management and extensions of the relational DBMS approach.

A major goal of this book is to convey a thorough understanding of how to organize information in a DBMS, and to maintain it and retrieve it efficiently, that is, how to *use* a DBMS effectively. Not surprisingly, many decisions about how to use a DBMS for a given application depend on what capabilities the DBMS supports efficiently. Thus in order to use a DBMS well, it is necessary to also understand how a DBMS *works*. The approach taken in this book is to cover DBMS implementation and architecture in sufficient detail to allow database design issues to be discussed in depth.

In the rest of this chapter, we provide an introduction to the the issues listed above. We begin by motivating the use of a DBMS in Section 1.2. In Section 1.3 we consider how information about an enterprise should be organized and stored in a DBMS. A user probably thinks about this information in high-level terms corresponding to the entities in the organization and their relationships, whereas the DBMS ultimately stores data in the form of (many, many) bits. The gap between how users think of their data and how the data is ultimately stored is bridged through several *levels of abstraction* supported by the DBMS. Intuitively, a user can begin by describing the data in fairly high-level terms, and then refine this description by considering additional storage and representation details as needed.

In Section 1.4 we consider how users can retrieve data stored in a DBMS, and the need for techniques to efficiently compute answers to questions involving such data. In Section 1.5 we provide an overview of how a DBMS supports concurrent access to data by several users, and how it protects the data in the event of system failures.

We then briefly describe the internal structure of a DBMS in Section 1.6, discuss the advantages of using a DBMS to manage data in Section 1.7, and mention various groups of people associated with the development and use of a DBMS in Section 1.8.

1.2   FILE SYSTEMS VERSUS A DBMS

To understand the need for a DBMS, let us consider a motivating scenario: A company has a large collection (say, 500 GB[1]) of data on employees, departments, products, sales, and so on. This data is accessed concurrently by several employees. Access to certain parts of the data (e.g., salaries) must be restricted; questions about the data must be answered quickly; and changes made to the data by different users must be applied consistently.

We can try to deal with this data management problem by storing the data in a collection of operating system files. This approach has many drawbacks, including the following:

- We probably do not have 500 GB of main memory to hold all the data; we must therefore store data in a storage device such as a disk or tape, and bring relevant parts into main memory for processing as needed.

- Even if we have 500 GB of main memory, on computer systems with 32-bit addressing, we cannot refer directly to more than about 4 GB of data! We have to program some method of identifying all data items.

- Operating systems provide only a password mechanism for security. This is not sufficiently flexible to enforce security policies in which different users have permission to access different subsets of the data.

- We have to write special programs to answer each question that users may want to ask about the data. These programs are likely to be complex because of the large volume of data to be searched.

- We must protect the data from inconsistent changes made by different users accessing the data concurrently. If programs that access the data are written with such concurrent access in mind, this adds greatly to their complexity.

- We must ensure that data is restored to a consistent state if the system crashes while changes are being made.

A DBMS is a piece of software that is designed to make the preceding tasks easier. By storing data in a DBMS, rather than as a collection of operating system files, we can use the DBMS's features to manage the data in a robust and efficient manner. As the volume of data and the number of users grow—hundreds of gigabytes of data and thousands of users are common in current corporate databases—DBMS support becomes indispensible.

---

[1] A kilobyte (KB) is 1024 bytes, a megabyte (MB) is 1024 KBs, a gigabyte (GB) is 1024 MBs, and a terabyte (TB) is 1024 GBs.

1.3   DESCRIBING AND STORING DATA IN A DBMS

The user of a DBMS is ultimately concerned with some real-world enterprise, and the data to be stored describes various aspects of this enterprise. For example, there are students, faculty and courses in a university, and the data in a university database describes these entities and their relationships.

A DBMS allows a user to define the data to be stored in terms of a **data model**, which is a collection of high-level data description constructs that hide many low-level storage details. Most database management systems today are based on the **relational data model** which we will focus on in this book.

While the data model of the DBMS hides many details, it is nonetheless closer to how the DBMS stores data than to how a user thinks about the underlying enterprise. To bridge this gap, several **semantic data models** have been proposed to assist in the process of database design. Semantic models allow the user to come up with a good initial description of the data in an enterprise. These models contain a wide variety of constructs that help describe a real application scenario. A DBMS is not intended to support all these constructs directly; it is typically built around a data model with just a few basic constructs, such as the relational model. A database design in terms of a semantic model serves as a useful starting point for a design in terms of the model the DBMS supports.

A widely used semantic data model called the entity-relationship (ER) model allows us to pictorially denote entities and the relationships amongst them. We cover the ER model in Chapter 14.

1.3.1   The Relational Model

In this section we provide a brief introduction to the relational model. The central data description construct in this model is a **relation**, which can be thought of as a set of **records**, each of which has the same number (and type) of fields.

A description of data in terms of a data model is called a **schema**. In the relational model, the schema for a relation specifies its name, the name of each **field** (or **attribute** or **column**), and the type of each field. As an example, student information in a university database may be stored in a relation with the following schema:

Students(*sid:* `string`, *name:* `string`, *login:* `string`, *age:* `integer`, *gpa:* `real`)

The preceding schema says that each row in the Students relation has five fields, with field names and types as indicated. An example instance of the Students relation appears in Figure 1.1.

sid	name	login	age	gpa
53666	Jones	jones@cs	18	3.4
53688	Smith	smith@ee	18	3.2
53650	Smith	smith@math	19	3.8
53831	Madayan	madayan@music	11	1.8
53832	Guldu	guldu@music	12	2.0

Figure 1.1   An Instance of the Students Relation

Each row in the Students relation describes a student. The description is not complete—for example, the student's height is not included—but is presumably adequate for the intended applications in the university database. Every row follows the schema of the Students relation, which can therefore be regarded as a template for describing a student.

We can make the description of a student more precise by specifying **integrity constraints**, which are conditions that the records in a relation must satisfy. For example, we could specify that every student has a unique *sid* value. Observe that we cannot capture this information by simply adding another field to the Students schema; thus the expressiveness of the constructs available for specifying integrity constraints is an important aspect of a data model.

Other Data Models

In addition to the relational data model (which is used in numerous systems, including DB2, Informix, Oracle, Sybase, Microsoft's Access, FoxBase, Paradox, Tandem and Teradata), other important data models include the hierarchical model (e.g., used in IBM's IMS DBMS), the network model (e.g., used in IDMS), the object-oriented model (e.g., used in Objectstore and Versant), and the object-relational model (e.g., used in Illustra, O2 and UniSQL). While there are many databases that use the hierarchical and network models, and systems based on the object-oriented and object-relational models are entering the marketplace, the dominant model today is the relational model.

In this book, we will focus on the relational model because of its wide use and importance. Indeed, the object-relational model, which is gaining in popularity, is an effort to combine the best features of the relational and object-oriented models, and a good grasp of the relational model is necessary to understand object-relational concepts. (We discuss the object-oriented and object-relational models in Chapter 21.)

1.3.2   Levels of Abstraction in a DBMS

The data in a DBMS is described at three levels of abstraction, as illustrated in Figure 1.2.

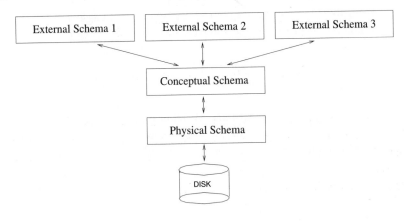

Figure 1.2   Levels of Abstraction in a DBMS

The *conceptual schema* describes the stored data in terms of the data model of the DBMS. The *physical schema* provides additional storage details. *External schemas* describe 'views' of the data tailored to different user groups. Information about the conceptual, external and physical schemas is stored in the **system catalogs**. (The catalogs also store information used in optimizing queries and checking whether users are authorized to access the data that they want to retrieve; see Chapter 3.)

A **data definition language** (DDL) is used to describe the external and conceptual schemas. We will discuss the DDL facilities of the most widely used database language, SQL, in Chapter 2.

We discuss the three levels of abstraction below.

Conceptual Schema

The **conceptual schema** (sometimes called the **logical schema**) describes the stored data in terms of the data model of the DBMS. In a relational DBMS, the conceptual schema describes all relations that are stored in the database. In our sample university database, these relations contain information about *entities*, such as students and faculty, and about *relationships*, such as students' enrollment in courses. All student entities can be described in a Students relation, as we saw earlier. In fact, each collection of entities and each collection of relationships can be described as a relation, leading to the following conceptual schema:

Students(*sid:* string, *name:* string, *login:* string,
        age: integer, *gpa:* real)
Faculty(*fid:* string, *fname:* string, *sal:* real)
Courses(*cid:* string, *cname:* string, *credits:* integer)
Rooms(*rno:* integer, *address:* string, *capacity:* integer)
Enrolled(*sid:* string, *cid:* string, *grade:* string)
Teaches(*fid:* string, *cid:* string)
Meets_In(*cid:* string, *rno:* integer, *time:* string)

The choice of relations, and the choice of fields for each relation, is not always obvious, and the process of arriving at a good conceptual schema is called **conceptual database design**. We discuss conceptual database design in Chapters 14 and 15.

Physical Schema

The **physical schema** specifies additional storage details such as the file organizations used and the auxiliary data structures used for fast retrieval. Essentially, the physical schema summarizes how the relations described in the conceptual schema are actually stored on secondary storage devices such as disks and tapes.

After the relations to be stored are chosen, decisions about how to store them must be made, and auxiliary data structures called **indexes** must be created to speed up important operations; that is, the physical schema must be determined. A sample physical schema for the university database follows:

- Store all relations as unsorted files of records. (A file in a DBMS is either a collection of records or a collection of pages, rather than a string of characters as in an operating system.)

- Create indexes (which are special data structures associated with a file in order to speed up certain queries on the indexed columns) on the first column of the Students, Faculty and Courses relations, the *sal* column of Faculty, and the *capacity* column of Rooms.

Decisions about the physical schema are based on an understanding of how the data is typically accessed. The process of arriving at a good physical schema

is called **physical database design**. We discuss physical database desig
Chapter 16.

External Schema

External schemas, which usually are also in terms of the data model of the
DBMS, allow data access to be customized (and authorized) at the level of individual users or groups of users. Any given database has exactly one conceptual
schema and one physical schema because it has just one set of stored relations,
but it may have several external schemas, each tailored to a particular group of
users. Each external schema consists of a collection of one or more **views** and
relations from the conceptual schema. A view is conceptually a set of records,
just like a relation, but the records in a view are not stored in the DBMS. Rather,
they are computed using a definition for the view, in terms of relations stored in
the DBMS. We discuss views in more detail in Chapter 10.

The external schema design is guided by end user requirements. For example, we
might want to allow students to find out the names of faculty members teaching
courses, as well as course enrollments. This can be done by defining the following
view:

$$\text{Courseinfo}(cid: \texttt{string}, \textit{fname}: \texttt{string}, \textit{enrollment}: \texttt{integer})$$

A user can treat a view just like a relation and ask questions about the records in
the view; even though the records in the view are not stored explicitly, they are
computed as needed. It is worth considering why we did not include Courseinfo in
the conceptual schema. The reason is that we can compute Courseinfo from the
relations in the conceptual schema, and to store it in addition would be redundant.
Such redundancy, in addition to the wasted space, could lead to inconsistencies;
for example, a tuple may be inserted into the Enrolled relation, indicating that a
particular student has enrolled in some course, without incrementing the value in
the *enrollment* field of the corresponding record of Courseinfo (if the latter also
is part of the conceptual schema and its tuples are stored in the DBMS).

1.3.3 Data Independence

A very important advantage of using a DBMS is that it offers **data independence**. That is, application programs are insulated from changes in the way the
data is structured and stored. Data independence is achieved through use of the
three levels of data abstraction; in particular, the conceptual schema and the
external schema provide distinct benefits in this area.

Relations in the external schema (view relations) are in principle generated on demand from the relations corresponding to the conceptual schema.[2] If the underlying data is reorganized, that is, the conceptual schema is changed, the definition of a view relation can be modified so that the same relation is computed as before. For example, suppose that the Faculty relation in our university database is replaced by the following two relations:

Faculty_public(*fid:* `string`, *fname:* `string`, *office:* `integer`)
Faculty_private(*fid:* `string`, *sal:* `real`)

Intuitively, some confidential information about faculty has been placed in a separate relation and information about offices has been added. The Courseinfo view relation can be redefined in terms of Faculty_public and Faculty_private, which together contain all the information in Faculty, so that a user who queries Courseinfo will get the same answers as before.

Thus users can be shielded from changes in the logical structure of the data, or changes in the choice of relations to be stored. This property is called **logical data independence**.

In turn, the conceptual schema insulates users from changes in the physical storage of the data. This property is referred to as **physical data independence**. The conceptual schema hides details such as how the data is actually laid out on disk, the file structure and the choice of indexes. As long as the conceptual schema remains the same, we can change these storage details without altering applications. (Of course, performance might be affected by such changes.)

1.4   QUERIES IN A DBMS

The ease with which information can be obtained from a database often determines its value to a user. In contrast to older database systems, relational database systems allow a rich class of questions to be posed easily; this feature has contributed greatly to their popularity. Consider the sample university database in Section 1.3.2. Here are examples of questions that a user might ask:

1. What is the name of the student with student id 123456?

2. What is the average salary of professors named Smith?

3. What is the average salary of professors who teach the course with cid CS564?

4. How many students are enrolled in course CS564?

---

[2] In practice, they could be precomputed and stored to speed up queries on view relations, but the computed view relations must be updated whenever the underlying relations are updated.

5. What fraction of students in course CS564 received a grade better than B?

6. Is any student with a GPA less than 3.0 enrolled in course CS564?

Such questions involving the data stored in a DBMS are called **queries**. A DBMS provides a specialized language, called the **query language**, in which queries can be posed. A very attractive feature of the relational model is that it supports powerful **query languages**. **Relational calculus** is a formal query language based on mathematical logic, and queries in this language have an intuitive, precise meaning. **Relational algebra** is another formal query language, based on a collection of **operators** for manipulating relations, which is equivalent in power to the calculus.

A DBMS takes great care to evaluate queries as efficiently as possible. We discuss query optimization and evaluation in Chapters 12 and 13. Of course, the efficiency of query evaluation is determined to a large extent by how the data is stored physically. Indexes can be used to speed up many queries—in fact, a good choice of indexes for the underlying relations can speed up each query in the preceding list. We discuss data storage and indexing in Chapters 3, 4, 5 and 6.

The query language of a DBMS is part of the **data manipulation language** (DML), which also provides constructs to insert, delete and modify data. We will discuss the DML features of SQL in Chapter 9. The DML and DDL are collectively referred to as the **data sublanguage** when embedded within a **host language** (e.g., C or COBOL).

1.5   CONCURRENT ACCESS AND CRASH RECOVERY

Consider a database that holds information about airline reservations. At any given instant, it is possible (and likely) that several travel agents are looking up information about available seats on various flights, and indeed, making new seat reservations. When several users access (and possibly modify) a database concurrently, the DBMS must order their requests carefully to avoid conflicts. For example, when one travel agent looks up Flight 100 on some given day and finds an empty seat, another travel agent may simultaneously be making a reservation for that seat, thereby making the information seen by the first agent obsolete.

Another example of concurrent use is a bank's database. While one user's application program is computing the total deposits, another application may transfer money from an account that the first application has just 'seen' to an account that has not yet been seen, thereby causing the total to appear larger than it should be. Clearly, such anomalies should not be allowed to occur. However, disallowing concurrent access can degrade performance.

An important task of a DBMS is to schedule concurrent accesses to data so that each user can safely ignore the fact that others are accessing the data concurrently. The importance of this task cannot be underestimated because a database is typically shared by a large number of users, who submit their requests to the DBMS independently, and simply cannot be expected to deal with arbitrary changes being made concurrently by other users. A DBMS allows users to think of their programs as if they were executing in isolation, and users need to think about other users' programs only to the extent that programs submitted concurrently could be executed in any order. For example, if a program that deposits cash into an account is submitted to the DBMS at the same time as another program that debits money from the same account, either of these programs could be run first by the DBMS, but their steps will not be interleaved in such a way that they interfere with each other.

Further, the DBMS must protect users from the effects of system failures by ensuring that all data (and the status of active applications) is restored to a consistent state when the system is restarted after a crash. For example, if a travel agent asks for a reservation to be made, and the DBMS responds saying that the reservation has been made, the reservation should not be lost if the system crashes. On the other hand, if the DBMS has not yet responded to the request, but is in the process of making the necessary changes to the data while the crash occurs, the partial changes should be undone when the system comes back up. For example, if the DBMS is in the middle of transferring money from account A to account B, and has debited the first account but not yet credited the second when the crash occurs, the money debited from acount A must be restored when the system comes back up after the crash.

A **transaction** is *any one execution* of a user program in a DBMS. (Executing the same program several times will generate several transactions.) A DBMS must ensure three important properties of transactions to correctly manage data, given concurrent access and the possibility of system failures:

1. **Isolation:** Users should be able to understand a transaction without considering the effect of other concurrently executing transactions, even if the DBMS interleaves the actions of several transactions for performance reasons.

2. **Atomicity:** Either all actions are carried out or none are. Users should not have to worry about the effect of incomplete transactions (say, when a system crash occurs).

3. **Durability:** Once the DBMS informs the user that a transaction has successfully completed, its effects should persist even if the system crashes before all its changes are reflected on disk.

Transaction isolation is ensured by guaranteeing that even though actions of several transactions might be interleaved, the net effect is identical to executing all transactions in some serial order. For example, if two transactions $T1$ and $T2$ are executed concurrently, the net effect is guaranteed to be equivalent to executing $T1$ followed by executing $T2$ or executing $T2$ followed by executing $T1$. (The DBMS provides no guarantees about which order is effectively chosen.)

A DBMS typically uses a **locking protocol** to achieve *isolation*. For example, suppose that two kinds of **locks** are supported by the DBMS: **shared locks** on an object can be held by two different transactions at the same time, but an **exclusive lock** on an object ensures that no other transactions hold *any* lock on this object. Suppose that every transaction begins by obtaining a shared lock on each data object that it needs to read and an exclusive lock on each data object that it needs to modify, and then releases all its locks after completing all actions. Consider two transactions $T1$ and $T2$ such that $T1$ wants to modify a data object and $T2$ wants to read the same object. Intuitively, if $T1$'s request for an exclusive lock on the object is granted first, $T2$ cannot proceed until $T1$ releases this lock, because $T2$'s request for a shared lock will not be granted by the DBMS until then. Thus all of $T1$'s actions will complete before any of $T2$'s actions are initiated. We consider locking in more detail in Chapter 17.

A DBMS ensures *transaction atomicity* by undoing the actions of incomplete transactions. In order to do so, the DBMS maintains a **log** of all writes to the database. A crucial property of the log is that each write action must be recorded in the log (on disk) *before* the corresponding change is reflected in the database itself—otherwise, if the system crashes just after making the change in the database but before the change is recorded in the log, the DBMS would be unable to detect and undo this change. This property is called **Write-Ahead Log** or **WAL**. To ensure this property, the DBMS must be able to selectively force a page in memory to disk. The log is also used to ensure *durability*, as explained in Chapter 18.

1.5.1 Points to Note

In summary, there are two points to remember with respect to DBMS support for concurrency control and recovery:

1. Every object that is read or written by a transaction is first locked in shared or exclusive mode, respectively. Placing a lock on an object restricts its availability to other transactions and thereby affects performance.

2. For efficient log maintenance, the DBMS must be able to selectively force a collection of pages in main memory to disk. Operating system support for this operation is not always satisfactory.

1.6   STRUCTURE OF A DBMS

Figure 1.3 shows the structure (with some simplification) of a typical DBMS based on the relational model of data.

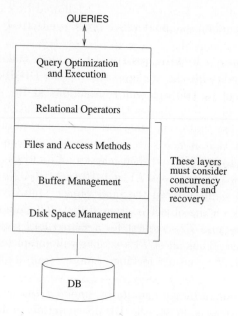

Figure 1.3   Architecture of a DBMS

The lowest layer of the software deals with management of space on disk, where the data is to be stored. Higher layers allocate, deallocate, read and write pages through (routines provided by) this layer, called the **disk space manager**. This layer is discussed in Chapter 3.

On top of the disk space manager, we have the **buffer manager**, which partitions the available main memory into a collection of pages or **frames**. The purpose of the buffer manager is to bring pages in from disk to main memory as needed in response to read requests from transactions. Buffer management is discussed in Chapter 3.

The next layer includes a variety of software for supporting the concept of a **file**, ich, in a DBMS, is a collection of pages or a collection of records. This layer ically supports a **heap file**, or file of unordered pages, as well as indexes. In lition to keeping track of the pages in a file, this layer organizes the information hin a page. File and page level storage issues are considered in Chapter 3. File anizations and indexes are considered in Chapter 4.

The code that implements relational operators sits on top of the file and access methods layer. These operators serve as the building blocks for evaluating queries posed against the data. The implementation of these operators is discussed in Chapter 12.

When a user issues a query, the query is presented to a **query optimizer**, which uses information about how the data is stored to produce an efficient execution plan for evaluating the query. An **execution plan** is usually represented as a tree of relational operators (with annotations that contain additional detailed information about which access methods to use, etc.). We discuss query optimization in Chapter 13.

The DBMS supports concurrency and crash recovery by carefully scheduling user requests, and maintaining a log of all changes to the database. For simplicity, we have not shown the components of the DBMS that implement **concurrency control** mechanisms and **crash recovery** in Figure 1.3. DBMS components associated with concurrency control and recovery include the **transaction manager**, which ensures that transactions request and release locks according to a suitable locking protocol and schedules the execution transactions, the **lock manager**, which keeps track of requests for locks and grants locks on database objects when they become available, and the **recovery manager**, which is responsible for maintaining a log, and restoring the system to a consistent state after a crash. The disk space management, buffer management and file and access method layers must interact with these components. We discuss concurrency control and recovery in detail in Chapter 17.

1.7   ADVANTAGES OF A DBMS

Using a DBMS to manage data has many advantages:

- **Data independence:** Application programs should be as independent as possible from details of data representation and storage. The DBMS can provide an abstract view of the data to insulate application code from such details, as discussed in Section 1.3.3.

- **Efficient data access:** A DBMS utilizes a variety of sophisticated techniques to store and retrieve data efficiently. This feature is especially important if the data is stored on external storage devices.

- **Data integrity and security:** If data is always accessed through the DBMS, the DBMS can enforce integrity constraints on the data. For example, before inserting salary information for an employee, the DBMS can check that the department budget is not exceeded. Also, the DBMS can enforce *access controls* that govern what data is visible to different classes of users.

- **Data administration:** When several users share the data, centralizing the administration of data can offer significant improvements. Experienced professionals who understand the nature of the data being managed, and how different groups of users use it, can be responsibile for organizing the data representation to minimize redundancy and for fine-tuning the storage of the data to make retrieval efficient.

- **Concurrent access and crash recovery:** As noted earlier, a DBMS schedules concurrent accesses to the data in such a manner that users can think of the data as being accessed by only one user at a time. Further, the DBMS protects users from the effects of system failures.

- **Reduced application development time:** Clearly, the DBMS supports many important functions that are common to many applications accessing data stored in the DBMS. This, in conjuction with the high-level interface to the data, facilitates quick development of applications. Such applications are also likely to be more robust than applications developed from scratch, because many important tasks are handled by the DBMS instead of being implemented by the application.

Given all these advantages, is there ever a reason *not* to use a DBMS? A DBMS is a complex piece of software, and the initial cost and hardware requirements, as well as the training required to use a DBMS, must be considered. In addition, the performance of a DBMS may not be adequate for certain applications; for example, applications with tight real-time constraints, or applications with just a few well-defined critical operations for which efficient custom code can be written. For reasons such as these, a specialized solution may sometimes be preferable to a DBMS, especially if the added benefits of a DBMS (e.g., flexible querying, security, concurrent access and crash recovery) are not required.

1.8 PEOPLE WHO DEAL WITH DATABASES

Quite a variety of people are associated with the creation and use of databases. Obviously, there are **database implementors**, who build DBMS software, and **end users** who wish to store and use data in a DBMS. Database implementors work for vendors such as IBM or Oracle. End users—fortunately for the database field!—come from a diverse and increasing number of fields. As data grows in complexity and volume, and is increasingly recognized as a major asset, the importance of maintaining it professionally in a DBMS is being widely accepted. Many end users simply use applications written by database application programmers (see below), and require little technical knowledge about DBMS software. Of course, sophisticated users who make more extensive use of a DBMS, for example, writing some queries of their own, require a deeper understanding of its features.

In addition to end users and implementors, two other classes of people are associated with a DBMS: *application programmers* and *database adminstrators* (DBAs).

Database application programmers develop packages that facilitate data access for end users, who are usually not computer professionals, using the host or data languages and software tools that DBMS vendors provide. (Such tools include report writers, spreadsheets, statistical packages, etc.) Application programs should ideally access data through the external schema. It is possible to write applications that access data at a lower level, but such applications would compromise data independence.

Although a personal database is typically maintained by the individual who owns it and uses it, corporate or enterprise-wide databases are typically important enough and complex enough that the task of designing and maintaining the database is entrusted to a professional called the **database administrator**. The DBA is responsible for many critical tasks:

- **Designing the conceptual and physical schemas:** The DBA is responsible for interacting with the users of the system to understand what data is to be stored in the DBMS and how it is likely to be used. Based on this knowledge, the DBA must design the conceptual schema (decide what relations to store), and the physical schema (decide how to store them). The DBA may also design widely used portions of the external schema, although users will probably augment this schema by creating additional views.

- **Security and authorization:** The DBA is responsible for ensuring that unauthorized data access is not permitted. In general, not everyone should be able to access all the data. In a relational DBMS, users can be granted permission to access only certain views and relations. For example, although you might allow students find out course enrollments and who teaches a given course, you would not want students to see faculty salaries or each others' grade information. The DBA can enforce this policy by giving students permission to read only the Courseinfo view.

- **Data availability and recovery from failures:** The DBA must take steps to ensure that in the event of a system failure, users can continue to access as much of the uncorrupted data as possible. The DBA must also work to restore the data to a consistent state. The DBMS provides software support for these functions, but the DBA is responible for implementing procedures to back up the data periodically and to maintain logs of system activity (to facilitate recovery from a crash).

- **Database tuning:** The needs of users are likely to evolve with time. The DBA is responsible for modifying the database, in particular the conceptual and physical schemas, to ensure adequate performance as user requirements change.

1.9   SUMMARY

A DBMS offers several features to support management of large datasets, including efficient access to data, data independence for applications, data integrity, security, quick application development, support for concurrent access, and recovery from system failures.

There are three levels of abstraction in a DBMS: external schema (or views), conceptual schema, and physical schema. The external schema describes the data as users see it, the conceptual schema describes what data is stored, and the physical schema describes how the data is stored. Designing a database for an enterprise and managing the database are important tasks, often performed by a database administrator.

Concurrency control and crash recovery are two important services that a DBMS provides. A DBMS views a user program, or transaction, as a series of reads and writes of data objects. The actions of several transactions are scheduled concurrently for performance reasons, because the system would otherwise be disk-bound. However, the DBMS ensures that transactions are atomic, and that the effect of a set of concurrently scheduled transactions is equivalent to running the transactions serially in some order. Thus users can understand their programs without thinking about other concurrently executing transactions. This property is usually achieved through a locking protocol according to which a transaction obtains a shared or exclusive lock on an object before reading or writing it.

Further, these properties (atomicity and serializability) are guaranteed even if the system crashes. The key to guaranteeing this property is the system log. The DBMS maintains a record of all changes to the data in the log, and uses the log to undo the effects of partial or aborted transactions. Each change must be recorded in the log (on disk) before the change is actually made to the data object.

The architecture of a relational DBMS typically consists of a layer that manages space on disk, a layer that manages available main memory and brings disk pages into memory as needed, a layer that supports the abstracts of files and index structures, a layer that implements relational operators, and a layer that parses and optimizes queries and produces an execution plan in terms of relational operators.

A database administrator designs a database for an enterprise, and manages the database. The DBA is responsible for security, bringing the system up after a failure, and periodically tuning the database to meet changing user needs. Application programmers develop applications that use DBMS functionality to access and manipulate data, and end users invoke these applications.

EXERCISES

Exercise 1.1 Why would you choose a database system instead of simply storing data in operating system files? When would it make sense *not* to use a database system?

Exercise 1.2 What is logical data independence and why is it important?

Exercise 1.3 Explain the difference between logical and physical data independence.

Exercise 1.4 Explain the difference between external, internal, and conceptual schemas. How are these different schema layers related to the concepts of logical and physical data independence?

Exercise 1.5 What are the responsibilities of a DBA? If we assume that the DBA is never interested in running his or her own queries, does the DBA still need to understand query optimization? Why?

Exercise 1.6 Scrooge McNugget wants to store information (names, addresses, descriptions of embarrassing moments, etc.) about the many ducks on his payroll. Not surprisingly, the volume of data compels him to buy a database system. To save money, he wants to buy one with the fewest possible features, and he plans to run it as a standalone application on his PC clone. Of course, Scrooge does not plan to share his list with anyone. Indicate which of the following DBMS features Scrooge should pay for; in each case also indicate why Scrooge should (or should not) pay for that feature in the system he buys.

1. A security facility.

2. Concurrency control.

3. Crash recovery.

4. A view mechanism.

5. A query language.

Exercise 1.7 Which of the following plays an important role in *representing* information about the real world in a database? Explain briefly.

1. The data definition language.

2. The data manipulation language.

3. The buffer manager.

4. The data model.

Exercise 1.8 Describe the structure of a DBMS. If your operating system is upgraded to support some new functions on OS files (e.g., the ability to force some sequence of bytes to disk), which layer(s) of the DBMS would you have to rewrite in order to take advantage of these new functions?

Exercise 1.9 Answer the following questions:

1. What is a transaction?

2. Why does a DBMS interleave the actions of different transactions, instead of executing transactions one after the other?

3. What must a user guarantee with respect to a transaction and database consistency? What should a DBMS guarantee with respect to concurrent execution of several transactions and database consistency?

4. Define *atomicity, isolation* and *durability*.

5. Explain the strict two-phase locking protocol.

6. What is the WAL property, and why is it important?

PROJECT-BASED EXERCISES

Exercise 1.10 Use a Web browser such as Mosaic or Netscape to look at the HTML documentation for Minibase. Try to get a feel for the overall architecture.

Exercise 1.11 If you are not experienced in C++, there are good on-line tutorials you can work through. Try the following URL, for example:

    http://uu-gna.mit.edu:8001/uu-gna/text/cc/index.html

BIBLIOGRAPHIC NOTES

The evolution of database management systems is traced in [206]. The use of data models for describing real-world data is discussed in [290], and [292] contains a taxonomy of data models. The three levels of abstraction were introduced in [134, 520]. The network data model is described in [134], and [569] discusses several commercial systems based on this model. [531] contains a good annotated collection of systems-oriented papers on database management.

Other texts covering database management systems include [146, 180, 234, 502, 413, 550, 562]. [146] provides a detailed discussion of the relational model from a conceptual standpoint, and is notable for its extensive annotated bibliography. [413] presents a performance-oriented perspective, with references to several commercial systems. [180] and [502] offer broad coverage of database system concepts, including a discussion of the hierarchical and network data models. [234] emphasizes the connection between database query languages and logic programming. [562] emphasizes data models. Of these texts, [550] provides the most detailed discussion of theoretical issues. Texts devoted to theoretical aspects include [35, 359, 4]. Handbook [547] includes a section on databases that contains introductory survey articles on a number of topics.

2

THE RELATIONAL MODEL

TABLE: An arrangement of words, numbers, or signs, or combinations of them, as in parallel columns, to exhibit a set of facts or relations in a definite, compact, and comprehensive form; a synopsis or scheme.

—Webster's *Dictionary of the English Language*

Codd proposed the relational model of data in 1970. At that time most database systems were based on one of two older data models (the hierarchical model and the network model); the relational model revolutionized the database field and largely supplanted these earlier models. Prototype relational database management systems were developed in pioneering research projects at IBM and UC-Berkeley by the mid-70s, and several vendors were offering relational database products shortly thereafter. Today, the relational model is by far the dominant data model, and is the foundation for the leading DBMS products, including IBM's DB2 family, Informix, Oracle, Sybase, Microsoft's Access and SQLServer, FoxBase and Paradox. Relational database systems are ubiquitous in the marketplace and represent a multibillion dollar industry.

The relational model is very simple and elegant; a database is a collection of one or more *relations*, where each relation is a table with rows and columns. This simple tabular representation enables even novice users to understand the contents of a database, and it permits the use of simple, high-level languages to query the data. Indeed, the major advantages of the relational model over the older data models are its simple data representation and the ease with which even complex queries can be expressed.

Consider the levels of abstraction that we discussed in Section 1.3.2. The *conceptual* (or *logical*) and the *external* schemas of a relational database are defined in terms of the relational model. The *physical* schema for a relational database describes how the relations in the conceptual schema are stored, in terms of the file organizations and indexes used; we will discuss file organizations and indexing in later chapters.

This chapter presents an overview of the relational model, along with an introduction to SQL, the most popular language for creating, modifying and querying relational databases; the discussion is based upon the current standard, SQL-92.

We discuss the concept of a relation in Section 2.1, and show how to create relations using the SQL language. An important component of a data model is the set of constructs it provides for specifying conditions that must be satisfied by the data. Such conditions, called *integrity constraints* (ICs), enable the DBMS to reject operations that might corrupt the data. We present integrity constraints in the relational model in Section 2.2, along with a discussion of SQL support for ICs. In Section 2.4 we turn to the mechanism for accessing and retrieving data from the database, *query languages*, and introduce the querying features of SQL, which we examine in greater detail in a later chapter.

2.1 RELATIONS

The main construct for representing data in the relational model is a **relation**. A relation consists of a **relation schema** and a **relation instance**. Intuitively, the relation instance is a table, and the relation schema describes the column heads for the table. We first describe the relation schema, and then the relation instance. The schema specifies the relation's name, the name of each **field** (or **column**, or **attribute**) and the **domain** of each field. A domain is referred to in a relation schema by the **domain name**, and has a set of associated **values**.

We can use the example of student information in a university database from Chapter 1 to illustrate the parts of a relation schema:

Students(*sid:* `string`, *name:* `string`, *login:* `string`, *age:* `integer`, *gpa:* `real`)

This says, for instance, that the field named *sid* has a domain named `string`. The set of values associated with domain `string` is the set of all character strings.

We now turn to the instances of a relation. An **instance** of a relation is a set of **tuples**, also called **records**, in which each tuple has the same number of fields as the relation schema. A relation instance can be thought of as a *table* in which each tuple is a *row*, and all rows have the same number of fields. (The term *relation instance* is often abbreviated to just *relation*, when there is no confusion with other aspects of a relation such as its schema.) An instance of the Students relation appears in Figure 2.1. Note that no two rows are identical. This is not happenstance, but a requirement of the relational model—each relation is defined to be a *set* of unique tuples or rows.[1] The order in which the rows are listed is not important. Figure 2.2 shows the same relation instance. If the fields are named, as in our schema definitions and figures depicting relation instances, the order of fields does not matter either. However, an alternative convention

---

[1] In practice, commercial systems allow tables to have duplicate rows, but we will assume that a relation is indeed a set of tuples unless otherwise noted.

sid	name	login	age	gpa
50000	Dave	dave@cs	19	3.3
53666	Jones	jones@cs	18	3.4
53688	Smith	smith@ee	18	3.2
53650	Smith	smith@math	19	3.8
53831	Madayan	madayan@music	11	1.8
53832	Guldu	guldu@music	12	2.0

Figure 2.1   An Instance *S*1 of the Students Relation

sid	name	login	age	gpa
53831	Madayan	madayan@music	11	1.8
53832	Guldu	guldu@music	12	2.0
53688	Smith	smith@ee	18	3.2
53650	Smith	smith@math	19	3.8
53666	Jones	jones@cs	18	3.4
50000	Dave	dave@cs	19	3.3

Figure 2.2   An Alternative Representation of Instance *S*1 of Students

is to list fields in a specific order, and to refer to a field by its position. Thus *sid* is field 1 of Students, *login* is field 3, and so on. If this convention is used, the order of fields is significant. Most database systems use a combination of these conventions. For example, in SQL the named fields convention is used in statements that retrieve records, and the ordered fields convention is commonly used when inserting records.

A relation schema specifies the domain of each field or column in the relation instance. These **domain constraints** in the schema specify an important condition that we want each instance of the relation to satisfy: The values that appear in a column must be drawn from the domain associated with that column. Thus the domain of a field is essentially the *type* of that field, in programming language terms, and restricts the values that can appear in the field.

More formally, let $R(f_1: \texttt{D1}, \ldots, f_n: \texttt{Dn})$ be a relation schema, and for each f_i, $1 \leq i \leq n$, let Dom_i be the set of values associated with the domain named $\texttt{Di}$. An instance of R that satisfies the domain constraints in the schema is a set of tuples with n fields:

$$\{ \langle f_1 : d_1, \ldots, f_n : d_n \rangle \mid d_1 \in Dom_1, \ldots, d_n \in Dom_n \}$$

The angular brackets $\langle \ldots \rangle$ identify the fields of a tuple, and the curly brackets $\{\ldots\}$ denote a set (of tuples, in this definition). The vertical bar | should be read 'such that,' the symbol $\in$ should be read 'in,' and the expression to the right of the vertical bar is a condition that must be satisfied by the field values of each tuple in the set.

Domain constraints are so fundamental in the relational model that we will henceforth consider only relation instances that satisfy them; therefore, *relation instance* means *relation instance that satisfies the domain constraints in the relation schema.*

The **cardinality** of a relation instance is the number of tuples in it. The **degree**, also called **arity**, of a relation is the number of fields. In Figure 2.1, the degree of the relation (the number of columns) is five, and the cardinality of this instance is six.

A **relational database** is a collection of relations with distinct relation names. The **relational database schema** is the set of schemas for the relations in the database. For example, in Chapter 1, we discussed a university database with relations called Students, Faculty, Courses, Rooms, Enrolled, Teaches and Meets_In. An **instance** of a relational database is a collection of relation instances, one per relation schema in the database schema; of course, each relation instance must satisfy the domain constraints in its schema.

2.1.1   Creating and Modifying Relations Using SQL-92

In SQL-92, there are several built-in types like `integer`, which are domains in terms of the relational model. There is a command that lets users define new domains, analogous to type definition commands in a programming language; we will discuss this in Section 9.9.

The `CREATE TABLE` statement is used to define a new table.[2] To create the Students relation, we can use the following statement:

```
CREATE TABLE Students ( sid    CHAR(20),
                        name   CHAR(20),
                        login  CHAR(10),
                        age    INTEGER,
                        gpa    REAL )
```

---

[2] SQL also provides statements to destroy tables and to change the columns associated with a table; we discuss these in Section 10.2.1.

Tuples are subsequently inserted using the INSERT command. We can insert a single tuple into the Students table as follows:

```
INSERT
INTO    Students S (sid, name, login, age, gpa)
VALUES  (53688, 'Smith', 'smith@ee', 18, 3.2)
```

We can optionally omit the list of column names in the INTO clause and list the values in the appropriate order, but it is good style to be explicit about column names.

We can delete tuples using the DELETE command. We can delete all Students tuples with *name* equal to Smith using the command:

```
DELETE
FROM    Students S
WHERE   S.name = 'Smith'
```

We can modify the column values in an existing row using the UPDATE command. For example, we can increment the age and decrement the gpa of the student with *sid* 53688:

```
UPDATE Students S
SET     S.age = S.age + 1, S.gpa = S.gpa - 1
WHERE   S.sid = 53688
```

These examples illustrate some important points. The WHERE clause is applied first and determines which rows are to be modified. The SET clause then determines how these rows are to be modified. If the column that is being modified is also used to determine the new value, the value used in the expression on the right side of equals (=) is the *old* value, that is, prior to the modification. To illustrate these points further, consider the following variation of the previous query:

```
UPDATE Students S
SET     S.age = S.age - 1
WHERE   S.age >= 18
```

If this query is applied on the instance S1 of Students shown in Figure 2.1, we obtain the instance shown in Figure 2.3.

2.2 INTEGRITY CONSTRAINTS

A database is only as good as the information stored in it, and a DBMS must therefore have some provision for preventing the entry of incorrect information.

sid	name	login	age	gpa
50000	Dave	dave@cs	18	3.3
53666	Jones	jones@cs	17	3.4
53688	Smith	smith@ee	17	3.2
53650	Smith	smith@math	18	3.8
53831	Madayan	madayan@music	11	1.8
53832	Guldu	guldu@music	12	2.0

Figure 2.3   Students Instance $S1$ after Update

An **integrity constraint (IC)** is a condition that is specified on a database schema, and restricts the data that can be stored in an instance of the database. If a database instance satisfies all the integrity constraints specified on the database schema, it is a **legal** instance. A DBMS **enforces** integrity constraints, in that it permits only legal instances to be stored in the database.

Integrity constraints are specified and enforced at different times:

1. When the DBA or end user defines a database schema, he or she specifies the ICs that must hold on any instance of this database.

2. When a database application is run, the DBMS checks for violations and disallows changes to the data that violate the specified ICs. (In some situations, rather than disallow the change, the DBMS might instead make some compensating changes to the data to ensure that the database instance satisfies all ICs. In any case, changes to the database are not allowed to create an instance that violates any IC.)

Many kinds of integrity constraints can be specified in the relational model. We have already seen one example of an integrity constraint in the *domain constraints* (Section 2.1) associated with a relation schema. In general, other kinds of constraints can be specified as well; for example, no two students have the same *sid* value. In this section we discuss the integrity constraints, other than domain constraints, that a DBA or user can specify in the relational model.

2.2.1   Key Constraints

Consider the Students relation and the constraint that no two students have the same student id. This IC is an example of a key constraint. A **key constraint** is a statement that a certain *minimal* subset of the fields of a relation is a unique identifier for a tuple. A set of fields that uniquely identifies a tuple according to a key constraint is called a **key** for the relation. In the case of the Students relation, the (set of fields containing just the) *sid* field is a key.

Let us take a closer look at the above definition of key. There are two parts to the definition:[3]

1. Two distinct tuples in a legal instance (an instance that satisfies all ICs, including the key constraint) cannot have identical values in all the fields of a key.

2. No subset of the set of fields in a key is a unique identifier for a tuple.

The first part of the definition means that in *any* legal instance, the values in the key fields uniquely identify a tuple in the instance. When specifying a key constraint, the DBA or user must be sure that this constraint will not prevent them from storing a 'correct' set of tuples. (Indeed, a similar comment applies to the specification of other kinds of ICs as well.) The notion of 'correctness' here depends upon the nature of the data being stored. For example, several students may have the same name, although each student has a unique student id. If the *name* field is declared to be a key, the DBMS will not allow the Students relation to contain two tuples describing different students with the same name!

The second part of the definition means, for example, that the set of fields {*sid, name*} is not a key for Students, because this set properly contains the key {*sid*}. The set {*sid, name*} is an example of a **superkey**, which is a set of fields that contains a key.

Look again at the instance of the Students relation in Figure 2.1. Observe that two different rows always have different *sid* values; *sid* is a key and uniquely identifies a tuple. However, this does not hold for nonkey fields. For example, the relation contains two rows with *Smith* in the *name* field.

Note that every relation is guaranteed to have a key. Since a relation is a set of tuples, the set of *all* fields is always a superkey. If other constraints hold, some subset of the fields may form a key, but if not, the set of all fields is a key.

A relation may have several keys. For example, the *login* and *age* fields of the Students relation may, taken together, also identify students uniquely. That is, {*login, age*} is also a key. It may seem that *login* is a key, since no two rows in the example instance have the same *login* value. However, the key must identify tuples uniquely in all possible legal instances of the relation. By stating that

---

[3] The term *key* is rather overworked. In the context of access methods, we speak of *search keys*, which are quite different.

{login, age} is a key, the user is declaring that two students may have the same login or age, but not both.

Out of all the available **candidate** keys, a database designer can identify a **primary** key. Intuitively, a tuple can be referred to from elsewhere in the database by storing the values of its primary key fields. For example, we can refer to a Students tuple by storing its *sid* value. As a consequence of referring to student tuples in this manner, tuples are frequently accessed by specifying their *sid* value. In principle, we can use any key, not just the primary key, to refer to a tuple. However, using the primary key is preferable because it is what the DBMS expects—this is the significance of designating a particular candidate key as a primary key—and optimizes for. For example, the DBMS may create an index with the primary key fields as the search key, to make the retrieval of a tuple given its primary key value efficient. The idea of referring to a tuple is developed further in the next section.

Specifying Key Constraints in SQL-92

In SQL we can declare that a subset of the columns of a table constitute a key by using the **UNIQUE** constraint. At most one of these 'candidate' keys can be declared to be a *primary key*, using the **PRIMARY KEY** constraint. (SQL does not require that such constraints be declared for all tables.)

Let us revisit our example table definition and specify key information:

```
CREATE TABLE Students ( sid    CHAR(20),
                        name   CHAR(20),
                        login  CHAR(10),
                        age    INTEGER,
                        gpa    REAL,
                        UNIQUE (login, age),
                        CONSTRAINT StudentsKey PRIMARY KEY (sid) )
```

This definition says that *sid* is the primary key and that the combination of *login* and *age* is also a key. The definition of the primary key also illustrates how we can name a constraint by preceding it with **CONSTRAINT** *constraint-name*. If the constraint is violated, the constraint name is returned and can be used to identify the error.

2.2.2 Foreign Key Constraints

Sometimes the information stored in a relation is linked to the information stored in another relation. If one of the relations is modified, the other must be checked, and perhaps modified, to keep the data consistent. An IC involving both relations must be specified if a DBMS is to make such checks. The most common IC involving two relations is a *foreign key* constraint.

Suppose that in addition to Students, we have a second relation:

Enrolled(*sid:* **string**, *cid:* **string**, *grade:* **string**)

To ensure that only bona fide students can enroll in courses, any value that appears in the *sid* field of an instance of the Enrolled relation should also appear in the *sid* field of some tuple in the Students relation. The *sid* field of Enrolled is called a **foreign key** and **refers** to Students.

This constraint is illustrated in Figure 2.4. As the figure shows, there may well be some students who are not referenced from Enrolled (e.g., the student with *sid=50000*). However, every *sid* value that appears in the instance of the Enrolled table appears in the primary key column of a row in the Students table.

Foreign key   Primary key

cid	grade	sid
Carnatic101	C	53831
Reggae203	B	53832
Topology112	A	53650
History105	B	53666

sid	name	login	age	gpa
50000	Dave	dave@cs	19	3.3
53666	Jones	jones@cs	18	3.4
53688	Smith	smith@ee	18	3.2
53650	Smith	smith@math	19	3.8
53831	Madayan	madayan@music	11	1.8
53832	Guldu	guldu@music	12	2.0

Enrolled (Referencing relation)   Students (Referenced relation)

Figure 2.4   Referential Integrity

If we try to insert the tuple ⟨*55555, Art104, A*⟩ into *E*1, the IC is violated because there is no tuple in *S*1 with the id 55555; the database system should reject such an insertion. Similarly, if we delete the tuple ⟨*53666, Jones, jones@cs, 18, 3.4*⟩ from *S*1, we violate the foreign key constraint because the tuple ⟨*53666, History105, B*⟩ in *E*1 contains *sid* value 53666, the *sid* of the deleted Students tuple. The DBMS should disallow the deletion or, perhaps, also delete the Enrolled tuple that refers to the deleted Students tuple. We discuss foreign key constraints and their impact on updates in Section 2.3.

Specifying Foreign Key Constraints in SQL-92

Let us define Enrolled(*sid:* **string**, *cid:* **string**, *grade:* **string**):

```
CREATE TABLE Enrolled ( sid    CHAR(20),
                        cid    CHAR(20),
                        grade CHAR(10),
                        PRIMARY KEY (sid, cid),
                        FOREIGN KEY (sid) REFERENCES Students )
```

The foreign key constraint states that every *sid* value in Enrolled must also appear in Students, that is, *sid* in Enrolled is a foreign key that references Students. Incidentally, the primary key constraint states that a student has exactly one grade for each course that he (or she) is enrolled in. If we want to record more than one grade per student per course, we should change the primary key constraint.

2.2.3 General Constraints

Domain, primary key and foreign key constraints are considered to be a fundamental part of the relational data model, and are given special attention in most commercial systems. Sometimes, however, it is necessary to specify more general constraints.

For example, we may require that student ages be within a certain range of values; given such an IC specification, the DBMS will reject inserts and updates that violate the constraint. This is very useful in preventing data entry errors. If we specify that all students must be at least 16 years old, the instance of Students shown in Figure 2.1 is illegal, because two students are underage. If we disallow the insertion of these two tuples, we have a legal instance, as shown in Figure 2.5.

sid	*name*	*login*	*age*	*gpa*
53666	Jones	jones@cs	18	3.4
53688	Smith	smith@ee	18	3.2
53650	Smith	smith@math	19	3.8

Figure 2.5   An Instance *S*2 of the Students Relation

The IC that students must be older than 16 can be thought of as an extended domain constraint, since we are essentially defining the set of permissible *age* values more stringently than is possible by simply using a standard domain such as `integer`. In general, however, constraints that go well beyond domain, key or foreign key constraints can be specified. For example, we could require that every student whose age is greater than 18 must have a gpa greater than 3. Current relational database systems support such general constraints; we discuss SQL support for general constraints, called *table constraints* and *assertions*, in Section 9.9.

2.3 ENFORCING INTEGRITY CONSTRAINTS

As we observed earlier, ICs are specified when a relation is created and enforced when a relation is modified. The impact of **PRIMARY KEY** and **UNIQUE** constraints is straightforward: if an insert, delete or update command causes a violation, it is rejected. Potential IC violation is generally checked at the end of each SQL statement execution, although it can be *deferred* until the end of the transaction executing the statement, as we will see in Chapter 17.

The impact of foreign key constraints is more complex because SQL sometimes makes an attempt to rectify a foreign key constraint violation instead of simply rejecting the change. We will discuss the **referential integrity enforcement steps** taken by the DBMS in terms of our Enrolled and Students tables, with the foreign key constraint that Enrolled.*sid* is a reference to (the primary key of) Students.

We must consider three basic questions:

1. *What should we do if an Enrolled row is inserted, with a* sid *column value that does not appear in any row of the Students table?*

   In this case the **INSERT** command is simply rejected.

2. *What should we do if a Students row is deleted?*

   The options are:

   ■ Delete all Enrolled rows that refer to the deleted Students row.

   ■ Disallow the deletion of the Students row if an Enrolled row refers to it.

   ■ Set the *sid* column to the *sid* of some (existing) 'default' student, for every Enrolled row that refers to the deleted Students row.

3. *What should we do if the primary key value of a Students row is updated?*

   The options here are similar to the previous case.

SQL allows us to choose any of the three options on **DELETE** and **UPDATE**. For example, we can specify that when a Students row is *deleted*, all Enrolled rows that refer to it are to be deleted as well, but that when the *sid* column of a Students row is *modified*, this update is to be rejected if an Enrolled row refers to the modified Students row:

```
CREATE TABLE Enrolled (  sid    CHAR(20),
                         cid    CHAR(20),
                         grade CHAR(10),
                         PRIMARY KEY (sid, cid),
                         FOREIGN KEY (sid) REFERENCES Students,
                              ON DELETE CASCADE,
                              ON UPDATE NO ACTION )
```

The options are specified as part of the foreign key declaration. The default option is NO ACTION, which means that the action (DELETE or UPDATE) is to be rejected. Thus the ON UPDATE clause in our example could be omitted, with the same effect. The CASCADE keyword says that if a Students row is deleted, all Enrolled rows that refer to it are to be deleted as well. If the UPDATE clause specified CASCADE, and the *sid* column of a Students row is updated, this update is also carried out in each Enrolled row that refers to the updated Students row.

If a Students row is deleted, we can switch the enrollment to a 'default' student by using ON DELETE SET DEFAULT. The default student is specified as part of the definition of the *sid* field in Enrolled; for example, *sid* CHAR(20) DEFAULT *'53666'*. Although the specification of a default value is appropriate in some situations (e.g., a default parts supplier if a particular supplier goes out of business), it is really not appropriate to switch enrollments to a default student. The correct solution in this example is to also delete all enrollment records for the deleted student (that is, CASCADE), or to reject the update.

For completeness, we remark that SQL also allows the use of a special value, called the **null** value, as the default, by specifying ON DELETE SET NULL. We will discuss *null* values in Chapter 9.

2.4   QUERY LANGUAGES

A **relational database query** is a question about the data, and the answer consists of a new relation containing the result. For example, we might want to find all students younger than 18 or all students enrolled in Reggae203. A **query language** is a specialized language for writing queries.

SQL is the most popular commercial query language for a relational DBMS. We now present some SQL examples that illustrate how easily relations can be queried. Consider the instance of the Students relation shown in Figure 2.1. We can retrieve rows corresponding to students who are younger than 18 with the following SQL query:

```
SELECT *
```

```
FROM    Students S
WHERE   S.age < 18
```

The symbol * means that we retain all fields of selected tuples in the result. To understand this query, think of S as a variable that is bound to each tuple in Students, one tuple after the other. The condition $S.age < 18$ in the WHERE clause specifies that we want to select only tuples in which the *age* field has a value less than 18. This query evaluates to the relation shown in Figure 2.6.

sid	name	login	age	gpa
53831	Madayan	madayan@music	11	1.8
53832	Guldu	guldu@music	12	2.0

Figure 2.6   Students with $age < 18$

This example illustrates that the domain of a field restricts the operations that are permitted on field values, in addition to restricting the values that can appear in the field. The condition $S.age < 18$ involves an arithmetic comparison of an *age* value with an integer and is permissible because the domain of *age* is the set of integers. On the other hand, a condition such as $S.age = S.sid$ does not make sense because it compares an integer value with a string value, and indeed, this comparison is defined to fail in SQL; a query containing this condition will produce no answer tuples.

In addition to selecting a subset of tuples, a query can extract a subset of the fields of each selected tuple. Thus we can compute the names and logins of students who are younger than 18 with the following query:

```
SELECT  S.name, S.login
FROM    Students S
WHERE   S.age < 18
```

Figure 2.7 shows the answer to this query; it is obtained by applying the selection to the instance $S1$ of Students (to get the relation shown in Figure 2.6), followed by removing unwanted fields. Note that the order in which we perform these operations does matter—if we remove unwanted fields first, we cannot check the condition $S.age < 18$, which involves one of those fields.

We can also combine information in the Students and Enrolled relations. If we want to obtain the names of all students who obtained an A and the id of the course in which they got an A, we could write the following query:

name	login
Madayan	madayan@music
Guldu	guldu@music

Figure 2.7   Names and Logins of Students under 18

```
SELECT  S.name, E.cid
FROM    Students S, Enrolled E
WHERE   S.sid = E.sid AND E.grade = 'A'
```

This query can be understood as follows: "If there is a Students tuple S and an Enrolled tuple E such that S.sid = E.sid (so that S describes the student who is enrolled in E) and E.grade = 'A', then print the student's name and the course id." When evaluated on the instances of Students and Enrolled in Figure 2.4, this query returns a single tuple, ⟨*Smith, Topology112*⟩.

2.5   SUMMARY

The relational model consists of a tabular representation for data called a *relation*, *integrity constraints* that can be specified on relations, and *query languages* for manipulating the data. A relation consists of a *relation schema*, which specifies the relation name, the name of each field, and the name of the domain associated with each field, and a *relation instance*, which is a set of tuples. The tuples in a relation have the same number of fields as the relation schema, and values in a field are required to be in the set of values associated with the domain for that field.

Integrity constraints are specified on the relation schema, and every instance of the relation that is stored in the database is required to satisfy all the ICs defined on the relation. Three important types of integrity constraints are *domain constraints*, *key constraints* and *foreign key constraints*.

SQL-92 includes constructs for creating tables; defining integrity constraints; and inserting, deleting and modifying rows in a table. Integrity constraints and commands that modify the data interact closely.

The simplicity of the tabular data representation makes the development of expressive and natural query languages possible. Indeed, the simplicity of the relational model is its greatest strength. It allows users to understand and manipulate the database easily, and comes with a rich theory of query optimization and database design, which we will study in later chapters.

EXERCISES

Exercise 2.1 Define the following terms: *relation schema, relational database schema, domain, relation instance, relation cardinality* and *relation degree.*

Exercise 2.2 How many distinct tuples are in a relation instance with cardinality 22?

Exercise 2.3 Does the relational model, as seen by an SQL query writer, provide physical and logical data independence? Explain.

Exercise 2.4 What is the difference between a candidate key and the primary key for a given relation? What is a superkey?

Exercise 2.5 Consider the instance of the Students relation shown in Figure 2.1.

1. Give an example of an attribute (or set of attributes) that you can deduce is *not* a candidate key, based on this instance being legal.

2. Give an example of an attribute (or set of attributes) that you can deduce *is* a candidate key, based on this instance being legal.

Exercise 2.6 What is a foreign key constraint? Why are such constraints important? What is referential integrity?

Exercise 2.7 Consider the relations Students, Faculty, Courses, Rooms, Enrolled, Teaches and Meets_In that were defined in Section 1.3.2.

1. List all the foreign key constraints among these relations.

2. Give an example of a (plausible) constraint involving one or more of these relations that is not a primary key or foreign key constraint.

Exercise 2.8 Answer each of the following questions briefly. The questions are based on the following relational schema:

> Emp(*eid:* **integer**, *ename:* **string**, *age:* **integer**, *salary:* **real**)
> Works(*eid:* **integer**, *did:* **integer**, *pct_time:* **integer**)
> Dept(*did:* **integer**, *dname:* **string**, *budget:* **real**, *managerid:* **integer**)

1. Give an example of a foreign key constraint that involves the Dept relation. What are the options for enforcing this constraint when a user attempts to delete a Dept tuple?

2. Write the SQL statements required to create the above relations, including appropriate versions of all primary and foreign key integrity constraints.

3. Define the Dept relation in SQL so that every department is guaranteed to have a manager.

4. Write an SQL statement to add 'John Doe' as an employee with $eid = 101$, $age = 32$ and $salary = 15,000$.

5. Write an SQL statement to give every employee a 10% raise.

6. Write an SQL statement to delete the 'Toy' department. Given the referential integrity constraints you chose for this schema, explain what happens when this statement is executed.

Exercise 2.9 Consider the SQL query whose answer is shown in Figure 2.6.

1. Modify this query so that only the *login* column is included in the answer.

2. If the clause WHERE *S.gpa* $>= 2$ is added to the original query, what is the set of tuples in the answer?

PROJECT-BASED EXERCISES

Exercise 2.10 Create the relations Students, Faculty, Courses, Rooms, Enrolled, Teaches and Meets_In in Minibase.

Exercise 2.11 Insert the tuples shown in Figures 2.1 and 2.4 into the relations Students and Enrolled. Create reasonable instances of the other relations.

Exercise 2.12 What integrity constraints are enforced by Minibase?

Exercise 2.13 Run the SQL queries presented in this chapter.

BIBLIOGRAPHIC NOTES

The relational model was proposed in a seminal paper by Codd [135]. Childs [126] and Kuhns [318] foreshadowed some of these developments. Gallaire and Minker's book [211] contains several papers on the use of logic in the context of relational databases. A system based on a variation of the relational model in which the entire database is regarded abstractly as a single relation, called the universal relation, is described in [549]. Extensions of the relational model to incorporate *null* values, which indicate an unknown or missing field value, are discussed by several authors; for example, [225, 268, 447, 555, 578].

Pioneering projects include System R [30, 111] at IBM San Jose Research Laboratory (now IBM Almaden Research Center), Ingres [525] at the University of California at Berkeley, PRTV [541] at the IBM UK Scientific Center in Peterlee, and QBE [588] at IBM T.J. Watson Research Center.

A rich theory underpins the field of relational databases. Texts devoted to theoretical aspects include those by Atzeni and DeAntonellis [35]; Maier [359]; and Abiteboul, Hull, and Vianu [4]. [285] is an excellent survey article.

Integrity constraints in relational databases have been discussed at length. [138] addresses semantic extensions to the relational model, but also discusses integrity, in particular referential integrity. [245], discuss semantic integrity constraints. [145] contains papers that address various aspects of integrity constraints, including in particular a detailed discussion of referential integrity. A vast literature deals with enforcing integrity constraints. [36] compares the cost of enforcing integrity constraints via compile-time, run-time and post-execution checks. [106] presents an SQL-based language for specifying integrity constraints, and identifies conditions under which integrity rules specified in this language can be violated. [521] discusses the technique of integrity constraint checking by query modification. [129] discusses real-time integrity constraints. Other papers on checking integrity constraints in databases include [62, 89, 99, 371]. [495] considers the approach of verifying the correctness of programs that access the database, instead of run-time checks. Note that this list of references is far from complete; in fact, it does not include any of the many papers on checking recursively specified integrity constraints. Some early papers in this widely studied area can be found in [211] and [210].

For references on SQL, see the bibliographic notes for Chapter 9. This book does not discuss specific products based on the relational model, but many fine books do discuss each of the major commercial systems; for example, Chamberlin's book on DB2 [110], Date and McGoveran's book on Sybase [149], and Koch and Loney's book on Oracle [310].

3

STORING DATA: DISKS AND FILES

Memory depends very much on the perspicuity, regularity, and order of our thoughts. Many complain of the want of memory, when the defect is in the judgment; and others, by grasping at all, retain nothing.

—Thomas Fuller

The preceding chapters introduced the basic concepts behind database systems and, in particular, relational database management systems (RDBMS). This chapter initiates a study of the internals of an RDBMS. In terms of the DBMS architecture presented in Section 1.6, it covers the disk space manager, the buffer manager, and the layer that supports the abstraction of a file of records. Later chapters cover auxiliary structures to speed retrieval of desired subsets of the data, and the implementation of a relational query language.

Data in a DBMS is stored on storage devices such as disks and tapes; we concentrate on disks and cover tapes briefly. The disk space manager is responsible for keeping track of available disk space. The file manager, which provides the abstraction of a file of records to higher levels of DBMS code, issues requests to the disk space manager to obtain and relinquish space on disk. The file management layer requests and frees disk space in units of a **page**; the size of a page is a DBMS parameter, and typical values are 4KB or 8KB. The file management layer is responsible for keeping track of the pages in a file, and for arranging records within pages.

When a record is needed for processing, it must be fetched from disk to main memory. The page on which the record resides is determined by the file manager. Sometimes, the file manager uses auxiliary data structures to quickly identify the page that contains a desired record. After identifying the required page, the file manager issues a a request for the page to a layer of DBMS code called the buffer manager. The buffer manager fetches requested pages from disk into a region of main memory called the buffer pool, and informs the file manager.

We cover the above points in detail in this chapter. Section 3.1 introduces disks and tapes. Section 3.2 discusses how a DBMS manages disk space, and Section 3.3 explains how a DBMS fetches data from disk into main memory. Section 3.4 covers alternative formats for storing individual records, and Section 3.5 covers different ways to arrange a collection of records on a page. Section 3.6 discusses how a collection of pages is organized into a file, and how auxiliary data structures can be built to speed up retrieval of records from a file. Section 3.7 examines how relations are stored as files of records, and how global information about all relations in a database is maintained in a relational DBMS.

3.1 THE MEMORY HIERARCHY

Memory in a computer system is arranged in a hierarchy. At the top, we have **primary storage**, which consists of cache and main memory, and provides very fast access to data. Then comes **secondary storage**, which consists of slower devices such as magnetic disks. **Tertiary storage** is the slowest class of storage devices; for example, tapes. Currently, the cost of a given amount of main memory is about 100 times the cost of the same amount of disk space, and tapes are even less expensive than disks. Slower storage devices such as tapes and disks play an important role in database systems because the amount of data is typically very large. Since buying enough main memory to store all data is prohibitively expensive, we must store data on tapes and disks and build database systems that can retrieve data from lower levels of the memory hierarchy into main memory as needed for processing.

There are reasons other than cost for storing data on secondary and tertiary storage. On systems with 32-bit addressing, only 2^{32} bytes can be directly referenced in main memory; the number of data objects may exceed this number! Further, data must be maintained across program executions. This requires storage devices that retain information when the computer is restarted (after a shutdown or a crash); we call such storage **nonvolatile**. Primary storage is usually volatile (although it is possible to make it nonvolatile by adding a battery backup feature), whereas secondary and tertiary storage is nonvolatile.

Tapes are relatively inexpensive and can store very large amounts of data. They are a good choice for *archival* storage, that is, when we need to maintain data for a long period but do not expect to access it very often. A Quantum DLT 4000 drive is a typical tape device; it stores 20 GB of data, and can store about twice as much by compressing the data. It records data on 128 *tape tracks*, which can be thought of as a linear sequence of adjacent bytes, and supports a sustained transfer rate of 1.5 MB/sec with uncompressed data (typically 3.0 MB/sec with compressed data). A single DLT 4000 tape drive can be used to access up to seven tapes in a stacked configuration, for a maximum compressed data capacity of about 280 GB.

The main drawback of tapes is that they are sequential access devices. We must essentially step through all the data in order, and cannot directly access a given location on tape. For example, to access the last byte on a tape, we would have to wind through the entire tape first. This makes tapes unsuitable for storing *operational data*, or data that is frequently accessed. Tapes are mostly used to back up operational data periodically.

3.1.1 Disks

Disks support direct access to a desired location, and are widely used for database applications. A DBMS provides seamless access to data on disk; applications need not worry about whether data is in main memory or disk. To understand how disks work, consider Figure 3.1, which shows the structure of a disk in simplified form.

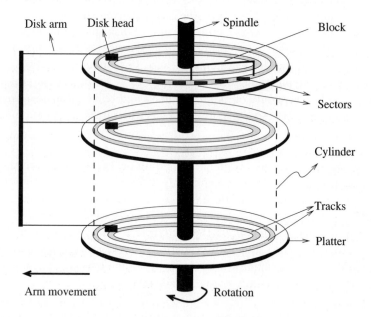

Figure 3.1   Structure of a Disk

Data is stored on disk in units called **disk blocks**. A disk block is a contiguous sequence of bytes and is the unit in which data is written to a disk and read from a disk. Blocks are arranged in concentric rings called **tracks**, on one or more **platters**. Tracks can be recorded on one or both surfaces of a platter; we refer to platters as single-sided or double-sided accordingly. The set of all tracks with the same diameter is called a **cylinder**, because the space occupied by these tracks is shaped like a cylinder; a cylinder contains one track per platter surface. Each track is divided into arcs called **sectors**, whose size is a characteristic of the disk and cannot be changed. The size of a disk block can be set when the disk is initialized as a multiple of the sector size.

An array of **disk heads**, one per platter, is moved as a unit; when one head is positioned over a block, the other heads are in identical positions with respect to their platters. To read or write a block, a disk head must be positioned on top of the block. Current systems typically allow at most one disk head to read or write at any one time.

It may come as a surprise that all the disk heads cannot read or write in parallel— after all, this technique would increase data transfer rates by a factor equal to the number of disk heads, and considerably speed up sequential scans. The reason is that it is very difficult to ensure that all the heads are perfectly aligned on the corresponding tracks. Current approaches are both expensive and more prone to faults as compared to disks with a single active head. In practice very few commercial products support this capability, and then only in a limited way; for example, two disk heads may be able to operate in parallel.

While direct access to any desired location in main memory takes approximately the same time, determining the time to access a location on disk is more complicated. The time to access a disk block has several components. **Seek time** is the time taken to move the disk heads to the track on which a desired block is located. **Rotational delay** is the waiting time for the desired block to rotate under the disk head; it is the time required for half a rotation on average and is usually less than seek time. **Transfer time** is the time to actually read or write the data in the block once the head is positioned, that is, the time for the disk to rotate over the block.

As an example, a Seagate Hawk 2XL is a 2.15GB disk with 5.55 msec average rotational delay. The average seek time is 9 msec. However, the time to seek from one track to the next is just 1 msec; the maximum seek time is 22 msec. There are 512 bytes per sector, 4569 cylinders, and four double-sided platters. The data transfer rate is about 5 MB/sec. A high-performance Barracuda drive can store nearly 9 GB of data, has a rotational delay of 4.1 msec, average seek time of about 8.5 msec, and a transfer rate of about 10 MB/sec. To put these numbers in perspective, observe that a disk access takes about 10 to 15 msecs, whereas accessing a main memory location typically takes less than 5 $\mu secs$!

3.1.2 Performance Implications of Disk Structure

Consider that:

1. Data must be in memory for the DBMS to operate on it.

2. The unit for data transfer between disk and main memory is a block; if a single item on a block is needed, the entire block is transferred. Reading or writing a disk block is called an **I/O** (for input/output) operation.

3. The time to read or write a block varies, depending on the location of the data:

$$access\ time\ =\ seek\ time\ +\ rotational\ delay\ +\ transfer\ time$$

These observations imply that the time taken for database operations is affected significantly by how data is stored on disks. The time for moving blocks to or from disk usually dominates the time taken for database operations. To minimize this time, it is necessary to locate data records strategically on disk, because of the geometry and mechanics of disks. In essence, if two records are frequently used together, we should place them close together. The 'closest' that two records can be on a disk is to be on the same block. In decreasing order of closeness, they could be on the same track, the same cylinder, or an adjacent cylinder.

To elaborate further, two records on the same block are obviously as close together as possible, because they are read or written as part of the same block. As the platter spins, other blocks on the track being read or written rotate under the active head. In current disk designs, all the data on a track can be read or written in one revolution. After a track is read or written, another disk head becomes active, and another track in the same cylinder is read or written. This process continues until all tracks in the current cylinder are read or written, and then the arm assembly moves (in or out) to an adjacent cylinder. Thus we have a natural notion of 'closeness' for blocks, which we can extend to a notion of *next* and *previous* blocks.

Exploiting this notion of next by arranging records so that they are read or written sequentially is very important for reducing the time spent in disk I/Os. Sequential access minimizes seek time and rotational delay and is much faster than random access. (This observation is reinforced and elaborated in Exercises 3.5 and 3.6, and the reader is urged to work through them.)

3.2 DISK SPACE MANAGEMENT

The lowest level of software in the DBMS architecture discussed in Section 1.6, called the **disk space manager**, manages space on disk. Abstractly, the disk space manager supports the concept of a page as a unit of data, and provides commands to allocate or deallocate a page and read or write a page. The size of a page is chosen to be the size of a disk block and pages are stored as disk blocks so that reading or writing a page can be done in one disk I/O.

It is often useful to allocate a sequence of pages as a *contiguous* sequence of blocks to hold data that is frequently accessed in sequential order. This capability is essential for exploiting the advantages of sequentially accessing disk blocks, which we discussed earlier in this chapter. Such a capability, if desired, must be provided by the disk space manager to higher-level layers of the DBMS.

Thus the disk space manager hides details of the underlying hardware (and possibly the operating system) and allows higher levels of the software to think of the data as a collection of pages.

3.2.1 Keeping Track of Free Blocks

A database grows and shrinks as records are inserted and deleted over time. The disk space manager keeps track of which disk blocks are in use, in addition to keeping track of which pages are on which disk blocks. Although it is likely that blocks are initially allocated sequentially on disk, subsequent allocations and deallocations could in general create 'holes.'

One way to keep track of block usage is to maintain a list of free blocks. As blocks are deallocated (by the higher-level software that requests and uses these blocks), we can add them to the free list for future use. A pointer to the first block on the free block list is stored in a known location on disk.

A second way is to maintain a bitmap with one bit for each disk block, which indicates whether a block is in use or not. A bitmap also allows very fast identification and allocation of contiguous areas on disk. This is difficult to accomplish with a linked list approach.

3.2.2 Using OS File Systems to Manage Disk Space

Operating systems also manage space on disk. Typically, an operating system supports the abstraction of a *file as a sequence of bytes*. The OS manages space on the disk and translates requests such as "Read byte i of file f" into corresponding low-level instructions: "Read block m of track t of cylinder c of disk d." A database disk space manager could be built using OS files. For example, the entire database could reside in one or more OS files for which a number of blocks are allocated (by the OS) and initialized. The disk space manager is then responsible for managing the space in these OS files.

Many database systems do not rely on the OS file system, and instead do their own disk management, either from scratch or by extending OS facilities. The reasons are practical as well as technical. One practical reason is that a DBMS vendor who wishes to support several OS platforms cannot assume features specific to any OS, for portability, and would therefore try to make the DBMS code as self-contained as possible. A technical reason is that on a 32-bit system, the largest file size is 4 GB, whereas a DBMS may want to access a single file larger than that. A related problem is that typical OS files cannot span disk devices, which is often desirable or even necessary in a DBMS. Additional technical reasons why a DBMS does not rely on the OS file system are outlined in Section 3.3.2.

3.3 BUFFER MANAGER

To understand the role of the buffer manager, consider a simple example. Suppose that the database contains 1,000,000 pages, but only 1000 pages of main memory are available for holding data. Consider a query that requires a scan of the entire file. Because all the data cannot be brought into main memory at one time, the DBMS must bring pages into main memory as they are needed, and in the process, decide what existing page in main memory to replace to make space for the new page.

In terms of the DBMS architecture presented in Section 1.6, the **buffer manager** is the software layer that is responsible for bringing pages from disk to main memory as needed. The buffer manager manages the available main memory by partitioning it into a collection of pages, which we collectively refer to as the **buffer pool**. The main memory pages in the buffer pool are called **frames**; it is convenient to think of them as slots that can hold a page (that usually resides on disk or other secondary storage media).

Higher levels of the DBMS code can be written without worrying about whether data pages are in memory or not; they ask the buffer manager for the page, and it is brought into a frame in the buffer pool if it is not already there. Of course, the higher-level code that requests a page must also release the page when it is no longer needed, by informing the buffer manager, so that the frame containing the page can be reused. The higher-level code must also inform the buffer manager if it modifies the requested page; the buffer manager then makes sure that the change is propagated to the copy of the page on disk. Buffer management is illustrated in Figure 3.2.

In addition to the buffer pool itself, the buffer manager maintains some book-keeping information, and two variables for each frame in the pool: *pin_count* and *dirty*. The number of times that the page currently in a given frame has been requested but not released, that is, the number of current users of the page, is recorded in the *pin_count* variable for that frame. The boolean variable *dirty* indicates whether the page has been modified since it was brought into the buffer pool from disk.

Initially, the *pin_count* for every frame is set to 0, and the *dirty* bits are turned off. When a page is requested the buffer manager does the following:

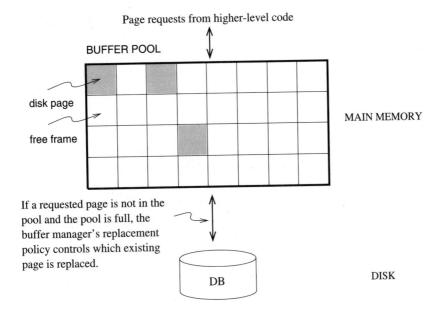

Figure 3.2   The Buffer Pool

1. Checks the buffer pool to see if it contains the requested page. If the page is not in the pool, the buffer manager brings it in as follows:

    (a) Chooses a frame for replacement, using the replacement policy.

    (b) If the *dirty* bit for the replacement frame is on, writes the page it contains to disk (that is, the disk copy of the page is overwritten with the contents of the frame).

    (c) Reads the requested page into the replacement frame.

2. Increments the *pin_count* of the frame containing the requested page, and returns its (main memory) address to the requestor.

Incrementing *pin_count* is often called **pinning** the requested page in its frame. When the code that calls the buffer manager and requests the page subsequently calls the buffer manager and releases the page, the *pin_count* of the frame containing the requested page is decremented. This is called **unpinning** the page. If the requestor has modified the page, it also informs the buffer manager of this at the time that it releases the page, and the *dirty* bit for the frame is set. The buffer manager will not read another page into a frame until its *pin_count* becomes 0, that is, until all requestors of the page have released it.

If a requested page is not in the buffer pool, and if a free frame is not available in the buffer pool, a frame with *pin_count* 0 is chosen for replacement. If there are many such frames, a frame is chosen according to the buffer manager's **replacement policy**. We discuss various replacement policies in Section 3.3.1.

When a page is eventually chosen for replacement, if the *dirty* bit is not set, it means that the page has not been modified since being brought into main memory. Thus there is no need to write the page back to disk; the copy on disk is identical to the copy in the frame, and it can simply be overwritten by the newly requested page. Otherwise, the modifications to the page must be propagated to the copy on disk. (The crash recovery protocol may impose further restrictions, as we saw in Section 1.5. For example, in the Write-Ahead Log (WAL) protocol, special log records are used to describe the changes made to a page. The log records pertaining to the page that is to be replaced may well be in the buffer; if so, the protocol requires that they be written to disk *before* the page is written to disk.)

If there is no page in the buffer pool with *pin_count* 0 and a page that is not in the pool is requested, the buffer manager must wait until some page is released before responding to the page request. In practice, the transaction requesting the page may simply be killed in this situation! So pages should be released—by the code that calls the buffer manager to request the page—as soon as possible.

A good question to ask at this point is "What if a page is requested by several different transactions?" That is, what if the page is requested by programs executing independently on behalf of different users? There is the potential for such programs to make conflicting changes to the page. The locking protocol (enforced by higher-level DBMS code, in particular the transaction manager) ensures that each transaction obtains a shared or exclusive lock before requesting a page to read or modify. Two different transactions cannot hold an exclusive lock on the same page at the same time; this is how conflicting changes are prevented. The buffer manager simply assumes that the appropriate lock has been obtained before a page is requested.

3.3.1   Buffer Replacement Policies

The policy that is used to choose an unpinned page for replacement can affect the time taken for database operations considerably. Many alternative policies exist, and each is suitable in different situations.

The best-known replacement policy is **least recently used** (LRU). This can be implemented in the buffer manager using a queue of pointers to frames with *pin_count* 0. A frame is added to the end of the queue when it becomes a candidate for replacement (that is, when the *pin_count* goes to 0). The page chosen for replacement is the one in the frame at the head of the queue.

A variant of LRU, called **clock** replacement, has similar behavior but less overhead. The idea is to choose a page for replacement using a *current* variable that takes on values 1 through N, where N is the number of buffer frames, in circular order. We can think of the frames being arranged in a circle, like a clock's face, and *current* as a clock hand moving across the face. In order to approximate LRU behavior, each frame also has an associated *referenced* bit, which is turned on when the page *pin_count* goes to 0.

The *current* frame is considered for replacement. If the frame is not chosen for replacement, *current* is incremented and the next frame is considered; this process is repeated until some frame is chosen. If the *current* frame has *pin_count* greater than 0, then it is not a candidate for replacement and *current* is incremented. If the *current* frame has the *referenced* bit turned on, the clock algorithm turns the *referenced* bit off and increments *current*—this way, a recently referenced page is less likely to be replaced. If the *current* frame has *pin_count* 0 and its *referenced* bit is off, then the page in it is chosen for replacement. If all frames are pinned in some sweep of the clock hand (that is, the value of *current* is incremented until it repeats), this means that no page in the buffer pool is a replacement candidate.

The LRU and clock policies are not always the best replacement strategies for a database system, particularly if many user requests require sequential scans of the data. Consider the following illustrative situation. Suppose that the buffer pool has 10 frames, and the file to be scanned has 10 or fewer pages. Assuming, for simplicity, that there are no competing requests for pages, only the first scan of the file does any I/O. Page requests in subsequent scans will always find the desired page in the buffer pool. On the other hand, suppose that the file to be scanned has 11 pages (which is one more than the number of available pages in the buffer pool). Using LRU, every scan of the file will result in reading every page of the file! In this situation, called **sequential flooding**, LRU is the *worst* possible replacement strategy.

Other replacement policies include **first in first out** (FIFO) and **most recently used** (MRU), which also entail overhead similar to LRU, and **random**, among others. The details of these policies should be evident from their names and the preceding discussion of LRU and clock.

Typically, the DBMS maintains a single shared buffer pool for all users. Most systems use a variant of clock or LRU, with some (usually ad hoc) modifications designed to address the problem of sequential flooding. Some systems (e.g., IBM's DB2/MVS) support sophisticated techniques in which the buffer pool is partitioned and different policies are used in different partitions. (The DBA has to make these decisions.) The drawback of such schemes is that they can lead to poor utilization of buffer space, in addition to being more complex.

3.3.2   Buffer Management in DBMS versus OS

Obvious similarities exist between virtual memory in operating systems and buffer management in database management systems. In both cases the goal is to provide access to more data than will fit in main memory, and the basic idea is to bring in pages from disk to main memory as needed, replacing pages that are no longer needed in main memory. Why can't we build a DBMS using the virtual memory capability of an OS? A DBMS can often predict the order in which pages will be accessed, or **page reference patterns**, much more accurately than is typical in an OS environment, and it is desirable to utilize this property. Further, a DBMS needs more control over when a page is written to disk than an OS typically provides.

A DBMS can often predict reference patterns because most page references are generated by higher-level operations (such as sequential scans or particular implementations of various relational algebra operators) with a known pattern of page accesses. This ability to predict reference patterns allows for a better choice of pages to replace, and makes the idea of specialized buffer replacement policies more attractive in the DBMS environment.

Even more important, being able to predict reference patterns enables the use of a simple and very effective strategy called **prefetching of pages**. The buffer manager can anticipate the next several page requests and fetch the corresponding pages into memory *before* the pages are requested. This strategy has two benefits. First, the pages are available in the buffer pool when they are requested. Second, reading in a contiguous block of pages is much faster than reading the same pages at different times in response to distinct requests. (Review the discussion of disk geometry to appreciate why this is so.) If the pages to be prefetched are not contiguous, recognizing that several pages need to be fetched can nonetheless lead to faster I/O because an order of retrieval can be chosen for these pages that minimizes seek times and rotational delays.

Incidentally, note that the I/O can typically be done concurrently with CPU computation. Once the prefetch request is issued to the disk, the disk is responsible for reading the requested pages into memory pages and the CPU can continue to do other work.

A DBMS also requires the ability to explicitly *force* a page to disk, that is, to ensure that the copy of the page on disk is updated with the copy in memory. As a related point, a DBMS must be able to ensure that certain pages in the buffer pool are written to disk *before* certain other pages are written, in order to implement the WAL protocol for crash recovery, as we saw in Section 1.5. Virtual memory implementations in operating systems cannot be relied upon to provide such control over when pages are written to disk; the OS command to write a page to disk may implemented by essentially recording the write request, and deferring the actual modification of the disk copy. If the system crashes in the interim, the effects can be catastrophic for a DBMS. (Crash recovery is discussed further in Chapter 18.)

3.4 RECORD FORMATS *

We[1] now turn our attention from the way pages are stored on disk and brought into main memory to the information stored within a page. The page abstraction is appropriate when dealing with I/O issues, but higher levels of the DBMS see data as a collection of records. In this section we discuss how to organize the fields of a record, and in Section 3.5 we consider how records can be organized on a page. While choosing a way to organize the fields of a record, we must take into account whether the fields of the record are of fixed or variable length, and consider the cost of various operations on the record, including retrieval and modification of fields.

Before discussing record formats, we note that in addition to storing individual records, information that is common to all records of a given record type (such as the number of fields and field types) is stored in the **system catalog**, which can be thought of as a description of the contents of a database, maintained by the DBMS (Section 3.7). This avoids repeated storage of the same information with each record of a given type.

3.4.1 Fixed-Length Records

In a fixed-length record, each field has a fixed length (that is, the value in this field is of the same length in all records), and the number of fields is also fixed. The fields of such a record can be stored consecutively, and given the address of the record, the address of a particular field can be calculated using information about the lengths of preceding fields, which is available in the system catalog. This record organization is illustrated in Figure 3.3.

---

[1] We remind the reader that omitting asterisked sections leaves approximately enough material in Chapters 1 through 17 for a typical one-semester course. No additional significance should be read into the asterisks.

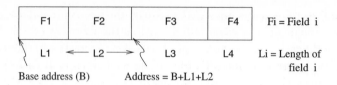

Figure 3.3   Organization of Records with Fixed-Length Fields

3.4.2   Variable-Length Records

In the relational model, every record in a relation contains the same number of fields. If the number of fields is fixed, a record is of variable length only because some of its fields are of variable length.

One possible organization is to store fields consecutively, separated by delimiters (which are special characters that do not appear in the data itself). This organization requires a scan of the record in order to locate a desired field.

An alternative is to reserve some space at the beginning of a record for use as an array of integer offsets—the ith integer in this array is the starting address of the ith field value relative to the start of the record. Note that we also store an offset to the end of the record; this offset is needed to recognize where the last field ends. Both alternatives are illustrated in Figure 3.4.

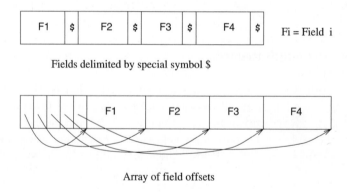

Figure 3.4   Alternative Record Organizations for Variable-Length Fields

The second approach is typically superior. For the overhead of the offset array, we get direct access to any field. We also get a clean way to deal with **null** values. A *null* value is a special value used to denote that the value for a field is unavailable or inapplicable. If a field contains a *null* value, the pointer to the end of the field is set to be the same as the pointer to the beginning of the field. That is, no space is used for representing the *null* value, and a comparison of the pointers to the beginning and the end of the field is used to determine that the value in the field is *null*.

Variable-length record formats can obviously be used to store fixed-length records as well; sometimes, the extra overhead is justified by the added flexibility, because issues such as supporting *null* values and adding fields to a record type arise with fixed-length records as well.

Having variable-length fields in a record can raise some subtle issues, especially when a record is modified.

- Modifying a field may cause it to grow, which requires us to shift all subsequent fields to make space for the modification in all three record formats presented above.

- A record that is modified may no longer fit into the space remaining on its page. If so, it may have to be moved to another page. If rids, which are used to 'point' to a record, include the page number (see Section 3.5), moving a record to another page causes a problem. We may have to leave a 'forwarding address' on this page identifying the new location of the record. And to ensure that space is always available for this forwarding address, we would have to allocate some minimum space for each record, regardless of its length.

- A record may grow so large that it no longer fits on *any* one page. We have to deal with this condition by breaking a record into smaller records. The smaller records could be chained together—part of each smaller record is a pointer to the next record in the chain—to enable retrieval of the entire original record.

3.5 PAGE FORMATS *

In this section, we consider how a collection of records can be arranged on a page. We can think of a page as a collection of **slots**, each of which contains a record. A record is identified by using the pair ⟨*page id, slot number*⟩. This identifier is called a **record id** (or **rid**), and serves as a 'pointer' to a record. (We remark that an alternative way to identify records is to assign each record a unique integer as its rid, and to maintain a table of that lists the page and slot of the corresponding record for each rid. Due to the overhead of maintaining this table, the approach of using ⟨*page id, slot number*⟩ as an rid is more common.)

We now consider some alternative approaches to managing slots on a page. The main considerations are how these approaches support operations such as searching, inserting or deleting records on a page.

3.5.1   Fixed-Length Records

If all records on the page are guaranteed to be of the same length, record slots are uniform and can be arranged consecutively within a page. At any instant, some slots are occupied by records, and others are unoccupied. When a record is inserted into the page, we must locate an empty slot and place the record there. The main issues are how we keep track of empty slots, and how we locate all records on a page. The alternatives hinge on how we handle the deletion of a record.

The first alternative is to store records in the first N slots (where N is the number of records on the page); whenever a record is deleted, we move the last record on the page into the vacated slot. This format allows us to locate the ith record on a page by a simple offset calculation, and all empty slots appear together at the end of the page. However, this approach does not work if there are external references to the record that is moved (because the rid contains the slot number, which is now changed).

The second alternative is to handle deletions by using an array of bits, one per slot, to keep track of free slot information. Locating records on the page requires scanning the bit array to find slots whose bit is on; when a record is deleted, its bit is turned off. The two alternatives for storing fixed-length records are illustrated in Figure 3.5. Note that in addition to the information about records on the page, a page usually contains additional file-level information (e.g., the id of the next page in the file). The figure does not show this additional information.

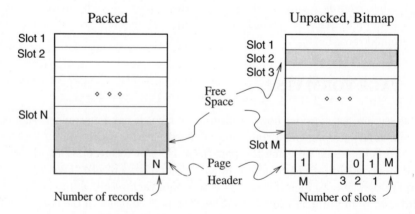

Figure 3.5   Alternative Page Organizations for Fixed-Length Records

The *slotted page* organization described for variable-length records in Section 3.5.2 can also be used for fixed-length records. It becomes attractive if we need to move records around on a page for reasons other than keeping track of space freed by deletions. A typical example is that we want to keep the records on a page sorted (according to the value in some field).

3.5.2   Variable-Length Records

If records are of variable length, then we cannot divide the page into a fixed collection of slots. The problem is that when a new record is to be inserted, we have to find an empty slot of 'just the right length'—if we use a slot that is too big, we waste space, and obviously we cannot use a slot that is smaller than the record length. Therefore, when a record is inserted, we must allocate just the right amount of space for it, and when a record is deleted, we must move records to fill the hole created by the deletion, in order to ensure that all the free space on the page is contiguous. Thus the ability to move records on a page becomes very important.

The most flexible organization for variable-length records is to maintain a **directory of slots** for each page, with a ⟨*record offset, record length*⟩ pair per slot. The first component (*record offset*) is a 'pointer' to the record, as shown in Figure 3.6; it is the offset in bytes from the start of the data area on the page to the start of the record. Deletion is readily accomplished by setting the record offset to -1. Records can be moved around on the page because the rid, which is the page number and slot number (that is, position in the directory), does not change when the record is moved; only the record offset stored in the slot changes.

The space available for new records must be managed carefully because the page is not preformatted into slots. One way to manage free space is to maintain a pointer (that is, offset from the start of the data area on the page) that indicates the start of the free space area. When a new record is too large to fit into the remaining free space, we have to move records on the page to reclaim the space freed by records that have been deleted earlier. The idea is to ensure that after reorganization, all records appear contiguously, followed by the available free space.

A subtle point to be noted is that the slot for a deleted record cannot always be removed from the slot directory, because slot numbers are used to identify records—by deleting a slot, we change (decrement) the slot number of subsequent slots in the slot directory, and thereby change the rid of records pointed to by subsequent slots. The only way to remove slots from the slot directory is to remove the last slot if the record that it points to is deleted. However, when a record is inserted, the slot directory should be scanned for an element that currently does not point to any record, and this slot should be used for the new record. A new slot is added to the slot directory only if all existing slots point to records. If inserts are much more common than deletes (as is typically the case), the number

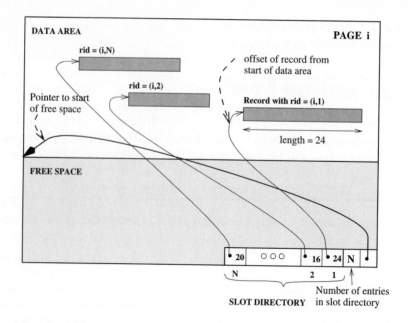

Figure 3.6   Page Organization for Variable-Length Records

of entries in the slot directory is likely to be very close to the actual number of records on the page.

This organization is also useful for fixed-length records if we need to move them around frequently; for example, when we want to maintain them in some sorted order. Indeed, when all records are the same length, instead of storing this common length information in the slot for each record, we can store it once in the system catalog.

In some special situations (e.g., the internal pages of a B+ tree, which we discuss in Chapter 5), we may not care about changing the rid of a record. In this case the slot directory can be compacted after every record deletion; this strategy guarantees that the number of entries in the slot directory is the same as the number of records on the page. If we do not care about modifying rids, we can also sort records on a page in an efficient manner by simply moving slot entries rather than actual records, which are likely to be much larger than slot entries.

A simple variation on the slotted organization is to maintain only record offsets in the slots. For variable-length records, the length is then stored with the record (say, in the first bytes). This variation makes the slot directory structure for pages with fixed-length records be the same as for pages with variable-length records.

3.6   FILES AND INDEXES

We have seen how pages can be stored on disk and brought into main memory as needed, and how the space on a page can be organized to store a collection of records. Higher levels of the DBMS code treat a page as effectively being a collection of records, ignoring the representation and storage details. In fact, the concept of a collection of records is not limited to the contents of a single page; a **file of records** is a collection of records that may reside on several pages. In this section, we consider how a collection of pages can be organized as a file.

The basic file structure that we consider stores records in random order, and supports retrieval of all records or retrieval of a particular record specified by its rid. Sometimes, we want to retrieve records by specifying some condition on the fields of desired records, for example, "Find all employee records with *age* 35." To speed up such selections, we can build auxiliary data structures that allow us to quickly find the rids of employee records that satisfy the given selection condition. Such an auxiliary structure is called an index; we introduce indexes in Section 3.6.2.

3.6.1   Heap Files *

The simplest file structure is an unordered file or **heap file**. The data in the pages of a heap file is not ordered in any way, and the only guarantee is that one can retrieve all records in the file by repeated requests for the next record. Every record in the file has a unique rid, and every page in a file is of the same size.

Supported operations on a heap file include *create* and *destroy* files, *insert* a record, *delete* a record with a given rid, *get* a record with a given rid, and *scan* all records in the file. To get or delete a record with a given rid, note that we must be able to find the id of the page containing the record, given the id of the record.

We must keep track of the pages in each heap file in order to support scans, and we must keep track of pages that contain free space in order to implement insertion efficiently. We discuss two alternative ways to maintain this information. In each of these alternatives, pages must hold two pointers (which are page ids) for file-level book-keeping in addition to the data.

Linked List of Pages

One possibility is to maintain a heap file as a doubly linked list of pages. The DBMS can remember where the first page is located by maintaining a table of

⟨*heap_file_name*, *page_1_addr*⟩ pairs in a known location on disk. We call the first page of the file the *header page*.

An important task is to maintain information about empty slots created by deleting a record from the heap file. This task has two distinct parts: how to keep track of free space within a page and how to keep track of pages that have some free space. We considered the first part in Section 3.5. The second part can be addressed by maintaining a doubly linked list of pages with free space, and a doubly linked list of full pages; together, these lists contain *all* pages in the heap file. This organization is illustrated in Figure 3.7; note that each pointer is really a page id.

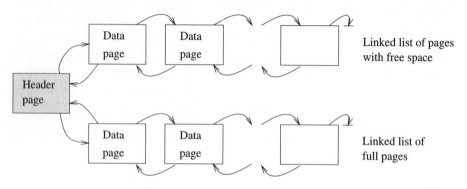

Figure 3.7   Heap File Organization with a Linked List

If a new page is required, it is obtained by making a request to the disk space manager and then added to the list of pages in the file (probably as a page with free space, because it is unlikely that the new record will take up all the space on the page). If a page is to be deleted from the heap file, it is removed from the list and the disk space manager is told to deallocate it. (Note that the scheme can easily be generalized to allocate or deallocate a sequence of several pages and maintain a doubly linked list of these page sequences.)

One disadvantage of this scheme is that virtually all pages in a file will be on the free list if records are of variable length, because it is likely that every page has at least a few free bytes. To insert a typical record, we must retrieve and examine several pages on the free list before we find one with enough free space. The directory-based heap file organization that we discuss next addresses this problem.

Directory of Pages

An alternative to a linked list of pages is to maintain a **directory of pages**. The DBMS must remember where the first directory page of each heap file is located. The directory is itself a collection of pages and is shown as a linked list in Figure 3.8. (Other organizations are possible for the directory itself, of course.)

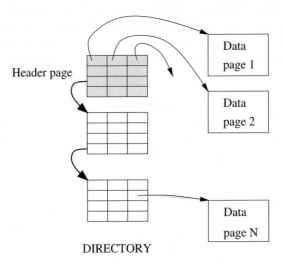

Figure 3.8   Heap File Organization with a Directory

Each directory entry identifies a page (or a sequence of pages) in the heap file. As the heap file grows or shrinks, the number of entries in the directory—and possibly the number of pages in the directory itself—grows or shrinks correspondingly. Note that since each directory entry is quite small in comparison to a typical page, the size of the directory is likely to be very small in comparison to the size of the heap file.

Free space can be managed by maintaining a bit per entry, indicating whether the corresponding page has any free space, or a count per entry, indicating the amount of free space on the page. If the file contains variable-length records, we can examine the free space count for an entry to determine if the record will fit on the page pointed to by the entry. Since several entries fit on a directory page, we can efficiently search for a data page with enough space to hold a record that is to be inserted.

3.6.2   Introduction to Indexes

Sometimes, we want to find all records that have a given value in a particular field. If we can find the rids of all such records, the heap file organization allows us to retrieve the records by specifying their rids; however, it does not help us to find the rids of such records. An **index** is an auxiliary data structure that is intended to help us find rids of records that meet a selection condition.

Consider how you locate a desired book in a library. You can search a collection of index cards, sorted on author name or book title, to find the call number for the book. Because books are stored according to call numbers, the call number enables you to walk to the shelf that contains the book you need. Observe that an index on author name cannot be used to locate a book by title, and vice versa; each index speeds up certain kinds of searches, but not all. This is illustrated in Figure 3.9.

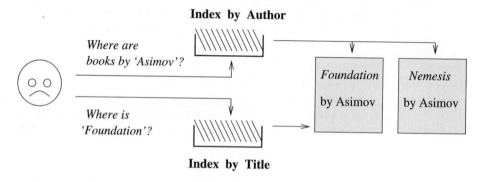

Figure 3.9   Indexes in a Library

The same ideas apply when we want to support efficient retrieval of a desired subset of the data in a file. From an implementation standpoint, an index is just another kind of file, containing records that direct traffic on requests for data records. Every index has an associated **search key**, which is a collection of one or more fields of the file of records for which we are building the index; any subset of the fields can be a search key. We sometimes refer to the file of records as the **indexed file**.

An index is designed to speed up equality or range selections on the search key. For example, if we wanted to build an index to improve the efficiency of queries about employees of a given age, we could build an index on the *age* attribute of the employee dataset. The records stored in an index file, which we refer to as **entries** to avoid confusion with data records, allow us to find data records with a given search key value. In our example the index might contain ⟨*age, rid*⟩ pairs, where *rid* identifies a data record.

The pages in the index file are organized in some way that allows us to quickly locate those entries in the index that have a given search key value. For example, we have to find entries with *age* ≥ 30 (and then follow the rids in the retrieved entries) in order to find employee records for employees who are older than 30. Organization techniques, or data structures, for index files are called **access methods**, and several are known, including B+ trees (Chapter 5) and hash-based structures (Chapter 6). B+ tree index files and hash-based index files are built using the page allocation and manipulation facilities provided by the disk space manager, just like heap files.

3.7   SYSTEM CATALOGS IN A RELATIONAL DBMS

In Chapter 2, we presented the relational data model, and in earlier sections of this chapter, we discussed the structure and implementation of files. In a relational DBMS, every relation is stored in a file. Each tuple is stored as a record in the file; the correspondence between tuples and records is straightforward.

We can store a relation using one of several alternative file structures, which we discuss in subsequent chapters, and we can create one or more indexes on each relation. Every relation or index is ultimately stored as a file of some kind; conversely, in a relational DBMS, every file contains either the tuples in a relation or the entries in an index. The collection of files corresponding to users' relations and indexes represents the *data* in the database.

A fundamental property of a database system is that it maintains a description of all the data that it contains. A relational DBMS maintains information about every relation and index that it contains. The DBMS also maintains information about views, for which no tuples are stored explicitly; rather, a definition of the view is stored and used to compute the tuples that belong in the view when the view is queried. This information is stored in a collection of relations, maintained by the system, called the **catalog relations**; an example of a catalog relation is shown in Figure 3.10. They are also called the **system catalog**, or *catalog* or the **data dictionary**. The system catalog is sometimes referred to as **metadata**; that is, not data, but descriptive information about the data.

Let us consider what is stored in the system catalog. At a minimum we have system-wide information, such as the size of the buffer pool and the page size, and the following information about individual relations, indexes and views:

- For each relation:
  - Its *relation name*, the *file name* (or some identifier), and the *file structure* (e.g., heap file) of the file in which it is stored.
  - The *attribute name* and *type* of each of its attributes.
  - The *index name* of each index on the relation.

- The *integrity constraints* (e.g., primary key and foreign key constraints) on the relation.

■ For each index:

- The *index name* and the *structure* (e.g., B+ tree) of the index.
- The *search key* attributes.

■ For each view:

- Its *view name* and *definition*.

In addition, there is usually information such as the number of tuples in a relation and the number of distinct search key values and the high-key and low-key values for an index. Such information is used by the query optimizer (Chapter 13). The catalogs also contain information about *users*, such as accounting information and *authorization* information (e.g., Joe User can modify the Enrolled relation, but only read the Faculty relation).

A very elegant aspect of a relational DBMS is that the system catalog is itself a collection of relations. For example, we might store information about the attributes of relations in a catalog relation called Attribute_Cat:

Attribute_Cat(*attr_name:* string, *rel_name:* string,
              type: string, *position:* integer)

Suppose that the database contains two relations:

Students(*sid:* string, *name:* string, *login:* string,
         age: integer, *gpa:* real)
Faculty(*fid:* string, *fname:* string, *sal:* real)

Figure 3.10 shows the tuples in the Attribute_Cat relation that describe the attributes of these two relations. Notice that in addition to the tuples describing Students and Faculty, other tuples (the first four listed) describe the four attributes of the Attribute_Cat relation itself! These other tuples illustrate an important point: the catalog relations describe all the relations in the database, *including* the catalog relations themselves. When information about a relation is needed, it is obtained from the system catalog. Of course, at the implementation level, whenever the DBMS needs to find the schema of a *catalog* relation, the code that retrieves this information must be handled specially. (Otherwise, this code would have to retrieve this information from the catalog relations without, presumably, knowing the schema of the catalog relations!)

The fact that the system catalog is also a collection of relations is very useful. For example, catalog relations can be queried just like any other relation, using

attr_name	rel_name	type	position
attr_name	Attribute_cat	string	1
rel_name	Attribute_cat	string	2
type	Attribute_cat	string	3
position	Attribute_cat	integer	4
sid	Students	string	1
name	Students	string	2
login	Students	string	3
age	Students	integer	4
gpa	Students	real	5
fid	Faculty	string	1
fname	Faculty	string	2
sal	Faculty	real	3

Figure 3.10   An Instance of the Attribute_Cat Relation

the query language of the DBMS! Further, all the techniques available for implementing and managing relations apply directly to catalog relations. The choice of catalog relations and their schemas is not unique and is made by the implementor of the DBMS. Real systems vary in their catalog schema design, but the catalog is always implemented as a collection of relations, and it essentially describes all the data stored in the database.[2]

3.8 SUMMARY

Disks provide inexpensive, nonvolatile storage with random access to pages. The time to access a page depends on its location on disk. The access time has three components: the time to move the disk arm to the desired track (*seek time*), the time to wait for the desired block to rotate under the disk head (*rotational delay*) and the time to transfer the data (*transfer time*). Careful placement of pages on the disk to exploit the geometry of a disk can minimize the seek time and rotational delay when pages are read sequentially.

The buffer manager brings pages into a main memory buffer pool from disk as needed. A requested page is kept in the buffer pool until it is released (unpinned) by all requestors. Subsequently, a page is written back to disk (if it has been

---

[2]Some systems may store additional information in a non-relational form. For example, a sytem with a sophisticated query optimizer may maintain histograms or other statistical information about the distribution of values in certain attributes of a relation. We can think of such information, when it is maintained, as a supplement to the catalog relations.

modified while in the buffer pool) when the frame containing it is chosen for replacement. The choice of frame to replace is based on the buffer manager's page replacement policy. A DBMS buffer manager can often predict the access pattern for disk pages; for example, because of relational operations that repeatedly scan a file. It takes advantage of such opportunities by issuing requests to the disk to *prefetch* several pages at a time. This technique minimizes disk arm movement and reduces I/O time.

Although operating systems provide disk space management and buffer management, a DBMS often reimplements these services because several features required by a DBMS are frequently unavailable. Such features include the ability to force a page to disk, to control the order in which buffer pages are written to disk, control over prefetching and replacement policies, and management of very large files that span disks. Even when a given OS provides some of these features, a DBMS may rely on its own implementation for reasons of portability.

Database pages are organized into files, and higher-level DBMS code views the data as a *collection of records*. Of the alternative formats available for storing a record, an organization with a directory of field offsets offers direct access to fields (which can be important if records are long and contain many fields) and support for *null* values. Of the alternative formats for storing pages, an organization with slotted pages allows records to be moved around on a page without altering the rid, which is a ⟨page id, slot number⟩ pair. This organization facilitates free space management on a page, especially with variable-length records, and makes it easy to sort records on a page.

The DBMS file layer keeps track of the pages in a file, and supports the abstraction of a collection of records. It keeps track of pages with free space by using linked lists or a page directory. Indexes can be constructed to support efficient retrieval of records based on the values in some fields.

The system catalog maintains global information (e.g., buffer pool size), and information about each relation, index and view. The information includes field names and types, statistics, authorizations, and so on. Essentially, all information that is common to a collection of records is stored in the catalog. In a relational DBMS, the catalog is itself stored as a collection of relations, and can be queried, for example, just like any other relations.

EXERCISES

Exercise 3.1 What is the most important difference between a disk and a tape?

Exercise 3.2 Explain the terms *seek time, rotational delay* and *transfer time.*

Exercise 3.3 Both disks and main memory support direct access to any desired location (page). On average, main memory accesses are faster, of course. What is the other important difference (from the perspective of the time required to access a desired page)?

Exercise 3.4 If you have a large file that is frequently scanned sequentially, explain how you would store the pages in the file on a disk.

Exercise 3.5 Consider a disk with a sector size of 512 bytes, 2000 tracks per surface, 50 sectors per track, 5 double-sided platters, average seek time of 10 msec.

1. What is the capacity of a track in bytes? What is the capacity of each surface? What is the capacity of the disk?

2. How many cylinders does the disk have?

3. Give examples of valid block sizes. Is 256 bytes a valid block size? 2048? 51,200?

4. If the disk platters rotate at 5400 rpm (revolutions per minute), what is the maximum rotational delay?

5. Assuming that one track of data can be transferred per revolution, what is the transfer rate?

Exercise 3.6 Consider again the disk specifications from Exercise 3.5 and suppose that a block size of 1024 bytes is chosen. Suppose that a file containing 100,000 records of 100 bytes each is to be stored on such a disk and that no record is allowed to span two blocks.

1. How many records fit onto a block?

2. How many blocks are required to store the entire file? If the file is arranged sequentially on disk, how many surfaces are needed?

3. How many records of 100 bytes each can be stored using this disk?

4. If pages are stored sequentially on disk, with page 1 on block 1 of track 1, what is the page stored on block 1 of track 1 on the next disk surface? How would your answer change if the disk were capable of reading/writing from all heads in parallel?

5. What is the time required to read a file containing 100,000 records of 100 bytes each sequentially? Again, how would your answer change if the disk were capable of reading/writing from all heads in parallel (and the data was arranged optimally)?

6. What is the time required to read a file containing 100,000 records of 100 bytes each in some random order? Note that in order to read a record, the block containing the record has to be fetched from disk. Assume that each block request incurs the average seek time and rotational delay.

Exercise 3.7 Explain what the buffer manager must do to process a read request for a page. What happens if the requested page is in the pool but not pinned?

Exercise 3.8 When does a buffer manager write a page to disk?

Exercise 3.9 What does it mean to say that a page is *pinned* in the buffer pool? Who is responsible for pinning pages? Who is responsible for unpinning pages?

Exercise 3.10 When a page in the buffer pool is modified, how does the DBMS ensure that this change is propagated to disk? (Explain the role of the buffer manager as well as the modifier of the page.)

Exercise 3.11 What happens if there is a page request when all pages in the buffer pool are dirty?

Exercise 3.12 What is *sequential flooding* of the buffer pool?

Exercise 3.13 Name an important capability of a DBMS buffer manager that is not supported by a typical operating system's buffer manager.

Exercise 3.14 Explain the term *prefetching*. Why is it important?

Exercise 3.15 Modern disks often have their own main memory caches, typically about 1MB, and use this to do prefetching of pages. The rationale for this technique is the empirical observation that if a disk page is requested by some (not necessarily database!) application, 80% of the time, the next page is requested as well. So the disk gambles by reading ahead.

1. Give a nontechnical reason that a DBMS may not want to rely on prefetching controlled by the disk.

2. Explain the impact on the disk's cache of several queries running concurrently, each scanning a different file.

3. Can the above problem be addressed by the DBMS buffer manager doing its own prefetching? Explain.

4. Modern disks support *segmented caches*, with about 4 to 6 segments, each of which is used to cache pages from a different file. Does this technique help, with respect to the above problem? Given this technique, does it matter whether the DBMS buffer manager also does prefetching?

Exercise 3.16 Describe two possible record formats. What are the trade-offs between them?

Exercise 3.17 Describe two possible page formats. What are the trade-offs between them?

Exercise 3.18 Consider the page format for variable-length records that uses a slot directory.

1. One approach to managing the slot directory is to use a maximum size (i.e., a maximum number of slots) and to allocate the directory array when the page is created. Discuss the pros and cons of this approach with respect to the approach discussed in the text.

2. Suggest a modification to this page format that would allow us to sort records (according to the value in some field) without moving records and without changing the record ids.

Exercise 3.19 Consider the two internal organizations for heap files (using lists of pages and a directory of pages) discussed in the text.

1. Describe them briefly and explain the trade-offs. Which organization would you choose if records are variable in length?

2. Can you suggest a single page format to implement both internal file organizations?

Exercise 3.20 Consider a list-based organization of the pages in a heap file in which two lists are maintained: a list of *all* pages in the file and a list of all pages with free space. In contrast, the list-based organization discussed in the text maintains a list of full pages and a list of pages with free space.

1. What are the trade-offs, if any? Is one of them clearly superior?

2. For each of these organizations, describe a page format that can be used to implement it.

Exercise 3.21 Modern disk drives store more sectors on the outer tracks than the inner tracks. Since the rotation speed is constant, the sequential data transfer rate is also higher on the outer tracks. The seek time and rotational delay are unchanged. Considering this information, explain good strategies for placing files with the following kinds of access patterns:

1. Frequent, random accesses to a small file (e.g., catalog relations).

2. Sequential scans of a large file (e.g., selection from a relation with no index).

3. Random accesses to a large file via an index (e.g., selection from a relation via the index).

4. Sequential scans of a small file.

PROJECT-BASED EXERCISES

Exercise 3.22 Study the public interfaces for the disk space manager, the buffer manager and the heap file layer in Minibase.

1. Are heap files with variable-length records supported?

2. What page format is used in Minibase heap files?

3. What happens if you insert a record whose length is greater than the page size?

4. How is free space handled in Minibase?

5. *Note to Instructors: See Appendix A for additional project-based exercises.*

BIBLIOGRAPHIC NOTES

Salzberg [467] and Wiederhold [570] discuss secondary storage devices and file organizations in detail. [424] proposes the use of a collection of small disks, called RAID (for Redundant Array of Inexpensive Disks).

The design and implementation of storage managers is discussed in [49, 97, 336, 526, 159]. With the exception of [159], these systems emphasize *extensibility*, and the papers contain much of interest from that standpoint as well. Other papers that cover storage management issues in the context of significant implemented prototype systems are [338] and [425]. The Dali storage manager, which is optimized for main memory databases, is described in [278]. Three techniques for implementing long fields are compared in [74].

Stonebraker discusses operating systems issues in the context of databases in [523]. Several buffer management policies for database systems are compared in [130]. Buffer management is also studied in [87, 123, 190, 171].

4

FILE ORGANIZATIONS AND INDEXES

If you don't find it in the index, look very carefully through the entire catalog.

—Sears, Roebuck, and Co., Consumers' Guide, 1897

A **file organization** is a way of arranging the records in a file when the file is stored on disk. A file of records is likely to be accessed and modified in a variety of ways, and different ways of arranging the records enable different operations over the file to be carried out efficiently. For example, if we want to retrieve employee records in alphabetical order, sorting the file by name is a good file organization. On the other hand, if we want to retrieve all employees whose salary is in a given range, sorting employee records by name is not a good file organization. A DBMS supports several file organization techniques, and an important task of a DBA is to choose a good organization for each file, based on its expected pattern of use.

We begin this chapter with a discussion of the cost model that we use in this book, in Section 4.1. In Section 4.2, we present a simplified analysis of three basic file organizations: *files of randomly ordered records* (i.e., heap files), *files sorted on some field*, and *files that are hashed on some fields*. Our objective is to emphasize the importance of choosing an appropriate file organization.

Each file organization makes certain operations efficient, but often we are interested in supporting more than one operation. For example, sorting a file of employee records on the *name* field makes it easy to retrieve employees in alphabetical order, but we may also want to retrieve all employees who are 55 years old; for this, we would have to scan the entire file. To deal with such situations, a DBMS builds an index, as we described in Section 3.6.2. An index on a file is designed to speed up operations that are not efficiently supported by the basic organization of records in that file. Later chapters cover several specific index data structures; in this chapter we focus on properties of indexes that do not depend on the specific index data structure used.

Section 4.3 introduces indexing as a general technique that can speed up retrieval of records with given values in the search field. Section 4.4 discusses some important properties of indexes, and Section 4.5 discusses DBMS commands to create an index.

4.1 COST MODEL

In this section we introduce a cost model that allows us to estimate the cost (in terms of execution time) of different database operations. We will use the following notation and assumptions in our analysis. There are B data pages with R records per page. The average time to read or write a disk page is D, and the average time to process a record (e.g., to compare a field value to a selection constant) is C. In the hashed file organization, we will use a function, called a *hash function*, to map a record into a range of numbers; the time required to apply the hash function to a record is H.

Typical values today are $D = 25$ milliseconds, C and $H = 1$ to 10 microseconds; we therefore expect the cost of I/O to dominate. This conclusion is supported by current hardware trends, in which CPU speeds are steadily rising, whereas disk speeds are not increasing at a similar pace. On the other hand, one should keep in mind that as main memory sizes increase, a much larger fraction of the needed pages are likely to fit in memory, leading to fewer I/O requests.

We therefore use the number of disk page I/Os as our cost metric in this book.

- We emphasize that real systems must consider other aspects of cost, such as CPU costs (and transmission costs in a distributed database). However, our goal is primarily to present the underlying algorithms and to illustrate how costs can be estimated. Therefore, for simplicity, we have chosen to concentrate on only the I/O component of cost. Given the fact that I/O is often (even typically) the dominant component of the cost of database operations, considering I/O costs gives us a good first approximation to the true costs.

- Even with our decision to focus on I/O costs, an accurate model would be too complex for our purposes of conveying the essential ideas in a simple way. We have therefore chosen to use a simplistic model in which we just count the number of pages that are read from or written to disk as a measure of I/O. We have ignored the important issue of **blocked access**—typically, disk systems allow us to read a block of contiguous pages in a single I/O request. The cost is equal to the time required to **seek** the first page in the block and to **transfer** all pages in the block. Such blocked access can be much cheaper than issuing one I/O request per page in the block, especially if these requests do not follow consecutively: We would have an additional seek cost for each page in the block.

This discussion of the cost metric we have chosen must be kept in mind when we discuss the cost of various algorithms in this chapter and in later chapters. We discuss the implications of the cost model whenever our simplifying assumptions are likely to affect the conclusions drawn from our analysis in an important way.

4.2 COMPARISON OF THREE FILE ORGANIZATIONS

We now compare the costs of some simple operations for three basic file organizations: *files of randomly ordered records, or heap files; files sorted on some field;* and *files that are hashed on some field.* Our goal is to emphasize how important the choice of an appropriate file organization can be. The operations that we consider are described below.

- **Scan:** Fetch all records in the file. The pages in the file must be fetched from disk into the buffer pool. There is also a CPU overhead per record for locating the record on the page (in the pool).

- **Search with Equality Selection:** Fetch all records that satisfy an equality selection, for example, "Find the Students record for the student with *sid* 23." Pages that contain qualifying records must be fetched from disk, and qualifying records must be located within retrieved pages.

- **Search with Range Selection:** Fetch all records that satisfy a range selection, for example, "Find all Students records with *name* alphabetically after 'Smith'."

- **Insert:** Insert a given record into the file. We must identify the page in the file into which the new record must be inserted, fetch that page from disk, modify it to include the new record, and then write back the modified page. Depending on the file organization, we may have to fetch, modify and write back other pages as well.

- **Delete:** Delete a record that is specified using its rid. We must identify the page that contains the record, fetch it from disk, modify it, and write it back. Depending on the file organization, we may have to fetch, modify and write back other pages as well.

4.2.1 Heap Files

Scan: The cost is $B(D + RC)$ because we must retrieve each of B pages taking time D per page, and for each page, process R records taking time C per record.

Search with Equality Selection: Suppose that we know in advance that exactly one record matches the desired equality selection, that is, the selection is specified on a candidate key. On average, we must scan half the file, assuming that the record exists and the distribution of values in the search field is uniform. For each retrieved data page (except possibly the last one retrieved), we must check all records on the page to see if it is the desired record. The cost is $0.5B(D+RC)$. If there is no record that satisfies the selection, however, we must scan the entire file to verify this.

If the selection is not on a candidate key field (e.g., "Find students aged 18"), we always have to scan the entire file because several records with $age = 18$ could be dispersed all over the file, and we have no idea how many such records exist.

Search with Range Selection: The entire file must be scanned because qualifying records could appear anywhere in the file, and we do not know how many qualifying records exist. The cost is $B(D + RC)$.

Insert: We assume that records are always inserted at the end of the file. We must fetch the last page in the file, add the record, and write the page back. The cost is $2D + C$.

Delete: We must find the record, remove the record from the page, and write the modified page back. We assume that no attempt is made to compact the file to reclaim the free space created by deletions, for simplicity.[1] The cost is the cost of searching plus $C + D$.

We assume that the record to be deleted is specified using the record id. Since the page id can easily be obtained from the record id, we can directly read in the page. The cost of searching is therefore D.

We remark that if the record to be deleted is specified using an equality or range condition on some fields, the cost of searching is given in our discussion of equality and range selections. The cost of deletion is also affected by the number of qualifying records, since all pages containing such records must be modified.

4.2.2   Sorted Files

Scan: The cost is $B(D + RC)$ because all pages must be examined. Note that this case is no better or worse than the case of unordered files. However, the order in which records are retrieved corresponds to the sort order.

Search with Equality Selection: We assume that the equality selection is specified on the field by which the file is sorted; if not, the cost is identical to that for a heap file. We can locate the first page containing the desired record or records, should any qualifying records exist, with a binary search in $log_2 B$ steps. Each step requires a disk I/O and two comparisons. Once the page is known, the first qualifying record can again be located by a binary search of the page at a

---

[1] In practice, a directory or other data structure is used to keep track of free space, and records are inserted into the first available free slot, as discussed in Chapter 3. This increases the cost of insertion and deletion a little, but not enough to affect our comparison of heap files, sorted files and hashed files.

cost of $Clog_2 R$. The cost is therefore $Dlog_2 B + Clog_2 R$, which is a significant improvement over searching heap files.

If there are several qualifying records (e.g., "Find all students aged 18"), they are guaranteed to be adjacent to each other due to the sorting on *age*, and so the cost of retrieving all such records is the cost of locating the first such record ($Dlog_2 B + Clog_2 R$) plus the cost of reading all the qualifying records in sequential order. Typically, all qualifying records fit on a single page. Observe that if there are no qualifying records, this is established by the search for the first qualifying record, which finds the page that would have contained a qualifying record, had one existed, and searches that page.

Search with Range Selection: Again assuming that the range selection is on the sort field, the first record that satisfies the selection is located as it is for search with equality. Subsequently, data pages are sequentially retrieved until a record is found that does not satisfy the range selection; this is similar to an equality search with many qualifying records.

The cost is the cost of search plus the cost of retrieving the set of records that satisfy the search. The cost of the search includes the cost of fetching the first page containing qualifying, or matching, records. For small range selections, all qualifying records appear on this page. For larger range selections, we have to fetch additional pages containing matching records.

Insert: To insert a record while preserving the sort order, we must first find the correct position in the file, add the record, and then fetch and rewrite all subsequent pages (because all the old records will be shifted by one slot, assuming that the file has no empty slots). On average, we can assume that the inserted record belongs in the middle of the file. Thus we must read the latter half of the file and then write it back after adding the new record. The cost is therefore the cost of searching to find the position of the new record plus $2 * (0.5B(D + RC))$, that is, search cost plus $B(D + RC)$.

Delete: We must search for the record, remove the record from the page, and write the modified page back. We must also read and write all subsequent pages because all records that follow the deleted record must be moved up to compact the free space.[2] The cost is therefore the same as for an insert, that is, search cost plus $B(D + RC)$. Given the rid of the record to delete, we can fetch the page containing the record directly.

---

[2] Unlike a heap file, there is no inexpensive way to manage free space, so we account for the cost of compacting a file when a record is deleted.

We remark that if records to be deleted are specified by an equality or range condition, the cost of deletion depends on the number of qualifying records. If the condition is specified on the sort field, qualifying records are guaranteed to be contiguous due to the sorting, and the first qualifying record can be located using binary search.

4.2.3 Hashed Files

We now describe a simple hashed file organization. A hashed file has an associated **search key**, which is a combination of one or more fields of the file. It enables us to locate records with a given search key value quickly, for example, "Find the Students record for Joe," if the file is hashed on the *name* field. Note that the search key for an index can be any combination of one or more fields; it need not uniquely identify records.

We note that there is an unfortunate overloading of the term *key* in the database literature. A *primary key* or *candidate key* (fields that uniquely identify a record; see Chapter 2) is unrelated to the concept of a search key.

The pages in a hashed file are grouped into **buckets**. The bucket to which a record belongs can be determined by applying a special function called a **hash function**, to the search field(s). On inserts, a record is inserted into the appropriate bucket, with additional 'overflow' pages allocated for the bucket if necessary; the overflow pages for each bucket are maintained in a linked list. To search for a record with a given search key value, we simply apply the hash function to identify the bucket to which such records belong, and look at all pages in that bucket. This organization is called a **static hashed file**; its main drawback is that long chains of overflow pages can develop. This can affect performance because all pages in a bucket have to be searched. Dynamic hash structures that address this problem are known, and we discuss them in Chapter 6; for the analysis in this chapter, we will simply assume that there are no overflow pages.

Scan: In a hashed file, pages are kept at about 80% occupancy (in order to leave some space for future insertions and minimize overflow pages as the file expands). This is achieved by adding a new page to a bucket when each existing page is 80% full, when records are initially organized into a hashed file structure. Thus the number of pages, and therefore the cost of scanning all the data pages, is about 1.25 times the cost of scanning an unordered file, that is, $1.25B(D + RC)$.

Search with Equality Selection: This operation is supported very efficiently if the selection is on the search key for the hashed file. (Otherwise, the entire file must be scanned.) The cost of identifying the page that contains qualifying records is H; assuming that this bucket consists of just one page (i.e., no overflow pages), retrieving it costs D. The cost is $H + D + 0.5RC$ if we assume that we find the record after scanning half the records on the page. This is even lower than the cost for sorted files. If there are several qualifying records, or none, we still have to retrieve just one page, but we must scan the entire page.

Note that the hash function associated with a hashed file maps a record to a bucket based on the values in *all* the search key fields; if the value for any one of these fields is not specified, we cannot tell which bucket the record belongs to. Thus if the selection is not an equality condition on all the search key fields, we have to scan the entire file.

Search with Range Selection: The hash structure offers no help at all; even if the range selection is on the search key, the entire file must be scanned. The cost is $1.25B(D + RC)$.

Insert: The appropriate page must be located, modified and then written back. The cost is thus the cost of search plus $C + D$.   *what happened to H?*

Delete: We must search for the record, remove it from the page, and write the modified page back. The cost is again the cost of search plus $C + D$ (for writing the modified page).

We remark that if records to be deleted are specified using an equality condition on the search key, all qualifying records are guaranteed to be in the same bucket, which can be identified by applying the hash function.

4.2.4 Choosing a File Organization

Figure 4.1 compares I/O costs for the three file organizations.

File Type	Scan	Equality Search	Range Search	Insert	Delete
Heap	BD	$0.5BD$	BD	$2D$	$Search + D$
Sorted	BD	$Dlog_2 B$	$Dlog_2 B + \#$ matches	$Search + BD$	$Search + BD$
Hashed	$1.25BD$	D	$1.25BD$	$2D$	$Search + D$

Figure 4.1   A Comparison of I/O Costs

A heap file has good storage efficiency, and supports fast scan, insertion, and deletion of records. However, it is slow for searches.

A sorted file also offers good storage efficiency, but insertion and deletion of records is slow. It is quite fast for searches, and in particular, it is the best structure for range selections. It is worth noting that in a real DBMS, a file is almost never kept fully sorted. A structure called a B+ tree, which we will discuss in Chapter 5, offers all the advantages of a sorted file *and* supports inserts and deletes efficiently. (There is a space overhead for these benefits, relative to a sorted file, but the trade-off is well worth it.)

Files are sometimes kept 'almost sorted' in that they are originally sorted, with some free space left on each page to accommodate future insertions, but once this space is used up, overflow pages are used to handle insertions. The cost of insertion and deletion is similar to a heap file, but the degree of sorting deteriorates as the file grows.

A hashed file does not utilize space quite as well as a sorted file, but insertions and deletions are fast, and equality selections are very fast. However, the structure offers no support for range selections, and full file scans are a little slower; the lower space utilization means that files contain more pages.

In summary, Figure 4.1 demonstrates that no one file organization is uniformly superior in all situations. An unordered file is best if only full file scans are desired. A hashed file is best if the most common operation is an equality selection. A sorted file is best if range selections are desired. The organizations that we have studied here can be improved on—the problems of overflow pages in static hashing can be overcome by using dynamic hashing structures, and the high cost of inserts and deletes in a sorted file can be overcome by using tree-structured indexes—but the main observation, that the choice of an appropriate file organization depends on how the file is commmonly used, remains valid.

4.3   OVERVIEW OF INDEXES

As we noted earlier, an index on a file is an auxiliary structure designed to speed up operations that are not efficiently supported by the basic organization of records in that file.

An index can be viewed as a collection of **data entries**, with an efficient way to locate all data entries with search key value k. Each such data entry, which we denote as $k*$, contains enough information to enable us to retrieve (one or more) data records with search key value k. Figure 4.2 shows an index with search key *sal* that contains ⟨*sal, rid*⟩ pairs as data entries. The *rid* component of a data entry in this index is a pointer to a record with search key value *sal*.

Two important questions to consider are:

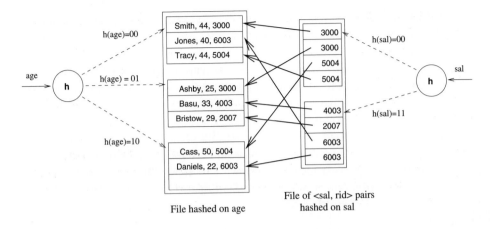

Figure 4.2 File Hashed on *age*, with Index on *sal*

- How are data entries organized in order to support efficient retrieval of data entries with a given search key value?

- Exactly what is stored as a data entry?

One way to organize data entries is to hash data entries on the search key. In this approach, we essentially treat the collection of data entries as a file of records, hashed on the search key. This is how the index on *sal* shown in Figure 4.2 is organized. The hash function *h* for this example is quite simple; it converts the search key value to its binary representation and uses the two least significant bits as the bucket identifier. Another way to organize data entries is to build a data structure that directs a search for data entries. Several index data structures are known that allow us to efficiently find data entries with a given search key value. We will study tree-based index structures in Chapter 5, and hash-based index structures in Chapter 6.

We consider what is stored in a data entry in the following section.

4.3.1 Alternatives for Data Entries in an Index

A data entry $k*$ allows us to retrieve one or more data records with key value k. We need to consider three main alternatives:

1. A data entry $k*$ is an actual data record (with search key value k).

2. A data entry is a $\langle k, rid \rangle$ pair, where rid is the record id of a data record with search key value k.

3. A data entry is a $\langle k, \textit{rid-list} \rangle$ pair, where *rid-list* is a list of record ids of data records with search key value k.

Observe that if an index uses Alternative (1), there is no need to store the data records separately, in addition to the contents of the index. We can think of such an index as a special file organization that can be used instead of a sorted file or a heap file organization. Figure 4.2 illustrates Alternatives (1) and (2). The file of employee records is hashed on *age*; we can think of this as an index structure in which a hash function is applied to the *age* value to locate the bucket for a record and Alternative (1) is used for data entries. The index on *sal* also uses hashing to locate data entries, which are now $\langle sal, \textit{rid of employee record} \rangle$ pairs; that is, Alternative (2) is used for data entries.

Alternatives (2) and (3), which contain data entries that point to data records, are independent of the file organization that is used for the indexed file (i.e., the file that contains the data records). Alternative (3) offers better space utilization than Alternative (2), but data entries are variable in length, depending on the number of data records with a given search key value.

If we want to build more than one index on a collection of data records, for example, we want to build indexes on both the *age* and the *sal* fields as illustrated in Figure 4.2, at most one of the indexes should use Alternative (1) because we want to avoid storing data records multiple times.

We note that different index data structures used to speed up searches for data entries with a given search key can be combined with any of the three alternatives for data entries.

4.4 PROPERTIES OF INDEXES

In this section, we discuss some important properties of an index that affect the efficiency of searches using the index.

4.4.1 Clustered versus Unclustered Indexes

When a file is organized so that the ordering of data records is the same as or close to the ordering of data entries in some index, we say that the index is **clustered**. An index that uses Alternative (1) is clustered, by definition. An index that uses Alternative (2) or Alternative (3) can be a clustered index only if the data records are sorted on the search key field. Otherwise, the order of the data records is random, defined purely by their physical order, and there is no reasonable way to arrange the data entries in the index in the same order. (Indexes based on hashing do not store data entries in sorted order by search key, and therefore a hash index is clustered only if it uses Alternative (1).)

Indexes that maintain data entries in sorted order by search key use a collection of *index entries*, organized into a tree structure, to guide searches for data entries, which are stored at the leaf level of the tree in sorted order. Clustered and unclustered tree indexes are illustrated in Figures 4.3 and 4.4; we discuss tree-structured indexes further in Chapter 5. For simplicity, in Figure 4.3 we assume that the underlying file of data records is fully sorted.

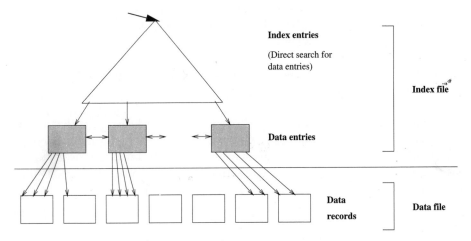

Figure 4.3 Clustered Tree Index Using Alternative (2)

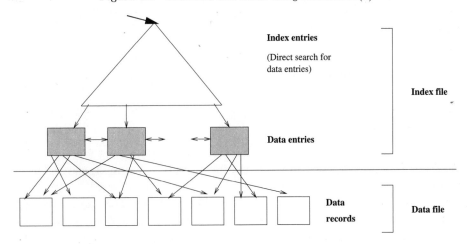

Figure 4.4 Unclustered Tree Index Using Alternative (2)

In practice, data records are rarely maintained in fully sorted order, unless data records are stored in an index using Alternative (1), because of the high overhead of moving data records around to preserve the sort order as records are inserted and deleted. Typically, the records are sorted initially and each page is left with some free space to absorb future insertions. If the free space on a page is subsequently used up (by records inserted after the initial sorting step), further insertions to this page are handled using a linked list of overflow pages. Thus after a while, the order of records only approximates the intended sorted order, and the file must be **reorganized** (i.e., sorted afresh) to ensure good performance.

Thus clustered indexes are relatively expensive to maintain when the file is updated. Another reason why clustered indexes are expensive to maintain is that data entries may have to be moved across pages, and if records are identified by a combination of page id and slot, as is often the case, all places in the database that point to a moved record (typically, entries in other indexes for the same collection of records) must also be updated to point to the new location; these additional updates can be very time-consuming.

A data file can be clustered on at most one search key, which means that we can have at most one clustered index on a data file. An index that is not clustered is called an **unclustered** index; we can have several unclustered indexes on a data file. Suppose that Students records are sorted by *age*; an index on *age* that stores data entries in sorted order by *age* is a clustered index. If in addition we have an index on the *gpa* field, the latter must be an unclustered index.

The cost of using an index to answer a range search query can vary tremendously based on whether the index is clustered. If the index is clustered, the rids in qualifying data entries point to a contiguous collection of records, as Figure 4.3 illustrates, and we need to retrieve only a few data pages. If the index is unclustered, each qualifying data entry could contain a rid that points to a distinct data page, leading to as many data page I/Os as the number of data entries that match the range selection! This point is discussed further in Chapters 7 and 16.

4.4.2   Dense versus Sparse Indexes

An index is said to be **dense** if it contains (at least) one data entry for every search key value that appears in a record in the indexed file.[3] A **non dense** or **sparse** index contains one entry for each page of records in the data file. Alternative (1) for data entries always leads to a dense index. Alternative (2) can be used to build either dense or sparse indexes. Alternative (3) is typically only used to build a dense index.

---

[3] We say 'at least' because several data entries could have the same search key value if there are duplicates and we use Alternative (2).

We illustrate sparse and dense indexes in Figure 4.5. A data file of records with three fields (*name, age* and *sal*) is shown with two simple indexes on it, both of which use Alternative (2) for data entry format. The first index is a sparse, clustered index on *name*. Notice how the order of data entries in the index corresponds to the order of records in the data file. There is one data entry per page of data records. The second index is a dense, unclustered index on the *age* field. Notice that the order of data entries in the index differs from the order of data records. There is one data entry in the index per record in the data file (because we use Alternative (1)).

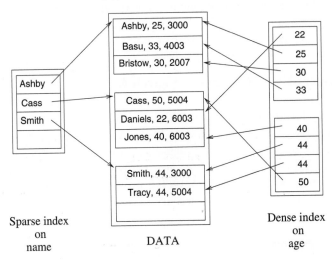

Figure 4.5   Sparse versus Dense Indexes

We cannot build a sparse index that is not clustered. Thus we can have at most one sparse index. A sparse index is typically much smaller than a dense index. On the other hand, some very useful optimization techniques rely on an index being dense (Chapter 16).

A data file is said to be **inverted** on a field if there is a dense secondary index on this field. A **fully inverted** file is one in which there is a dense secondary index on each field that does not appear in the primary key.[4]

4.4.3   Primary and Secondary Indexes

An index on a set of fields that includes the *primary key* is called a **primary index**. An index that is not a primary index is called a **secondary** index. (The

---

[4]This terminology arises from the observation that these index structures allow us to take the value in a non key field and get the values in key fields, which is the inverse of the more intuitive case in which we use the values of the key fields to locate the record.

terms *primary index* and *secondary index* are sometimes used with a different meaning: An index that uses Alternative (1) is called a primary index, and one that uses Alternatives (2) or (3) is called a secondary index. We will be consistent with the definitions presented earlier, but the reader should be aware of this lack of standard terminology in the literature.)

Two data entries are said to be **duplicates** if they have the same value for the search key field associated with the index. A primary index is of course guaranteed not to contain duplicates, but an index on other (collections of) fields can contain duplicates. Thus in general, a secondary index contains duplicates. If we know that no duplicates exist, that is, we know that the search key contains some candidate key, we call the index a **unique** index.

4.4.4   Indexes Using Composite Search Keys

The search key for an index can contain several fields; such keys are called **composite search keys** or **concatenated keys**. As an example, consider a collection of employee records, with fields *name, age,* and *sal*, stored in sorted order by *name*. Figure 4.6 illustrates the difference between a composite index with key ⟨*age, sal*⟩, a composite index with key ⟨*sal, age*⟩, an index with key *age* and an index with key *sal*. All indexes shown in the figure use Alternative (2) for data entries.

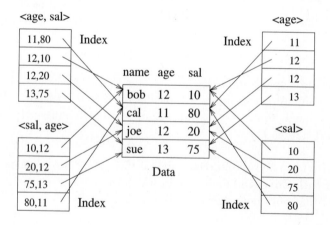

Figure 4.6   Composite Key Indexes

If the search key is composite, an **equality query** is one in which *each* field in the search key is bound to a constant. For example, we can ask to retrieve all data entries with *age* = 20 and *sal* = 10. The hashed file organization supports only equality queries, since a hash function identifies the bucket containing desired records only if a value is specified for each field in the search key.

A **range query** is one in which not all fields in the search key are bound to constants. For example, we can ask to retrieve all data entries with $age = 20$; this query implies that any value is acceptable for the *sal* field. As another example of a range query, we can ask to retrieve all data entries with $age < 30$ and $sal > 40$.

4.5 INDEX SPECIFICATION IN SQL-92

The SQL-92 standard does *not* include any statement for creating or dropping index structures. In fact, the standard does not even require SQL implementations to support indexes! In practice, of course, every commercial relational DBMS supports one or more kinds of indexes. The following command to create a B+ tree index—we discuss B+ tree indexes in Chapter 5—is illustrative:

```
CREATE INDEX IndAgeRating ON Students
      WITH  STRUCTURE = BTREE,
            KEY = (age, gpa)
```

This specifies that a B+ tree index is to be created on the Students table using the concatenation of the *age* and *gpa* columns as the key. Thus key values are pairs of the form $\langle age, gpa \rangle$, and there is a distinct entry for each such pair. Once the index is created, it is automatically maintained by the DBMS adding/removing entries in response to inserts/deletes on Students.

4.6 SUMMARY

Various file and index organizations have their own advantages and disadvantages. The choice of appropriate structures for a given dataset can have a significant impact on performance. If equality and range searches are frequent, sorting the file or building an index is important. An *index* is a collection of data entries with support for efficiently retrieving data entries that have a given search key value. Data entries can be actual data records, $\langle$*search-key, rid*$\rangle$ pairs, or $\langle$*search-key, rid-list*$\rangle$ pairs. Each of these alternatives can be combined with any index data structures. A given file of data records can have several indexes, each with a different search key.

Hash-based indexes are good only for equality selections; they are useful for implementing relational operations in which equality selections are used extensively. Sorted files and tree-based indexes are best for range selections, and they are also good for equality selections.

Indexes can be classified as clustered versus unclustered, primary versus secondary, and dense versus sparse. The differences have important performance implications. These variations, like the alternative formats for data entries, are independent of the index data structure used to locate data entries.

EXERCISES

Exercise 4.1 What are the main conclusions that you can draw from the discussion of the three file organizations?

Exercise 4.2 Consider a delete specified using an equality condition. What is the cost if no record qualifies? What is the cost if the condition is not on a key?

Exercise 4.3 Which of the three basic file organizations would you choose for a file where the most frequent operations are as follows?

1. Search for records based on a range of field values.

2. Perform inserts and scans where the order of records does not matter.

3. Search for a record based on a particular field value.

Exercise 4.4 Explain the difference between each of the following:

1. Primary versus secondary indexes.

2. Dense versus sparse indexes.

3. Clustered versus unclustered indexes.

If you were about to create an index on a relation, what considerations would guide your choice with respect to each pair of properties listed above?

Exercise 4.5 Consider a relation stored as a randomly ordered file for which the only index is an unclustered index on a field called *sal*. If you want to retrieve all records with *sal* > 20, is using the index always the best alternative? Explain.

Exercise 4.6 If an index contains data records as 'data entries,' is it clustered or unclustered? Dense or sparse?

Exercise 4.7 Consider Alternatives (1), (2) and (3) for 'data entries' in an index, as discussed in Section 4.3.1. Are they all suitable for secondary indexes? Explain.

Exercise 4.8 Consider the following instance of the Students relation, sorted by *age*: For the purposes of this question, assume that these tuples are stored in a sorted file in the order shown; the first tuple is in page 1, slot 1; the second tuple is in page 1, slot 2; and so on Each page can store up to three data records. You can use ⟨*page-id, slot*⟩ to identify a tuple.

List the data entries in each of the following indexes. If the order of entries is significant, say so and explain why. If such an index cannot be constructed, say so and explain why.

sid	name	login	age	gpa
53831	Madayan	madayan@music	11	1.8
53832	Guldu	guldu@music	12	2.0
53666	Jones	jones@cs	18	3.4
53688	Smith	smith@ee	19	3.2
53650	Smith	smith@math	19	3.8

Figure 4.7 An Instance of the Students Relation, Sorted by *age*

1. A dense index on *age* using Alternative (1).

2. A dense index on *age* using Alternative (2).

3. A dense index on *age* using Alternative (3).

4. A sparse index on *age* using Alternative (1).

5. A sparse index on *age* using Alternative (2).

6. A sparse index on *age* using Alternative (3).

7. A dense index on *gpa* using Alternative (1).

8. A dense index on *gpa* using Alternative (2).

9. A dense index on *gpa* using Alternative (3).

10. A sparse index on *gpa* using Alternative (1).

11. A sparse index on *gpa* using Alternative (2).

12. A sparse index on *gpa* using Alternative (3).

PROJECT-BASED EXERCISES

Exercise 4.9 Answer the following questions:

1. What indexing techniques are supported in Minibase?

2. What alternatives for data entries are supported?

3. Are clustered indexes supported? Are sparse indexes supported?

BIBLIOGRAPHIC NOTES

Several books discuss file organizations in detail [23, 218, 309, 380, 467, 507, 569].

TREE-STRUCTURED INDEXING

I think that I shall never see
A billboard lovely as a tree.
Perhaps unless the billboards fall
I'll never see a tree at all.

—Ogden Nash, *Song of the Open Road*

We now consider two index data structures, called ISAM and B+ trees, based on tree organizations. These structures provide efficient support for range searches, including sorted file scans as a special case. Unlike sorted files, these index structures support efficient insertion and deletion. They also provide support for equality selections, although they are not as efficient in this case as hash-based indexes, which are discussed in Chapter 6.

An ISAM[1] tree is a static structure that is effective when the file is not frequently updated, but is unsuitable for files that grow and shrink a lot. We discuss ISAM in Section 5.1. The B+ tree is a dynamic structure that adjusts to changes in the file gracefully. It is the most widely used index structure because it adjusts well to changes and supports both equality and range queries. We introduce B+ trees in Section 5.2. We cover B+ trees in detail in the remaining sections. Section 5.3 describes the format of a tree node. Section 5.4 considers how to search for records by using a B+ tree index. Section 5.5 presents the algorithm for inserting records into a B+ tree, and Section 5.6 presents the deletion algorithm. Section 5.7 discusses how duplicates are handled. We conclude with a discussion of some practical issues concerning B+ trees in Section 5.8.

Notation: In the ISAM and B+ tree structures, leaf pages contain *data entries*, according to the terminology introduced in Chapter 4. For convenience, we will denote a data entry with search key value k as $k*$. Non leaf pages contain **index entries** of the form ⟨*search key value, page id*⟩, and are used to direct the search for a desired data entry (which is stored in some leaf). We will often simply use *entry* where the context makes the nature of the entry (index or data) clear.

---

[1] ISAM stands for Indexed Sequential Access Method.

5.1　INDEXED SEQUENTIAL ACCESS METHOD (ISAM) *

To understand the motivation for the ISAM technique, it is useful to begin with a simple sorted file. Consider a file of Students records sorted by *gpa*. To answer a range selection such as "Find all students with a gpa higher than 3.0," we must identify the first such student by doing a binary search of the file and then scan the file from that point on. If the file is large, the initial binary search can be quite expensive; can we improve upon this method?

One idea is to create a second file with one record per page in the original (data) file, of the form ⟨*first key on page, pointer to page*⟩, again sorted by the key attribute (which is *gpa* in our example). The format of a page in the second *index* file is illustrated in Figure 5.1.

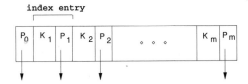

Figure 5.1　Format of an Index Page

We refer to pairs of the form ⟨*key, pointer*⟩ as *entries*. Notice that each index page contains one pointer more than the number of keys—each key serves as a *separator* for the contents of the pages pointed to by the pointers to its left and right. This structure is illustrated in Figure 5.2.

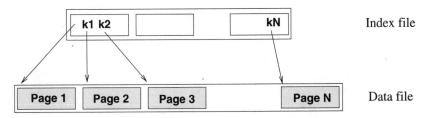

Figure 5.2　One-Level Index Structure

We can do a binary search of the index file to identify the page containing the first key (*gpa*) value that satisfies the range selection (in our example, the first student with *gpa* over 3.0), and follow the pointer to the page containing the first data record with that key value. We can then scan the data file sequentially to retrieve other qualifying records. This example uses the index to find the first data page containing a Students record with *gpa* greater than 3.0, and the data file is scanned from that point on to retrieve other such Students records.

Because the size of an entry in the index file (key value and page id) is likely to be much smaller than the size of a page, and only one such entry exists per page of the data file, the index file is likely to be much smaller than the data file; thus a binary search of the index file is much faster than a binary search of the data file. However, binary search of the index file could still be fairly expensive, and the index file is typically still large enough to make inserts and deletes expensive.

The potential large size of the index file motivates the ISAM idea: Why not apply the previous step of building an auxiliary file on the *index* file, and indeed, so on recursively until the final auxiliary file fits on one page? This repeated construction of a one-level index leads to a structure that is illustrated in Figure 5.3. In addition, some systems carefully organize the layout of pages so that page boundaries correspond closely to the physical characteristics of the underlying storage device. The ISAM structure is completely static (except for the overflow pages, of which it is hoped, there will be few) and therefore facilitates such low-level optimizations.

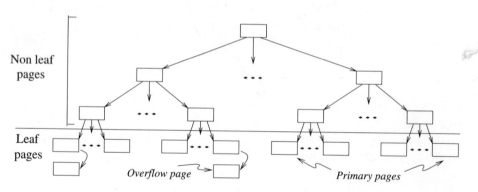

Figure 5.3   ISAM Index Structure

Each tree node is a disk page, and all the data resides in the leaf pages. This corresponds to an index that uses Alternative (1) for data entries, in terms of the alternatives described in Chapter 4; we can create an index with Alternative (2) by storing the data records in a separate file and storing ⟨*key, rid*⟩ pairs in the leaf pages of the ISAM index. When the file is created, all leaf pages are allocated sequentially and sorted on the search key value. (If Alternatives (2) or (3) are used, the data records are created and sorted before allocating the leaf pages of the ISAM index.) The non leaf level pages are then allocated. If there are several inserts to the file subsequently, so that more entries are inserted into a leaf than will fit onto a single page, additional pages are needed because the index structure is static. These additional pages are allocated from an overflow area. The allocation of pages is illustrated in Figure 5.4.

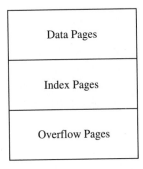

Figure 5.4   Page Allocation in ISAM

The basic operations of insertion, deletion and search are all quite straightforward. For an equality selection search, we start at the root node and determine which subtree to search by comparing the value in the search field of the given record with the key values in the node. (The search algorithm is identical to that for a B+ tree; we present this algorithm in more detail later.) For a range query, the starting point in the data (or leaf) level is determined similarly, and data pages are then retrieved sequentially. For inserts and deletes, the appropriate page is determined as for a search, and the record is inserted or deleted with overflow pages added if necessary.

The following example illustrates the ISAM index structure. Consider the tree shown in Figure 5.5. All searches begin at the root. For example, to locate a record with the key value 27, we start at the root and follow the left pointer, since 27 < 40. We then follow the middle pointer, since 20 <= 27 < 33. For a range search, we find the first qualifying data entry as for an equality selection and then retrieve primary leaf pages sequentially (also retrieving overflow pages as needed by following pointers from the primary pages). The primary leaf pages are assumed to be allocated sequentially—this assumption is reasonable because the number of such pages is known when the tree is created and does not change subsequently under inserts and deletes—and so no 'next leaf page' pointers are needed.

We assume that each leaf page can contain two entries. If we now insert a record with key value 23, the entry 23* belongs in the second data page, which already contains 20* and 27* and has no more space. We deal with this situation by adding an *overflow* page and putting 23* in the overflow page. Chains of overflow pages can easily develop. For instance, inserting 48*, 41* and 42* leads to an overflow chain of two pages. The tree of Figure 5.5 with all these insertions is shown in Figure 5.6.

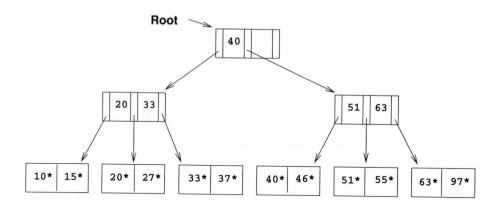

Figure 5.5   Sample ISAM Tree

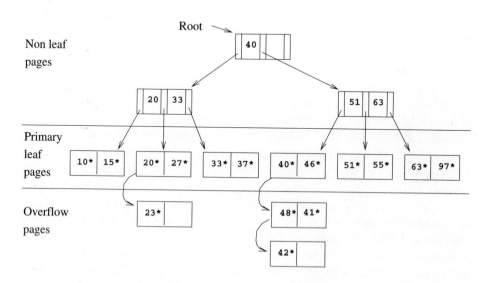

Figure 5.6   ISAM Tree after Inserts

The deletion of an entry $k*$ is handled by simply removing the entry. If this entry is on an overflow page and the overflow page becomes empty, the page can be removed. If the entry is on a primary page and deletion makes the primary page empty, the simplest approach is to simply leave the empty primary page as it is; it serves as a placeholder for possibly non empty overflow pages. Thus the number of primary leaf pages is fixed at file creation time. Notice that deleting entries could lead to a situation in which key values that appear in the index levels do not appear in the leaves! Since index levels are used only to direct a search to the correct leaf page, this situation is not a problem. The tree of Figure 5.6 is shown in Figure 5.7 after deletion of the entries 42*, 51* and 97*. Note that after deleting 51*, the key value 51 continues to appear in the index level. A subsequent search for 51* would go to the correct leaf page and determine that the entry is not in the tree.

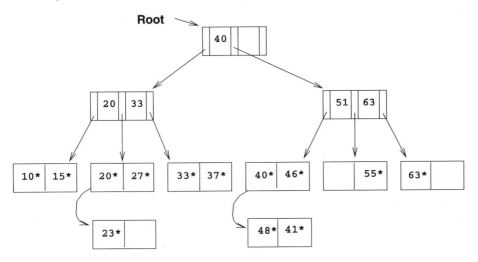

Figure 5.7   ISAM Tree after Deletes

The non leaf pages direct a searcher to the correct leaf page. The number of disk I/Os is equal to the number of levels of the tree and is $log_F N$, where N is the number of primary leaf pages and F (the *fan-out*) is the number of entries per index page. This number is considerably less than the number of disk I/Os for binary search, which is $log_2 N$; in fact, it is reduced further by pinning the root page in memory. The cost of access via a one-level index is $log_2(N/F)$. If we consider a file with 1,000,000 records, 10 records per leaf page, and 100 entries per index page, the cost (in page I/Os) of a file scan is 100,000, a binary search of the sorted data file is 17, a binary search of a one-level index is 10, and the ISAM file (assuming no overflow) is 3.

Note that once the ISAM file is created, inserts and deletes affect only the contents of leaf pages. A consequence of this design is that long overflow chains could develop if a number of inserts are made to the same leaf. These chains can significantly affect the time to retrieve a record because the overflow chain has to be searched as well when the search gets to this leaf. (Although data in the overflow chain can be kept sorted, it usually is not, in order to make inserts fast.) To alleviate this problem, the tree is initially created so that about 20% of each page is free. However, once the tree fills up, unless space is freed again through deletes, overflow chains can be eliminated only by a complete reorganization of the file.

The fact that only leaf pages are modified also has an important advantage with respect to concurrent access. When a page is accessed, it is typically 'locked' by the requestor to ensure that it is not concurrently modified by other users of the page. To modify a page, it must be locked in 'exclusive' mode, which is permitted only when no one else holds a lock on the page. Locking can lead to queues of users (*transactions*, to be more precise) waiting to get access to a page. Queues can be a significant performance bottleneck, especially for heavily accessed pages near the root of an index structure. In the ISAM structure, since we know that index-level pages are never modified, we can safely omit the locking step. Not locking index-level pages is an important advantage of ISAM over a dynamic structure like a B+ tree. If the data distribution and size is relatively static, which means overflow chains are rare, ISAM might be preferable to B+ trees due to this advantage.

5.2   B+ TREES: A DYNAMIC INDEX STRUCTURE

A static structure such as the ISAM index suffers from the problem that long overflow chains can develop as the file grows, leading to poor performance. This problem motivated the development of more flexible, dynamic structures that adjust gracefully to inserts and deletes. The **B+ tree** search structure, which is widely used in practice, is a balanced tree in which the internal nodes direct the search and the leaf nodes contain the data entries. Since the tree structure grows and shrinks dynamically, it is not feasible to allocate the leaf pages sequentially as in ISAM, where the set of primary leaf pages was static. In order to retrieve all leaf pages efficiently, we have to link them using page pointers. By organizing them into a doubly linked list, we can easily traverse the sequence of leaf pages (sometimes called the **sequence set**) in either direction. This structure is illustrated in Figure 5.8.

The following are some of the main characteristics of a B+ tree:

- Operations (insert, delete) on the tree keep it balanced.

- A minimum occupancy of 50% is guaranteed for each node except the root if the deletion algorithm discussed in Section 5.6 is implemented. However,

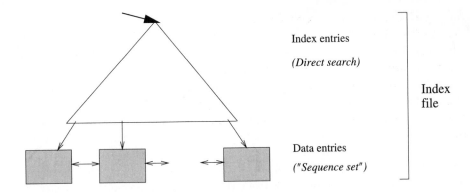

Figure 5.8 Structure of a B+ Tree

deletion is often implemented by simply locating the data entry and removing it, without adjusting the tree as needed to guarantee the 50% occupancy, because files typically grow rather than shrink.

■ Searching for a record requires just a traversal from the root to the appropriate leaf. We will refer to the length of a path from the root to a leaf—any leaf, because the tree is balanced—as the **height** of the tree. For example, a tree with only a leaf level and a single index level, such as the tree shown in Figure 5.10, has height 1. Because of high fan-out, the height of a B+ tree is rarely more than 3 or 4.

We will study B+ trees in which every node contains m entries, where $d \leq m \leq 2d$. The value d is a parameter of the B+ tree, called the **order** of the tree, and is a measure of the capacity of a tree node. The root node is the only exception to this requirement on the number of entries; for the root it is simply required that $1 \leq m \leq 2d$.

If a file of records is updated frequently and sorted access is important, maintaining a B+ tree index with data records stored as data entries is almost always superior to maintaining a sorted file. For the space overhead of storing the index entries, we obtain all the advantages of a sorted file plus efficient insertion and deletion algorithms. B+ trees typically maintain 67% space occupancy. B+ trees are usually also preferable to ISAM indexing because inserts are handled gracefully without overflow chains. However, if the dataset size and distribution remain fairly static, overflow chains may not be a major problem. In this case, two factors favor ISAM: the leaf pages are allocated in sequence (making scans over a large range more efficient than in a B+ tree, in which pages are likely to get out of sequence on disk over time, even if they were in sequence after bulk-loading), and the locking overhead of ISAM is lower than that for B+ trees. As a general rule, however, B+ trees are likely to perform better than ISAM.

5.3   FORMAT OF A NODE

The format of a node is the same as for ISAM and is shown in Figure 5.1. Non leaf nodes with m *index entries* contain $m + 1$ pointers to children. Pointer P_i points to a subtree in which all key values K are such that $K_i \leq K < K_{i+1}$. As special cases, P_0 points to a tree in which all key values are less than K_1, and P_m points to a tree in which all key values are greater than or equal to K_m. For leaf nodes, entries are denoted as $k*$, as usual. Just as in ISAM, leaf nodes (and *only* leaf nodes!) contain *data entries*. In the common case that Alternative (2) or (3) is used, leaf entries are $\langle K, I(K) \rangle$ pairs, just like non leaf entries. Regardless of the alternative chosen for leaf entries, the leaf pages are chained together in a doubly linked list. Thus the leaves form a sequence, which can be used to answer range queries efficiently.

The reader should carefully consider how such a node organization can be achieved using the record formats presented in Section 3.4; after all, each key–pointer pair can be thought of as a record. If the field being indexed is of fixed length, these index entries will be of fixed length; otherwise, we have variable-length records. In either case the B+ tree can itself be viewed as a file of records. If the leaf pages do not contain the actual data records, then the B+ tree is indeed a file of records that is distinct from the file that contains the data. If the leaf pages contain data records, then a file contains the B+ tree as well as the data.

5.4   SEARCH

The algorithm for search finds the leaf node in which a given data entry belongs. A pseudocode sketch of the algorithm is given in Figure 5.9. We use the notation **ptr* to denote the value pointed to by a pointer variable *ptr*, and *& (value)* to denote the address of *value*. Note that finding i in *tree_search* requires us to search within the node, which can be done with either a linear search or a binary search (e.g., depending on the number of entries in the node).

In discussing the search, insertion and deletion algorithms for B+ trees, we will assume that there are no *duplicates*. That is, no two data entries are allowed to have the same key value. Of course, duplicates arise whenever the search key does not contain a candidate key and must be dealt with in practice. We consider how duplicates can be handled in Section 5.7.

Consider the sample B+ tree shown in Figure 5.10. This B+ tree is of order d=2. That is, each node contains between 2 and 4 entries. Each non leaf entry is a $\langle key\ value,\ nodepointer \rangle$ pair; at the leaf level, the entries are data records that we denote by $k*$. To search for entry 5*, we follow the left-most child pointer, since 5 < 13. To search for the entries 14* or 15*, we follow the second pointer,

func *find* (search key value K) **returns** nodepointer
// *Given a search key value, finds its leaf node*
return tree_search(root, K);   // searches from root
endfunc

func *tree_search* (nodepointer, search key value K) **returns** nodepointer
// *Searches tree for entry*
if *nodepointer is a leaf, return nodepointer;
else,
    if $K < K_1$ then return tree_search(P_0, K);
    else,
        if $K \geq K_m$ then return tree_search(P_m, K);   // $m = $ # entries
        else,
            find i such that $K_i \leq K < K_{i+1}$;
            return tree_search(P_i, K)
endfunc

Figure 5.9   Algorithm for Search

since $13 \leq 14 < 17$, and $13 \leq 15 < 17$. (We don't find 15* on the appropriate leaf, and we can therefore conclude that it is not present in the tree.) To find 24*, we follow the fourth child pointer, since $24 \leq 24 < 30$.

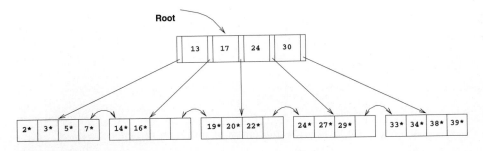

Figure 5.10   Example of a B+ Tree, Order d=2

5.5 INSERT

The algorithm for insertion takes an entry, finds the leaf node where it belongs, and inserts it there. Pseudocode for the B+ tree insertion algorithm is given in Figure 5.11. The basic idea behind the algorithm is that we recursively insert the entry by calling the insert algorithm on the appropriate child node. Usually, this procedure results in going down to the leaf node where the entry belongs, placing the entry there, and returning all the way back to the root node. Occasionally a node is full and it must be split. When the node is split, an entry pointing to the node created by the split must be inserted into its parent; this entry is pointed to by the pointer variable *newchildentry*. If the (old) root is split, a new root node is created and the height of the tree increases by one.

proc *insert* (nodepointer, entry, newchildentry)
// *Inserts entry into subtree with root '*nodepointer'; degree is d;*
// *'newchildentry' is null initially, and null upon return unless child is split*

if *nodepointer is a non leaf node, say N,
    find i such that $K_i \le$ entry's key value $< K_{i+1}$;   // choose subtree
    insert(P_i, entry, newchildentry);   // *recursively,* insert entry
    if newchildentry is null, return;   // usual case; didn't split child
    else,   // we split child, must insert *newchildentry in N
        if N has space,   // usual case
            put *newchildentry on it, set newchildentry to null, return;
        else,   // note difference wrt splitting of leaf page!
            split N: // $2d + 1$ key values and $2d + 2$ nodepointers
            first d key values and $d + 1$ nodepointers stay,
            last d keys and $d + 1$ pointers move to new node, $N2$;
            // *newchildentry set to guide searches between N and $N2$
            newchildentry = & ($\langle$smallest key value on $N2$, pointer to N2$\rangle$);
            if N is the root,   // root node was just split
                create new node with $\langle$pointer to N, *newchildentry$\rangle$;
                make the tree's root-node pointer point to the new node;
            return;

if *nodepointer is a leaf node, say L,
    if L has space,   // usual case
    put entry on it, set newchildentry to null, and return;
    else,   // once in a while, the leaf is full
        split L: first d entries stay, rest move to brand new node $L2$;
        newchildentry = & ($\langle$smallest key value on $L2$, pointer to $L2$$\rangle$);
        set sibling pointers in L and $L2$;
        return;
endproc

Figure 5.11   Algorithm for Insertion into B+ Tree of Order d

To illustrate insertion, let us continue with the sample tree shown in Figure 5.10. If we insert entry 8*, it belongs in the left-most leaf, which is already full. This insertion causes a split of the leaf page; the split pages are shown in Figure 5.12. The tree must now be adjusted to take the new leaf page into account, so we insert an entry consisting of the pair ⟨5, *pointer to new page*⟩ into the parent node. Notice how the key 5, which discriminates between the split leaf page and its newly created sibling, is 'copied up.' We cannot just 'push up' 5, because every data entry must appear in a leaf page.

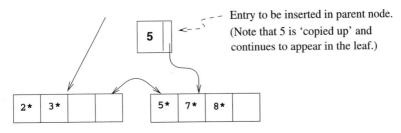

Figure 5.12   Split Leaf Pages during Insert of Entry 8*

Since the parent node is also full, another split occurs. In general we have to split a non leaf node when it is full, containing $2d$ keys and $2d+1$ pointers, and we have to add another index entry to account for a child split. We now have $2d + 1$ keys and $2d + 2$ pointers, yielding two minimally full non leaf nodes, each containing d keys and $d + 1$ pointers, and an extra key, which we choose to be the 'middle' key. This key and a pointer to the second non leaf node constitute an index entry that must be inserted into the parent of the split non leaf node. The middle key is thus 'pushed up' the tree, in contrast to the case for a split of a leaf page.

The split pages in our example are shown in Figure 5.13. The index entry pointing to the new non leaf node is the pair ⟨17, *pointer to new index-level page*⟩; notice that the key value 17 is 'pushed up' the tree, in contrast to the splitting key value 5 in the leaf split, which was 'copied up.'

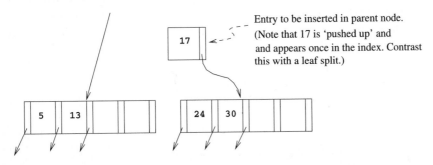

Figure 5.13   Split Index Pages during Insert of Entry 8*

The difference in handling leaf-level and index-level splits arises from the B+ tree requirement that all data entries $k*$ must reside in the leaves. This requirement prevents us from 'pushing up' 5 and leads to the slight redundancy of having some key values appearing in the leaf level as well as in some index level. However, range queries can be efficiently answered by just retrieving the sequence of leaf pages; the redundancy is a small price to pay for efficiency. In dealing with the index levels, we have more flexibility, and we 'push up' 17 to avoid having two copies of 17 in the index levels.

Now, since the split node was the old root, we need to create a new root node to hold the entry that distinguishes the two split index pages. The tree after completing the insertion of the entry 8* is shown in Figure 5.14.

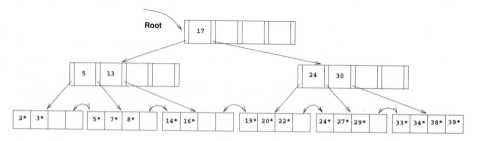

Figure 5.14   B+ Tree after Inserting Entry 8*

One variation of the insert algorithm tries to redistribute entries of a node N with a sibling before splitting the node; this improves average occupancy. The **sibling** of a node N, in this context, is a node that is immediately to the left or right of N *and has the same parent as N.*

To illustrate redistribution, reconsider insertion of entry 8* into the tree shown in Figure 5.10. The entry belongs in the left-most leaf, which is full. However, the (only) sibling of this leaf node contains only two entries and can thus accommodate more entries. We can therefore handle the insertion of 8* with a redistribution. Note how the entry in the parent node that points to the second leaf has a new key value; we 'copy up' the new low key value on the second leaf. This process is illustrated in Figure 5.15.

To determine whether redistribution is possible, we have to retrieve the sibling. If the sibling happens to be full, we have to split the node anyway. On average, checking whether redistribution is possible increases I/O for index node splits, especially if we check both siblings. (Checking whether redistribution is possible may reduce I/O if the redistribution succeeds whereas a split propagates up the tree, but this case is very infrequent.) If the file is growing, average occupancy will probably not be affected much even if we do not redistribute. Taking these

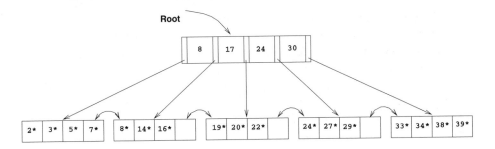

Figure 5.15 B+ Tree after Inserting Entry 8* Using Redistribution

considerations into account, *not* redistributing entries at non leaf levels usually pays off.

If a split occurs at the leaf level, however, we have to retrieve a neighbor in order to adjust the previous and next-neighbor pointers with respect to the newly created leaf node. Therefore, a limited form of redistribution makes sense: If a leaf node is full, fetch a neighbor node; if it has space, and has the same parent, redistribute entries. Otherwise (neighbor has different parent, i.e., is not a sibling; or is also full) split the leaf node and adjust the previous and next-neighbor pointers in the split node, the newly created neighbor, and the old neighbor.

5.6 DELETE *

The algorithm for deletion takes an entry, finds the leaf node where it belongs, and deletes it. Pseudocode for the B+ tree deletion algorithm is given in Figure 5.16. The basic idea behind the algorithm is that we recursively delete the entry by calling the delete algorithm on the appropriate child node. We usually go down to the leaf node where the entry belongs, remove the entry from there, and return all the way back to the root node. Occasionally a node is at minimum occupancy before the deletion, and the deletion causes it to go below the occupancy threshold. When this happens, we must either redistribute entries from an adjacent sibling, or merge the node with a sibling, in order to maintain minimum occupancy. If entries are redistributed between two nodes, their parent node must be updated to reflect this; the key value in the index entry pointing to the second node must be changed to be the lowest search key in the second node. If two nodes are merged, their parent must be updated to reflect this by deleting the index entry for the second node; this index entry is pointed to by the pointer variable *oldchildentry* when the delete call returns to the parent node. If the last entry in the root node is deleted in this manner because one of its children was deleted, the height of the tree decreases by one.

proc *delete* (parentpointer, nodepointer, entry, oldchildentry)
// Deletes entry from subtree with root '*nodepointer'; degree is d;
// 'oldchildentry' null initially, and null upon return unless child deleted
if *nodepointer is a non leaf node, say N,

    find i such that $K_i \leq$ entry's key value $< K_{i+1}$;   // choose subtree
    delete(nodepointer, P_i, entry, oldchildentry);   // *recursive* delete
    if oldchildentry is null, return;   // usual case: child not deleted
    else,   // we discarded child node (see discussion)

        remove *oldchildentry from N, // next, check minimum occupancy
        if N has entries to spare,   // usual case
            set oldchildentry to null, return;   // delete doesn't go further
        else,   // note difference wrt merging of leaf pages!

            get a sibling S of N: // parentpointer arg used to find S
            if S has extra entries,

                redistribute evenly between N and S *through* parent;
                set oldchildentry to null, return;
            else, *merge* N and S // call node on rhs M
                oldchildentry = & (current entry in parent for M);
                pull splitting key from parent down into node on left;
                move all entries from M to node on left;
                discard empty node M, return;

if *nodepointer is a leaf node, say L,
    if L has entries to spare,   // usual case
        remove entry, set oldchildentry to null, and return;
    else,   // once in a while, the leaf becomes underfull
        get a sibling S of L;   // parentpointer used to find S
        if S has extra entries,

            redistribute evenly between L and S;
            find entry in parent for node on right;   // call it M
            replace key value in parent entry by new low-key value in M;
            set oldchildentry to null, return;
        else, *merge* L and S // call node on rhs M
            oldchildentry = & (current entry in parent for M);
            move all entries from M to node on left;
            discard empty node M, adjust sibling pointers, return;
endproc

Figure 5.16 Algorithm for Deletion from B+ Tree of Order d

To illustrate deletion, let us consider the sample tree shown in Figure 5.14. To delete entry 19*, we simply remove it from the leaf page on which it appears, and we are done because the leaf still contains two entries. If we subsequently delete 20*, however, the leaf contains only one entry after the deletion. The (only) sibling of the leaf node that contained 20* has three entries, and we can therefore deal with the situation by redistribution; we move entry 24* to the leaf page that contained 20* and 'copy up' the new splitting key (27, which is the new low key value of the leaf from which we borrowed 24*) into the parent. This process is illustrated in Figure 5.17.

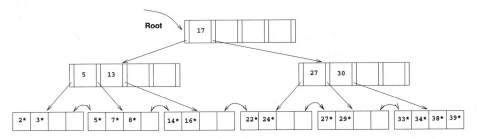

Figure 5.17   B+ Tree after Deleting Entries 19* and 20*

Suppose that we now delete entry 24*. The affected leaf contains only one entry (22*) after the deletion, and the (only) sibling contains just two entries (27* and 29*). Therefore, we cannot redistribute entries. However, these two leaf nodes together contain only three entries and can therefore be merged. While merging, we can 'toss' the entry (⟨*27, pointer to second leaf page*⟩) in the parent, which pointed to the second leaf page, because the second leaf page is empty after the merge and can be discarded. The right subtree of Figure 5.17 after this step in the deletion of entry 24* is shown in Figure 5.18.

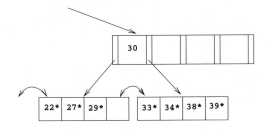

Figure 5.18   Partial B+ Tree during Deletion of Entry 24*

Deleting the entry ⟨*27, pointer to second leaf page*⟩ has created a non leaf-level page with just one entry, which is below the minimum of d=2. To fix this problem, we must either redistribute or merge. In either case we must fetch a sibling. The only sibling of this node contains just two entries (with key values 5 and 13), and so redistribution is not possible; we must therefore merge.

The situation when we have to merge two non leaf nodes is exactly the opposite of the situation when we have to split a non leaf node. We have to split a non leaf node when it contains $2d$ keys and $2d + 1$ pointers, and we have to add another key–pointer pair. Since we resort to merging two non leaf nodes only when we cannot redistribute entries between them, the two nodes must be minimally full; that is, each must contain d keys and $d + 1$ pointers prior to the deletion. After merging the two nodes and removing the key–pointer pair to be deleted, we have $2d - 1$ keys and $2d + 1$ pointers: Intuitively, the left-most pointer on the second merged node lacks a key value. To see what key value must be combined with this pointer to create a complete index entry, consider the parent of the two nodes being merged. The index entry pointing to one of the merged nodes must be deleted from the parent because the node is about to be discarded. The key value in this index entry is precisely the key value we need to complete the new merged node: The entries in the first node being merged, followed by the splitting key value that is 'pulled down' from the parent, followed by the entries in the second non leaf node gives us a total of $2d$ keys and $2d + 1$ pointers, which is a full non leaf node. Notice how the splitting key value in the parent is 'pulled down,' in contrast to the case of merging two leaf nodes.

Consider the merging of two non leaf nodes in our example. Together, the non leaf node and the sibling to be merged contain only three entries, and they have a total of five pointers to leaf nodes. To merge the two nodes, we also need to 'pull down' the index entry in their parent that currently discriminates between these nodes. This index entry has key value 17, and so we create a new entry ⟨*17, left-most child pointer in sibling*⟩. Now we have a total of four entries and five child pointers, which can fit on one page in a tree of order d=2. Notice that pulling down the splitting key 17 means that it will no longer appear in the parent node following the merge. After we merge the affected non leaf node and its sibling by putting all the entries on one page and discarding the empty sibling page, the new node is the only child of the old root, which can therefore be discarded. The tree after completing all these steps in the deletion of entry 24* is shown in Figure 5.19.

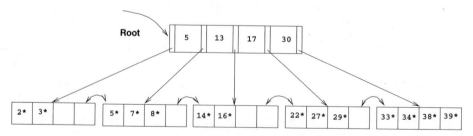

Figure 5.19   B+ Tree after Deleting Entry 24*

The previous examples illustrated redistribution of entries across leaves and merging of both leaf-level and non leaf-level pages. The remaining case is that of redistribution of entries between non leaf-level pages. To understand this case, consider the intermediate right subtree shown in Figure 5.18. We would arrive at the same intermediate right subtree if we try to delete 24* from a tree similar to the one shown in Figure 5.17 but with the left subtree and root key value as shown in Figure 5.20. The tree in Figure 5.20 illustrates an intermediate stage during the deletion of 24*. (Try and construct the initial tree.)

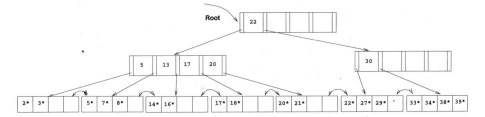

Figure 5.20   A B+ Tree during a Deletion

In contrast to the case when we deleted 24* from the tree of Figure 5.17, the non leaf level node containing key value 30 now has a sibling that can spare entries (the entries with key values 17 and 20). We move these entries[2] over from the sibling. Notice that in doing so, we essentially 'push' them through the splitting entry in their parent node (the root), which takes care of the fact that 17 becomes the new low key value on the right and therefore must replace the old splitting key in the root (the key value 22). The tree with all these changes is shown in Figure 5.21.

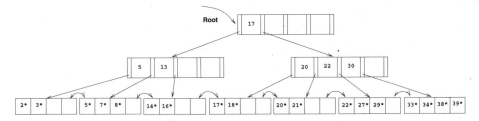

Figure 5.21   B+ Tree after Deletion

In concluding our discussion of deletion, we note that we retrieve only one sibling of a node. If this node has spare entries, we use redistribution; otherwise, we merge. If the node has a second sibling, it may be worth retrieving that sibling as well to check for the possibility of redistribution. Chances are high that redistribution will be possible, and unlike merging, redistribution is guaranteed to

---

[2]It is sufficient to move over just the entry with key value 20, but we are moving over two entries to illustrate what happens when several entries are redistributed.

propagate no further than the parent node. Also, the pages have more space on them, which reduces the likelihood of a split on subsequent insertions. (Remember, files typically grow, not shrink!) However, the number of times that this case arises (node becomes less than half-full and first sibling can't spare an entry) is not very high, so it is not essential to implement this refinement of the basic algorithm that we have presented.

5.7   DUPLICATES *

The search, insertion and deletion algorithms that we have presented ignore the issue of **duplicate keys**, that is, several data entries with the same key value. We now discuss how duplicates can be handled.

The basic search algorithm assumes that all entries with a given key value reside on a single leaf page. One way to satisfy this assumption is to use *overflow pages* to deal with duplicates. (In ISAM, of course, we have overflow pages in any case, and duplicates are easily handled.)

Typically, however, we use an alternative approach for duplicates. We handle them just like any other entries and several leaf pages may contain entries with a given key value. To retrieve all data entries with a given key value, we must search for the *left-most* data entry with the given key value and then possibly retrieve more than one leaf page (using the leaf sequence pointers). Modifying the search algorithm to find the left-most data entry in an index with duplicates is an interesting exercise (in fact, it is Exercise 5.11).

One problem with this approach is that when a record is deleted, if we use Alternative (2) for data entries, finding the corresponding data entry to delete in the B+ tree index could be inefficient because we may have to check several duplicate entries ⟨key, rid⟩ with the same *key* value. This problem can be addressed by considering the *rid* value in the data entry to be *part of the search key*, for purposes of positioning the data entry in the tree. This solution effectively turns the index into a *unique* index (i.e., no duplicates). Remember that a search key can be any sequence of fields—in this variant, the rid of the data record is essentially treated as another field while constructing the search key.

Alternative (3) for data entries leads to a natural solution for duplicates, but if we have a large number of duplicates, a single data entry could span multiple pages. And of course, when a data record is deleted, finding the rid to delete from the corresponding data entry can be inefficient. The solution to this problem is similar to the one discussed above for Alternative (2): We can maintain the list of rids within each data entry in sorted order (say, by page number and then slot number if a rid consists of a page id and a slot id).

5.8 B+ TREES IN PRACTICE *

In this section we discuss several important pragmatic issues.

5.8.1 Key Compression

The height of a B+ tree depends on the *number of data entries* and the *size of index entries*. The size of index entries determines the number of index entries that will fit on a page, and therefore, the *fan-out* of the tree. Since the height of the tree is proportional to $log_{fan-out}$ *(# of data entries)*, it is clearly important to maximize the fan-out, to minimize the height.

An index entry contains a search key value and a page pointer. Thus the size primarily depends on the size of the search key value. If search key values are very long (for instance, the name Devarakonda Venkataramana Sathyanarayana Seshasayee Yellamanchali Murthy), not many index entries will fit on a page; fan-out is low, and the height of the tree is large.

On the other hand, search key values in index entries are used only to direct traffic to the appropriate leaf. When we want to locate data entries with a given search key value, we compare this search key value with the search key values of index entries (on a path from the root to the desired leaf). During the comparison at an index-level node, we want to identify two index entries with search key values k_1 and k_2 such that the desired search key value k falls between k_1 and k_2. To accomplish this, we do not need to store search key values in their entirety in index entries.

For example, suppose that we have two adjacent index entries in a node, with search key values 'David Smith' and 'Devarakonda ...' To discriminate between these two values, it is sufficient to store the abbreviated forms 'Da' and 'De.' More generally, the meaning of the entry 'David Smith' in the B+ tree is that every value in the subtree pointed to by the pointer to the left of 'David Smith' is less than 'David Smith,' and every value in the subtree pointed to by the pointer to the right of 'David Smith' is (greater than or equal to 'David Smith' and) less than 'Devarakonda ...'

To ensure that this semantics for an entry is preserved, while compressing the entry with key 'David Smith,' we must examine the largest key value in the subtree to the left of 'David Smith' and the smallest key value in the subtree to the right of 'David Smith,' not just the index entries ('Daniel Lee' and 'Devarakonda ...') that are its neighbors. This point is illustrated in Figure 5.22; the value 'Davey Jones' is greater than 'Dav,' and thus, 'David Smith' can only be abbreviated to 'Davi,' not to 'Dav.'

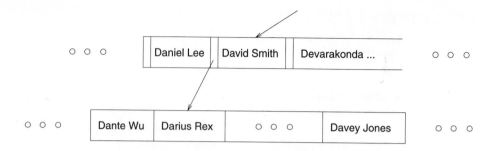

Figure 5.22   Example Illustrating Prefix Key Compression

This technique is called **prefix key compression**, or simply **key compression**, and is supported in many commercial implementations of B+ trees. It can substantially increase the fan-out of a tree. We will not discuss the details of the insertion and deletion algorithms in the presence of key compression.

5.8.2   Bulk-Loading a B+ Tree

Entries are added to a B+ tree in two ways. First, we may have an existing collection of data records with a B+ tree index on it; whenever a record is added to the collection, a corresponding entry must be added to the B+ tree as well. (Of course, a similar comment applies to deletions.) Second, we may have a collection of data records for which we want to create a B+ tree index on some key field(s). In this situation, we can of course start with an empty tree and insert an entry for each data record, one at a time, using the standard insertion algorithm. However, this approach is likely to be quite expensive because each entry requires us to start from the root and go down to the appropriate leaf page. Even though the index-level pages are likely to stay in the buffer pool between successive requests, the overhead is still considerable.

For this reason many systems provide a *bulk-loading* utility for creating a B+ tree index on an existing collection of data records. The first step is to sort the data entries $k*$ to be inserted into the (to be created) B+ tree according to the search key k. (If the entries are key–pointer pairs, sorting them does not mean sorting the data records that are pointed to, of course.) We will use a running example to illustrate the bulk-loading algorithm. We will assume that each data page can hold only two entries, and that each index page can hold two entries and an additional pointer (i.e., the B+ tree is assumed to be of order d=1).

After the data entries have been sorted, we allocate an empty page to serve as the root and insert a pointer to the first page of (sorted) entries into it. We illustrate this process in Figure 5.23, using a sample set of nine sorted pages of data entries.

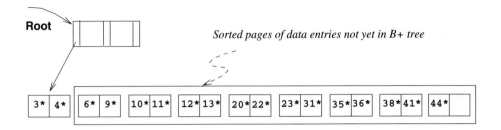

Figure 5.23 Initial Step in B+ Tree Bulk-Loading

We then add one entry to the root page for each page of the sorted data entries. The new entry consists of ⟨*low key value on page, pointer to page*⟩. We proceed until the root page is full; see Figure 5.24.

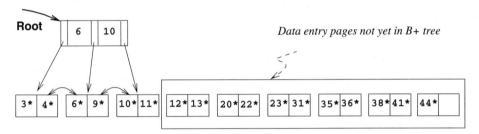

Figure 5.24 Root Page Fills up in B+ Tree Bulk-Loading

To insert the entry for the next page of data entries, we must split the root and create a new root page. We show this step in Figure 5.25.

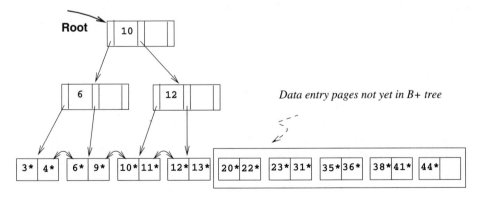

Figure 5.25 Page Split during B+ Tree Bulk-Loading

We have redistributed the entries evenly between the two children of the root, in anticipation of the fact that the B+ tree is likely to grow. Although it is difficult

(!) to illustrate these options when at most two entries fit on a page, we could also have just left all the entries on the old page or filled up some desired fraction of that page (say, 80%). These alternatives are simple variants of the basic idea.

To continue with the bulk-loading example, entries for the leaf pages are always inserted into the right-most index page just above the leaf level. When the right-most index page above the leaf level fills up, it is split. This action may, in turn, cause a split of the right-most index page one step closer to the root, as illustrated in Figures 5.26 and 5.27.

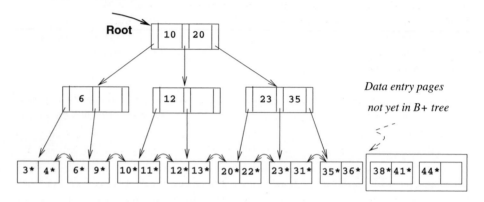

Figure 5.26   Before Adding Entry for Leaf Page Containing 38*

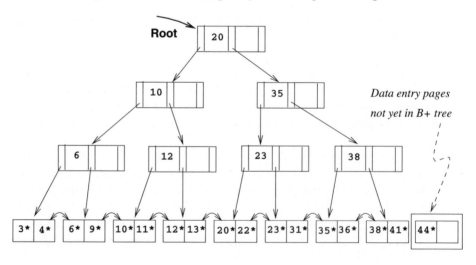

Figure 5.27   After Adding Entry for Leaf Page Containing 38*

Note that splits occur only on the right-most path from the root to the leaf level. We leave the completion of the bulk-loading example as a simple exercise.

Let us consider the cost of creating an index on an existing collection of records. This operation consists of three steps: (1) creating the data entries to insert in the index, (2) sorting the data entries, and (3) building the index from the sorted entries. The first step involves scanning the records and writing out the corresponding data entries; the cost is $(R + E)$ I/Os, where R is the number of pages containing records and E is the number of pages containing data entries. Sorting is discussed in Chapter 7; you will see that the index entries can be generated in sorted order at a cost of about $3E$ I/Os. These entries can then be inserted into the index as they are generated, using the bulk-loading algorithm discussed in this section. The cost of the third step, that is, inserting the entries into the index, is then just the cost of writing out all index pages.

5.8.3   The Order Concept

We have presented B+ trees using the parameter d to denote minimum occupancy. It is worth noting that the concept of *order* (i.e., the parameter d), while useful for teaching B+ tree concepts, must usually be relaxed in practice and replaced by a physical space criterion; for example, that nodes must be kept at least half-full.

One reason for this is that leaf nodes and non leaf nodes can usually hold different numbers of entries. Recall that B+ tree nodes are disk pages and that non leaf nodes contain only search keys and node pointers, while leaf nodes can contain the actual data records. Obviously, the size of a data record is likely to be quite a bit larger than the size of a search entry, so many more search entries than records will fit on a disk page.

A second reason for relaxing the order concept is that the search key may contain a character string field (e.g., the *name* field of Students) whose size varies from record to record; such a search key leads to variable-size data entries and index entries, and the number of entries that will fit on a disk page becomes variable.

Finally, even if the index is built on a fixed-size field, several records may still have the same search key value (e.g., several Students records may have the same *gpa* or *name* value). This situation can also lead to variable-size leaf entries (if we use Alternative (3) for data entries). Because of all of these complications, the concept of order is typically replaced by a simple physical criterion (e.g., merge if possible when more than half of the space in the node is unused).

5.8.4   The Effect of Inserts and Deletes on Rids

If the leaf pages contain data records—that is, the B+ tree is a clustered index— then operations such as splits, merges and redistributions can have the effect of changing rids. Recall that a typical representation for a rid is some combination of (physical) page number and slot number. This scheme allows us to move records within a page if an appropriate page format is chosen, but not across pages, as is the case with operations such as splits. So unless rids are chosen to be independent of page numbers, an operation such as split or merge in a clustered B+ tree may require compensating updates to other indexes on the same data.

A similar comment holds for any dynamic clustered index, regardless of whether it is tree-based or hash-based. Of course, the problem does not arise with non-clustered indexes because only index entries are moved around.

5.9   MULTIDIMENSIONAL INDEXES

A B+ tree supports range queries efficiently because it imposes an order on the data entries. Other ways of ordering the data entries lead to different kinds of index structures:

- **One-dimensional indexes:** A linear order is imposed on the set of search key values, and data entries are stored according to this order. The B+ tree is an example of such an index structure.

- **Multidimensional indexes:** A linear order is not imposed. Rather, some kind of a **spatial** relationship is utilized in organizing data entries, with each key value seen as a point in a k-dimensional space, where k is the number of fields in the composite key.

In a one-dimensional index, the 2-dimensional space of $\langle age,\ sal \rangle$ values is linearized by sorting on age first and then on sal. For example, $\langle age,\ sal \rangle$ pairs are maintained in the following sorted order in a B+ tree index with key $\langle age,\ sal \rangle$: $\langle 11,\ 80 \rangle$, $\langle 12,\ 10 \rangle$, $\langle 12,\ 20 \rangle$, $\langle 13,\ 75 \rangle$.

Range queries on the first field (age) can be answered efficiently because qualifying data entries are close to each other, but range queries on sal can be quite expensive. Thus retrieving all data entries with $age < 12$ is easy, but retrieving all entries with $sal < 20$ requires us to consider all data entries. We could also sort on sal first and then age, that is, use the composite key $\langle sal,\ age \rangle$; then, range queries on sal would be cheap but range queries on age would be expensive.

A multidimensional index stores data entries based on their proximity in the underlying k dimensional space. For example, $\langle 12,\ 10 \rangle$ and $\langle 12,\ 20 \rangle$ might be stored together, and $\langle 11,\ 80 \rangle$ and $\langle 13,\ 75 \rangle$ might be stored together, based on proximity. Figure 5.28 illustrates this. In a B+ tree, the data entries are stored in the order shown by the dotted line. In a multidimensional index, data entries are stored together as shown by the dotted boxes. The multidimensional index must also provide a way to locate the desired boxes in response to a query; this is not shown in the figure. This is usually accomplished by having index entries organized into a tree, similar to a B+ tree, although there are differences in how the children of a node are related to the node.

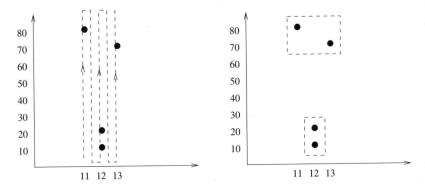

Figure 5.28 Clustering of Data Entries in 1-D vs. k-D Indexes

In a multidimensional index, all the fields in the search key are treated symmetrically. Queries like *age* < 12 and *sal* < 20 are both evaluated quite efficiently. Multidimensional indexes are ideal for queries such as "Find the 10 nearest neighbors of a given point," and "Find all points within a certain distance of a given point." The drawback with respect to a one-dimensional index is that if (almost) all data entries are to be retrieved in *age* order, a multidimensional index is likely to be slower than a one-dimensional index in which *age* is the first field in the search key.

Many multidimensional tree-structured indexes have been proposed; the R Tree is an example. R Trees can be used to store geometric objects such as lines and regions (more precisely, bounding boxes that enclose geometric objects) in addition to points. They are therefore widely used in DBMSs designed to store geographical data (e.g., information on roads, maps, etc.). However, few relational DBMSs currently support multidimensional indexes. Multidimensional indexes will probably become more widely used, but in this book, we will not discuss them further.

5.10 SUMMARY

Tree-structured indexes are ideal for range selections, and also support equality selections quite efficiently. ISAM is a static tree-structured index in which only leaf pages are modified by inserts and deletes. As the file grows, overflow pages are added. Unless the size of the dataset and the data distribution remain ap-

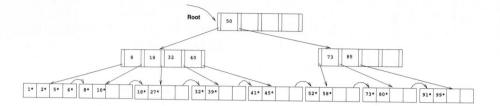

Figure 5.29   Tree for Exercise 5.1

proximately the same over the lifetime of the ISAM index, overflow chains could become long and degrade performance.

The B+ tree structure is a widely used indexing mechanism that addresses the problem of overflow chains in ISAM. It is a dynamic, height-balanced structure that grows and shrinks gracefully. Inserts and deletes have a cost proportional to the height of the tree, which is likely to be small even for very large datasets because of the balanced nature of the tree and the high fan-out.

Key compression is an important optimization that increases the fan-out of a tree index, and is widely used. Most systems also provide a utility for *bulk-loading* a large dataset and creating an index. Using such a utility is faster than the alternative, which is simply to create the index by repeatedly inserting one data entry per data record. Further, leaf pages can be allocated in sequence, and pages can be filled to a desired level of occupancy.

Several variations on the B+ tree (such as the B tree and the B* tree) have been described in the literature, but the B+ tree variant remains the most popular due to its relative simplicity and good performance.

EXERCISES

Exercise 5.1 Consider the B+ tree index of order $d = 2$ shown in Figure 5.29.

1. Show the tree that would result from inserting a data entry with key 9 into this tree.

2. Show the B+ tree that would result from inserting a data entry with key 3 into the original tree. How many page reads and page writes will the insertion require?

3. Show the B+ tree that would result from deleting the data entry with key 8 from the original tree, assuming that the left sibling is checked for possible redistribution.

4. Show the B+ tree that would result from deleting the data entry with key 8 from the original tree, assuming that the right sibling is checked for possible redistribution.

5. Show the B+ tree that would result from starting with the original tree, inserting a data entry with key 46 and then deleting the data entry with key 52.

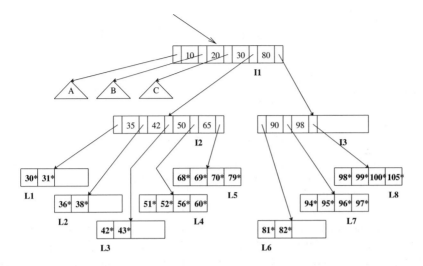

Figure 5.30 Tree for Exercise 5.2

6. Show the B+ tree that would result from deleting the data entry with key 91 from the original tree.

7. Show the B+ tree that would result from starting with the original tree, inserting a data entry with key 59 and then deleting the data entry with key 91.

8. Show the B+ tree that would result from successively deleting the data entries with keys 32, 39, 41, 45 and 73 from the original tree.

Exercise 5.2 Consider the B+ tree index shown in Figure 5.30, which uses Alternative (1) for data entries. Each intermediate node can hold up to five pointers and four key values. Each leaf can hold up to four records, and leaf nodes are doubly linked as usual, although these links are not shown in the figure.

Answer the following questions.

1. Name all the tree nodes that must be fetched to answer the following query: "Get all records with search key greater than 38."

2. Insert a record with search key 109 into the tree.

3. Delete the record with search key 81 from the (original) tree.

4. Name a search key value such that inserting it into the (original) tree would cause an increase in the height of the tree.

5. Note that subtrees A, B and C are not fully specified. Nonetheless, what can you infer about the contents and the shape of these trees?

6. How would your answers to the above questions change if this were an ISAM index?

7. Suppose that this is an ISAM index. What is the minimum number of insertions needed to create a chain of three overflow pages?

Exercise 5.3 Answer the following questions.

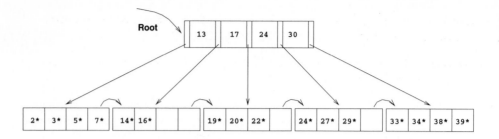

Figure 5.31   Tree for Exercise 5.5

1. What is the minimum space utilization for a B+ tree index?

2. What is the minimum space utilization for an ISAM index?

3. If your database system supported both a static and a dynamic tree index (say, ISAM and B+ trees), would you ever consider using the *static* index in preference to the *dynamic* index?

Exercise 5.4 Suppose that a page can contain at most four data values and that all data values are integers. Using only B+ trees of order 2, give examples of each of the following:

1. A B+ tree whose height changes from 2 to 3 when the value 25 is inserted. Show your structure before and after the insertion.

2. A B+ tree in which the deletion of the value 25 leads to a redistribution. Show your structure before and after the deletion.

3. A B+ tree in which the deletion of the value 25 causes a merge of two nodes, but without altering the height of the tree.

4. An ISAM structure with four buckets, none of which has an overflow page. Further, every bucket has space for exactly one more entry. Show your structure before and after inserting two additional values, chosen so that an overflow page is created.

Exercise 5.5 Consider the B+ tree shown in Figure 5.31.

1. Identify a list of data entries such that:

    (a) Inserting the entries in the order shown and then deleting them in the opposite order (e.g., insert *a*, insert *b*, delete *b*, delete *a*) results in the original tree.

    (b) Inserting the entries in the order shown and then deleting them in the opposite order (e.g., insert *a*, insert *b*, delete *b*, delete *a*) results in a different tree.

2. What is the minimum number of insertions of data entries with distinct keys that will cause the height of the (original) tree to change from its current value (of 1) to 3?

3. Would the minimum number of insertions that will cause the original tree to increase to height 3 change if you were allowed to insert duplicates (multiple data entries with the same key), assuming that overflow pages are not used for handling duplicates?

Exercise 5.6 Answer Exercise 5.5 assuming that the tree is an ISAM tree! (Some of the examples asked for may not exist—if so, explain briefly.)

Exercise 5.7 Suppose that you have a sorted file, and you want to construct a dense primary B+ tree index on this file.

1. One way to accomplish this task is to scan the file, record by record, inserting each one using the B+ tree insertion procedure. What performance and storage utilization problems are there with this approach?

2. Explain how the bulk-loading algorithm described in the text improves upon the above scheme.

Exercise 5.8 Assume that you have just built a dense B+ tree index using Alternative (2) on a heap file containing 20,000 records. The key field for this B+ tree index is a 40-byte string, and it is a candidate key. Pointers (i.e., record ids and page ids) are (at most) 10-byte values. The size of one disk page is 1000 bytes. The index was built in a bottom-up fashion using the bulk-loading algorithm, and the nodes at each level were filled up as much as possible.

1. How many levels does the resulting tree have?

2. For each level of the tree, how many nodes are at that level?

3. How many levels would the resulting tree have if key compression is used and it reduces the average size of each key in an entry to 10 bytes?

4. How many levels would the resulting tree have without key compression, but with all pages 70% full?

Exercise 5.9 The algorithms for insertion and deletion into a B+ tree are presented as recursive algorithms. In the code for *insert*, for instance, there is a call made at the parent of a node N to insert into (the subtree rooted at) node N, and when this call returns, the current node is the parent of N. Thus, we do not maintain any 'parent pointers' in nodes of B+ tree. Such pointers are not part of the B+ tree structure for a good reason, as this exercise will demonstrate. An alternative approach that uses parent pointers—again, remember that such pointers are *not* part of the standard B+ tree structure!—in each node appears to be simpler:

> Search to the appropriate leaf using the search algorithm; then insert the entry and split if necessary, with splits propagated to parents if necessary (using the parent pointers to find the parents).

Consider this (unsatisfactory) alternative approach:

1. Suppose that an internal node N is split into nodes N and N2. What can you say about the parent pointers in the children of the original node N?

2. Suggest two ways of dealing with the inconsistent parent pointers in the children of node N.

3. For each of the above suggestions, identify a potential (major) disadvantage.

4. What conclusions can you draw from this exercise?

sid	name	login	age	gpa
53831	Madayan	madayan@music	11	1.8
53832	Guldu	guldu@music	12	3.8
53666	Jones	jones@cs	18	3.4
53901	Jones	jones@toy	18	3.4
53902	Jones	jones@physics	18	3.4
53903	Jones	jones@english	18	3.4
53904	Jones	jones@genetics	18	3.4
53905	Jones	jones@astro	18	3.4
53906	Jones	jones@chem	18	3.4
53902	Jones	jones@sanitation	18	3.8
53688	Smith	smith@ee	19	3.2
53650	Smith	smith@math	19	3.8
54001	Smith	smith@ee	19	3.5
54005	Smith	smith@cs	19	3.8
54009	Smith	smith@astro	19	2.2

Figure 5.32   An Instance of the Students Relation

Exercise 5.10 Consider the instance of the Students relation shown in Figure 5.32. Show a B+ tree of order 2 in each of these cases, assuming that duplicates are handled using overflow pages. Clearly indicate what the data entries are (i.e., do not use the '$k*$' convention).

1. A dense B+ tree index on *age* using Alternative (1) for data entries.

2. A sparse B+ tree index on *age* using Alternative (1) for data entries.

3. A dense B+ tree index on *gpa* using Alternative (2) for data entries. For the purposes of this question, assume that these tuples are stored in a sorted file in the order shown in the figure: the first tuple is in page 1, slot 1; the second tuple is in page 1, slot 2; and so on. Each page can store up to three data records. You can use ⟨*page-id, slot*⟩ to identify a tuple.

Exercise 5.11 Suppose that duplicates are handled using the approach without over-flow pages discussed in Section 5.7. Describe an algorithm to search for the left-most occurrence of a data entry with search key value K.

Exercise 5.12 Answer Exercise 5.10 assuming that duplicates are handled without using overflow pages, using the alternative approach suggested in Section 5.7.

PROJECT-BASED EXERCISES

Exercise 5.13 Compare the public interfaces for heap files, B+ tree indexes and linear hashed indexes. What are the similarities and differences? Explain why these similarities and differences exist.

Exercise 5.14 This exercise involves using Minibase to explore the earlier (non project) exercises further.

1. Create the trees shown in earlier exercises and visualize them using the B+ tree visualizer in Minibase.

2. Verify your answers to exercises that require insertion and deletion of data entries by doing the insertions and deletions in Minibase and looking at the resulting trees using the visualizer.

Exercise 5.15 (*Note to instructors: Additional details must be provided if this question is assigned; see Appendix A.*) Implement B+ trees on top of the lower-level code in Minibase.

BIBLIOGRAPHIC NOTES

The original version of the B+ tree was presented by Bayer and McCreight [51]. The B+ tree is described in [309] and [142]. B tree indexes for skewed data distributions are studied in [189]. The VSAM indexing structure is described in [563]. Various tree structures for supporting range queries are surveyed in [60]. An early paper on multiattribute search keys is [356].

Several multidimensional indexing techniques have been proposed. These include Bang Files [203], Grid Files [408], the hB Tree [349], Quad Trees [468] and R Trees [238]. Several variations of these, and several other distinct techniques, have also been proposed; Samet's text [469] deals with many of them. [254] proposes a generalized tree index that can be specialized to obtain many of the specific tree indexes mentioned earlier.

References for concurrent access to B trees are in the bibliography for Chapter 17.

HASH-BASED INDEXING

Not chaos-like, together crushed and bruised,
But, as the world harmoniously confused:
Where order in variety we see.

—Alexander Pope, *Windsor Forest*

In this chapter we consider file organizations that are excellent for equality selections. The basic idea is to use a *hashing function*, which maps values in a search field into a range of *bucket numbers* to find the page on which a desired data entry belongs. We use a simple scheme called *Static Hashing* to introduce the idea. This scheme suffers from the problem of long overflow chains, which can affect performance. Two solutions to the problem are presented. The *Extendible Hashing* scheme uses a directory to support inserts and deletes efficiently without any overflow pages. The *Linear Hashing* scheme uses a clever policy for creating new buckets and supports inserts and deletes efficiently without the use of a directory. Although overflow pages are used, the length of overflow chains is rarely more than two.

Hash-based indexing techniques cannot support range searches, unfortunately. Tree-based indexing techniques, discussed in Chapter 5, can support range searches efficiently and are almost as good as hash-based indexing for equality selections. Thus many commercial systems choose to support only tree-based indexes. Nonetheless, hashing techniques prove to be very useful in implementing relational operations such as joins, as we will see in Chapter 12. In particular, the Index Nested Loops join method generates many equality selection queries, and the difference in cost between a hash-based index and a tree-based index can become significant in this context.

The rest of this chapter is organized as follows. Section 6.1 presents Static Hashing. Like ISAM, its drawback is that performance degrades as the data grows and shrinks. We discuss a dynamic hashing technique called Extendible Hashing in Section 6.2, and another dynamic technique, called Linear Hashing, in Section 6.3. We compare Extendible and Linear Hashing in Section 6.4.

6.1   STATIC HASHING

The Static Hashing scheme is illustrated in Figure 6.1. The pages containing the data can be viewed as a collection of **buckets**, with one **primary** page and possibly additional **overflow** pages per bucket. A file consists of buckets 0 through $N - 1$, with one primary page per bucket initially. Buckets contain *data entries*, which can be any of the three alternatives discussed in Chapter 4.

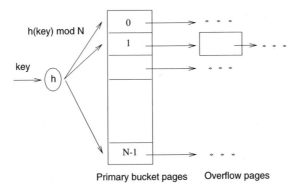

Primary bucket pages   Overflow pages

Figure 6.1   Static Hashing

To search for a data entry, we apply a **hash function h** to identify the bucket to which it belongs and then search this bucket. To speed the search of a bucket, we can maintain data entries in sorted order by search key value; in this chapter, we do not sort entries, and the order of entries within a bucket has no significance. In order to insert a data entry, we use the hash function to identify the correct bucket and then put the data entry there. If there is no space for this data entry, we allocate a new *overflow* page, put the data entry on this page, and add the page to the **overflow chain** of the bucket. To delete a data entry, we use the hashing function to identify the correct bucket, locate the data entry by searching the bucket, and then remove it. If this data entry is the last in an overflow page, the overflow page is removed from the overflow chain of the bucket and added to a list of *free pages*.

The hash function is an important component of the hashing approach. It must distribute values in the domain of the search field uniformly over the collection of buckets. If we have N buckets, numbered 0 through $N - 1$, a hash function h of the form $h(value) = (a * value + b)$ works well in practice. (The bucket identified is $h(value)$ *mod* N.) The constants a and b can be chosen to 'tune' the hash function.

Since the number of buckets in a static hashed file is known when the file is created, the primary pages can be stored on successive disk pages. Thus a search ideally requires just one disk I/O, and insert and delete operations require two I/Os (read and write the page), although the cost could be higher in the presence of overflow pages. As the file grows, long overflow chains can develop. Since searching a bucket requires us to search (in general) all pages in its overflow chain, it is easy to see how performance can deteriorate. By initially keeping pages 80% full, we can avoid overflow pages if the file doesn't grow too much, but in general the only way to get rid of overflow chains is to create a new file with more buckets.

The main problem with Static Hashing is that the number of buckets is fixed. If a file shrinks greatly, a lot of space is wasted; more importantly, if a file grows a lot, long overflow chains develop, resulting in poor performance. One alternative is to periodically 'rehash' the file to restore the ideal situation (no overflow chains, about 80% occupancy). However, rehashing takes time and the index cannot be used while rehashing is in progress. Another alternative is to use **dynamic hashing** techniques such as Extendible and Linear Hashing, which deal with inserts and deletes gracefully. We consider these techniques in the rest of this chapter.

6.1.1 Notation and Conventions

In the rest of this chapter, we use the following conventions. The first step in searching for, inserting, or deleting a data entry $k*$ (with search key k) is always to apply a hash function h to the search field, and we will denote this operation as $h(k)$. The value $h(k)$ identifies a bucket. We will often denote the data entry $k*$ by using the hash value, as $h(k)*$. Note that two different keys can have the same hash value.

6.2 EXTENDIBLE HASHING *

To understand Extendible Hashing, let us begin by considering a static hashed file. If we have to insert a new data entry into a full bucket, we need to add an overflow page. If we don't want to add overflow pages, one solution is to reorganize the file at this point by doubling the number of buckets and redistributing the entries across the new set of buckets. This solution suffers from one major defect—the entire file has to be read, and twice as many pages have to be written, to achieve the reorganization. This problem, however, can be overcome by a simple idea: use a **directory** of pointers to buckets, and double the size of the number of buckets by doubling just the directory and splitting *only* the bucket that overflowed.

To understand the idea, consider the sample file shown in Figure 6.2. The directory consists of an array of size 4, with each element being a pointer to a bucket. (The *global depth* and *local depth* fields will be discussed shortly; ignore them for now.) To locate a data entry, we apply a hash function to the search field and take the last two bits of its binary representation to get a number between 0 and 3. The pointer in this array position gives us the desired bucket; we assume that each bucket can hold four data entries. Thus to locate a data entry with hash value 5 (binary 101), we look at directory element 01 and follow the pointer to the data page (bucket B in the figure).

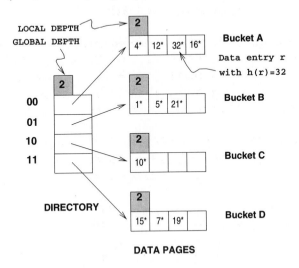

Figure 6.2 Example of an Extendible Hashed File

To insert a data entry, we search to find the appropriate bucket. For example, to insert a data entry with hash value 13 (denoted as 13*), we would examine directory element 01 and go to the page containing data entries 1*, 5* and 21*. Since the page has space for an additional data entry, we are done after we insert the entry (Figure 6.3).

Next, let us consider insertion of a data entry into a full bucket. The essence of the Extendible Hashing idea lies in how we deal with this case. Consider the insertion of data entry 20* (binary 10100). Looking at directory element 00, we are led to bucket A, which is already full. We must first **split** the bucket by allocating a new bucket[1] and redistributing the contents (including the new entry to be inserted) across the old bucket and its 'split image.' To redistribute entries across the old bucket and its split image, we consider the last *three* bits of $h(r)$; the last two bits are 00, indicating a data entry that belongs to one of these two buckets, and the third bit discriminates between these buckets. The redistribution of entries is illustrated in Figure 6.4.

---

[1]Since there are no overflow pages in Extendible Hashing, a bucket can be thought of as a single page.

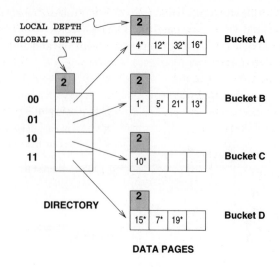

LOCAL DEPTH
GLOBAL DEPTH

2 | 4* | 12* | 32* | 16*   **Bucket A**

2

00

01

10

11

2 | 1* | 5* | 21* | 13*   **Bucket B**

2 | 10* | | | **Bucket C**

DIRECTORY

2 | 15* | 7* | 19* | **Bucket D**

DATA PAGES

Figure 6.3   After Inserting Entry r with $h(r)=13$

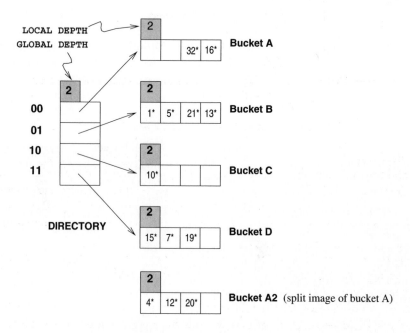

LOCAL DEPTH
GLOBAL DEPTH

2 | | | 32* | 16*   **Bucket A**

2

00

01

10

11

2 | 1* | 5* | 21* | 13*   **Bucket B**

2 | 10* | | | **Bucket C**

DIRECTORY

2 | 15* | 7* | 19* | **Bucket D**

2 | 4* | 12* | 20* | **Bucket A2** (split image of bucket A)

Figure 6.4   While Inserting Entry r with $h(r)=20$

Notice a problem that we must now resolve—we need three bits to discriminate between two of our data pages (A and A2), but the directory has only enough slots to store all two-bit patterns. The solution is to *double the directory*. Elements that differ only in the third bit from the end are said to 'correspond': *corresponding elements* of the directory point to the same bucket with the exception of the elements corresponding to the split bucket. In our example, bucket 0 was split; so, new directory element 000 points to one of the split versions and new element 100 points to the other. The sample file after completing all steps in the insertion of 20* is shown in Figure 6.5.

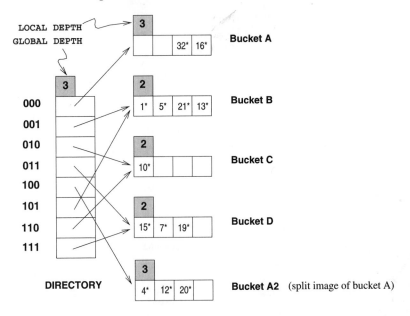

Figure 6.5   After Inserting Entry r with $h(r)=20$

Thus doubling the file requires allocating a new bucket page, writing both this page and the old bucket page that is being split, and doubling the directory array. The directory is likely to be much smaller than the file itself because each element is just a page-id, and can be doubled by simply copying it over (and adjusting the elements for the split buckets). The cost of doubling is now quite acceptable.

We observe that the basic technique used in Extendible Hashing is to treat the result of applying a hash function h as a binary number and to interpret the last d bits, where d depends on the size of the directory, as an offset into the directory. In our example d is originally 2 because we only have four buckets; after the split, d becomes 3 because we now have eight buckets. A corollary is that when distributing entries across a bucket and its split image, we should do so on the basis of the dth bit. (Note how entries are redistributed in our example; see Figure 6.5.) The number d is called the **global depth** of the hashed file and is kept as part of the header of the file. It is used every time we need to locate a data entry.

An important point that arises is whether splitting a bucket necessitates a directory doubling. Consider our example, as shown in Figure 6.5. If we now insert 9*, it belongs in bucket B; this bucket is already full. We can deal with this situation by splitting the bucket and using directory elements 001 and 101 to point to the bucket and its split image, as shown in Figure 6.6.

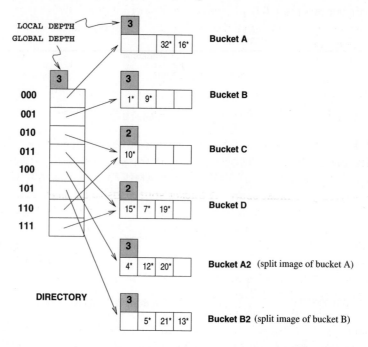

Figure 6.6   After Inserting Entry *r* with *h(r)*=9

Thus a bucket split does not necessarily require a directory doubling. However, if either bucket A or A2 grows full and an insert then forces a bucket split, we are forced to double the directory again.

In order to differentiate between these cases, and determine whether a directory doubling is needed, we maintain a **local depth** for each bucket. If a bucket whose local depth is equal to the global depth is split, the directory must be doubled. Going back to the example, when we inserted 9* into the index shown in Figure 6.5, it belonged to bucket B with local depth 2, whereas the global depth was 3. Even though the bucket was split, the directory did not have to be doubled. Buckets A and A2, on the other hand, have local depth equal to the global depth, and if they grow full and are split, the directory must then be doubled.

Initially, all local depths are equal to the global depth (which is the number of bits needed to express the total number of buckets). We increment the global depth by 1 each time the directory doubles, of course. Also, whenever a bucket is split (whether or not the split leads to a directory doubling), we increment by 1 the local depth of the split bucket and assign this same (incremented) local depth to its (newly created) split image. Intuitively, if a bucket has local depth l, the hash values of data entries in it agree upon the last l bits; further, no data entry in any other bucket of the file has a hash value with the same last l bits. A total of 2^{d-l} directory elements point to a bucket with local depth l; if $d = l$, exactly one directory element is pointing to the bucket, and splitting such a bucket requires directory doubling.

A final point to note is that we can also use the first d bits (the *most significant* bits) instead of the last d (*least significant* bits), but in practice the *last d* bits are used. The reason is that a directory can then be doubled simply by copying it.

In summary, a data entry can be located by computing its hash value, taking the last d bits, and looking in the bucket pointed to by this directory element. For inserts, the data entry is placed in the bucket to which it belongs and the bucket is split if necessary to make space. A bucket split leads to an increase in the local depth, and if the local depth becomes greater than the global depth as a result, to a directory doubling (and an increase in the global depth) as well.

For deletes, the data entry is located and removed. If the delete leaves the bucket empty, it can be merged with its split image, although this step is often omitted in practice. Merging buckets decreases the local depth. If each directory element points to the same bucket as its split image (i.e., 0 and 2^{d-1} point to the same bucket, namely A; 1 and $2^{d-1} + 1$ point to the same bucket, namely B, which may or may not be identical to A; etc.), we can halve the directory and reduce the global depth, although this step is not necessary for correctness.

The insertion examples can be worked out backwards as examples of deletion. (Start with the structure shown after an insertion and delete the inserted element. In each case the original structure should be the result.)

If the directory fits in memory, an equality selection can be answered in a single disk access, as for Static Hashing (in the absence of overflow pages), but otherwise, two disk I/Os are needed. As a typical example, a 100 MB file with 100 bytes per data entry and a page size of 4 KB contains 1,000,000 data entries and only about 25,000 elements in the directory. (Each page/bucket contains roughly 40 data entries, and we have one directory element per bucket.) Thus, although equality selections can be twice as slow as for static hashed files, chances are high that the directory will fit in memory and performance is the same as for static hashed files.

On the other hand, the directory grows in spurts and can become large for *skewed data distributions* (where our assumption that data pages contain roughly equal numbers of data entries is not valid). In the context of hashed files, a **skewed data distribution** is one in which the distribution of *hash-values of search field values* (rather than the distribution of search field values themselves) is skewed (very 'bursty' or non uniform). Even if the distribution of search values is skewed, the choice of a good hashing function typically yields a fairly uniform distribution of hash-values; skew is therefore not a problem in practice.

Further, **collisions**, or data entries with the same hash value, cause a problem and must be handled specially. We have not discussed this issue; in essence, consider what happens when more data entries than will fit on a page have the same hash value. We may need overflow pages to deal with this case.

6.3 LINEAR HASHING *

Linear Hashing is a dynamic hashing technique, like Extendible Hashing, adjusting gracefully to inserts and deletes. In contrast to Extendible Hashing, it does not require a directory, deals naturally with collisions, and offers a lot of flexibility with respect to the timing of buckets splits (thus allowing us to trade off slightly greater overflow chains for higher average space utilization). If the data distribution is very skewed, however, overflow chains could cause Linear Hashing performance to be worse than that of Extendible Hashing.

The scheme utilizes a *family* of hash functions h_0, h_1, h_2, ..., with the property that each function's range is twice that of its predecessor. That is, if h_i maps a data entry into one of M buckets, h_{i+1} maps a data entry into one of $2M$ buckets. Such a family is typically obtained by choosing a hash function h and an initial number N of buckets,[2] and defining $h_i(value) = h(value) \ mod \ (2^i N)$. If N is chosen to be a power of 2, then we apply h and look at the last d_i bits; d_0 is the number of bits needed to represent N, and $d_i = d_0 + i$. Typically we choose h to be a function that maps a data entry to some integer. Suppose that we set the initial number N of buckets to be 32. In this case d_0 is 5, and h_0 is therefore $h \ mod \ 32$, that is, a number in the range 0 to 31. The value of d_1 is $d_0 + 1 = 6$, and h_1 is $h \ mod \ (2 * 32)$, that is, a number in the range 0 to 63. h_2 yields a number in the range 0 to 127, and so on.

The idea is best understood in terms of **rounds** of splitting. During round number *Level*, only hash functions h_{Level} and $h_{Level+1}$ are in use. The buckets in the file at the beginning of the round are split, one by one from the first to the last bucket, thereby doubling the number of buckets. At any given point within a

---

[2] Note that 0 to $N - 1$ is *not* the range of h!

round, therefore, we have buckets that have been split, buckets that are yet to be split, and buckets created by splits in this round, as illustrated in Figure 6.7.

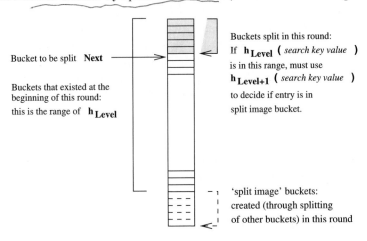

Figure 6.7 includes the following labels:

Bucket to be split **Next**

Buckets that existed at the beginning of this round: this is the range of h_{Level}

Buckets split in this round: If h_{Level} (*search key value*) is in this range, must use $h_{Level+1}$ (*search key value*) to decide if entry is in split image bucket.

'split image' buckets: created (through splitting of other buckets) in this round

Figure 6.7   Buckets during a Round in Linear Hashing

Consider how we search for a data entry with a given search key value. We apply hash function h_{Level}, and if this leads us to one of the unsplit buckets, we simply look there. If it leads us to one of the split buckets, the entry may be there or it may have been moved to the new bucket created earlier in this round by splitting this bucket; to determine which of these two buckets contains the entry, we apply $h_{Level+1}$.

Unlike Extendible Hashing, when an insert triggers a split, the bucket into which the data entry is inserted is not necessarily the bucket that is split. An overflow page is added to store the newly inserted data entry (which triggered the split), as in Static Hashing. However, since the bucket to split is chosen in round-robin fashion, eventually all buckets are split, thereby redistributing the data entries in overflow chains before the chains get to be more than one or two pages long.

We now describe Linear Hashing in more detail. A counter *Level* is used to indicate the current round number and is initialized to 0. The bucket to split is denoted by *Next* and is initially bucket 0 (the first bucket). We denote the number of buckets in the file at the beginning of round *Level* by N_{Level}. We can easily verify that $N_{Level} = N * 2^{Level}$. Let the number of buckets at the beginning of round 0, denoted by N_0, be N. We show a small linear hashed file in Figure 6.8. Each bucket can hold four data entries, and the file initially contains four buckets, as shown in the figure.

We have considerable flexibility in how to trigger a split, thanks to the use of overflow pages. We can split whenever a new overflow page is added, or we can

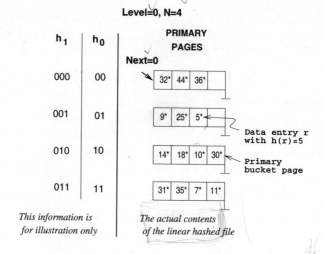

Figure 6.8 Example of a Linear Hashed File

impose additional conditions based on conditions such as space utilization. For our examples, a split is 'triggered' when inserting a new data entry causes the creation of an overflow page.

Whenever a split is triggered the *Next* bucket is split, and hash function $h_{Level+1}$ redistributes entries between this bucket (say bucket number b) and its split image; the split image is therefore bucket number $b + N_{Level}$. After splitting a bucket, the value of *Next* is incremented by 1. In the example file, insertion of data entry 43* triggers a split. The file after completing the insertion is shown in Figure 6.9.

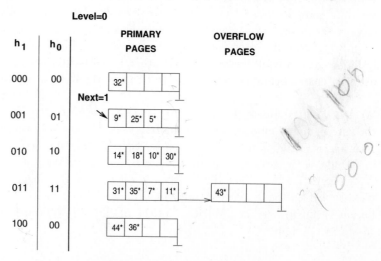

Figure 6.9 After Inserting Record r with $h(r)=43$

At any time in the middle of a round *Level*, all buckets above bucket *Next* have been split, and the file contains buckets that are their split images, as illustrated in Figure 6.7. Buckets *Next* through N_{Level} have not yet been split. If we use h_{Level} on a data entry and obtain a number b in the range *Next* through N_{Level}, the data entry belongs to bucket b. For example, $h_0(18)$ is 2 (binary 10); since this value is between the current values of *Next* $(= 1)$ and N_1 $(= 4)$, this bucket has not been split. However, if we obtain a number b in the range 0 through *Next*, the data entry may be in this bucket or in its split image (which is bucket number $b + N_{Level}$); we have to use $h_{Level+1}$ to determine which of these two buckets the data entry belongs to. In other words, we have to look at one more bit of the data entry's hash value. For example, $h_0(32)$ and $h_0(44)$ are both 0 (binary 00). Since *Next* is currently equal to 1, which indicates a bucket that has been split, we have to apply h_1. We have $h_1(32) = 0$ (binary 000) and $h_1(44) = 4$ (binary 100). Thus 32 belongs in bucket A and 44 belongs in its split image, bucket A2.

Not all insertions trigger a split, of course. If we insert 37* into the file shown in Figure 6.9, the appropriate bucket has space for the new data entry. The file after the insertion is shown in Figure 6.10.

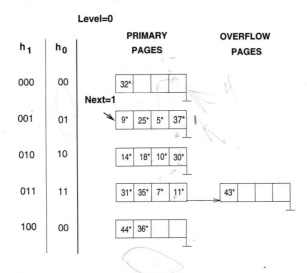

Figure 6.10   After Inserting Record r with $h(r)=37$

Sometimes, the bucket pointed to by *Next* (the current candidate for splitting) is full, and a new data entry should be inserted in this bucket. In this case a split is triggered, of course, but we do not need a new overflow bucket. This situation is illustrated by inserting 29* into the file shown in Figure 6.10. The result is shown in Figure 6.11.

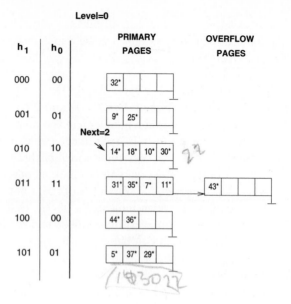

Figure 6.11   After Inserting Record *r* with *h(r)*=29

When *Next* is equal to $N_{Level} - 1$ and a split is triggered, we split the last of the buckets that were present in the file at the beginning of round *Level*. The number of buckets after the split is twice the number at the beginning of the round, and we start a new round with *Level* incremented by 1 and *Next* reset to 0. Incrementing *Level* amounts to doubling the effective range into which keys are hashed. Consider the example file in Figure 6.12, which was obtained from the file of Figure 6.11 by inserting 22*, 66*, and 34*. (The reader is encouraged to try to work out the details of these insertions.) Inserting 50* causes a split that leads to incrementing *Level*, as discussed above; the file after this insertion is shown in Figure 6.13.

In summary, an equality selection costs just one disk I/O unless the bucket has overflow pages; in practice, the cost on average is about 1.2 disk accesses for reasonably uniform data distributions. (The cost can be considerably worse—linear in the number of data entries in the file—if the distribution is very skewed. The space utilization is also very poor with skewed data distributions.) Inserts require reading and writing a single page, unless a split is triggered.

We will not discuss deletion in detail, but it is essentially the inverse of insertion. If the last bucket in the file is empty, it can be removed and *Next* can be decremented. (If *Next* is 0 and the last bucket becomes empty, *Next* is made to point to bucket $(M/2) - 1$, where M is the current number of buckets, Level is decremented, and the empty bucket is removed.) If we wish, we can combine the last bucket with its split image even when it is not empty, using some criterion to trigger this merging,

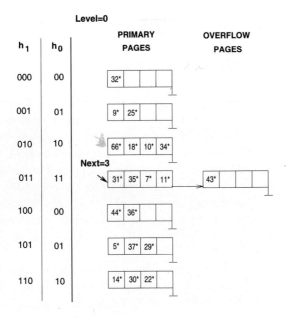

Figure 6.12 After Inserting Records with $h(r)$=22, 66 and 34

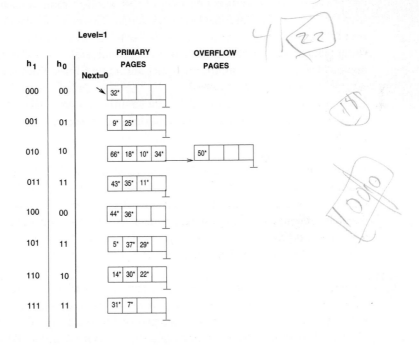

Figure 6.13 After Inserting Record r with $h(r)$=50

in essentially the same way. The criterion is typically based on the occupancy of the file, and merging can be done to improve space utilization.

6.4   EXTENDIBLE HASHING VERSUS LINEAR HASHING *

To understand the relationship between Linear Hashing and Extendible Hashing, imagine that we also have a directory in Linear Hashing with elements 0 to $N-1$. The first split is at bucket 0, and so we add directory element N. In principle, we may imagine that the entire directory has been doubled at this point; however because element 1 is the same as element $N+1$, element 2 is the same as element $N+2$, and so on, we can avoid the actual copying for the rest of the directory. The second split occurs at bucket 1; now directory element $N+1$ becomes significant and is added. At the end of the round, all the original N buckets are split, and the directory is doubled in size (because all elements point to distinct buckets).

We observe that the choice of hashing functions is actually very similar to what goes on in Extendible Hashing—in effect, moving from h_i to h_{i+1} in Linear Hashing corresponds to doubling the directory in Extendible Hashing. Both operations double the effective range into which key values are hashed; but whereas the directory is doubled in a single step of Extendible Hashing, moving from h_i to h_{i+1}, along with a corresponding doubling in the number of buckets, occurs gradually over the course of a round in Linear Hashing. The new idea behind Linear Hashing is that a directory can be avoided by a clever choice of the bucket to split. On the other hand, by always splitting the appropriate bucket, Extendible Hashing may lead to a reduced number of splits and higher bucket occupancy.

The directory analogy is useful for understanding the ideas behind Extendible and Linear Hashing. However, we note that the directory structure can indeed be avoided for Linear Hashing (but not for Extendible Hashing) by allocating primary bucket pages consecutively, which would allow us to locate the page for bucket i by a simple offset calculation. For uniform distributions, this implementation of Linear Hashing has a lower average cost for equality selections (because the directory level is eliminated). For skewed distributions, this implementation could result in any empty or nearly empty buckets, each of which is allocated at least one page, leading to poor performance relative to Extendible Hashing, which is likely to have higher bucket occupancy.

A different implementation of Linear Hashing, in which a directory is actually maintained, offers the flexibility of not allocating one page per bucket; *null* directory elements can be used as in Extendible Hashing. However, this implementation introduces the overhead of a directory level and could prove costly for large, uniformly distributed files. (Also, although this implementation alleviates the potential problem of low bucket occupancy by not allocating pages for empty buckets, it is not a complete solution because we can still have many pages with very few entries.)

6.5 SUMMARY

Static Hashing can answer equality queries with a single disk I/O, in the absence of overflow chains. As the file grows, however, Static Hashing suffers from long overflow chains and performance deteriorates. The dynamic hashing schemes address this problem.

Extendible Hashing avoids overflow pages by splitting a full bucket when a new data entry must be added to it. A directory is used to keep track of the buckets, and this directory has to be doubled in size periodically. The directory can get to be large if the data distribution is skewed, which causes a lot of bucket splits. In this context a skewed data distribution is one in which the hash values of data entries are not uniformly distributed, rather than a data distribution in which the search key values are not uniformly distributed—the choice of a good hash function can often compensate for a non uniform distribution of search key values.

If the directory does not fit in memory, finding the directory page requires an additional I/O. Doubling the directory can also be a significant overhead if the distribution is very skewed. If several data entries have the same hash value, they may not fit into one page; in this case, overflow pages must be added to handle such 'collisions.' In practice, therefore, overflow pages must be supported!

The intuition behind Linear Hashing is similar to Extendible Hashing, but the use of a directory is avoided by splitting the buckets in a round-robin fashion. Overflow pages are required, but overflow chains are unlikely to be long because of the round-robin splitting. An obvious advantage is that collisions are handled easily.

The disadvantage of Linear Hashing relative to Extendible Hashing is that space utilization could be lower, especially for skewed distributions, because the bucket splits are not concentrated where the data density is highest, as they are in Extendible Hashing. A directory-based implementation can improve space occupancy, but it is still likely to be inferior to Extendible Hashing in extreme cases. We can address this problem by adjusting the criterion used to trigger splits; in effect, we can trade off slightly longer overflow chains for better space utilization.

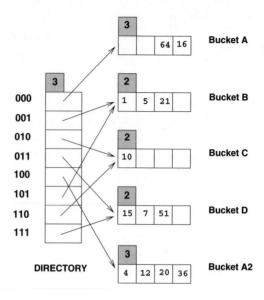

Figure 6.14   Figure for Exercise 6.1

EXERCISES

Exercise 6.1 Consider the Extendible Hashing index shown in Figure 6.14. Answer the following questions about this index:

1. What can you say about the last entry that was inserted into the index?

2. What can you say about the last entry that was inserted into the index if you know that there have been no deletions from this index so far?

3. Suppose that you are told that there have been no deletions from this index so far. What can you say about the last entry whose insertion into the index caused a split?

4. Show the index after inserting an entry with hash value 68.

5. Show the original index after inserting entries with hash values 17 and 69.

6. Show the original index after deleting the entry with hash value 21. (Assume that the full deletion algorithm is used.)

7. Show the original index after deleting the entry with hash value 10. Is a merge triggered by this deletion? If not, explain why. (Assume that the full deletion algorithm is used.)

Exercise 6.2 Consider the Extendible Hashing index shown in Figure 6.15. Answer the following questions about this index:

1. What can you say about the last entry that was inserted into the index?

2. What can you say about the last entry that was inserted into the index if you know that there have been no deletions from this index so far?

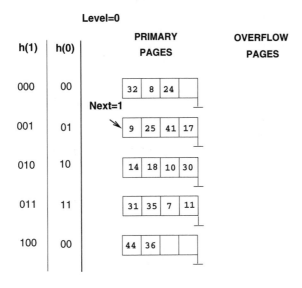

Figure 6.15 Figure for Exercise 6.2

3. Suppose that you know that there have been no deletions from this index so far. What can you say about the last entry whose insertion into the index caused a split?

4. Show the index after inserting an entry with hash value 4.

5. Show the original index after inserting an entry with hash value 15.

6. Show the original index after deleting the entries with hash values 36 and 44. (Assume that the full deletion algorithm is used.)

7. Find a list of entries whose insertion into the original index would lead to a bucket with two overflow pages. Use as few entries as possible to accomplish this. What is the maximum number of entries that can be inserted into this bucket before a split occurs that reduces the length of this overflow chain?

Exercise 6.3 Answer the following questions about Extendible Hashing:

1. Explain why local depth and global depth are needed.

2. After an insertion that causes the directory size to double, how many buckets have exactly one directory entry pointing to them? If an entry is then deleted from one of these buckets, what happens to the directory size? Explain your answers briefly.

3. Does Extendible Hashing guarantee at most one disk access to retrieve a record with a given key value?

4. If the hash function distributes data entries over the space of bucket numbers in a very skewed (non uniform) way, what can you say about the size of the directory? What can you say about the space utilization in data pages (i.e., non directory pages)?

5. Does doubling the directory require us to examine all buckets with local depth equal to global depth?

6. Why is handling duplicate key values in Extendible Hashing harder than in ISAM?

Exercise 6.4 Answer the following questions about Linear Hashing.

1. How does Linear Hashing provide an average-case search cost of only slightly more than one disk I/O, given that overflow buckets are part of its data structure?

2. Does Linear Hashing guarantee at most one disk access to retrieve a record with a given key value?

3. If a Linear Hashing index using Alternative (1) for data entries contains N records, with P records per page and an average storage utilization of 80%, what is the worst-case cost for an equality search? Under what conditions would this cost be the actual search cost?

4. If the hash function distributes data entries over the space of bucket numbers in a very skewed (non uniform) way, what can you say about the space utilization in data pages?

Exercise 6.5 Give an example of when you would use each element (A or B) for each of the following 'A versus B' pairs:

1. A hashed index using Alternative (1) versus heap file organization.

2. Extendible Hashing versus Linear Hashing.

3. Static Hashing versus Linear Hashing.

4. Static Hashing versus ISAM.

5. Linear Hashing versus B+ trees.

Exercise 6.6 Give examples of the following:

1. A Linear Hashing index and an Extendible Hashing index with the same data entries, such that the Linear Hashing index has more pages.

2. A Linear Hashing index and an Extendible Hashing index with the same data entries, such that the Extendible Hashing index has more pages.

Exercise 6.7 Consider a relation R(a, b, c, d) containing 1,000,000 records, where each page of the relation holds 10 records. R is organized as a heap file with dense secondary indexes, and the records in R are randomly ordered. Assume that attribute a is a candidate key for R, with values lying in the range 0 to 999,999. For each of the following queries, name the approach that would most likely require the fewest I/Os for processing the query. The approaches to consider follow:

■ Scanning through the whole heap file for R.

■ Using a B+ tree index on attribute R.a.

■ Using a hash index on attribute R.a.

The queries are:

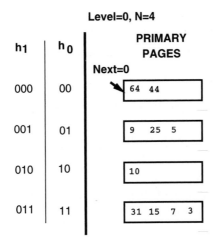

Figure 6.16 Figure for Exercise 6.9

1. Find all R tuples.

2. Find all R tuples such that $a < 50$.

3. Find all R tuples such that $a = 50$.

4. Find all R tuples such that $a > 50$ and $a < 100$.

Exercise 6.8 How would your answers to Exercise 6.7 change if attribute a is not a candidate key for R? How would they change if we assume that records in R are sorted on a?

Exercise 6.9 Consider the snapshot of the Linear Hashing index shown in Figure 6.16. Assume that a bucket split occurs whenever an overflow page is created.

1. What is the *maximum* number of data entries that can be inserted (given the best possible distribution of keys) before you have to split a bucket? Explain very briefly.

2. Show the file after inserting a *single* record whose insertion causes a bucket split.

3. (a) What is the *minimum* number of record insertions that will cause a split of all four buckets? Explain very briefly.

   (b) What is the the value of *Next* after making these insertions?

   (c) What can you say about the number of pages in the fourth bucket shown after this series of record insertions?

Exercise 6.10 Consider the data entries in the Linear Hashing index for Exercise 6.9.

1. Show an Extendible Hashing index with the same data entries.

2. Answer the questions in Exercise 6.9 with respect to this index.

Exercise 6.11 In answering the following questions, assume that the full deletion algorithm is used. Assume that merging is done when a bucket becomes empty.

1. Give an example of an Extendible Hashing index in which deleting an entry reduces the global depth.

2. Give an example of a Linear Hashing index in which deleting an entry causes *Next* to be decremented but leaves *Level* unchanged. Show the file before and after the entry is deleted.

3. Give an example of a Linear Hashing index in which deleting an entry causes *Level* to be decremented. Show the file before and after the entry is deleted.

4. Give an example of an Extendible Hashing index and a list of entries e_1, e_2, e_3 such that inserting the entries in order leads to three splits, and deleting them in the reverse order yields the original index. If such an example does not exist, explain.

5. Give an example of a Linear Hashing index and a list of entries e_1, e_2, e_3 such that inserting the entries in order leads to three splits, and deleting them in the reverse order yields the original index. If such an example does not exist, explain.

PROJECT-BASED EXERCISES

Exercise 6.12 (*Note to instructors: Additional details must be provided if this question is assigned. See Appendix A.*) Implement Linear Hashing or Extendible Hashing in Minibase.

BIBLIOGRAPHIC NOTES

Hashing is discussed in detail in [309]. Extendible Hashing is proposed in [188]. Litwin proposed Linear Hashing in [341]. A generalization of Linear Hashing for distributed environments is described in [345].

There has been extensive research into hash-based indexing techniques. Larson describes two variations of Linear Hashing in [331] and [332]. Ramakrishna presents an analysis of hashing techniques in [437]. Hash functions that do not produce bucket overflows are studied in [438]. Order-preserving hashing techniques are discussed in [342] and [217]. Partitioned-hashing, in which each field is hashed to obtain some bits of the bucket address, extends hashing for the case of queries in which equality conditions are specified only for some of the key fields. This approach was proposed by Rivest [452] and is discussed in [550]; a further development is described in [444].

EXTERNAL SORTING

Good order is the foundation of all things.

—Edmund Burke

Sorting a collection of records on some (search) key is a very useful operation. The key can be a single attribute or an ordered list of attributes, of course. Sorting is required in a variety of situations, including the following important ones:

- Users may want answers in some order; for example, by increasing age (Section 9.1).

- Sorting records is the first step in *bulk loading* a tree index (Section 5.8.2).

- Sorting is useful for eliminating *duplicate* copies in a collection of records (Chapter 12).

- A widely used algorithm for performing a very important relational algebra operation, called *join*, requires a sorting step (Section 12.5.2).

Although main memory sizes are increasing, as usage of database systems increases, increasingly larger datasets are becoming common as well. When the data to be sorted is too large to fit into available main memory, we need to use an *external sorting* algorithm. Such algorithms seek to minimize the cost of disk accesses.

We introduce the idea of external sorting by considering a very simple algorithm in Section 7.1; using repeated passes over the data, even very large datasets can be sorted with a small amount of memory. This is algorithm generalized to develop a realistic external sorting algorithm in Section 7.2. Three important refinements are discussed. The first, discussed in Section 7.2.1, enables us to reduce the number of passes. The next two refinements, covered in Section 7.3, require us to consider a more detailed model of I/O costs than the number of page I/Os. Section 7.3.1 discusses the effect of *blocked* I/O, that is, reading and writing several pages at a time; and Section 7.3.2 considers how to use a technique called double buffering to minimize the time spent waiting for an I/O operation to complete. Section 7.4 discusses the use of B+ trees for sorting.

With the exception of Section 7.3, we consider only I/O costs, which we approximate by counting the number of pages read or written, as per the cost model discussed in Chapter 4. Our goal is to use a simple cost model to convey the main ideas, rather than to provide a detailed analysis.

7.1   A SIMPLE TWO-WAY MERGE SORT

We begin by presenting a simple algorithm to illustrate the idea behind external sorting. This algorithm utilizes only three pages of main memory, which is very unrealistic, and it is presented only for pedagogical purposes. In the course of sorting a file, several sorted subfiles are typically generated in intermediate steps. In this chapter, we will refer to each sorted subfile as a **run**.

The basic idea is that even if the entire file does not fit into the available main memory, we can sort it by breaking it into smaller subfiles, sorting these subfiles, and then merging them using a minimal amount of main memory at any given time. In the first pass the pages in the file are read in one at a time. When a page is read in, the records on it are sorted and the sorted page (a sorted run one page long) is written out. Quicksort or any other in-memory sorting technique can be used to sort the records on a page. In subsequent passes pairs of runs from the output of the previous pass are read in and *merged* to produce runs that are twice as long. This algorithm is shown in Figure 7.1.

> **proc** *sort2* (file)
> // *Given a file on disk, sorts it using three buffer pages*
> // Produce runs that are one page long: Pass 0
> Read each page into memory, sort it, write it out.
> // Merge pairs of runs to produce longer runs until only
> // one run (containing all records of input file) is left
> While the number of runs at end of previous pass is > 1:
>   // Pass i = 1, 2, ...
>   While there are runs to be merged from previous pass:
>   Choose next two runs (from previous pass).
>   Read each run into an input buffer; page at a time.
>   Merge the runs and write to the output buffer;
>   force output buffer to disk one page at a time.
>
> **endproc**

Figure 7.1   Two-Way Merge Sort

If the number of pages in the input file is 2^k, for some k:

> Pass 0 produces 2^k sorted runs of one page each,
> Pass 1 produces 2^{k-1} sorted runs of two pages each,
> Pass 2 produces 2^{k-2} sorted runs of four pages each,
> and so on, until
> Pass k produces one sorted run of 2^k pages.

In each pass we read every page in the file, process it, and write it out. Thus we have two disk I/Os per page, per pass. The number of passes is $\lceil log_2 N \rceil + 1$, where N is the number of pages in the file. Thus the cost is $2N(\lceil log_2 N \rceil + 1)$ I/Os.

The algorithm is illustrated on an example input file containing seven pages in Figure 7.2. The sort takes a total of four passes, and in each pass we read and write seven pages, for a total of 56 I/Os. This result agrees with the preceding analysis because $2 * 7(\lceil log_2 7 \rceil + 1) = 56$. The dark pages in the figure illustrate what would happen on a file of eight pages; the number of passes remains at four ($\lceil log_2 8 \rceil + 1 = 4$), but we read and write an additional page in each pass for a total of 64 I/Os. (Try to work out what would happen on a file with, say, five pages.)

This algorithm requires just three buffer pages in main memory, as Figure 7.3 illustrates. This observation raises an important point: even if we have more buffer space available, this simple algorithm cannot utilize it effectively. The external merge sort algorithm that we discuss next addresses this problem.

7.2 EXTERNAL MERGE SORT

Suppose that B buffer pages are available in memory and that we need to sort a large file with N pages. How can we improve upon the two-way merge sort presented in the previous section? The intuition behind the generalized algorithm that we now present is to retain the basic structure of making multiple passes while trying to minimize the number of passes. There are two important modifications to the two-way merge sort algorithm:

1. In Pass 0, read in B pages at a time and sort internally to produce $\lceil N/B \rceil$ runs of B pages each (except for the last run, which may contain fewer pages). This modification is illustrated in Figure 7.4, using the input file from Figure 7.2 and a buffer pool with four pages.

2. In passes i=1,2, ... , use $B - 1$ buffer pages for input, and use the remaining page for output; thus you do a $(B-1)$-way merge in each pass. The utilization of buffer pages in the merging passes is illustrated in Figure 7.5.

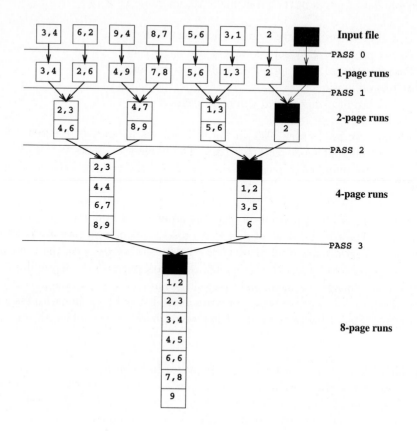

Figure 7.2 Two-Way Merge Sort of a Seven-Page File

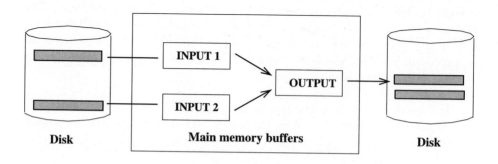

Figure 7.3 Two-Way Merge Sort with Three Buffer Pages

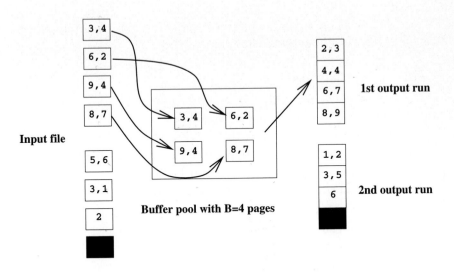

Figure 7.4   External Merge Sort with B Buffer Pages: Pass 0

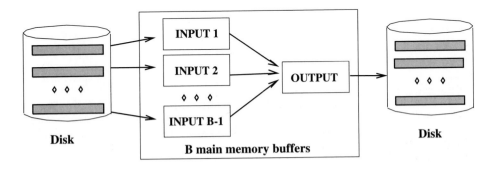

Figure 7.5   External Merge Sort with B Buffer Pages: Pass $i > 0$

The first refinement reduces the number of runs produced by Pass 0 to $N1 = \lceil N/B \rceil$, versus N for the two-way merge.[1] The second refinement is even more important. By doing a $(B - 1)$-way merge, the number of passes is reduced dramatically—including the initial pass, it becomes $\lceil log_{B-1} N1 \rceil + 1$ versus $\lceil log_2 N \rceil + 1$ for the two-way merge algorithm presented earlier. Because B is typically quite large, the savings can be substantial.

> **proc** *extsort* (file)
> // *Given a file on disk, sorts it using three buffer pages*
> // Produce runs that are B pages long: Pass 0
> Read B pages into memory, sort them, write out a run.
> // Merge $B - 1$ runs at a time to produce longer runs until only
> // one run (containing all records of input file) is left
> While the number of runs at end of previous pass is > 1:
>   // Pass i = 1, 2, ...
>   While there are runs to be merged from previous pass:
>   Choose next $B - 1$ runs (from previous pass).
>   Read each run into an input buffer; page at a time.
>   Merge the runs and write to the output buffer;
>   force output buffer to disk one page at a time.
>
> **endproc**

Figure 7.6   External Merge Sort

As an example, suppose that we have five buffer pages available, and want to sort a file with 108 pages.

> Pass 0 produces $\lceil 108/5 \rceil = 22$ sorted runs of five pages each, except for the last run, which is only three pages long.
> Pass 1 does a four-way merge to produce $\lceil 22/4 \rceil =$ six sorted runs of 20 pages each, except for the last run, which is only eight pages long.
> Pass 2 produces $\lceil 6/4 \rceil =$ two sorted runs; one with 80 pages and one with 28 pages.
> Pass 3 merges the two runs produced in Pass 2 to produce the sorted file.

In each pass we read and write 108 pages; thus the total cost is $2 * 108 * 4 = 864$ I/Os. Applying our formula, we have $N1 = \lceil 108/5 \rceil = 22$ and cost $= 2 * N * (\lceil log_{B-1} N1 \rceil + 1) = 2 * 108 * (\lceil log_4 22 \rceil + 1) = 864$, as expected.

---

[1] Incidentally, note that the technique used for sorting data in buffer pages is orthogonal to external sorting. You could use, say, Quicksort for sorting data in buffer pages.

To emphasize the potential gains in using all available buffers, in Figure 7.7 we show the number of passes, computed using our formula, for several values of N and B. To obtain the cost, the number of passes should be multiplied by $2N$. In practice, one would expect to have more than 257 buffers, but this table illustrates the importance of a high fan-in during merging.

N	B=3	B=5	B=9	B=17	B=129	B=257
100	7	4	3	2	1	1
1000	10	5	4	3	2	2
10,000	13	7	5	4	2	2
100,000	17	9	6	5	3	3
1,000,000	20	10	7	5	3	3
10,000,000	23	12	8	6	4	3
100,000,000	26	14	9	7	4	4
1,000,000,000	30	15	10	8	5	4

Figure 7.7 Number of Passes of External Merge Sort

Of course, the CPU cost of a multiway merge can be greater than that for a two-way merge, but in general the I/O costs tend to dominate. In doing a $(B-1)$-way merge, we have to repeatedly pick the 'lowest' record in the $B - 1$ runs being merged and write it to the output buffer. This operation can be implemented simply by examining the first (remaining) element in each of the $B - 1$ input buffers. In practice, for large values of B, more sophisticated techniques can be used, although we will not discuss them here. Further, as we will see shortly, there are other ways to utilize buffer pages in order to reduce I/O costs; these techniques involve allocating additional pages to each input (and output) run, thereby making the number of runs merged in each pass considerably smaller than the number of buffer pages B.

7.2.1 Minimizing the Number of Runs *

In Pass 0 we read in B pages at a time and sorted internally to produce $\lceil N/B \rceil$ runs of B pages each (except for the last run, which may contain fewer pages). With a more aggressive implementation, we can write out runs of approximately $2 * B$ internally sorted pages on average.

This improvement is achieved as follows. We begin by reading in pages of the file of tuples to be sorted, say R, until the buffer is full, reserving (say) one page for use as an input buffer and (say) one page for use as an output buffer. We will refer to the $B - 2$ pages of R tuples that are not in the input or output buffer as the *current set*. Suppose that the file is to be sorted in ascending order on some search key k. Tuples are appended to the output in ascending order by k value.

The idea is to repeatedly pick the tuple in the current set with the smallest k value that is still greater than the largest k value in the output buffer, and append it to the output buffer. The idea is to repeatedly pick a tuple in the current set and append it to the output buffer. In order for the output buffer to remain sorted, the chosen tuple must satisfy the condition that its k value be greater than the largest k value currently in the output buffer; of all tuples in the current set that satisfy this condition, we pick the one with the smallest k value, and append it to the output buffer. Moving this tuple to the output buffer creates some space in the current set, which we use to add the next input tuple to the current set. (We assume for simplicity that all tuples are the same size.) This process is illustrated in Figure 7.8. The tuple in the current set that is going to be appended to the output next is highlighted, as is the most recently appended output tuple.

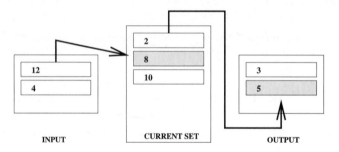

Figure 7.8   Generating Longer Runs

When all tuples in the input buffer have been consumed in this manner, the next page of the file is read in. Of course, the output buffer is written out when it is full, thereby extending the current run (which is gradually built up on disk).

The important question is this: When do we have to terminate the current run and start a new run? As long as some tuple t in the current set has a bigger k value than the most recently appended output tuple, we can append t to the output buffer, and the current run can be extended.[2] In Figure 7.8, although a tuple ($k = 2$) in the current set has a smaller k value than the largest output tuple ($k = 5$), the current run can be extended because the current set also has a tuple ($k = 8$) that is larger than the largest output tuple.

When every tuple in the current set is smaller than the largest tuple in the output buffer, the output buffer is written out and becomes the last page in the current

---

[2]If B is large, the CPU cost of finding such a tuple t can be significant unless appropriate in-memory data structures are used to organize the tuples in the buffer pool. We will not discuss this issue further.

run. We then start a new run and continue the cycle of writing tuples from the input buffer to the current set to the output buffer. It is known that this algorithm produces runs that are about $2 * B$ pages long, on average.

7.3 MINIMIZING I/O COST VERSUS NUMBER OF I/OS

We have thus far used the number of page I/Os as a cost metric. This metric is only an approximation to true I/O costs because it ignores the effect of *blocked I/O*—issuing a single request to read (or write) several consecutive pages can be much cheaper than reading (or writing) the same number of pages through independent I/O requests, as discussed in Chapter 4. This difference turns out to have some very important consequences for our external sorting algorithm.

Further, the time taken to perform I/O is only part of the time taken by the algorithm; we must consider CPU costs as well. Even if the time taken to do I/O accounts for most of the total time, the time taken for processing records is nontrivial and is definitely worth reducing. In particular, we can use a technique called *double buffering* to keep the CPU busy while an I/O operation is in progress.

In this section we consider how the external sorting algorithm can be refined using blocked I/O and double buffering. The motivation for these optimizations requires us to look beyond the number of I/Os as a cost metric. These optimizations can also be applied to other I/O intensive operations such as joins, which we will study in Chapter 12.

7.3.1 Blocked I/O *

If the number of page I/Os is taken to be the cost metric, the goal is clearly to minimize the number of passes in the sorting algorithm because each page in the file is read and written in each pass. It therefore makes sense to maximize the fan-in during merging by allocating just one buffer pool page per run (which is to be merged) and one buffer page for the output of the merge. Thus we can merge $B - 1$ runs, where B is the number of pages in the buffer pool. If we take into account the effect of blocked access, which reduces the average cost to read or write *a single page*, we are led to consider whether it might be better to read and write in units of more than one page.

Suppose that we decide to read and write in units, which we call **buffer blocks**, of b pages. We must now set aside one buffer block per input run and one buffer block for the output of the merge, which means that we can merge at most $\lfloor \frac{B-b}{b} \rfloor$ runs in each pass. For example, if we have 10 buffer pages, we can either merge nine runs at a time with 1-page input and output buffer blocks, or we can merge four runs at a time with 2-page input and output buffer blocks. If we choose larger buffer blocks, however, the number of passes increases, while we continue to read and write every page in the file in each pass! In the example each merging pass reduces the number of runs by a factor of 4, rather than a factor of 9. Therefore, the number of page I/Os increases. This is the price we pay for decreasing the per-page I/O cost and is a trade-off that we must take into account when designing an external sorting algorithm.

In practice, however, current main memory sizes are large enough that all but the largest files can be sorted in just two passes, even using blocked I/O. Suppose that we have B buffer pages and choose to use a blocking factor of b pages. That is, we read and write b pages at a time, and our input and output buffer blocks are all b pages long. The first pass produces about $N2 = \lceil N/2B \rceil$ sorted runs, each of length $2B$ pages, if we use the optimization described in Section 7.2.1, and about $N1 = \lceil N/B \rceil$ sorted runs, each of length B pages, otherwise. For the purposes of this section, we will assume that the optimization is used.

In subsequent passes we can merge $F = \lfloor B/b \rfloor - 1$ runs at a time. The number of passes is therefore $1 + \lceil log_F N2 \rceil$, and in each pass we read and write all pages in the file. Figure 7.9 shows the number of passes needed to sort files of various sizes N, given B buffer pages, using a blocking factor b of 32 pages. It is quite reasonable to expect 5000 pages to be available for sorting purposes; with 4KB pages, 5000 pages is only 20MB. (With 10,000 buffer pages, we can do 311-way merges, with 5000 buffer pages, we can do 155-way merges, and with 1000 buffer pages, we can do 30-way merges.)

N	B=1000	B=5000	B=10,000
100	1	1	1
1000	1	1	1
10,000	2	2	1
100,000	3	2	2
1,000,000	3	2	2
10,000,000·	4	3	3
100,000,000	5	3	3
1,000,000,000	5	4	3

Figure 7.9   Number of Passes of External Merge Sort with Block Size $b = 32$

To compute the I/O cost, we need to calculate the number of 32-page blocks read or written, and multiply this number by the cost of doing a 32-page block I/O. To find the number of block I/Os, we can find the total number of page I/Os (number of passes multiplied by the number of pages in the file) and divide by the block size, 32. The cost of a 32-page block I/O is the seek time and rotational delay for the first page, plus transfer time for all 32 pages, as discussed in Chapter 4. The reader is invited to calculate the total I/O cost of sorting files of the sizes mentioned in Figure 7.9 with 5000 buffer pages, for different block sizes (say, $b = 1$, 32 and 64) to get a feel for the benefits of using blocked I/O.

7.3.2 Double Buffering *

Consider what happens in the external sorting algorithm when all the tuples in an input block have been consumed: an I/O request is issued for the next block of tuples in the corresponding input run, and the execution is forced to suspend until the I/O is complete. That is, for the duration of the time taken for reading in one block, the CPU remains idle (assuming that no other jobs are running). The overall time taken by an algorithm can be increased considerably because the CPU is repeatedly forced to wait for an I/O operation to complete. This effect becomes more and more important as CPU speeds increase relative to I/O speeds, which is a long-standing trend in relative speeds. It is therefore desirable to keep the CPU busy while an I/O request is being carried out, that is, to overlap CPU and I/O processing. Current hardware supports such overlapped computation, and it is therefore desirable to design algorithms to take advantage of this capability.

In the context of external sorting, we can achieve this overlap by allocating extra pages to each input buffer. Suppose that a block size of $b = 32$ is chosen. The idea is to allocate an additional 32-page block to every input (and the output) buffer. Now, when all the tuples in a 32-page block have been consumed, the CPU can process the next 32 pages of the run by switching to the second, 'double,' block for this run. Meanwhile, an I/O request is issued to fill the empty block. Thus assuming that the time to consume a block is greater than the time to read in a block, the CPU is never idle! On the other hand, the number of pages allocated to a buffer is doubled (for a given block size, which means the total I/O cost stays the same). This technique is called **double buffering**, and it can considerably reduce the total time taken to sort a file. The use of buffer pages is illustrated in Figure 7.10.

Note that although double buffering can considerably reduce the response time for a given query, it may not have a significant impact on throughput, because the CPU can be kept busy by working on other queries while waiting for one query's I/O operation to complete.

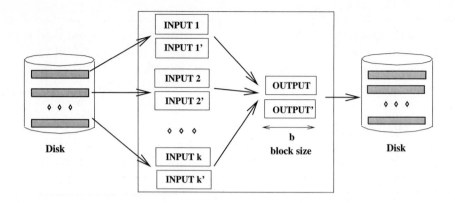

Figure 7.10   Double Buffering

7.4   USING B+ TREES FOR SORTING

Suppose that we have a B+ tree index on the (search) key to be used for sorting a file of records. Instead of using an external sorting algorithm, we could use the B+ tree index to retrieve the records in search key order by traversing the sequence set (i.e., the sequence of leaf pages). Whether this is a good strategy depends on the nature of the index.

7.4.1   Clustered Index

If the B+ tree index is clustered, then the traversal of the sequence set is very efficient. The search key order corresponds to the order in which the data records are stored, and for each page of data records that we retrieve, we can read all the records on it in sequence. This correspondence between search key ordering and data record ordering is illustrated in Figure 7.11, with the assumption that data entries are ⟨*key, rid*⟩ pairs (i.e., Alternative (2) is used for data entries).

The cost of using the clustered B+ tree index to retrieve the data records in search key order is the cost to traverse the tree from root to the left-most leaf (which is usually less than four I/Os) plus the cost of retrieving the pages in the sequence set, plus the cost of retrieving the (say N) pages containing the data records. Note that no data page is retrieved twice, thanks to the ordering of data entries being the same as the ordering of data records. The number of pages in the sequence set is likely to be much smaller than the number of data pages because data entries are likely to be smaller than typical data records. Thus the strategy of using a clustered B+ tree index to retrieve the records in sorted order is a good one and should be used whenever such an index is available.

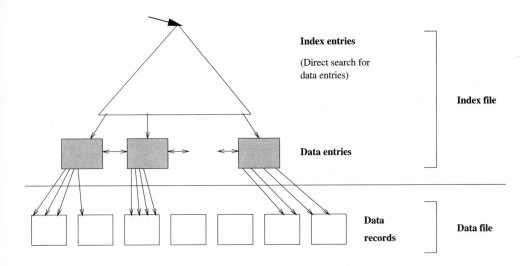

Figure 7.11 Clustered B+ Tree for Sorting

What if Alternative (1) is used for data entries? Then the leaf pages would contain the actual data records, and retrieving the pages in the sequence set (a total of N pages) would be the only cost. (Note that the space utilization is about 67% in a B+ tree; thus the number of leaf pages is greater than the number of pages needed to hold the data records in a sorted file, where, in principle, 100% space utilization can be achieved.) In this case the choice of the B+ tree for sorting is excellent!

7.4.2 Unclustered Index

What if the B+ tree index on the key to be used for sorting is unclustered? This is illustrated in Figure 7.12, with the assumption that data entries are ⟨*key, rid*⟩.

In this case each rid in a leaf page could point to a different data page. Should this happen, the cost (in disk I/Os) of retrieving all data records could equal the number of data records. That is, the worst-case cost is equal to the number of data records because fetching each record could require a disk I/O. This cost is in addition to the cost of retrieving leaf pages of the B+ tree to get the data entries (which point to the data records).

If p is the average number of records per data page and there are N data pages, the number of data records is $p * N$. If we take f to be the ratio of the size of a data entry to the size of a data record, we can approximate the number of leaf pages in the tree by $f * N$. The total cost of retrieving records in sorted order

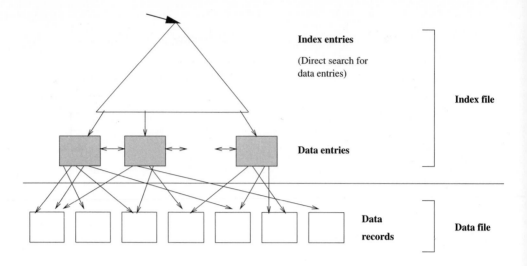

Figure 7.12   Unclustered B+ Tree for Sorting

using a unclustered B+ tree is therefore $(f + p) * N$. Since f is usually 0.1 or smaller and p is typically much larger than 10, $p * N$ is a good approximation.

In practice, the cost may be somewhat less because some rids in a leaf page will lead to the same data page, and further, some pages will be found in the buffer pool, thereby avoiding an I/O. Nonetheless, the usefulness of an unclustered B+ tree index for sorted retrieval is highly dependent on the extent to which the order of data entries corresponds—and this is just a matter of chance—to the physical ordering of data records.

We illustrate the cost of sorting a file of records using external sorting and unclustered B+ tree indexes in Figure 7.13. The costs shown for the unclustered index are worst-case numbers and are based on the approximate formula $p * N$. For comparison, note that the cost for a clustered index is approximately equal to N, the number of pages of data records.

Keep in mind that p is likely to be closer to 100 and that B is likely to be higher than 1000 in practice. The ratio of the cost of sorting versus the cost of using an unclustered index is likely to be even lower than is indicated by Figure 7.13 because the I/O for sorting is in 32-page buffer blocks, whereas the I/O for the unclustered indexes is one page at a time. The value of p is determined by the page size and the size of a data record; for p to be 10, with 4KB pages, the average data record size must be about 400 bytes. In practice, p is likely to be greater than 10.

N	Sorting	$p=1$	$p=10$	$p=100$
100	200	100	1000	10,000
1000	2000	1000	10,000	100,000
10,000	40,000	10,000	100,000	1,000,000
100,000	600,000	100,000	1,000,000	10,000,000
1,000,000	8,000,000	1,000,000	10,000,000	100,000,000
10,000,000	80,000,000	10,000,000	100,000,000	1,000,000,000

Figure 7.13   Cost of External Sorting ($B=1000$, $b=32$) versus Unclustered Index

For even modest file sizes, therefore, sorting by using an unclustered index is clearly inferior to external sorting. Indeed, even if we want to retrieve only about 10 to 20% of the data records, for example, in response to a range query such as "Find all sailors whose rating is greater than 7," sorting the file may prove to be more efficient than using an unclustered index!

7.5 SUMMARY

External sorting plays an important role in a DBMS; so much so that systems often dedicate a part of the buffer pool for sorting purposes. Sorting is required for ordering answers as per user requests, for bulk loading B+ tree indexes, for eliminating duplicate tuples, and as part of a widely used join algorithm.

The focus in external sorting is to minimize the cost of disk I/Os, and the key is to use the available main memory as effectively as possible. In the first pass the data is repeatedly read in and sorted in memory to create *runs* of length equal to the number of main memory pages. In each subsequent pass, runs are read into memory in units of pages called *buffer blocks*. As many blocks (one per run) full of data are read in as is possible, given the available main memory. The blocks are merged to produce larger runs, which are similarly merged in later passes. For all but the largest files, a single merging pass is sufficient.

If the data to be sorted has a clustered B+ tree index with a search key equal to the fields to be sorted by, then we can simply scan the sequence set to produce the records in sorted order. This technique is clearly superior to using an external sorting algorithm. However, if the index is not clustered, an external sorting algorithm will almost certainly be cheaper than using the index. Of course, a hash-based index is of no use for sorting purposes.

EXERCISES

Exercise 7.1 Suppose that you have a file with 10,000 pages and that you have 3 buffer pages. Answer the following questions for each of these scenarios, assuming that our most general external sorting algorithm is used:

(a) A file with 10,000 pages and 3 available buffer pages.

(b) A file with 20,000 pages and 5 available buffer pages.

(c) A file with 2,000,000 pages and 17 available buffer pages.

1. How many runs will you produce in the first pass?

2. How many passes will it take to sort the file completely?

3. What is the total I/O cost of sorting the file?

4. How many buffer pages do you need to sort the file completely in just 2 passes?

Exercise 7.2 Answer Exercise 7.1 assuming that a 2-way external sort is used.

Exercise 7.3 Suppose that you just finished inserting several records into a heap file, and now you want to sort those records. Assume that the DBMS uses external sort and makes efficient use of the available buffer space when it sorts a file. Here is some potentially useful information about the newly loaded file and the DBMS software that is available to operate on it:

> The number of records in the file is 4500. The sort key for the file is 4 bytes long. You can assume that rids are 8 bytes long and page ids are 4 bytes long. Each record is a total of 48 bytes long. The page size is 512 bytes. Each page has 12 bytes of control information on it. Four buffer pages are available.

1. How many sorted subfiles will there be after the initial pass of the sort, and how long will each subfile be?

2. How many passes (including the initial pass considered above) will be required to sort this file?

3. What will be the total I/O cost for sorting this file?

4. What is the largest file, in terms of the number of records, that you can sort with just 4 buffer pages in 2 passes? How would your answer change if you had 257 buffer pages?

5. Suppose that you have a B+ tree index with the search key being the same as the desired sort key. Find the cost of using the index to retrieve the records in sorted order for each of the following cases:

   ■ The index uses Alternative (1) for data entries.

   ■ The index uses Alternative (2) and is not clustered. (You can compute the worst-case cost in this case.)

   ■ How would the costs of using the index change if the file is the largest that you can sort in two passes of external sort with 257 buffer pages? Give your answer for both clustered and unclustered indexes.

Exercise 7.4 Consider a disk with an average seek time of 10ms, average rotational delay of 5ms, and a transfer time of 1ms for a 4K page. Assume that the cost of reading/writing a page is the sum of these values (i.e., 16ms) unless a *sequence* of pages is read/written. In this case the cost is the average seek time plus the average rotational delay (to find the first page in the sequence) plus 1ms per page (to transfer data). You are given 320 buffer pages and asked to sort a file with 10,000,000 pages.

1. Why is it a bad idea to use the 320 pages to support virtual memory, that is, to 'new' 10,000,000*4K bytes of memory, and to use an in-memory sorting algorithm such as Quicksort?

2. Assume that you begin by creating sorted runs of 320 pages each in the first pass. Evaluate the cost of the following approaches for the subsequent merging passes:

   (a) Do 319-way merges.

   (b) Create 256 'input' buffers of 1 page each, create an 'output' buffer of 64 pages, and do 256-way merges.

   (c) Create 16 'input' buffers of 16 pages each, create an 'output' buffer of 64 pages, and do 16-way merges.

   (d) Create 8 'input' buffers of 32 pages each, create an 'output' buffer of 64 pages, and do 8-way merges.

   (e) Create 4 'input' buffers of 64 pages each, create an 'output' buffer of 64 pages, and do 4-way merges.

Exercise 7.5 Consider the refinement to the external sort algorithm that produces runs of length $2B$ on average, where B is the number of buffer pages. This refinement was described in Section 7.2.1 under the assumption that all records are the same size. Explain why this assumption is required and extend the idea to cover the case of variable length records.

PROJECT-BASED EXERCISES

Exercise 7.6 (*Note to instructors: Additional details must be provided if this question is assigned; see Appendix A.*) Implement external sorting in Minibase.

BIBLIOGRAPHIC NOTES

Knuth's text [309] is the classic reference for sorting algorithms. A number of papers discuss parallel external sorting algorithms, including [50, 53, 163, 352, 409, 466].

8

RELATIONAL ALGEBRA
AND CALCULUS

> Stand firm in your refusal to remain conscious during algebra. In real life, I
> assure you, there is no such thing as algebra.
>
> —Fran Lebowitz, *Social Studies*

This chapter presents two formal query languages associated with the relational
model. **Query languages** are specialized languages for asking questions, or
queries, that involve the data in a database. After covering some preliminaries
in Section 8.1, we discuss *relational algebra* in Section 8.2. Queries in algebra are
composed using a collection of operators, and each query describes a step-by-step
procedure for computing the desired answer; that is, queries are specified in an
operational manner. In Section 8.3 we discuss **relational calculus**, in which a
query describes the desired answer without specifying how the answer is to be
computed; this nonprocedural style of querying is called *declarative*. We compare
the expressive power of algebra and calculus in Section 8.4. These formal query
languages have greatly influenced commercial query languages such as SQL, which
we will discuss in later chapters.

8.1 PRELIMINARIES

To set the stage for a detailed look at relational queries and query languages,
we begin by clarifying some important points. The inputs and outputs for a
query are relations. A query is evaluated using *instances* of each input relation,
and produces an instance of the output relation. In Section 2.4, we used field
names to refer to fields because this notation makes queries more readable. An
alternative is to always list the fields of a given relation in the same order and to
refer to fields by position rather than by field name.

In defining relational algebra and calculus, the alternative of referring to fields
by position is more convenient than referring to fields by name: Queries often
involve the computation of intermediate results, which are themselves relation
instances, and if we use field names to refer to fields, the definition of query
language constructs must specify the names of fields for all intermediate relation
instances. This can be tedious, and is really a secondary issue because we can

refer to fields by position anyway. On the other hand, field names make queries more readable.

Due to these considerations, we use the positional notation to formally define relational algebra and calculus. We also introduce simple conventions that allow intermediate relations to 'inherit' field names, for convenience.

We present a number of sample queries using the following schema:

> Sailors(*sid:* `integer`, *sname:* `string`, *rating:* `integer`, *age:* `real`)
> Boats(*bid:* `integer`, *bname:* `string`, *color:* `string`)
> Reserves(*sid:* `integer`, *bid:* `integer`, *day:* `dates`)

The key fields are underlined, and the domain of each field is listed after the field name. Thus *sid* is the key for Sailors, *bid* is the key for Boats, and all three fields together form the key for Reserves. Fields in an instance of one of these relations will be referred to by name, or positionally, using the order in which they are listed above.

In several examples, we will use the instances $S1$ and $S2$ (of Sailors) and $R1$ (of Reserves) shown in Figures 8.1, 8.2, and 8.3, respectively.

sid	sname	rating	age
22	dustin	7	45.0
31	lubber	8	55.5
58	rusty	10	35.0

Figure 8.1 An Instance $S1$ of Sailors

sid	sname	rating	age
28	yuppy	9	35.0
31	lubber	8	55.5
44	guppy	5	35.0
58	rusty	10	35.0

Figure 8.2 An Instance $S2$ of Sailors

sid	bid	day
22	101	10/10/96
58	103	11/12/96

Figure 8.3 An Instance $R1$ of Reserves

8.2 RELATIONAL ALGEBRA

Relational algebra is one of the two formal query languages associated with the relational model. Queries in algebra are composed using a collection of operators. A fundamental property is that every operator in the algebra accepts (one or two) relation instances as arguments and returns a relation instance as the result. This property makes it easy to *compose* operators to form a complex query—a **relational algebra expression** is recursively defined to be a relation, a unary algebra operator applied to a single expression, or a binary algebra operator applied to two expressions. We describe the basic operators of the algebra (selection, projection, union, cross-product and difference), as well as some additional operators that can be defined in terms of the basic operators but arise frequently enough to warrant special attention, in the following sections.

Each relational query describes a step-by-step procedure for computing the desired answer, based on the order in which operators are applied in the query. The procedural nature of the algebra allows us to think of an algebra expression as a recipe, or a plan, for evaluating a query, and relational systems in fact use algebra expressions to represent query evaluation plans.

8.2.1   Selection and Projection

Relational algebra provides operators to *select* rows from a relation (σ) and to *project* columns (π). These operations allow us to manipulate data in a single relation. Consider the instance of the Sailors relation shown in Figure 8.2, denoted as *S2*. We can retrieve rows corresponding to expert sailors by using the σ operator. The expression

$$\sigma_{rating>8}(S2)$$

evaluates to the relation shown in Figure 8.4. The subscript *rating>8* specifies the selection criterion to be applied while retrieving tuples.

sname	rating
yuppy	9
lubber	8
guppy	5
rusty	10

sid	sname	rating	age
28	yuppy	9	35.0
58	rusty	10	35.0

Figure 8.4 $\sigma_{rating>8}(S2)$ **Figure 8.5** $\pi_{sname,rating}(S2)$

The selection operator σ specifies the tuples to retain through a *selection condition*. In general, the selection condition is a boolean combination (i.e., an expression using the logical connectives $\wedge$ and $\vee$) of *terms* that have the form *attribute op constant* or *attribute1 op attribute2*, where *op* is one of the comparison operators $<, <=, =, \neq, >=$ or $>$. The reference to an attribute can be by position (of the form *.i* or *i*) or by name (of the form *.name* or *name*). The schema of the result of a selection is the schema of the input relation instance.

The projection operator π allows us to extract columns from a relation; for example, we can find out all sailor names and ratings by using π. The expression

$$\pi_{sname,rating}(S2)$$

evaluates to the relation shown in Figure 8.5. The subscript *sname, rating* specifies the fields to be retained; the other fields are 'projected out.' The schema of the result of a projection is determined by the fields that are projected in the obvious way.

Suppose that we wanted to find out only the ages of sailors. The expression

$$\pi_{age}(S2)$$

evaluates to the relation shown in Figure 8.6. The important point to note is that although three sailors are aged 35, a single tuple with *age=35.0* appears in the result of the projection. This follows from the definition of a relation as a *set* of tuples. In practice, real systems often omit the expensive step of eliminating *duplicate tuples*, leading to relations that are multisets. However, our discussion of relational algebra and calculus assumes that duplicate elimination is always done so that relations are sets of tuples.

Since the result of a relational algebra expression is always a relation, we can substitute an expression wherever a relation is expected. For example, we can compute the names and ratings of highly rated sailors by combining two of the preceding queries. The expression

$$\pi_{sname,rating}(\sigma_{rating>8}(S2))$$

produces the result shown in Figure 8.7. It is obtained by applying the selection to $S2$ (to get the relation shown in Figure 8.4) and then applying the projection.

age
35.0
55.5

sname	rating
yuppy	9
rusty	10

Figure 8.6 $\pi_{age}(S2)$

Figure 8.7 $\pi_{sname,rating}(\sigma_{rating>8}(S2))$

8.2.2 Set-Operations

The following standard operations on sets are also available in relational algebra: *union* ($\cup$), *intersection* ($\cap$), *set-difference* ($-$), and *cross-product* ($\times$).

- **Union:** $R \cup S$ returns a relation instance containing all tuples that occur in *either* relation instance R or relation instance S (or both). R and S must be *union-compatible*, and the schema of the result is defined to be identical to the schema of R.

Two relation instances are said to be **union-compatible** if the following conditions hold:

- they have the same number of the fields, and

- corresponding fields, taken in order from left to right, have the same *domains*.

Note that field names are not used in defining union-compatibility. For convenience, we will assume that the fields of $R \cup S$ inherit names from R, if the fields of R have names. (This assumption is implicit in defining the schema of $R \cup S$ to be identical to the schema of R, as stated earlier.)

- **Intersection:** $R \cap S$ returns a relation instance containing all tuples that occur in *both* R and S. The relations R and S must be union-compatible, and the schema of the result is defined to be identical to the schema of R.

- **Set-difference:** $R - S$ returns a relation instance containing all tuples that occur in R but not in S. The relations R and S must be union-compatible, and the schema of the result is defined to be identical to the schema of R.

- **Cross-product:** $R \times S$ returns a relation instance whose schema contains all the fields of R (in the same order as they appear in R) followed by all the fields of S (in the same order as they appear in S). The result of $R \times S$ contains one tuple $\langle r,\ s \rangle$ for each pair of tuples $r \in R$, $s \in S$. (We use $\langle r,\ s \rangle$ to denote a tuple obtained by concatenating the tuples r and s.)

  We will use the convention that the fields of $R \times S$ inherit names from the corresponding fields of R and S. It is possible for both R and S to contain one or more fields having the same name; this situation creates a *naming conflict*. The corresponding fields in $R \times S$ are unnamed and are referred to solely by position.

In the preceding definitions, note that each operator can be applied to relation instances that are computed using a relational algebra (sub)expression.

We now illustrate these definitions through several examples. The union of $S1$ and $S2$ is shown in Figure 8.8. Fields are listed in order; field names are also inherited from $S1$. $S2$ has the same field names, of course, since it is also an instance of Sailors. In general, fields of $S2$ may have different names; recall that we require only domains to match. Note that the result is a *set* of tuples. Tuples that appear in both $S1$ and $S2$ appear only once in $S1 \cup S2$. Also, $S1 \cup R1$ is not well-defined because the two relations are not union-compatible. The intersection of $S1$ and $S2$ is shown in Figure 8.9, and the set-difference $S1 - S2$ is shown in Figure 8.10.

sid	sname	rating	age
22	dustin	7	45.0
31	lubber	8	55.5
58	rusty	10	35.0
28	yuppy	9	35.0
44	guppy	5	35.0

Figure 8.8 $S1 \cup S2$

sid	sname	rating	age
31	lubber	8	55.5
58	rusty	10	35.0

Figure 8.9 $S1 \cap S2$

sid	sname	rating	age
22	dustin	7	45.0

Figure 8.10 $S1 - S2$

The result of the cross-product $S1 \times R1$ is shown in Figure 8.11. Because $R1$ and $S1$ both have a field named *sid*, by our convention on field names, the corresponding two fields in $S1 \times R1$ are unnamed, and referred to solely by the position in which they appear in Figure 8.11. The fields in $S1 \times R1$ have the same domains as the corresponding fields in $R1$ and $S1$. In Figure 8.11 *sid* is listed in parentheses to emphasize that it is not an inherited field name; only the corresponding domain is inherited.

(sid)	sname	rating	age	(sid)	bid	day
22	dustin	7	45.0	22	101	10/10/96
22	dustin	7	45.0	58	103	11/12/96
31	lubber	8	55.5	22	101	10/10/96
31	lubber	8	55.5	58	103	11/12/96
58	rusty	10	35.0	22	101	10/10/96
58	rusty	10	35.0	58	103	11/12/96

Figure 8.11 $S1 \times R1$

8.2.3 Renaming

We have been careful to adopt field name conventions that ensure that the result of a relational algebra expression inherits field names from its argument (input) relation instances in a natural way whenever possible. However, name conflicts can arise in some cases; for example, in $S1 \times R1$. It is therefore convenient to be able to give names to the fields of a relation instance that is defined by a relational algebra expression. In fact, it is often convenient to give the instance itself a name so that we can break a large algebra expression into smaller pieces by giving names to the results of subexpressions.

We introduce a **renaming** operator ρ for this purpose. The expression $\rho(R(\overline{F}), E)$ takes an arbitrary relational algebra expression E and returns an instance of a (new) relation called R. R contains the same tuples as the result of E, and has the same schema as E, but some fields are renamed. The field names in relation R are the same as in E, except for fields renamed in the *renaming list* $\overline{F}$, which is a list of terms having the form *oldname* $\rightarrow$ *newname* or *position* $\rightarrow$ *newname*. For ρ to be well-defined, references to fields (in the form of *oldnames* or *positions* in the renaming list) may be unambiguous, and no two fields in the result must have the same name. Sometimes we only want to rename fields or to (re)name the relation; we will therefore treat both R and $\overline{F}$ as optional in the use of ρ. (Of course, it is meaningless to omit both.)

As an example, the expression $\rho(C(1 \rightarrow sid1, 5 \rightarrow sid2), S1 \times R1)$ returns a relation that contains the tuples shown in Figure 8.11 and has the following schema: C(*sid1:* integer, *sname:* string, *rating:* integer, *age:* real, *sid2:* integer, *bid:* integer, *day:* dates).

It is customary to include some additional operators in the algebra, but they can all be defined in terms of the operators that we have defined thus far. (In fact, the renaming operator is only needed for syntactic convenience, and even the $\cap$ operator is redundant; $R \cap S$ can be defined as $R - (R - S)$.) We will consider these additional operators, and their definition in terms of the basic operators, in the next two subsections.

8.2.4 Joins

The *join* operation is one of the most useful operations in relational algebra and is the most commonly used way to combine information from two or more relations. Although a join can be defined as a cross-product followed by selections and projections, joins arise much more frequently in practice than plain cross-products. Further, the result of a cross-product is typically much larger than the result of a join, and it is very important to recognize joins and implement them without materializing the underlying cross-product (by applying the selections and projections 'on-the-fly'). For these reasons, joins have received a lot of attention, and there are in fact several variants of the join operation.[1]

---

[1] Indeed, there are more variants of joins than the ones discussed in this chapter. An important class of joins called *outer joins* is discussed in Chapter 9.

Condition Joins

The most general version of the join operation accepts a *join condition c* and a pair of relation instances as arguments, and returns a relation instance. The *join condition* is identical to a *selection condition* in form. The operation is defined as follows:

$$R \bowtie_c S \ = \ \sigma_c(R \times S)$$

Thus $\bowtie$ is defined to be a cross-product followed by a selection. Note that the condition c can (and typically *does*) refer to attributes of both R and S. The reference to an attribute of a relation, say R, can be by position (of the form $R.i$) or by name (of the form $R.name$).

As an example, the result of $S1 \bowtie_{S1.sid<R1.sid} R1$ is shown in Figure 8.12. Because *sid* appears in both $S1$ and $R1$, the corresponding fields in the result of the cross-product $S1 \times R1$ (and therefore in the result of $S1 \bowtie_{S1.sid<R1.sid} R1$) are unnamed. Domains are inherited from the corresponding fields of $S1$ and $R1$.

(sid)	sname	rating	age	(sid)	bid	day
22	dustin	7	45.0	58	103	11/12/96
31	lubber	8	55.5	58	103	11/12/96

Figure 8.12 $S1 \bowtie_{S1.sid<R1.sid} R1$

Equijoin

A common special case of the join operation $R \bowtie S$ is when the *join condition* consists solely of equalities of the form $R.name1 = S.name2$, that is, equalities between two fields in R and S. In this case, obviously, there is some redundancy in retaining both attributes in the result. For join conditions that contain only such equalities, the join operation is refined by doing an additional projection in which $S.name2$ is dropped. The join operation with this refinement is called *equijoin*.

The schema of the result of an equijoin contains the fields of R (with the same names and domains as in R) followed by the fields of S that do not appear in the join conditions. If this set of fields in the result relation includes two fields that inherit the same name from R and S, they are unnamed in the result relation.

We illustrate $S1 \bowtie_{R.sid=S.sid} R1$ in Figure 8.13. Notice that only one field called *sid* appears in the result.

sid	sname	rating	age	bid	day
22	dustin	7	45.0	101	10/10/96
58	rusty	10	35.0	103	11/12/96

Figure 8.13 $S1 \bowtie_{R.sid=S.sid} R1$

Natural Join

A further special case of the join operation $R \bowtie S$ is an equijoin in which equalities are specified on *all* fields having the same name in R and S. In this case, we can simply omit the join condition; the default is that the join condition is a collection of equalities on all common fields. We call this special case a *natural join*, and it has the nice property that the result is guaranteed not to have two fields with the same name.

The equijoin expression $S1 \bowtie_{R.sid=S.sid} R1$ is actually a natural join and can simply be denoted as $S1 \bowtie R1$, since the only common field is *sid*. If the two relations have no attributes in common, $S1 \bowtie R1$ is simply the cross-product.

8.2.5   Division

The division operator is useful for expressing certain kinds of queries, for example: "Find the names of sailors who have reserved all boats." Understanding how to use the basic operators of the algebra to define division is a useful exercise. However, the division operator does not have the same importance as the other operators— it is not needed as often, and database systems do not try to exploit the semantics of division by implementing it as a distinct operator (as, for example, is done with the join operator).

We discuss division through an example. Consider two relation instances A and B in which A has (exactly) two fields x and y and B has just one field y, with the same domain as in A. We define the *division* operation A/B as the set of all x values (in the form of unary tuples) such that for *every* y value in (a tuple of) B, there is a tuple $\langle x, y \rangle$ in A.

Another way to understand division is as follows. For each x value in (the first column of) A, consider the set of y values that appear in (the second field of) tuples of A with that x value. If this set contains (all y values in) B, the x value is in the result of A/B.

An analogy with integer division may also help to understand division. For integers A and B, A/B is an integer Q such that $Q*B \le A$. For relation instances A and B, A/B is a relation instance Q such that $Q \times B \subseteq A$.

Division is illustrated in Figure 8.14. It helps to think of A as a relation listing the parts supplied by suppliers, and of the B relations as listing parts. A/Bi computes suppliers who supply *all* parts listed in relation instance Bi.

A	sno	pno
	s1	p1
	s1	p2
	s1	p3
	s1	p4
	s2	p1
	s2	p2
	s3	p2
	s4	p2
	s4	p4

B1	pno
	p2

B2	pno
	p2
	p4

B3	pno
	p1
	p2
	p4

A/B1	sno
	s1
	s2
	s3
	s4

A/B2	sno
	s1
	s4

A/B3	sno
	s1

Figure 8.14   Examples Illustrating Division

Expressing A/B in terms of the basic algebra operators is an interesting exercise, and the reader should try to do this before reading further. The basic idea is to compute all x values in A that are not *disqualified*. An x value is *disqualified* if by attaching a y value from B, we obtain a tuple $\langle x,y \rangle$ that is not in A. We can compute disqualified tuples using the algebra expression

$$\pi_x((\pi_x(A) \times B) - A)$$

Thus we can define A/B as

$$\pi_x(A) - \pi_x((\pi_x(A) \times B) - A)$$

To understand the division operation in full generality, we have to consider the case when both x and y are replaced by a set of attributes. The generalization is straightforward and is left as an exercise for the reader.

8.2.6   More Examples of Relational Algebra Queries

We now present several examples to illustrate how to write queries in relational algebra. We use the Sailors, Reserves and Boats schema for all our examples in this section. We will use parentheses as needed to make our algebra expressions unambiguous.

Find the names of sailors who have reserved boat 103.

This query can be written as follows:

$$\pi_{sname}((\sigma_{bid=103}Reserves) \bowtie Sailors)$$

We first compute the set of tuples in Reserves with $bid = 103$ and then take the natural join of this set with Sailors. This expression can be evaluated on instances of Reserves and Sailors. Evaluated on the instances $R1$ and $S1$, it yields a relation that contains just one field, called *sname*, and one tuple $\langle rusty \rangle$. We can break this query into smaller pieces using the renaming operator ρ:

$$\rho(Temp1, \sigma_{bid=103}Reserves)$$
$$\rho(Temp2, Temp1 \bowtie Sailors)$$
$$\pi_{sname}(Temp2)$$

Notice that because we are only using ρ to give names to intermediate relations, the renaming list is optional and is omitted. *Temp1* denotes an intermediate relation that identifies reservations of boat 103. *Temp2* is another intermediate relation, and it denotes sailors who have made a reservation in the set *Temp1*. The instances of these relations when evaluating this query on the instances $S1$ and $R1$ are illustrated in Figures 8.15 and 8.16. Finally, we extract the *sname* column from *Temp2*.

sid	bid	day
58	103	11/12/96

sid	sname	rating	age	bid	day
58	rusty	10	35	103	11/12/96

Figure 8.15   Instance of *Temp1*   **Figure 8.16**   Instance of *Temp2*

The version of the query using ρ is essentially the same as the original query; the use of ρ is just syntactic sugar. However, there are indeed several distinct ways to write a query in relational algebra. Here is another way to write this query:

$$\pi_{sname}(\sigma_{bid=103}(Reserves \bowtie Sailors))$$

In this version we first compute the natural join of Reserves and Sailors and then apply the selection and the projection. In fact, a good query optimizer can transform the second version of this query into the first (which is likely to be less expensive to compute because the sizes of intermediate relations are smaller, thanks to the early use of selection).

Find names of sailors who have reserved a red boat.

$$\pi_{sname}((\sigma_{color='red'}Boats) \bowtie Reserves \bowtie Sailors)$$

This query involves a series of two joins. First we choose (tuples describing) red boats. Then we join this set with Reserves (natural join, with equality specified on the *bid* column) to identify reservations of red boats. Next we join the resulting intermediate relation with Sailors (natural join, with equality specified on the *sid* column) to retrieve the names of sailors who have made reservations of red boats. Finally, we project the sailors' names. An equivalent expression is:

$$\pi_{sname}(\pi_{sid}((\pi_{bid}\sigma_{color='red'}Boats) \bowtie Reserves) \bowtie Sailors)$$

The reader is invited to rewrite both of these queries by using ρ to make the intermediate relations explicit, and to compare the schemas of the intermediate relations. The second expression generates intermediate relations with fewer fields (and is therefore likely to result in intermediate relation instances with fewer tuples, as well). A relational query optimizer would try to identify the second expression if it is given the first.

Find the colors of boats reserved by Bob.

$$\pi_{color}((\sigma_{sname='Bob'}Sailors) \bowtie Reserves \bowtie Boats)$$

This query is very similar to the query we used to compute sailors who reserved red boats.

Find the names of sailors who have reserved at least one boat.

$$\pi_{sname}(Sailors \bowtie Reserves)$$

The join of Sailors and Reserves creates an intermediate relation in which tuples consist of a Sailors tuple 'attached to' a Reserves tuple. A Sailors tuple appears in (some tuple of) this intermediate relation only if at least one Reserves tuple has the same *sid* value, that is, the sailor has made some reservation. At this point it is worth remarking on how frequently the natural join operation is used in our examples. This frequency is more than just a happenstance based on the set of queries that we have chosen to discuss; the natural join is indeed a very natural and widely used operation.

Find the names of sailors who have reserved a red or a green boat.

$$\rho(Tempboats, (\sigma_{color='red'}Boats) \cup (\sigma_{color='green'}Boats))$$
$$\pi_{sname}(Tempboats \bowtie Reserves \bowtie Sailors)$$

We identify the set of all boats that are either red or green (Tempboats). Then we join with Reserves to get *sids* of sailors who have reserved one of these boats and join with Sailors to find the names of Sailors with these *sids*. Another equivalent definition is the following:

$$\rho(Tempboats, (\sigma_{color='red'\vee color='green'}Boats))$$
$$\pi_{sname}(Tempboats \bowtie Reserves \bowtie Sailors)$$

Let us now consider a very similar query:

Find the names of sailors who have reserved a red and a green boat. It is tempting to try to do this by simply replacing $\cup$ by $\cap$ in the definition of Tempboats:

$$\rho(Tempboats2, (\sigma_{color='red'}\, Boats) \cap (\sigma_{color='green'}\, Boats))$$

$$\pi_{sname}(Tempboats2 \bowtie Reserves \bowtie Sailors)$$

However, this solution is incorrect—it instead tries to compute sailors who have reserved a boat that is both red and green. (Since *bid* is a key for Boats, a boat can be only one color; this query will always return an empty answer set.) The correct approach is to find sailors who have reserved a red boat, then sailors who have reserved a green boat, and then take the intersection of these two sets:

$$\rho(Tempred, \pi_{sid}((\sigma_{color='red'}\, Boats) \bowtie Reserves))$$

$$\rho(Tempgreen, \pi_{sid}((\sigma_{color='green'}\, Boats) \bowtie Reserves))$$

$$\pi_{sname}((Tempred \cap Tempgreen) \bowtie Sailors)$$

There are several points worth making. The two temporary relations compute the *sids* of sailors, and their intersection identifies sailors who have reserved both red and green boats. Obviously, $\cap$ can be replaced by $\cup$ to find sailors who have reserved red or green boats. More important, the fact that *sid* is a key for Sailors is being utilized. Consider the following variation of the query:

$$\rho(Tempred, \pi_{sname}((\sigma_{color='red'}\, Boats) \bowtie Reserves \bowtie Sailors))$$

$$\rho(Tempgreen, \pi_{sname}((\sigma_{color='green'}\, Boats) \bowtie Reserves \bowtie Sailors))$$

$$Tempred \cap Tempgreen$$

This variation is incorrect for a rather subtle reason. Two distinct sailors with the same name, say *Bob*, may have reserved red and green boats, respectively, and if so, the name *Bob* will (incorrectly) be included in the answer even if no one individual called Bob has reserved a red boat and a green boat. The cause of this error is that *sname* is being used to identify sailors in this version of the query, and *sname* is not a key.

Find the names of sailors who have reserved at least two boats.

$$\rho(Reservations, \pi_{sid,sname,bid}(Sailors \bowtie Reserves))$$

$$\rho(Reservationpairs(1 \rightarrow sid1, 2 \rightarrow sname1, 3 \rightarrow bid1, 4 \rightarrow sid2,$$

$$5 \rightarrow sname2, 6 \rightarrow bid2), Reservations \times Reservations)$$

$$\pi_{sname1}\sigma_{(sid1=sid2)\wedge(bid1\neq bid2)} Reservationpairs$$

First we compute tuples of the form $\langle sid, sname, bid \rangle$, where sailor *sid* has made a reservation for boat *bid*; this set of tuples is the temporary relation Reservations. Next we find all pairs of Reservations tuples where the same sailor has made both reservations and the boats involved are distinct. Here is the central idea: In order to show that a sailor has reserved two boats, we must find two Reservations tuples involving the same sailor but distinct boats. Finally, we project the names of such sailors to obtain the answer. Notice that we included *sid* in Reservations because it is the key field; in addition, we need it to check that two Reservations tuples involve the same sailor. As noted in the previous example, we can't use *sname* for this purpose.

Find the sids of sailors with age over 20 who have not reserved a red boat.

$$\pi_{sid}(\sigma_{age>20}Sailors) -$$
$$\pi_{sid}((\sigma_{color='red'}Boats) \bowtie Reserves \bowtie Sailors)$$

This query illustrates the use of the set-difference operator. Again, we use the fact that *sid* is the key for Sailors. We first identify sailors aged over 20 (using their *sid*s) and then discard those who have reserved a red boat. If we want to compute the names of such sailors, we must first compute their *sid*s (as shown above), and then join with Sailors and project the *sname* values.

Find the names of sailors who have reserved all boats. The use of the word *all* (or *every*) is a good indication that the division operation might be applicable:

$$\rho(Tempsids, (\pi_{sid,bid}Reserves)/(\pi_{bid}Boats))$$
$$\pi_{sname}(Tempsids \bowtie Sailors)$$

The intermediate relation Tempsids is defined using division, and computes the set of *sid*s of sailors who have reserved every boat. Notice how we define the two relations that the division operator (/) is applied to—the first relation has the schema *(sid,bid)* and the second has the schema *(bid)*. Division then returns all *sid*s such that there is a tuple $\langle sid,bid \rangle$ in the first relation for each *bid* in the second.

Find the names of sailors who have reserved all boats called Interlake.

$$\rho(Tempsids, (\pi_{sid,bid}Reserves)/(\pi_{bid}(\sigma_{bname='Interlake'}Boats)))$$
$$\pi_{sname}(Tempsids \bowtie Sailors)$$

The only difference with respect to the previous query is that now we apply a selection to Boats, to ensure that we compute only *bid*s of boats named *Interlake* in defining the second argument to the division operator.

8.3 RELATIONAL CALCULUS

Relational calculus is an alternative to relational algebra. In contrast to the algebra, which is procedural, the calculus is nonprocedural, or *declarative*, in that it allows us to describe the set of answers without being explicit about how they should be computed. Relational calculus has had a big influence on the design of commercial query languages such as SQL and, especially, Query-by-Example (QBE).

The variant of the calculus that we present in detail is called the tuple relational calculus (TRC). In another variant, called the domain relational calculus (DRC), the variables range over field values. TRC has had more of an influence on SQL, while DRC has strongly influenced QBE. We discuss DRC in Section 8.3.2. [2]

8.3.1   Tuple Relational Calculus

A **tuple variable** is a variable that takes on tuples of a particular relation schema as values. That is, every value assigned to a given tuple variable has the same number and type of fields. A tuple relational calculus query has the form $\{\ T\ |\ p(T)\ \}$, where T is a tuple variable and $p(T)$ denotes a *formula* that describes T; we will shortly define formulas and queries rigorously. The result of this query is the set of all tuples t for which the formula $p(T)$ evaluates to **true** with $T = t$. The language for writing formulas $p(T)$ is thus at the heart of TRC and is essentially a simple subset of *first-order logic*. As a simple example, consider the following query.

Find all sailors with a rating above 7.

$$\{S \mid S \in Sailors \land S.rating > 7\}$$

This query can be evaluated on an instance of the Sailors relation. The tuple variable S is instantiated successively to each tuple in this instance of Sailors, and the test *S.rating>7* is applied. The answer contains those instances of S that pass this test.

Syntax of TRC Queries

We now define these concepts formally, beginning with the notion of a formula. Let *Rel* be a relation name, R and S be tuple variables, a an attribute of R, and b an attribute of S. Let **op** denote an operator in the set $\{<, >, =, \leq, \geq, \neq\}$. An **atomic formula** is one of the following:

- $R \in Rel$

- $R.a$ **op** $S.b$

---

[2] The material on DRC is referred to in the chapter on QBE; with the exception of this chapter, the material on DRC and TRC can be omitted without loss of continuity.

- $R.a$ **op** *constant*, or *constant* **op** $R.a$

A **formula** is recursively defined to be one of the following, where p and q are themselves formulas, and $p(R)$ denotes a formula in which the variable R appears:

- any atomic formula

- $\neg p$, $p \wedge q$, $p \vee q$, or $p \Rightarrow q$

- $\exists R(p(R))$, where R is a tuple variable

- $\forall R(p(R))$, where R is a tuple variable

In the last two clauses above, the **quantifiers** $\exists$ and $\forall$ are said to **bind** the variable R. A variable is said to be **free** in a formula or *subformula* (a formula contained in a larger formula) if the (sub)formula does not contain an occurrence of a quantifier that binds it.[3]

We observe that every variable in a TRC formula appears in a subformula that is atomic, and that every relation schema specifies a domain for each field; this observation ensures that each variable in a TRC formula has a well-defined domain from which values for the variable are drawn. That is, each variable has a well-defined *type*, in the programming language sense. Informally, an atomic formula $R \in Rel$ gives R the type of tuples in *Rel*, and comparisons such as $R.a$ **op** $S.b$ and $R.a$ **op** *constant* induce type restrictions on the field $R.a$. If a variable R does not appear in an atomic formula of the form $R \in Rel$ (i.e., it appears only in atomic formulas that are comparisons), we will follow the convention that the type of R is a tuple whose fields include all (and only) fields of R that appear in the formula.

We will not define types of variables formally, but the type of a variable should be clear in most cases, and the important point to note is that comparisons of values having different types should always fail. (In discussions of relational calculus, the simplifying assumption is often made that there is a single domain of constants and that this is the domain associated with each field of each relation.)

A **TRC query** is defined as an expression of the form $\{T \mid p(T)\}$, where T is the only free variable in the formula p.

---

[3] We will make the assumption that each variable in a formula is either free or bound by exactly one occurrence of a quantifier, to avoid worrying about details such as nested occurrences of quantifiers that bind some, but not all, occurrences of variables.

Semantics of TRC Queries

What does a TRC query mean? More precisely, what is the set of answers for a given TRC query? The **answer** to a TRC query $\{T \mid p(T)\}$, as we noted earlier, is the set of all tuples t for which the formula $p(T)$ evaluates to **true** with variable T assigned the tuple value t. To complete this definition, we must state which assignments of tuple values to the free variables in a formula make the formula evaluate to **true**.

A query is evaluated on a given instance of the database. Let each free variable in a formula F be bound to a tuple value. For the given assignment of tuples to variables, with respect to the given database instance, F evaluates to (or simply 'is') **true** if one of the following holds:

- F is an atomic formula $R \in Rel$, and R is assigned a tuple in the instance of relation Rel.

- F is a comparison $R.a$ **op** $S.b$, $R.a$ **op** *constant*, or *constant* **op** $R.a$, and the tuples assigned to R and S have field values $R.a$ and $S.b$ that make the comparison **true**.

- F is of the form $\neg p$, and p is not **true**; or of the form $p \wedge q$, and both p and q are **true**; or of the form $p \vee q$, and one of them is **true**, or of the form $p \Rightarrow q$ and q is **true** whenever[4] p is **true**.

- F is of the form $\exists R(p(R))$, and there is some assignment of tuples to the free variables in $p(R)$, including the variable R,[5] that makes the formula $p(R)$ **true**.

- F is of the form $\forall R(p(R))$, and there is some assignment of tuples to the free variables in $p(R)$ that makes the formula $p(R)$ **true** no matter what tuple is assigned to R.

Examples of TRC Queries

We now illustrate the calculus through several examples. We will use parentheses as needed to make our formulas unambiguous. Often, a formula $p(R)$ includes a condition $R \in Rel$, and the meaning of the phrases *some tuple R* and *for all tuples R* is intuitive. We will use the notation $\exists R \in Rel(p(R))$ for $\exists R(R \in Rel \wedge p(R))$. Similarly, we use the notation $\forall R \in Rel(p(R))$ for $\forall R(R \in Rel \Rightarrow p(R))$.

---

[4]'Whenever' should be read more precisely as 'for all assignments of tuples to the free variables.'

[5]Note that some of the free variables in $p(R)$ (e.g., the variable R itself) may be bound in F.

Find the names and ages of sailors with a rating above 7.

$$\{S \mid \exists S1 \in Sailors(S1.rating > 7 \wedge S.name = S1.sname \wedge S.age = S1.age)\}$$

This query illustrates a useful convention: S is considered to be a tuple variable with exactly two fields, which are called *name* and *age*, because these are the only fields of S that are mentioned and S does not range over any of the relations in the query; that is, there is no subformula of the form $S \in Relname$. The result of this query is a relation with two fields, *name* and *age*. The atomic formulas *S.name* = *S1.sname* and *S.age* = *S1.age* give values to the fields of an answer tuple S.

Print the sailor name, boat id, and reservation date for each reservation.

$$\{P \mid \exists R \in Reserves(\exists S \in Sailors$$
$$(R.sid = S.sid \wedge P.bid = R.bid \wedge P.day = R.day \wedge P.sname = S.sname))\}$$

For each Reserves tuple, we look for a tuple in Sailors with the same *sid*. Given a pair of such tuples, we construct an answer tuple P with fields *sname, bid* and *day* by copying the corresponding fields from these two tuples. This query illustrates how we can combine values from different relations in an answer tuple.

Find all sailors with a rating above 7 who have reserved boat 103.

$$\{S \mid S \in Sailors \wedge S.rating > 7$$
$$\wedge \exists R \in Reserves(R.sid = S.sid \wedge R.bid = 103)\}$$

This query can be read as follows: "Retrieve all sailor tuples with a rating greater than 7 for which there exists a tuple in Reserves, having the same value in the *sid* field, and with *bid* = 103." That is, for each sailor tuple with rating greater than 7, we look for a tuple in Reserves that shows that this sailor has reserved boat 103.

Find all sailors with a rating above 7 who have reserved a red boat.

$$\{S \mid S \in Sailors \wedge S.rating > 7$$
$$\wedge \exists R \in Reserves(R.sid = S.sid$$
$$\wedge \exists B \in Boats(B.bid = R.bid \wedge B.color =' red'))\}$$

This query can be read as follows: "Retrieve all sailor tuples S with a rating greater than 7 for which there exist tuples R in Reserves and B in Boats such that $S.sid = R.sid$, $R.bid = B.bid$, and $B.color =' red'$." The three tuples S, R and B can be regarded as a 'proof-by-example' that sailor S has reserved a red boat. Another way to write this query, which corresponds more closely to this reading, is as follows:

$$\{S \mid S \in Sailors(S.rating > 7 \wedge \exists R \in Reserves \ \exists B \in Boats$$
$$(R.sid = S.sid \wedge B.bid = R.bid \wedge B.color =\,'red')\}$$

Find sailors who have reserved at least two boats.

$$\{S \mid S \in Sailors \wedge \exists R1 \in Reserves \ \exists R2 \in Reserves$$
$$(S.sid = R1.sid \wedge R1.sid = R2.sid \wedge R1.bid \neq R2.bid)\}$$

Contrast this query with the algebra version and see how much simpler the calculus version is. In part, this difference is due to the cumbersome renaming of fields in the algebra version, but the calculus version really is simpler.

Find sailors who have reserved all boats.

$$\{S \mid S \in Sailors \wedge \forall B \in Boats$$
$$(\exists R \in Reserves(S.sid = R.sid \wedge R.bid = B.bid))\}$$

This query was expressed using the division operator in relational algebra. Notice how easily it is expressed in the calculus. The calculus query directly reflects how we might express the query in English: "Find sailors S such that for all boats B, there is a Reserves tuple showing that sailor S has reserved boat B."

Find sailors who have reserved all red boats.

$$\{S \mid S \in Sailors \wedge \forall B \in Boats$$
$$(B.color =\,'red' \Rightarrow (\exists R \in Reserves(S.sid = R.sid \wedge R.bid = B.bid)))\}$$

For each candidate (sailor), if a boat is red, the sailor must have reserved it. That is, for a candidate sailor, a boat being red must imply the sailor having reserved it. We can write this query without using implication, by observing that an expression of the form $p \Rightarrow q$ is logically equivalent to $\neg p \vee q$:

$$\{S \mid S \in Sailors \wedge \forall B \in Boats$$
$$(B.color \neq\,'red' \vee (\exists R \in Reserves(S.sid = R.sid \wedge R.bid = B.bid)))\}$$

This query should be read as follows: "Find sailors S such that for all boats B, either the boat is not red or a Reserves tuple shows that sailor S has reserved boat B."

8.3.2   Domain Relational Calculus

A **domain variable** is a variable that ranges over the values in the domain of some attribute (e.g., the variable can be assigned an integer if it appears in an attribute whose domain is the set of integers). A DRC query has the form $\{\langle x_1, x_2, \ldots, x_n \rangle \mid p(\langle x_1, x_2, \ldots, x_n \rangle)\}$, where each x_i is either a *domain variable* or a constant and $p(\langle x_1, x_2, \ldots, x_n \rangle)$ denotes a **DRC formula** whose only free variables are the variables among the x_i, $1 \leq i \leq n$. The result of this query is the set of all tuples $\langle x_1, x_2, \ldots, x_n \rangle$ for which the formula evaluates to `true`.

A DRC formula is defined in a manner that is very similar to the definition of a TRC formula. The main difference is that the variables are now domain variables. Let op denote an operator in the set $\{<, >, =, \leq, \geq, \neq\}$ and let X and Y be domain variables. An **atomic formula** in DRC is one of the following:

- $\langle x_1, x_2, \ldots, x_n \rangle \in Rel$, where Rel is a relation with n attributes; each x_i, $1 \leq i \leq n$ is either a variable or a constant.

- X op Y

- X op *constant*, or *constant* op X

A **formula** is recursively defined to be one of the following, where p and q are themselves formulas, and $p(X)$ denotes a formula in which the variable X appears:

- any atomic formula

- $\neg p$, $p \wedge q$, $p \vee q$, or $p \Rightarrow q$

- $\exists X (p(X))$, where X is a domain variable

- $\forall X (p(X))$, where X is a domain variable

The reader is invited to compare this definition with the definition of TRC formulas and see how closely these two definitions correspond. We will not define the semantics of DRC formulas formally; this is left as an exercise for the reader.

Examples of DRC Queries

We now illustrate DRC through several examples. The reader is invited to compare these with the TRC versions.

Find all sailors with a rating above 7.

$$\{\langle I, N, T, A \rangle \mid \langle I, N, T, A \rangle \in Sailors \wedge T > 7\}$$

This differs from the TRC version in giving each attribute a (variable) name. The condition $\langle I, N, T, A \rangle \in Sailors$ ensures that the domain variables I, N, T and A

are restricted to be fields of the *same* tuple. Thus in comparison with the TRC query, we can say $T > 7$ instead of *S.rating* > 7, but we must specify the tuple $\langle I, N, T, A \rangle$ in the result, rather than just S.

Find all sailors with a rating above 7 who have reserved boat 103.

$$\{\langle I, N, T, A \rangle \mid \langle I, N, T, A \rangle \in Sailors \wedge T > 7$$
$$\wedge \exists Ir, Br, D(\langle Ir, Br, D \rangle \in Reserves \wedge Ir = I \wedge Br = 103)\}$$

Note that we use the notation $\exists Ir, Br, D(\ldots)$ as a shorthand for $\exists Ir(\exists Br(\exists D(\ldots)))$. Very often, all the quantified variables appear in a single relation, as in this example. An even more compact notation in this case is $\exists \langle Ir, Br, D \rangle \in Reserves$. With this notation, which we will use henceforth, the above query would be as follows:

$$\{\langle I, N, T, A \rangle \mid \langle I, N, T, A \rangle \in Sailors \wedge T > 7$$
$$\wedge \exists \langle Ir, Br, D \rangle \in Reserves(Ir = I \wedge Br = 103)\}$$

The comparison with the corresponding TRC formula should now be straightforward. This query can also be written as follows; notice the repetition of variable I and the use of the constant 103:

$$\{\langle I, N, T, A \rangle \mid \langle I, N, T, A \rangle \in Sailors \wedge T > 7$$
$$\wedge \exists D(\langle I, 103, D \rangle \in Reserves)\}$$

Find the names of all sailors with a rating above 7 who have reserved a red boat.

$$\{\langle N \rangle \mid \exists I, T, A(\langle I, N, T, A \rangle \in Sailors \wedge T > 7$$
$$\wedge \exists \langle Ir, Br, D \rangle \in Reserves(Ir = I$$
$$\wedge \exists \langle B, BN, 'red' \rangle \in Boats(B = Br)))\}$$

Notice that only the *sname* field is retained in the answer and that only N is a free variable.

Find sailors who have reserved at least two boats.

$$\{\langle I, N, T, A \rangle \mid \langle I, N, T, A \rangle \in Sailors \wedge$$
$$\exists Br1, Br2, D1, D2(\langle I, Br1, D1 \langle \in Reserves \wedge \langle I, Br2, D2 \rangle \in Reserves \wedge Br1 \neq Br$$

Notice how the repeated use of variable I ensures that the same sailor has reserved both the boats in question.

Find sailors who have reserved all boats.

$$\{\langle I, N, T, A \rangle \mid \langle I, N, T, A \rangle \in Sailors \wedge$$
$$\forall B, BN, C(\neg(\langle B, BN, C \rangle \in Boats) \vee$$
$$(\exists \langle Ir, Br, D \rangle \in Reserves(I = Ir \wedge Br = B)))\}$$

This query can be read as follows: "Find all tuples $\langle I, N, T, A \rangle$ in Sailors such that for every $\langle B, BN, C \rangle$, either this is not a tuple in Boats or there is some tuple $\langle Ir, Br, D \rangle$ in Reserves that proves that Sailor I has reserved boat B." The $\forall$ quantifier allows the domain variables B, BN and C to range over all values in their respective attribute domains, and the expression $\neg(\langle B, BN, C \rangle \in Boats) \vee$ is necessary to restrict attention to those values that appear in tuples of Boats. This pattern is common in DRC formulas, and the notation $\forall \langle B, BN, C \rangle \in Boats$ can be used as a shorthand instead. This is similar to the notation introduced earlier for $\exists$. With this notation the query would be written as follows:

$$\{\langle I, N, T, A \rangle \mid \langle I, N, T, A \rangle \in Sailors \wedge \forall \langle B, BN, C \rangle \in Boats$$
$$(\exists \langle Ir, Br, D \rangle \in Reserves(I = Ir \wedge Br = B))\}$$

Find sailors who have reserved all red boats.

$$\{\langle I, N, T, A \rangle \mid \langle I, N, T, A \rangle \in Sailors \wedge \forall \langle B, BN, C \rangle \in Boats$$
$$(C =' red' \Rightarrow \exists \langle Ir, Br, D \rangle \in Reserves(I = Ir \wedge Br = B))\}$$

Here, we find all sailors such that for every red boat there is a tuple in Reserves that shows the sailor has reserved it.

8.4 EXPRESSIVE POWER OF ALGEBRA AND CALCULUS *

We have presented two formal query languages for the relational model. Are they equivalent in power? Can every query that can be expressed in relational algebra also be expressed in relational calculus? The answer is yes, it can. Can every query that can be expressed in relational calculus also be expressed in relational algebra? Before we answer this question, we consider a major problem with the calculus as we have presented it.

Consider the query $\{S \mid \neg(S \in Sailors)\}$. This query is syntactically correct. However, it asks for all tuples S such that S is not in (the given instance of) Sailors. The set of such S tuples is obviously infinite, in the context of infinite domains like the set of all integers. This simple example illustrates an *unsafe* query. It is desirable to restrict relational calculus to disallow unsafe queries.

We now sketch how calculus queries are restricted to be safe. Consider a set I of relation instances, with one instance per relation that appears in the query Q. Let $Dom(Q, I)$ be the set of all constants that appear in these relation instances I or in the formulation of the query Q itself. Since we only allow finite instances I, $Dom(Q, I)$ is also finite.

For a calculus formula Q to be considered safe, at a minimum we want to ensure that for any given I, the set of answers for Q contains only values that are in

$Dom(Q, I)$. While this restriction is obviously required, it is not enough. Not only do we want the set of answers to be composed of constants in $Dom(Q, I)$, we wish to *compute* the set of answers by only examining tuples that contain constants in $Dom(Q, I)$! This wish leads to a subtle point associated with the use of quantifiers $\forall$ and $\exists$: Given a TRC formula of the form $\exists R(p(R))$, we want to find all values for variable R that make this formula `true` by checking only tuples that contain constants in $Dom(Q, I)$. Similarly, given a TRC formula of the form $\forall R(p(R))$, we want to find any values for variable R that make this formula `false` by checking only tuples that contain constants in $Dom(Q, I)$.

We therefore define a *safe* TRC formula Q to be a formula such that:

1. For any given I, the set of answers for Q contains only values that are in $Dom(Q, I)$.

2. For each subexpression of the form $\exists R(p(R))$ in Q, if a tuple r (assigned to variable R) makes the formula `true`, then r contains only constants in $Dom(Q, I)$.

3. For each subexpression of the form $\forall R(p(R))$ in Q, if a tuple r (assigned to variable R) contains a constant that is not in $Dom(Q, I)$, then r must make the formula `true`.

Note that this definition is not *constructive*, that is, it does not tell us how to check if a query is safe.

The query $Q = \{S \mid \neg(S \in \textit{Sailors})\}$ is unsafe by this definition. Dom(Q,I) is the set of all values that appear in (an instance I of) Sailors. Consider the instance $S1$ shown in Figure 8.1. The answer to this query obviously includes values that do not appear in $Dom(Q, S1)$.

Returning to the question of expressiveness, we can show that every query that can be expressed using a *safe* relational calculus query can also be expressed as a relational algebra query. The expressive power of relational algebra is often used as a metric of how powerful a relational database query language is. If a query language can express all the queries that we can express in relational algebra, it is said to be **relationally complete**. A practical query language is expected to be relationally complete; in addition, commercial query languages typically support features that allow us to express some queries that cannot be expressed in relational algebra.

8.5 SUMMARY

The relational model supports algebraic and calculus query languages for manipulating the data. The calculus provides a *declarative*, nonoperational language in which users can specify *what* answers they want. The algebra provides a more operational language that can be used to represent the steps to be taken to compute answers. Commercial query languages such as SQL have borrowed elements from both the calculus and the algebra, although the influence of the calculus is perhaps more significant. Internally, database systems use some variant of the algebra to represent query evaluation plans.

Relational algebra consists of a collection of operators. *Selection* and *projection* are unary operators that choose a subset of the rows or columns of the input relation. *Cross-product, union, intersection* and *set-difference* are the usual binary set-operations from mathematics. Additional operators are defined for convenience, and these include *division* and several versions of *join*. Algebra expressions can be composed naturally to write complex queries. Relational calculus is essentially a restricted subset of first-order predicate logic. In tuple relational calculus, the variables take on tuple values, and in domain relational calculus, the variables take on field values, but the two versions of the calculus are very similar.

All relational algebra queries can be expressed in relational calculus. With some simple restrictions on the calculus, the converse also holds. An important criterion for commercial query languages is that they should be *relationally complete* in the sense that they can express all relational algebra queries.

EXERCISES

Exercise 8.1 Explain the statement that relational algebra operators can be *composed*. Why is the ability to compose operators important?

Exercise 8.2 Given two relations $R1$ and $R2$, where $R1$ contains N1 tuples, $R2$ contains N2 tuples, and N2 > N1 > 0, give the minimum and maximum possible sizes (in tuples) for the result relation produced by each of the following relational algebra expressions. In each case, state any assumptions about the schemas for $R1$ and $R2$ that are needed to make the expression meaningful.

1. $R1 \cup R2$
2. $R1 \cap R2$
3. $R1 - R2$
4. $R1 \times R2$
5. $\sigma_{a=5}(R1)$
6. $\pi_a(R1)$
7. $R1/R2$

Exercise 8.3 Consider the following schema:

> Suppliers(*sid:* integer, *sname:* string, *address:* string)
> Parts(*pid:* integer, *pname:* string, *color:* string)
> Catalog(*sid:* integer, *pid:* integer, *cost:* real)

The key fields are underlined, and the domain of each field is listed after the field name. Thus *sid* is the key for Suppliers, *pid* is the key for Parts, and *sid* and *pid* together form the key for Catalog. The Catalog relation lists the prices charged for parts by Suppliers. Write the following queries in relational algebra, tuple relational calculus, and domain relational calculus:

1. Find the *names* of suppliers who supply some red parts.
2. Find the *sids* of suppliers who supply some red or green part.
3. Find the *sids* of suppliers who supply some red part or whose address is 221 Packer Street.
4. Find the *sids* of suppliers who supply some red part and some green part.
5. Find the *sids* of suppliers who supply every part.
6. Find the *sids* of suppliers who supply every red part.
7. Find the *sids* of suppliers who supply every red or green part.
8. Find the *sids* of suppliers who supply every red part or supply every green part.
9. Find pairs of *sids* such that the supplier with the first *sid* charges more for some part than the supplier with the second *sid*.
10. Find the *pids* of parts that are supplied by at least two different suppliers.
11. Find the *pids* of the most expensive parts supplied by suppliers named Yosemite Sham.
12. Find the *pids* of parts supplied by every supplier at a price less than 200 dollars. (If any supplier either does not supply the part or charges more than 200 dollars for it, the part should not be selected.)

Exercise 8.4 Consider the Supplier-Parts-Catalog schema from the previous question. State what the following queries compute:

1. $\pi_{sname}(\pi_{sid}(\sigma_{color='red'}Parts) \bowtie (\sigma_{cost<100}Catalog) \bowtie Suppliers)$

2. $\pi_{sname}(\pi_{sid}((\sigma_{color='red'}Parts) \bowtie (\sigma_{cost<100}Catalog) \bowtie Suppliers))$

3. $(\pi_{sname}((\sigma_{color='red'}Parts) \bowtie (\sigma_{cost<100}Catalog) \bowtie Suppliers)) \cap$

   $(\pi_{sname}((\sigma_{color='green'}Parts) \bowtie (\sigma_{cost<100}Catalog) \bowtie Suppliers))$

4. $(\pi_{sid}((\sigma_{color='red'}Parts) \bowtie (\sigma_{cost<100}Catalog) \bowtie Suppliers)) \cap$

   $(\pi_{sid}((\sigma_{color='green'}Parts) \bowtie (\sigma_{cost<100}Catalog) \bowtie Suppliers))$

5. $\pi_{sname}((\pi_{sid,sname}((\sigma_{color='red'}Parts) \bowtie (\sigma_{cost<100}Catalog) \bowtie Suppliers)) \cap$

   $(\pi_{sid,sname}((\sigma_{color='green'}Parts) \bowtie (\sigma_{cost<100}Catalog) \bowtie Suppliers)))$

Exercise 8.5 Consider the following relations containing airline flight information:

> Flights(*flno:* integer, *from:* string, *to:* string,
>   *distance:* integer, *departs:* time, *arrives:* time)
> Aircraft(*aid:* integer, *aname:* string, *cruisingrange:* integer)
> Certified(*eid:* integer, *aid:* integer))
> Employees(*eid:* integer, *ename:* string, *salary:* integer)

Note that the Employees relation describes pilots and other kinds of employees as well; every pilot is certified for some aircraft (otherwise, he or she would not qualify as a pilot), and only pilots are certified to fly.

Write the following queries in relational algebra, tuple relational calculus, and domain relational calculus. Note that some of these queries may not be expressible in relational algebra (and therefore, also not expressible in tuple and domain relational calculus)! For such queries, informally explain why they cannot be expressed. (*See the exercises at the end of Chapter 9 for additional queries over the airline schema.*)

1. Find the *eid*s of pilots certified for some Boeing aircraft.
2. Find the *name*s of pilots certified for some Boeing aircraft.
3. Find the *aid*s of all aircraft that can be used on non stop flights from L.A. to N.Y.
4. Identify the flights that can be piloted by every pilot whose salary is more than 100,000.
5. Find the names of pilots who can operate planes with a range greater than 3000 miles but are not certified on any Boeing aircraft.
6. Find the *eid*s of employees who make the highest salary.
7. Find the *eid*s of employees who make the second highest salary.
8. Find the *eid*s of employees who are certified for the largest number of aircraft.
9. Find the *eid*s of employees who are certified for exactly three aircraft.
10. Find the total amount paid to employees as salaries.
11. Is there a sequence of flights from Madison to Timbuktu? Each flight in the sequence is required to depart from the city that is the destination of the previous flight; the first flight must leave Madison, the last flight must reach Timbuktu, and there is no restriction on the number of intermediate flights. Your query must determine whether a sequence of flights from Madison to Timbuktu exists for *any* input Flights relation instance.

Exercise 8.6 What is *relational completeness*? If a query language is relationally complete, can you write any desired query in that language?

Exercise 8.7 What is an *unsafe* query? Give an example and explain why it is important to disallow such queries.

BIBLIOGRAPHIC NOTES

Relational algebra was proposed by Codd in [135], and he showed the equivalence of relational algebra and TRC in [137]. Earlier, Kuhns [318] considered the use of logic to pose queries. LaCroix and Pirotte discussed DRC in [323]. Klug generalized the algebra and calculus to include aggregate operations in [306]. Extensions of the algebra and calculus to deal with aggregate functions are also discussed in [417]. Merrett proposed an extended relational algebra with quantifiers such as *the number of*, which go beyond just universal and existential quantification [379]. Such generalized quantifiers are discussed at length in [37].

SQL: THE QUERY LANGUAGE

What men or gods are these? What maidens loth?
What mad pursuit? What struggle to escape?
What pipes and timbrels? What wild ecstasy?

—John Keats, *Ode on a Grecian Urn*

What is the average salary in the Toy department?

—Anonymous SQL user

Structured Query Language (SQL) is the most widely used commercial relational database language. It was originally developed at IBM in the SEQUEL-XRM and System-R projects (1974–1977). Almost immediately, other vendors introduced DBMS products based on SQL, and it is now a defacto standard. SQL continues to evolve in response to changing needs in the database area. Our presentation follows the current ANSI/ISO standard for SQL, which is called SQL-92. The SQL language has several parts:

- **The Data Manipulation Language (DML):** This subset of SQL allows users to pose queries and to insert, delete and modify rows. The query language features of SQL are strongly influenced by relational algebra and calculus.

- **The Data Definition Language (DDL):** This subset of SQL supports the creation, deletion and modification of definitions for tables and views. *Integrity constraints* can be defined on tables, either when the table is created or later. The DDL also provides commands for specifying *access rights* or *privileges* to tables and views. Although the standard does not discuss indexes, commercial implementations also provide commands for creating and deleting indexes. We covered the DDL features of SQL in Chapter 2.

- **Embedded and dynamic SQL:** Embedded SQL features allow SQL code to be called from a host language such as C or COBOL. Dynamic SQL features allow a query to be constructed (and executed) at run-time.

- **Security:** SQL provides mechanisms to control users' access to data objects such as tables and views.

- **Transaction management:** Various commands allow a user to explicitly control aspects of how a transaction is to be executed.

- **Client-server execution and remote database access:** These commands control how a *client* application program can connect to an SQL database *server*, or access data from a database over a network.

This chapter covers the data retrieval features of SQL, including the query language and facilities for embedding SQL commands in a host language. The ease of expressing queries in SQL has played a major role in the success of relational database systems. Although this material can be read independently of the preceding chapters, relational algebra and calculus (which we covered in Chapter 8) provide a formal foundation for a large subset of the SQL query language. Much of the power and elegance of the SQL query language can be attributed to this foundation.

We will continue our presentation of SQL in Chapter 10, where we discuss aspects of SQL that are related to security. In particular, we present the concept of *views* in Chapter 10, even though the use of views is not limited to enforcing security, since the commands related to security interact with view definitions. We discuss SQL's support for the *transaction* concept in Chapter 17.

The rest of this chapter is organized as follows. We present basic SQL queries in Section 9.1 and introduce SQL's set-operators in Section 9.2. We discuss nested queries, in which a relation referred to in the query is itself defined within the query, in Section 9.3. We cover aggregate operators, which allow us to write SQL queries that are not expressible in relational algebra, in Section 9.4. We discuss *null* values, which are special values used to indicate unknown or nonexistent field values, in Section 9.5. We consider how SQL commands can be embedded in a host language in Section 9.6 and in Section 9.7, where we discuss how relations can be accessed one tuple at a time through the use of *cursors*. In Section 9.8 we describe how queries can be constructed at run-time using dynamic SQL.

Finally, in Section 9.9, we consider how complex integrity constraints can be specified by using the power of SQL queries. This topic is technically part of the SQL DDL, which we covered in Chapter 2, but we cover this material here because it requires knowledge of the query language features.

We will present a number of sample queries using the following table definitions:

Sailors(*sid:* **integer**, *sname:* **string**, *rating:* **integer**, *age:* **real**)
Boats(*bid:* **integer**, *bname:* **string**, *color:* **string**)
Reserves(*sid:* **integer**, *bid:* **integer**, *day:* **dates**)

9.1   THE FORM OF A BASIC SQL QUERY

This section presents the syntax of a simple SQL query and explains its meaning through a hypothetical evaluation strategy. The basic form of an SQL query is as follows:

SELECT   [DISTINCT] **select-list**
FROM   **from-list**
WHERE   **qualification**

Such a query intuitively corresponds to a relational algebra expression involving selections, projections and cross-products. Every query must have a SELECT clause, which specifies columns to be retained in the result, and a FROM clause, which specifies a cross-product of tables. The optional WHERE clause specifies selection conditions on the tables mentioned in the FROM clause. Let us consider a simple query.

Find the names and ages of all sailors.

SELECT DISTINCT S.sname, S.age
FROM   Sailors S

The answer is a *set* of rows, each of which is a pair ⟨*sname, age*⟩, even if two or more sailors have the same name and age. This query is equivalent to applying the projection operator of relational algebra. If we omit the keyword DISTINCT, we would get a copy of the row ⟨*s,a*⟩ for each sailor with name *s* and age *a*; the answer would be a *multiset* of rows. (A **multiset** is similar to a set in that it is an unordered collection of elements, but there could be several copies of each element, and the number of copies is significant—two multisets could have the same elements and yet be different because the number of copies is different for some elements.)

As another example, let us choose sailors younger than 18.

SELECT S.sid, S.sname, S.rating, S.age
FROM   Sailors AS S
WHERE   S.age < 18

This query is equivalent to an application of the selection operator of relational algebra. This query uses the optional keyword AS to introduce a range variable. Incidentally, when we want to retrieve all columns, as in this query, SQL provides a convenient shorthand: We can simply write SELECT *. This notation is useful for interactive querying, but it is poor style for queries that are intended to be reused and maintained.

As these two examples illustrate, the SELECT clause is actually used to do *projection*, whereas *selections* in the relational algebra sense are expressed using the WHERE clause! This mismatch between the naming of the selection and projection operators in relational algebra and the syntax of SQL is an unfortunate historical accident.

We now consider the syntax of a basic SQL query in more detail.

- The **from-list** in the FROM clause is a list of table names. A table name can be followed by a **range variable**; a range variable is particularly useful when the same table name appears more than once in the from-list.

- The **select-list** is a list of (expressions involving) column names of tables named in the from-list. Column names can be prefixed by a range variable.

- The **qualification** in the WHERE clause is a Boolean combination (i.e., an expression using the logical connectives AND , OR and NOT) of conditions of the form *expression op expression*, where op is one of the comparison operators $\{<, <=, =, <>, >=, >\}$.[1] An *expression* is a *column* name, a *constant*, or an (arithmetic or string) expression.

- The DISTINCT keyword is optional. It indicates that the table computed as an answer to this query should not contain *duplicates*, that is, two copies of the same row. The default is that duplicates are not eliminated.

Although the preceding rules describe (informally) the syntax of a basic SQL query, they don't tell us the *meaning* of a query. The answer to a query is itself a relation—which is a *multiset* of rows in SQL!—whose contents can be understood by considering the following hypothetical evaluation strategy:

1. Compute the cross-product of the tables in the **from-list**.

2. Delete those rows in the cross-product that fail the **qualification** conditions.

3. Delete all columns that do not appear in the **select-list**.

4. If DISTINCT is specified, eliminate duplicate rows.

This straightforward hypothetical evaluation strategy makes explicit the rows that must be present in the answer to the query. However, it is likely to be quite inefficient. We will consider how a DBMS actually evaluates queries in Chapters 12 and 13; for now, our purpose is simply to explain the meaning of a query. We illustrate the hypothetical evaluation strategy using the following query:

---

[1]Expressions with NOT can always be replaced by equivalent expressions without NOT given the set of comparison operators listed above.

Find the names of sailors who have reserved boat number 103.

It can be expressed in SQL as follows.

> SELECT S.sname
> FROM   Sailors S, Reserves R
> WHERE   S.sid = R.sid AND R.bid=103

Let us compute the answer to this query on the instances of Reserves and Sailors shown in Figures 9.1 and 9.2.

sid	sname	rating	age
22	dustin	7	45.0
31	lubber	8	55.5
58	rusty	10	35.0

sid	bid	day
22	101	10/10/96
58	103	11/12/96

Figure 9.1   Instance *Reserves1* of Reserves   **Figure 9.2**   Instance *Sailors1* of Sailors

The first step is to construct the cross-product *Sailors*1 × *Reserves*1, which is shown in Figure 9.3.

sid	sname	rating	age	sid	bid	day
22	dustin	7	45.0	22	101	10/10/96
22	dustin	7	45.0	58	103	11/12/96
31	lubber	8	55.5	22	101	10/10/96
31	lubber	8	55.5	58	103	11/12/96
58	rusty	10	35.0	22	101	10/10/96
58	rusty	10	35.0	58	103	11/12/96

Figure 9.3   *Sailors1 × Reserves1*

The second step is to apply the qualification *S.sid = R.sid* AND *R.bid=103*. This step eliminates all but the last row from the instance shown in Figure 9.3. The third step is to eliminate unwanted columns; only *sname* appears in the SELECT clause. This step leaves us with the result shown in Figure 9.4, which is a table with a single column, and as it happens, just one row.

9.1.1   Examples of Basic SQL Queries

We now present several example queries, many of which were expressed earlier in relational algebra and calculus (Chapter 8). Our first example illustrates that the use of range variables is optional, unless they are needed to resolve an ambiguity.

Figure 9.4   Answer to Example Query

The query that we discussed in the previous section can also be expressed as follows:

```
SELECT sname
FROM    Sailors S, Reserves R
WHERE   S.sid = R.sid AND bid=103
```

Only the occurrences of *sid* have to be qualified, since this column appears in both the Sailors and Reserves tables. An equivalent way to write this query is:

```
SELECT sname
FROM    Sailors, Reserves
WHERE   Sailors.sid = Reserves.sid AND bid=103
```

This query shows that table names can be used implicitly as row variables. Range variables need to be introduced explicitly only when the **FROM** clause contains more than one occurrence of a relation.[2]

However, we recommend the explicit use of range variables and full qualification of all occurrences of columns with a range variable to improve the readability of your programs. We will follow this convention in all our examples.

Find the sids of sailors who have reserved a red boat.

```
SELECT    R.sid
FROM      Boats B, Reserves R
WHERE     R.bid = B.bid AND B.color = 'red'
```

This query contains a join of two tables, followed by a selection on the color of boats. We can think of B and R as rows in the corresponding tables that 'prove' that a sailor with sid R.sid reserved a red boat B.bid. If we want the names of sailors, we must also consider the Sailors relation, since Reserves does not contain this information, as the next example illustrates.

Find the names of sailors who have reserved a red boat.

---

[2]However, the use of the table name as an implicit range variable is illegal once a range variable is introduced for the relation.

```
SELECT    S.sname
FROM      Sailors S, Boats B, Reserves R
WHERE     S.sid = R.sid AND R.bid = B.bid AND B.color = 'red'
```

This query contains a join of three tables followed by a selection on the color of boats. The join with Sailors allows us to find the name of the sailor who, according to Reserves tuple R, has reserved a red boat described by tuple B.

Find the colors of boats reserved by sailors named Bob.

```
SELECT  B.color
FROM    Sailors S, Boats B, Reserves R
WHERE   S.sid = R.sid AND R.bid = B.bid AND S.sname = 'Bob'
```

This query is very similar to the previous one. Notice that there may be more than one sailor called 'Bob' (since *sname* is not a key for Sailors); this query is still correct.

Find the names of sailors who have reserved at least one boat.

```
SELECT  S.sname
FROM    Sailors S, Reserves R
WHERE   S.sid = R.sid
```

The join of Sailors and Reserves ensures that for each selected *sname*, the sailor has indeed made some reservation. (If a sailor has not made a reservation, the second step in the hypothetical evaluation strategy would eliminate all rows in the cross-product that involve this sailor.)

9.1.2 Expressions and Strings in the SELECT Command

SQL supports a more general version of the **column-list** than just a list of columns. Each item in a **column-list** can be of the form *expression* **AS** *column_name*, where *expression* is any arithmetic or string expression over column names (possibly prefixed by range variables) and constants. It can also contain *aggregates* such as *sum* and *count*, which we will discuss shortly. The SQL-92 standard also includes expressions over date and time values, which we will not discuss. Although not part of the SQL-92 standard, many implementations also support the use of built-in functions such as *sqrt*, *sin* and *mod*.

The following query increments the ratings of persons who have sailed two different boats on the same day.

```
SELECT  S.sname, S.rating+1 AS  rating
```

```
FROM    Sailors S, Reserves R1, Reserves R2
WHERE   S.sid = R1.sid AND S.sid = R2.sid
        AND R1.day = R2.day AND R1.bid <> R2.bid
```

Also, each item in a *qualification* can be as general as *expression1 = expression2*.

```
SELECT S1.sname AS name1, S2.sname AS name2
FROM   Sailors S1, Sailors S2
WHERE  2*S1.rating = S2.rating-1
```

For string comparisons, we can use the comparison operators $(=, <, >,$ etc.) with the ordering of strings determined alphabetically as usual. In fact, SQL-92 supports a general concept of a **character set** with an associated **collation**, or sort order, which provides great flexibility in string manipulation.

In addition, SQL provides support for pattern matching through the LIKE operator, along with the use of the wild-card symbols % (which stands for zero or more arbitrary characters) and _ (which stands for exactly one, arbitrary, character). Thus, '_AB%' denotes a pattern that will match every string that contains at least three characters, with the second and third characters being A and B respectively. Note that unlike the other comparison operators, blanks can be significant for the LIKE operator (depending on the collation for the underlying character set). Thus *'Jeff' = 'Jeff '* could be true while *'Jeff'* LIKE *'Jeff '* is false. An example of the use of LIKE in a query is given below.

Find the ages of sailors whose name begins and ends with B and has at least three characters.

```
SELECT S.age
FROM   Sailors S
WHERE  S.sname LIKE 'B_%B'
```

9.2   UNION, INTERSECT AND EXCEPT

SQL provides three set-manipulation constructs that extend the basic query form presented earlier. Since the answer to a query is a set of rows, it is natural to consider the use of set-operations such as union, intersection and difference; SQL supports these operations under the names UNION, INTERSECT and EXCEPT.[3] SQL also provides other set-operations: IN (to check if an element is in a given

---

[3]Note that although the SQL-92 standard includes these operations, many systems currently support only UNION.

set), op **ANY** , op **ALL** (to compare a value with the elements in a given set, using comparison operator op), and **EXISTS** (to check if a set is empty). **IN** and **EXISTS** can be prefixed by **NOT**, with the obvious modification to their meaning. We cover **UNION, INTERSECT** and **EXCEPT** in this section, and the other operations in Section 9.3.

Consider the following query:

Find the names of sailors who have reserved a red or a green boat.

```
SELECT  S.sname
FROM    Sailors S, Boats B, Reserves R
WHERE   S.sid = R.sid AND R.bid = B.bid
        AND (B.color = 'red' OR B.color = 'green')
```

This query is easily expressed using the **OR** connective in the **WHERE** clause. However, the following query, which is identical except for the use of and rather than or in the English version, turns out to be much more difficult:

Find the names of sailors who have reserved both a red and a green boat.

If we were to just replace the use of **OR** in the previous query by **AND**, in analogy to the English statements of the two queries, we would retrieve the names of sailors who have reserved a reddish green boat! A correct statement of this query using **AND** is the following:

```
SELECT  S.sname
FROM    Sailors S, Boats B1, Reserves R1, Boats B2, Reserves R2
WHERE   S.sid = R1.sid AND R1.bid = B1.bid
        AND S.sid = R2.sid AND R2.bid = B2.bid
        AND B1.color='red' AND B2.color = 'green'
```

We can think of R1 and B1 as rows that prove that sailor S.Sid has reserved a red boat. R2 and B2 similarly prove that the same sailor has reserved a green boat. S.sname is not included in the result unless five such rows S, R1, B1, R2, and B2 are found.

The previous query is difficult to understand (and also quite inefficient, as it turns out). In particular, the similarity to the previous **OR** query is completely lost. A better solution for these two queries is to use **UNION** and **INTERSECT**.

The **OR** query can be rewritten as follows:

```
SELECT  S.sname
```

```
FROM    Sailors S, Boats B, Reserves R
WHERE   S.sid = R.sid AND R.bid = B.bid AND B.color = 'red'
UNION
SELECT  S2.sname
FROM    Sailors S2, Boats B2, Reserves R2
WHERE   S2.sid = R2.sid AND R2.bid = B2.bid AND B2.color = 'green'
```

This query says, naturally, that we want the union of the set of sailors who have reserved red boats and the set of sailors who have reserved green boats. In complete symmetry, the AND query can be rewritten as follows:

```
SELECT  S.sname
FROM    Sailors S, Boats B, Reserves R
WHERE   S.sid = R.sid AND R.bid = B.bid AND B.color = 'red'
INTERSECT
SELECT  S2.sname
FROM    Sailors S2, Boats B2, Reserves R2
WHERE   S2.sid = R2.sid AND R2.bid = B2.bid AND B2.color = 'green'
```

This query actually contains a subtle bug—if there are two sailors called Bob, one of whom has reserved a red boat and the other has reserved a green boat, the name Bob is returned, even though no one individual called Bob has reserved both a red and a green boat. Thus the query actually computes sailor names such that some sailor with this name has reserved a red boat and some sailor with the same name (perhaps a different sailor) has reserved a green boat. The problem arises because we are using *sname* to identify sailors, and *sname* is not a key for Sailors! If we select *sid* instead of *sname* in the previous query, we would compute the set of *sid*s of sailors who have reserved both red and green boats. (To compute the names of such sailors requires a nested query; we will return to this example in Section 9.3.4.)

If we want the *sid*s of all sailors who have reserved red boats but not green boats, we can use the following query:

```
SELECT  S.sid
FROM    Sailors S, Boats B, Reserves R
WHERE   S.sid = R.sid AND R.bid = B.bid AND B.color = 'red'
EXCEPT
SELECT  S2.sid
FROM    Sailors S2, Boats B2, Reserves R2
WHERE   S2.sid = R2.sid AND R2.bid = B2.bid AND B2.color = 'green'
```

Indeed, since the Reserves relation contains sid information, there is no need to look at the Sailors relation, and we can use the following simpler query:

```
SELECT  R.sid
FROM    Boats B, Reserves R
WHERE   R.bid = B.bid AND B.color = 'red'
EXCEPT
SELECT  R2.sid
FROM    Boats B2, Reserves R2
WHERE   R2.bid = B2.bid AND B2.color = 'green'
```

Note that UNION, INTERSECT, and EXCEPT can be used on *any* two tables that are union-compatible, that is, have the same number of columns and the columns, taken in order, have the same types. For example, we can write the following query:

Find all sids of sailors who have a rating of 10 or have reserved boat 111.

```
SELECT  S.sid
FROM    Sailors S
WHERE   S.rating = 10
UNION
SELECT  R.sid
FROM    Reserves R
WHERE   R.bid = 111
```

A final point to note about UNION, INTERSECT, and EXCEPT follows. In contrast to the default that duplicates are not eliminated unless DISTINCT is specified in the basic query form, the default for UNION queries is that duplicates *are* eliminated! To retain duplicates, UNION ALL must be used; if so, the number of copies of a row in the result is $m + n$, where m and n are the numbers of times that the row appears in the two input tables. Similarly, one version of INTERSECT retains duplicates—the number of copies of a row in the result is $min(m, n)$—and one version of EXCEPT also retains duplicates—the number of copies of a row in the result is $m - n$, where m corresponds to the first relation.

9.3   NESTED QUERIES

One of the most powerful features of SQL is nested queries. A **nested query** is a query that has another query embedded within it; the embedded query is called a **subquery**. When writing a query, we sometimes need to express a condition that refers to a table that must itself be computed. The query used to compute this subsidiary table is a subquery, and appears as part of the main query. A subquery typically appears within the WHERE clause of a query. Subqueries can sometimes appear in the FROM clause or the HAVING clause (which we present in Section 9.4). This section discusses only subqueries that appear in the WHERE clause.

The treatment of subqueries appearing elsewhere is quite similar; examples of subqueries that appear in the FROM clause are discussed in Section 9.4.1.

9.3.1   Introduction to Nested Queries

As an example, let us rewrite the following query, which we discussed earlier, using a nested subquery:

Find the names of sailors who have reserved boat number 103.

```
SELECT  S.sname
FROM    Sailors S
WHERE   S.sid IN ( SELECT  R.sid
                   FROM    Reserves R
                   WHERE   R.bid = 103 )
```

The nested subquery computes the set of *sid*s for sailors who have reserved boat 103, and the top-level query retrieves the names of sailors in this set. The IN operator allows us to test whether a value is in a given set of elements; an SQL query is used to generate the set to be tested. Notice that it is very easy to modify this query to find all sailors who have *not* reserved boat 103—we can just replace IN by NOT IN!

The best way to understand a nested query is to think of it in terms of a nested loop evaluation strategy. In our example the strategy consists of a loop that examines rows in Sailors, and for each such row, evaluates the subquery over Reserves. In general the hypothetical evaluation strategy that we presented for defining the semantics of a query can be extended to cover nested queries as follows: Construct the cross-product of the tables in the FROM clause of the top-level query as before. For each row in the cross-product, while testing the qualification in the WHERE clause, (re)compute the subquery.[4] Of course, the subquery might itself contain another nested subquery, in which case we apply the same idea one more time, leading to an evaluation strategy with several levels of nested loops.

As an example of a multiply-nested query, let us rewrite the following query.

Find the names of sailors who have reserved a red boat.

```
SELECT    S.sname
FROM      Sailors S
```

---

[4]Since the inner subquery in our example does not depend on the 'current' row from the outer query in any way, you might wonder why we have to recompute the subquery for each outer row. For an answer, see Section 9.3.2.

```
WHERE      S.sid IN ( SELECT R.sid
                      FROM    Reserves R
                      WHERE   R.bid IN ( SELECT B.bid
                                         FROM   Boats B
                                         WHERE  B.color = 'red' )
```

The innermost subquery finds the set of *bid*s of red boats. The subquery one level above finds the set of *sid*s of sailors who have reserved one of these boats. The top-level query finds the names of such sailors.

It is interesting to consider how the query is modified if we replace the two occurrences of **IN** by **NOT IN**. To find the names of sailors who have not reserved a red boat, we replace the outermost occurrence of **IN**.

*Find the names of sailors who have **not** reserved a red boat.*

```
SELECT    S.sname
FROM      Sailors S
WHERE     S.sid NOT IN ( SELECT R.sid
                         FROM    Reserves R
                         WHERE   R.bid IN ( SELECT B.bid
                                            FROM   Boats B
                                            WHERE  B.color = 'red' )
```

If we replace the inner occurrence of **IN** with **NOT IN**, we get the names of sailors who have reserved a boat, but not a red boat. Note the difference between these queries. (What do we get if we replace both occurrences of **IN** with **NOT IN**?)

9.3.2 Correlated Nested Queries

In the nested queries that we have seen thus far, the inner subquery has been completely independent of the outer query. In general the inner subquery could depend on the row that is currently being examined in the outer query (in terms of our hypothetical evaluation strategy). Let us rewrite the following query once more:

Find the names of sailors who have reserved boat number 103.

```
SELECT S.sname
FROM   Sailors S
WHERE  EXISTS ( SELECT *
                FROM   Reserves R
                WHERE  R.bid = 103
                AND    S.sid = R.sid )
```

The EXISTS operator is another set comparison operator, like IN. It allows us to test whether a set is nonempty. Thus, for each Sailor row S, we test whether the set of Reserves rows R such that $R.bid = 103$ AND $S.sid = R.sid$ is nonempty. If so, sailor S has reserved boat 103, and we retrieve the name. The subquery clearly depends on the current row S and must be re-evaluated for each row in Sailors. The occurrence of S in the subquery (in the form of the literal $S.sid$) is called a *correlation*, and such queries are called *correlated* queries.

This query also illustrates the use of the special symbol * in situations where all we want to do is to check that a qualifying row exists, and don't really want to retrieve any columns from the row. This is one of the two uses of * in the SELECT clause that is good programming style; the other is as an argument of the COUNT aggregate operation, which we will describe shortly.

As a further example, by using NOT EXISTS instead of EXISTS, we can compute the names of sailors who have not reserved a red boat. Closely related to EXISTS is the UNIQUE predicate. When we apply UNIQUE to a subquery, it returns true if no row appears twice in the answer to the subquery, that is, there are no duplicates; in particular, it returns true if the answer is empty. (And of course, there is a version NOT UNIQUE.)

9.3.3 Set-Comparison Operators

We have already seen the set-comparison operators EXISTS, IN and UNIQUE, along with their negated versions. SQL also supports op ANY and op ALL, where op is one of the arithmetic comparison operators $\{<, <=, =, <>, >=, >\}$. (SOME is also available, but it is just a synonym for ANY.)

Find sailors whose rating is better than Horatio's.

```
SELECT  S.sid
FROM    Sailors S
WHERE   S.rating > ANY ( SELECT  S2.rating
                         FROM    Sailors S2
                         WHERE   S2.sname = 'Horatio' )
```

If there are several sailors called Horatio, this query finds all sailors whose rating is better than that of *some* sailor called Horatio. What if there is *no* sailor called Horatio? In this case the comparison $S.rating >$ ANY ... is defined to return false. To understand comparisons involving ANY, it is useful to think of the comparison being carried out repeatedly. In the example above, $S.rating$ is successively compared with each rating value that is an answer to the nested query. Intuitively, the subquery must return a row that makes the comparison true, in order for *S.rating* > ANY ... to return true.

By replacing ANY with ALL in this query, we can retrieve all sailors whose rating is better than that of *every* sailor called Horatio. If there is no sailor called Horatio, the comparison *S.rating* > ALL ... is defined to return true! Again, it is useful to think of the comparison being carried out repeatedly. Intuitively, if the subquery returns a row, the comparison must be true for that row (for every returned row), in order for *S.rating* > ALL ... to return true.

As another illustration of ALL, consider the following query:

Find the sailors with the highest rating.

```
SELECT  S.sid
FROM    Sailors S
WHERE   S.rating >= ALL ( SELECT  S2.rating
                          FROM    Sailors S2 )
```

Note that IN and NOT IN are equivalent to = ANY and <> ALL, respectively.

9.3.4 More Examples of Nested Queries

Let us revisit a query that we considered earlier using the INTERSECT operator.

Find the names of sailors who have reserved both a red and a green boat.

```
SELECT  S.sname
FROM    Sailors S, Boats B, Reserves R
WHERE   S.sid = R.sid AND R.bid = B.bid AND B.color = 'red'
        AND S.sid IN ( SELECT  S2.sid
                       FROM    Sailors S2, Boats B2, Reserves R2
                       WHERE   S2.sid = R2.sid AND R2.bid = B2.bid
                               AND B2.color = 'green' )
```

This query can be understood as follows: "Find all sailors who have reserved a red boat and, further, have sailor ids that are included in the set of *sids* of sailors who have reserved a green boat." Thus queries using INTERSECT can be rewritten using IN, which is useful to know if your system does not support INTERSECT. Queries using EXCEPT can be similarly rewritten by using NOT IN. To find the sids of sailors who have reserved red boats but not green boats, we can simply replace the keyword IN in the previous query by NOT IN.

In contrast, writing this query with INTERSECT is more complicated:

ne
S3
[N ((SELECT R.sid
        FROM   Boats B, Reserves R
        WHERE   R.bid = B.bid AND B.color = 'red')
        INTERSECT
        (SELECT R2.sid
        FROM   Boats B2, Reserves R2
        WHERE   R2.bid = B2.bid AND B2.color = 'green'))

ates how the *division* operation in relational algebra can

Find the names of sailors who have reserved all boats (possibly on different days).

```
SELECT  S.sname
FROM    Sailors S
WHERE   NOT EXISTS (( SELECT  B.bid
                      FROM    Boats B )
                      EXCEPT
                      (SELECT R.bid
                      FROM    Reserves R
                      WHERE   R.sid = S.sid ))
```

Notice that this query is correlated—for each sailor S, we check to see that the set of boats reserved by S includes all boats. An alternative way to do this query without using **EXCEPT** follows:

```
SELECT  S.sname
FROM    Sailors S
WHERE   NOT EXISTS ( SELECT  B.bid
                     FROM    Boats B
                     WHERE   NOT EXISTS ( SELECT  R.bid
                                          FROM    Reserves R
                                          WHERE   R.bid = B.bid
                                          AND R.sid = S.sid ))
```

9.4 AGGREGATE OPERATORS

In addition to simply retrieving data, we often want to perform some computation or summarization. As we noted earlier in this chapter, SQL allows the use of arithmetic expressions. We now consider a powerful class of constructs for computing *aggregate values* like **MIN** and **SUM**. These features represent a significant extension of relational algebra. SQL supports five aggregate operations, which can be applied on any column, say A, of a relation:

1. COUNT ([DISTINCT] A): The number of (unique) values in the A column.

2. SUM ([DISTINCT] A): The sum of all (unique) values in the A column.

3. AVG ([DISTINCT] A): The average of all (unique) values in the A column.

4. MAX (A): The maximum value in the A column.

5. MIN (A): The minimum value in the A column.

Note that it does not make sense to specify DISTINCT in conjunction with MIN or MAX (although SQL-92 does not preclude this).

Find the average age of sailors.

```
SELECT AVG (S.age)
FROM    Sailors S
```

Of course, the WHERE clause can be used to restrict the sailors who are considered in computing the average age.

Find the average age of sailors with a rating of 10.

```
SELECT AVG (S.age)
FROM    Sailors S
WHERE   S.rating = 10
```

MIN (or MAX) can be used instead of AVG in the above queries to find the age of the youngest (oldest) sailor. However, finding both the name and the age of the oldest sailor is more tricky. Consider the query:

```
SELECT S.sname, MAX (S.age)
FROM    Sailors S
```

The intent is for this query to return not only the maximum age but also the name of the sailors having that age. However, this query is illegal in SQL—if the SELECT clause uses an aggregate operation, then it must use *only* aggregate operations unless the query contains a GROUP BY clause! (The intuition behind this restriction should become clear when we discuss the GROUP BY clause in Section 9.4.1.) Thus we cannot use MAX (S.age) as well as S.sname. We have to use a nested query to compute the desired answer:

```
SELECT  S.sname, S.age
FROM    Sailors S
WHERE   S.age = ( SELECT MAX (S2.age)
                  FROM Sailors S2 )
```

Observe that we have used the result of an aggregate operation in the subquery as an argument to a comparison operation. Strictly speaking, we are comparing an age value with the result of the subquery, which is a relation. However, because of the use of the aggregate operation, the subquery is guaranteed to return a single tuple with a single field, and SQL converts such a relation to a field value for the sake of the comparison. The following equivalent query is legal in the SQL-92 standard, but is not supported in many systems:

```
SELECT  S.sname, S.age
FROM    Sailors S
WHERE   ( SELECT MAX (S2.age)
          FROM Sailors S2 ) = S.age
```

We can count the number of sailors using COUNT:

```
SELECT COUNT (*)
FROM   Sailors S
```

This example illustrates the use of * as an argument to COUNT, which is useful when we want to count all rows. We can think of * as shorthand for all the columns (in the cross-product of the from-list in the FROM clause). Contrast this query with the following query, which computes the number of distinct sailor names. (Remember that *sname* is not a key!)

```
SELECT COUNT ( DISTINCT S.sname )
FROM   Sailors S
```

If DISTINCT is omitted, this query is the same as the previous query. However, the use of COUNT (*) is better querying style when it is applicable.

Aggregate operations offer an alternative to the ANY and ALL constructs. For example, consider the following query:

Find the names of sailors who are older than the oldest sailor with a rating of 10.

```
SELECT  S.sname
FROM    Sailors S
WHERE   S.age > ( SELECT MAX ( S2.age )
```

```
            FROM    Sailors S2
            WHERE   S2.rating = 10 )
```

Using **ALL**, this query could alternatively be written as follows:

```
    SELECT  S.sname
    FROM    Sailors S
    WHERE   S.age > ALL ( SELECT S2.age
                          FROM    Sailors S2
                          WHERE   S2.rating = 10 )
```

However, the **ALL** query is more error prone—one could easily (and incorrectly!) use **ANY** instead of **ALL**, and retrieve sailors who are older than *some* sailor with a rating of 10. The use of **ANY** intuitively corresponds to the use of **MIN**, instead of **MAX**, in the previous query.

9.4.1   The GROUP BY and HAVING Clauses

Thus far, we have applied aggregate operations to all (qualifying) rows in a relation. Often we want to apply aggregate operations to each of a number of **groups** of rows in a relation, where the number of groups depends on the relation instance (i.e., is not known in advance). For example, consider the following query.

Find the age of the youngest sailor for each rating level.

If we know that ratings are integers in the range 1 to 10, we could write 10 queries of the form:

```
    SELECT  MIN (S.age)
    FROM    Sailors S
    WHERE   S.rating = i
```

where $i = 1, 2, \ldots, 10$. Writing such a query in this fashion is tedious. More importantly, we may not know what rating levels exist in advance.

To write such queries, we need a major extension to the basic SQL query form, namely, the **GROUP BY** clause. In fact, the extension also includes an optional **HAVING** clause that can be used to specify qualifications over groups (for example, we may only be interested in rating levels > 6). The general form of an SQL query with these extensions is:

```
    SELECT   [ DISTINCT ] select-list
    FROM     from-list
```

```
WHERE     qualification
GROUP BY  grouping-list
HAVING    group-qualification
```

Let us consider some important points concerning the new clauses:

- The **select-list** in the `SELECT` clause consists of (1) a list of column names and (2) a list of terms having the form **aggop** (*column-name*) `AS` *new-name*. The optional `AS` *new-name* term gives this column a name in the table that is the result of the query. Any of the aggregation operators can be used for **aggop**.

  Every column that appears in (1) must also appear in **grouping-list**. The reason is that each row in the result of the query corresponds to one *group*, which is a collection of rows that agree on the values of columns in grouping-list. If a column appears in list (1), but not in **grouping-list**, it is not clear what value should be assigned to it in an answer row.

- The expressions appearing in the **group-qualification** in the `HAVING` clause must have a *single* value per group. The intuition is that the `HAVING` clause determines whether an answer row is to be generated for a given group. Therefore, a column appearing in the **group-qualification** must appear as the argument to an aggregation operator, or it must also appear in **grouping-list**.

- If the `GROUP BY` clause is omitted, the entire table is regarded as a single group.

We will explain the semantics of such a query through an example. Consider the query:

Find the age of the youngest sailor who is eligible to vote (i.e., is at least 18 years old) for each rating level with at least two such sailors.

```
SELECT    S.rating, MIN (S.age) AS minage
FROM      Sailors S
WHERE     S.age >= 18
GROUP BY  S.rating
HAVING    COUNT (*) > 1
```

The instance of Sailors on which this query is to be evaluated is shown in Figure 9.5. Extending the hypothetical evaluation strategy presented in Section 9.1, we proceed as follows. The first step is to construct the cross-product of tables in **from-list**. Because the only relation is Sailors, the result is just the instance shown in Figure 9.5.

sid	sname	rating	age
22	dustin	7	45.0
31	lubber	8	55.5
32	andy	8	25.5
85	art	3	25.5
95	bob	3	63.5
58	rusty	10	35.0
29	brutus	1	33.0
64	horatio	7	35.0
71	zorba	10	16.0

Figure 9.5   An Instance *Sailors2* of Sailors

The second step is to apply the qualification in the **WHERE** clause *S.age* $>= 18$. This step eliminates the row $\langle 71, zorba, 10, 16 \rangle$. The third step is to eliminate unwanted columns. Only columns mentioned in the **SELECT** clause, the **GROUP BY** clause, or the **HAVING** clause are necessary, which means we can eliminate *sid* and *sname* in our example. The result is shown in Figure 9.6. The fourth step is to sort the table according to the **GROUP BY** clause to identify the groups. The result of this step is shown in Figure 9.7.

rating	age
7	45.0
8	55.5
8	25.5
3	25.5
3	63.5
10	35.0
1	33.0
7	35.0

Figure 9.6   After Evaluation Step 3

rating	age
1	33.0
3	25.5
3	63.5
7	45.0
7	35.0
8	55.5
8	25.5
10	35.0

Figure 9.7   After Evaluation Step 4

The fifth step is to apply the group-qualification in the **HAVING** clause, that is, the condition **COUNT** (*) > 1. This step eliminates the groups with *rating* equal to 1 and 10. Observe that the order in which the **WHERE** and **GROUP BY** clauses are considered is significant: If the **WHERE** clause were not considered first, the group with *rating=10* would have met the group-qualification in the **HAVING** clause. The sixth step is to generate one answer row per remaining group. The answer row corresponding to a group consists of a subset of the grouping columns, plus one or more columns generated by applying an aggregation operator. In our example, each answer row has a *rating* column and a *minage* column, which is computed by applying MIN to the values in the *age* column of the corresponding group. The result of this step is shown in Figure 9.8.

rating	minage
3	25.5
7	35.0
8	25.5

Figure 9.8   Final Result in Sample Evaluation

If the query contains DISTINCT in the SELECT clause, duplicates are eliminated in an additional, and final, step.

9.4.2   More Examples of Aggregate Queries

For each red boat, find the number of reservations for this boat.

```
SELECT     B.bid, COUNT (*) AS sailorcount
FROM       Boats B, Reserves R
WHERE      R.bid = B.bid AND B.color = 'red'
GROUP BY   B.bid
```

Note that the number of reservations is not the same as the number of sailors who have reserved this boat, since a sailor may have reserved the boat many times. It is interesting to observe that the following version of the above query is illegal:

```
SELECT     B.bid, COUNT (*) AS sailorcount
FROM       Boats B, Reserves R
WHERE      R.bid = B.bid
GROUP BY   B.bid
HAVING     B.color = 'red'
```

Even though the group-qualification *B.color = 'red'* is single-valued per group, since *bid* is a key for Boats, SQL disallows this query. Only columns that appear in the GROUP BY clause can appear in the HAVING clause, unless they appear as arguments to an aggregate operator.

Find the average age of sailors for each rating level that has at least two sailors.

```
SELECT     S.rating, AVG ( S.age ) AS avgage
```

```
FROM      Sailors S
GROUP BY  S.rating
HAVING    1 < ( SELECT COUNT (*)
                FROM    Sailors S2
                WHERE   S.rating = S2.rating )
```

This example illustrates that the **HAVING** clause can have a nested subquery, just like the **WHERE** clause.

A variation of the previous query is:

Find the average age of sailors who are of voting age (i.e., at least 18 years old) for each rating level that has at least two sailors.

```
SELECT    S.rating, AVG ( S.age ) AS avgage
FROM      Sailors S
WHERE     S. age > 18
GROUP BY  S.rating
HAVING    1 < ( SELECT COUNT (*)
                FROM    Sailors S2
                WHERE   S.rating = S2.rating )
```

A further variation is the following query:

*Find the average age of sailors who are of voting age (i.e., at least 18 years old) for each rating level that has at least two **such** sailors.*

```
SELECT    S.rating, AVG ( S.age ) AS avgage
FROM      Sailors S
WHERE     S. age > 18
GROUP BY  S.rating
HAVING    1 < ( SELECT COUNT (*)
                FROM    Sailors S2
                WHERE   S.rating = S2.rating AND  S2.age > 18 )
```

A much simpler alternative follows:

```
SELECT    S.rating, AVG ( S.age ) AS avgage
FROM      Sailors S
WHERE     S. age > 18
GROUP BY  S.rating
HAVING    COUNT (*) > 1
```

This query takes advantage of the fact that the **WHERE** clause is applied before grouping is done; thus only sailors with *age*> 18 are left when grouping is done. It is instructive to consider yet another way of writing this query:

```
SELECT  Temp.rating, Temp.avgage
FROM    ( SELECT     S.rating, AVG ( S.age ) AS avgage,
                     COUNT (*) AS ratingcount
          FROM       Sailors S
          WHERE      S. age > 18
          GROUP BY   S.rating ) AS Temp
WHERE   Temp.ratingcount > 1
```

This alternative brings out several interesting points. First, the **FROM** clause can also contain a nested subquery according to the SQL-92 standard.[5] Second, the **HAVING** clause is not needed at all. Any query with a **HAVING** clause can be rewritten without one, but many queries are simpler to express with the **HAVING** clause. Finally, when a subquery appears in the **FROM** clause, using the **AS** keyword to give it a name is necessary (since otherwise we could not express, for instance, the condition *Temp.ratingcount > 1*).

Find those ratings for which the average age of sailors is the minimum over all ratings.

We use this query to illustrate that aggregate operations cannot be nested. One might consider writing it as follows:

```
SELECT     S.rating
FROM       Sailors S
WHERE      AVG (S.age) = ( SELECT     MIN (AVG (S2.age))
                           FROM       Sailors S2
                           GROUP BY   S2.rating )
```

A little thought shows that this query will not work even if the expression **MIN** (**AVG** (S2.age), which is illegal, were allowed. In the nested query, Sailors is partitioned into groups by rating, and the average age is computed for each rating value. For each group, applying **MIN** to this average age value for the group will return the same value! A correct version of the above query follows. It essentially computes a temporary table containing the average age for each rating value and then finds the rating(s) for which this average age is the minimum.

```
SELECT  Temp.rating, Temp.avgage
FROM    ( SELECT     S.rating, AVG (S.age) AS avgage,
```

---

[5]Not all systems currently support nested queries in the **FROM** clause.

```
            FROM        Sailors S
            GROUP BY S.rating) AS Temp
    WHERE   Temp.avgage = ( SELECT MIN (Temp.avgage) FROM Temp )
```

As an exercise, the reader should consider whether the following query computes the same answer, and if not, why:

```
    SELECT   Temp.rating, MIN ( Temp.avgage )
    FROM     ( SELECT    S.rating, AVG (S.age) AS avgage,
               FROM       Sailors S
               GROUP BY S.rating ) AS Temp
    GROUP BY Temp.rating
```

9.5   NULL VALUES *

Thus far, we have assumed that column values in a row are always known. In practice column values can be **unknown**. For example, when a sailor, say Bob, first joins a yacht club, he may not yet have a rating assigned. Since the definition for the Sailors table has a *rating* column, what row should we insert for Bob? Intuitively, what is needed here is a special value that denotes *unknown*. As another example, suppose that the Sailor table definition was modified to also include a *maiden-name* column. However, only married women who take their husband's last name have a maiden name. For single women and for men, the *maiden-name* column is *inapplicable*. Again, what value do we include in this column for the row representing Bob?

SQL provides a special column value called *null* to use in such situations. Thus we use *null* when the column value is either *unknown* or *inapplicable*. Using our Sailor table definition, we might enter the row ⟨98, *Bob, null*, 39⟩ to represent Bob. The presence of *null* values complicates many issues, and we consider the impact of *null* values on the SQL query language in the rest of this section.

9.5.1   Comparisons Using Null Values

Consider a comparison such as *rating = 8*. If this is applied to the row for Bob, is this condition true or false? Since Bob's rating is unknown, it is reasonable to say that this comparison should evaluate to the value **unknown**. In fact, this is the case for the comparisons *rating> 8* and *rating< 8* as well. Perhaps less obviously, if we compare two *null* values using $<, >, =$, and so on, the result is always **unknown**. For example, if we have *null* in two distinct rows of the sailor relation, any comparison returns **unknown**.

SQL also provides a special comparison operator to test whether a column value is *null*; for example, we can say *rating* IS NULL, which would evaluate to true on the row representing Bob. We can also say *rating* IS NOT NULL, which would evaluate to false on the row for Bob.

9.5.2 Logical Connectives AND, OR and NOT

Now, what about boolean expressions such as *rating*= 8 OR *age*< 40 and *rating*= 8 AND *age*< 40? Considering the row for Bob again, because *age*< 40, the first expression evaluates to true regardless of the value of *rating*, but what about the second? We can only say unknown.

But this example raises an important point—once we have *null* values, we must define the logical operators AND, OR and NOT using a *three-valued* logic in which expressions evaluate to true, false, or unknown. We extend the usual interpretations of AND, OR, and NOT to cover the case when one of the arguments is unknown as follows. The expression NOT unknown is defined to be unknown. OR of two arguments evaluates to true if either argument evaluates to true, and to unknown if one argument evaluates to false and the other evaluates to unknown. (If both arguments are false, of course, it evaluates to false.) AND of two arguments evaluates to false if either argument evaluates to false, and to unknown if one argument evaluates to unknown and the other evaluates to true or unknown. (If both arguments are true, of course, it evaluates to true.)

9.5.3 Impact on SQL Constructs

Boolean expressions arise in many contexts in SQL, and the impact of *null* values must be recognized. For example, the *qualification* in the WHERE clause eliminates rows (in the cross-product of tables named in the FROM clause) for which the *qualification* does not evaluate to true. Therefore, in the presence of *null* values, any row that evaluates to false or to unknown is eliminated. Eliminating rows that evaluate to unknown has a subtle but significant impact on queries, especially nested queries involving EXISTS or UNIQUE.

Another issue in the presence of *null* values is the definition of when two rows in a relation instance are regarded as *duplicates*. The SQL definition is that two rows are duplicates if corresponding columns are either equal, or both contain *null*. Contrast this definition with the fact that if we compare two *null* values using =, the result is unknown! In the context of duplicates, this comparison is implicitly treated as true, which is an anomaly.

As expected, the arithmetic operations $+, -, *$, and $/$ all return *null* if one of their arguments is *null*. However, nulls can cause some unexpected behavior with aggregate operations. COUNT(*) handles *null* values just like other values, that is, they get counted. All the other aggregate operations (COUNT, SUM, AVG, MIN, MAX, and variations using DISTINCT) simply discard *null* values—thus SUM cannot be understood as just the addition of all values in the (multi)set of values that it is applied to; a preliminary step of discarding all *null* values must also be accounted for. As a special case, if one of these operators—other than COUNT—is applied to *only* null values, the result is again *null*.

9.5.4 Outer Joins

Some interesting variants of the join operation that rely on *null* values, called **outer joins**, are supported in SQL. Consider the join of two tables, say Sailors $\bowtie_c$ Reserves. Tuples of Sailors that do not match some row in Reserves according to the join condition c do not appear in the result. In an outer join, on the other hand, Sailor rows without a matching Reserves row appear exactly once in the result, with the result columns inherited from Reserves assigned *null* values.

In fact, there are several variants of the outer join idea. In a **left outer join**, Sailor rows without a matching Reserves row appear in the result, but not vice versa. In a **right outer join**, Reserves rows without a matching Sailors row appear in the result, but not vice versa. In a **full outer join**, both Sailors and Reserves rows without a match appear in the result. (Of course, rows with a match always appear in the result, for all these variants, just like the usual joins (sometimes called *inner* joins) presented earlier in Chapter 8.)

SQL-92 allows the desired type of join to be specified in the FROM clause. For example, the following query lists ⟨*sid,bid*⟩ pairs corresponding to sailors and boats they have reserved:

```
SELECT  Sailors.sid, Reserves.bid
FROM    Sailors NATURAL LEFT OUTER JOIN Reserves R
```

The NATURAL keyword specifies that the join condition is equality on all common attributes (in this example, *sid*), and the WHERE clause is not required (unless we want to specify additional, non join, conditions). On the instances of Sailors and Reserves shown in Figure 9.1, this query computes the result shown in Figure 9.9.

sid	sid
22	101
31	null
58	103

Figure 9.9   Left Outer Join of *Sailor1* and *Reserves1*

9.5.5   Disallowing Null Values

We can disallow *null* values by specifying NOT NULL as part of the field definition, for example, *sname* CHAR(20) NOT NULL. In addition, the fields in a primary key are not allowed to take on *null* values. Thus there is an implicit NOT NULL constraint for every field listed in a PRIMARY KEY constraint.

We conclude our coverage of *null* values with the remark that our discussion is far from complete. The interested reader should consult one of the many books devoted to SQL for a more detailed treatment of the topic.

9.6   EMBEDDED SQL *

We have looked at a wide range of SQL query constructs, treating SQL as an independent language in its own right. Indeed, a relational DBMS supports an *interactive SQL* interface, and users can directly enter SQL commands. This simple approach is perfectly fine as long as the task at hand can be accomplished entirely with SQL commands. In practice we often encounter situations in which we need the greater flexibility of a general-purpose programming language such as C or COBOL, in addition to the data manipulation facilities provided by SQL. For example, we may want to ask a query that cannot be expressed in SQL—see Chapter 20 for examples of such queries—or interact with the user through a graphical interface.

To deal with such situations, the SQL standard defines how SQL commands can be executed from within a program in a **host language** such as C or COBOL. The use of SQL commands within a host language program is called **embedded SQL**. Details of embedded SQL also depend on the host language; although similar capabilities are supported for a variety of host languages, the syntax sometimes varies.

Conceptually, embedding SQL commands in a host language program is straightforward. SQL statements (i.e., not declarations) can be used wherever a statement in the host language is allowed (with a few restrictions). Of course, SQL statements must be clearly marked so that a preprocessor can deal with them before invoking the compiler for the host language. Also, any host language variables used to pass arguments into an SQL command must be declared in SQL, and certain variables *must* be declared in this manner (so that, for example, any error conditions arising during SQL execution can be communicated back to the main application program in the host language).

There are, however, two complications to bear in mind. First, the data types recognized by SQL may not be recognized by the host language, and vice versa. This mismatch is typically addressed by casting data values appropriately before passing them to or from SQL commands. (SQL, like C and other programming languages, provides an operator to cast values of one type into values of another type.) The second complication has to do with the fact that SQL is **set-oriented**; commands operate on and produce tables, which are sets (or multisets) of rows. Programming languages do not typically have a data type that corresponds to sets or multisets of rows. Thus, although SQL commands deal with tables, the interface to the host language is constrained to be one row at a time. The *cursor* mechanism is introduced to deal with this problem; we discuss cursors in Section 9.7.

In our discussion of embedded SQL, we assume that the host language is C for concreteness, because minor differences exist in how SQL statements are embedded in different host languages.

9.6.1 Declaring Variables and Exceptions

SQL statements can refer to variables defined in the host program. Such variables must be prefixed by a colon (:) in SQL statements and must be declared between the commands `EXEC SQL BEGIN DECLARE SECTION` and `EXEC SQL END DECLARE SECTION`. The declarations are similar to how they would look in a C program, and as usual in C, are separated by semicolons. For example, we can declare variables *c_sname*, *c_sid*, *c_rating* and *c_age* (with the initial *c* used as a naming convention to emphasize that these are host language variables) as follows:

```
EXEC SQL BEGIN DECLARE SECTION
char c_sname[20];
long c_sid;
short c_rating;
float c_age;
EXEC SQL END DECLARE SECTION
```

The first question that arises is which SQL types correspond to the various C types, since we have just declared a collection of C variables whose values are intended to be read (and possibly set) in an SQL run-time environment when an SQL statement that refers to them is executed. The SQL-92 standard defines such a correspondence between the host language types and SQL types for a number of host languages. In our example *c_sname* has the type CHARACTER(20) when referred to in an SQL statement, *c_sid* has the type INTEGER, *c_rating* has the type SMALLINT, and *c_age* has the type REAL.

An important point to consider is that SQL needs some way to report what went wrong if an error condition arises when executing an SQL statement. The SQL-92 standard recognizes two special variables for reporting errors, SQLCODE and SQLSTATE. SQLCODE is the older of the two and is defined to return some negative value when an error condition arises, without specifying further just what error a particular negative integer denotes. SQLSTATE, introduced in the SQL-92 standard for the first time, associates predefined values with several common error conditions, thereby introducing some uniformity to how errors are reported. One of these two variables *must* be declared. The appropriate C type for SQLCODE is long and the appropriate C type for SQLSTATE is char[6], that is, a character string that is five characters long. (Recall the null-terminator in C strings!) In this chapter, we will assume that SQLSTATE is declared.

9.6.2   Embedding SQL Statements

All SQL statements that are embedded within a host program must be clearly marked, with the details dependent on the host language; in C, SQL statements must be prefixed by EXEC SQL. An SQL statement can essentially appear in any place in the host language program where a host language statement can appear.

As a simple example, the following embedded SQL statement inserts a row, whose column values are based on the values of the host language variables contained in it, into the Sailors relation:

    EXEC SQL INSERT INTO Sailors VALUES (:*c_sname*, :*c_sid*, :*c_rating*, :*c_age*);

Observe that a semicolon terminates the command, as per the convention for terminating statements in C.

The SQLSTATE variable should be checked for errors and exceptions after each embedded SQL statement. SQL provides the WHENEVER command to simplify this tedious task:

    EXEC SQL WHENEVER [SQLERROR | NOT FOUND] [CONTINUE | GOTO *stmt*]

The intent is that after each embedded SQL statement is executed, the value of SQLSTATE should be checked. If SQLERROR is specified and the value of SQLSTATE

indicates an exception, control is transferred to *stmt*, which is presumably responsible for error/exception handling. Control is also transferred to *stmt* if **NOT
FOUND** is specified and the value of **SQLSTATE** is 02000, which denotes **NO DATA**.

9.7 CURSORS *

A major problem in embedding SQL statements in a host language like C is that
an *impedance mismatch* occurs because SQL operates on *sets* of records, whereas
languages like C do not cleanly support a set-of-records abstraction. The solution
is to essentially provide a mechanism that allows us to retrieve rows one at a time
from a relation.

This mechanism is called a **cursor**. We can declare a cursor on any relation, or
indeed, on any SQL query (because every query returns a set of rows). Once a
cursor is declared, we can **open** it (which positions the cursor just before the
first row); **fetch** the next row; **move** the cursor (to the next row, to the row
after the next *n*, to the first row, or to the previous row, etc., by specifying
additional parameters for the **FETCH** command); or **close** the cursor. Thus a
cursor essentially allows us to retrieve the rows in a table by positioning the
cursor at a particular row and reading its contents.

9.7.1 Basic Cursor Definition and Usage

Cursors enable us to examine in the host language program a collection of rows
computed by an embedded SQL statement:

■   We usually need to open a cursor if the embedded statement is a **SELECT** (i.e.,
    a query). However, we can avoid opening a cursor if the answer contains a
    single row, as we will see shortly.

■   **INSERT**, **DELETE** and **UPDATE** statements typically don't require a cursor, al-
    though some variants of **DELETE** and **UPDATE** do use a cursor.

As an example, we can find the name and age of a sailor, specified by assigning a
value to the host variable *c_sid*, declared earlier, as follows:

```
EXEC SQL SELECT  S.sname, S.age
         INTO    :c_sname, :c_age
         FROM    Sailors S
         WHERE   S.sid = :c_sid;
```

The **INTO** clause allows us to assign the columns of the single answer row to the
host variables *c_sname* and *c_age*. Thus we do not need a cursor to embed this

query in a host language program. But what about the following query, which computes the names and ages of all sailors with a rating greater than the current value of the host variable *c_minrating*?

```
SELECT  S.sname, S.age
FROM    Sailors S
WHERE   S.rating > :c_minrating
```

This query returns a collection of rows, not just one row. When executed interactively, the answers are printed on the screen. If we embed this query in a C program by prefixing the command with **EXEC SQL**, how can the answers be bound to host language variables? The **INTO** clause is not adequate because we must deal with several rows. The solution is to use a cursor:

```
DECLARE sinfo CURSOR FOR
SELECT  S.sname, S.age
FROM    Sailors S
WHERE   S.rating > :c_minrating;
```

This code can be included in a C program, and once it is executed, the cursor *sinfo* is defined. Subsequently, we can open the cursor:

```
OPEN  sinfo;
```

The value of *c_minrating* in the SQL query associated with the cursor is the value of this variable when we open the cursor. (The cursor declaration is processed at compile time, and the **OPEN** command is executed at run-time.)

A cursor can be thought of as 'pointing' to a row in the collection of answers to the query associated with it. When a cursor is opened, it is positioned just before the first row. We can use the **FETCH** command to read the first row of cursor *sinfo* into host language variables:

```
FETCH sinfo INTO :c_sname, :c_age;
```

When the **FETCH** statement is executed, the cursor is positioned to point at the next row (which is the first row in the table when **FETCH** is executed for the first time after opening the cursor) and the column values in the row are copied into the corresponding host variables. By repeatedly executing this **FETCH** statement (say, in a **while** loop in the C program), we can read all the rows computed by the query, one row at a time. Additional parameters to the **FETCH** command allow us to position a cursor in very flexible ways, but we will not discuss them.

How do we know when we have looked at all the rows associated with the cursor? By looking at the special variables **SQLCODE** or **SQLSTATE**, of course. **SQLSTATE**, for example, is set to the value 02000, which denotes **NO DATA**, to indicate that there are no more rows if the **FETCH** statement positions the cursor after the last row.

When we are done with a cursor, we can close it:

> **CLOSE** sinfo;

It can be opened again if needed, and the value of : *c_minrating* in the SQL query associated with the cursor would be the value of the host variable *c_minrating* at that time.

9.7.2   Properties of Cursors

The general form of a cursor declaration is:

> **DECLARE** *cursorname* [INSENSITIVE] [SCROLL] **CURSOR FOR**
>   *some query*
>   [**ORDER BY** order-item-list]
>   [**FOR READ ONLY** | **FOR UPDATE**]

A cursor can be declared to be a **read-only cursor** (FOR READ ONLY) or, if it is a cursor on a base relation or an updatable view, to be an **updatable cursor** (FOR UPDATE). If it is updatable, simple variants of the **UPDATE** and **DELETE** commands allow us to update or delete the row on which the cursor is positioned. For example, if *sinfo* is an updatable cursor and is open, we can execute the following statement:

> **UPDATE** Sailors S
> **SET**   S.rating = S.rating - 1
> **WHERE**   **CURRENT** of sinfo;

This embedded SQL statement modifies the *rating* value of the row currently pointed to by cursor *sinfo*; similarly, we can delete this row by executing the next statement:

> **DELETE** Sailors S
> **WHERE**   **CURRENT** of sinfo;

A cursor is updatable by default unless it is a scrollable or insensitive cursor (see below), in which case it is read-only by default.

If the keyword **SCROLL** is specified, the cursor is **scrollable**, which means that variants of the **FETCH** command can be used to position the cursor in very flexible ways; otherwise, only the basic **FETCH** command, which retrieves the next row, is allowed.

If the keyword **INSENSITIVE** is specified, the cursor behaves as if it is ranging over a private copy of the collection of answer rows. Otherwise, and by default, other actions of some transaction could modify these rows, creating unpredictable behavior. For example, while we are fetching rows using the *sinfo* cursor, we might modify *rating* values in Sailor rows by concurrently executing the command:

```
UPDATE Sailors S
SET     S.rating = S.rating - 1
```

Consider a Sailor row such that: (1) it has not yet been fetched, and (2) its original *rating* value would have met the condition in the **WHERE** clause of the query associated with *sinfo*, but the new *rating* value does not. Do we fetch such a Sailor row? If **INSENSITIVE** is specified, the behavior is as if all answers were computed and stored when *sinfo* was opened; thus the update command has no effect on the rows fetched by *sinfo* if it is executed after *sinfo* is opened. If **INSENSITIVE** is not specified, the behavior is implementation dependent in this situation.

Finally, in what order do **FETCH** commands retrieve rows? In general this order is unspecified, but the optional **ORDER BY** clause can be used to specify a sort order. Note that columns mentioned in the **ORDER BY** clause cannot be updated through the cursor!

The **order-item-list** is a list of **order-items**; an order-item is a column name, optionally followed by one of the keywords **ASC** or **DESC**. Every column mentioned in the **ORDER BY** clause must also appear in **select-list** of the query associated with the cursor; otherwise it is not clear what columns we should sort on. The keywords **ASC** or **DESC** that follow a column control whether the result should be sorted—with respect to that column—in ascending or descending order; the default is **ASC**. This clause is applied as the last step in evaluating the query.

Consider the query discussed in Section 9.4.1, and the answer shown in Figure 9.8. Suppose that a cursor is opened on this query, with the clause:

```
ORDER BY minage ASC, rating DESC
```

The answer is sorted first in ascending order by *minage*, and if several rows have the same *minage* value, these rows are sorted further in descending order by *rating*. The cursor would fetch the rows in the order shown in Figure 9.10.

rating	minage
8	25.5
3	25.5
7	35.0

Figure 9.10   Order in which Tuples are Fetched

9.8   DYNAMIC SQL *

Consider an application like a spreadsheet or a graphical front-end that needs to access data from a DBMS. Such an application must accept commands from a user, and based on what the user needs, generate appropriate SQL statements to retrieve the necessary data. In such situations, we may not be able to predict in advance just what SQL statements need to be executed, even though there is (presumably) some algorithm by which the application can construct the necessary SQL statements once a user's command is issued.

SQL provides some facilities to deal with such situations; these are referred to as **dynamic SQL**. There are two main commands, **PREPARE** and **EXECUTE**, which we illustrate through a simple example:

```
char c_sqlstring[] = {"DELETE FROM Sailors WHERE rating>5"};
EXEC SQL PREPARE readytogo FROM :c_sqlstring;
EXEC SQL EXECUTE readytogo;
```

The first statement declares the C variable *c_sqlstring* and initializes its value to the string representation of an SQL command. The second statement results in this string being parsed and compiled as an SQL command, with the resulting executable bound to the SQL variable *readytogo*. (Since *readytogo* is an SQL variable, just like a cursor name, it is not prefixed by a colon.) The third statement executes the command.

Many situations require the use of dynamic SQL. However, note that the preparation of a dynamic SQL command occurs at run-time and is a run-time overhead. Interactive and embedded SQL commands can be prepared once and for all at compile time and then re-executed as often as desired. Consequently you should limit the use of dynamic SQL to situations in which it is essential.

There are many more things to know about dynamic SQL—how can we pass parameters from the host langugage program to the SQL statement being prepared, for example?—but we will not discuss it further; readers interested in using dynamic SQL should consult one of the many good books devoted to SQL.

9.9   QUERIES IN COMPLEX INTEGRITY CONSTRAINTS *

In this section we discuss the specification of complex integrity constraints in
SQL-92, utilizing the full power of SQL query constructs. The features discussed
in this section complement the integrity constraint features of SQL presented in
Chapter 2.

9.9.1   Constraints over a Single Table

We can specify complex constraints over a single table using **table constraints**,
which have the form **CHECK** *conditional-expression*. For example, to ensure that
rating must be an integer in the range 1 to 10, we could use:

```
CREATE TABLE Sailors ( sid     INTEGER,
                       sname  CHAR(10),
                       rating INTEGER,
                       age     REAL,
                       PRIMARY KEY (sid),
                       CHECK ( rating >= 1 AND rating <= 10 ))
```

To enforce the constraint that Interlake boats cannot be reserved, we could use:

```
CREATE TABLE Reserves (  sid     INTEGER,
                         bid     INTEGER,
                         day     DATE,
                         FOREIGN KEY (sid) REFERENCES Students
                         FOREIGN KEY (bid) REFERENCES Boats
                         CONSTRAINT noInterlakeRes
                         CHECK ( 'Interlake' <>
                                  ( Select B.bname
                                    FROM  Boats B
                                    WHERE B.bid = Reserves.bid )))
```

When a row is inserted into Reserves or an existing row is modified, the *conditional
expression* in the **CHECK** constraint is evaluated. If it evaluates to **false**, the
command is rejected.

9.9.2   Domain Constraints

A user can define a new domain using the **CREATE DOMAIN** statement, which makes
use of **CHECK** constraints.

```
CREATE DOMAIN ratingval INTEGER DEFAULT 0
```

$$\texttt{CHECK (VALUE >= 1 AND VALUE <= 10)}$$

INTEGER is the **base type** for the domain `ratingval`, and every `ratingval` value must be of this type. Values in `ratingval` are further restricted by using a CHECK constraint; in defining this constraint, we use the keyword VALUE to refer to a value in the domain. By using this facility, we can constrain the values that belong to a domain using the full power of SQL queries. Once a domain is defined, the name of the domain can be used to restrict column values in a table; we can use the following line in a schema declaration, for example:

        rating   ratingval

The optional DEFAULT keyword is used to associate a default value with a domain. If the domain `ratingval` is used for a column in some relation, and no value is entered for this column in an inserted tuple, the default value 0 associated with `ratingval` is used. (If a default value is specified for the column as part of the table definition, this takes precedence over the dafault value associated with the domain.) This feature can be used to minimize data entry errors; common default values are automatically filled in rather than being typed in.

SQL-92's support for the concept of a domain is limited in an important respect. For example, we can define two domains called Studentid and Boatclass, each using INTEGER as a base type. The intent is to force a comparison of a Studentid value with a Boatclass value to always fail (since they are drawn from different domains); however, since they both have the same base type, INTEGER, the comparison will succeed in SQL-92.

9.9.3   Assertions: ICs over Several Tables

Table constraints are associated with a single table, although the conditional expression in the CHECK clause can refer to other tables. Table constraints are required to hold *only* if the associated table is nonempty. Thus, when a constraint involves two or more tables, the table constraint mechanism is sometimes cumbersome, and not quite what is desired. To cover such situations, SQL supports the creation of **assertions**, which are constraints not associated with any one table.

As an example, suppose that we wish to enforce the constraint that the number of boats plus the number of sailors should be less than 100. (This condition might be required, say, to qualify as a 'small' sailing club.) We could try the following table constraint:

```
CREATE TABLE Sailors ( sid     INTEGER,
                       sname  CHAR(10),
```

```
rating  INTEGER,
age     REAL,
PRIMARY KEY (sid),
CHECK ( rating >= 1 AND rating <= 10)
CHECK ( ( SELECT COUNT (S.sid) FROM Sailors S )
            + ( SELECT COUNT (B.bid) FROM Boats B )
        < 100 )
```

This solution suffers from two drawbacks. It is associated with Sailors, although it involves Boats in a completely symmetric way. More important, if the Sailors table is empty, this constraint is defined (as per the semantics of table constraints) to always hold, even if we have more than 100 rows in Boats! We could extend this constraint specification to check that Sailors is nonempty, but this approach becomes very cumbersome. The best solution is to create an assertion, as follows:

```
CREATE ASSERTION smallClub
CHECK (( SELECT COUNT (S.sid) FROM Sailors S )
         + ( SELECT COUNT (B.bid) FROM Boats B)
       < 100 )
```

9.10   SUMMARY

We have highlighted the central data retrieval features in SQL-92. The SQL language was an important factor in the early acceptance of the relational model, since users found it much more natural and easy to use than earlier, more procedural query languages. SQL is relationally complete, and features such as aggregate operators, grouping, nested queries, and null values extend the expressive power of SQL beyond relational algebra in significant ways. For example, we cannot compute the average age of sailors in relational algebra. Even for queries that are expressible in relational algebra, the rich set of constructs in SQL often enables us to find a more natural, direct formulation of a query. In fact, the variety of alternatives can sometimes be downright confusing! We remark that some queries cannot be expressed in SQL-92; this is discussed further in Chapter 20.

We also discussed how SQL commands can be executed from within a host language such as C. Conceptually, the main issue is that of data type mismatches between SQL and the host language, in particular, the fact that typical programming languages do not have a data type that corresponds to a collection of records (i.e., tables). The *cursor* mechanism addresses this problem by allowing us to retrieve rows one at a time.

The query capabilities of SQL can be used to specify a rich class of integrity constraints. We discussed domain constraints, **CHECK** constraints (which are appropriate for expressing conditions over a single table), and assertions (which are appropriate for expressing conditions involving more than one table).

EXERCISES

Exercise 9.1 Consider the following relations:

> Student(*snum:* integer, *sname:* string, *major:* string, *level:* string, *age:* integer)
> Class(*name:* string, *meets_at:* time, *room:* string, *fid:* integer)
> Enrolled(*snum:* integer, *cname:* string)
> Faculty(*fid:* integer, *fname:* string, *deptid:* integer)

The meaning of these relations is straightforward; for example, Enrolled has one record per student-class pair such that the student is enrolled in the class.

Write the following queries in SQL. No duplicates should be printed in any of the answers.

1. Find the names of all Juniors (Level = JR) who are enrolled in a class taught by I. Teach.

2. Find the age of the oldest student who is either a History major or is enrolled in a course taught by I. Teach.

3. Find the names of all classes that either meet in room R128 or have five or more students enrolled.

4. Find the names of all students who are enrolled in two classes that meet at the same time.

5. Find the names of faculty members who teach in every room in which some class is taught.

6. Find the names of faculty members for whom the combined enrollment of the courses that they teach is less than five.

7. Print the Level and the average age of students for that Level, for each Level.

8. Print the Level and the average age of students for that Level, for all Levels except JR.

9. Find the names of students who are enrolled in the maximum number of classes.

10. Find the names of students who are not enrolled in any class.

11. For each age value that appears in Students, find the level value that appears most often. For example, if there are more FR level students aged 18 than SR, JR or SO students aged 18, you should print the pair (18, FR).

Exercise 9.2 Consider the following schema:

> Suppliers(*sid:* integer, *sname:* string, *address:* string)
> Parts(*pid:* integer, *pname:* string, *color:* string)
> Catalog(*sid:* integer, *pid:* integer, *cost:* real)

The Catalog relation lists the prices charged for parts by Suppliers. Write the following queries in SQL:

1. Find the *pnames* of parts for which there is some supplier.
2. Find the *snames* of suppliers who supply every part.
3. Find the *snames* of suppliers who supply every red part.
4. Find the *pnames* of parts supplied by Acme Widget Suppliers and by no one else.
5. Find the *sids* of suppliers who charge more for some part than the average cost of that part (averaged over all the suppliers who supply that part).
6. For each part, find the *sname* of the supplier who charges the most for that part.
7. Find the *sids* of suppliers who supply only red parts.
8. Find the *sids* of suppliers who supply a red part and a green part.
9. Find the *sids* of suppliers who supply a red part or a green part.

Exercise 9.3 The following relations keep track of airline flight information:

> Flights(*flno:* integer, *from:* string, *to:* string, *distance:* integer,
>   *departs:* time, *arrives:* time, *price:* integer)
> Aircraft(*aid:* integer, *aname:* string, *cruisingrange:* integer)
> Certified(*eid:* integer, *aid:* integer))
> Employees(*eid:* integer, *ename:* string, *salary:* integer)

Note that the Employees relation describes pilots and other kinds of employees as well; every pilot is certified for some aircraft, and only pilots are certified to fly. Write each of the following queries in SQL. (*Additional queries using the same schema are listed in the exercises for Chapter 8.*)

1. Find the names of aircraft such that all pilots certified to operate them earn more than 80,000.
2. For each pilot who is certified for more than three aircraft, find the *pilotid* and the maximum *cruisingrange* of the aircraft that he (or she) is certified for.
3. Find the names of pilots whose *salary* is less than the price of the cheapest route from L.A. to Honolulu.
4. For all aircraft with *cruisingrange* over 1000, find the name of the aircraft and the average salary of all pilots certified for this aircraft.
5. Find the names of pilots certified for some Boeing aircraft.
6. Find the *aircraftids* of all aircraft that can be used on routes from L.A. to Chicago.
7. Identify the routes that can be piloted by every pilot who makes more than 100,000.
8. Print the *enames* of pilots who can operate planes with *cruisingrange* greater than 3000 miles, but are not certified on any Boeing aircraft.
9. A customer wants to travel from Madison to N.Y. with no more than two changes of flight. List the choice of departure times from Madison if the customer wants to arrive in N.Y. by 6 p.m.

sid	sname	rating	age
18	jones	3	30.0
41	jonah	6	56.0
22	ahab	7	44.0
63	moby	*null*	15.0

Figure 9.11 An Instance of Sailors

10. Compute the difference between the average salary of a pilot and the average salary of all employees (including pilots).

11. Print the name and salary of every non pilot whose salary is more than the average salary for pilots.

Exercise 9.4 Consider the following relational schema. An employee can work in more than one department; the *pct_time* field of the Works relation shows the percentage of time that a given employee works in a given department.

> Emp(*eid:* integer, *ename:* string, *age:* integer, *salary:* real)
> Works(*eid:* integer, *did:* integer, *pct_time:* integer)
> Dept(*did:* integer, *budget:* real, *managerid:* integer)

Write the following queries in SQL:

1. Print the names and ages of each employee who works in both the Hardware department and the Software department.

2. For each department with more than 20 full-time-equivalent employees (i.e., where the part-time and full-time employees add up to at least that many full-time employees), print the *did* together with the number of employees that work in that department.

3. Print the name of each employee whose salary exceeds the budget of all of the departments that he or she works in.

4. Find the *managerids* of managers who manage only departments with budgets greater than 1,000,000.

5. Find the *enames* of managers who manage the departments with the largest budget.

6. If a manager manages more than one department, he or she *controls* the sum of all the budgets for those departments. Find the *managerids* of managers who control more than 5,000,000.

7. Find the *managerids* of managers who control the largest amount.

Exercise 9.5 Consider the instance of the Sailors relation shown in Figure 9.11.

1. Write SQL queries to compute the average rating, using AVG; the sum of the ratings, using SUM; and the number of ratings, using COUNT.

2. If you divide the sum computed above by the count, would the result be the same as the average? How would your answer change if the above steps were carried out with respect to the *age* field instead of *rating*?

3. Consider the following query: *Find the names of sailors with a higher rating than all sailors with age < 21.* The following two SQL queries attempt to obtain the answer to this question. Do they both compute the result? If not, explain why. Under what conditions would they compute the same result?

```
SELECT  S.sname
FROM    Sailors S
WHERE   NOT EXISTS ( SELECT *
                     FROM   Sailors S2
                     WHERE  S2.age < 21
                            AND S.rating <= S2.rating )
SELECT  *
FROM    Sailors S
WHERE   S.rating > ANY ( SELECT S2.rating
                         FROM   Sailors S2
                         WHERE  S2.age < 21 )
```

4. Consider the instance of Sailors shown in Figure 9.11. Let us define instance S1 of Sailors to consist of the first two tuples, instance S2 to be the last two tuples and S to be the given instance.

   (a) Show the left outer join of S with itself, with the join condition being *sid=sid*.

   (b) Show the right outer join of S with itself, with the join condition being *sid=sid*.

   (c) Show the full outer join of S with itself, with the join condition being *sid=sid*.

   (d) Show the left outer join of S1 with S2, with the join condition being *sid=sid*.

   (e) Show the right outer join of S1 with S2, with the join condition being *sid=sid*.

   (f) Show the full outer join of S1 with S2, with the join condition being *sid=sid*.

Exercise 9.6 Answer the following questions.

1. Explain the term *impedance mismatch* in the context of embedding SQL commands in a host language such as C.

2. How can the value of a host language variable be passed to an embedded SQL command?

3. Explain the WHENEVER command's use in error and exception handling.

4. Explain the need for cursors.

5. Give an example of a situation that calls for the use of embedded SQL, that is, interactive use of SQL commands is not enough, and some host language capabilities are needed.

6. Write a C program with embedded SQL commands to address your example in the previous answer.

7. Write a C program with embedded SQL commands to find the standard deviation of sailors' ages.

8. Extend the previous program to find all sailors whose age is within one standard deviation of the average age of all sailors.

9. Explain how you would write a C program to compute the transitive closure of a graph, represented as an SQL relation Edges(*from, to*), using embedded SQL commands. (You don't have to write the program; just explain the main points to be dealt with.)

10. Explain the following terms with respect to cursors: *updatability, sensitivity* and *scrollability.*

11. Define a cursor on the Sailors relation that is updatable, scrollable, and returns answers sorted by *age.* Which fields of Sailors can such a cursor *not* update? Why?

12. Give an example of a situation that calls for dynamic SQL, that is, even embedded SQL is not sufficient.

Exercise 9.7 Consider the following relational schema and briefly answer the questions that follow:

> Emp(*eid:* integer, *ename:* string, *age:* integer, *salary:* real)
> Works(*eid:* integer, *did:* integer, *pct_time:* integer)
> Dept(*did:* integer, *budget:* real, *managerid:* integer)

1. Define a table constraint on Emp that will ensure that every employee makes at least 10,000.

2. Define a table constraint on Dept that will ensure that all managers have *age* > 30.

3. Define an assertion on Dept that will ensure that all managers have *age* > 30. Compare this assertion with the equivalent table constraint. Explain which is better.

4. Write SQL statements to delete all information about employees whose salaries exceed that of the manager of one or more departments that they work in. Be sure to ensure that all the relevant integrity constraints are satisfied after your updates.

Exercise 9.8 Consider the following relations:

> Student(*snum:* integer, *sname:* string, *major:* string,
>   *level:* string, *age:* integer)
> Class(*name:* string, *meets_at:* time, *room:* string, *fid:* integer)
> Enrolled(*snum:* integer, *cname:* string)
> Faculty(*fid:* integer, *fname:* string, *deptid:* integer)

The meaning of these relations is straightforward; for example, Enrolled has one record per student-class pair such that the student is enrolled in the class.

1. Write the SQL statements required to create the above relations, including appropriate versions of all primary and foreign key integrity constraints.

2. Express each of the following integrity constraints in SQL unless it is implied by the primary and foreign key constraint; if so, explain how it is implied. If the constraint cannot be expressed in SQL, say so. For each constraint, state what operations (inserts, deletes, and updates on specific relations) must be monitored to enforce the constraint.

   (a) Every class has a minimum enrollment of 5 students and a maximum enrollment of 30 students.

   (b) At least one class meets in each room.

   (c) Every faculty member must teach at least two courses.

   (d) Only faculty in the department with *deptid=33* teach more than three courses.

   (e) Every student must be enrolled in the course called Math101.

   (f) The room in which the earliest scheduled class (i.e., the class with the smallest *meets_at* value) meets should not be the same as the room in which the latest scheduled class meets.

   (g) Two classes cannot meet in the same room at the same time.

   (h) The department with the most faculty members must have fewer than twice the number of faculty members in the department with the fewest faculty members.

   (i) No department can have more than 10 faculty members.

   (j) A student cannot add more than two courses at a time (i.e., in a single update).

   (k) The number of CS majors must be more than the number of Math majors.

   (l) The number of distinct courses in which CS majors are enrolled is greater than the number of distinct courses in which Math majors are enrolled.

   (m) The total enrollment in courses taught by faculty in the department with *deptid=33* is greater than the number of Math majors.

   (n) There must be at least one CS major if there are any students whatsoever.

   (o) Faculty members from different departments cannot teach in the same room.

PROJECT-BASED EXERCISES

Exercise 9.9 Identify the subset of SQL-92 queries that are supported in Minibase.

BIBLIOGRAPHIC NOTES

The original version of SQL was developed as the query language for IBM's System R project, and its early development can be traced in [81, 112]. SQL has since become the most widely used relational query language, and its development is now subject to an international standardization process.

A very readable and comprehensive treatment of SQL-92 is presented by Melton and Simon in [375]; we refer readers to this book and to [147] for more a more detailed treatment. Date offers an insightful critique of SQL in [144]. Although some of the problems have been addressed in SQL-92, others remain. A formal semantics for a large subset of SQL queries is presented in [406]. SQL-92 is the current International Standards Organization (ISO) and American National Standards Institute (ANSI) standard. Melton is the editor of the ANSI document on the SQL-92 standard, document X3.135-1992. The corresponding ISO document is ISO/IEC 9075:1992. A successor, called SQL3, that builds on SQL-92 is being actively developed and is likely to include procedural language extensions, user-defined types, row ids, a call-level interface, multimedia data types, recursive queries, and other enhancements.

SECURITY, VIEWS, AND SQL

I know that's a secret, for it's whispered everywhere.

—*William Congreve*

Database management systems are increasingly being used to store information about all aspects of an enterprise. Thus the data stored in a DBMS is often vital to the business interests of the organization and is regarded as a corporate asset. In addition to protecting the intrinsic value of the data, corporations must consider ways to ensure privacy and to control access to data that must not be revealed to certain groups of users for various reasons.

In this chapter we discuss the concepts underlying access control and security in a DBMS. After introducing database security issues in Section 10.1, we present the view mechanism in Section 10.2. **Views** are tables that are defined in terms of queries over other tables. The view mechanism can be used to create a 'window' on a collection of data that is appropriate for some group of users. Views are very useful from a security standpoint because they allow us to limit access to sensitive data by instead providing access to a restricted version of that data (which is defined as a view). It is important to note that views are very useful quite independently of security considerations because they allow us to create several presentations of the same data, each of which is tailored to the needs of a different group of users, without actually replicating the data. SQL-92 provides commands for creating, querying, and even updating views.

After discussing views, we consider two distinct approaches, called *discretionary* and *mandatory*, to specifying and managing access controls. An **access control** mechanism is a way to control the data that is accessible to a given user. After introducing access controls in Section 10.3 we cover discretionary access control, which is supported in SQL-92, in Section 10.4. We briefly cover mandatory access control, which is not supported in SQL-92, in Section 10.5.

In Section 10.6 we discuss several additional aspects of security, such as security in a statistical database, the role of the database administrator, and the use of techniques such as encryption and audit trails.

10.1   INTRODUCTION TO DATABASE SECURITY

There are three main objectives to consider while designing a secure database application:

1. **Secrecy:** Information should not be disclosed to unauthorized users. For example, a student should not be allowed to examine other students' grades.

2. **Integrity:** Only authorized users should be allowed to modify data. For example, students may be allowed to see their grades, yet not allowed (obviously!) to modify them.

3. **Availability:** Authorized users should not be denied access. For example, an instructor who wishes to change a grade should be allowed to do so.

To achieve these objectives, a clear and consistent **security policy** should be developed to describe what security measures must be enforced. In particular, we must determine what part of the data is to be protected and which users get access to which portions of the data. Next, the **security mechanisms** of the underlying DBMS (and OS, as well as external mechanisms such as securing access to buildings etc.) must be utilized to enforce the policy. We emphasize that security measures must be taken at several levels. Security leaks in the operating system or network connections can circumvent database security mechanisms. For example, such leaks could allow an intruder to log on as the database administrator with all the attendant DBMS access rights! Human factors are another source of security leaks. For example, a user may choose a password that is easy to guess, or a user who is authorized to see sensitive data may misuse it. Such errors in fact account for a large percentage of security breaches. We will not discuss these aspects of security despite their importance because they are not specific to database management systems.

We use the following schemas in our examples:

Sailors(*sid:* `integer`, *sname:* `string`, *rating:* `integer`, *age:* `real`)
Boats(*bid:* `integer`, *bname:* `string`, *color:* `string`)
Reserves(*sname:* `string`, *bid:* `integer`, *day:* `dates`)

Notice that Reserves has been modified to use *sname*, rather than *sid*.

10.2   VIEWS

The view mechanism is a very powerful feature of a relational DBMS. In addition to its use for enhancing access control, it provides **logical data independence**. That is, it can be used to mask changes in the conceptual schema of the database

from applications. In our discussion of views, therefore, we will not limit ourselves
to security aspects.

To understand the concept of a view, consider this example. Suppose that we
are often interested in finding the names and ages of sailors with a rating greater
than 6 who have made at least one reservation, along with the dates on which
they have made reservations. We can define a **view** for this purpose:

```
CREATE VIEW ActiveSailors (name, age, day)
     AS SELECT S.sname, S.age, R.day
        FROM    Sailors S, Reserves R
        WHERE   S.sname = R.sname AND S.rating > 6
```

A view is a table whose rows are not explicitly stored in the database, but computed as needed from a **view definition**. The view ActiveSailors, whose definition is listed above, has three columns called *name*, *age*, and *day* with the same
domains as the columns *sname* and *age* in *Sailors* and *day* in Reserves. (If the
arguments *name*, *age*, and *day* are omitted, the column names *sname*, *age* and
day are inherited.) This view can be used just like a **base**, or explicitly stored,
table in defining new queries or views.

10.2.1   Destroying/Altering Tables and Views

If we decide that we no longer need a base table and want to destroy it (i.e.,
delete all the rows *and* remove the table definition information), we can use
the DROP TABLE command. For example, DROP TABLE Sailors RESTRICT destroys
the Sailors table unless some view or integrity constraint refers to Sailors; if so,
the command fails. If the keyword RESTRICT is replaced by CASCADE, Sailors
is dropped and any referencing views or integrity constraints are (recursively)
dropped as well; one of these two keywords must always be specified. A view can
be dropped using the DROP VIEW command, which is just like DROP TABLE.

ALTER TABLE modifies the structure of an existing table. To add a column called
maiden-name to Sailors, for example, we would use the following command:

```
ALTER TABLE Sailors
    ADD COLUMN maiden-name CHAR(10)
```

The definition of Sailors is modified to add this column, and all existing rows are
padded with *null* values in this column. ALTER TABLE can also be used to delete
columns and to add or drop integrity constraints on a table; we will not discuss
these aspects of the command beyond remarking that dropping columns is treated
very similarly to dropping tables or views.

10.2.2   Queries on Views

Once a view is defined, we can write queries or new view definitions that use it. In this respect a view is just like a base table. Consider a query on ActiveSailors, where we want the name and most recent reservation date for all ActiveSailors:

```
SELECT    A.name, MAX (A.day)
FROM      ActiveSailors A
GROUP BY  A.name
```

While the SQL-92 standard does not specify how to evaluate queries on views, it is useful to think in terms of a process called **query modification**. The idea is to replace the occurrence of ActiveSailors in the query by the view definition. The result on the above query is:

```
SELECT    name, MAX (A.day)
FROM      ( SELECT S.sname AS name, S.age, R.day
            FROM    Sailors S, Reserves R
            WHERE   S.sname = R.sname AND S.rating > 6 ) AS  A
GROUP BY  A.name
```

Incidentally, note how the *sname* column has been renamed to *name* for consistency with the schema of ActiveSailors. As another example, let us define view NumReservations as follows:

```
CREATE VIEW NumReservations (name, numres)
     AS SELECT S.sname, COUNT (*)
        FROM    Sailors S, Reserves R
        WHERE   S.sname = R.sname
        GROUP BY S.sname
```

Consider the following query, which is intended to find the highest number of reservations made by some one sailor (actually, by sailors with some one name, since *name* is not a key for Sailors!):

```
SELECT    MAX (N.numres)
FROM      NumReservations N
```

It is modified as follows:

```
SELECT    MAX (N.numres)
FROM      ( SELECT S.sname AS name, COUNT (*) AS  numres
            FROM    Sailors S, Reservations R
            WHERE   S.sname = R.sname
            GROUP BY S.sname ) AS N
```

10.2.3   Updates on Views *

The motivation behind the view mechanism is that we can tailor how users see the data. Users should not have to worry about the view versus base table distinction; this goal is indeed achieved in the case of queries on views. It is natural to want to specify updates on views as well. Here, unfortunately, the distinction between a view and a base table must be kept in mind. Consider the instances of Sailors and Reserves shown in Figures 10.1 and 10.2. (Note the use of *sname* to refer to sailors in the Reserves table; earlier chapters used *sid*. Be sure that you understand why the change is necessary for the purposes of this example!)

sid	sname	rating	age
22	dustin	7	45.0
31	lubber	8	55.5
58	rusty	10	35.0
62	rusty	8	25.0

sname	bid	day
dustin	101	10/10/94
rusty	103	11/12/94
rusty	104	12/15/94

Figure 10.1   An Instance S of Sailors

Figure 10.2   An Instance R of Reserves

When evaluated using the instances R and S, ActiveSailors contains the rows shown in Figure 10.3.

name	age	day
dustin	45.0	10/10/94
rusty	35.0	11/12/94
rusty	25.0	11/12/94
rusty	35.0	12/15/94
rusty	25.0	12/15/94

Figure 10.3   Instance of ActiveSailors

Now suppose that we want to delete the row $\langle rusty,25.0,11/12/94 \rangle$ from Active-Sailors. How are we to do this? ActiveSailors rows are not stored explicitly, but computed as needed from the Sailors and Reserves tables using the view definition. So we must change either Sailors or Reserves (or both) in such a way that evaluating the view definition on the modified instance does not produce $\langle rusty,25.0,11/12/94 \rangle$. This task can be accomplished in one of two ways: by either deleting the row $\langle 62,rusty,8,25.0 \rangle$ from Sailors or deleting the row $\langle rusty,103,11/12/94 \rangle$ from Reserves. But neither solution is satisfactory. Removing the Sailors row has the effect of also deleting the row $\langle rusty,25.0,12/15/94 \rangle$ from the view ActiveSailors. Removing the Reserves row has the effect of also deleting the row $\langle rusty,35.0,11/12/94 \rangle$ from the view ActiveSailors. Neither of these side-effects is desirable. In fact, the only reasonable solution is to *disallow* such updates on views.

In essence the SQL-92 standard allows updates to be specified only on views that are defined on a single base table using just selection and projection, with no use of aggregate operations; such views are called **updatable views**. This definition is oversimplified, but it captures the spirit of the restrictions. An update on such a restricted view can always be implemented by updating the underlying base table in an unambiguous way. Consider the following view:

```
CREATE VIEW YoungSailors (sid, age, rating)
    AS SELECT S.sid, S.age, S.rating
       FROM    Sailors S
       WHERE   S.age < 18
```

We can implement a command to modify the rating of a YoungSailors row by modifying the corresponding row in Sailors. We can delete a YoungSailors row by deleting the corresponding row from Sailors. (In general, if the view did not include a key for the underlying table, several rows in the table could 'correspond' to a single row in the view. A command that affects a row in the view would also affect all corresponding rows in the table.)

We can insert a YoungSailors row by inserting a row into Sailors, using *null* values in columns of Sailors that do not appear in YoungSailors (e.g., *sname*). Note that primary key columns are not allowed to contain *null* values. Therefore, if we attempt to insert rows through a view that does not contain the primary key of the underlying table, the insertions will be rejected. For example, if Young-Sailors contained *sname* but not *sid*, we could not insert rows into Sailors through insertions to YoungSailors.

An important observation is that an **INSERT** or **UPDATE** may change the underlying base table so that the resulting (i.e., inserted or modified) row is not in the view! For example, if we try to insert a row $\langle bryan, 22, 7 \rangle$ into the view, this row can be added to the underlying Sailors table, but it will not appear in the view because it does not satisfy the view condition *age* < 18. The default is to allow this insertion, but we can disallow it by adding the clause **WITH CHECK OPTION** to the definition of the view.

The reader should note that when a view is defined in terms of another view, the interaction between these definitions with respect to updates and the **CHECK OPTION** clause can be complex; we will not go into the details.

10.3   ACCESS CONTROL

A database for an enterprise contains a great deal of information and usually has several users, and indeed, several groups of users. Most users need to access only a small part of the database to carry out their tasks. Allowing users unrestricted access to all the data can be undesirable, and a DBMS should therefore provide mechanisms to control access to data.

A DBMS offers two main approaches to access control. **Discretionary access control** is based on the concept of access rights, or **privileges**, and mechanisms for giving users such privileges. A privilege allows a user to access some data object in a certain manner (e.g., to read or to modify). A user who creates a database object such as a table or a view automatically gets all applicable privileges on that object. The DBMS subsequently keeps track of how these privileges are granted to other users, and possibly revoked, and ensures that at all times only users with the necessary privileges can access an object. SQL-92 supports discretionary access control through the `GRANT` and `REVOKE` commands. The `GRANT` command gives privileges to users, and the `REVOKE` command takes away privileges. We discuss discretionary access control in Section 10.4.

Discretionary access control mechanisms, while generally effective, have certain weaknesses. In particular, a devious unauthorized user can trick an authorized user into disclosing sensitive data. **Mandatory access control** is based on system wide policies that cannot be changed by individual users. In this approach each database object is assigned a *security class*, each user is assigned *clearance* for a security class, and rules are imposed on reading and writing of database objects by users. The DBMS determines whether a given user can read or write a given object based on certain rules that involve the security level of object and the clearance of the user. These rules seek to ensure that sensitive data can never be 'passed on' to a user without the necessary clearance. The SQL-92 standard does not include any support for mandatory access control. We discuss mandatory access control in Section 10.5.

10.4   DISCRETIONARY ACCESS CONTROL *

SQL-92 supports discretionary access control through the `GRANT` and `REVOKE` commands. The `GRANT` command gives users privileges to base tables and views. The syntax of this command is as follows:

GRANT **privileges** ON **object** TO **users** [WITH GRANT OPTION]

For our purposes **object** is either a base table or a view. SQL recognizes certain other kinds of objects, but we will not discuss them. Several privileges can be specified, including these:

- **SELECT**: The right to access (read) all columns of the table specified as the **object**, *including columns added later* through **ALTER TABLE** commands.

- **INSERT**(*column-name*): The right to insert rows with (non *null* or non default) values in the named column of the table named as **object**. If this right is to be granted with respect to all columns, including columns that might be added later, we can simply use **INSERT**. **UPDATE**(*column-name*) and **UPDATE** are similar.

- **DELETE**: The right to delete rows from the table named as **object**.

- **REFERENCES**(*column-name*): The right to define foreign keys (in other tables) that refer to the specified column of the table **object**. **REFERENCES** denotes this right with respect to all columns, including any that are added later.

If a user has a privilege with the **grant option**, he or she can pass it to another user (with or without the grant option) by using the **GRANT** command. A user who creates a base table automatically has all applicable privileges on it, along with the right to grant these privileges to other users. A user who creates a view has precisely those privileges on the view that he or she has on *every* one of the view or base tables used to define the view. The user creating the view must have the **SELECT** privilege on each underlying table, of course, and so is always granted the **SELECT** privilege on the view. The creator of the view has the **SELECT** privilege with the grant option only if he or she has the **SELECT** privilege with the grant option on every underlying table. In addition, if the view is updatable and the user holds **INSERT**, **DELETE** or **UPDATE** privileges (with or without the grant option) on the (single) underlying table, the user automatically gets the same privileges on the view.

We remark that only the owner of a schema can execute the data definition statements **CREATE**, **ALTER** and **DROP** on that schema. The right to execute these statements cannot be granted or revoked.

In conjunction with the **GRANT** and **REVOKE** commands, views are an important component of the security mechanisms provided by a relational DBMS. By defining views on the base tables, we can present needed information to a user while *hiding* other information that the user should not be given access to. For example, a user who can access ActiveSailors, but not Sailors or Reserves, cannot find out the *bid*s of boats reserved by a given sailor.

Suppose that user Joe has created the tables Boats, Reserves, and Sailors. Incidentally, privileges are assigned in SQL-92 to **authorization ids**, which can denote a single user or a group of users; a user must specify an authorization id and, in many systems, a corresponding *password* before the DBMS accepts any commands from him or her. So, technically, *Joe, Michael,* and so on are authorization ids rather than user names in the following examples.

Some examples of the `GRANT` command that Joe can now execute are listed below:

```
GRANT INSERT, DELETE ON Reserves TO Yuppy WITH GRANT OPTION
GRANT SELECT ON Sailors TO Michael
GRANT SELECT ON Reserves TO Michael
GRANT SELECT ON Sailors TO Michael WITH GRANT OPTION
GRANT UPDATE (rating) ON Sailors TO Leah
GRANT REFERENCES (bid) ON Boats TO Bill
```

Yuppy can insert or delete Reserves rows and can authorize someone else to do the same. Michael can execute `SELECT` queries on Sailors and Reserves, and he can pass this privilege to others for Sailors, but not for Reserves. With the `SELECT` privilege, Michael can create a view that accesses the Sailors and Reserves tables (for example, the ActiveSailors view) but he cannot grant `SELECT` on Active-Sailors to others. If Michael creates the YoungSailors view, on the other hand, the only underlying table is Sailors, for which he has `SELECT` with the grant option. He therefore has `SELECT` with the grant option on YoungSailors, but he cannot insert rows, for instance, because he does not hold the `INSERT` privilege on the underlying Sailors table. Michael can pass on the `SELECT` privilege on YoungSailors to Eric and Guppy:

```
GRANT SELECT ON YoungSailors TO Eric, Guppy
```

Eric and Guppy can now execute `SELECT` queries on the view YoungSailors—note, however, that Eric and Guppy do *not* have the right to execute `SELECT` queries directly on the underlying Sailors or Reserves tables.

Michael can also define constraints based on the information in the Sailors and Reserves tables. For example, Michael can define the following table, which has an associated table constraint:

```
CREATE TABLE Sneaky (maxrating   INTEGER,
                CHECK ( maxrating >=
                            ( SELECT MAX (S.rating )
                            FROM    Sailors S )))
```

By repeatedly inserting rows with gradually increasing *maxrating* values into the Sneaky table until an insertion finally succeeds, Michael can find out the highest *rating* value in the Sailors table! This example illustrates why SQL requires the creator of a table constraint that refers to Sailors to possess the SELECT privilege on Sailors.

Returning to the privileges granted by Joe, Leah can update only the *rating* column of Sailors rows. She can execute the following command, which sets all ratings to 8:

    UPDATE Sailors S
    SET   S.rating = 8

However, she cannot execute the same command if the SET clause is changed to be SET *S.age = 25*, because she is not allowed to update the *age* field. A more subtle point is illustrated by the following command, which decrements the rating of all sailors:

    UPDATE Sailors S
    SET   S.rating = S.rating - 1

Leah cannot execute this command because it requires the SELECT privilege on the *S.rating* column and Leah does not have this privilege!

Bill can refer to the *bid* column of Boats as a foreign key in another table. For example, Bill can create the Reserves table through the following command:

    CREATE TABLE Reserves (sname CHAR(10) NOT NULL ,
                            bid   INTEGER,
                            day   DATE,
                            PRIMARY KEY (bid, day),
                            UNIQUE (sname),
                            FOREIGN KEY (bid) REFERENCES Boats)

If Bill did not have the REFERENCES privilege on the *bid* column of Boats, he would not be able to execute this CREATE statement because the FOREIGN KEY clause requires this privilege.

It is worth emphasizing that specifying just the INSERT (similarly, REFERENCES etc.) privilege in a GRANT command is not the same as specifying SELECT(*column-name*) for each column currently in the table. Consider the following command over the Sailors table, which has columns *sid, sname, rating,* and *age*:

    GRANT INSERT ON Sailors TO Michael

Suppose that this command is executed and then a column is added to the Sailors table (by executing an ALTER TABLE command). Note that Michael has the

INSERT privilege with respect to the newly added column! If we had executed the following GRANT command, instead of the previous one, Michael would not have the INSERT privilege on the new column:

GRANT   INSERT ON Sailors(*sid*), Sailors(*sname*), Sailors(*rating*),
        Sailors(*age*), TO Michael

There is a complementary command to GRANT that allows the withdrawal of privileges. The syntax of the REVOKE command is as follows:

REVOKE [GRANT OPTION FOR] **privileges**
        ON object FROM users { RESTRICT | CASCADE }

The command can be used to revoke either a privilege or just the grant option on a privilege (by using the optional GRANT OPTION FOR clause). One of the two alternatives, RESTRICT or CASCADE, must be specified; we will see what this choice means shortly.

The intuition behind the GRANT command is clear: The creator of a base table or a view is given all the appropriate privileges with respect to it and is allowed to pass these privileges—including the right to pass along a privilege!—to other users. The REVOKE command is, as expected, intended to achieve the reverse: A user who has granted a privilege to another user may change his mind and want to withdraw the granted privilege. The intuition behind exactly what effect a REVOKE command has is complicated by the fact that a user may be granted the same privilege multiple times, possibly by different users.

When a user executes a REVOKE command with the CASCADE keyword, the effect is to withdraw the named privileges or grant option from all users who currently hold these privileges *solely* through a GRANT command that was previously executed by the same user who is now executing the REVOKE command. If these users received the privileges with the grant option and passed it along, those recipients will also lose their privileges as a consequence of the REVOKE command unless they also received these privileges independently.

We illustrate the REVOKE command through several examples. First, consider what happens after the following sequence of commands, where Joe is the creator of Sailors.

GRANT SELECT ON Sailors TO Art WITH GRANT OPTION   *(executed by Joe)*
GRANT SELECT ON Sailors TO Bob WITH GRANT OPTION   *(executed by Art)*
REVOKE SELECT ON Sailors FROM Art CASCADE   *(executed by Joe)*

Art loses the SELECT privilege on Sailors, of course. Then Bob, who received this privilege from Art, and only Art, also loses this privilege. Bob's privilege is said to be **abandoned** when the privilege that it was derived from (Art's `SELECT` privilege with grant option, in this example) is revoked. When the `CASCADE` keyword is specified, all abandoned privileges are also revoked (possibly causing privileges held by other users to become abandoned, and thereby revoked recursively). If the `RESTRICT` keyword is specified in the `REVOKE` command, the command is rejected if revoking the privileges *just* from the users specified in the command would result in other privileges becoming abandoned.

Consider the following sequence, as another example:

> `GRANT SELECT ON` Sailors `TO` Art `WITH GRANT OPTION`   *(executed by Joe)*
> `GRANT SELECT ON` Sailors `TO` Bob `WITH GRANT OPTION`   *(executed by Joe)*
> `GRANT SELECT ON` Sailors `TO` Bob `WITH GRANT OPTION`   *(executed by Art)*
> `REVOKE SELECT ON` Sailors `FROM` Art `CASCADE`   *(executed by Joe)*

As before, Art loses the `SELECT` privilege on Sailors. But what about Bob? Bob received this privilege from Art, but he also received it independently (coincidentally, directly from Joe). Thus Bob retains this privilege. Consider a third example:

> `GRANT SELECT ON` Sailors `TO` Art `WITH GRANT OPTION`   *(executed by Joe)*
> `GRANT SELECT ON` Sailors `TO` Art `WITH GRANT OPTION`   *(executed by Joe)*
> `REVOKE SELECT ON` Sailors `FROM` Art `CASCADE`   *(executed by Joe)*

Since Joe granted the privilege to Art twice and only revoked it once, does Art get to keep the privilege? As per the SQL-92 standard, no. Even if Joe absentmindedly granted the same privilege to Art several times, he can revoke it with a single `REVOKE` command.

It is possible to revoke just the grant option on a privilege:

> `GRANT SELECT ON` Sailors `TO` Art `WITH GRANT OPTION`   *(executed by Joe)*
> `REVOKE GRANT OPTION FOR SELECT ON` Sailors
>   `FROM` Art `CASCADE`   *(executed by Joe)*

This command would leave Art with the `SELECT` privilege on Sailors, but Art no longer has the grant option on this privilege and therefore cannot pass it on to other users.

These examples bring out the intuition behind the `REVOKE` command, but they also highlight the complex interaction between `GRANT` and `REVOKE` commands. When a `GRANT` is executed, a **privilege descriptor** is added to a table of such descriptors maintained by the DBMS. The privilege descriptor specifies the following: the *grantor* of the privilege, the *grantee* who receives the privilege, the *granted privilege* (including the name of the object involved), and whether the grant option is included. When a user creates a table or view and 'automatically' gets certain privileges, a privilege descriptor with *system* as the grantor is entered into this table.

The effect of a series of `GRANT` commands can described in terms of an **authorization graph** in which the nodes are users—technically, they are authorization ids—and the arcs indicate how privileges are passed. There is an arc from (the node for) user 1 to user 2 if user 1 executed a `GRANT` command giving a privilege to user 2; the arc is labeled with the descriptor for the `GRANT` command. A `GRANT` command has no effect if the same privileges have already been granted to the same grantee by the same grantor. The following sequence of commands illustrates the semantics of `GRANT` and `REVOKE` commands when there is a *cycle* in the authorization graph:

```
GRANT SELECT ON Sailors TO Art WITH GRANT OPTION    (executed by Joe)
GRANT SELECT ON Sailors TO Bob WITH GRANT OPTION    (executed by Art)
GRANT SELECT ON Sailors TO Art WITH GRANT OPTION    (executed by Bob)
GRANT SELECT ON Sailors TO Cal WITH GRANT OPTION    (executed by Joe)
GRANT SELECT ON Sailors TO Bob WITH GRANT OPTION    (executed by Cal)
REVOKE SELECT ON Sailors FROM Art CASCADE           (executed by Joe)
```

The authorization graph for this example is shown in Figure 10.4. Note that we indicate how Joe, the creator of Sailors, acquired the `SELECT` privilege from the DBMS by introducing a *System* node and drawing an arc from this node to Joe's node.

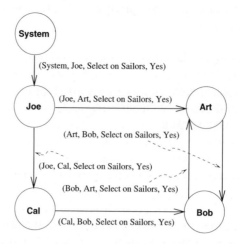

Figure 10.4 Example Authorization Graph

As the graph clearly indicates, Bob's grant to Art and Art's grant to Bob (of the same privilege) creates a cycle. Bob is subsequently given the same privilege by Cal, who received it independently from Joe. At this point Joe decides to revoke the privilege that he granted to Art.

Let us trace the effect of this revocation. The arc from Joe to Art is removed because it corresponds to the granting action that is revoked. All remaining nodes have the following property: *If node N has an outgoing arc labeled with a privilege, there is a path from the System node to node N in which each arc label contains the same privilege plus the grant option.* That is, any remaining granting action is justified by a privilege received (directly or indirectly) from the System. The execution of Joe's `REVOKE` command therefore stops at this point, with everyone continuing to hold the `SELECT` privilege on Sailors.

This result may seem unintuitive because Art continues to have the privilege only because he received it from Bob, and at the time that Bob granted the privilege to Art, he had received it only from Art! Although Bob acquired the privilege through Cal subsequently, shouldn't the effect of his grant to Art be undone when executing Joe's `REVOKE` command? The effect of the grant from Bob to Art is *not* undone in SQL-92. In effect, if a user acquires a privilege multiple times from different grantors, SQL-92 treats each of these grants to the user as having occurred *before* that user passed on the privilege to other users. This implementation of `REVOKE` is convenient in many real-world situations. For example, if a manager is fired after passing on some privileges to subordinates (who may in turn have passed the privileges to others), we can ensure that only the manager's privileges are removed by first redoing all of the manager's granting actions and then revoking his or her privileges. That is, we need not recursively redo the subordinates' granting actions.

To return to the the saga of Joe and his friends, let us suppose that Joe decides to revoke Cal's `SELECT` privilege as well. Clearly, the arc from Joe to Cal corresponding to the grant of this privilege is removed. The arc from Cal to Bob is removed as well, since there is no longer a path from System to Cal that gives Cal the right to pass the `SELECT` privilege on Sailors to Bob. The authorization graph at this intermediate point is shown in Figure 10.5.

The graph now contains two nodes (Art and Bob) for which there are outgoing arcs with labels containing the `SELECT` privilege on Sailors; thus these users have granted this privilege. However, although each node contains an incoming arc carrying the same privilege, *there is no such path from System to either of these nodes*; thus these users' right to grant the privilege has been abandoned. We therefore remove the outgoing arcs as well. In general, these nodes might have other arcs incident upon them, but in this example, they now have no incident

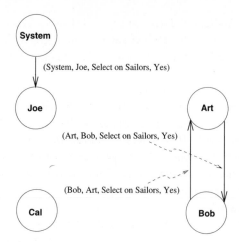

Figure 10.5   Example Authorization Graph during Revocation

arcs. Joe is left as the only user with the **SELECT** privilege on Sailors; Art and Bob have lost their privileges.

10.4.1   Grant and Revoke on Views and Integrity Constraints

The privileges held by the creator of a view (with respect to the view) change over time as he or she gains or loses privileges on the underlying tables. If the creator loses a privilege held with the grant option, users who were given that privilege on the view will lose it as well. There are some subtle aspects to the **GRANT** and **REVOKE** commands when they involve views or integrity constraints. We will consider some examples that highlight the following important points:

1. A view may be dropped because a **SELECT** privilege is revoked from the user who created the view.

2. If the creator of a view gains additional privileges on the underlying tables, he or she automatically gains additional privileges on the view.

3. The distinction between the **REFERENCES** and **SELECT** privileges is important.

Suppose that Joe created Sailors, gave Michael the **SELECT** privilege on it with the grant option, and Michael then created the view YoungSailors and gave Eric the **SELECT** privilege on YoungSailors. Eric now defines a view called FineYoung-Sailors:

    CREATE VIEW FineYoungSailors (name, age, rating)

```
AS SELECT S.sname, S.age, S.rating
FROM     YoungSailors S
WHERE    S.rating > 6
```

What happens if Joe revokes the **SELECT** privilege on Sailors from Michael? Michael no longer has the authority to execute the query used to define Young-Sailors because the definition refers to Sailors. Therefore, the view YoungSailors is dropped (i.e., destroyed). In turn, FineYoungSailors is dropped as well. Both these view definitions are removed from the system catalogs; even if a remorseful Joe decides to give back the **SELECT** privilege on Sailors to Michael, the views are gone and must be created afresh if they are required.

On a more happy note, suppose that everything proceeds as described above until Eric defines FineYoungSailors; then, instead of revoking the **SELECT** privilege on Sailors from Michael, Joe decides to also give Michael the **INSERT** privilege on Sailors. Michael's privileges on the view YoungSailors are upgraded to what he would have if he were to create the view *now*. Thus he acquires the **INSERT** privilege on YoungSailors as well. (Note that this view is updatable.) What about Eric? His privileges are unchanged.

Whether or not Michael has the **INSERT** privilege on YoungSailors with the grant option depends on whether or not Joe gives him the **INSERT** privilege on Sailors with the grant option. To understand this situation, consider Eric again. If Michael has the **INSERT** privilege on YoungSailors with the grant option, he can pass this privilege to Eric. Eric could then insert rows into the Sailors table because inserts on YoungSailors are effected by modifying the underlying base table, Sailors. Clearly, we don't want Michael to be able to authorize Eric to make such changes unless Michael has the **INSERT** privilege on Sailors with the grant option.

The **REFERENCES** privilege is very different from the **SELECT** privilege, as the following example illustrates. Suppose that Joe is the creator of Boats. He can authorize another user, say Fred, to create Reserves with a foreign key that refers to the *bid* column of Boats by giving Fred the **REFERENCES** privilege with respect to this column. On the other hand, if Fred has the **SELECT** privilege on the *bid* column of Boats but not the **REFERENCES** privilege, Fred *cannot* create Reserves with a foreign key that refers to Boats. If Fred creates Reserves with a foreign key column that refers to *bid* in Boats, and later loses the **REFERENCES** privilege on the *bid* column of boats, the foreign key constraint in Reserves is dropped; however, the Reserves table is *not* dropped.

To understand why the SQL-92 standard chose to introduce the **REFERENCES** privilege, rather than to simply allow the **SELECT** privilege to be used in this situation, consider what happens if the definition of Reserves specified the **NO**

ACTION option with the foreign key—Joe, the owner of Boats, may be prevented from deleting a row from Boats because a row in Reserves refers to this Boats row! Giving Fred, the creator of Reserves, the right to constrain updates on Boats in this manner goes beyond simply allowing him to read the values in Boats, which is all that the SELECT privilege authorizes.

10.5   MANDATORY ACCESS CONTROL *

Discretionary access control mechanisms, while generally effective, have certain weaknesses. In particular they are susceptible to *Trojan horse* schemes whereby a devious unauthorized user can trick an authorized user into disclosing sensitive data. For example, suppose that student Tricky Dick wants to break into the grade tables of instructor Trustin Justin. Dick does the following:

■ He creates a new table called MineAllMine and gives INSERT privileges on this table to Justin (who is blissfully unaware of all this attention, of course).

■ He modifies the code of some DBMS application that Justin uses often to do a couple of additional things: first, read the Grades table, and next, write the result into MineAllMine.

Then he sits back and waits for the grades to be copied into MineAllMine, and later undoes the modifications to the application to ensure that Justin does not somehow find out later that he has been cheated. Thus in spite of the DBMS enforcing all discretionary access controls—only Justin's authorized code was allowed to access Grades—sensitive data is disclosed to an intruder. The fact that Dick could surreptitiously modify Justin's code is outside the scope of the DBMS's access control mechanism.

Mandatory access control mechanisms are aimed at addressing such loopholes in discretionary access control. The popular model for mandatory access control, called the Bell-LaPadula model, is described in terms of **objects** (e.g., tables, views, rows, columns); **subjects** (e.g., users, programs); **security classes**; and **clearances**. Each database object is assigned a *security class*, and each subject is assigned *clearance* for a security class; we will denote the class of an object or subject A as *class(A)*. The security classes in a system are organized according to a partial order, with a **most secure class** and a **least secure class**. For simplicity, we will assume that there are four classes: *top secret (TS), secret (S), confidential (C) and unclassified (U)*. In this system, $TS > S > C > U$, where $A > B$ means that class A data is more sensitive than class B data.

The Bell-LaPadula model imposes two restrictions on all reads and writes of database objects:

1. **Simple Security Property:** Subject S is allowed to read object O only if *class(S)* $\geq$ *class(O)*. For example, a user with TS clearance can read a table with C clearance, but a user with C clearance is not allowed to read a table with TS classification.

2. ***-Property:** Subject S is allowed to write object O only if *class(S)* $\leq$ *class(O)*. For example, a user with S clearance can only write objects with S or TS classification.

If discretionary access controls are also specified, these rules represent additional restrictions. Thus to read or write a database object, a user must have the necessary privileges (obtained via **GRANT** commands) *and* the security classes of the user and the object must satisfy the preceding restrictions. Let us consider how such a mandatory control mechanism might have foiled Tricky Dick. The Grades table could be classified as S, Justin could be given clearance for S, and Tricky Dick could be given a lower clearance (C). Dick can only create objects of C or lower classification; thus the table MineAllMine can have at most the classification C. When the application program running on behalf of Justin (and therefore with clearance S) tries to copy Grades into MineAllMine, it is not allowed to do so because *class(MineAllMine)* < *class(application)*, and the *-Property is violated.

10.5.1 Multilevel Relations and Polyinstantiation

In order to apply mandatory access control policies in a relational DBMS, a security class must be assigned to each database object. The objects can be at the granularity of tables, rows, or even individual column values. Let us assume that each row is assigned a security class. This situation leads to the concept of a **multilevel table**, which is a table with the surprising property that users with different security clearances will see a different collection of rows when they access the same table.

Consider the instance of the Boats table shown in Figure 10.6. Users with S and TS clearance will get both rows in the answer when they ask to see all rows in Boats. A user with C clearance will get only the second row, and a user with U clearance will get no rows at all.

The Boats table is defined to have *bid* as the primary key. Suppose that a user with clearance C wishes to enter the row $\langle 101, Picante, Scarlet, C \rangle$. We have a dilemma here:

- If the insertion is permitted, two distinct rows in the table will have the key value 101.

bid	bname	color	Security Class
101	Salsa	Red	S
102	Pinto	Brown	C

Figure 10.6 An Instance *B1* of Boats

- If the insertion is not permitted because the primary key constraint is violated, the user trying to insert the new row, who has clearance C, can infer that there is a boat with *bid=101* whose security class is higher than C. This situation compromises the principle that users should not be able to infer any information about objects that have a higher security classification.

This dilemma is resolved by effectively treating the security classification as part of the key. Thus the insertion is allowed to continue, and the table instance is modified as shown in Figure 10.7.

bid	bname	color	Security Class
101	Salsa	Red	S
101	Picante	Scarlet	C
102	Pinto	Brown	C

Figure 10.7 Instance *B1* after Insertion

Users with clearance C or U see just the rows for Picante and Pinto, but users with clearance S or TS see all four rows. The two rows with *bid=101* can be interpreted in one of two ways: only the row with the higher classification (Salsa, with classification S) actually exists, or both exist and their presence is revealed to users according to their clearance level. The choice of interpretation is up to application developers and users.

The presence of data objects that appear to have different values to users with different clearances (for example, the boat with *bid* 10) is called **polyinstantiation**. If we consider security classifications associated with individual columns, the intuition underlying polyinstantiation can be generalized in a straightforward manner, but some additional details must be addressed. We remark that the main drawback of mandatory access control schemes is their rigidity; policies are set by system administrators, and the classification mechanisms are not flexible enough. A satisfactory combination of discretionary and mandatory access controls is yet to be achieved.

10.5.2   Covert Channels, DOD Security Levels

Even if a DBMS enforces the mandatory access control scheme discussed above, it is possible that information can flow from a higher classification level to a lower classification level through indirect means, called **covert channels**. For example, if a transaction accesses data at more than one site in a distributed DBMS, the actions at the two sites must be coordinated. The process at one site may have a lower clearance (say C) than the process at another site (say S), and both processes have to agree to commit before the transaction can be committed. This requirement can be exploited to pass information with an S classification to the process with a C clearance: The transaction is repeatedly invoked, and the process with the C clearance always agrees to commit, whereas the process with the S clearance agrees to commit if it wants to transmit a 1 bit and does not agree if it wants to transmit a 0 bit.

In this (admittedly tortuous) manner, information with an S clearance can be sent to a process with a C clearance as a stream of bits. This covert channel is an indirect violation of the intent behind the *-Property. Additional examples of covert channels can be found readily in statistical databases, which we discuss in Section 10.6.2.

DBMS vendors have recently started implementing mandatory access control mechanisms (although they are not part of the SQL-92 standard) because the United States Department of Defense (DoD) requires such support for its systems. The DoD requirements can be described in terms of **security levels** A, B, C, and D of which A is the most secure and D is the least secure.

Level C requires support for discretionary access control. It is divided into sublevels $C1$ and $C2$; $C2$ also requires some degree of accountability through procedures such as login verification and audit trails. Level B requires support for mandatory access control. It is subdivided into levels $B1$, $B2$, and $B3$. Level $B2$ additionally requires the identification and elimination of covert channels. Level $B3$ additionally requires maintenance of audit trails and the designation of a **security administrator** (usually, but not necessarily, the DBA). Level A, the most secure level, requires a mathematical proof that the security mechanism enforces the security policy!

Commercial systems are available that support discretionary controls at the $C2$ level and mandatory controls at the $B1$ level.

10.6 ADDITIONAL ISSUES RELATED TO SECURITY *

Security is a broad topic, and our coverage is necessarily limited. This section briefly touches on some additional important issues.

10.6.1 Role of the Database Administrator

The database administrator (DBA) plays an important role in enforcing the security-related aspects of a database design. In conjunction with the owners of the data, the DBA will probably also contribute to developing a security policy. The DBA has a special account, which we will call the **system account**, and is responsible for the overall security of the system. In particular the DBA deals with the following:

1. **Creating new accounts:** Each new user or group of users must be assigned an authorization id and a password. Note that application programs that access the database have the same authorization id as the user executing the program.

2. **Mandatory control issues:** If the DBMS supports mandatory control—some customized systems for applications with very high security requirements (for example, military data) provide such support—the DBA must assign security classes to each database object and assign security clearances to each authorization id in accordance with the chosen security policy.

The DBA is also responsible for maintaining the **audit trail**, which is essentially the log of updates with the authorization id (of the user who is executing the transaction) added to each log entry. This log is just a minor extension of the log mechanism used to recover from crashes. Additionally, the DBA may choose to maintain a log of *all* actions, including reads, performed by a user. Analyzing such histories of how the DBMS was accessed can help prevent security violations by identifying suspicious patterns before an intruder finally succeeds in breaking in, or help track down an intruder after a violation has been detected.

10.6.2 Security in Statistical Databases

A **statistical database** is one that contains specific information on individuals or events but is intended to permit only statistical queries. For example, if we maintained a statistical database of information about sailors, we would allow statistical queries about average ratings, maximum age, and so on, but would not want to allow queries about individual sailors. Security in such databases poses some new problems because it is possible to **infer** protected information (such as an individual sailor's rating) from answers to permitted statistical queries.

Such inference opportunities represent covert channels that can compromise the security policy of the database.

Suppose that sailor Sneaky Pete wants to know the rating of Admiral Horntooter, the esteemed chairman of the sailing club, and happens to know that Horntooter is the oldest sailor in the club. Pete repeatedly asks queries of the form "How many sailors are there whose age is greater than X?" for various values of X, until the answer is 1. Obviously, this sailor is Horntooter, the oldest sailor. Note that each of these queries is a valid statistical query, and is permitted. Let the value of X at this point be, say, 65. Pete now asks the query "What is the maximum rating of all sailors whose age is greater than 65?" Again, this query is permitted because it is a statistical query. However, the answer to this query reveals Horntooter's rating to Pete, and the security policy of the database is violated.

One approach to preventing such violations is to require that each query must involve at least some minimum number, say N, of rows. With a reasonable choice of N, Pete would not be able to isolate the information about Horntooter, because the query about the maximum rating would fail. This restriction, however, is easy to overcome. By repeatedly asking queries of the form "How many sailors are there whose age is greater than X?" until the system rejects one such query, Pete identifies a set of N sailors, including Horntooter. Let the value of X at this point be 55. Now, Pete can ask two queries:

- "What is the sum of the ratings of all sailors whose age is greater than 55?" Since N sailors have age greater than 55, this query is permitted.

- "What is the sum of the ratings of all sailors, other than Horntooter, whose age is greater than 55, and sailor Pete?" Since the set of sailors whose ratings are added up now includes Pete instead of Horntooter, but is otherwise the same, the number of sailors involved is still N, and this query is also permitted.

From the answers to these two queries, say A_1 and A_2, Pete, who knows his rating, can easily calculate Horntooter's rating as $A_1 - A_2 + $ *Pete's rating.*

Pete succeeded because he was able to ask two queries that involved many of the same sailors. The number of rows examined in common by two queries is called their **intersection**. If a limit were to be placed on the amount of intersection permitted between any two queries issued by the same user, Pete could be foiled. Actually, a truly fiendish (and patient) user can generally find out information about specific individuals even if the system places a minimum number of rows bound (N) and a maximum intersection bound (M) on queries, but the number of queries required to do this grows in proportion to N/M. We can try to additionally limit the total number of queries that a user is allowed to ask, but two users could still conspire to breach security. By maintaining a log of all activity (including read-only accesses), such query patterns can be detected, hopefully before a security violation occurs. This discussion should make it clear, however, that security in statistical databases is difficult to enforce.

10.6.3 Encryption

A DBMS can use *encryption* to protect information in certain situations where the normal security mechanisms of the DBMS are not adequate. For example, an intruder may steal tapes containing some data or tap a communication line. By storing and transmitting data in an encrypted form, the DBMS ensures that such stolen data is not intelligible to the intruder.

The basic idea behind encryption is to apply an **encryption algorithm**, which may well be accessible to the intruder, to the original data, and a user-specified or DBA-specified **encryption key**, which is kept secret. The output of the algorithm is the encrypted version of the data. There is also a **decryption algorithm**, which takes the encrypted data and the encryption key as input and then returns the original data. Without the correct encryption key, the decryption algorithm produces gibberish. This approach forms the basis for the **Data Encryption Standard** (DES), which has been in use since 1977, with an encryption algorithm that consists of character substitutions and permutations. The main weakness of this approach is that authorized users must be told the encryption key, and the mechanism for communicating this information is vulnerable to clever intruders.

Another approach to encryption, called **public-key encryption**, has become increasingly popular in recent years. The encryption scheme proposed by Rivest, Shamir and Adleman, called RSA, is a well-known example of public-key encryption. Each authorized user has a **public encryption key**, known to everyone, and a *private* **decryption key** (used by the decryption algorithm), chosen by the user and known only to him or her. The encryption and decryption algorithms themselves are assumed to be publicly known. Consider a user called Sam. Anyone can send Sam a secret message by encrypting the message using Sam's publicly known encryption key. Only Sam can decrypt this secret message because the decryption algorithm requires Sam's decryption key, known only to Sam. Since users choose their own decryption keys, the weakness of DES is avoided.

The main issue for public-key encryption is how encryption and decryption keys are chosen. Technically, public-key encryption algorithms rely on the existence of **one-way functions**, which are functions whose inverse is computationally very hard to determine. The RSA algorithm, for example, is based on the observation that although checking whether a given number is prime is easy, determining the prime factors of a non prime number is extremely hard. (Determining the prime factors of a number with over 100 digits can take years of CPU-time on the fastest available computers today.)

We now sketch the intuition behind the RSA algorithm, assuming that the data to be encrypted is an integer I. To choose an encryption key and a decryption key, our friend Sam would first choose a very large integer *limit*, which we assume is larger than the largest integer that he will ever need to encode. Sam chooses *limit* to be the product of two (large!) distinct prime numbers, say $p * q$. Sam then chooses some prime number e, chosen to be larger than both p and q, as his encryption key. Both *limit* and e are made public and are used by the encryption algorithm.

Now comes the clever part: Sam chooses the decryption key d in a special way based on p, q and e.[1] The essential point of the scheme is that it is easy to compute d given e, p and q, but *very* hard to compute d given just e and *limit*. In turn, this difficulty depends on the fact that it is hard to determine the prime factors of *limit*, which happen to be p and q.

A very important property of the encryption and decryption algorithms in this scheme is that given the corresponding encryption and decryption keys, the algorithms are inverses of each other—not only can data be encrypted and then decrypted, we can apply the decryption algorithm first and then the encryption algorithm, and still get the original data back! This property can be exploited by two users, say Elmer and Sam, to exchange messages in such a way that if Elmer gets a message that is supposedly from Sam, he can indeed verify that it is from Sam (in addition to being able to decrypt the message), and further, *prove* that it is from Sam. This feature has obvious practical value. For example, suppose that Elmer's company accepts orders for its products over the Internet and stores these orders in a DBMS. The requirements are:

1. Only the company (Elmer) should be able to understand an order. A customer (say Sam) who orders jewelry frequently may want to keep the orders private (perhaps because he does not want to become a popular attraction for burglars!).

2. The company should be able to verify that an order that supposedly was placed by customer Sam was indeed placed by Sam, and not by an intruder claiming to be Sam. By the same token, Sam should not be able to claim that the company forged an order from him—an order from Sam must *provably* come from Sam.

---

[1] In case you are curious, d is chosen such that $d * e = 1 \ \mathbf{mod} \ ((p - 1) * (q - 1))$.

The company asks each customer to choose an encryption key (Sam chooses e_{Sam}) and a decryption key (d_{Sam}) and to make the encryption key public. It also makes its own encryption key (e_{Elmer}) public. The company's decryption key (d_{Elmer}) is kept secret, and customers are expected to keep their decryption keys secret as well.

Now let's see how the two requirements can be met. To place an order, Sam could just encrypt the order using encryption key e_{Elmer}, and Elmer could decrypt this using decryption key d_{Elmer}. This simple approach satisfies the first requirement because d_{Elmer} is known only to Elmer. However, since e_{Elmer} is known to everyone, someone who wishes to play a prank could easily place an order on behalf of Sam without informing Sam. From the order itself, there is no way for Elmer to verify that it came from Sam. (Of course, one way to handle this is to give each customer an account and to rely on the login procedure to verify the identity of the user placing the order—the user would have to know the password for Sam's account—but the company may have thousands of customers and may not want to give each of them an account.)

A clever use of the encryption scheme, however, allows Elmer to verify whether the order was indeed placed by Sam. Instead of encrypting the order using e_{Elmer}, Sam first applies his *decryption algorithm*, using d_{Sam}, known only to Sam (and not even to Elmer!), to the original order. Since the order was not encrypted first, this produces gibberish, but as we shall see, there is a method in this madness. Next, Sam encrypts the result of the previous step using e_{Elmer} and registers the result in the database.

When Elmer examines such an order, he first decrypts it using d_{Elmer}. This step yields the gibberish that Sam generated from his order, because the encryption and decryption algorithm are inverses when applied with the right keys. Next, Elmer applies the *encryption algorithm* to this gibberish, using Sam's encryption key e_{Sam}, which is known to Elmer (and indeed, is public). This step yields the original unencrypted order, again because the encryption and decryption algorithm are inverses!

If the order had been forged, the forger could not have known Sam's decryption key d_{Sam}; the final result would have been nonsensical, rather than the original order. Further, because the company does not know d_{Sam}, Sam cannot claim that a genuine order was forged by the company.

The use of public-key cryptography is not limited to database systems, but it is likely to find increasing application in the DBMS context thanks to the use of the DBMS as a repository for the records of sensitive commercial transactions. Internet commerce, as in the example above, could well be a driving force in this respect.

10.7 SUMMARY

This chapter presented the concept of a *view*, which is a powerful mechanism for customizing data for different groups of users and for hiding sensitive information while revealing part of the data. Views play an important role in database security.

Security in a DBMS must be enforced in conjunction with related layers such as the operating system and network gateways. Within a DBMS, specifically, there are two main approaches to security, called *discretionary* and *mandatory* access control. Discretionary controls are based on *granting* (and *revoking* from) users *privileges* to data objects. Mandatory controls are based on assigning each database object a *security class*, and each user *clearance* for a security class, and enforcing rules that prevent information from flowing from a higher to a lower security class. SQL-92 supports discretionary access controls, but not mandatory access controls. Some commercial systems support mandatory access control mechanisms as well.

The database administrator is responsible for the overall security of the system. In addition to enforcing the database's *security policy*, namely, decisions about who can access what, in terms of DBMS security mechanisms, the DBA must also consider ways in which these mechanisms can be defeated and take additional steps as warranted (such as maintaining a record of all accesses) to minimize security violations.

Statistical databases present some particularly difficult security challenges because clever users can infer information about specific individuals from the answers to valid statistical queries. Finally, encryption techniques are important tools that enable database users and designers to develop truly secure systems.

EXERCISES

Exercise 10.1 Briefly answer the following questions based on this schema:

> Emp(*eid:* integer, *ename:* string, *age:* integer, *salary:* real)
> Works(*eid:* integer, *did:* integer, *pct_time:* integer)
> Dept(*did:* integer, *budget:* real, *managerid:* integer)

1. Suppose you have a view SeniorEmp defined as follows:

> CREATE VIEW SeniorEmp (sname, sage, salary)
>   AS SELECT E.ename, E.age, E.salary
>   FROM   Emp E
>   WHERE E.age > 50

Explain what the system will do to process the following query:

```
SELECT  S.sname
FROM    SeniorEmp S
WHERE   S.salary > 100,000
```

2. Give an example of a view on Emp that could be automatically updated by updating Emp.

3. Give an example of a view on Emp that would be impossible to update (automatically) and explain why your example presents the update problem that it does.

4. Consider the following view definition:

```
CREATE VIEW DInfo (did, manager, numemps, totsals)
       AS SELECT   D.did, D.managerid, COUNT (*), SUM (E.salary)
          FROM     Emp E, Works W, Dept D
          WHERE    E.eid = W.eid AND W.did = D.did
          GROUP BY D.did, D.managerid
```

   (a) Give an example of a view update on DInfo that could (in principle) be implemented automatically by updating one or more of the relations Emp, Works and Dept. Does SQL-92 allow such a view update?

   (b) Give an example of a view update on DInfo that cannot (even in principle) be implemented automatically by updating one or more of the relations Emp, Works and Dept. Explain why.

   (c) How could the view DInfo help in enforcing security?

Exercise 10.2 You are the DBA for the VeryFine Toy Company, and you create a relation called Employees with fields *ename*, *dept* and *salary*. For authorization reasons, you also define views EmployeeNames (with *ename* as the only attribute) and DeptInfo with fields *dept* and *avgsalary*. The latter lists the average salary for each department, of course.

1. Show the view definition statements for EmployeeNames and DeptInfo.

2. What privileges should be granted to a user who needs to know only average department salaries for the Toy and CS departments?

3. You want to authorize your secretary to fire people (you'll probably tell him whom to fire, but you want to be able to delegate this task), to check on who is an employee, and to check on average department salaries. What privileges should you grant?

4. Continuing with the preceding scenario, you don't want your secretary to be able to look at the salaries of individuals. Does your answer to the previous question ensure this? Be specific: Can your secretary possibly find out salaries of *some* individuals (depending on the actual set of tuples), or can your secretary always find out the salary of any individual that he wants to?

5. You want to give your secretary the authority to allow other people to read the EmployeeNames view. Show the appropriate command.

6. Your secretary defines two new views using the EmployeeNames view. The first is called AtoRNames and simply selects names that begin with a letter in the range A to R. The second is called HowManyNames and counts the number of names. You

are so pleased with this achievement that you decide to give your secretary the right to insert tuples into the EmployeeNames view. Show the appropriate command, and describe what privileges your secretary has after this command is executed.

7. Your secretary allows Todd to read the EmployeeNames relation, and later quits. You then revoke the secretary's privileges. What happens to Todd's privileges?

8. Give an example of a view update on the above schema that cannot be implemented through updates to Employees.

9. You decide to go on an extended vacation, and to make sure that emergencies can be handled, you want to authorize your boss Joe to read and modify the Employees relation and the EmployeeNames relation. Show the appropriate SQL statements. Can Joe read the DeptInfo view?

10. After returning from your (wonderful) vacation, you see a note from Joe, indicating that he authorized his secretary Mike to read the Employees relation. You want to revoke Mike's SELECT privilege on Employees, but you don't want to revoke the rights that you gave to Joe, even temporarily. Can you do this in SQL?

11. Later you realize that Joe has been quite busy. He has defined a view called All-Names using the view EmployeeNames, defined another relation called StaffNames that he has access to (but that you can't access), and given his secretary Mike the right to read from the AllNames view. Mike has passed this right on to his friend Susan. You decide that even at the cost of annoying Joe by revoking some of his privileges, you simply have to take away Mike and Susan's rights to see your data. What REVOKE statement would you execute? What rights does Joe have on Employees after this statement is executed? What views are dropped as a consequence?

Exercise 10.3 Briefly answer the following questions.

1. Explain the intuition behind the two rules in the Bell-LaPadula model for mandatory access control.

2. Give an example of how covert channels can be used to defeat the Bell-LaPadula model.

3. Give an example of polyinstantiation.

4. Describe a scenario in which mandatory access controls prevent a breach of security that cannot be prevented through discretionary controls.

5. Describe a scenario in which discretionary access controls are required to enforce a security policy that cannot be enforced using only mandatory controls.

6. If a DBMS already supports discretionary and mandatory access controls, is there a need for encryption?

7. Explain the need for each of the following limits in a statistical database system:

    (a) A maximum on the number of queries a user can pose.

    (b) A minimum on the number of tuples involved in answering a query.

    (c) A maximum on the intersection of two queries (i.e., on the number of tuples that both queries examine).

8. Explain the use of an audit trail, with special reference to a statistical database system.

9. What is the role of the DBA with respect to security?

10. What is public-key encryption? How does it differ from the encryption approach taken in the Data Encryption Standard (DES), and in what ways is it better than DES?

11. What are one-way functions, and what role do they play in public-key encryption?

12. Explain how a company offering services on the Internet could use public-key encryption to make its order-entry process secure. Describe how you would use DES encryption for the same purpose, and contrast the public-key and DES approaches.

PROJECT-BASED EXERCISES

Exercise 10.4 Is there any support for views or authorization in Minibase?

BIBLIOGRAPHIC NOTES

[521] discusses how queries on views can be converted to queries on the underlying tables through query modification. [247] compares the performance of query modification versus immediate and deferred view maintenance. [515] presents an analytical model of materialized view maintenance algorithms. A number of papers discuss how materialized views can be incrementally maintained as the underlying relations are changed. This area has become very active recently, in part because of the interest in *data warehouses*, which can be thought of as collections of views over relations from various sources. The following partial list should provide pointers for additional reading: [78, 140, 141, 237, 251, 412, 434, 457, 479, 513, 586]. Several papers consider the problem of translating updates specified on views into updates on the underlying table [44, 151, 289, 330, 572]. [208] is a good survey on this topic.

The authorization mechanism of System R, which greatly influenced the GRANT and REVOKE paradigm in SQL-92, is described in [235]. A good general treatment of security and cryptography is presented in [155], and an overview of database security can be found in [101] and [329]. Security in statistical databases is investigated in several papers, including [154] and [128]. Multilevel security is discussed in several papers, including [281, 357, 506, 518].

11

QUERY-BY-EXAMPLE (QBE)

Example is always more efficacious than precept.

—Samuel Johnson

11.1 INTRODUCTION

Query-by-Example (QBE) is another language for querying (and, like SQL, for creating and modifying) relational data. It is different from SQL, and in fact from most other database query languages, in having a graphical user interface that allows users to write queries by creating *example tables* on the screen. A user needs minimal information to get started and the whole language contains relatively few concepts. QBE is especially suited for queries that are not too complex, and can be expressed in terms of a few tables.

QBE, like SQL, was developed at IBM and QBE is an IBM trademark, but a number of other companies sell QBE-like interfaces, including Paradox. Some systems, such as Microsoft Access, offer partial support for form-based queries and reflect the influence of QBE. Often a QBE-like interface is offered in addition to SQL, with QBE serving as a more intuitive user-interface for simpler queries and the full power of SQL available for more complex queries. Thus an appreciation of the features of QBE offers insight into the more general, and widely used, paradigm of tabular query interfaces for relational databases.

This presentation is based on IBM's Query Management Facility (QMF) and the QBE version that it supports (Version 2, Release 4). The purpose of this chapter is to explain how a tabular interface can provide the expressive power of relational calculus (and more) in a user-friendly form. The reader should concentrate on the connection between QBE and domain relational calculus (DRC), and the role of various important constructs (e.g., the conditions box), rather than on QBE-specific details. We note that every QBE query can be expressed in SQL; in fact, QMF supports a command called **CONVERT** that generates an SQL query from a QBE query.

We will present a number of example queries using the following schema:

Sailors(*sid:* integer, *sname:* string, *rating:* integer, *age:* real)

255

Boats(*bid:* integer, *bname:* string, *color:* string)
Reserves(*sid:* integer, *bid:* integer, *day:* dates)

The key fields are underlined, and the domain of each field is listed after the field name.

We introduce QBE queries in Section 11.2 and consider queries over multiple relations in Section 11.3. We consider queries with set-difference in Section 11.4 and queries with aggregation in Section 11.5. We discuss how to specify complex constraints in Section 11.6. We show how additional computed fields can be included in the answer in Section 11.7. We discuss update operations in QBE in Section 11.8. Finally, we consider relational completeness of QBE and illustrate some of the subtleties of QBE queries with negation in Section 11.9.

11.2   BASIC QBE QUERIES

A user writes queries by creating *example tables*. QBE uses *domain variables*, as in the DRC, to create example tables. The domain of a variable is determined by the column in which it appears, and variable symbols are prefixed with underscore (_) to distinguish them from constants. Constants, including strings, appear unquoted, in contrast to SQL. The fields that should appear in the answer are specified by using the command P., which stands for *print*. The fields containing this command are analogous to the *target-list* in the SELECT clause of an SQL query.

In this section we introduce QBE (fittingly enough!) through example queries involving just one relation. To print the names and ages of all sailors, we would create the following example table:

Sailors	sid	sname	rating	age
		P._N		P._A

A variable that appears only once can be omitted; QBE supplies a unique new name internally. Thus the previous query could also be written by omitting the variables _N and _A, leaving just P. in the *sname* and *age* columns. The query corresponds to the following DRC query, obtained from the QBE query by introducing existentially quantified domain variables for each field.

$$\{\langle N, A \rangle \mid \exists I, T(\langle I, N, T, A \rangle \in Sailors)\}$$

A large class of QBE queries can be translated to DRC in a direct manner. (Of course, queries containing features such as aggregate operators cannot be expressed in DRC.) We will present DRC versions of several QBE queries. Although we will not define the translation from QBE to DRC formally, the idea should be clear from the examples; intuitively, there is a term for each row, and the terms are connected using $\wedge$.[1]

A convenient shorthand notation is that if we want to print all fields in some relation, we can place `P.` under the name of the relation. This notation is like the `SELECT` * convention in SQL. It is equivalent to placing a `P.` in every field:

Sailors	sid	sname	rating	age
P.				

Selections are expressed by placing a constant in some field:

Sailors	sid	sname	rating	age
P.			10	

Placing a constant, say 10, in a column is the same as placing the condition $=10$. This query is very similar to the DRC query

$$\{\langle I, N, 10, A\rangle \mid \langle I, N, 10, A\rangle \in Sailors\}$$

We can use other comparison operations ($<, >, <=, >=, \neg$) as well. For example, we could say < 10 to retrieve sailors with a rating less than 10 or say $\neg 10$ to retrieve sailors whose rating is not equal to 10. The expression $\neg 10$ in an attribute column is the same as $\neq 10$. As we will see shortly, $\neg$ under the relation name denotes (a limited form of) $\neg \exists$ in the relational calculus sense.

11.2.1   Other Features: Duplicates, Ordering Answers *

We can explicitly specify whether duplicate tuples in the answer are to be eliminated (or not) by putting `UNQ.` (respectively `ALL.`) under the relation name.

We can order the presentation of the answers through the use of the `.AO` (for *ascending order*) and `.DO` commands in conjunction with `.P`. An optional integer argument allows us to sort on more than one field. For example, we can display the names, ages and ratings of all sailors in ascending order by age, and for each age, in ascending order by rating as follows:

---

[1] The semantics of QBE is unclear when there are several rows containing `P.` or if there are rows that are not linked via shared variables to the row containing `P.`. We will discuss such queries in Section 11.6.1.

Sailors	sid	sname	rating	age
		P.	P.AO(2)	P.AO(1)

11.3   QUERIES OVER MULTIPLE RELATIONS

To find sailors with a reservation, we have to combine information from the Sailors and the Reserves relations. In particular we have to select tuples from the two relations with the same value in the join column *sid*. We do this by placing the same variable in the *sid* columns of the two example relations.

Sailors	sid	sname	rating	age		Reserves	sid	bid	date
	_Id	P._S					_Id		

To find sailors who have reserved a boat for 8/24/96 and who are older than 25, we could write:[2]

Sailors	sid	sname	rating	age		Reserves	sid	bid	date
	_Id	P._S		> 25			_Id		'8/24/96'

Extending this example, we could try to find the colors of Interlake boats reserved by sailors who have reserved a boat for 8/24/96 and who are older than 25:

Sailors	sid	sname	rating	age
	_Id			> 25

Reserves	sid	bid	date		Boats	bid	bname	color
	_Id	_B	'8/24/96'			_B	Interlake	P.

As another example, the following query prints the names and ages of sailors who have reserved some boat that is also reserved by the sailor with id 22:

Sailors	sid	sname	rating	age		Reserves	sid	bid	date
	_Id	P._N					_Id	_B	
							22	_B	

---

[2]Incidentally, note that we have quoted the date value. In general constants are not quoted in QBE. The exceptions to this rule include date values and string values with embedded blanks or special characters.

Each of the queries in this section can be expressed in DRC. For example, the previous query can be written as follows:

$$\{\langle N \rangle \mid \exists Id, T, A, B, D1, D2(\langle Id, N, T, A \rangle \in Sailors$$
$$\wedge \langle Id, B, D1 \rangle \in Reserves \wedge \langle 22, B, D2 \rangle \in Reserves)\}$$

Notice how the only free variable (N) is handled and how Id and B are repeated, as in the QBE query.

11.4 NEGATION IN THE RELATION-NAME COLUMN

We can print the names of sailors who do *not* have a reservation by using the ¬ command in the relation name column:

Sailors	sid	sname	rating	age		Reserves	sid	bid	date
	_Id	P._S				¬	_Id		

This query can be read as follows: "Print the *sname* field of Sailors tuples such that there is *no* tuple in Reserves with the same value in the *sid* field." Note the importance of *sid* being a key for Sailors. In the relational model, keys are the only available means for *unique identification* (of sailors, in this case). (Consider how the meaning of this query would change if the Reserves schema contained *sname*—which is not a key!—rather than *sid*, and we used a common variable in this column to effect the join.)

All variables in a negative row (i.e., a row that is preceded by ¬) must also appear in positive rows (i.e., rows not preceded by ¬). Intuitively, variables in positive rows can be instantiated in many ways, based on the tuples in the input instances of the relations, and each negative row involves a simple check to see if the corresponding relation contains a tuple with certain given field values.

The use of ¬ in the relation-name column gives us a limited form of the set-difference operator of relational algebra. For example, we can easily modify the previous query to find sailors who are not (both) younger than 30 and rated higher than 4:

Sailors	sid	sname	rating	age		Sailors	sid	sname	rating	age
	_Id	P._S				¬	_Id		> 4	< 30

This mechanism is not as general as set-difference, because there is no way to control the order in which occurrences of ¬ are considered if a query contains more than one occurrence of ¬. To capture full set-difference, views can be used. (The issue of QBE's relational completeness, and in particular the ordering problem, is discussed further in Section 11.9.)

11.5 AGGREGATES

Like SQL, QBE supports the aggregate operations `AVG.`, `COUNT.`, `MAX.`, `MIN.`, and `SUM.` By default, these aggregate operators do *not* eliminate duplicates, with the exception of `COUNT.`, which does eliminate duplicates. To eliminate duplicate values, the variants `AVG.UNQ.` and `SUM.UNQ.` must be used. (Of course, this is irrelevant for `MIN.` and `MAX.`) Curiously, there is no variant of `COUNT.` that does *not* eliminate duplicates.

Consider the instance of Sailors shown in Figure 11.1. On this instance the fol-

sid	sname	rating	age
22	dustin	7	45.0
58	rusty	10	35.0
44	horatio	7	35.0

Figure 11.1   An Instance of Sailors

lowing query prints the value 38.3:

Sailors	sid	sname	rating	age	
				_A	P.AVG._A

Thus the value 35.0 is counted twice in computing the average. To count each age only once, we could specify `P.AVG.UNQ.` instead, and we would get 40.0.

QBE supports *grouping*, as in SQL, through the use of the `G.` command. To print average ages by rating, we could use:

Sailors	sid	sname	rating	age	
			G.P.	_A	P.AVG._A

To print the answers in sorted order by rating, we could use `G.P.AO` or `G.P.DO.` instead. When an aggregate operation is used in conjunction with `P.`, or there is a use of the `G.` operator, every column to be printed must specify either an aggregate operation or the **G.** operator. (Note that SQL has a similar restriction.) If **G.** appears in more than one column, the result is similar to placing each of these column names in the **GROUP BY** clause of an SQL query. If we place **G.** in the *sname* and *rating* columns, all tuples in each group have the same *sname* value and also the same *rating* value.

We consider some more examples using aggregate operations after introducing the conditions box feature.

11.6 THE CONDITIONS BOX

Simple conditions can be expressed directly in columns of the example tables. For more complex conditions QBE provides a feature called a **conditions box**.

Conditions boxes are used to do the following:

- *Express a condition involving two or more columns*, such as $\_R/\_A > 0.2$.

- *Express a condition involving an aggregate operation on a group*, for example, **AVG.**$\_A > 30$. Notice that this use of a conditions box is similar to the **HAVING** clause in SQL. The following query prints those ratings for which the average age is more than 30:

Sailors	sid	sname	rating	age		Conditions
			G.P.	_A		AVG._A > 30

As another example, the following query prints the *sids* of sailors who have reserved all boats for which there is some reservation:

Sailors	sid		sname	rating	age
	P.G._Id				

Reserves	sid	bid	date		Conditions
	_Id	_B1			COUNT._B1 = COUNT._B2
		_B2			

For each _Id value (notice the **G.** operator), we count all _B1 values to get the number of (distinct) *bid* values reserved by sailor _Id. We compare this count against the count of all _B2 values, which is simply the total number of (distinct) *bid* values in the Reserves relation (i.e., the number of boats with reservations). If these counts are equal, the sailor has reserved all boats for which there is some reservation. Incidentally, the following query, intended to print the names of such sailors, is incorrect:

Sailors	sid	sname	rating	age
	P.G._Id	P.		

Reserves	sid	bid	date
	_Id	_B1	
		_B2	

Conditions
COUNT._B1 = COUNT._B2

The problem is that in conjunction with **G.**, only columns with either **G.** or an aggregate operation can be printed. This limitation is a direct consequence of the SQL definition of **GROUPBY**, which we discussed in Section 9.4.1; QBE is typically implemented by translating queries into SQL. If **P.G.** replaces **P.** in the *sname* column, the query is legal, and we then group by both *sid* and *sname*, which results in the same groups as before because *sid* is a key for Sailors.

- *Express conditions involving the **AND** and **OR** operators.* We can print the names of sailors who are younger than 20 *or* older than 30 as follows:

Sailors	sid	sname	rating	age	Conditions
		P.		_A	_A < 20 OR 30 < _A

We can print the names of sailors who are both younger than 20 *and* older than 30 by simply replacing the condition with *_A < 20 **OR** 30 < _A*; of course, the set of such sailors is always empty! We can print the names of sailors who are either older than 20 *or* have a rating equal to 8 by using the condition *20 < _A **OR** _R = 8*, and placing the variable _R in the *rating* column of the example table.

11.6.1 And/Or Queries *

It is instructive to consider how queries involving **AND** and **OR** can be expressed in QBE without using a conditions box. We can print the names of sailors who are younger than 30 *or* older than 20 by simply creating two example rows:

Sailors	sid	sname	rating	age
		P.		< 30
		P.		> 20

To translate a QBE query with several rows containing **P.**, we create subformulas for each row with a **P.** and connect the subformulas through ∨. If a row containing **P.** is linked to other rows through shared variables (which is not the case in this example), the subformula contains a term for each linked row, all connected using $\wedge$. Notice how the answer variable N, which must be a free variable, is handled:

$$\{\langle N \rangle \mid \exists I1, N1, T1, A1, I2, N2, T2, A2($$
$$\langle I1, N1, T1, A1 \rangle \in Sailors(A1 < 30 \wedge N = N1)$$
$$\vee \langle I2, N2, T2, A2 \rangle \in Sailors(A2 > 20 \wedge N = N2))\}$$

To print the names of sailors who are both younger than 30 *and* older than 20, we use the same variable in the key fields of both rows:

Sailors	sid	sname	rating	age
	_Id	P.		< 30
	_Id			> 20

In terms of DRC, we can write this query as follows:

$$\{\langle N \rangle \mid \exists I1, N1, T1, A1, I2, N2, T2, A2$$
$$(\langle I1, N1, T1, A1 \rangle \in Sailors(A1 < 30 \wedge N = N1)$$
$$\wedge \langle I2, N2, T2, A2 \rangle \in Sailors(A2 > 20 \wedge N = N2))\}$$

Compare this DRC query with the DRC version of the previous query to see how closely they are related (and how closely QBE follows DRC). In contrast to the previous query, however, both rows are linked through *Id*, and there is just one row with a P. The formula for this row contains a term for each linked row, and these terms are connected using $\wedge$.

11.7 UNNAMED COLUMNS

If we want to display some information in addition to fields retrieved from a relation, we can create *unnamed columns* for display.[3] As an example—admittedly, a silly one!—we could print the name of each sailor along with the ratio *rating/age* as follows:

Sailors	sid	sname	rating	age	
		P.	_R	_A	P._R / _A

All our examples thus far have included P. commands in exactly one table. This is not a coincidence, but a QBE restriction. If we want to display fields from more than one table, we can use unnamed columns. To print the names of sailors along with the dates on which they have a boat reserved, we could use the following:

---

[3]A QBE facility includes simple commands for drawing empty example tables, adding fields, and so on. We do not discuss these features but assume that they are available.

Sailors	sid	sname	rating	age	
	_Id	P.			P._D

Reserves	sid	bid	date
	_Id		_D

Note that unnamed columns should not be used for expressing *conditions* such as _D >8/9/96; a conditions box should be used instead.

11.8 UPDATES

Insertion, deletion and modification of a tuple are specified through the commands I., D. and U., respectively. We can insert a new tuple into the Sailors relation as follows:

Sailors	sid	sname	rating	age
I.	74	Janice	7	41

We can insert several tuples, computed essentially through a query, into the Sailors relation as follows:

Sailors	sid	sname	rating	age
I.	_Id	_N		_A

Students	sid	name	login	age	Conditions
	_Id	_N		_A	_A > 18 OR _N LIKE 'C%'

We insert one tuple for each student older than 18 or with a name that begins with C. (QBE's LIKE operator is similar to the SQL version.) The *rating* field of every inserted tuple contains a *null* value. The following query is very similar to the previous query, but differs in a subtle way:

Sailors	sid	sname	rating	age
I.	_Id1	_N1		_A1
I.	_Id2	_N2		_A2

Students	sid	name	login	age
	_Id1	_N1		_A1 > 18
	_Id2	_N2 LIKE 'C%'		_A2

The difference is that a student older than 18 with a name that begins with 'C' is now inserted *twice* into Sailors. (The second insertion would be rejected by the integrity constraint enforcement mechanism because *sid* is a key for Sailors. However, if this integrity constraint is not declared, we would find two copies of such a student in the Sailors relation.)

We can delete all tuples with *rating* > 5 from the Sailors relation as follows:

Sailors	sid	sname	rating	age
D.			> 5	

We can delete all reservations for sailors with *rating* < 4 by using:

Sailors	sid	sname	rating	age	Reserves	sid	bid	date
	_Id		< 4		D.	_Id		

We can update the age of the sailor with *sid* 74 to be 42 years by using:

Sailors	sid	sname	rating	age
	74			U.42

The fact that *sid* is the key is significant here; we cannot update the key field, but we can use it to identify the tuple to be modified (in other fields). We can also change the age of sailor 74 from 41 to 42 by incrementing the age value:

Sailors	sid	sname	rating	age
	74			U._A+1

11.8.1 Restrictions on Update Commands

There are some restrictions on the use of the I., D. and U. commands. First, we cannot mix these operators in a single example table (or combine them with P.). Second, we cannot specify I., D. or U. in an example table that contains G. Third, we cannot insert, update, or modify tuples based on values in fields of other tuples in the same table. Thus the following update is incorrect:

Sailors	sid	sname	rating	age
		john		U._A+1
		joe		_A

This update seeks to change John's age based on Joe's age. Since *sname* is not a key, the meaning of such a query is ambiguous—should we update *every* John's age, and if so, based on *which* Joe's age? QBE avoids such anomalies using a rather broad restriction. For example, if *sname* were a key, this would be a reasonable request, even though it is disallowed.

11.9 DIVISION AND RELATIONAL COMPLETENESS *

In Section 11.6 we saw how division can be expressed in QBE using COUNT. It is instructive to consider how division can be expressed in QBE without the use of aggregate operators. If we don't use aggregate operators, we cannot express division in QBE without using the update commands to create a temporary relation or view. However, taking the update commands into account, QBE is relationally complete, even without the aggregate operators. Although we will not prove these claims, the example that we discuss below should bring out the underlying intuition.

We use the following query in our discussion of division:

Find sailors who have reserved all boats.

In Chapter 8 we saw that this query can be expressed in DRC as:

$$\{\langle I, N, T, A\rangle \mid \langle I, N, T, A\rangle \in Sailors \wedge \forall \langle B, BN, C\rangle \in Boats$$
$$(\exists \langle Ir, Br, D\rangle \in Reserves(I = Ir \wedge Br = B))\}$$

The ∀ quantifier is not available in QBE, so let us rewrite the above without ∀:

$$\{\langle I, N, T, A\rangle \mid \langle I, N, T, A\rangle \in Sailors \wedge \neg\exists \langle B, BN, C\rangle \in Boats$$
$$(\neg\exists \langle Ir, Br, D\rangle \in Reserves(I = Ir \wedge Br = B))\}$$

This calculus query can be read as follows: "Find Sailors tuples (with *sid* I) for which there is no Boats tuple (with *bid* B) such that no Reserves tuple indicates that sailor I has reserved boat B." We might try to write this query in QBE as follows:

Sailors	sid	sname	rating	age
	_Id	P._S		

Boats	bid	bname	color	Reserves	sid	bid	date
¬	_B			¬	_Id	_B	

This query is illegal because the variable _B does not appear in any positive row. Going beyond this technical objection, this QBE query is ambiguous with respect to the *ordering* of the two uses of ¬. It could denote either the calculus query that we want to express or the following calculus query, which is not what we want:

$$\{\langle I, N, T, A \rangle \mid \langle I, N, T, A \rangle \in \mathit{Sailors} \land \neg \exists \langle Ir, Br, D \rangle \in \mathit{Reserves}$$
$$(\neg \exists \langle B, BN, C \rangle \in \mathit{Boats}(I = Ir \land Br = B))\}$$

There is no mechanism in QBE to control the order in which the ¬ operations in a query are applied. (Incidentally, the above query finds all Sailors who have made reservations only for boats that exist in the Boats relation.)

One way to achieve such control is to break the query into several parts by using temporary relations or views. As we saw in Chapter 8, we can accomplish division in two logical steps: first, identify *disqualified* candidates, and then remove this set from the set of all candidates. In the query at hand, we have to first identify the set of *sids* (called, say, BadSids) of sailors who have not reserved some boat (i.e., for each such sailor, we can find a boat not reserved by that sailor), and then we have to remove BadSids from the set of *sids* of all sailors. This process will identify the set of sailors who've reserved all boats. The view BadSids can be defined as follows:

Sailors	sid	sname	rating	age		Reserves	sid	bid	date
	_Id					¬	_Id	_B	

Boats	bid	bname	color		BadSids	sid
	_B				I.	_Id

Given the view BadSids, it is a simple matter to find sailors whose *sids* are not in this view.

The ideas in this example can be extended to show that QBE is *relationally complete*.

11.10 SUMMARY

QBE is an elegant, user-friendly query language that is strongly influenced by the domain relational calculus. It was one of the first database query languages with a graphical interface. It is a remarkable demonstration of how expressive such a graphical language can be; QBE is relationally complete, taking into account its querying and view creation features. In addition to the query and update features that we have discussed, QBE provides support for tasks such as data definition and authorization, like SQL.

A QBE query consists of one or more *example rows*, over one or more relations. Simple visual conventions are used to express selections, projections, grouping, sorting, and so on. Joins are accomplished by using the same variable in multiple locations. The use of negation is restricted in QBE in comparison to DRC, but overall, the translation from QBE to DRC is very straightforward (for queries that do not involve aggregate operations or grouping, of course, since DRC does not support these features).

Although QBE is a name used only by IBM, several other products, such as Paradox, are very similar to QBE. Other database products, such as Microsoft Access, support graphical query interfaces that are influenced by QBE. Understanding the ideas behind QBE offers insight into the general paradigm of tabular query interfaces, which are widely used.

EXERCISES

Exercise 11.1 Consider the following relational schema. An employee can work in more than one department.

> Emp(*eid:* integer, *ename:* string, *salary:* real)
> Works(*eid:* integer, *did:* integer)
> Dept(*did:* integer, *dname:* string, *managerid:* integer, *floornum:* integer)

Write the following queries in QBE. Be sure to underline your variables to distinguish them from your constants.

1. Print the names of all employees who work on the 10th floor and make less than 50,000.

2. Print the names of all managers who manage three or more departments on the same floor.

3. Give every employee who works in the Toy department a 10% raise.

4. Print the names of the departments that employee Santa works in.

5. Print the names and salaries of employees who work in both the Toy department and the Candy department.

6. Print the names of employees who earn a salary that is either less than 10,000 or more than 100,000.

7. Print all of the attributes for employees who work in some department that employee Santa also works in.

8. Fire Santa.

9. Print the names of employees who make more than 20,000 and work in either the Video department or the Toy department.

10. Print the names of all employees who work on the floor(s) where Jane Dodecahedron works.

11. Print the name of each employee who earns more than the manager of the department that he or she works in.

12. Print the name of each department that has a manager whose last name is Psmith and who is neither the highest-paid nor the lowest-paid employee in the department.

Exercise 11.2 Write the following queries in QBE, based on this schema:

> Suppliers(*sid:* integer, *sname:* string, *city:* string)
> Parts(*pid:* integer, *pname:* string, *color:* string)
> Orders(*sid:* integer, *pid:* integer, *quantity:* integer)

1. For each supplier from whom all of the following things have been ordered in quantities of at least 150, print the name and city of the supplier: a blue gear, a red crankshaft and a yellow bumper.

2. Print the names of the purple parts that have been ordered from suppliers located in Madison, Milwaukee or Waukesha.

3. Print the names and cities of suppliers who have an order for more than 150 units of a yellow or purple part.

4. Print the *pid*s of parts that have been ordered from a supplier named American but which have also been ordered from some supplier with a different name in a quantity that is greater than the American order by at least 100 units.

5. Print the names of the suppliers located in Madison. Could there be any duplicates in the answer?

6. Print all available information about suppliers that supply green parts.

7. For each order of a red part, print the quantity and the name of the part.

8. Print the names of the parts that come in both blue and green. (Assume that no two distinct parts can have the same name and color.)

9. Print (in ascending order alphabetically) the names of parts supplied both by a Madison supplier and by a Berkeley supplier.

10. Print the names of parts supplied by a Madison supplier, but not supplied by any Berkeley supplier. Could there be any duplicates in the answer?

11. Print the total number of orders.

12. Print the largest quantity per order for each *sid* such that the minimum quantity per order for that supplier is greater than 100.

13. Print the average quantity per order of red parts.

14. Can you write this query in QBE? If so, how?
    Print the sid*s of suppliers from whom every part has been ordered.*

Exercise 11.3 Answer the following questions:

1. Describe the various uses for unnamed columns in QBE.

2. Describe the various uses for a conditions box in QBE.

3. What is unusual about the treatment of duplicates in QBE?

4. Is QBE based upon relational algebra, tuple relational calculus, or domain relational calculus? Explain briefly.

5. Is QBE relationally complete? Explain briefly.

6. What restrictions does QBE place on update commands?

PROJECT-BASED EXERCISES

Exercise 11.4 Minibase's version of QBE, called MiniQBE, tries to preserve the spirit of QBE but cheats occasionally. Try the queries shown in this chapter and in the exercises, and identify the ways in which MiniQBE differs from QBE. For each QBE query you try in MiniQBE, examine the SQL query that it is translated into by MiniQBE.

BIBLIOGRAPHIC NOTES

The QBE project was led by Moshe Zloof [588], and resulted in the first visual database query language, whose influence is seen today in products such as Borland's Paradox and, to a lesser extent, Microsoft's Access. QBE was also one of the first relational query languages to support the computation of transitive closure, through a special operator, anticipating much subsequent research into extensions of relational query languages to support recursive queries. A successor called Office-by-Example [587] sought to extend the QBE visual interaction paradigm to applications such as electronic mail integrated with database access. Klug presented a version of QBE that dealt with aggregate queries in [305].

12

EVALUATION OF RELATIONAL OPERATORS

Now, *here*, you see, it takes all the running you can do, to keep in the same place. If you want to get somewhere else, you must run at least twice as fast as that!

—Lewis Carroll, *Through the Looking Glass*

The relational operators serve as the building blocks for query evaluation. Queries, written in a language such as SQL, are presented to a *query optimizer*, which uses information about how the data is stored (available in the system catalogs) to produce an efficient *execution plan* for evaluating the query. Finding a good execution plan for a query consists of more than just choosing an implementation for each of the relational operators that appear in the query. For example, the order in which operators are applied can influence the cost. Issues in finding a good plan that go beyond implementation of individual operators are discussed in Chapter 13.

This chapter considers the implementation of individual relational operators. Section 12.1 provides an introduction to query processing, highlighting some common themes that recur throughout this chapter, and discusses how tuples are retrieved from relations while evaluating various relational operators. We present implementation alternatives for the selection operator in Sections 12.2 and 12.3. It is instructive to see the variety of alternatives, and the wide variation in performance of these alternatives, for even such a simple operator. In Section 12.4 we consider the other unary operator in relational algebra, namely, projection.

We then discuss the implementation of binary operators, beginning with joins in Section 12.5. Joins are among the most expensive operators in a relational database system, and their implementation has a big impact on performance. After discussing the join operator, we consider implementation of the binary operators cross-product, intersection, union, and set-difference in Section 12.6. We discuss the implementation of grouping and aggregate operators, which are extensions of relational algebra, in Section 12.7. We conclude with a discussion of how buffer management affects operator evaluation costs in Section 12.8.

The discussion of each operator is largely independent of the discussion of other operators. Several alternative implementation techniques are presented for each operator; the reader who wishes to cover this material in less depth can skip some of these alternatives without loss of continuity.

12.1 INTRODUCTION TO QUERY PROCESSING

One of the virtues of a relational DBMS is that queries are composed of a few basic operators, and the implementation of these operators can (and should!) be carefully optimized for good performance. There are several alternative algorithms for implementing each relational operator, and for most operators there is no universally superior technique. Which algorithm is best depends on several factors, including the sizes of the relations involved, existing indexes and sort orders, the size of the available buffer pool, and the buffer replacement policy.

The algorithms for various relational operators actually have a lot in common. As this chapter will demonstrate, a few simple techniques are used to develop algorithms for each operator:

- **Iteration:** Examine all tuples in input relations iteratively. Sometimes, instead of examining tuples, we can examine index data entries (which are smaller) that contain all necessary fields.

- **Indexing:** If a selection or join condition is specified, use an index to examine just the tuples that satisfy the condition.

- **Partitioning:** By partitioning tuples on a sort key, we can often decompose an operation into a less expensive collection of operations on partitions. *Sorting* and *hashing* are two commonly used partitioning techniques.

12.1.1   Access Paths

All the algorithms discussed in this chapter have to retrieve tuples from one or more input relations. There is typically more than one way to retrieve tuples from a relation, because of the availability of indexes and the (possible) presence of a selection condition in the query that restricts the subset of the relation we need. (The selection condition can come from a selection operator or from a join.) The alternative ways to retrieve tuples from a relation are called **access paths**.

An *access path* is either (1) a file scan, or (2) an index plus a **matching** selection condition. Intuitively, a selection condition *matches* an index if the index can be used to retrieve just the tuples that satisfy the condition. Consider a simple selection of the form *attr* **op** *value*, where **op** is one of the comparison operators $<, \leq, =, \neq, \geq$, or $>$. Such a selection matches an index if the index search key is *attr* and either (1) the index is a tree index, or (2) the index is a hash index and **op** is equality. We consider when more complex selection conditions match an index in Section 12.3.

The **selectivity** of an access path is the number of pages retrieved (index pages plus data pages) if we use this access path to retrieve all desired tuples. If a relation contains an index that matches a given selection, there are at least two access paths, namely, the index and a scan of the data file. The **most selective** access path is the one that retrieves the fewest pages; using the most selective access path minimizes the cost of data retrieval.

12.1.2   Preliminaries: Examples and Cost Calculations

We will present a number of example queries using the following schema:

Sailors(*sid:* `integer`, *sname:* `string`, *rating:* `integer`, *age:* `real`)
Reserves(*sid:* `integer`, *bid:* `integer`, *day:* `dates`, *rname:* `string`)

This schema is a variant of the one that we used in Chapter 9; we have added a string field *rname* to Reserves. Intuitively, this field is the name of the person who has made the reservation (and may be different from the name of the sailor *sid* for whom the reservation was made; indeed, a reservation may be made by a person who is not a sailor on behalf of a sailor). The addition of this field gives us more flexibility in choosing illustrative examples. We will assume that each tuple of Reserves is 40 bytes long, that a page can hold 100 Reserves tuples, and that we have 1000 pages of such tuples. Similarly, we will assume that each tuple of Sailors is 50 bytes long, that a page can hold 80 Sailors tuples, and that we have 500 pages of such tuples.

Two points must be kept in mind to understand our discussion of costs:

- As discussed in Chapter 4, we consider only I/O costs, and measure I/O cost in terms of the number of page I/Os. We also make use of big-O notation to express the complexity of an algorithm in terms of an input parameter, and assume that the reader is familiar with this notation. For example, the cost of a file scan is $O(M)$, where M is the size of the file.

- We discuss several alternate algorithms for each operation. Since each alternative incurs the same cost in writing out the result, should this be necessary, we will uniformly ignore this cost in comparing alternatives.

12.2   THE SELECTION OPERATION

In this section we describe various algorithms to evaluate the selection operator. To motivate the discussion, consider the selection query shown in Figure 12.1, which has the selection condition *rname='Joe'*.

```
SELECT *
FROM    Reserves R
WHERE   R.rname='Joe'
```

Figure 12.1   Simple Selection Query

We can evaluate this query by scanning the entire relation, checking the condition on each tuple, and adding the tuple to the result if the condition is satisfied. The cost of this approach is 1000 I/Os, since Reserves contains 1000 pages. If there are only a few tuples with *rname='Joe'*, this approach is expensive because it does not utilize the selection to reduce the number of tuples retrieved in any way. How can we improve on this approach? The key is to utilize information in the selection condition and to use an index if a suitable index is available. For example, a B+ tree index on *rname* could be used to answer this query considerably faster, but an index on *bid* would not be useful.

In the rest of this section we consider various situations with respect to the file organization used for the relation and the availability of indexes, and discuss appropriate algorithms for the selection operation. We discuss only simple selection operations of the form $\sigma_{R.attr\ \boldsymbol{op}\ value}(R)$ until Section 12.3, where we consider general selections. In terms of the general techniques listed in Section 12.1, the algorithms for selection use either iteration or indexing.

12.2.1   No Index, Unsorted Data

Given a selection of the form $\sigma_{R.attr\ \boldsymbol{op}\ value}(R)$, if there is no index on *R.attr* and *R* is not sorted on *R.attr*, we have to scan the entire relation. Thus the most selective access path is a file scan. For each tuple, we must test the condition *R.attr op value* and add the tuple to the result if the condition is satisfied.

The cost of this approach is M I/Os, where M is the number of pages in R. In the example selection from Reserves (Figure 12.1), the cost is 1000 I/Os.

12.2.2   No Index, Sorted Data*

Given a selection of the form $\sigma_{R.attr\ \boldsymbol{op}\ value}(R)$, if there is no index on *R.attr*, but *R* is physically sorted on *R.attr*, we can utilize the sort order by doing a binary search to locate the first tuple that satisfies the selection condition. Further, we can then retrieve all tuples that satisfy the selection condition by starting at this location and scanning R until the selection condition is no longer satisfied. The access method in this case is a sorted-file scan with selection condition $\sigma_{R.attr \; op \; value}(R)$.

For example, suppose that the selection condition is $R.attr1 > 5$, and that R is sorted on $attr1$ in ascending order. After a binary search to locate the position in R corresponding to 5, we simply scan all remaining records.

The cost of the binary search is $O(log_2 M)$. In addition, we have the cost of the scan to retrieve qualifying tuples. The cost of the scan depends on the number of such tuples and can vary from zero to M. In our selection from Reserves (Figure 12.1), the cost of the binary search is $log_2 1000 \approx 10$ I/Os.

In practice, it is unlikely that a relation will be kept sorted if the DBMS supports Alternative (1) for index data entries, that is, allows data records to be stored as index data entries. If the ordering of data records is important, a better way to maintain it is through a B+ tree index that uses Alternative (1).

12.2.3   B+ Tree Index

If a B+ tree index is available on $R.attr$, the best strategy for selection conditions $\sigma_{R.attr \; op \; value}(R)$ in which op is not equality is to use the index. This strategy is also a good access path for equality selections, although a hash index on $R.attr$ would be a little better.

We can use the index as follows: We search the tree to find the first index entry that points to a qualifying tuple of R. Then we scan the leaf pages of the index to retrieve all entries in which the key value satisfies the selection condition. For each of these entries, we retrieve the corresponding tuple of R.

The cost of identifying the starting leaf page for the scan is typically two or three I/Os. The cost of scanning the leaf level page for qualifying entries depends on the number of such entries. The cost of retrieving qualifying tuples from R depends on the number of such tuples and on whether the B+ tree index is clustered; our comments above on hash-based indexes apply here as well, and with additional force, since range queries are likely to have many more qualifying tuples than equality queries. (Clustered and unclustered B+ tree indexes are illustrated in Figures 7.11 and 7.12. In fact, the figures should give the reader a feel for the impact of clustering, regardless of the type of index involved.)

Consider a selection of the form *rname* < *'C%'* on the Reserves relation. Assuming that names are uniformly distributed with respect to the initial letter, for simplicity, we estimate that roughly 10% of Reserves tuples are in the result. This is a total of 10,000 tuples, or 100 pages. If we have a clustered B+ index on the *rname* field of Reserves, we can retrieve the qualifying tuples with 100 I/Os (plus a few I/Os to traverse from the root to the appropriate leaf page to start the scan). However, if the index is unclustered, we could have up to 10,000 I/Os in the worst case, since each tuple could cause us to read a page. If we sort the rids of Reserves tuples by the page number and then retrieve pages of Reserves, we will avoid retrieving the same page multiple times; nonetheless, the tuples to be retrieved are likely to be scattered across many more than 100 pages. Therefore, the use of an unclustered index for a range selection could be expensive; it might be cheaper to simply scan the entire relation (which is 1000 pages in our example).

12.2.4   Hash Index, Equality Selection

If a hash index is available on $R.attr$ and **op** is equality, the best way to implement the selection $\sigma_{R.attr\ \textbf{op}\ value}(R)$ is obviously to use the index to retrieve qualifying tuples.

The cost includes a few (typically one or two) I/Os to retrieve the appropriate bucket page in the index, plus the cost of retrieving qualifying tuples from R. Since **op** is equality, there is exactly one qualifying tuple if $R.attr$ is a (candidate) key for the relation. Otherwise, we could have several tuples with the same value in this attribute. The cost of retrieving qualifying tuples depends on two factors:

- The number of qualifying tuples.

- Whether the index is clustered.

If the index is clustered, the cost of retrieving qualifying tuples is probably just one page I/O (since it is likely that all such tuples are contained in a single page). If the index is not clustered, each index entry could point to a qualifying tuple on a different page, and the cost of retrieving qualifying tuples in a straightforward way could be one page I/O per qualifying tuple (unless we get lucky with buffering). We can significantly reduce the number of I/Os to retrieve qualifying tuples from R by first sorting the rids (in the index's data entries) by their *page-id* component. This sort ensures that when we bring in a page of R, all qualifying tuples on this page are retrieved one after the other. The cost of retrieving qualifying tuples is now the number of pages of R that contain qualifying tuples.

Consider the selection in Figure 12.1. Suppose that there is an unclustered hash index on the *rname* attribute, that we have 10 buffer pages, and that there are 100 reservations made by people named Joe. The cost of retrieving the index page containing the rids of such reservations is one or two I/Os. The cost of retrieving the 100 Reserves tuples can vary between 1 and 100, depending on how these records happen to be distributed across pages of Reserves and the order in which we retrieve these records. If these 100 records are contained in, say, some five pages of Reserves, we have just five additional I/Os if we sort the rids by their page component. Otherwise, it is possible that we bring in one of these five pages, then look at some of the other pages, and find that the first page has been paged out when we need it again. (Remember that several users and DBMS operations share the buffer pool.) This situation could cause us to retrieve the same page several times.

12.3 GENERAL SELECTION CONDITIONS *

In our discussion of the selection operation thus far, we have considered selection conditions of the form $\sigma_{R.attr \ \mathbf{op} \ value}(R)$. In general a selection condition is a boolean combination (i.e., an expression using the logical connectives $\wedge$ and $\vee$) of **terms** that have the form *attribute* **op** *constant* or *attribute1* **op** *attribute2*. For example, if the **WHERE** clause in the query shown in Figure 12.1 contained the condition $R.rname = 'Joe'$ **AND** $R.bid = r$, the equivalent algebra expression would be $\sigma_{R.rname = 'Joe' \wedge R.bid = r}(R)$.

In Section 12.3.1 we introduce a standard form for general selection conditions and define when such a condition matches an index. We consider algorithms for applying selection conditions without disjunction in Section 12.3.2, and then discuss conditions with disjunction in Section 12.3.3.

12.3.1 CNF and Index Matching

To process a selection operation with a general selection condition, we first express the condition in **conjunctive normal form (CNF)**, that is, as a collection of *conjuncts* that are connected through the use of the $\wedge$ operator. Each **conjunct** consists of one or more *terms* (of the form described above) connected by $\vee$.[1] Conjuncts that contain $\vee$ are said to be **disjunctive**, or to contain **disjunction**.

As an example, suppose that we have a selection on Reserves with the condition $(day < 8/9/94 \ \wedge \ rname = 'Joe') \ \vee \ bid=5 \ \vee \ sid=3$. We can rewrite this in

---

[1] Every selection condition can be expressed in CNF. We refer the reader to any standard text on mathematical logic for the details.

conjunctive normal form as *(day < 8/9/94 ∨ bid=5 ∨ sid=3) ∧ (rname = 'Joe' ∨ bid=5 ∨ sid=3)*.

We now turn to the issue of when a general selection condition, represented in CNF, *matches* an index. The following examples provide some intuition:

- If we have a hash index on the search key ⟨*rname,bid,sid*⟩, we can use the index to retrieve just the tuples that satisfy the condition *rname='Joe' ∧ bid=5 ∧ sid=3*. The entire condition *rname='Joe' ∧ bid=5 ∧ sid=3* is said to *match* the index. On the other hand, if the selection condition is *rname='Joe' ∧ bid=5*, or some condition on *date*, this index does not match. That is, it cannot be used to retrieve just the tuples that satisfy these conditions.

  In contrast, if the index were a B+ tree, it would match both *rname='Joe' ∧ bid=5 ∧ sid=3* and *rname='Joe' ∧ bid=5*. However, it would not match *bid=5 ∧ sid=3* (since tuples are sorted primarily by *rname*).

- If we have an index (hash or tree) on the search key ⟨*bid,sid*⟩ and the selection condition *rname='Joe' ∧ bid=5 ∧ sid=3*, we can use the index to retrieve tuples that satisfy *bid=5 ∧ sid=3*, but the additional condition on *rname* must then be applied to each retrieved tuple and will eliminate some of the retrieved tuples from the result. In this case only a part of the selection condition (the part *bid=5 ∧ sid=3*) matches the index.

- If we have an index on the search key ⟨*bid, sid*⟩ and we also have a B+ tree index on *day*, the selection condition *day < 8/9/94 ∧ bid=5 ∧ sid=3* offers us a choice. Both indexes match (part of) the selection condition, and we can use either to retrieve Reserves tuples. Whichever index we use, the terms in the selection condition that don't match the index (e.g., *bid=5 ∧ sid=3* if we use the B+ tree index on *day*) must be checked for each retrieved tuple.

Generalizing the intuition behind these examples, the following rules define when an index **matches** a selection condition:

- A hash index matches a selection condition that is a conjunction of terms of the form *attribute=value* if the condition contains exactly one such term for each attribute in the index's search key.

- A tree index matches a selection condition that is a conjunction of terms of the form *attribute op value* if the condition contains exactly one such term for each attribute in a *prefix* of the index's search key. (⟨*a*⟩ and ⟨*a, b*⟩ are prefixes of key ⟨*a, b, c*⟩, but ⟨*a, c*⟩ and ⟨*b, c*⟩ are not.) Note that *op* can be any comparison; it is not restricted to be equality as it is for matching selections on a hash index.

As we observed in the examples, some subset of the terms in a selection condition (in CNF) could match an index, even though the entire condition does not match it. We will refer to the terms that match the index as the **primary** terms in the selection.

The selectivity of an access path obviously depends on the selectivity of the primary terms in the selection condition (with respect to the index involved).

12.3.2 Selections without Disjunction

We have two options to consider when no conjunct in the selection condition contains disjunction, that is, the selection is a conjunction of terms:

- We can retrieve tuples using a file scan or a single index that matches some terms (and which we estimate to be the most selective access path) and apply all non-primary terms in the selection to each retrieved tuple. This approach is very similar to how we use indexes for simple selection conditions, and we will not discuss it further. (We emphasize that the number of tuples retrieved depends on the selectivity of the primary terms in the selection, and the remaining terms only serve to reduce the cardinality of the result of the selection.)

- We can try to utilize several indexes. We examine this approach in the rest of this section.

If several (conjunctions of) terms in the selection match indexes in which the data entries contain rids (i.e., Alternatives (2) or (3)), we can use these indexes to compute sets of rids of candidate tuples. We can then intersect these sets of rids, typically by first sorting them, and then retrieve those records whose rids are in the intersection. If additional terms are present in the selection, we can then apply these terms to discard some of the candidate tuples from the result.

As an example, given the condition *day < 8/9/94 ∧ bid=5 ∧ sid=3*, we can retrieve the rids of records that meet the condition *day < 8/9/94* by using a B+ tree index on *day*, retrieve the rids of records that meet the condition *sid=3* by using a hash index on *sid*, and intersect these two sets of rids. (If we sort these sets by the page id component to do the intersection, a side benefit is that the rids in the intersection are obtained in sorted order by the pages that contain the corresponding tuples, which ensures that we do not fetch the same page twice while retrieving tuples using their rids.) We can now retrieve the necessary pages of Reserves to retrieve tuples, and check *bid=5* to obtain tuples that meet the condition *day < 8/9/94 ∧ bid=5 ∧ sid=3*.

12.3.3   Selections with Disjunction

Now let us consider the case that one of the conjuncts in the selection condition is a *disjunction of terms*. If even one of these terms requires a file scan because suitable indexes or sort orders are unavailable, testing this conjunct by itself (i.e., without taking advantage of other conjuncts) requires a file scan. For example, suppose that the only available indexes are a hash index on *rname* and a hash index on *sid*, and that the selection condition contains just the (disjunctive) conjunct *(day < 8/9/94 ∨ rname='Joe')*. We can retrieve tuples satisfying the condition *rname='Joe')* by using the index on *rname*. However, *day < 8/9/94* requires a file scan. So we might as well do a file scan and check the condition *rname='Joe'* for each retrieved tuple. Thus the most selective access path in this example is a file scan.

On the other hand, if the selection condition is *(day < 8/9/94 ∨ rname='Joe')* ∧ *sid=3*, the conjunct *sid=3* matches the index on *sid*. We can use this index to find qualifying tuples and apply *day < 8/9/94 ∨ rname='Joe'* to just these tuples. The best access path in this example is the index on *sid* with the primary selection *sid=3*.

Finally, if every term in a disjunction matches an index, we can retrieve candidate tuples using the indexes and then take the union. For example, if the selection condition is the conjunct *(day < 8/9/94 ∨ rname='Joe')* and we have B+ tree indexes on *day* and *rname*, we can retrieve all tuples such that *day < 8/9/94* using the index on *day*, retrieve all tuples such that *rname='Joe'* using the index on *rname*, and then take the union of the retrieved tuples. If all the matching indexes use Alternative (2) or (3) for data entries, a better approach is to take the union of rids and sort them before retrieving the qualifying data records. Thus in the example, we can find rids of tuples such that *day < 8/9/94* using the index on *day*, find rids of tuples such that *rname='Joe'* using the index on *rname*, take the union of these sets of rids and sort them by page number, and then retrieve the actual tuples from Reserves. This strategy can be thought of as a (complex) access path that matches the selection condition *(day < 8/9/94 ∨ rname='Joe')*.

We remark that most current systems do not handle selection conditions with disjunction efficiently, and concentrate on optimizing selections without disjunction.

12.4   THE PROJECTION OPERATION *

Consider the query shown in Figure 12.2. The optimizer translates this query into the relational algebra expression $\pi_{sid,bid}Reserves$. In general the projection operator is of the form $\pi_{attr1,attr2,...,attrm}(R)$.

```
SELECT DISTINCT R.sid, R.bid
FROM     Reserves R
```

Figure 12.2 Simple Projection Query

To implement projection, we have to do the following:

1. Remove unwanted attributes (i.e., those not specified in the projection).

2. Eliminate any duplicate tuples that are produced.

The second step is the difficult one. There are two basic algorithms, one based on sorting and one based on hashing. In terms of the general techniques listed in Section 12.1, both algorithms are instances of partitioning. While the technique of using an index to identify a subset of useful tuples is not applicable for projection, the sorting or hashing algorithms can be applied to data entries in an index, instead of to data records, under certain conditions described in Section 12.4.4.

12.4.1 Projection Based on Sorting

The algorithm based on sorting has the following steps (at least conceptually):

1. Scan R and produce a set of tuples that contain only the desired attributes.

2. Sort this set of tuples using the combination of all its attributes as the key for sorting.

3. Scan the sorted result, comparing adjacent tuples, and discard duplicates.

If we use temporary relations at each step, the first step costs M I/Os to scan R, where M is the number of pages of R, and T I/Os to write the temporary relation, where T is the number of pages of the temporary; T is $O(M)$. (The exact value of T depends on the number of fields that are retained and the sizes of these fields.) The second step costs $O(TlogT)$ (which is also $O(MlogM)$, of course). The final step costs T. The total cost is therefore $O(MlogM)$. The first and third steps are straightforward and relatively inexpensive. (As noted in the chapter on sorting, the complexity of sorting is really linear in practice, given typical dataset sizes and main memory sizes.)

Consider the projection on Reserves shown in Figure 12.2. We can scan Reserves at a cost of 1000 I/Os. If we assume that each tuple in the temporary relation created in the first step is 10 bytes long, the cost of writing this temporary relation is 250 I/Os. Suppose that we have 20 buffer pages. We can sort the temporary relation in two passes at a cost of $2 * 2 * 250 = 1000$ I/Os. The scan required in the third step costs an additional 250 I/Os. The total cost is 2500 I/Os.

This approach can be improved on by modifying the sorting algorithm to do projection with duplicate elimination. Recall the structure of the external sorting algorithm that we presented in Chapter 7. The very first pass (Pass 0) involves a scan of the records that are to be sorted to produce the initial set of (internally) sorted runs. Subsequently one or more passes merge runs. Two important modifications to the sorting algorithm adapt it for projection:

- We can project out unwanted attributes during the first pass (Pass 0) of sorting. If B buffer pages are available, we can read in B pages of R and write out $(T/M) * B$ *internally sorted* pages of the temporary relation. In fact, with a more aggressive implementation, we can write out approximately $2 * B$ internally sorted pages of the temporary relation on average. (The idea is similar to the refinement of external sorting that is discussed in Section 7.2.1.)

- We can eliminate duplicates during the merging passes. In fact, this modification will reduce the cost of the merging passes since fewer tuples are written out in each pass. (Most of the duplicates will be eliminated in the very first merging pass.)

Let us consider our example again. In the first pass we scan Reserves, at a cost of 1000 I/Os and write out 250 pages. With 20 buffer pages, the 250 pages are written out as seven internally sorted runs, each (except the last) about 40 pages long. In the second pass we read the runs, at a cost of 250 I/Os, and merge them. The total cost is 1500 I/Os, which is much lower than the cost of the first approach used to implement projection.

12.4.2   Projection Based on Hashing

If we have a fairly large number (say, B) of buffer pages relative to the number of pages of R, a hash-based approach is worth considering. There are two phases: *partitioning* and *duplicate elimination*.

In the *partitioning* phase we have one *input* buffer page and $B - 1$ *output* buffer pages. The relation R is read into the input buffer page, one page at a time. The input page is processed as follows: For each tuple, we project out the unwanted attributes and then apply a hash function $h1$ to the combination of all remaining attributes. The function $h1$ is chosen so that tuples are distributed uniformly to one of $B - 1$ partitions; there is one output page per partition. After the projection the tuple is written to the output buffer page that it is hashed to by $h1$.

At the end of the partitioning phase, we have $B - 1$ partitions, each of which contains a collection of tuples that share a common hash value (computed by applying $h1$ to all fields), and have only the desired fields. The partitioning phase is illustrated in Figure 12.3.

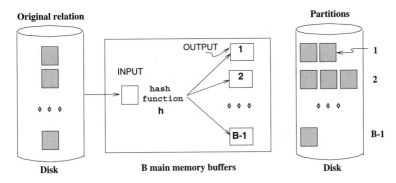

Figure 12.3   Partitioning Phase of Hash-Based Projection

Two tuples that belong to different partitions are guaranteed not to be duplicates because they have different hash values. Thus if two tuples are duplicates, they are in the same partition. In the *duplicate elimination* phase, we read in the $B - 1$ partitions one at a time to eliminate duplicates. The basic idea is to build an in-memory hash table as we process tuples in order to detect duplicates.

For each partition produced in the first phase:

1. Read in the partition one page at a time. Hash each tuple by applying hash function $h2$ ($\neq h1$!) to the combination of all fields and then insert it into an in-memory hash table. If a new tuple hashes to the same value as some existing tuple, compare the two to check whether the new tuple is a duplicate. Discard duplicates as they are detected.

2. After the entire partition has been read in, write the tuples in the hash table (which is free of duplicates) to the result file. Then clear the in-memory hash table to prepare for the next partition.

Note that $h2$ is intended to distribute the tuples in a partition across many buckets, in order to minimize *collisions* (two tuples having the same $h2$ values). Since all tuples in a given partition have the same $h1$ value, $h1$ cannot be the same as $h2$!

This hash-based projection strategy will not work well if the size of the hash table for a partition (produced in the partitioning phase) is greater than the number of available buffer pages B. One way to handle this *partition overflow* problem is to recursively apply the hash-based projection technique to eliminate the duplicates in each partition that overflows. That is, we divide an overflowing partition into subpartitions, then read each subpartition into memory to eliminate duplicates.

If we assume that $h1$ distributes the tuples with perfect uniformity and that the number of pages of tuples *after* the projection (but before duplicate elimination) is T, each partition contains $\frac{T}{B-1}$ pages. (Note that the number of partitions is $B-1$ because one of the buffer pages is used to read in the relation during the partitioning phase.) The size of a partition is therefore $\frac{T}{B-1}$, and the size of a hash table for a partition is $\frac{T}{B-1} * f$; the number of buffer pages B must be greater than this number to avoid partition overflow. This observation implies that we require approximately $B > \sqrt{f * T}$ buffer pages.

Now let us consider the cost of hash-based projection. In the partitioning phase, we read R, at a cost of M I/Os. We also write out the projected tuples, a total of T pages, where T is some fraction of M, depending on the fields that are projected out. The cost of this phase is therefore $M + T$ I/Os; the cost of hashing is a CPU cost, and we do not take it into account. In the duplicate elimination phase, we have to read in every partition. The total number of pages in all partitions is T. We also write out the in-memory hash table for each partition after duplicate elimination; this hash table is part of the result of the projection, and we ignore the cost of writing out result tuples, as usual. Thus the total cost of both phases is $M + 2T$. In our projection on Reserves (Figure 12.2), this cost is $1000 + 2 * 250 = 1500$ I/Os.

12.4.3 Sorting versus Hashing for Projections

The sorting-based approach is superior to hashing if we have many duplicates or if the distribution of (hash) values is very nonuniform. In this case, some partitions could be much larger than average, and a hash table for such a partition would not fit in memory during the duplicate elimination phase. Also, a useful side-effect of using the sorting-based approach is that the result is sorted. Further, since external sorting is required for a variety of reasons, most database systems have a sorting utility, which can be used to implement projection relatively easily. For these reasons, sorting is the standard approach for projection. And perhaps due to a simplistic use of the sorting utility, unwanted attribute removal and duplicate elimination are separate steps in many systems (i.e., the basic sorting algorithm is often used without the refinements that we outlined).

We observe that if we have $B > \sqrt{T}$ buffer pages, where T is the size of the projected relation before duplicate elimination, both approaches have the same I/O cost. Sorting takes two passes. In the first pass we read M pages of the original relation and write out T pages. In the second pass we read the T pages, and output the result of the projection. Using hashing, in the partitioning phase we read M pages and write T pages' worth of partitions. In the second phase, we read T pages, and output the result of the projection. Thus considerations such as CPU costs, desirability of sorted order in the result, and skew in the distribution of values drive the choice of projection method.

12.4.4 Use of Indexes for Projections

Neither the hashing nor the sorting approach utilizes any existing indexes. An existing index is useful if the key includes all the attributes that we wish to retain in the projection. In this case, we can simply retrieve the key values from the index—without ever accessing the actual relation—and apply our projection techniques to this (much smaller) set of pages. This technique is called an **index-only scan**. If we have an ordered (i.e., a tree) index whose search key includes the wanted attributes as a *prefix*, we can do even better: Just retrieve the data entries in order, discarding unwanted fields, and compare adjacent entries to check for duplicates. The index-only scan technique is discussed further in Section 13.10.

12.5 THE JOIN OPERATION

Consider the following query:

```
SELECT *
FROM    Reserves R, Sailors S
WHERE   R.sid = S.sid
```

This query can be expressed in relational algebra using the join operation: $R \bowtie S$. The *join* operation is one of the most useful operations in relational algebra and is the primary means of combining information from two or more relations.

Although a join can be defined as a cross-product followed by selections and projections, joins arise much more frequently in practice than plain cross-products. Further, the result of a cross-product is typically much larger than the result of a join, so it is very important to recognize joins and implement them without materializing the underlying cross-product (by applying the selections and projections as tuples in the cross-product are generated, and materializing only the subset of the cross-product that contributes to the join result). Joins have therefore received a lot of attention.

We will consider several alternative techniques for implementing joins. We begin by discussing two algorithms (simple nested loops and block nested loops) that essentially enumerate all tuples in the cross-product and discard tuples that do not meet the join conditions. These algorithms are instances of the simple iteration technique mentioned in Section 12.1.

The remaining join algorithms avoid enumerating the cross-product. They are instances of the indexing and partitioning techniques mentioned in Section 12.1. Intuitively, if the join condition consists of equalities, tuples in the two relations can be thought of as belonging to *partitions* such that only tuples in the same partition can join with each other; the tuples in a partition contain the same values in the join columns. Index nested loops join scans one of the relations and, for each tuple in it, uses an index on the (join columns of the) second relation to locate tuples in the same partition. Thus only a subset of the second relation is compared with a given tuple of the first relation, and the entire cross-product is not enumerated. The last two algorithms (sort-merge join and hash join) also take advantage of join conditions to partition tuples in the relations to be joined, and compare only tuples in the same partition while computing the join, but they do not rely on a pre-existing index. Instead, they either sort or hash the relations to be joined to achieve the partitioning.

We discuss the join of two relations R and S, with the join condition $R_i = S_j$, using positional notation. (If we have more complex join conditions, the basic idea behind each algorithm remains essentially the same. We discuss the details in Section 12.5.4.) We assume that there are M pages in R with p_R tuples per page, and N pages in S with p_S tuples per page. We will use R and S in our presentation of the algorithms, and the Reserves and Sailors relations for specific examples.

12.5.1   Nested Loops Join

The simplest join algorithm is a tuple-at-a-time nested loops evaluation.

> **foreach** tuple $r \in R$ **do**
>   **foreach** tuple $s \in S$ **do**
>   **if** $r_i == s_j$ **then** add $\langle r, s \rangle$ to result

Figure 12.4   Simple Nested Loops Join

We scan the *outer* relation R, and for each tuple $r \in R$, we scan the entire *inner* relation S. The cost of scanning R is M I/Os. We scan S a total of $p_R * M$ times, and each scan costs N I/Os. Thus the total cost is $M + p_R * M * N$.

Suppose that we choose R to be Reserves and S to be Sailors. The value of M is then 1000, p_R is 100, and N is 500. The cost of simple nested loops join is $1000 + 100 * 1000 * 500$ page I/Os (plus the cost of writing out the result; we remind the reader one last time that we will uniformly ignore this component of the cost). The cost is staggering: $1000 + (5 * 10^7)$ I/Os. Note that each I/O costs about 10ms on current hardware, which means that this join will take about 140 hours!

A simple refinement is to do this join *page-at-a-time*: For each page of R, we can retrieve each page of S and write out tuples $\langle r, s \rangle$ for all qualifying tuples $r \in R$-*page* and $s \in S$-*page*. This way, the cost is M to scan R, as before. However, S is scanned only M times, and so the total cost is $M + M * N$. Thus the page-at-a-time refinement gives us an improvement of a factor of p_R. In the example join of the Reserves and Sailors relations, the cost is reduced to $1000 + 1000 * 500 = 501,000$ I/Os, and would take about 1.4 hours. This dramatic improvement underscores the importance of page-oriented operations for minimizing disk I/O.

From these cost formulas a straightforward observation is that we should choose the outer relation R to be the smaller of the two relations ($R \bowtie B = B \bowtie R$, as long as we keep track of field names). This choice does not change the costs significantly, however. If we choose the smaller relation, Sailors, as the outer relation, the cost of the page-at-a-time algorithm is $500 + 500 * 1000 = 500,500$ I/Os, which is only marginally better than the cost of page-oriented simple nested loops join with Reserves as the outer relation.

Block Nested Loops Join

The simple nested loops join algorithm does not effectively utilize buffer pages. Suppose that we have enough memory to hold the smaller relation, say R, with at least two extra buffer pages left over. We can read in the smaller relation and use one of the extra buffer pages to scan the larger relation S. For each tuple $s \in S$, we check R and output a tuple $\langle r, s \rangle$ for qualifying tuples s (i.e., $r_i = s_j$). The second extra buffer page is used as an output buffer. Each relation is scanned just once, for a total I/O cost of $M + N$, which is optimal.

If enough memory is available, an important refinement is to build an in-memory *hash table* for the smaller relation R. The I/O cost is still $M + N$, but the CPU cost is typically much lower with the hash table refinement.

What if we do not have enough memory to hold the entire smaller relation? We can generalize the preceding idea by breaking the relation R into *blocks* that can fit into the available buffer pages and scanning all of S for each block of R. R is the *outer* relation, since it is scanned only once, and S is the *inner* relation, since it is scanned multiple times. If we have B buffer pages, we can read in $B - 2$ pages of the outer relation R and scan the inner relation S using one of the two remaining pages. We can write out tuples $\langle r, s \rangle$, where $r \in R$-*block* and $s \in S$-*page* and $r_i = s_j$, using the last buffer page for output.

An efficient way to find **matching** pairs of tuples (i.e., tuples satisfying the join condition $r_i = s_j$) is to build a main-memory hash table for the block of R. Because a hash table for a set of tuples takes a little more space than just the tuples themselves, building a hash table involves a trade-off: the effective block size of R, in terms of the number of tuples per block, is reduced. In practice building a hash table is well worth the effort. The block nested loops algorithm is described in Figure 12.5. Buffer usage in this algorithm is illustrated in Figure 12.6.

> **foreach** block of $B - 2$ pages of R do
>   **foreach** page of S do {
>   for all matching in-memory tuples $r \in R\text{-}block$ and $s \in S\text{-}page$,
>   add $\langle r, s \rangle$ to result
>   }

Figure 12.5   Block Nested Loops Join

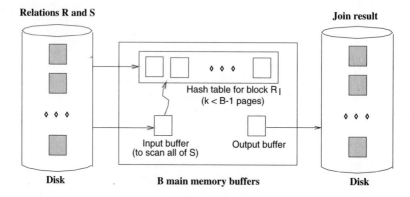

Figure 12.6   Buffer Usage in Block Nested Loops Join

The cost of this strategy is M I/Os for reading in R (which is scanned only once). S is scanned a total of $\lceil \frac{M}{B-2} \rceil$ times—ignoring the extra space required per page due to the in-memory hash table—and each scan costs N I/Os. The total cost is thus $M + N * \lceil \frac{M}{B-2} \rceil$.

Consider the join of the Reserves and Sailors relations. Let us choose Reserves to be the outer relation R and assume that we have enough buffers to hold an in-memory hash table for 100 pages of Reserves (with at least two additional buffers, of course). We have to scan Reserves, at a cost of 1000 I/Os. For each 100 page block of Reserves, we have to scan Sailors. Thus we perform 10 scans of Sailors, each costing 500 I/Os. The total cost is $1000 + 10 * 500 = 6000$ I/Os. If we had only enough buffers to hold 90 pages of Reserves, we would have to scan Sailors $\lceil 1000/90 \rceil = 12$ times, and the total cost would be $1000 + 12 * 500 = 7000$ I/Os.

Suppose we choose Sailors to be the outer relation R instead. Scanning Sailors costs 500 I/Os. We would scan Reserves $\lceil 500/100 \rceil = 5$ times. The total cost is $500 + 5 * 1000 = 5500$ I/Os. If instead we have only enough buffers for 90 pages of Sailors, we would scan Reserves a total of $\lceil 500/90 \rceil = 6$ times. The total cost in this case is $500 + 6 * 1000 = 6500$ I/Os. We note that block nested loops join takes a little over a minute on our running example, assuming 10ms per I/O as before.

Impact of Blocked Access

It is worth remarking that if we take into account the effect of blocked access to several pages, there is a fundamental change in the way we allocate buffers for blocked nested loops. Rather than using just one buffer page for the inner relation, the best approach is to split the buffer pool evenly between the two relations. This allocation results in more passes over the inner relation, leading to more page fetches. However, the time spent on *seeking* for pages is dramatically reduced.

The technique of double buffering (discussed in Chapter 7 in the context of sorting) can also be used, but we will not discuss it further.

Index Nested Loops Join

If there is an index on one of the relations on the join attribute(s), we can take advantage of the index by making the indexed relation be the inner relation. Suppose that we have a suitable index on S; Figure 12.7 describes the index nested loops join algorithm.

> **foreach** tuple $r \in R$ **do**
>   **foreach** tuple $s \in S$ **where** $r_i == s_j$
>   add $\langle r, s \rangle$ to result

Figure 12.7 Index Nested Loops Join

For each tuple $r \in R$, we use the index to retrieve matching tuples of S. Intuitively, we compare r only with tuples of S that are in the same *partition*, in that they have the same value in the join column. Unlike the other nested loops join algorithms, therefore, index nested loops join does not enumerate the cross-product of R and S. The cost of scanning R is M, as before. The cost of retrieving matching S

tuples depends on the kind of index and the number of matching tuples; for each R tuple, the cost is as follows:

1. If the index on S is a B+ tree index, the cost to find the appropriate leaf is typically 2 to 4 I/Os. If the index is a hash index, the cost to find the appropriate bucket is 1 or 2 I/Os.

2. Once we find the appropriate leaf or bucket, the cost of retrieving matching S tuples depends on whether the index is clustered. If it is, the cost per outer tuple $r \in R$ is typically just one more I/O. If it is not clustered, the cost could be one I/O per matching S-tuple (since each of these could be on a different page in the worst case).

As an example, suppose that we have a hash-based index using Alternative (2) on the *sid* attribute of Sailors and that it takes about 1.2 I/Os on average[2] to retrieve the appropriate page of the index. Since *sid* is a key for Sailors, we have at most one matching tuple. Indeed, *sid* in Reserves is a foreign key referring to Sailors, and therefore we have *exactly* one matching Sailors tuple for each Reserves tuple. Let us consider the cost of scanning Reserves and using the index to retrieve the matching Sailors tuple for each Reserves tuple. The cost of scanning Reserves is 1000. There are $100 * 1000$ tuples in Reserves. For each of these tuples, retrieving the index page containing the rid of the matching Sailors tuple costs 1.2 I/Os (on average); in addition, we have to retrieve the Sailors page containing the qualifying tuple. Thus we have $100,000 * (1 + 1.2)$ I/Os to retrieve matching Sailors tuples. The total cost is 221,000 I/Os.

As another example, suppose that we have a hash-based index using Alternative (2) on the *sid* attribute of Reserves. Now we can scan Sailors (500 I/Os) and for each tuple, use the index to retrieve matching Reserves tuples. We have a total of $80 * 500$ Sailors tuples, and each tuple could match with either zero or more Reserves tuples; a sailor may have no reservations, or several. For each Sailors tuple, we can retrieve the index page containing the rids of matching Reserves tuples (assuming that we have at most one such index page, which is a reasonable guess) in 1.2 I/Os on average. The total cost thus far is $500 + 40,000 * 1.2 = 48,500$ I/Os.

In addition, we have the cost of retrieving matching Reserves tuples. Since we have 100,000 reservations for 40,000 Sailors, assuming a uniform distribution we can estimate that each Sailors tuple matches with 2.5 Reserves tuples on average. If the index on Reserves is clustered, and these matching tuples are typically on the same page of Reserves for a given sailor, the cost of retrieving them is just one I/O per Sailor tuple, which adds up to 40,000 extra I/Os. If the index is not

---

[2]This is a typical cost for hash-based indexes.

clustered, each matching Reserves tuple may well be on a different page, leading to a total of $2.5 * 40,000$ I/Os for retrieving qualifying tuples. Thus the total cost can vary from $48,500 + 40,000 = 88,500$ to $48,500 + 100,000 = 148,500$ I/Os. Assuming 10ms per I/O, this would take about 15 to 25 minutes.

Thus even with an unclustered index, if the number of matching inner tuples for each outer tuple is small (on average), the cost of index nested loops join is likely to be much less than the cost of a simple nested loops join. So much so that some systems build an index on the inner relation at run-time if one does not already exist, and do index nested loops join using the newly created index.

12.5.2 Sort-Merge Join *

The basic idea behind the **sort-merge join** algorithm is to *sort* both relations on the join attribute, and to then look for qualifying tuples $r \in R$ and $s \in S$ by essentially *merging* the two relations. The sorting step groups all tuples with the same value in the join column together, and thus makes it easy to identify partitions, or groups of tuples with the same value in the join column. We exploit this partitioning by comparing the R tuples in a partition with only the S tuples in the same partition (rather than with all S tuples), thereby avoiding enumeration of the cross-product of R and S. (This partition-based approach only works for equality join conditions.)

The external sorting algorithm discussed in Chapter 7 can be used to do the sorting, and of course, if a relation is already sorted on the join attribute, we need not sort it again. We now consider the merging step in detail: We scan the relations R and S, looking for qualifying tuples (i.e., tuples Tr in R and Ts in S such that $Tr_i = Ts_j$). The two scans start at the first tuple in each relation. We advance the scan of R as long as the current R tuple is less than the current S tuple (with respect to the values in the join attribute). Similarly, we then advance the scan of S as long as the current S tuple is less than the current R tuple. We alternate between such advances until we find an R tuple Tr and a S tuple Ts with $Tr_i = Ts_j$.

When we find tuples Tr and Ts such that $Tr_i = Ts_j$, we need to output the joined tuple. In fact, we could have several R tuples and several S tuples with the same value in the join attributes as the current tuples Tr and Ts. We refer to these tuples as the *current R partition* and the *current S partition*. For each tuple r in the current R partition, we scan all tuples s in the current S partition and output the joined tuple $\langle r, s \rangle$. We then resume scanning R and S, beginning with the first tuples that follow the partitions of tuples that we just processed.

The sort-merge join algorithm is shown in Figure 12.8. We assign only tuple values to the variables Tr, Ts and Gs and use the special value eof to denote that there are no more tuples in the relation being scanned. Subscripts identify fields, for example, Tr_i denotes the ith field of tuple Tr. If Tr has the value eof, any comparison involving Tr_i is defined to evaluate to `false`.

proc $smjoin(R, S, `R_i = S'_j)$

if R not sorted on attribute i, sort it;
if S not sorted on attribute j, sort it;

Tr = first tuple in R;   // ranges over R
Ts = first tuple in S;   // ranges over S
Gs = first tuple in S;   // start of current S-partition

while $Tr \neq eof$ and $Gs \neq eof$ do {

    while $Tr \neq eof$ and $Tr_i < Gs_j$ do
      Tr = next tuple in R after Tr;   // continue scan of R

    while $Gs \neq eof$ and $Tr_i > Gs_j$ do
      Gs = next tuple in S after Gs // continue scan of S

    while $Tr \neq eof$ and $Tr_i == Gs_j$ do {   // process current R partition
      $Ts = Gs$;   // reset S partition scan
      while $Ts \neq eof$ and $Ts_j == Tr_i$ do {   // process current R tuple
        add $\langle Tr, Ts \rangle$ to result;   // output joined tuples
        Ts = next tuple in S after Ts;}   // advance S partition scan
      Tr = next tuple in R after Tr;   // advance scan of R
    }   // done with current R partition

    $Gs = Ts$;   // initialize search for next S partition

}

Figure 12.8   Sort-Merge Join

We illustrate sort-merge join on the Sailors and Reserves instances shown in Figures 12.9 and 12.10, with the join condition being equality on the *sid* attributes.

These two relations are already sorted, and the merging phase of sort-merge join begins with the scans positioned at the first tuple of each relation instance. We advance the scan of Sailors, since its *sid* value, now 22, is less than the *sid* value

sid	sname	rating	age
22	dustin	7	45.0
28	yuppy	9	35.0
31	lubber	8	55.5
36	lubber	6	36.0
44	guppy	5	35.0
58	rusty	10	35.0

sid	bid	day	rname
28	103	12/04/96	guppy
28	103	11/03/96	yuppy
31	101	10/10/96	dustin
31	102	10/12/96	lubber
31	101	10/11/96	lubber
58	103	11/12/96	dustin

Figure 12.9 An Instance of Sailors

Figure 12.10 An Instance of Reserves

of Reserves, which is now 28. The second Sailors tuple has $sid = 28$, which is equal to the sid value of the current Reserves tuple. Therefore, we now output a result tuple for each pair of tuples, one from Sailors and one from Reserves, in the current partition (i.e., with $sid = 28$). Since we have just one Sailors tuple with $sid = 28$, and two such Reserves tuples, we write two result tuples. After this step, we position the scan of Sailors at the first tuple after the partition with $sid = 28$, which has $sid = 31$. Similarly, we position the scan of Reserves at the first tuple with $sid = 31$. Since these two tuples have the same sid values, we have found the next matching partition, and we must write out the result tuples generated from this partition (there are three such tuples). After this, the Sailors scan is positioned at the tuple with $sid = 36$, and the Reserves scan is positioned at the tuple with $sid = 58$. The rest of the merge phase proceeds similarly.

In general, we have to scan a partition of tuples in the second relation as often as the number of tuples in the corresponding partition in the first relation. The first relation in the example, Sailors, has just one tuple in each partition. (This is not happenstance, but a consequence of the fact that sid is a key—this example is a key–foreign key join.) In contrast, suppose that the join condition is changed to be *sname=rname*. Now, both relations contain more than one tuple in the partition with *sname=rname='lubber'*. The tuples with *rname='lubber'* in Reserves have to be scanned for each Sailors tuple with *sname='lubber'*.

Cost of Sort-Merge Join

The cost of sorting R is $O(MlogM)$ and the cost of sorting S is $O(NlogN)$. The cost of the merging phase is $M + N$ if no S partition is scanned multiple times (or the necessary pages are found in the buffer after the first pass). This approach is especially attractive if at least one relation is already sorted on the join attribute or has a clustered index on the join attribute.

Consider the join of the relations Reserves and Sailors. Assuming that we have 100 buffer pages (roughly the same number that we assumed were available in our discussion of block nested loops join), we can sort Reserves in just two passes. The first pass produces 10 internally sorted runs of 100 pages each. The second pass merges these 10 runs to produce the sorted relation. Because we read and write Reserves in each pass, the sorting cost is $2*2*1000 = 4000$ I/Os. Similarly, we can sort Sailors in two passes, at a cost of $2*2*500 = 2000$ I/Os. In addition, the second phase of the sort-merge join algorithm requires an additional scan of both relations. Thus the total cost is $4000+2000+1000+500 = 7500$ I/Os, which is similar to the cost of the block nested loops algorithm.

Suppose that we have only 35 buffer pages. We can still sort both Reserves and Sailors in two passes, and the cost of sort-merge join remains at 7500 I/Os. However, the cost of block nested loops join is more than 15,000 I/Os. On the other hand, if we have 300 buffer pages, the cost of sort-merge join remains at 7500 I/Os, whereas the cost of block nested loops join drops to 2500 I/Os. (We leave it to the reader to verify these numbers.)

We note that multiple scans of a partition of the second relation are potentially expensive. In our example, if the number of Reserves tuples in a repeatedly scanned partition is small (say, just a few pages), the likelihood of finding the entire partition in the buffer pool on repeated scans is very high, and the I/O cost remains essentially the same as for a single scan. However, if there are many pages of Reserves tuples in a given partition, the first page of such a partition may no longer be in the buffer pool when we request it a second time (after first scanning all pages in the partition; remember that each page is unpinned as the scan moves past it). In this case, the I/O cost could be as high as the number of pages in the Reserves partition times the number of tuples in the corresponding Sailors partition!

In the worst-case scenario, the merging phase could require us to read all of the second relation for each *tuple* in the first relation, and the number of I/Os is $O(M*N)$ I/Os! (This scenario occurs when all tuples in both relations contain the same value in the join attribute; it is extremely unlikely.)

In practice the I/O cost of the merge phase is typically just a single scan of each relation. A single scan can be guaranteed if at least one of the relations involved has no duplicates in the join attribute; this is the case, fortunately, for key–foreign key joins, which are very common.

An Important Refinement

We have assumed that the two relations are sorted first and then merged in a distinct pass. It is possible to improve sort-merge join by combining the merging phase of sorting with the merging phase of the join. First we produce sorted runs of size B for both R and S. If $B > \sqrt{L}$, where L is the size of the larger relation, the number of runs per relation is less than $\sqrt{L}$. Suppose that the number of buffers available for the merging phase is at least $2\sqrt{L}$, that is, more than the total number of runs for R and S. We allocate one buffer page for each run of R *and* one for each run of S. We then merge the runs of R (to generate the sorted version of R), merge the runs of S, and merge the resulting R and S streams as they are generated; we apply the join condition as we merge the R and S streams, and discard tuples in the cross-product that do not meet the join condition.

This idea has the drawback that it increases the number of buffers required to $2\sqrt{L}$. However, by using the technique discussed in Section 7.2.1 we can produce sorted runs of size approximately $2 * B$ for both R and S. Consequently we have fewer than $\sqrt{L}/2$ runs of each relation, given the assumption that $B > \sqrt{L}$. Thus the total number of runs is less than $\sqrt{L}$, that is, less than B, and we can combine the merging phases with no need for additional buffers.

This approach allows us to perform sort-merge join at the cost of reading and writing R and S in the first pass, and of reading R and S in the second pass. The total cost is thus $3 * (M + N)$. In our example the cost goes down from 7500 to 4500 I/Os.

Blocked Access and Double-Buffering

We remark that the blocked I/O and double-buffering optimizations, discussed in Chapter 7 in the context of sorting, can be used to speed up the merging pass, as well as the sorting of the relations to be joined; we will not discuss these refinements.

12.5.3   Hash Join *

The **hash join** algorithm, like sort-merge join, identifies partitions in R and S and subsequently compares tuples in an R partition only with tuples in the corresponding S partition for testing equality join conditions. Unlike sort-merge join, hash join uses hashing to identify partitions, rather than sorting.

The idea is to hash *both* relations on the join attribute, using the *same* hash function h. If we hash each relation (hopefully uniformly) into k partitions, we are assured that R tuples in partition i can join only with S tuples in the same partition i. This observation can be used to good effect: We can read in a (complete) partition of the smaller relation R, and scan just the corresponding partition of S for matches. We never need to consider these R and S tuples again. Thus once R and S are partitioned, we can perform the join by reading in R and

S just once, provided that enough memory is available to hold all the tuples in any given partition of R.

In practice we build an in-memory hash table for the R partition, using a hash function $h2$ that is different from h (since $h2$ is intended to distribute tuples in a partition based on h!), in order to reduce CPU costs. We need enough memory to hold this hash table, which is a little larger than the R partition itself.

The hash join algorithm is presented in Figure 12.11. (We note that there are several variants on this idea; the version that we present is called *Grace hash join* in the literature.)

```
// Partition R into k partitions
foreach tuple r ∈ R do
     read r and add it to buffer page h(rᵢ);            // flushed as page fills

// Partition S into k partitions
foreach tuple s ∈ S do
     read s and add it to buffer page h(sⱼ);            // flushed as page fills

// Probing Phase
for l = 1,...,k do {

     // Build in-memory hash table for Rₗ, using h2
     foreach tuple r ∈ partition Rₗ do
          read r and insert into hash table using h2(rᵢ) ;

     // Scan Sₗ and probe for matching Rₗ tuples
     foreach tuple s ∈ partition Sₗ do {
          read s and probe table using h2(sⱼ);
          for matching R tuples r, output ⟨r, s⟩ };

     clear hash table to prepare for next partition;
     }
```

Figure 12.11   Hash Join

The **partitioning** (also called **building**) phase of hash join is similar to the partitioning in hash-based projection, and is illustrated in Figure 12.3. The **probing** (sometimes called **matching**) phase is illustrated in Figure 12.12.

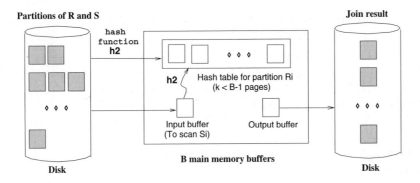

Figure 12.12   Probing Phase of Hash Join

Consider the cost of the hash join algorithm. In the partitioning phase we have to scan both R and S once and write them both out once. The cost of this phase is therefore $2(M + N)$. In the second phase we scan each partition once, assuming no partition overflows, at a cost of $M + N$ I/Os. The total cost is therefore $3(M + N)$, given our assumption that each partition fits into memory in the second phase. On our example join of Reserves and Sailors, the total cost is $3 * (500 + 1000) = 4500$ I/Os, and assuming 10ms per I/O, hash join takes under a minute. Compare this with simple nested loops join, which took about 140 *hours*—this difference underscores the importance of using a good join algorithm.

Memory Requirements and Overflow Handling

To increase the chances of a given partition fitting into available memory in the probing phase, we must minimize the size of a partition by maximizing the number of partitions. In the partitioning phase, to partition R (similarly, S) into k partitions, we need at least k output buffers and one input buffer. Thus, given B buffer pages, the maximum number is of partitions is $k = B - 1$. Assuming that partitions are equal in size, this means that the size of each R partition is $\frac{M}{B-1}$ (as usual, M is the number of pages of R). The number of pages in the (in-memory) hash table built during the probing phase for a partition is thus $\frac{f*M}{B-1}$, where f is a *fudge factor* used to capture the (small) increase in size between the partition and a hash table for the partition.

During the probing phase, in addition to the hash table for the R partition, we require a buffer page for scanning the S partition, and an output buffer. Therefore, we require $B > \frac{f*M}{B-1} + 2$. *Therefore, we need approximately $B > \sqrt{f * M}$ for hash join to perform well.*

Since the partitions of R are likely to be close in size, but not identical, the largest partition will be somewhat larger than $\frac{M}{B-1}$, and the number of buffer pages required is a little more than $B > \sqrt{f * M}$. There is also the risk that if the hash function h does not partition R uniformly, the hash table for one or more R partitions may not fit in memory during the probing phase. This situation can significantly degrade performance.

One way to handle this *partition overflow* problem is to recursively apply the hash join technique to the join of the overflowing R partition with the corresponding S partition. That is, we first divide the R and S partitions into subpartitions. Then we join the subpartitions pairwise. All subpartitions of R will probably fit into memory; if not, we apply the hash join technique recursively.

Utilizing Extra Memory: Hybrid Hash Join

The minimum amount of memory required for hash join is $B > \sqrt{f * M}$. If more memory is available, a variant of hash join called **hybrid hash join** offers better performance. Suppose that $B > f * (M/k)$, for some integer k. This means that if we divide R into k partitions of size M/k, an in-memory hash table can be built for each partition. To partition R (similarly, S) into k partitions, we need k output buffers and one input buffer, that is, $k + 1$ pages. This leaves us with $B - (k + 1)$ extra pages during the partitioning phase.

Suppose that $B - (k + 1) > f * (M/k)$. That is, we have enough extra memory during the partitioning phase to hold an in-memory hash table for a partition of R. The idea behind hybrid hash join is to build an in-memory hash table for the first partition of R during the partitioning phase, which means that we don't write this partition to disk. Similarly, while partitioning S, rather than write out the tuples in the first partition of S, we can directly probe the in-memory table for the first R partition and write out the results. At the end of the partitioning phase, we have therefore completed the join of the first partitions of R and S, in addition to partitioning the two relations; in the probing phase, we join the remaining partitions as in hash join.

The savings realized through hybrid hash join is that we avoid writing the first partitions of R and S to disk during the partitioning phase, and reading them in again during the probing phase. Consider our example, with 500 pages in R and 1000 pages in S. If we have $B = 300$ pages, we can easily build an in-memory hash table for the first R partition while partitioning R into two partitions. During the partitioning phase of R, we scan R and write out one partition; the cost is $500 + 250$ if we assume that the partitions are of equal size. We then scan S and write out one partition; the cost is $1000 + 500$. In the probing phase, we scan the second partition of R and of S; the cost is $250 + 500$. The total cost is $750 + 1500 + 750 = 3000$. In contrast, the cost of hash join is 4500.

If we have enough memory to hold an in-memory hash table for all of R, the savings are even greater. For example, if $B > f * M + 2$, that is, $k = 1$, we can build an in-memory hash table for all of R. This means that we only read R once, to build this hash table, and read S once, to probe the R hash table. The cost is $500 + 1000 = 1500$.

Hash Join versus Block Nested Loops Join

While presenting the block nested loops join algorithm, we briefly discussed the idea of building an in-memory hash table for the inner relation. We now compare this (more CPU-efficient) version of block nested loops join with hybrid hash join.

If a hash table for the entire smaller relation fits in memory, the two algorithms are identical. If both relations are large relative to the available buffer size, we require several passes over one of the relations in block nested loops join; hash join is a more effective application of hashing techniques in this case. The I/O that is saved in this case by using the hash join algorithm in comparison to block nested loops join is illustrated in Figure 12.13. In the latter, we read in all of S for each block of R; the I/O cost corresponds to the whole rectangle. In the hash join algorithm, for each block of R, we read only the corresponding block of S; the I/O cost corresponds to the the shaded areas in the figure. This difference in I/O due to scans of S is highlighted in the figure.

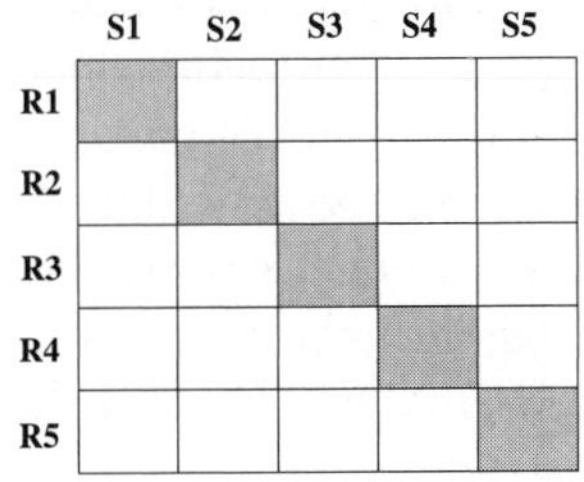

Figure 12.13   Hash Join versus Block Nested Loops for Large Relations

We note that this picture is rather simplistic. It does not capture the cost of scanning R in block nested loops join, and the cost of the partitioning phase in hash join, and focuses on the cost of the probing phase.

Hash Join versus Sort-Merge Join

Let us compare hash join with sort-merge join. If we have $B > \sqrt{M}$ buffer pages, where M is the number of pages in the *smaller* relation, and we assume uniform partitioning, the cost of hash join is $3(M + N)$ I/Os. If we have $B > \sqrt{N}$ buffer pages, where N is the number of pages in the *larger* relation, the cost of sort-merge join is also $3(M + N)$, as discussed in Section 12.5.2. A choice between these techniques is therefore governed by other factors, notably:

- If the partitions in hash join are not uniformly sized, hash join could cost more. Sort-merge join is less sensitive to such data skew.

- If the available number of buffers falls between $\sqrt{M}$ and $\sqrt{N}$, hash join costs less than sort-merge join, since we need only enough memory to hold partitions of the smaller relation, whereas in sort-merge join the memory requirements depend on the size of the larger relation. The larger the difference in size between the two relations, the more important this factor becomes.

- Additional considerations include the fact that the result is sorted in sort-merge join.

12.5.4   General Join Conditions *

We have discussed several join algorithms for the case of a simple equality join condition. Other important cases include a join condition that involves equalities over several attributes and inequality conditions. To illustrate the case of several equalities, we consider the join of Reserves R and Sailors S with the join condition $R.sid=S.sid \wedge R.rname=S.sname$:

- For index nested loops join, we can build an index on Reserves on the combination of fields $\langle R.sid, R.rname \rangle$ and treat Reserves as the inner relation. We can also use an existing index on this combination of fields, or on $R.sid$, or on $R.rname$. (Similar remarks hold for the choice of Sailors as the inner relation, of course.)

- For sort-merge join, we sort Reserves on the combination of fields $\langle sid, rname \rangle$ and Sailors on the combination of fields $\langle sid, sname \rangle$. Similarly, for hash join, we partition on these combinations of fields.

- The other join algorithms that we discussed are essentially unaffected.

If we have an inequality comparison, for example, a join of Reserves R and Sailors S with the join condition $R.rname < S.sname$:

- For index nested loops join, we require a B+ tree index.

- Hash join and sort-merge join are not applicable.

- The other join algorithms that we discussed are essentially unaffected.

Of course, regardless of the algorithm, the number of qualifying tuples in an inequality join is likely to be much higher than in an equality join.

We conclude our presentation of joins with the observation that there is no join algorithm that is uniformly superior to the others. The choice of a good algorithm depends on the sizes of the relations being joined, available access methods, and the size of the buffer pool. This choice can have a considerable impact on performance because the difference between a good and a bad algorithm for a given join can be enormous.

12.6 THE SET OPERATIONS *

We now briefly consider the implementation of the set operations $R \cap S$, $R \times S$, $R \cup S$, and $R - S$. From an implementation standpoint, intersection and cross-product can be seen as special cases of join (with equality on all fields as the join condition for intersection, and with no join condition for cross-product). Therefore, we will not discuss them further.

The main point to address in the implementation of union is the elimination of duplicates. Set-difference can also be implemented using a variation of the techniques for duplicate elimination. (Union and difference queries on a single relation can be thought of as a selection query with a complex selection condition. The techniques discussed in Section 12.3 are applicable for such queries.)

There are two implementation algorithms for union and set-difference, again based on sorting and hashing. Both algorithms are instances of the partitioning technique mentioned in Section 12.1.

12.6.1 Sorting for Union and Difference

To implement $R \cup S$:

1. Sort R using the combination of all fields; similarly, sort S.

2. Scan the sorted R and S in parallel and merge them, eliminating duplicates.

As a refinement, we can produce sorted runs of R and S and merge these runs in parallel. (This refinement is similar to the one discussed in detail for projection.) The implementation of $R - S$ is similar. During the merging pass, we write only tuples of R to the result, after checking that they do not appear in S.

12.6.2 Hashing for Union and Difference

To implement $R \cup S$:

1. Partition R and S using a hash function h.

2. Process each partition l as follows:

   - Build an in-memory hash table (using hash function $h2 \neq h$) for S_l.

   - Scan R_l. For each tuple, probe the hash table for S_l. If the tuple is in the hash table, discard it; otherwise, add it to the table.

   - Write out the hash table and then clear it to prepare for the next partition.

To implement $R - S$, we proceed similarly. The difference is in the processing of a partition. After building an in-memory hash table for S_l, we scan R_l. For each R_l tuple, we probe the hash table; if the tuple is not in the table, we write it to the result.

12.7 AGGREGATE OPERATIONS *

The SQL query shown in Figure 12.14 involves an *aggregate operation*, AVG. The other aggregate operations supported in SQL-92 are MIN, MAX, SUM, and COUNT.

```
SELECT  AVG(S.age)
FROM    Sailors S
```

Figure 12.14 Simple Aggregation Query

The basic algorithm for aggregate operators consists of scanning the entire Sailors relation, and maintaining some *running information* about the scanned tuples; the details are straightforward. The running information for each aggregate operation is shown in Figure 12.15. The cost of this operation is the cost of scanning all Sailors tuples.

Aggregate operators can also be used in combination with a GROUP BY clause. If we add GROUP BY *rating* to the query in Figure 12.14, we would have to compute the average age of sailors for each *rating* group. For queries with grouping, there are two good evaluation algorithms that do not rely on an existing index; one algorithms is based on sorting and the other is based on hashing. Both algorithms are instances of the partitioning technique mentioned in Section 12.1.

The *sorting* approach is simple—we sort the relation on the grouping attribute (*rating*) and then scan it again to compute the result of the aggregate operation

Aggregate Operation	Running Information
SUM	*Total* of the values retrieved
AVG	⟨*Total, Count*⟩ of the values retrieved
COUNT	*Count* of values retrieved
MIN	Smallest value retrieved
MAX	Largest value retrieved

Figure 12.15   Running Information for Aggregate Operations

for each group. The second step is similar to the way we implement aggregate operations without grouping, with the only additional point being that we have to watch for group boundaries. (It is possible to refine the approach by doing aggregation as part of the sorting step; we leave this as an exercise for the reader.) The I/O cost of this approach is just the cost of the sorting algorithm.

In the *hashing* approach we build a hash table (in main memory if possible) on the grouping attribute. The entries have the form ⟨*grouping-value, running-info*⟩. The running information depends on the aggregate operation, as per the discussion of aggregate operations without grouping. As we scan the relation, for each tuple, we probe the hash table to find the entry for the group to which the tuple belongs and update the running information. When the hash table is complete, the entry for a grouping value can be used to compute the answer tuple for the corresponding group in the obvious way. If the hash table fits in memory, which is likely because each entry is quite small and there is only one entry per grouping value, the cost of the hashing approach is $O(M)$, where M is the size of the relation.

If the relation is so large that the hash table does not fit in-memory, we can partition the relation using a hash function h on *grouping-value*. Since all tuples with a given grouping-value are in the same partition, we can then process each partition independently by building an in-memory hash table for the tuples in it.

12.7.1   Implementing Aggregation by Using an Index

The technique of using an index to select a subset of useful tuples is not applicable for aggregation. However, under certain conditions we can evaluate aggregate operations efficiently by using the data entries in an index instead of the data records:

- If the search key for the index includes all the attributes needed for the aggregation query, we can apply the techniques described earlier in this section to the set of data entries in the index, rather than to the collection of data records, and thereby avoid fetching data records.

■ If the `GROUP BY` clause attribute list forms a prefix of the index search key
   and the index is a tree index, we can retrieve data entries (and data records,
   if necessary) in the order required for the grouping operation, and thereby
   avoid a sorting step.

A given index may support one or both of these techniques; both are examples
of *index-only* plans. We discuss the use of indexes for queries with grouping and
aggregation in the context of queries that also include selections and projections
in Section 13.10.

12.8 THE IMPACT OF BUFFERING

In implementations of relational operators, effective use of the buffer pool is very
important, and we explicitly considered the size of the buffer pool in determining
algorithm parameters for several of the algorithms that we discussed. There are
three main points to note:

1. If several operations execute concurrently, they share the buffer pool. This
   effectively reduces the number of buffer pages available for each operation.

2. If tuples are accessed using an index, especially an unclustered index, the
   likelihood of finding a page in the buffer pool if it is requested multiple times
   depends (in a rather unpredictable way, unfortunately) on the size of the
   buffer pool and the replacement policy. Further, if tuples are accessed using
   an unclustered index, each tuple retrieved is likely to require us to bring in
   a new page; thus the buffer pool fills up quickly, leading to a high level of
   paging activity.

3. If an operation has a *pattern* of repeated page accesses, we can increase
   the likelihood of finding a page in memory by a good choice of replacement
   policy or by *reserving* a sufficient number of buffers for the operation (if the
   buffer manager provides this capability). Several examples of such patterns
   of repeated access follow:

   ■ Consider simple nested loops join. For each tuple of the outer relation,
      we repeatedly scan all pages in the inner relation. If we have enough
      buffer pages to hold the entire inner relation, the replacement policy is
      irrelevant. Otherwise, the replacement policy becomes critical. With
      LRU we will *never* find a page when it is requested, because it is paged
      out. With MRU we obtain the best buffer utilization—the first $B - 2$
      pages of the inner relation always remain in the buffer pool. (B is the
      number of buffer pages; we use one page for scanning the outer relation,[3]
      and always replace the last page used for scanning the inner relation.)

---

[3] Think about the sequence of pins and unpins used to achieve this.

- In block nested loops join, for each block of the outer relation, we scan the entire inner relation. However, since only one unpinned page is available for the scan of the inner relation, the replacement policy makes no difference.

- In index nested loops join, for each tuple of the outer relation, we use the index to find matching inner tuples. If several tuples of the outer relation have the same value in the join attribute, there is a repeated pattern of access on the inner relation; we can maximize the repetition by sorting the outer relation on the join attributes.

12.9 SUMMARY

This chapter covered the implementation of individual relational operators. The alternatives for selection are scanning all tuples or fetching tuples by using indexes that match a selection condition. Projection can be implemented by scanning all tuples or scanning the data entries in some index whose search key includes all desired fields. An important issue in implementing projection is how duplicate tuples are eliminated from the answer. Sorting or hashing can be used for this purpose.

There are several algorithms for computing joins. The nested loops algorithms compare every tuple in the first relation with every tuple in the second relation. Block nested loops join carries out this comparison in a way that minimizes the number of disk accesses. Index nested loops join refines this idea by fetching only matching tuples from the second relation for each tuple of the first relation, by using an index. Sort-merge join and hash join partition the tuples in the two relations and only compare tuples within the same partition.

The same techniques that underlie the algorithms for selection, projection, and join can be applied to evaluate set-operations such as union, intersection, and set-difference. The idea of partitioning also allows us to compute aggregate operations efficiently. We note that the cost of a relational operator depends on the amount of main memory available, which is influenced by the number of operators being evaluated concurrently, and by how the buffer pool is managed.

EXERCISES

Exercise 12.1 Briefly answer the following questions:

1. Consider the three basic techniques, *iteration*, *indexing*, and *partitioning*; and the relational algebra operators *selection*, *projection*, and *join*. For each technique–operator pair, describe an algorithm based on the technique for evaluating the operator.

2. Define the term *most selective access path for a query.*

3. Describe *conjunctive normal form*, and explain why it is important in the context of relational query evaluation.

4. When does a general selection condition *match* an index? What is a *primary term* in a selection condition with respect to a given index?

5. How does hybrid hash join improve upon the basic hash join algorthm?

6. Discuss the pros and cons of hash join, sort-merge join and block nested loops join.

7. If the join condition is not equality, can you use sort-merge join? Can you use hash join? Can you use index nested loops join? Can you use block nested loops join?

8. Describe how to evaluate a grouping query with aggregation operator MAX using a sorting-based approach.

9. Suppose that you are building a DBMS and want to add a new aggregate operator called SECOND LARGEST, which is a variation of the MAX operator. Describe how you would implement it.

10. Give an example of how buffer replacement policies can affect the performance of a join algorithm.

Exercise 12.2 Consider a relation R(a,b,c,d,e) containing 5,000,000 records, where each data page of the relation holds 10 records. R is organized as a sorted file with dense secondary indexes. Assume that $R.a$ is a candidate key for R, with values lying in the range 0 to 4,999,999, and that R is stored in $R.a$ order. For each of the following relational algebra queries, state which of the following three approaches is most likely to be the cheapest:

- Access the sorted file for R directly.

- Use a (clustered) B+ tree index on attribute $R.a$.

- Use a linear hashed index on attribute $R.a$.

1. $\sigma_{a<50,000}(R)$

2. $\sigma_{a=50,000}(R)$

3. $\sigma_{a>50,000 \land a<50,010}(R)$

4. $\sigma_{a\neq50,000}(R)$

Exercise 12.3 Consider processing the following SQL projection query:

SELECT DISTINCT E.title, E.ename FROM Executives E

You are given the following information:

Executives has attributes *ename*, *title*, *dname*, and *address*; all are string fields of the same length.
The *ename* attribute is a candidate key.
The relation contains 10,000 pages.
There are 10 buffer pages.

Consider the optimized version of the sorting-based projection algorithm: The initial sorting pass reads the input relation and creates sorted runs of tuples containing only attributes *ename* and *title*. Subsequent merging passes eliminate duplicates while merging the initial runs to obtain a single sorted result (as opposed to doing a separate pass to eliminate duplicates from a sorted result containing duplicates).

1. How many sorted runs are produced in the first pass? What is the average length of these runs? (Assume that memory is utilized well and that any available optimization to increase run size is used.) What is the I/O cost of this sorting pass?

2. How many additional merge passes will be required to compute the final result of the projection query? What is the I/O cost of these additional passes?

3. (a) Suppose that a clustered B+ tree index on *title* is available. Is this index likely to offer a cheaper alternative to sorting? Would your answer change if the index were unclustered? Would your answer change if the index were a hash index?

   (b) Suppose that a clustered B+ tree index on *ename* is available. Is this index likely to offer a cheaper alternative to sorting? Would your answer change if the index were unclustered? Would your answer change if the index were a hash index?

   (c) Suppose that a clustered B+ tree index on ⟨*ename, title*⟩ is available. Is this index likely to offer a cheaper alternative to sorting? Would your answer change if the index were unclustered? Would your answer change if the index were a hash index?

4. Suppose that the query is as follows:

   SELECT E.title, E.ename **FROM** Executives E

   That is, you are not required to do duplicate elimination. How would your answers to the previous questions change?

Exercise 12.4 Consider the join $R\bowtie_{R.a=S.b}S$, given the following information about the relations to be joined. The cost metric is the number of page I/Os unless otherwise noted, and the cost of writing out the result should be uniformly ignored.

Relation R contains 10,000 tuples and has 10 tuples per page.
Relation S contains 2000 tuples and also has 10 tuples per page.
Attribute *b* of relation S is the primary key for S.
Both relations are stored as simple heap files.
Neither relation has any indexes built on it.
52 buffer pages are available.

1. What is the cost of joining R and S using page-oriented simple nested loops join? What is the minimum number of buffer pages required for this cost to remain unchanged?

2. What is the cost of joining R and S using block nested loops join? What is the minimum number of buffer pages required for this cost to remain unchanged?

3. What is the cost of joining R and S using sort-merge join? What is the minimum number of buffer pages required for this cost to remain unchanged?

4. What is the cost of joining R and S using hash join? What is the minimum number of buffer pages required for this cost to remain unchanged?

5. What would be the lowest possible I/O cost for joining R and S using *any* join algorithm, and how much buffer space would be needed to achieve this cost? Explain briefly.

6. How many tuples will the join of R and S produce, at most, and how many pages would be required to store the result of the join back on disk?

7. Would your answers to any of the previous questions in this exercise change if you are told that $R.a$ is a foreign key that refers to $S.b$?

Exercise 12.5 Consider the join of R and S described in Exercise 12.4.

1. With 52 buffer pages, if unclustered B+ indexes existed on $R.a$ and $S.b$, would either provide a cheaper alternative for performing the join (using index nested loops join) than block nested loops join? Explain.

   (a) Would your answer change if only five buffer pages were available?

   (b) Would your answer change if S contained only 10 tuples instead of 2000 tuples?

2. With 52 buffer pages, if *clustered* B+ indexes existed on $R.a$ and $S.b$, would either provide a cheaper alternative for performing the join (using the *index nested loops* algorithm) than a block nested loops join? Explain.

   (a) Would your answer change if only five buffer pages were available?

   (b) Would your answer change if S contained only 10 tuples instead of 2000 tuples?

3. If only 15 buffers were available, what would be the cost of sort-merge join? What would be the cost of hash join?

4. If the size of S were increased to also be 10,000 tuples, but only 15 buffer pages were available, what would be the cost of sort-merge join? What would be the cost of hash join?

5. If the size of S were increased to also be 10,000 tuples, and 52 buffer pages were available, what would be the cost of sort-merge join? What would be the cost of hash join?

Exercise 12.6 Answer each of the questions—if some question is inapplicable, explain why—in Exercise 12.4 again, but using the following information about R and S:

Relation R contains 200,000 tuples and has 20 tuples per page.
Relation S contains 4,000,000 tuples and also has 20 tuples per page.
Attribute a of relation R is the primary key for R.
Each tuple of R joins with exactly 20 tuples of S.
1002 buffer pages are available.

Exercise 12.7 We described variations of the join operation called *outer joins* in Section 9.5.4. One approach to implementing an outer join operation is to first evaluate the corresponding (inner) join, and then add additional tuples padded with *null* values to the result in accordance with the semantics of the given outer join operator. However, this requires us to compare the result of the inner join with the input relations to determine the additional tuples to be added. The cost of this comparison can be avoided by modifying the join algorithm to add these extra tuples to the result while input tuples are processed during the join. Consider the following join algorithms: *block nested loops join, index nested loop join, sort-merge join,* and *hash join.* Describe how you would modify each of these algorithms to compute the following operations on the Sailors and Reserves tables discussed in this chapter:

1. Sailors `NATURAL LEFT OUTER JOIN` Reserves

2. Sailors `NATURAL RIGHT OUTER JOIN` Reserves

3. Sailors `NATURAL FULL OUTER JOIN` Reserves

PROJECT-BASED EXERCISES

Exercise 12.8 (*Note to instructors: Additional details must be provided if this question is assigned; see Appendix A.*) Implement the various join algorithms described in this chapter in Minibase. (As additional exercises, you may want to implement selected algorithms for the other operators as well.)

BIBLIOGRAPHIC NOTES

The implementation techniques used for relational operators in System R are discussed in [79]. The implementation techniques used in PRTV, which utilized relational algebra transformations and a form of multiple-query optimization, are discussed in [244]. The techniques used for aggregate operations in Ingres are described in [181]. [221] is an excellent survey of algorithms for implementing relational operators and is recommended for further reading.

Hash-based techniques are investigated (and compared with sort-based techniques) in [82], [162] and [490]. Duplicate elimination was discussed in [77]. [198] discusses secondary storage access patterns arising in join implementations. Parallel algorithms for implementing relational operations are discussed in [77, 122, 160, 164, 169, 209, 381].

RELATIONAL
QUERY OPTIMIZATION

> This very remarkable man
> Commends a most practical plan:
> You can do what you want
> If you don't think you can't,
> So don't think you can't if you can.
>
> —Charles Inge

Consider a simple selection query asking for all reservations made by sailor Joe. As we saw in the previous chapter, there are many ways to evaluate even this simple query, each of which is superior in certain situations, and the DBMS must consider these alternatives and choose the one with the least estimated cost. Queries that consist of several operations have many more evaluation options, and finding a good plan represents a significant challenge.

A more detailed view of the query optimization and execution layer in the DBMS architecture presented in Section 1.6 is shown in Figure 13.1. Queries are parsed and then presented to a **query optimizer**, which is responsibe for identifying an efficient execution plan for evaluating the query. The optimizer generates alternative plans and chooses the plan with the least estimated cost. To estimate the cost of a plan, the optimizer uses information in the system catalogs.

This chapter covers query optimization in detail. Section 13.1 lays the foundation for our discussion. It introduces query evaluation plans, which are composed of relational operators; considers alternative techniques for passing results between relational operators in a plan; and describes an *iterator* interface that makes it easy to combine code for individual relational operators into an executable plan. Section 13.2 shows how SQL queries are converted into units called *blocks*, and how blocks are translated into (extended) relational algebra expressions; the central task of an optimizer is to find a good plan for evaluating such expressions. Since the costs of alternative plans for a given query can vary by orders of magnitude, the choice of query evaluation plan can have a dramatic impact on execution time. We illustrate the differences in cost between alternative plans through a detailed motivating example in Section 13.3.

Optimizing a relational algebra expression involves two basic steps:

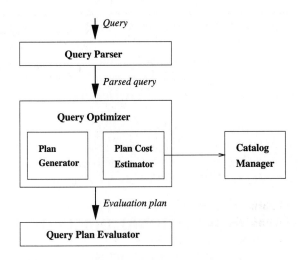

Figure 13.1 Query Parsing, Optimization, and Execution

- Enumerating alternative plans for evaluating the expression; typically, an optimizer considers a subset of all possible plans because the number of possible plans is very large.

- Estimating the cost of each enumerated plan, and choosing the plan with the least estimated cost.

To estimate the cost of a plan, we must estimate the cost of individual relational operators in the plan, using information about properties (e.g., size, sort order) of the argument relations, and we must estimate the properties of the result of an operator (in order to be able to compute the cost of any operator that uses this result as input). We discussed the cost of individual relational operators in Chapter 12. We discuss how to use system statistics to estimate the properties of the result of a relational operation, in particular result sizes, in Section 13.4.

After discussing how to estimate the cost of a given plan, we describe the space of plans considered by a typical relational query optimizer in Sections 13.5 and 13.6. Exploring all possible plans is prohibitively expensive because of the large number of alternative plans for even relatively simple queries. Thus optimizers have to somehow narrow down the space of alternative plans that they consider.

We discuss how nested SQL queries are handled in Section 13.7. This chapter concentrates on an exhaustive, dynamic-programming approach to query optimization. Although this approach is currently the most widely used, it cannot satisfactorily handle complex queries. We conclude with a short discussion of other approaches to query optimization in Section 13.8.

We will consider a number of example queries using the following schema:

Sailors(*sid:* `integer`, *sname:* `string`, *rating:* `integer`, *age:* `real`) 50 bytes
Boats(*bid:* `integer`, *bname:* `string`, *color:* `string`)
Reserves(*sid:* `integer`, *bid:* `integer`, *day:* `dates`, *rname:* `string`) 40 bytes

As in Chapter 12, we will assume that each tuple of Reserves is 40 bytes long, that a page can hold 100 Reserves tuples, and that we have 1000 pages of such tuples. Similarly, we will assume that each tuple of Sailors is 50 bytes long, that a page can hold 80 Sailors tuples, and that we have 500 pages of such tuples.

13.1 OVERVIEW OF RELATIONAL QUERY OPTIMIZATION

The goal of a query optimizer is to find a good evaluation plan for a given query. In this section we lay the foundation for our discussion of query optimization by introducing evaluation plans (Section 13.1.1) and the technique of pipelining results between two or more operators in a plan (Section 13.1.2). We also explain how a uniform *iterator* interface is used to combine code implementing algorithms for individual operators into an executable plan in Section 13.1.3. We end this section by highlighting some important design choices made in typical relational optimizers, which can be traced back to IBM's System R optimizer.

13.1.1 Query Evaluation Plans

A **query evaluation plan** (or simply **plan**) consists of an extended relational algebra tree, with additional annotations at each node indicating the access methods to use for each relation and the implementation method to use for each relational operator.

Consider the following SQL query:

```
SELECT  S.sname
FROM    Reserves R, Sailors S
WHERE   R.sid = S.sid
        AND R.bid = 100 AND S.rating > 5
```

This query can be expressed in relational algebra as follows:

$$\pi_{sname}(\sigma_{bid=100 \wedge rating>5}(Reserves \bowtie_{sid=sid} Sailors))$$

This expression is shown in the form of a tree in Figure 13.2. The algebra expression partially specifies how to evaluate the query—we first compute the natural

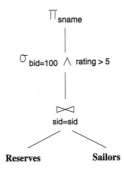

Figure 13.2   Query Expressed as a Relational Algebra Tree

join of Reserves and Sailors, then perform the selections, and finally project the *sname* field.

To obtain a fully specified evaluation plan, we must decide on an implementation for each of the algebra operations involved. For example, we can use a page-oriented simple nested loops join with Reserves as the outer relation and apply selections and projections to each tuple in the result of the join as it is produced; the result of the join prior to the selections and projections is never stored in its entirety. This query evaluation plan is shown in Figure 13.3.

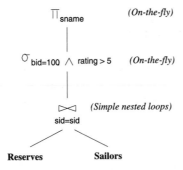

Figure 13.3   Query Evaluation Plan for Sample Query

In drawing the query evaluation plan, we have used the convention that the *outer relation* is the *left child* of the join operator. We will adopt this convention henceforth.

13.1.2   Pipelined Evaluation

When a query is composed of several operators, the result of one operator is sometimes **pipelined** to another operator without creating a temporary relation

to hold the intermediate result; the plan in Figure 13.3 pipelines the output of
the join of Sailors and Reserves into the selections and projections that follow.
Pipelining the output of an operator into the next operator saves the cost of
writing out the intermediate result and reading it back in, and the cost savings
can be significant. If the output of an operator is saved in a temporary relation
for processing by the next operator, we say that the tuples are **materialized**;
pipelined evaluation has lower overhead costs than materialization and is chosen
whenever the algorithm for the operator evaluation permits it.

There are many opportunities for pipelining in typical query plans, even simple
plans that only involve selections. Consider a selection query in which only part
of the selection condition matches an index. We can think of such a query as
containing *two* instances of the selection operator: The first contains the primary,
or matching, part of the original selection condition, and the second contains
the rest of the selection condition. We can evaluate such a query by applying
the primary selection and writing the result to a temporary relation, and then
applying the second selection to the temporary relation. In contrast, a pipelined
evaluation consists of applying the second selection to each tuple in the result of
the primary selection as it is produced, and adding tuples that qualify to the final
result. When the input relation to a unary operator (e.g., selection or projection)
is pipelined, we sometimes say that the operator is applied **on-the-fly**.

As a second and more general example, consider a join of the form $(A \bowtie B) \bowtie C$,
shown in Figure 13.4 as a tree of join operations.

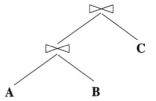

Figure 13.4   A Query Tree Illustrating Pipelining

Both joins can be evaluated in pipelined fashion using some version of nested
loops join. Conceptually, the evaluation is initiated from the root, and the node
joining A and B produces tuples as and when they are requested by its parent
node. When the root node gets a page of tuples from its left child (the outer
relation), all the matching inner tuples are retrieved (using either an index or
a scan) and joined with matching outer tuples; the current page of outer tuples
is then discarded. A request is then made to the left child for the next page of
tuples, and the process is repeated. Pipelined evaluation is thus a *control strategy*
governing the rate at which different joins in the plan proceed. It has the great

virtue of not writing the result of intermediate joins to a temporary file because the results are produced, consumed, and discarded one page at a time.

13.1.3 The Iterator Interface for Operators and Access Methods

A query evaluation plan is a tree of relational operators, and is executed by calling the operators in some (possibly interleaved) order. Each operator has one or more inputs and an output, which are also nodes in the plan, and tuples must be passed between operators according to the plan's tree structure.

In order to simplify the code that is responsible for coordinating the execution of a plan, the relational operators that form the nodes of a plan tree (which is to be evaluated using pipelining) typically support a uniform **iterator** interface, hiding the internal implementation details of each operator. The iterator interface for an operator includes the functions *open*, *get_next*, and *close*. The *open* function initializes the state of the iterator by allocating buffers for its inputs and output, and is also used to pass in arguments such as selection conditions that modify the behavior of the operator. The code for the *get_next* function calls the *get_next* function on each input node, and calls operator-specific code to process the input tuples. The output tuples generated by the processing are placed in the output buffer of the operator, and the state of the iterator is updated to keep track of how much input has been consumed. When all output tuples have been produced through repeated calls to *get_next*, the *close* function is called (by the code that initiated execution of this operator) to deallocate state information.

The iterator interface supports pipelining of results naturally; the decision to pipeline or materialize input tuples is encapsulated in the operator-specific code that processes input tuples. If the algorithm implemented for the operator allows input tuples to be processed completely when they are received, input tuples are not materialized and the evaluation is pipelined. If the algorithm repeatedly examines input tuples, they are materialized. This decision, like other details of the operator's implementation, is hidden by the iterator interface for the operator.

The iterator interface is also used to encapsulate access methods such as B+ trees and hash-based indexes; externally, access methods can be viewed simply as operators that produce a stream of output tuples. In this case, the *open* function can be used to pass the selection conditions that match the access path.

13.1.4 The System R Optimizer

Current relational query optimizers have been greatly influenced by choices made in the design of IBM's System R query optimizer. Important design choices in the System R optimizer include:

1. The use of *statistics* about the database instance to estimate the cost of a query evaluation plan.

2. A decision to consider only plans with binary joins in which the inner relation is a base relation (i.e., not a temporary relation). This heuristic reduces the (potentially very large) number of alternative plans that must be considered.

3. A decision to focus optimization on the class of SQL queries without nesting, and to treat nested queries in a relatively ad hoc way.

4. A decision not to perform duplicate elimination for projections (except as a final step in the query evaluation when required by a `DISTINCT` clause).

5. A model of cost that accounted for CPU costs as well as I/O costs.

Our discussion of optimization reflects these design choices, except for the last point in the preceding list, which we ignore in order to retain our simple cost model based on the number of page I/Os.

13.2 TRANSLATING SQL QUERIES INTO ALGEBRA

SQL queries are optimized by decomposing them into a collection of smaller units called *blocks*. A typical relational query optimizer concentrates on optimizing a single block at a time. In this section we describe how a query is decomposed into blocks, and how the optimization of a single block can be understood in terms of plans composed of relational algebra operators.

13.2.1 Decomposition of a Query into Blocks

When a user submits an SQL query, the query is parsed into a collection of query blocks and then passed on to the query optimizer. A **query block** (or simply **block**) is an SQL query with no nesting and exactly one `SELECT` clause and one `FROM` clause; and at most one `WHERE` clause, `GROUP BY` clause, and `HAVING` clause. The `WHERE` clause is assumed to be in conjunctive normal form, as per the discussion in Section 12.3. We will use the following query as a running example:

For each sailor with the highest rating (over all sailors), and at least two reservations for red boats, find the sailor id and the earliest date on which the sailor has a reservation for a red boat.

The SQL version of this query is shown in Figure 13.5. This query has two query

SELECT	S.sid, MIN (R.day)
FROM	Sailors S, Reserves R, Boats B
WHERE	S.sid = R.sid AND R.bid = B.bid AND B.color = 'red' AND
	S.rating = (SELECT MAX (S2.rating)
	FROM Sailors S2)
GROUP BY	S.sid
HAVING	COUNT (*) > 2

Figure 13.5 Sailors Reserving Red Boats

blocks. The **nested block** is:

SELECT MAX	(S2.rating)
FROM	Sailors S2

The nested block computes the highest sailor rating. The **outer block** is shown in Figure 13.6. Every SQL query can be decomposed into a collection of query blocks without nesting.

SELECT	S.sid, MIN (R.day)
FROM	Sailors S, Reserves R, Boats B
WHERE	S.sid = R.sid AND R.bid = B.bid AND B.color = 'red' AND
	S.rating = *Reference to nested block*
GROUP BY	S.sid
HAVING	COUNT (*) > 2

Figure 13.6 Outer Block of Red Boats Query

The optimizer examines the **system catalogs** to retrieve information about the types and lengths of fields, statistics about the referenced relations, and the access paths (indexes) available for them. The optimizer then considers each query block and chooses a query evaluation plan for that block. We will mostly focus on optimizing a single query block and defer a discussion of nested queries to Section 13.7.

13.2.2 A Query Block as a Relational Algebra Expression

The first step in optimizing a query block is to express it as a relational algebra expression. For uniformity, let us assume that GROUP BY and HAVING are also operators in the extended algebra used for plans, and that aggregate operations are allowed to appear in the argument list of the projection operator. The meaning of the operators should be clear from our discussion of SQL. The SQL query of Figure 13.6 can be expressed in the extended algebra as:

$$\pi_{S.sid,MIN(R.day)}($$
$$HAVING_{COUNT(*)>2}($$
$$GROUP\ \ BY_{S.sid}($$
$$\sigma_{S.sid=R.sid \wedge R.bid=B.bid \wedge B.color='red' \wedge S.rating=value\_from\_nested\_block}($$
$$Sailors \times Reserves \times Boats))))$$

For brevity, we've used S, R and B (rather than Sailors, Reserves and Boats) to prefix attributes. Intuitively, the selection is applied to the cross-product of the three relations. Then the qualifying tuples are grouped by $S.sid$, and the HAVING clause condition is used to discard some groups. For each remaining group, a result tuple containing the attributes (and count) mentioned in the projection list is generated. Finally, the result tuples are ordered by S.sname. This algebra expression is a faithful summary of the semantics of an SQL query, which we discussed in Chapter 9.

Every SQL query block can be expressed as an extended algebra expression having this form. The SELECT clause corresponds to the projection operator, the WHERE clause corresponds to the selection operator, the FROM clause corresponds to the cross-product of relations, and the remaining clauses are mapped to corresponding operators in a straightforward manner.

The alternative plans examined by a typical relational query optimizer can be understood by recognizing that *a query is essentially treated as a $\sigma\pi\times$ algebra expression*, with the remaining operations (if any, in a given query) carried out on the result of the $\sigma\pi\times$ expression. The $\sigma\pi\times$ expression for the query in Figure 13.6 is:

$$\pi_{S.sid,R.day}($$
$$\sigma_{S.sid=R.sid \wedge R.bid=B.bid \wedge B.color='red' \wedge S.rating=value\_from\_nested\_block}($$
$$Sailors \times Reserves \times Boats))$$

To make sure that the GROUP BY and HAVING operations in the query can be carried out, the attributes mentioned in these clauses are added to the projection list. Further, since aggregate operations in the SELECT clause, such as the MIN*(R.day)* operation in our example, are computed after first computing the $\sigma\pi\times$ part of the query, aggregate expressions in the projection list are replaced by the names of the attributes that they refer to. Thus the optimization of the $\sigma\pi\times$ part of the query essentially ignores these aggregate operations.

The optimizer finds the best plan for the $\sigma\pi\times$ expression obtained in this manner from a query. This plan is evaluated and the resulting tuples are then sorted (alternatively, hashed) to implement the `GROUP BY` clause. The `HAVING` clause is applied to eliminate some groups, and aggregate expressions in the `SELECT` clause are computed for each remaining group. This procedure is summarized in the following extended algebra expression:

$$\pi_{S.sid,MIN(R.day)} ($$
$$HAVING_{COUNT(*)>2} ($$
$$GROUP \ BY_{S.sid} ($$
$$\pi_{S.sid,S.sname,R.day} ($$
$$\sigma_{S.sid=R.sid \wedge R.bid=B.bid \wedge B.color='red' \wedge S.rating=value\_from\_nested\_block} ($$
$$Sailors \times Reserves \times Boats)))))$$

Some optimizations are possible if the `FROM` clause contains just one relation and the relation has some indexes that can be used to carry out the grouping operation. We discuss this situation further in Section 13.6.1.

To a first approximation therefore, the alternative plans examined by a typical optimizer can be understood in terms of the plans considered for $\sigma\pi\times$ queries. An optimizer enumerates plans by applying several equivalences between relational algebra expressions, which we present in Section 13.5. We discuss the space of plans enumerated by an optimizer in Section 13.6.

13.3 ALTERNATIVE PLANS: A MOTIVATING EXAMPLE

Consider the example query from Section 13.1. Let us consider the cost of evaluating the plan shown in Figure 13.3. The cost of the join is $1000 + 1000 * 500 = 501,000$ page I/Os. The selections and the projection are done on-the-fly, and are do not incur additional I/Os. Following the cost convention described in Section 12.1.2, we ignore the cost of writing out the final result. The total cost of this plan is therefore 501,000 page I/Os. This plan is admittedly naive; however, it is possible to be even more naive by treating the join as a cross-product followed by a selection!

We now consider several alternative plans for evaluating this query. Each alternative improves on the original plan in a different way and introduces some optimization ideas that are examined in more detail in the rest of this chapter.

13.3.1 Pushing Selections

A join is a relatively expensive operation, and a good heuristic is to reduce the sizes of the relations to be joined as much as possible. One approach is to apply selections early; if a selection operator appears after a join operator, it is worth examining whether the selection can be 'pushed' ahead of the join. As an example, the selection *bid=100* involves only the attributes of Reserves and can be applied to Reserves *before* the join. Similarly, the selection *rating*> 5 involves only attributes of Sailors, and can be applied to Sailors before the join. Let us suppose that the selections are performed using a simple file scan, that the result of each selection is written to a temporary relation on disk, and that the temporary relations are then joined using sort-merge join. The resulting query evaluation plan is shown in Figure 13.7.

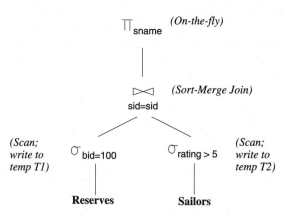

Figure 13.7 A Second Query Evaluation Plan

Let us assume that five buffer pages are available and estimate the cost of this query evaluation plan. (It is likely that more buffer pages will be available in practice. We have chosen a small number simply for illustration purposes in this example.) The cost of applying *bid=100* to Reserves is the cost of scanning Reserves (1000 pages) plus the cost of writing the result to a temporary relation, say T1. Note that the cost of writing the temporary relation cannot be ignored— we can only ignore the cost of writing out the *final* result of the query, which is the only component of the cost that is the same for all plans, according to the convention described in Section 12.1.2. To estimate the size of T1, we require some additional information. For example, if we assume that the maximum number of reservations of a given boat is one (note that this assumption is *not* consistent with the key field information for Reserves!), just one tuple appears in the result. Alternatively, if we know that there are 100 boats, we can assume that reservations are spread out uniformly across all boats and estimate the number of pages in T1 to be 10. For concreteness, let us assume that the number of pages in T1 is indeed 10.

The cost of applying *rating*> 5 to Sailors is the cost of scanning Sailors (500 pages) plus the cost of writing out the result to a temporary relation, say T2. If we assume that ratings are uniformly distributed over the range 1 to 10, we can approximately estimate the size of T2 as 250 pages.

To do a sort-merge join of T1 and T2, let us assume that a straightforward implementation is used in which the two relations are first completely sorted and then merged. Since five buffer pages are available, we can sort T1 (which has 10 pages) in two passes. Two runs of five pages each are produced in the first pass and these are merged in the second pass. In each pass, we read and write 10 pages; thus the cost of sorting T1 is $2 * 2 * 10 = 40$ page I/Os. We need three passes to sort T2, which has 250 pages. The cost is $2 * 3 * 250 = 1500$ page I/Os. To merge the sorted versions of T1 and T2, we need to scan these relations, and the cost of this step is $10 + 250 = 260$. The final projection is done on-the-fly, and by convention we ignore the cost of writing the final result.

The total cost of the plan shown in Figure 13.7 is the sum of the cost of the selection ($1000 + 10 + 500 + 250 = 1760$) and the cost of the join ($40 + 1500 + 260 = 1800$), that is, 3560 page I/Os.

Sort-merge join is one of several join methods. We may be able to reduce the cost of this plan by choosing a different join method. As an alternative, suppose that we used block nested loops join instead of sort-merge join. Using T1 as the outer relation, for every three-page block of T1, we scan all of T2; thus we scan T2 four times. The cost of the join is therefore the cost of scanning T1 (10) plus the cost of scanning T2 ($4 * 250 = 1000$). The cost of the plan is now $1760 + 1010 = 2770$ page I/Os.

A further refinement is to push the projection, just like we pushed the selections past the join. Observe that only the *sid* attribute of T1 and the *sid* and *sname* attributes of T2 are really required. As we scan Reserves and Sailors to do the selections, we could also eliminate unwanted columns. This on-the-fly projection reduces the sizes of the temporary relations T1 and T2. The reduction in the size of T1 is substantial because only an integer field is retained. In fact, T1 will now fit within three buffer pages, and we can perform block nested loops join with a single scan of T2. The cost of the join step thus drops to under 250 page I/Os, and the total cost of the plan drops to about 2000 I/Os.

13.3.2 Using Indexes

If indexes are available on the Reserves and Sailors relations, even better query evaluation plans may be available. For example, suppose that we have a clustered static hash index on the *bid* field of Reserves and another hash index on the *sid* field of Sailors. We can then use the query evaluation plan shown in Figure 13.8.

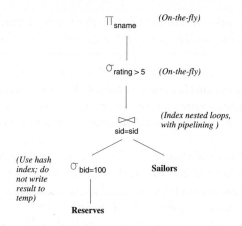

Figure 13.8   A Query Evaluation Plan Using Indexes

The selection $bid=100$ is performed on Reserves by using the hash index on bid to retrieve only matching tuples. As before, if we know that 100 boats are available and assume that reservations are spread out uniformly across all boats, we can estimate the number of selected tuples to be $100,000/100 = 1000$. Since the index on bid is clustered, these 1000 tuples appear consecutively within the same bucket; thus the cost is 10 page I/Os.

For each selected tuple, we retrieve matching Sailors tuples using the hash index on the sid field; selected Reserves tuples are not materialized and the join is pipelined. For each tuple in the result of the join, we perform the selection $rating>5$ and the projection of $sname$ on-the-fly. There are several important points to note here:

1. Since the result of the selection on Reserves is not materialized, the optimization of projecting out fields that are not needed subsequently is unnecessary (and is not used in the plan shown in Figure 13.8).

2. The join field sid is a key for Sailors. Therefore, at most one Sailors tuple matches a given Reserves tuple. The cost of retrieving this matching tuple depends on whether the directory of the hash index on the sid column of Sailors fits in memory and on the presence of overflow pages (if any). However, the cost does *not* depend on whether this index is clustered because there is at most one matching Sailors tuple and requests for Sailors tuples are made in random order by sid (because Reserves tuples are considered in random order by sid). For a good dynamic hash index, 1.2 page I/Os (on average) is a good estimate of the cost for retrieving a matching Sailors tuple.

3. We have chosen not to push the selection $rating>5$ ahead of the join, and there is an important reason for this decision. If we performed the selection before the join, the selection would involve scanning Sailors, assuming that

no index is available on the *rating* field of Sailors. Further, whether or not such an index is available, once we apply such a selection, we do not have an index on the *sid* field of the result of the selection (unless we choose to build such an index solely for the sake of the subsequent join). Thus pushing selections ahead of joins is a good heuristic, but not always the best strategy. Typically, as in this example, the existence of useful indexes is the reason that a selection is *not* pushed. (Otherwise, selections are pushed.)

Let us estimate the cost of this plan. The selection of Reserves tuples costs 10 I/Os, as we saw earlier. There are 1000 such tuples, and for each the cost of finding the matching Reserves tuple is 1.2 I/Os, on average. The cost of this step (the join) is therefore 1200 I/Os. All remaining selections and projections are performed on-the-fly. Thus the total cost of the plan is 1210 I/Os.

As noted earlier, this plan does not utilize clustering of the Sailors index. The plan can be further refined if the index on the *sid* field of Sailors is clustered. Suppose we materialize the result of performing the selection *bid*=100 on Reserves and sort this temporary relation. This relation contains 10 pages. Selecting the tuples costs 10 page I/Os (as before), writing out the result to a temporary relation costs another 10 I/Os, and with five buffer pages, sorting this temporary costs $2 * 2 * 10 = 40$ I/Os. (The cost of this step is reduced if we push the projection on *sid*. The *sid* column of materialized Reserves tuples requires only three pages and can be sorted in memory with five buffer pages.) The selected Reserves tuples can now be retrieved in order by *sid*. If a sailor has reserved the same boat many times, all corresponding Reserves tuples are now retrieved consecutively; the matching Sailors tuple will be found in the buffer pool on all but the first request for it. This improved plan also demonstrates that pipelining is not always the best strategy.

The combination of pushing selections and using indexes that is illustrated by this plan is very powerful. If the selections on the outer relation identify a single tuple, the join operation may become trivial, and the performance gains with respect to the naive plan are even more dramatic. The following variant of our example query illustrates this situation:

```
SELECT  S.sname
FROM    Reserves R, Sailors S
WHERE   R.sid = S.sid
        AND R.bid = 100 AND S.rating > 5
        AND R.day = '8/9/94'
```

A slight variant of the plan shown in Figure 13.8, designed to answer this query, is shown in Figure 13.9. The selection *day='8/9/94'* is applied on-the-fly to the result of the selection *bid=100* on the Reserves relation.

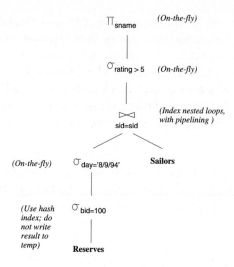

Figure 13.9   A Query Evaluation Plan for the Second Example

Suppose that *bid* and *day* form a key for Reserves. (Note that this assumption differs from the schema presented earlier in this chapter.) Let us estimate the cost of the plan shown in Figure 13.9. The selection *bid=100* costs 10 page I/Os, as before, and the additional selection *day='8/9/94'* is applied on-the-fly, eliminating all but (at most) one Reserves tuple. There is at most one matching Sailors tuple, and this is retrieved in 1.2 I/Os (an average number!). The selection on *rating* and the projection on *sname* are then applied on-the-fly at no additional cost. The total cost is thus about 11 I/Os. In contrast, if we modify the naive plan to perform the additional selection on *day* along with the selection *bid=100*, the cost remains at 501,000 I/Os.

13.4 ESTIMATING THE COST OF A PLAN

For each enumerated plan, we have to estimate its cost. There are two parts to estimating the cost of an evaluation plan for a query block:

1. For each node in the tree, we must *estimate the cost* of performing the corresponding operation. Costs are affected significantly by whether pipelining is used or temporary relations are created to pass the output of an operator to its parent.

2. For each node in the tree, we must *estimate the size of the result,* and whether it is sorted. This result is the input for the operation that corresponds to the parent of the current node, and the size and sort order will in turn affect the estimation of size, cost and sort order for the parent.

We discussed the cost of implementation techniques for relational operators in Chapter 12. As we saw there, estimating costs requires knowledge of various parameters of the input relations, such as the number of pages and available indexes. Such statistics are maintained in the DBMS's system catalogs. In this section we describe the statistics maintained by a typical DBMS, and discuss how result sizes are estimated. As in Chapter 12, we will use the number of page I/Os as the metric of cost, and ignore issues such as blocked access, for the sake of simplicity.

The estimates used by a DBMS for result sizes and costs are at best approximations to actual sizes and costs. It is therefore unrealistic to expect an optimizer to find the very best plan; it is more important to avoid the worst plans and to find a good plan.

13.4.1 Statistics Maintained by a DBMS *

Statistics about relations and indexes are stored in the system catalogs and updated periodically (*not* every time the underlying relations are modified). The following information is commonly stored:

- **Cardinality:** The number of tuples *NTuples(R)* for each relation *R*.

- **Size:** The number of pages *NPages(R)* for each relation *R*.

- **Index Cardinality:** Number of distinct key values *NKeys(I)* for each index *I*.

- **Index Size:** The number of pages *INPages(I)* for each index *I*. (For a B+ tree index *I*, we will take *INPages* to be the number of leaf pages.)

- **Index Height:** The number of non leaf levels *IHeight(I)* for each tree index *I*.

- **Index Range:** The minimum present key value *ILow(I)* and the maximum present key value *IHigh(I)* for each index *I*.

We will assume that the database architecture presented in Chapter 3 is used. In particular, in our earlier discussion of files, we assumed that each file of records was implemented as a separate file of pages. Other file organizations are possible, of course. For example, in System R a page file can contain pages that store records from more than one record file. (System R uses different names for these abstractions and in fact uses somewhat different abstractions.) If such a file organization is used, additional statistics must be maintained, such as the fraction of pages in a file that contain records from a given collection of records.

13.4.2   Estimating Result Sizes *

We now discuss how a typical optimizer estimates the size of the result computed by an operator on given inputs. Size estimation plays an important role in cost estimation as well because the output of one operator can be the input to another operator, and the cost of an operator depends on the size of its inputs.

Consider a query block of the form:

> SELECT   *attribute list*
> FROM   *relation list*
> WHERE $term_1 \wedge term_2 \wedge \ldots \wedge term_n$

The maximum number of tuples in the result of this query (without duplicate elimination) is the product of the cardinalities of the relations in the FROM clause. Every term in the WHERE clause, however, eliminates some of these potential result tuples. We can model the effect of the WHERE clause on the result size by associating a **reduction factor** with each term. The actual size of the result can be estimated as the maximum size times the product of the reduction factors for the terms in the WHERE clause. Of course, this estimate reflects the—unrealistic, but simplifying—assumption that the conditions tested by each term are statistically independent.

We now consider how reduction factors can be computed for different kinds of terms in the WHERE clause by using the statistics available in the catalogs. As we will see, these estimates for reduction factors are at best approximations that rely on assumptions such as uniform distribution of values and independent distribution of values in different columns. In recent years more sophisticated techniques based on sampling or on storing more detailed statistics (e.g., histograms of the values in a column) have been proposed and are finding their way into commercial systems. We follow the approximations used in System R, however, for concreteness; reasonable approximations often suffice in practice to differentiate good plans from bad ones.

- *column = value*: For a term of this form, the reduction factor can be approximated by $\frac{1}{NKeys(I)}$ if there is an index I on *column* for the relation in question. This formula assumes even distribution of tuples among the index key values; this uniform distribution assumption is frequently made in arriving at cost estimates in a typical relational query optimizer. If there is no index on *column*, the System R optimizer arbitrarily assumes that the reduction factor is $\frac{1}{10}$! Of course, it is possible to maintain statistics such as the number of distinct values present for any attribute whether or not there is an index on that attribute. If such statistics are maintained, we can do better than the arbitrary choice of $\frac{1}{10}$.

- *column1 = column2*: In this case the reduction factor can be approximated by $\frac{1}{\mathbf{MAX}\ (NKeys(I1),NKeys(I2))}$ if there are indexes $I1$ and $I2$ on *column1* and *column2*, respectively. This formula assumes that each key value in the smaller index, say $I1$, has a matching value in the other index. Given a value for *column1*, we assume that each of the $NKeys(I2)$ values for *column2* is equally likely. Thus the number of tuples that have the same value in *column2* as a given value in *column1* is $\frac{1}{NKeys(I2)}$. If only one of the two columns has an index I, we take the reduction factor to be $\frac{1}{NKeys(I)}$; if neither column has an index, we approximate it by the ubiquitous $\frac{1}{10}$. By the way, note that these formulas are used whether or not the two columns appear in the same relation.

- *column > value*: The reduction factor is approximated by $\frac{High(I)\ -\ value}{High(I)\ -\ Low(I)}$ if there is an index I on *column*. If the column is not of an arithmetic type or there is no index, a fraction less than half is arbitrarily chosen. Similar formulas for the reduction factor can be derived for other range selections.

- *column* **IN** *(list of values)*: The reduction factor is taken to be the reduction factor for *column = value* multiplied by the number of items in the list. However, it is allowed to be at most half, reflecting the heuristic belief that each selection eliminates at least half the candidate tuples.

Reduction factors can also be approximated for terms of the form *column* **IN** *subquery* (ratio of the estimated size of the subquery result to the number of distinct values in *column* in the outer relation); **NOT** *condition* ($1-$reduction factor for *condition*); *value1<column<value2*; the disjunction of two conditions; and so on, but we will not discuss such reduction factors.

To summarize, regardless of the plan chosen, we can estimate the size of the final result by taking the product of the sizes of the relations in the **FROM** clause and the reduction factors for the terms in the **WHERE** clause. We can similarly estimate the size of the result of each operator in a plan tree by using reduction factors, since the subtree rooted at that operator's node is itself a query block.

Note that the number of tuples in the result is not affected by projections if duplicate elimination is not performed. However, projections reduce the number of pages because tuples in the result of a projection are smaller than the original tuples; the ratio of tuple sizes can be used as a **reduction factor for projection** to estimate the result size in pages, given the size of the input relation.

13.5 RELATIONAL ALGEBRA EQUIVALENCES *

In this section we present several equivalences among relational algebra expressions, and in Section 13.6 we discuss the space of alternative plans considered by a optimizer. Relational algebra equivalences play a central role in identifying alternative plans. Consider the query discussed in Section 13.3. As we saw earlier, pushing the selection in that query ahead of the join yielded a dramatically better evaluation plan; pushing selections ahead of joins is based on relational algebra equivalences involving the selection and cross-product operators.

Our discussion of equivalences is aimed at explaining the role that such equivalences play in a System R style optimizer. In essence, a basic SQL query block can be thought of as an algebra expression consisting of the cross-product of all relations in the **FROM** clause, the selections in the **WHERE** clause, and the projections in the **SELECT** clause. Algebra equivalences allow us to convert cross-products to joins, to choose different join orders, and to push selections and projections ahead of joins. For simplicity, we will assume that naming conflicts never arise and that we do not need to consider the renaming operator ρ.

13.5.1 Selections

There are two important equivalences that involve the selection operation. The first one involves **cascading of selections**:

$$\sigma_{c1 \wedge c2 \wedge \ldots cn}(R) \equiv \sigma_{c1}(\sigma_{c2}(\ldots(\sigma_{cn}(R))\ldots))$$

Going from the right side to the left, this equivalence allows us to combine several selections into one selection. Intuitively, we can test whether a tuple meets each of the conditions $c1 \ldots cn$ at the same time. In the other direction, this equivalence allows us to take a selection condition involving several conjuncts and to replace it with several smaller selection operations. Replacing a selection with several smaller selections turns out to be very useful in combination with other equivalences, especially commutation of selections with joins or cross-products, which we will discuss shortly. Intuitively, such a replacement is useful in cases where only part of a complex selection condition can be pushed.

The second equivalence states that selections are **commutative**:

$$\sigma_{c1}(\sigma_{c2}(R)) \equiv \sigma_{c2}(\sigma_{c1}(R))$$

In other words, we can test the conditions $c1$ and $c2$ in either order.

13.5.2 Projections

The rule for **cascading projections** says that successively eliminating columns from a relation is equivalent to simply eliminating all but the columns retained by the final projection:

$$\pi_{a1}(R) \equiv \pi_{a1}(\pi_{a2}(\ldots(\pi_{an}(R))\ldots))$$

Each ai is a set of attributes of relation R, and $ai \subseteq ai + 1$ for $i = 1 \ldots n - 1$. This equivalence is useful in conjunction with other equivalences such as commutation of projections with joins.

13.5.3 Cross-Products and Joins

There are two important equivalences involving cross-products and joins. We present them in terms of natural joins for simplicity, but they hold for general joins as well.

First, assuming that fields are identified by name rather than position, these operations are **commutative**:

$$R \times S \equiv S \times R$$

$$R \bowtie S \equiv S \bowtie R$$

This property is very important. It allows us to choose which relation is to be the inner and which the outer in a join of two relations.

The second equivalence states that joins and cross-products are **associative**:

$$R \times (S \times T) \equiv (R \times S) \times T$$

$$R \bowtie (S \bowtie T) \equiv (R \bowtie S) \bowtie T$$

Thus we can either join R and S first and then join T to the result, or join S and T first and then join R to the result. The intuition behind associativity of cross-products is that regardless of the order in which the three relations are considered, the final result contains the same columns. Join associativity is based on the same intuition, with the additional observation that the selections specifying the join conditions can be cascaded. Thus the same rows appear in the final result, regardless of the order in which the relations are joined.

Together with commutativity, associativity essentially says that we can choose to join any pair of these relations, then join the result with the third relation, and always obtain the same final result. For example, let us verify that

$$R \bowtie (S \bowtie T) \equiv (T \bowtie R) \bowtie S$$

From commutativity, we have:

$$R \bowtie (S \bowtie T) \equiv R \bowtie (T \bowtie S)$$

From associativity, we have:

$$R \bowtie (T \bowtie S) \equiv (R \bowtie T) \bowtie S$$

Using commutativity again, we have:

$$(R \bowtie T) \bowtie S \equiv (T \bowtie R) \bowtie S$$

In other words, when joining several relations, we are free to join the relations in any order that we choose. This order-independence is fundamental to how a query optimizer generates alternative query evaluation plans.

13.5.4   Selects, Projects and Joins

Some important equivalences involve two or more operators.

We can **commute** a selection with a projection if the selection operation involves only attributes that are retained by the projection:

$$\pi_a(\sigma_c(R)) \equiv \sigma_c(\pi_a(R))$$

Every attribute mentioned in the selection condition c must be included in the set of attributes a.

We can **combine** a selection with a cross-product to form a join, as per the definition of join:

$$R \bowtie_c S \equiv \sigma_c(R \times S)$$

We can **commute** a selection with a cross-product or a join if the selection condition involves only attributes of one of the arguments to the cross-product or join:

$$\sigma_c(R \times S) \equiv \sigma_c(R) \times S$$
$$\sigma_c(R \bowtie S) \equiv \sigma_c(R) \bowtie S$$

The attributes mentioned in c must appear only in R, and not in S. Similar equivalences hold if c involves only attributes of S and not R, of course.

In general a selection σ_c on $R \times S$ can be replaced by a cascade of selections σ_{c1}, σ_{c2} and σ_{c3} such that $c1$ involves attributes of both R and S, $c2$ involves only attributes of R, and $c3$ involves only attributes of S:

$$\sigma_c(R \times S) \equiv \sigma_{c1 \wedge c2 \wedge c3}(R \times S)$$

Using the cascading rule for selections, this expression is equivalent to

$$\sigma_{c1}(\sigma_{c2}(\sigma_{c3}(R \times S)))$$

Using the rule for commuting selections and cross-products, this expression is equivalent to

$$\sigma_{c1}(\sigma_{c2}(R) \times \sigma_{c3}(S)).$$

Thus we can push part of the selection condition c ahead of the cross-product. This observation also holds for selections in combination with joins, of course.

We can **commute** a projection with a cross-product:

$$\pi_a(R \times S) \equiv \pi_{a1}(R) \times \pi_{a2}(S)$$

$a1$ is the subset of attributes in a that appear in R, and $a2$ is the subset of attributes in a that appear in S. We can also **commute** a projection with a join if the join condition involves only attributes retained by the projection:

$$\pi_a(R \bowtie_c S) \equiv \pi_{a1}(R) \bowtie_c \pi_{a2}(S)$$

$a1$ is the subset of attributes in a that appear in R, and $a2$ is the subset of attributes in a that appear in S. Further, every attribute mentioned in the join condition c must appear in a.

Intuitively, we need to retain only those attributes of R and S that are either mentioned in the join condition c or included in the set of attributes a retained by the projection. Clearly, if a includes all attributes mentioned in c, the commutation rules above hold. If a does *not* include all attributes mentioned in c, we can generalize the commutation rules by first projecting out attributes that are not mentioned in c or a, performing the join, and then projecting out all attributes that are not in a:

$$\pi_a(R \bowtie_c S) \equiv \pi_a(\pi_{a1}(R) \bowtie_c \pi_{a2}(S))$$

Now $a1$ is the subset of attributes of R that appear in either a or c, and $a2$ is the subset of attributes of S that appear in either a or c.

We can in fact derive the more general commutation rule by using the rule for cascading projections and the simple commutation rule. Using the cascading rule, we have

$$\pi_a(R \bowtie_c S) \equiv \pi_a(\pi_{a1}(\pi_{a2}(R \bowtie_c S)))$$

where $a1$ is the subset of attributes of R that appear in either a or c and $a2$ is the subset of attributes of S that appear in either a or c. It is now straightforward to obtain the general commutation rule from the simple commutation rule.

13.5.5 Others

Additional equivalences hold when we consider operations such as set-difference, union and intersection. Union and intersection are associative and commutative.

Selections and projections can be commuted with each of the set operations (set-difference, union and intersection). We will not discuss these equivalences further.

13.6 ENUMERATION OF ALTERNATIVE PLANS *

We now come to an issue that is at the heart of an optimizer, namely, the space of alternative plans that is considered for a given query. Given a query, an optimizer essentially enumerates a certain set of plans and chooses the plan with the least estimated cost; the discussion in Section 13.4.1 indicated how the cost of a plan is estimated. The algebraic equivalences discussed in Section 13.5 form the basis for generating alternative plans, in conjunction with the choice of implementation technique for the relational operators (e.g., joins) present in the query. However, not all algebraically equivalent plans are considered because doing so would make the cost of optimization prohibitively expensive for all but the simplest queries. This section describes the subset of the plan space that is enumerated by a typical optimizer.

There are two important cases to consider: queries in which the `FROM` clause contains a single relation and queries in which the `FROM` clause contains two or more relations.

13.6.1 Single-Relation Queries

If the query contains a single relation in the `FROM` clause, only selection, projection, grouping, and aggregate operations are involved; there are no joins. If we have just one selection or projection or aggregate operation applied to a relation, the alternative implementation techniques and cost estimates discussed in Chapter 12 cover all the plans that must be considered. We now consider how to optimize queries that involve a combination of several such operations, using the following query as an example:

For each rating greater than 5, print the rating and the number of 20-year-old sailors with that rating, provided that there are at least two such sailors with different names.

The SQL version of this query is shown in Figure 13.10.

Using the extended algebra notation introduced in Section 13.2.2, we can write this query as:

$$\pi_{S.rating,COUNT(*)} \big($$
$$HAVING_{COUNTDISTINCT(S.sname)>2} \big($$

```
SELECT    S.rating, COUNT (*)
FROM      Sailors S
WHERE     S.rating > 5 AND S.age = 20
GROUP BY  S.rating
HAVING    COUNT DISTINCT (S.sname) > 2
```

Figure 13.10   A Single-Relation Query

$$GROUP\ BY_{S.rating}($$
$$\pi_{S.rating,S.sname}($$
$$\sigma_{S.rating>5 \land S.age=20}($$
$$Sailors)))))$$

Notice that *S.sname* is added to the projection list, even though it is not in the SELECT clause, because it is required to test the HAVING clause condition.

We are now ready to discuss the plans that an optimizer would consider. The main decision to be made is which access path to use in retrieving Sailors tuples. If we considered only the selections, we would simply choose the most selective access path based on which available indexes *match* the conditions in the WHERE clause (as per the definition in Section 12.3.1). Given the additional operators in this query, we must also take into account the cost of subsequent sorting steps and consider whether these operations can be performed without sorting by exploiting some index. We first discuss the plans generated when there are no suitable indexes and then examine plans that utilize some index.

Plans without Indexes

The basic approach in the absence of a suitable index is to scan the Sailors relation and apply the selection and projection (without duplicate elimination) operations to each retrieved tuple, as indicated by the following algebra expression:

$$\pi_{S.rating,S.sname}($$
$$\sigma_{S.rating>5 \land S.age=20}($$
$$Sailors))$$

The resulting tuples are then sorted according to the GROUP BY clause (in the sample query, on *rating*), and one answer tuple is generated for each group that meets the condition in the HAVING clause. The computation of the aggregate functions in the SELECT and HAVING clauses is done for each group, using one of the techniques described in Section 12.7.

The cost of this approach consists of the costs of each of these steps:

1. Performing a file scan to retrieve tuples and apply the selections and projections.

2. Writing out tuples after the selections and projections.

3. Sorting these tuples to implement the GROUP BY clause.

Note that the HAVING clause does not cause additional I/O. The aggregate computations can be done for free (with respect to I/O) as we generate the tuples in each group at the end of the sorting step for the GROUP BY clause.

In the sample query the cost includes the cost of a file scan on Sailors plus the cost of writing out ⟨S.rating, S.sname⟩ pairs plus the cost of sorting as per the GROUP BY clause. The cost of the file scan is *NPages(Sailors)*, which is 500 I/Os, and the cost of writing out ⟨S.rating, S.sname⟩ pairs is *NPages(Sailors)* times the ratio of the size of such a pair to the size of a Sailors tuple. In our example this ratio is about 0.8, and the cost of this step is 400 I/Os. The cost of sorting this intermediate relation (which we will call Temp) can be estimated as *3*NPages(Temp)*, which is 1200 I/Os, if we assume that enough pages are available in the buffer pool to sort it in two passes. (Relational optimizers often assume that a relation can be sorted in two passes, to simplify the estimation of sorting costs. If this assumption is not met at run-time, the actual cost of sorting may well be higher than the estimate!) The total cost of the sample query is therefore 500+400+1200 = 2100 I/Os.

Plans Utilizing an Index

Indexes can be utilized in several ways and can lead to plans that are significantly faster than any plan that does not utilize indexes.

1. **Single-index access path:** If several indexes match the selection conditions in the WHERE clause, each matching index offers an alternative access path. An optimizer can choose the access path that it estimates will result in retrieving the fewest pages, apply any projections and non primary selection terms (i.e., parts of the selection condition that do not match the index), and then proceed to compute the grouping and aggregation operations (by sorting on the GROUP BY attributes).

2. **Multiple-index access path:** If several indexes using Alternatives (2) or (3) for data entries match the selection condition, each such index can be used to retrieve a set of rids. We can *intersect* these sets of rids, then sort the result by page id (assuming that the rid representation includes the page id) and retrieve tuples that satisfy the primary selection terms of all the matching indexes. Any projections and non matching selection terms can then be applied, followed by grouping and aggregation operations.

3. **Sorted index access path:** If the list of grouping attributes is a prefix of a tree index, the index can be used to retrieve tuples in the order required by the GROUP BY clause. All selection conditions can be applied on each retrieved tuple, unwanted fields can be removed, and aggregate operations computed for each group. This strategy works well for clustered indexes.

4. **Index-Only Access Path:** If all the attributes mentioned in the query (in the SELECT, WHERE, GROUP BY, or HAVING clauses) are included in the search key for some *dense* index on the relation in the FROM clause, an **index-only scan** can be used to compute answers. Because the data entries in the index contain all the attributes of a tuple that are needed for this query, and there is one index entry per tuple, we never need to retrieve actual tuples from the relation. Using just the data entries from the index, we can carry out the following steps as needed in a given query: apply selection conditions, remove unwanted attributes, sort the result to achieve grouping, and compute aggregate functions within each group. This *index-only* approach works even if the index does not match the selections in the WHERE clause. If the index matches the selection, we need only examine a subset of the index entries; otherwise, we must scan all index entries. In either case, we can avoid retrieving actual data records; therefore, the cost of this strategy does not depend on whether the index is clustered.

   In addition, if the index is a tree index and the list of attributes in the GROUP BY clause forms a prefix of the index key, we can retrieve data entries in the order needed for the GROUP BY clause and thereby avoid sorting!

We now illustrate each of these four cases, using the query shown in Figure 13.10 as a running example. We will assume that the following indexes, all using Alternative (2) for data entries, are available: a B+ tree index on *rating*, a hash index on *age*, and a B+ tree index on ⟨*rating, sname, age*⟩. For brevity, we will not present detailed cost calculations, but the reader should be able to calculate the cost of each plan. The steps in these plans are scans (a file scan, a scan retrieving tuples by using an index, or a scan of only index entries), sorting, and writing temporary relations, and we have already discussed how to estimate the costs of these operations.

As an example of the first case, we could choose to retrieve Sailors tuples such that *S.age*=20 using the hash index on *age*. The cost of this step is the cost of retrieving the index entries plus the cost of retrieving the corresponding Sailors tuples, which depends on whether the index is clustered. We can then apply the condition *S.rating*> 5 to each retrieved tuple; project out fields not mentioned in the SELECT, GROUP BY, and HAVING clauses; and write the result to a temporary relation. In the example, only the *rating* and *sname* fields need to be retained. The temporary relation is then sorted on the *rating* field to identify the groups, and some groups are eliminated by applying the HAVING condition.

As an example of the second case, we can retrieve rids of tuples satisfying *rating*>5 using the index on *rating*, retrieve rids of tuples satisfying *age*=20 using the index on *age*, sort the retrieved rids by page number, and then retrieve the corresponding Sailors tuples. We can retain just the *rating* and *name* fields and write the result to a temporary relation, which we can sort on *rating* to implement the `GROUP BY` clause. (A good optimizer might pipeline the projected tuples to the sort operator without creating a temporary relation.) The `HAVING` clause is handled as before.

As an example of the third case, we can retrieve Sailors tuples such that *S.rating*> 5, ordered by *rating*, using the B+ tree index on *rating*. We can compute the aggregate functions in the `HAVING` and `SELECT` clauses on-the-fly because tuples are retrieved in *rating* order.

As an example of the fourth case, we can retrieve *data entries* from the ⟨*rating, sname, age*⟩ index such that *rating*> 5. These entries are sorted by *rating* (and then by *sname* and *age*, although this additional ordering is not relevant for this query). We can choose entries with *age=20* and compute the aggregate functions in the `HAVING` and `SELECT` clauses on-the-fly because the data entries are retrieved in *rating* order. In this case, in contrast to the previous case, we do not retrieve any Sailors tuples. This property of not retrieving data records makes the index-only strategy especially valuable with unclustered indexes.

13.6.2   Multiple-Relation Queries

Query blocks that contain two or more relations in the `FROM` clause require joins (or cross-products). Finding a good plan for such queries is very important because these queries can be quite expensive. Regardless of the plan chosen, the size of the final result can be estimated by taking the product of the sizes of the relations in the `FROM` clause and the reduction factors for the terms in the `WHERE` clause. But depending on the order in which relations are joined, intermediate relations of widely varying sizes can be created, leading to plans with very different costs.

In this section we consider how multiple-relation queries are optimized. We first introduce the class of plans considered by a typical optimizer, and then describe how all such plans are enumerated.

Left-Deep Plans

Consider a query of the form $A \bowtie B \bowtie C \bowtie D$, that is, the natural join of four relations. Two relational algebra operator trees that are equivalent to this query are shown in Figure 13.11.

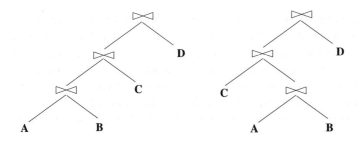

Figure 13.11   Two Linear Join Trees

We note that the left child of a join node is the outer relation and the right child is the inner relation, as per our convention. By adding details such as the join method for each join node, it is straightforward to obtain several query evaluation plans from these trees. Also, the equivalence of these trees is based on the relational algebra equivalences that we discussed earlier, particularly the associativity and commutativity of joins and cross-products.

The *form* of these trees is important in understanding the space of alternative plans explored by the System R query optimizer. Both the trees in Figure 13.11 are called **linear** trees. In a linear tree, at least one child of a join node is a base relation. The first tree is an example of a **left-deep** tree—the *right* child of each join node is a base relation. An example of a join tree that is not linear is shown in Figure 13.12; such trees are called **bushy** trees.

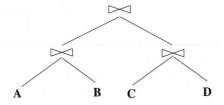

Figure 13.12   A Nonlinear Join Tree

A fundamental heuristic decision in the System R optimizer is to examine only left-deep trees in constructing alternative plans for a join query. Of course, this decision rules out many alternative plans that may well be of lower cost than the best plan using a left-deep tree; we have to live with the fact that the optimizer will never find such plans. There are two main reasons for this decision to concentrate on **left-deep plans**, or plans based on left-deep trees:

1. As the number of joins increases, the number of alternative plans increases rapidly and some pruning of the space of alternative plans becomes necessary.

2. Left-deep trees allow us to generate all **fully pipelined** plans, that is, plans in which the joins are all evaluated using pipelining. Inner relations must always be materialized fully because we must examine the entire inner relation for each tuple of the outer relation. Thus a plan in which an inner relation is the result of a join forces us to materialize the result of that join. This observation motivates the heuristic decision to consider only left-deep trees. Of course, not all plans using left-deep trees are fully pipelined. For example, a plan that uses a sort-merge join may require the outer tuples to be retrieved in a certain sorted order, which may force us to materialize the outer relation.

Enumeration of Left-Deep Plans

Consider a query block of the form:

> SELECT   *attribute list*
> FROM   *relation list*
> WHERE $term_1 \wedge term_2 \wedge \ldots \wedge term_n$

A System R style query optimizer enumerates all left-deep plans, with selections and projections considered (but not necessarily applied!) as early as possible. The enumeration of plans can be understood as a multiple-pass algorithm in which we proceed as follows:

Pass 1: We enumerate all single-relation plans (over some relation in the FROM clause). Intuitively, each single-relation plan is a partial left-deep plan for evaluating the query in which the given relation is the first (in the linear join order). When considering plans involving a relation A, we identify those selection terms in the WHERE clause that mention only attributes of A. These are the selections that can be performed when first accessing A, before any joins that involve A. We also identify those attributes of A that are not mentioned in the SELECT clause or in terms in the WHERE clause involving attributes of other relations. These attributes can be projected out when first accessing A, before any joins that involve A. We choose the best access method for A to carry out these selections and projections, as per the discussion in Section 13.6.1.

For each relation, if we find plans that produce tuples in different orders, we retain the cheapest plan for each such ordering of tuples. An ordering of tuples could prove useful at a subsequent step, say for a sort-merge join or for implementing a GROUP BY or ORDER BY clause.

Pass 2: We generate all two-relation plans by considering each single-relation plan that is retained after Pass 1 as the outer relation and (successively) every other relation as the inner relation. Suppose that A is the outer relation and

B the inner relation for a particular two-relation plan. We examine the list of selections in the WHERE clause and identify:

1. Selections that involve only attributes of B and can be applied before the join.

2. Selections that serve to define the join (i.e., are conditions involving attributes of both A and B and no other relation).

3. Selections that involve attributes of other relations and can be applied only after the join.

The first two groups of selections can be considered while choosing an access path for the inner relation B. We also identify the attributes of B that do not appear in the SELECT clause or in any selection conditions in the second or third group above, and can therefore be projected out before the join.

Notice that our identification of attributes that can be projected out before the join and selections that can be applied before the join is based on the relational algebra equivalences discussed earlier. In particular, we are relying on the equivalences that allow us to push selections and projections ahead of joins. As we will see, whether we actually perform these selections and projections ahead of a given join depends on cost considerations. The only selections that are really applied *before* the join are those that match the chosen access paths for A and B. The remaining selections and projections are done on-the-fly as part of the join.

An important point to note is that tuples generated by the outer plan are assumed to be *pipelined* into the join. That is, we avoid having the outer plan write its result to a file that is subsequently read by the join (to obtain outer tuples). For some join methods, the join operator might require materializing the outer tuples. For example, a hash join would partition the incoming tuples, and a sort-merge join would sort them if they are not already in the appropriate sort order. Nested loops joins, however, can use outer tuples as they are generated and avoid materializing them. Similarly, sort-merge joins can use outer tuples as they are generated if they are generated in the sorted order required for the join. We include the cost of materializing the outer, should this be necessary, in the cost of the join. The adjustments to the join costs discussed in Chapter 12 to reflect the use of pipelining or materialization of the outer are straightforward.

For each single-relation plan for A retained after Pass 1, for each join method that we consider, we must determine the best access method to use for B. The access method chosen for B will retrieve, in general, a subset of the tuples in B, possibly with some fields eliminated, as discussed below. Consider B. We have a collection of selections (some of which are the join conditions) and projections on a single relation, and the choice of the best access method is made as per the discussion in Section 13.6.1. The only additional consideration is that the join method might require tuples to be retrieved in some order. For example, in a sort-merge join we want the inner tuples in sorted order on the join column(s). If a given access method does not retrieve inner tuples in this order, we must add the cost of an additional sorting step to the cost of the access method.

Pass 3: We generate all three-relation plans. We proceed as in Pass 2, except that we now consider plans retained after Pass 2 as outer relations, instead of plans retained after Pass 1.

Additional passes: This process is repeated with additional passes until we produce plans that contain all the relations in the query. We now have the cheapest overall plan for the query, as well as the cheapest plan for producing the answers in some interesting order.

If a multiple-relation query contains a `GROUP BY` clause and aggregate functions such as `MIN`, `MAX` and `SUM` in the `SELECT` clause, these are dealt with at the very end. If the query block includes a `GROUP BY` clause, a set of tuples is computed based on the rest of the query, as described above, and this set is sorted as per the `GROUP BY` clause. Of course, if there is a plan according to which the set of tuples is produced in the desired order, the cost of this plan is compared with the cost of the cheapest plan (assuming that the two are different) plus the sorting cost. Given the sorted set of tuples, partititions are identified and any aggregate functions in the `SELECT` clause are applied on a per-partition basis, as per the discussion in Chapter 12.

Examples of Multiple-Relation Query Optimization

Consider the query tree shown in Figure 13.2. Figure 13.13 shows the same query, taking into account how selections and projections are considered early.

In looking at this figure, it is worth emphasizing that the selections shown on the leaves are not necessarily done in a distinct step that precedes the join—rather, as we have seen, they are considered as potential matching predicates when considering the available access paths on the relations.

Suppose that we have the following indexes: a B+ tree index on the *rating* field of Sailors, a hash index on the *sid* field of Sailors, and a B+ tree index on the *bid* field of Reserves. In addition, we assume that we can do a sequential scan of both Reserves and Sailors. Let us consider how the optimizer proceeds.

In Pass 1 we consider three access methods for Sailors (B+ tree, hash index, and sequential scan), taking into account the selection $\sigma_{rating>5}$. This selection

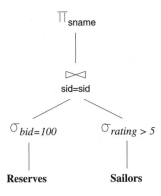

Figure 13.13   A Query Tree

matches the B+ tree on *rating* and therefore reduces the cost for retrieving tuples that satisfy this selection. The cost of retrieving tuples using the hash index and the sequential scan is likely to be much higher than the cost of using the B+ tree. So the plan retained for Sailors is access via the B+ tree index, and it retrieves tuples in sorted order by *rating*. Similarly, we consider two access methods for Reserves taking into account the selection $\sigma_{bid=100}$. This selection matches the B+ tree index on Reserves, and the cost of retrieving matching tuples via this index is likely to be much lower than the cost of retrieving tuples using a sequential scan; access through the B+ tree index is therefore the only plan retained for Reserves after Pass 1.

In Pass 2 we consider taking the (relation computed by the) plan for Reserves and joining it (as the outer) with Sailors. In doing so, we recognize that now, we need only Sailors tuples that satisfy $\sigma_{rating>5}$ and $\sigma_{sid=value}$, where *value* is some value from an outer tuple. The selection $\sigma_{sid=value}$ matches the hash index on the *sid* field of Sailors, and the selection $\sigma_{rating>5}$ matches the B+ tree index on the *rating* field. Since the equality selection has a much lower reduction factor, the hash index is likely to be the cheaper access method. In addition to the preceding consideration of alternative access methods, we consider alternative join methods. All available join methods are considered. For example, consider a sort-merge join. The inputs must be sorted by *sid*; since neither input is sorted by *sid* or has an access method that can return tuples in this order, the cost of the sort-merge join in this case must include the cost of storing the two inputs in temporary relations and sorting them. Sort-merge join provides results in sorted order by *sid*, but this is not an interesting order in this example because the projection π_{sname} is applied (on-the-fly) to the result of the join, thereby eliminating the *sid* field from the answer. Thus, the plan using sort-merge join will be retained after Pass 2 only if it is the least expensive plan involving Reserves and Sailors.

Similarly, we also consider taking the plan for Sailors retained after Pass 1 and joining it (as the outer) with Reserves. Now we recognize that we need only Reserves tuples that satisfy $\sigma_{bid=100}$ and $\sigma_{sid=value}$, where *value* is some value from an outer tuple. Again, we consider all available join methods.

We finally retain the cheapest plan overall.

As another example, illustrating the case when more than two relations are joined, consider the following query:

SELECT	S.sid, COUNT(*) AS numres
FROM	Boats B, Reserves R, Sailors S
WHERE	R.sid = S.sid AND B.bid=R.bid AND B.color = 'red'
GROUP BY	S.sid

This query finds the number of red boats reserved by each sailor. This query is shown in the form of a tree in Figure 13.14.

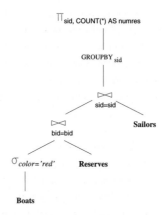

Figure 13.14   A Query Tree

Suppose that the following indexes are available: for Reserves, a B+ tree on the *sid* field and a clustered B+ tree on the *bid* field; for Sailors, a B+ tree index on the *sid* field and a hash index on the *sid* field; and for Boats, a B+ tree index on the *color* field and a hash index on the *color* field. (The list of available indexes is contrived to create a relatively simple, illustrative example.) Let us consider how this query is optimized. The initial focus is on the SELECT, FROM and WHERE clauses.

Pass 1: The best plan is found for accessing each relation, regarded as the first relation in an execution plan. For Reserves and Sailors, the best plan is obviously a file scan because there are no selections that match an available index. The best plan for Boats is to use the hash index on *color*, which matches the selection

B.color = *'red'*. Although the B+ tree on *color* also matches this selection, the hash index is cheaper.

Pass 2: For each of the plans generated in Pass 1, taken as the outer, we consider joining another relation as the inner. Thus we consider each of the following joins: file scan of Reserves (outer) with Boats (inner), file scan of Reserves (outer) with Sailors (inner), file scan of Sailors (outer) with Boats (inner), file scan of Sailors (outer) with Reserves (inner), Boats accessed via hash index on *color* (outer) with Boats (inner), and Boats accessed via hash index on *color* (outer) with Sailors (inner).

For each such pair, we consider each join method, and for each join method, we consider every available access path for the inner relation. For each pair of relations, we retain the cheapest of the plans considered for each sorted order in which the tuples are generated. For example, with Boats accessed via the hash index on *color* as the outer relation, index nested loops join accessing Reserves via the B+ tree index on *bid* is likely to be a good plan; observe that there is no hash index on this field of Reserves. Another plan for joining Reserves and Boats is to access Boats using the hash index on *color*, access Reserves using the B+ tree on *bid*, and use a sort-merge join; this plan, in contrast to the previous one, generates tuples in sorted order by *bid*. It is therefore retained even if the previous plan is cheaper, unless there is an even cheaper plan that produces the tuples in sorted order by *bid*! However, the previous plan, which produces tuples in no particular order, would not be retained if this plan is cheaper.

Pass 3: For each plan retained in Pass 2, taken as the outer, we consider how to join the remaining relation as the inner. An example of a plan generated at this step is the following: Access Boats via the hash index on *color*, access Reserves via the B+ tree index on *bid*, and join them using a sort-merge join; then take the result of this join as the outer and join with Sailors using a sort-merge join, accessing Sailors via the B+ tree index on the *sid* field. Notice that since the result of the first join is produced in sorted order by *bid*, whereas the second join requires its inputs to be sorted by *sid*, the result of the first join must be sorted by *sid* before being used in the second join. The tuples in the result of the second join are generated in sorted order by *sid*.

The **GROUP BY** clause is considered next, and it requires sorting on the *sid* field. For each plan retained in Pass 3, if the result is not sorted on *sid*, we add the cost of sorting on the *sid* field. The sample plan generated in Pass 3 produces tuples in *sid* order; therefore it may be the cheapest plan for the query even if a cheaper plan joins all three relations, but does not produce tuples in *sid* order.

13.7   NESTED SUBQUERIES *

The unit of optimization in a typical system is a *query block*, and nested queries are dealt with using some form of nested loops evaluation. Consider the following nested query in SQL: *Find the names of sailors with the highest rating.*

```
SELECT  S.sname
FROM    Sailors S
WHERE   S.rating = ( SELECT MAX (S2.rating)
                     FROM    Sailors S2 )
```

In this simple query the nested subquery can be evaluated just once, yielding a single value. This value is incorporated into the top-level query as if it had been part of the original statement of the query. For example, if the highest rated sailor has a rating of 8, the **WHERE** clause is effectively modified to **WHERE** *S.rating = 8.*

However, the subquery may sometimes return a relation, or more precisely, a table in the SQL sense (i.e., possibly with duplicate rows). Consider the following query: *Find the names of sailors who have reserved boat number 103.*

```
SELECT  S.sname
FROM    Sailors S
WHERE   S.sid IN ( SELECT  R.sid
                   FROM    Reserves R
                   WHERE   R.bid = 103 )
```

Again, the nested subquery can be evaluated just once, yielding a collection of *sid*s. For each tuple of Sailors, we must now check whether the *sid* value is in the computed collection of *sid*s; this check entails a join of Sailors and the computed collection of *sid*s, and in principle we have the full range of join methods to choose from. For example, if there is an index on the *sid* field of Sailors, an index nested loops join with the computed collection of *sid*s as the outer relation and Sailors as the inner might well be the most efficient join method. However, in many systems, the query optimizer is not smart enough to find this strategy—a common approach is to always do a nested loops join in which the inner relation is the collection of *sid*s computed from the subquery (and this collection may not be indexed).

The motivation for this approach is that it is a simple variant of the technique used to deal with **correlated queries** such as the following version of the previous query:

```
SELECT  S.sname
FROM    Sailors S
```

```
WHERE   EXISTS ( SELECT *
                 FROM    Reserves R
                 WHERE   R.bid = 103
                 AND  S.sid = R.sid )
```

This query is *correlated*—the tuple variable S from the top-level query appears in the nested subquery. Therefore, we cannot evaluate the subquery just once. In this case the typical evaluation strategy is to evaluate the nested subquery for each tuple of Sailors.

An important point to note about nested queries is that a typical optimizer is likely to do a poor job, because of the limited approach to nested query optimization. This is highlighted below:

- In a nested query with correlation, the join method is effectively index nested loops, with the inner relation typically a subquery (and therefore potentially expensive to compute). This approach creates two distinct problems. First, the nested subquery is evaluated once per outer tuple; if the same value appears in the correlation field (S.sid in our example) of several outer tuples, the same subquery is evaluated many times. The second problem is that the approach to nested subqueries is not *set-oriented*. In effect, a join is seen as a scan of the outer relation with a selection on the inner subquery for each outer tuple. This precludes consideration of alternative join methods such as sort-merge join or hash join, which could well lead to far superior plans.

- Even if index nested loops is the appropriate join method, nested query evaluation may be inefficient. For example, if there is an index on the *sid* field of Reserves, a good strategy might be to do an index nested loops join with Sailors as the outer relation and Reserves as the inner relation, and to apply the selection on *bid* on-the-fly. However, this option is not considered when optimizing the version of the query that uses **IN** because the nested subquery is fully evaluated as a first step; that is, Reserves tuples that meet the *bid* selection are retrieved first.

- Opportunities for finding a good evaluation plan may also be missed because of the implicit ordering imposed by the nesting. For example, if there is an index on the *sid* field of Sailors, an index nested loops join with Reserves as the outer relation and Sailors as the inner might well be the most efficient plan for our sample correlated query. However, this join ordering is never considered by an optimizer.

A nested query often has an equivalent query without nesting, and a correlated query often has an equivalent query without correlation. We have already seen correlated and uncorrelated versions of the sample nested query. There is also an equivalent query without nesting:

```
SELECT  S.sname
FROM    Sailors S, Reserves R
WHERE   S.sid = R.sid AND R.bid=103
```

A typical SQL optimizer is likely to find a much better evaluation strategy if it is given the non nested version of the sample query than it would if it were given either of the nested versions of the query. Many current optimizers cannot recognize the equivalence of these queries and transform one of the nested versions to the non nested form. This is, unfortunately, up to the educated user. From an efficiency standpoint, users are well-advised to consider such alternative formulations of a query.

We conclude our discussion of nested queries by observing that there could be several levels of nesting. In general the approach that we have sketched is extended by evaluating such queries from the innermost to the outermost level, in order, in the absense of correlation. A correlated subquery must be evaluated for each candidate tuple of the higher-level (sub)query that refers to it. The basic idea is thus similar to the case of one-level nested queries; we omit the details.

13.8   OTHER APPROACHES TO QUERY OPTIMIZATION *

We have described query optimization based on an exhaustive search of a large space of plans for a given query. The space of all possible plans grows rapidly with the size of the query expression, in particular with respect to the number of joins, because join-order optimization is a central issue. Therefore, heuristics are used to limit the space of plans considered by an optimizer. A widely used heuristic is that only left-deep plans are considered, which works well for most queries. However, once the number of joins becomes greater than about 15, the cost of optimization using this exhaustive approach becomes prohibitively high, even if we only consider left-deep plans.

Such complex queries are becoming important in decision-support environments, and other approaches to query optimization have been proposed. These include **rule-based optimizers**, which use a set of rules to guide the generation of candidate plans, and **randomized plan generation**, which use probabilistic algorithms such as *simulated annealing* to explore a large space of plans quickly, with a reasonable likelihood of finding a good plan.

Current research in this area also involves techniques for estimating the size of intermediate relations more accurately; **parametrized query optimization**, which seeks to find good plans for a given query for each of several different conditions that might be encountered at run-time; and **multiple-query opti-**

mization, in which the optimizer takes concurrent execution of several queries into account.

13.9 SUMMARY

Query optimization is one of the most important tasks of a relational DBMS. One of the strengths of relational query language is the wide variety of ways in which a user can express a query. Although this flexibility makes the languages more natural to use, it makes the quality of the query optimizer a very important determinant of performance—there are many ways to evaluate a given query, and the difference in cost between the best and worst plans may be several orders of magnitude.

A relational query optimizer uses relational algebra equivalences to consider many equivalent expressions for a given query. For each such equivalent version of the query, all available implementation techniques are considered for the relational operators involved. A relational algebra expression of the query together with a choice of implementation methods for each operator that it contains is called a *plan*; the goal of an optimizer is to find a good plan. Of course, the lower the estimated cost of a plan, the better we expect it to be. To estimate the cost of a plan, an optimizer relies on statistics about the relation instances, which are available in the system catalogs. Realistically, we cannot expect to find the best plan, but we do expect to find a plan that is quite good.

The space of all possible plans for a query is very large, and typical current optimizers reduce this space through the use of heuristics. An important and widely used heuristic is that only the space of left-deep plans is considered. Over this space of plans, an exhaustive search can be carried out using dynamic programming techniques, and this approach works well for most queries. When the query expression is large—for example, the query contains 15 or more joins—the cost of optimization using this approach becomes prohibitive. Alternative optimization techniques, which we have not discussed, have also been proposed.

EXERCISES

Exercise 13.1 Briefly answer the following questions.

1. Describe the advantages of *pipelining*.
2. Give an example in which pipelining *cannot* be used.
3. Describe the *iterator* interface and explain its advantages.
4. In the context of query optimization, what is an *SQL query block*?
5. What role do statistics gathered from the database play in query optimization?

6. Define the term *reduction factor*.

7. Describe a situation in which projection should precede selection in processing a project-select query, and describe a situation where the opposite processing order is better. (Assume that duplicate elimination for projection is done via sorting.)

8. If there are dense, unclustered (secondary) B+ tree indexes on both *R.a* and *S.b*, the join $R \bowtie_{a=b} S$ could be processed by doing a sort-merge type of join—without doing any sorting—by using these indexes.

    (a) Would this be a good idea if R and S each have only one tuple per page, or would it be better to ignore the indexes and sort R and S? Explain.

    (b) What if R and S each have many tuples per page? Again, explain.

9. Why does the System R optimizer consider only left-deep join trees? Give an example of a plan that would not be considered because of this restriction.

10. Explain the role of *interesting orders* in the System R optimizer.

Exercise 13.2 Consider a relation with this schema:

$$Employees(\underline{eid:\ \texttt{integer}},\ ename:\ \texttt{string},\ sal:\ \texttt{integer},\ title:\ \texttt{string},\ age:\ \texttt{integer})$$

Suppose that the following indexes, all using Alternative (2) for data entries, exist: a hash index on *eid*, a B+ tree index on *sal*, a hash index on *age*, and a clustered B+ tree index on ⟨*age, sal*⟩. Each Employees record is 100 bytes long, and you can assume that each index data entry is 20 bytes long. The Employees relation contains 10,000 pages.

1. Consider each of the following selection conditions and, assuming that the reduction factor (RF) for each term that matches an index is 0.1, compute the cost of the most selective access path for retrieving all Employees tuples that satisfy the condition:

    (a) $sal > 100$

    (b) $age = 25$

    (c) $age > 20$

    (d) $eid = 1000$

    (e) $sal > 200 \land age > 30$

    (f) $sal > 200 \land age = 20$

    (g) $sal > 200 \land title = 'CFO'$

    (h) $sal > 200 \land age > 30 \land title = 'CFO'$

2. Suppose that for each of the preceding selection conditions, you want to retrieve the average salary of qualifying tuples. For each selection condition, describe the least expensive evaluation method and state its cost.

3. Suppose that for each of the preceding selection conditions, you want to compute the average salary for each *age* group. For each selection condition, describe the least expensive evaluation method and state its cost.

4. Suppose that for each of the preceding selection conditions, you want to compute the average age for each *sal* level (i.e., group by *sal*). For each selection condition, describe the least expensive evaluation method and state its cost.

5. For each of the following selection conditions, describe the best evaluation method:

   (a) $sal > 200 \lor age = 20$

   (b) $sal > 200 \lor title = 'CFO'$

   (c) $title = 'CFO' \land ename = 'Joe'$

Exercise 13.3 For each of the following SQL queries, for each relation involved, list the attributes that must be examined in order to compute the answer. All queries refer to the following relations:

Emp(*eid:* integer, *did:* integer, *sal:* integer, *hobby:* char(20))
Dept(*did:* integer, *dname:* char(20), *floor:* integer, *budget:* real)

1. SELECT * FROM Emp

2. SELECT * FROM Emp, Dept

3. SELECT * FROM Emp E, Dept D WHERE E.did = D.did

4. SELECT E.eid, D.dname FROM Emp E, Dept D WHERE E.did = D.did

5. SELECT COUNT(*) FROM Emp E, Dept D WHERE E.did = D.did

6. SELECT MAX(E.sal) FROM Emp E, Dept D WHERE E.did = D.did

7. SELECT MAX(E.sal) FROM Emp E, Dept D WHERE E.did = D.did AND D.floor = 5

8. SELECT E.did, COUNT(*) FROM Emp E, Dept D WHERE E.did = D.did GROUP BY D.did

9. SELECT D.floor, AVG(D.budget) FROM Dept D GROUP BY D.floor HAVING COUNT(*) > 2

10. SELECT D.floor, AVG(D.budget) FROM Dept D GROUP BY D.floor ORDER BY D.floor

Exercise 13.4 You are given the following information:

Executives has attributes *ename, title, dname,* and *address*; all are string fields of the same length.
The *ename* attribute is a candidate key.
The relation contains 10,000 pages.
There are 10 buffer pages.

1. Consider the following query:

   SELECT E.title, E.ename FROM Executives E WHERE E.title='CFO'

   Assume that only 10% of Executives tuples meet the selection condition.

   (a) Suppose that a clustered B+ tree index on *title* is (the only index) available. What is the cost of the best plan? (In this and subsequent questions, be sure to describe the plan that you have in mind.)

   (b) Suppose that an unclustered B+ tree index on *title* is (the only index) available. What is the cost of the best plan?

    (c) Suppose that a clustered B+ tree index on *ename* is (the only index) available. What is the cost of the best plan?

    (d) Suppose that a clustered B+ tree index on *address* is (the only index) available. What is the cost of the best plan?

    (e) Suppose that a clustered B+ tree index on $\langle ename, title \rangle$ is (the only index) available. What is the cost of the best plan?

2. Suppose that the query is as follows:

    SELECT E.ename FROM Executives E WHERE E.title='CFO' AND E.dname='Toy'

Assume that only 10% of Executives tuples meet the condition $E.title = 'CFO'$, only 10% meet $E.dname = 'Toy'$, and that only 5% meet both conditions.

    (a) Suppose that a clustered B+ tree index on *title* is (the only index) available. What is the cost of the best plan?

    (b) Suppose that a clustered B+ tree index on *dname* is (the only index) available. What is the cost of the best plan?

    (c) Suppose that a clustered B+ tree index on $\langle title, dname \rangle$ is (the only index) available. What is the cost of the best plan?

    (d) Suppose that a clustered B+ tree index on $\langle title, ename \rangle$ is (the only index) available. What is the cost of the best plan?

    (e) Suppose that a clustered B+ tree index on $\langle dname, title, ename \rangle$ is (the only index) available. What is the cost of the best plan?

    (f) Suppose that a clustered B+ tree index on $\langle ename, title, dname \rangle$ is (the only index) available. What is the cost of the best plan?

3. Suppose that the query is as follows:

    SELECT E.title, COUNT(*) FROM Executives E GROUP BY E.title

    (a) Suppose that a clustered B+ tree index on *title* is (the only index) available. What is the cost of the best plan?

    (b) Suppose that an unclustered B+ tree index on *title* is (the only index) available. What is the cost of the best plan?

    (c) Suppose that a clustered B+ tree index on *ename* is (the only index) available. What is the cost of the best plan?

    (d) Suppose that a clustered B+ tree index on $\langle ename, title \rangle$ is (the only index) available. What is the cost of the best plan?

    (e) Suppose that a clustered B+ tree index on $\langle title, ename \rangle$ is (the only index) available. What is the cost of the best plan?

4. Suppose that the query is as follows:

    SELECT E.title, COUNT(*) FROM Executives E
    WHERE E.dname > 'W%' GROUP BY E.title

Assume that only 10% of Executives tuples meet the selection condition.

(a) Suppose that a clustered B+ tree index on *title* is (the only index) available. What is the cost of the best plan? If an additional index (on any search key that you want) is available, would it help to produce a better plan?

(b) Suppose that an unclustered B+ tree index on *title* is (the only index) available. What is the cost of the best plan?

(c) Suppose that a clustered B+ tree index on *dname* is (the only index) available. What is the cost of the best plan? If an additional index (on any search key that you want) is available, would it help to produce a better plan?

(d) Suppose that a clustered B+ tree index on ⟨*dname, title*⟩ is (the only index) available. What is the cost of the best plan?

(e) Suppose that a clustered B+ tree index on ⟨*title, dname*⟩ is (the only index) available. What is the cost of the best plan?

Exercise 13.5 Consider the query $\pi_{A,B,C,D}(R \bowtie_{A=C} S)$. Suppose that the projection routine is based on sorting and is smart enough to eliminate all but the desired attributes during the initial pass of the sort, and also to toss out duplicate tuples on-the-fly while sorting, thus eliminating two potential extra passes. Finally, assume that you know the following:

R is 10 pages long, and R tuples are 300 bytes long.
S is 100 pages long, and S tuples are 500 bytes long.
C is a key for S, and A is a key for R.
The page size is 1024 bytes.
Each R tuple joins with exactly one S tuple (and vice versa).
The combined size of attributes A, B, C and D is 450 bytes.
A and B are in R and have a combined size of 200 bytes; C and D are in S.

1. What is the cost of writing out the final result? (As usual, you should ignore this cost in answering subsequent questions.)

2. Suppose that three buffer pages are available, and the only join method that is implemented is simple (page-oriented) nested loops.

   (a) Compute the cost of doing the projection followed by the join.

   (b) Compute the cost of doing the join followed by the projection.

   (c) Compute the cost of doing the join first and then the projection on-the-fly.

   (d) Would your answers change if 11 buffer pages were available?

3. Suppose that there are three buffer pages available, and the only join method that is implemented is block nested loops.

   (a) Compute the cost of doing the projection followed by the join.

   (b) Compute the cost of doing the join followed by the projection.

   (c) Compute the cost of doing the join first and then the projection on-the-fly.

   (d) Would your answers change if 11 buffer pages were available?

Exercise 13.6 Briefly answer the following questions.

1. Explain the role of relational algebra equivalences in the System R optimizer.

2. Consider a relational algebra expression of the form $\sigma_c(\pi_l(R \times S))$. Suppose that the equivalent expression with selections and projections pushed as much as possible, taking into account only relational algebra equivalences, is in one of the following forms. In each case give an illustrative example of the selection conditions and the projection lists $(c, l, c1, l1, \text{etc.})$.

   (a) *Equivalent maximally pushed form:* $\pi_{l1}(\sigma_{c1}(R) \times S)$.

   (b) *Equivalent maximally pushed form:* $\pi_{l1}(\sigma_{c1}(R) \times \sigma_{c2}(S))$.

   (c) *Equivalent maximally pushed form:* $\sigma_c(\pi_{l1}(\pi_{l2}(R) \times S))$.

   (d) *Equivalent maximally pushed form:* $\sigma_{c1}(\pi_{l1}(\sigma_{c2}(\pi_{l2}(R)) \times S))$.

   (e) *Equivalent maximally pushed form:* $\sigma_{c1}(\pi_{l1}(\pi_{c2}(\sigma_{l2}(R)) \times S))$.

   (f) *Equivalent maximally pushed form:* $\pi_l(\sigma_{c1}(\pi_{l1}(\pi_{c2}(\sigma_{l2}(R)) \times S)))$.

Exercise 13.7 Consider the following relational schema and SQL query. The schema captures information about employees, departments, and company finances (organized on a per department basis).

Emp(*eid:* `integer`, *did:* `integer`, *sal:* `integer`, *hobby:* `char(20)`)
Dept(*did:* `integer`, *dname:* `char(20)`, *floor:* `integer`, *phone:* `char(10)`)
Finance(*did:* `integer`, *budget:* `real`, *sales:* `real`, *expenses:* `real`)

Consider the following query:

```
SELECT  D.dname, F.budget
FROM    Emp E, Dept D, Finance F
WHERE   E.did=D.did AND D.did=F.did AND D.floor=1
        AND E.sal ≥ 59000 AND E.hobby = 'yodeling'
```

1. Identify a relational algebra tree (or a relational algebra expression if you prefer) that reflects the order of operations that a decent query optimizer would choose.

2. List the join orders (i.e., orders in which pairs of relations can be joined together to compute the query result) that a relational query optimizer will consider. (Assume that the optimizer follows the heuristic of never considering plans that require the computation of cross-products.) Briefly explain how you arrived at your list.

3. Suppose that the following additional information is available: Unclustered B+ tree indexes exist on *Emp.did, Emp.sal, Dept.floor, Dept.did,* and *Finance.did.* The system's statistics indicate that employee salaries range from 10,000 to 60,000, employees enjoy 200 different hobbies, and the company owns two floors in the building. There are a total of 50,000 employees and 5000 departments (each with corresponding financial information) in the database. The DBMS used by the company has just one join method available, namely, index nested loops.

   (a) For each of the query's base relations (Emp, Dept and Finance) estimate the number of tuples that would be initially selected from that relation if all of the non join predicates on that relation were applied to it before any join processing begins.

(b) Given your answer to the preceding question, which of the join orders that are considered by the optimizer has the least estimated cost?

Exercise 13.8 Consider the following relational schema and SQL query:

Suppliers(*sid:* integer, *sname:* char(20), *city:* char(20))
Supply(*did:* integer, *pid:* integer)
Parts(*pid:* integer, *pname:* char(20), *price:* real)

```
SELECT  S.sname, P.pname
FROM    Suppliers S, Parts P, Supply Y
WHERE   S.sid = Y.sid AND Y.pid = P.pid AND
        S.city = 'Madison' AND P.price ≤ 1000
```

1. What information about these relations will the query optimizer need to select a good query execution plan for the given query?

2. How many different join orders, assuming that cross-products are disallowed, will a System R style query optimizer consider when deciding how to process the given query? List each of these join orders.

3. What indexes might be of help in processing this query? Explain briefly.

4. What impact would adding DISTINCT to the SELECT clause have on the plans that are produced?

5. What impact would adding ORDER BY *sname* to the query have on the plans that are produced?

6. What impact would adding GROUP BY *sname* to the query have on the plans that are produced?

Exercise 13.9 Consider the following scenario:

Emp(*eid:* integer, *sal:* integer, *age:* real, *did:* integer)
Dept(*did:* integer, *projid:* integer, *budget:* real, *status:* char(10))
Proj(*projid:* integer, *code:* integer, *report:* varchar)

Assume that each Emp record is 20 bytes long, each Dept record is 40 bytes long, and each Proj record is 2000 bytes long on average. There are 20,000 tuples in Emp, 5000 tuples in Dept (note that *did* is not a key), and 1000 tuples in Proj. Each department, identified by *did*, has 10 projects on average. The file system supports 4000 byte pages, and 12 pages are available in the buffer. The following questions are all based on this information. You can assume uniform distribution of values whenever necessary. State any additional assumptions. The cost metric to use is *the number of page I/Os*. Ignore the cost of writing out the final result.

1. Consider the following two queries: "Find all employees with *age* = 30" and "Find all projects with *code* = 20." Assume that the number of qualifying tuples is the same in each case. If you are building indexes on the selected attributes to speed up these queries, for which query is a *clustered* index (in comparison to an *unclustered* index) more important?

2. Consider the following query: "Find all employees with $age > 30$." Assume that there is an unclustered index on age. Let the number of qualifying tuples be N. For what values of N is a sequential scan cheaper than using the index?

3. Consider the following query:

   ```
   SELECT *
   FROM   Emp E, Dept D
   WHERE  E.did=D.did
   ```

   (a) Suppose that there is a clustered hash index on did on Emp. List all the plans that are considered and identify the plan with the least estimated cost.

   (b) Assume that both relations are sorted on the join column. List all the plans that are considered and show the plan with the least estimated cost.

   (c) Suppose that there is a clustered B+ tree index on did on Emp and that Dept is sorted on did. List all the plans that are considered and identify the plan with the least estimated cost.

4. Consider the following query:

   ```
   SELECT    D.did, COUNT(*)
   FROM      Dept D, Proj P
   WHERE     D.projid=P.projid
   GROUP BY  D.did
   ```

   (a) Suppose that no indexes are available. Show the plan with the least estimated cost.

   (b) Suppose that there is a hash index on $P.projid$. Show the plan with the least estimated cost.

   (c) Suppose that there is a hash index on $D.projid$. Show the plan with the least estimated cost.

   (d) Suppose that there is a hash index on $D.projid$ and $P.projid$. Show the plan with the least estimated cost.

   (e) Suppose that there is a clustered B+ tree index on $D.did$ and a hash index on $P.projid$. Show the plan with the least estimated cost.

   (f) Suppose that there is a clustered B+ tree index on $D.did$, a hash index on $D.projid$, and a hash index on $P.projid$. Show the plan with the least estimated cost.

   (g) Suppose that there is a clustered B+ tree index on $\langle D.did, D.projid \rangle$ and a hash index on $P.projid$. Show the plan with the least estimated cost.

   (h) Suppose that there is a clustered B+ tree index on $\langle D.projid, D.did \rangle$ and a hash index on $P.projid$. Show the plan with the least estimated cost.

5. Consider the following query:

   ```
   SELECT    D.did, COUNT(*)
   FROM      Dept D, Proj P
   WHERE     D.projid=P.projid AND  D.budget>99000
   GROUP BY  D.did
   ```

Assume that department budgets are uniformly distributed in the range 0 to 100,000.

(a) Suppose that no indexes are available. Show the plan with the least estimated cost.

(b) Suppose that there is a hash index on *P.projid*. Show the plan with the least estimated cost.

(c) Suppose that there is a hash index on *D.budget*. Show the plan with the least estimated cost.

(d) Suppose that there is a hash index on *D.projid* and *D.budget*. Show the plan with the least estimated cost.

(e) Suppose that there is a clustered B+ tree index on ⟨*D.did,D.budget*⟩ and a hash index on *P.projid*. Show the plan with the least estimated cost.

(f) Suppose that there is a clustered B+ tree index on *D.did*, a hash index on *D.budget*, and a hash index on *P.projid*. Show the plan with the least estimated cost.

(g) Suppose that there is a clustered B+ tree index on ⟨*D.did, D.budget, D.projid*⟩ and a hash index on *P.projid*. Show the plan with the least estimated cost.

(h) Suppose that there is a clustered B+ tree index on ⟨*D.did, D.projid, D.budget*⟩ and a hash index on *P.projid*. Show the plan with the least estimated cost.

6. Consider the following query:

```
SELECT E.eid, D.did, P.projid
FROM   Emp E, Dept D, Proj P
WHERE  E.sal=50,000 AND D.budget>20,000
       E.did=D.did AND D.projid=P.projid
```

Assume that employee salaries are uniformly distributed in the range 10,009 to 110,008 and that project budgets are uniformly distributed in the range 10,000 to 30,000. There is a clustered index on *sal* for Emp, a clustered index on *did* for Dept, and a clustered index on *projid* for Proj.

(a) List all the one-relation, two-relation and three-relation subplans considered in optimizing this query.

(b) Show the plan with the least estimated cost for this query.

(c) If the index on Proj were unclustered, would the cost of the preceding plan change substantially? What if the index on Emp or on Dept were unclustered?

PROJECT-BASED EXERCISES

Exercise 13.10 (*Note to instructors: This question can be made more specific by providing additional details about the queries and the catalogs. See Appendix A.*) Minibase has a nice query optimizer visualization tool that lets you see how a query is optimized. Try initializing the catalogs to reflect various scenarios (perhaps taken from the chapter or the other exercises) and optimizing different queries. Using the graphical interface, you can look at each enumerated plan at several levels of detail, toggle (i.e., turn on/off) the availability of indexes, join methods, and so on.

BIBLIOGRAPHIC NOTES

Query optimization is critical in a relational DBMS, and it has therefore been extensively studied. We have concentrated in this chapter on the approach taken in System R, as described in [483], although our discussion incorporated subsequent refinements to the approach. [575] describes query optimization in Ingres. Good surveys can be found in [282] and [271]. [301] contains several articles on query processing and optimization.

From a theoretical standpoint, [114] showed that determining whether two *conjunctive queries* (queries involving only selections, projections and cross-products) are equivalent is an NP-complete problem; if relations are *multisets*, rather than sets of tuples, it is not known whether the problem is decidable, although it is Π_2^p hard. The equivalence problem was shown to be decidable for queries involving selections, projections, cross-products and unions in [464]; surprisingly, this problem is undecidable if relations are multisets [276]. Equivalence of conjunctive queries in the presence of integrity constraints is studied in [24], and equivalence of conjunctive queries with inequality selections is studied in [307].

An important problem in query optimization is estimating the size of the result of a query expression. Approaches based on sampling are explored in [240, 241, 258, 339, 411]. The use of detailed statistics, in the form of histograms, to estimate size is studied in [277, 404, 431]. Unless care is exercised, errors in size estimation can quickly propagate and make cost estimates worthless for expressions with several operators. This problem is examined in [272]. [367] surveys several techniques for estimating result sizes and correlations between values in relations. There are a number of other papers in this area, for example, [20, 124, 429, 533], and our list is far from complete.

Semantic query optimization is based on transformations that preserve equivalence only when certain integrity constraints hold. The idea was introduced in [304] and developed further in [496, 109, 501].

In recent years, there has been increasing interest in complex queries for decision support applications. Optimization of nested SQL queries is discussed in [560, 213, 293, 297, 403]. The use of the Magic Sets technique for optimizing SQL queries is studied in [399, 401, 400, 488, 485]. Rule-based query optimizers are studied in [204, 222, 348, 385, 430]. Finding a good join order for queries with a large number of joins is studied in [317, 273, 274, 534]. Optimization of multiple queries for simultaneous execution is considered in [422, 455, 484]. Determining query plans at run-time is discussed in [223, 275].

CONCEPTUAL DESIGN AND THE ER MODEL

PICTURE, n. A representation in two dimensions of something wearisome in three.

—Ambrose Bierce, *The Devil's Dictionary*

Database design is an important and challenging task. Good design requires a thorough understanding the data associated with an enterprise and how it is used, as well as a good grasp of the features supported by the DBMS.

We begin this chapter with an overview of database design in Section 14.1. We introduce the *entity-relationship (ER) data model*, which is used to develop a first-cut database design, in Section 14.2. Additional features of the ER model are discussed in Section 14.3. We discuss the use of the ER model for database design in Section 14.4, and consider how its features should be used in different situations to model the data faithfully. We conclude by discussing some of the challenges in designing databases for very large enterprises in Section 14.5.

14.1 OVERVIEW OF DATABASE DESIGN

The very first step in designing a database application is to understand what information the database must store for the given enterprise and what *integrity constraints* or *business rules* apply to the data. This first step is called **requirements analysis** and is typically an informal process that involves discussions with user groups, a study of the current operating environment and how it is expected to change, analysis of any available documentation on existing applications that are expected to be replaced or complemented by the database, and so on. Several methodologies have been proposed for organizing and presenting the information gathered in this phase, and some automated tools have been developed to support this process.

The information gathered from this process is used to develop a high-level description of the data to be stored in the database, along with the constraints that are known to hold over this data. We will refer to this step as **conceptual design**, and it is often carried out using the ER model, which allows us to describe the data at a high level of abstraction. There are no database systems that directly support the ER model; we must translate an ER model description of data into a collection of relations if we want to use a relational DBMS. In this chapter we will focus on conceptual design.

The next stage of the design process is to refine the collection of relations, taking into account all the available information about integrity constraints. We call this step **schema refinement**. In contrast to the initial step of conceptual design, which is essentially a subjective process, schema refinement can be guided by some elegant and powerful theory. The theory of *normalizing* relations—restructuring them to ensure some desirable properties—is discussed in Chapter 15.

The third step in database design is **physical database design**. In this step we must consider typical expected workloads that our database must support and further refine the database design to ensure that it meets desired performance criteria. This step may simply involve building indexes on some relations or involve a substantial redesign of parts of the database schema obtained from the first two design steps. In general, our division of the design process into three steps should be seen as a classification of the *kinds* of steps involved in design. Realistically, although we might begin with conceptual design, followed by schema refinement, followed by physical design, a complete database design will probably require a subsequent **tuning** phase in which all three kinds of design steps are interleaved and iterated. We discuss physical design and database tuning in Chapter 16.

In preceding chapters, we examined the concepts and techniques that underlie a relational DBMS. While this material is clearly useful to someone who wants to implement or maintain the internals of a database system, it is important to recognize that serious users and DBAs must also know how a DBMS works. A good understanding of database system internals is essential for a user who wishes to take full advantage of a DBMS and design a good database; this is especially true of physical design and database tuning.

14.2   THE ENTITY-RELATIONSHIP (ER) DATA MODEL

The **ER data model** is built around the basic concepts of **entities**, **attributes** and **relationships**. We discuss these concepts below, and also introduce pictorial representations for them that allow us to describe a database in terms of **ER diagrams**. As we present each construct in the ER model, we also discuss how it can be translated into the relational model (or indicate why it cannot be translated). We note that many variations of ER diagrams are in use, and no widely accepted standards prevail. The presentation in this chapter is representative of the family of ER models and includes a selection of the most popular features.

14.2.1   Entities, Attributes and Entity Sets

An **entity** is an object in the real world that is distinguishable from other objects. Examples include the following: the Green Dragonzord toy, the toy department, the manager of the toy department, the home address of the manager of the toy department. It is often useful to identify a collection of similar entities. Such a collection is called an **entity set**. Note that entity sets need not be disjoint; the collection of toy department employees and the collection of appliance department employees may both contain employee John Doe (who happens to work in both departments). We could also define an entity set called Employees that contains both the toy and appliance department employee sets.

An entity is described in the database using a set of **attributes**. All entities in a given entity set have the same attributes; this is essentially what we mean by *similar*. (This statement is an oversimplification, as we will see when we discuss inheritance hierarchies in Section 14.3.4, but it suffices for now and highlights the main idea.) Our choice of attributes reflects the level of detail at which we wish to represent information about entities. For example, the Employees entity set could use name, social security number (ssn), and parking lot (lot) as attributes. In this case we will store the name, social security number, and lot number for each employee. However, we will not store, say, an employee's address (or gender or age).

For each attribute associated with an entity set, we must identify a **domain** of possible values. For example, the domain associated with the attribute name of Employees might be the set of 20-character strings.[1] Further, for each entity set, we choose a **key**. The concept of a key here is intuitively the same as the one we discussed in Chapter 2. A key is a minimal set of attributes whose values uniquely identify an entity in the set. There could be more than one **candidate** key; if so, we designate one of them as the **primary** key. For now we will assume that each entity set contains at least one set of attributes that uniquely identify an entity in the set; that is, the set of attributes contains a key. We will revisit this point in Section 14.3.3.

The Employees entity set with attributes *ssn, name* and *lot* is shown in Figure 14.1. An entity set is represented by a rectangle, and an attribute is represented by an oval. Each attribute in the primary key is underlined. The domain information could be listed along with the attribute name, but we omit this to keep the figures compact. The key is *ssn*.

---

[1] To avoid confusion, we will assume that attribute names do not repeat across entity sets. This is not a real limitation because we can always use the entity set name to resolve ambiguities if the same attribute name is used in more than one entity set.

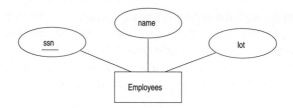

Figure 14.1   The Employees Entity Set

Translation to the Relational Model

An entity set is mapped to a relation in a straightforward way: each attribute of the entity set becomes an attribute of the relation. Note that we know both the domain of each attribute and the (primary) key of the entity set.

A possible instance of the Employees entity set, containing three Employees entities, is shown in Figure 14.2 in a relational format.

ssn	name	lot
123-22-3666	Attishoo	48
231-31-5368	Smiley	22
131-24-3650	Smethurst	35

Figure 14.2   An Instance of the Employees Entity Set

The following SQL statement captures the preceding information, including the domain and key constraints:

```
CREATE TABLE Employees ( ssn      CHAR(11),
                         name     CHAR(20),
                         lot      INTEGER,
                         PRIMARY KEY (ssn) )
```

14.2.2   Relationships and Relationship Sets

A **relationship** is an association among two or more entities. For example, we may have the relationship that Attishoo works in the Pharmacy department. As with entities, we may wish to collect a set of similar relationships into a **relationship set**. A relationship set can be thought of as a set of n-tuples:

$$\{(e_1, \ldots, e_n) \mid e_1 \in E_1, \ldots, e_n \in E_n\}$$

Each n-tuple denotes a relationship involving n entities e_1 through e_n, where entity e_i is in entity set E_i. In Figure 14.3 we show the relationship set Works_In, in which each relationship indicates a department in which an employee works. Note that several relationship sets might involve the same entity sets. For example, we could also have a Manages relationship set involving Employees and Departments.

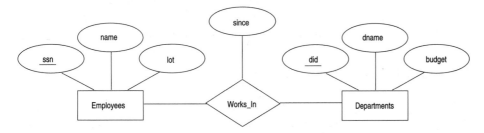

Figure 14.3 The Works_In Relationship Set

A relationship can also have **descriptive attributes**. Descriptive attributes are used to record information about the relationship, rather than about any one of the participating entities; for example, we may wish to record that Attishoo works in the pharmacy department as of January 1991. This information is captured in Figure 14.3 by adding an attribute, *since*, to Works_In. A relationship must be uniquely identified by the participating entities, without reference to the descriptive attributes.

As another example of an ER diagram, suppose that each department has offices in several locations and we want to record the locations at which each employee works. This relationship is **ternary** because we must record an association between an employee, a department and a location. The ER diagram for this variant of Works_In, which we call Works_In2, is shown in Figure 14.4.

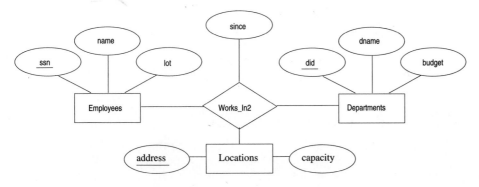

Figure 14.4 A Ternary Relationship Set

The entity sets that participate in a relationship set need not be distinct; sometimes a relationship might involve two entities in the same entity set. For example, consider the Reports_To relationship set that is shown in Figure 14.5. Since employees report to other employees, every relationship in Reports_To is of the form (emp_1, emp_2), where both emp_1 and emp_2 are entities in Employees. However, they play different **roles**: emp_1 reports to the managing employee emp_2, which is reflected in the **role indicators** *supervisor* and *subordinate* in Figure 14.5. If an entity set plays more than one role, the role indicator concatenated with an attribute name from the entity set gives us a unique name for each attribute in the relationship set.

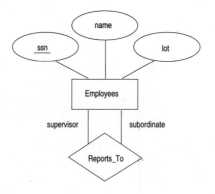

Figure 14.5   The Reports_To Relationship Set

Translation to the Relational Model

A relationship set, like an entity set, is mapped to a relation in the relational model. To represent a relationship, we must be able to identify each participating entity and give values to the descriptive attributes of the relationship. Thus the attributes of the relation include:

- The primary key attributes of each participating entity set, as foreign key fields.

- The descriptive attributes of the relationship set.

The set of nondescriptive attributes is a superkey for the relation. If there are no key constraints (see Section 14.3.1), this set of attributes is a candidate key.

A possible instance of the Works_In relationship set, containing four relationships, is shown in Figure 14.6 in a relational format. The key is *ssn, did*.

ssn	did	since
123-22-3666	51	1/1/91
123-22-3666	56	3/3/93
231-31-5368	51	2/2/92
131-24-3650	60	3/1/92

Figure 14.6   An Instance of the Works_In Relationship Set

All the available information about the Works_In relation is captured by the following SQL definition:

```
CREATE TABLE Works_In ( ssn      CHAR(11),
                        did      INTEGER,
                        since    DATE,
                        PRIMARY KEY (ssn, did),
                        FOREIGN KEY (ssn) REFERENCES Employees,
                        FOREIGN KEY (did) REFERENCES Departments )
```

Note that the *did* and *ssn* fields cannot take on *null* values. Because these fields are part of the primary key for Works_In, a **NOT NULL** constraint is implicit for each of these fields. This constraint ensures that these fields indeed identify a department and an employee in each tuple of Works_In. We can also specify that a particular action is desired when a referenced Employees or Departments tuple is deleted, as explained in the discussion of integrity constraints in Chapter 2. In this chapter we assume that the default action is appropriate except for situations in which the semantics of the ER diagram construct require some other action.

The **CREATE** statement for the Works_In2 relationship set is similar:

```
CREATE TABLE Works_In2 ( ssn      CHAR(11),
                         did      INTEGER,
                         address  CHAR(20),
                         since    DATE,
                         PRIMARY KEY (ssn, did, address),
                         FOREIGN KEY (ssn) REFERENCES Employees,
                         FOREIGN KEY (address) REFERENCES Locations,
                         FOREIGN KEY (did) REFERENCES Departments )
```

Note that the primary key is now ⟨*ssn, did, address*⟩. The definition of Locations is straightforward, and we omit it. The **CREATE** statement for Reports_To uses the role names to generate meaningful field names:

```
CREATE TABLE Reports_To (
```

```
supervisor_ssn   CHAR(11),
subordinate_ssn  CHAR(11),
PRIMARY KEY (supervisor_ssn, subordinate_ssn),
FOREIGN KEY (supervisor_ssn) REFERENCES Employees,
FOREIGN KEY (subordinate_ssn) REFERENCES Employees )
```

14.3   ADDITIONAL FEATURES OF THE ER MODEL

We now look at some of the constructs in the ER model that allow us to draw important distinctions about the data. These features allow us to capture more of the semantics of the enterprise being modeled than is possible with the relational model. The expressiveness of the ER model is a big reason for its widespread use in conceptual design.

14.3.1   Key Constraints

Consider the Works_In relationship shown in Figure 14.3. An employee can work in several departments, and a department can have several employees, as illustrated in Figure 14.6. Employee 123-22-3666 has worked in Department 51 since 1/1/91 and in Department 56 since 3/3/93. Department 51 has two employees.

Now consider another relationship set called Manages between the Employees and Departments entity sets such that each department has at most one manager, although a single employee is allowed to manage more than one department. The restriction that each department has at most one manager is an example of a **key constraint**, and it implies that each Departments entity appears in at most one Manages relationship in any allowable instance of Manages.

The relation corresponding to Manages has the same attributes as the relation corresponding to Works_In: *ssn, did, since*. However, because each department has at most one manager, no two tuples can have the same *did* value but differ on the *ssn* value. A consequence of this observation is that *did* is itself a key for Manages; indeed, the set *did, ssn* is not a key (because it is not minimal).

Such a relationship set is sometimes said to be **one-to-many**, to indicate that *one* employee can be associated with *many* departments (in the capacity of a manager), whereas each department can be associated with at most one employee as its manager. In contrast, the Works_In relationship set, in which an employee is allowed to work in several departments and a department is allowed to have several employees, is said to be **many-to-many**. These concepts are illustrated in Figure 14.7, which shows typical instances of a one-to-one relationship set, a one-to-many relationship set, a many-to-one relationship set, and a many-to-many relationship set.

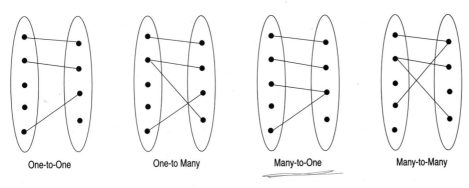

| One-to-One | One-to Many | Many-to-One | Many-to-Many |

Figure 14.7   Typical Instances of Relationship Sets

Continuing with our example, the key constraint means that the relation instance shown in Figure 14.6 is not a legal instance of the relation for Manages; however, we obtain a legal instance by deleting a row, as shown in Figure 14.8. The

ssn	did	since
123-22-3666	51	1/1/91
123-22-3666	56	3/3/93
131-24-3650	60	3/1/92

Figure 14.8   An Instance of the Manages Relationship Set

ER diagram in Figure 14.9 indicates that each Departments entity participates in at most one Manages relationship by using an arrow from Departments to Manages. Intuitively, the arrow suggests that given a Departments entity, we can uniquely determine the Manages relationship in which it appears. We can extend this convention—and the underlying key constraint concept—to relationship sets involving three or more entity sets: If an entity set E has a key constraint in a relationship set R, each entity in an instance of E appears in at most one relationship in (a corresponding instance of) R.

An example of a ternary relationship set (Manages3) with a key constraint is discussed later in this chapter, and an example instance of that relationship set is shown in Figure 14.19.

Translation to the Relational Model

If a relationship set involves n entity sets and some m of them are linked via arrows in the ER diagram, the key for any one of these m entity sets constitutes a key for the relation to which the relationship set is mapped. Thus we have m

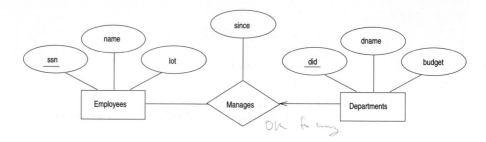

Figure 14.9   Key Constraint on Manages

candidate keys, and one of these should be designated as the primary key. The translation discussed in Section 14.2.2 from relationship sets to a relation can be used in the presence of key constraints, taking into account this point about keys.

The Manages relation can be defined using the following SQL statement:

```
CREATE TABLE Manages (   ssn      CHAR(11),
                         did      INTEGER,
                         since    DATE,
                         PRIMARY KEY (did),
                         FOREIGN KEY (ssn) REFERENCES Employees,
                         FOREIGN KEY (did) REFERENCES Departments )
```

Note the similarity between this statement and the one defining Works_In; the only difference is in the definition of the primary key.

A second approach to translating a relationship set with key constraints is often superior; it avoids creating a distinct relation for the relationship set and 'folds' the information into the relation corresponding to one of the participating entity sets with a key constraint. The idea is quite simple: Because a department has at most one manager, we can add the key fields of the Employees tuple denoting the manager and the *since* attribute to the Departments record.

This approach eliminates the need for a separate Manages relation, and queries asking for a department's manager can be answered without a join. The only drawback to this approach is that space could be wasted if several departments have no managers. In this case the added fields would have to be filled with *null* values. The first translation avoids this inefficiency, but some important queries require joins.

The following SQL statement defining a Dept_Mgr relation that essentially captures the information in both Departments and Manages illustrates this approach:

```
CREATE TABLE Dept_Mgr ( did     INTEGER,
                        dname   CHAR(20),
                        budget  REAL,
                        ssn     CHAR(11),
                        since   DATE,
                        PRIMARY KEY (did),
                        FOREIGN KEY (ssn) REFERENCES Employees )
```

Note that *ssn* can take on *null* values.

This idea can be extended to deal with relationship sets involving more than two entity sets. In general, if a relationship set involves n entity sets and some m of them are linked via arrows in the ER diagram, the relation corresponding to any of the m sets can be augmented to capture the relationship.

We discuss the relative merits of the two translation approaches further after introducing participation constraints.

14.3.2 Participation Constraints

The key constraint on Manages tells us that a department has at most one manager. A natural question to ask is whether every department has a manager. Let us say that every department is required to have a manager. This requirement is an example of a **participation constraint**; the participation of the entity set Departments in the relationship set Manages is said to be **total**. In terms of the Manages relation, this constraint means that every *did* value that appears in the Departments relation must also appear in at least one row of the Manages relation with a non *null* value in the *ssn* field. In conjunction with the key constraint that a department has at most one manager, it is easy to see that each department is required to have one and only one manager. A participation that is not total is said to be **partial**. As an example, the participation of the entity set Employees in Manages is partial, since not every employee gets to manage a department.

Revisiting the Works_In relationship set, it is natural to expect that each employee works in at least one department and that each department has at least one employee. This means that the participation of both Employees and Departments in Works_In is total. The ER diagram in Figure 14.10 shows both the Manages and Works_In relationship sets and all the given constraints. If the participation of an entity set in a relationship set is total, the two are connected by a thick line; independently, the presence of an arrow indicates a key constraint.

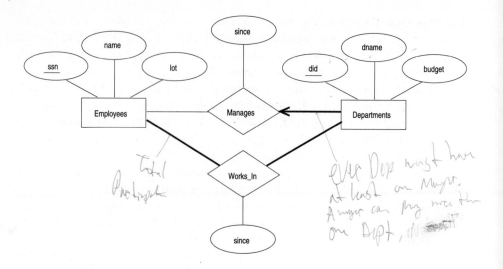

Figure 14.10   Manages and Works_In

Translation to the Relational Model

The constraint that every department must have a manager is captured in the following SQL statement, which reflects the second translation approach discussed in Section 14.3.1:

```
CREATE TABLE Dept_Mgr (  did      INTEGER,
                         dname    CHAR(20),
                         budget   REAL,
                         ssn      CHAR(11) NOT NULL,
                         since    DATE,
                         PRIMARY KEY (did),
                         FOREIGN KEY (ssn) REFERENCES Employees,
                         ON DELETE NO ACTION )
```

Because *ssn* cannot take on *null* values, each tuple of Dept_Mgr identifies a tuple in Employees (who is the manager), thereby ensuring that the participation constraint holds. The NO ACTION specification, which is the default and need not be explicitly specified, ensures that an Employees record cannot be deleted while it is pointed to by a Dept_Mgr record. If we wish to delete such an Employees record, we must first change the Dept_Mgr record to have a new employee as manager. (We could have specified CASCADE instead of NO ACTION, but deleting all information about a department just because its manager has been fired seems a bit extreme!)

The constraint that every department must have a manager cannot be captured using the first translation approach discussed in Section 14.3.1. (Look at the definition of Manages and think about what effect it would have if we added **NOT NULL** constraints to the *ssn* and *did* fields. *Hint:* The constraint would prevent the firing of a manager, but does not ensure that a manager is initially appointed for each department!) This situation is a strong argument in favor of using the second approach for one-to-many relationships such as Manages, especially when the entity set with the key constraint also has a total participation constraint.

Unfortunately, there are many participation constraints that we cannot capture using SQL-92, short of using *table constraints* or *assertions.* Table constraints and assertions can be specified using the full power of the SQL query language (as discussed in Section 9.9) and are very expressive, but also very expensive to check and enforce. For example, we cannot enforce the participation constraints on the Works_In relation without using these general constraints. To see why, consider the Works_In relation obtained by translating the ER diagram into relations. It contains fields *ssn* and *did*, which are foreign keys referring to Employees and Departments. To ensure total participation of Departments in Works_In, we have to guarantee that every *did* value in Departments appears in a tuple of Works_In. We could try to guarantee this condition by declaring that *did* in Departments is a foreign key referring to Works_In, but this is not a valid foreign key constraint because *did* is not a candidate key for Works_In.

To ensure total participation of Departments in Works_In using SQL-92, we need an assertion. We have to guarantee that every *did* value in Departments appears in a tuple of Works_In; further, this tuple of Works_In must also have non *null* values in the fields that are foreign keys referencing other entity sets involved in the relationship (in this example, the *ssn* field). We can ensure the second part of this constraint by imposing the stronger requirement that *ssn* in Works_In cannot contain *null* values. The reader is invited to write an SQL assertion to ensure that the participation of Departments in Works_In is total, proceeding along the lines sketched in this paragraph. (Ensuring that the participation of Employees in Works_In is total is symmetric.)

Another constraint that requires assertions to express in SQL is the requirement that each Employees entity (in the context of the Manages relationship set) must manage at least one department.

In fact, the Manages relationship set exemplifies most of the participation constraints that we can capture using key and foreign key constraints. Manages is a binary relationship set in which exactly one of the entity sets (Departments) has a key constraint, and the total participation constraint is expressed on that entity set.

We can also capture participation constraints using key and foreign key constraints in one other special situation: a relationship set in which all participating entity sets have key constraints and total participation. The best translation approach in this case is to map all the entities as well as the relationship into a single table; the details are straightforward.

14.3.3 Weak Entities *

Thus far, we have assumed that the attributes associated with an entity set include a key. This assumption does not always hold. For example, suppose that employees can purchase insurance policies to cover their dependents. We wish to record information about policies, including who is covered by each policy, but this information is really our only interest in the dependents of an employee. If an employee quits, any policy owned by the employee is terminated and we want to delete all the relevant policy and dependent information from the database.

We might choose to identify a dependent by name alone in this situation, since it is reasonable to expect that the dependents of a given employee have different names. Thus the attributes of the Dependents entity set might be *pname* and *age*. The attribute *pname* does *not* identify a dependent uniquely. Recall that the key for Employees is *ssn*; thus we might have two employees called Smethurst, and each might have a son called Joe.

Dependents is an example of a **weak entity set**. A weak entity can be identified uniquely only by considering some of its attributes in conjunction with the primary key of another entity, which is called the **identifying owner**.

The following restrictions must hold:

- The owner entity set and the weak entity set must participate in a one-to-many relationship set (one owner entity is associated with one or more weak entities, but each weak entity has a single owner). This relationship set is called the **identifying relationship set** of the weak entity set.

- The weak entity set must have total participation in the identifying relationship set.

For example, a Dependents entity can be identified uniquely only if we take the key of the *owning* Employees entity and the *pname* of the Dependents entity. The set of attributes of a weak entity set that uniquely identify a weak entity for a given owner entity is called a *partial key* of the weak entity set. In our example *pname* is a partial key for Dependents.

The Dependents weak entity set and its relationship to Employees is shown in Figure 14.11. The total participation of Dependents in Policy is indicated by linking them with a dark line. The arrow from Dependents to Policy indicates that each Dependents entity appears in at most one (indeed, exactly one, because of the participation constraint) Policy relationship. However, note that Dependents has only a partial key. If we translate Policy into a table, there may well be two rows with the same *pname* value.

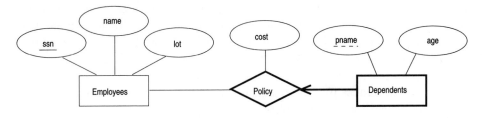

Figure 14.11   A Weak Entity Set

To underscore the fact that Dependents is a weak entity and Policy is its identifying relationship, we draw both with dark lines. To indicate that *pname* is a partial key for Dependents, we underline it using a broken line.

Translation to the Relational Model

A weak entity set always participates in a one-to-many binary relationship, and has a key constraint and total participation. The second translation approach discussed in Section 14.3.1 is ideal in this case, but we must take into account the fact that the weak entity has only a partial key. Also, when an owner entity is deleted, we want all owned weak entities to be deleted.

In our example we can capture the desired semantics with the following definition of the Dep_Policy relation:

```
CREATE TABLE Dep_Policy ( pname   CHAR(20),
                          age     INTEGER,
                          cost    REAL,
                          ssn     CHAR(11) NOT NULL,
                          PRIMARY KEY (pname, ssn),
                          FOREIGN KEY (ssn) REFERENCES Employees,
                          ON DELETE CASCADE )
```

Note that the primary key is ⟨*pname, ssn*⟩, since Dependents is a weak entity. This constraint is a change with respect to the translation discussed in Section 14.3.1. The **NOT NULL** constraint ensures that every Dependents entity is associated with an Employees entity (the owner), as per the total participation constraint on Dependents. The CASCADE option ensures that information about an employee's policy and dependents is deleted if the corresponding Employees record is deleted.

14.3.4   Class Hierarchies *

Sometimes it is natural to classify the entities in an entity set into subclasses. For example, we might want to talk about an Hourly_Emps entity set and a Contract_Emps entity set to distinguish the basis on which they are paid. We might have attributes *hours_worked* and *hourly_wage* defined for Hourly_Emps and an attribute *contractid* defined for Contract_Emps.

We want the semantics that every entity in one of these sets is also an Employees entity, and as such must have all of the attributes of Employees defined. Thus the attributes defined for an Hourly_Emps entity are the attributes for Employees plus Hourly_Emps; the attributes for the entity set Employees are *inherited* by the entity set Hourly_Emps. In addition—and in contrast to class hierarchies in programming languages such as C++—there is an inclusion constraint: A query that asks for all Employees entities must consider all Hourly_Emps and Contract_Emps entities as well. Figure 14.12 illustrates the class hierarchy.

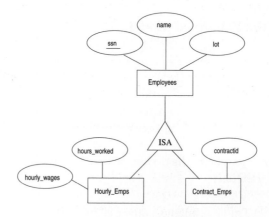

Figure 14.12   Class Hierarchy

The entity set Employees may also be classified using a different criterion. For example, we might identify a subset of employees as Senior_Emps. We can modify Figure 14.12 to reflect this change by adding a second ISA (read *is a*) node as a child of Employees, and making Senior_Emps a child of this node. Each of these entity sets might be classified further, creating a multilevel ISA hierarchy.

A class hierarchy can be viewed in one of two ways:

- Employees is **specialized** into subclasses. Specialization is the process of identifying subsets of an entity set (the **superclass**) that share some distinguishing characteristic. Typically the superclass is defined first, the subclasses are defined next, and subclass-specific attributes and relationship sets are then added.

- Hourly_Emps and Contract_Emps are **generalized** by Employees. As another example, two entity sets Motorboats and Cars may be generalized into an entity set Motor_Vehicles. Generalization consists of identifying some common characteristics of a collection of entity sets and creating a new entity set that contains entities possessing these common characteristics. Typically the subclasses are defined first, the superclass is defined next, and any relationship sets that involve the superclass are then defined.

There are two kinds of constraints that we can specify with respect to ISA hierarchies, namely, *overlap* and *covering* constraints. **Overlap constraints** determine whether two subclasses are allowed to contain the same entity. For example, can Attishoo be both an Hourly_Emps entity and a Contract_Emps entity? Intuitively, no. Can he be both a Contract_Emps entity and a Senior_Emps entity? Intuitively, yes.

Covering constraints determine whether the entities in the subclasses collectively include all entities in the superclass. For example, does every Employees entity have to belong to one of its subclasses? Intuitively, no. Does every Motor_Vehicles entity have to be either a Motorboats entity or a Cars entity? Intuitively, yes; a characteristic property of generalization hierarchies is that every instance of a superclass is an instance of a subclass.

There are two basic reasons for identifying subclasses (by specialization or generalization):

1. We might want to add descriptive attributes that make sense only for the entities in a subclass. For example, *hourly_wages* does not make sense for a Contract_Emps entity, whose pay is determined by an individual contract.

2. We might want to identify the set of entities that participate in some relationship. For example, we might wish to define the Manages relationship so that the participating entity sets are Senior_Emps and Departments, to ensure that only senior employees can be managers. As another example, Motorboats and Cars may have different descriptive attributes (say, tonnage and number of doors), but as Motor_Vehicles entities, they must be licensed. The licensing information can be captured by a Licensed_To relationship between Motor_Vehicles and an entity set called Owners.

Translation to the Relational Model

We present the two basic approaches to handling ISA hierarchies by applying them to the ER diagram shown in Figure 14.12:

1. We can map each of the entity sets Employees, Hourly_Emps and Contract_Emps to a distinct relation. The Employees relation is created as in Section 14.2.1. We discuss Hourly_Emps here; Contract_Emps is handled similarly. The relation for Hourly_Emps includes the *hourly_wages* and *hours_worked* attributes of Hourly_Emps. It also contains the key attributes of the superclass (*ssn*, in this example), which serve as the primary key for Hourly_Emps, as well as a foreign key referencing the superclass (Employees). For each Hourly_Emps entity, the value of the *name* and *lot* attributes are stored in the corresponding row of the superclass (Employees). Note that if the superclass tuple is deleted, the delete must be cascaded to Hourly_Emps.

2. Alternatively, we can create just two relations, corresponding to Hourly_Emps and Contract_Emps. The relation for Hourly_Emps includes all the attributes of Hourly_Emps as well as all the attributes of Employees (i.e., *ssn, name, lot, hourly_wages, hours_worked*).

The first approach is general and is always applicable. Queries in which we want to examine all employees and do not care about the attributes specific to the subclasses are handled easily using the Employees relation. However, queries in which we want to examine, say, hourly employees, may require a join with Employees to retrieve *name* and *lot*.

The second approach is not applicable if we have employees who are neither hourly employees nor contract employees, since there is no way to store such employees. Also, if an employee is both an Hourly_Emps and a Contract_Emps entity, then the *name* and *lot* values are stored twice. This duplication can lead to some of the anomalies that we discuss in Chapter 15. A query that needs to examine all employees must now examine two relations. On the other hand, a query that needs to examine only hourly employees can now do so without the need for a join. The choice between these approaches clearly depends on the semantics of the data and the frequency of common operations.

In general, overlap and covering constraints can be expressed in SQL-92 only by using assertions.

14.3.5 Aggregation *

As we have defined it thus far, a relationship set is an association between entity sets. Sometimes we have to model a relationship between a collection of entities and *relationships.* To do so, we require a concept called **aggregation**. Suppose that we have an entity set called Projects and that each Projects entity is sponsored by one or more departments. The Sponsors relationship set captures this information. A department that sponsors a project might assign employees to monitor it. Intuitively, Monitors should be a relationship set that associates a Sponsors relationship with an Employees entity. This association is accomplished using aggregation, which effectively allows us to view Sponsors as an entity set for purposes of participation in other relationship sets. This is illustrated in Figure 14.13, with a dashed box used to denote aggregation.

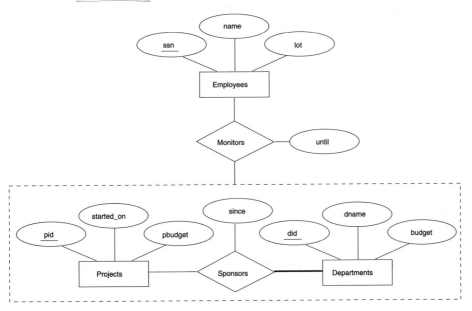

Figure 14.13   Aggregation

When should we use aggregation? Intuitively, when we need to express a relationship among relationships. But can't we express relationships involving other relationships without using aggregation? In our example, why not make Sponsors a ternary relationship? The answer is that there are really two distinct relationships, Sponsors and Monitors, each possibly with attributes of its own. For instance, the Monitors relationship has an attribute *until* that records the date until when the employee is appointed as the sponsorship monitor. Compare this attribute with the attribute *since* of Sponsors, which is the date since when the sponsorship has been in effect. The use of aggregation versus a ternary relationship may also be guided by certain integrity constraints, as explained in Section 14.4.4.

Translation to the Relational Model

Translating aggregation into the relational model is easy because there is no real distinction between entities and relationships in the relational model. The Employees, Projects and Departments entity sets and the Sponsors relationship set are mapped as described in previous sections. For the Monitors relationship set, we create a relation with the following attributes: the key attributes of Employees (*ssn*), the key attributes of Sponsors (*did, pid*), and the descriptive attributes of Monitors (*until*). This translation is essentially the standard mapping for a relationship set, as described in Section 14.2.2.

There is a special case in which this translation can be refined further by dropping the Sponsors relation. Consider this relation. It has attributes *pid, did* and *since*, and in general we need it (in addition to Monitors) for two reasons:

1. We have to record the descriptive attributes (in our example, *since*) of the Sponsors relationship.

2. Not every sponsorship has a monitor, and thus some ⟨*pid, did*⟩ pairs in the Sponsors relation may not appear in the Monitors relation.

However, if Sponsors has no descriptive attributes and has total participation in Monitors, every possible instance of the Sponsors relation can be obtained by projecting the ⟨*pid, did*⟩ columns of the Monitors relation. Thus we need not store the Sponsors relation in this case.

14.4 CONCEPTUAL DESIGN USING THE ER MODEL

In this section we consider some important issues related to the use of the ER model in conceptual database design. The first step in designing a database is to understand the enterprise to be modeled and the information that is to be stored. Once a designer has a thorough grasp of the data and its usage, conceptual design can be carried out using ER design (or other conceptual design methodologies, which we do not discuss). There are several important issues to bear in mind while developing an ER diagram, and we discuss some of them in this section.

The first point to observe is that developing an ER diagram presents several choices. Some important choices appear in the following list; the last choice was discussed briefly when we presented aggregation, and the others will be discussed further in this section.

■   Should a concept be modeled as an entity or an attribute?

■   Should a concept be modeled as an entity or a relationship?

- What are the relationships? Should we use binary or ternary relationships?

- Should we use aggregation?

The second point to note is that the ER diagram is just an approximate description of the data—we may not always be able to capture all the semantics relevant to our application. In particular the constraints expressible in the ER model may not be adequate to express important data constraints. This problem is compounded by the fact that the relational model cannot express some constraints in ER diagrams! Fortunately, SQL-92 allows us to express a broad range of constraints using table constraints and assertions, although this approach can be expensive.

Finally, ER modeling is sometimes regarded as a complete approach to designing a database schema; this is incorrect. It is important to appreciate why the relations obtained by translating an ER diagram may need to be further refined.

14.4.1 Entity versus Attribute

While identifying the attributes of an entity set, it is sometimes not clear whether a property should be modeled as an attribute or as an entity set (and related to the first entity set using a relationship set). For example, consider adding address information to the Employees entity set. One option is to use an attribute *address*. This option is appropriate if we need to record only one address per employee, and it suffices to think of an address as a string. An alternative is to create an entity set called Addresses and to record associations between employees and addresses using a relationship (say, Has_Address). This more complex alternative is necessary in two situations:

- We have to record more than one address for an employee.

- We want to capture the structure of an address in our ER diagram. For example, we might break down an address into city, state, country, and zip code, in addition to a string for street information. By representing an address as an entity with these attributes, we can support queries such as "Find all employees with an address in Madison, WI."

As another example of when to model a concept as an entity set rather than as an attribute, consider the relationship set (called Works_In2) shown in Figure 14.14.

It differs from the Works_In relationship set of Figure 14.3 only in that it has attributes *from* and *to*, instead of *since*. Intuitively, it records the interval during which an employee works for a department. Now suppose that it is possible for an employee to work in a given department over more than one period, as illustrated in Figure 14.15. This instance is *illegal* because there are two distinct rows with

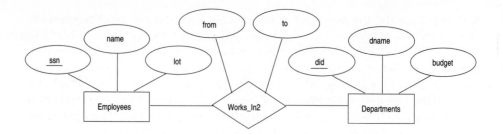

Figure 14.14   The Works_In2 Relationship Set

ssn	did	from	to
123-22-3666	51	1/1/91	2/2/92
123-22-3666	56	3/3/93	3/5/94
131-24-3650	60	3/1/92	12/12/92
123-22-3666	56	5/7/95	3/5/96

Figure 14.15   An *Illegal* Instance of Works_In2

the same *ssn* and *did* values. Thus ⟨*ssn, did*⟩ (the union of key attributes of all participating entity sets) does not constitute a key for Works_In2.

The problem is that we want to record several values for the descriptive attributes of Works_In2 for each instance of this relationship. (This situation is analogous to wanting to record several addresses for each employee.) We can address this problem by introducing an entity set called, say, Duration, with attributes *from* and *to*, as shown in Figure 14.16. The illegal instance of Works_In2 shown in Figure 14.15 is a legal instance of Works_In3.

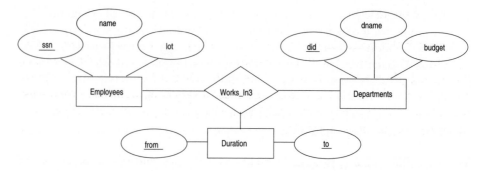

Figure 14.16   The Works_In3 Relationship Set

In some versions of the ER model, attributes are allowed to take on sets as values. Given this feature, we could make Duration an attribute of Works_In, rather than an entity set; associated with each Works_In relationship, we would have a set of intervals. This approach is perhaps more intuitive than modeling Duration as an entity set. Nonetheless, when such set-valued attributes are translated into the relational model, which does not support set-valued attributes, the resulting relational schema is very similar to what we get by regarding Duration as an entity set.

14.4.2 Entity versus Relationship

Consider the relationship set called Manages in Figure 14.9. Suppose that each department manager is given a discretionary budget (*dbudget*), as shown in Figure 14.17, in which we have also renamed the relationship set to Manages2.

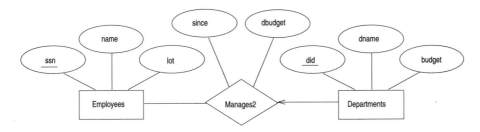

Figure 14.17 Entity versus Relationship

There is at most one employee managing a department, but a given employee could manage several departments; we store the starting date and discretionary budget for each manager-department pair. This approach is natural if we assume that a manager receives a separate discretionary budget for each department that he or she manages.

But what if the discretionary budget is a sum that covers *all* departments managed by that employee? In this case each Manages2 relationship that involves a given employee will have the same value in the *dbudget* field. In general such redundancy could be significant and could cause a variety of problems. (We discuss redundancy and its attendant problems in Chapter 15.) Another problem with this design is that it is misleading.

We can address these problems by associating *dbudget* with the appointment of the employee as manager of a *group* of departments. In this approach, we model the appointment as an entity set, say Mgr_Appt, and use a ternary relationship, say Manages3, to relate a manager, an appointment, and a department. The details of an appointment (such as the discretionary budget) are not repeated for

each department that is included in the appointment now, although there is still
one Manages3 relationship instance per such department. Further, note that each
department has at most one manager, as before, because of the key constraint.
This approach is illustrated in Figure 14.18.

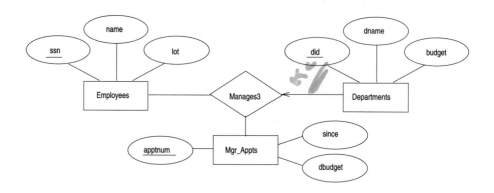

Figure 14.18 Entity Set versus Relationship

A legal instance of Manages3 is shown in Figure 14.19, and a corresponding instance of Mgr_Appts is shown in Figure 14.20. Notice how the information about
the appointment of employee 123-22-3666 as the manager of departments 63 and
64 is stored just once in Mgr_Appts.

ssn	did	apptnum
123-22-3666	51	3
123-22-3666	56	4
131-24-3650	60	7
123-22-3666	63	8
123-22-3666	64	8

apptnum	since	dbudget
3	1/1/91	10000
4	3/3/93	10000
7	3/1/92	12000
8	4/4/95	30000

Figure 14.19 An Instance of the Manages3
Relationship Set

Figure   14.20 An   Instance   of   the
Mgr_Appts Entity Set

14.4.3   Binary versus Ternary Relationships *

Consider the ER diagram shown in Figure 14.21. It models a situation in which an
employee can own several policies, each policy can be owned by several employees,
and each dependent can be covered by several policies.

Suppose that we have the following additional requirements:

■   A policy cannot be owned jointly by two or more employees.

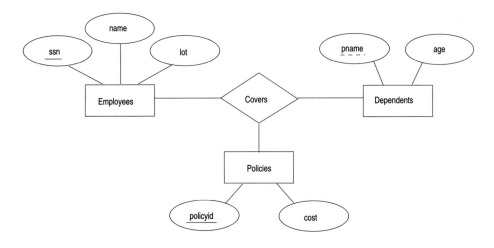

Figure 14.21 Policies as an Entity Set

- Every policy must be owned by some employee.

- Dependents is a weak entity set, and each dependent entity is uniquely identified by taking *pname* in conjunction with the *policyid* of a policy entity (which, intuitively, covers the given dependent).

The first requirement suggests that we impose a key constraint on Policies with respect to Covers, but this constraint has the unintended side effect that a policy can cover only one dependent. The second requirement suggests that we impose a total participation constraint on Policies. This solution is acceptable if each policy covers at least one dependent. The third requirement forces us to introduce an identifying relationship that is binary (in our version of ER diagrams, although there are versions in which this is not the case).

Even ignoring the third point above, the best way to model this situation is to use two binary relationships, as shown in Figure 14.22.

We can translate this ER diagram into the relational model as follows, taking advantage of the key constraints to combine Purchaser information with Policies and Beneficiary information with Dependents:

```
CREATE TABLE Policies (    policyid INTEGER,
                           cost     REAL,
                           ssn      CHAR(11) NOT NULL,
                           PRIMARY KEY (policyid),
                           FOREIGN KEY (ssn) REFERENCES Employees,
                           ON DELETE CASCADE)
```

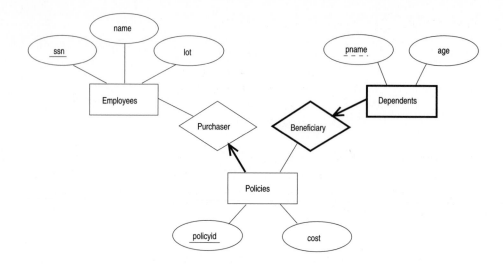

Figure 14.22   Policy Revisited

```
CREATE TABLE Dependents (  pname    CHAR(20),
                           age      INTEGER,
                           policyid INTEGER,
                           PRIMARY KEY (pname, policyid),
                           FOREIGN KEY (policyid) REFERENCES Policies,
                           ON DELETE CASCADE )
```

Notice how the deletion of an employee leads to the deletion of all policies owned by the employee and all dependents who are beneficiaries of those policies. Further, each dependent is required to have a covering policy—because *policyid* is part of the primary key of Dependents, there is an implicit **NOT NULL** constraint. This model accurately reflects the participation constraints in the ER diagram and the intended actions when an employee entity is deleted.

Before concluding our discussion of this example, it is worth making an interesting point about weak entity sets. In general there could be a chain of identifying relationships for weak entity sets. For example, we assumed that *policyid* uniquely identifies a policy. Suppose that *policyid* only distinguishes the policies owned by a given employee; that is, *policyid* is only a partial key and Policies should be modeled as a weak entity set. This new assumption about *policyid* does not cause much to change in the preceding discussion. In fact, the only changes are that the primary key of Policies becomes ⟨*policyid, ssn*⟩, and as a consequence, the definition of Dependents changes—an *ssn* field is added, and becomes part of both the primary key of Dependents and the foreign key referencing Policies:

```
CREATE TABLE Dependents (pname   CHAR(20),
                         ssn     CHAR(11),
                         age     INTEGER,
                         policyid INTEGER NOT NULL,
                         PRIMARY KEY (pname, policyid, ssn),
                         FOREIGN KEY (policyid, ssn) REFERENCES Policies,
                         ON DELETE CASCADE)
```

This example really had two relationships involving Policies, and our attempt to use a single ternary relationship (Figure 14.21) was inappropriate. There are situations, however, where a relationship inherently associates more than two entities. We have already seen such an example (Figure 14.4, and also Figures 14.16 and 14.18).

As another good example of a ternary relationship, consider entity sets Parts, Suppliers, and Departments, and a relationship set Contracts (with descriptive attribute *qty*) that involves all of them. A contract specifies that a supplier will supply (some quantity of) a part to a department. This relationship cannot be adequately captured by a collection of binary relationships (without the use of aggregation). With binary relationships, we can denote that a supplier 'can supply' certain parts, that a department 'needs' some parts, or that a department 'deals with' a certain supplier. No combination of these relationships expresses the meaning of a contract adequately, for at least two reasons:

■   The facts that supplier S can supply part P, that department D needs part P, and that D will buy from S do not necessarily imply that department D indeed buys part P from supplier S!

■   We cannot represent the *qty* attribute of a contract cleanly.

Let us examine the first point in more detail. Consider the instance of Contracts shown in Figure 14.23.

sid	*pid*	*did*	*qty*
s1	p1	d1	10
s2	p1	d2	20
s1	p2	d2	30
s2	p2	d1	40

sid	*pid*
s1	p1
s2	p1
s1	p2
s2	p2

Figure 14.23   An Instance of Contracts   **Figure 14.24**   Supplier-Part Pairs

We cannot represent $\langle sid, pid, did \rangle$ relationships by storing any collection of binary relationships ($\langle sid, pid \rangle$, $\langle sid, did \rangle$, or $\langle did, pid \rangle$). Even if we stored all three binary

pid	did
p1	d1
p1	d2
p2	d2
p2	d1

sid	did
s1	d1
s2	d2
s1	d2
s2	d1

Figure 14.25   Part-Department Pairs   **Figure 14.26**   Supplier-Department Pairs

relationship sets, shown in Figures 14.24, 14.25 and 14.26, we would not be able to reconstruct the exact set of relationships in the Contracts instance. For example, we cannot tell that $\langle s1, p1, d2 \rangle$ is not in the given instance of Contracts. Clearly, we must represent the information in Contracts using a ternary relationship set.

14.4.4   Aggregation versus Ternary Relationships *

As we noted in Section 14.3.5, the choice between using aggregation or a ternary relationship is mainly determined by the existence of a relationship that relates a *relationship set* to an entity set (or second relationship set). The choice may also be guided by certain integrity constraints that we want to express. For example, consider the ER diagram shown in Figure 14.13. According to this diagram, a project can be sponsored by any number of departments, a department can sponsor one or more projects, and each sponsorship is monitored by one or more employees. If we don't need to record the *until* attribute of Monitors, then we might reasonably use a ternary relationship, say, Sponsors2, as shown in Figure 14.27.

Consider the constraint that each sponsorship (of a project by a department) be monitored by at most one employee. We cannot express this constraint in terms of the Sponsors2 relationship set. On the other hand, we can easily express the constraint by drawing an arrow from the aggregated relationship Sponsors to the relationship Monitors in Figure 14.27. Thus the presence of such a constraint serves as another reason for using aggregation rather than a ternary relationship set. If we also make the participation of Sponsors in Monitors be total, the optimized translation into the relational model (outlined in Section 14.3.5) will produce just the Monitors relation, with the appropriate primary key, and discard the redundant Sponsors relation.

14.4.5   Constraints beyond the ER Model *

In our discussion of the ER model, we have carefully noted the integrity constraints implied by constructs in the model. We have also discussed how to express these constraints using SQL when translating an ER diagram into the relational

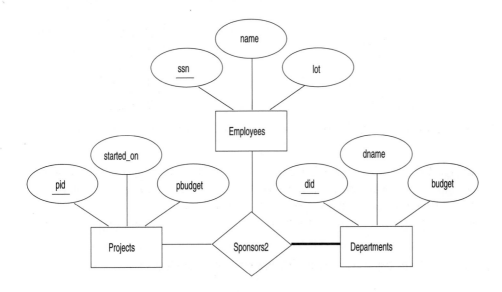

Figure 14.27 Using a Ternary Relationship instead of Aggregation

model. It is important use primary and foreign key constraints whenever possible (for clarity and efficiency), although as we have seen, some constraints can only be expressed using the table constraints or assertions in SQL.

Although we have concentrated on constraints that can be expressed using ER model constructs, there are constraints that cannot be expressed in this model. We should also identify such constraints during the design phase, and we should consider the use of table constraints or assertions (or application program logic, if that is more appropriate) to enforce them. Some examples of such constraints follow.

- Consider the ternary relationship set Contracts between the entity sets Parts, Suppliers and Departments (Section 14.4.3). There might be a policy that a department should not order two different parts from the same supplier. This constraint implies that the key attributes of Suppliers and Departments constitute a key for Contracts, but we cannot express this constraint easily in the ER model. As another example, we might have a policy that a department must place all of its contracts with a single supplier. Again, we cannot express this policy easily in the ER model. These constraints are examples of *functional dependencies*, which we discuss in Chapter 15.

  It is worth considering the conditions under which such a constraint can be expressed in the ER model. In the Contracts example, we have to break Contracts into two relationship sets and relate them using aggregation. The discussion of Sponsors (Figure 14.13) versus Sponsors2 (Figure 14.27) in Section 14.4.4 illustrates one solution. Clearly, it is complicated and becomes more so as the arity of the relationship set and the number of functional dependencies over it increase.

- Consider the Manages and Reports_To relationship sets (Section 14.2.2). We might require that all manager entities have someone reporting to them; that is, the set of *ssn* values in the Manages relation instance must be a subset of the set of *supervisor_ssn* values in the Reports_To relation instance in any allowable state of the database. This example illustrates an **inclusion dependency**. Inclusion dependencies generalize the concept of foreign keys, and in general they cannot be expressed in the ER model, although certain special cases can indeed be expressed.

  Foreign keys are an important special case of inclusion dependencies; every value that apears in a foreign key field must also appear in the primary key of the relation that is referenced. This special case, fortunately, can usually be captured in ER diagrams—each edge that links a relationship set to an entity set implicitly specifies such an inclusion. The example inclusion dependency between the *ssn* field of Manages and the *supervisor_ssn* field of Reports_To cannot be expressed in the ER model in this manner because it does not arise from a relationship-set-to-entity-set edge. In fact, this inclusion dependency is *not* a foreign key constraint because *supervisor_ssn* is not a key for Reports_To.

  Although we will not discuss inclusion dependencies in detail, they arise frequently in practice, especially inclusion dependencies that involve only key attributes, and have been widely studied.

- Many examples of complex constraints go beyond functional and inclusion dependencies. We might require that an employee can report only to another employee in the same department. This constraint is intuitively similar to an inclusion dependency but is even more general. As additional examples, an employee who monitors the sponsorship of a project for a department (Section 14.3.5) may be required to be a senior employee in that department, or a manager's discretionary budget may be required to be less than 10% of the combined budgets of all the departments that he or she manages.

14.4.6 Need for Further Refinement

Database design is sometimes presented as the task of developing an ER diagram and translating it into a collection of SQL **CREATE TABLE** statements. The fact that the ER model cannot express many important kinds of constraints on data suggests that this approach of just creating ER diagrams and translating them into relations is not sufficient; we must take additional constraints that are not expressed in the ER model into account.

But can we do anything concrete, beyond keeping these constraints in mind while developing an ER diagram? With very complex constraints, the best we can do is to consider the cost of checking these constraints while examining alternative database designs. However, we can do much more with functional dependencies (and certain other kinds of specialized constraints on relations) because there is a rich design theory based on these dependencies.

In particular, complex relationships among several entities (or even complex entities!) can lead to relations with a large number of attributes. The theory of *normalization*, which we discuss in Chapter 15, allows us to refine such relations by using information about certain kinds of constraints, especially functional dependencies.

14.5   CONCEPTUAL DESIGN FOR LARGE ENTERPRISES

We have thus far concentrated on the constructs available in the ER model for describing various application concepts and relationships. The process of conceptual design consists of more than just describing small fragments of the application in terms of ER diagrams. For a large enterprise, the design may well require the efforts of more than one designer, and span data and application code used by a number of user groups. Using a high-level, semantic data model such as ER diagrams for conceptual design in such an environment offers the additional advantage that the high-level design can be diagrammatically represented and is easily understood by the many people who must provide input to the design process.

An important aspect of the design process is the methodology used to structure the development of the overall design and to ensure that the design takes into account all user requirements and is consistent. The usual approach is that the requirements of various user groups are taken into account, any conflicting requirements are somehow resolved, and a single set of global requirements is generated at the end of the requirements analysis phase. Generating a single set of global requirements is a difficult task, but it allows the conceptual design phase to proceed with the development of a logical schema that spans all the data and applications throughout the enterprise.

An alternative approach is to develop separate conceptual schemas for different user groups and to then *integrate* these conceptual schemas. To integrate multiple conceptual schemas, we must establish correspondences between entities, relationships and attributes, and we must resolve numerous kinds of conflicts (e.g., naming conflicts, domain mismatches, differences in measurement units). This task is difficult in its own right. In some situations schema integration cannot be avoided—for example, when one organization merges with another, existing databases may have to be integrated. Schema integration is also increasing in importance as users demand access to *heterogeneous* data sources, often maintained by different organizations.

14.6   SUMMARY

Conceptual database design follows a *requirements analysis* phase in which a detailed understanding of the enterprise is first developed. Conceptual design should produce a high-level description of the data that is to be stored in the database. The ER model is popular as a tool for conceptual design because it provides a collection of expressive constructs that are close to the terms in which people think about their applications.

The basic constructs in the ER model include *entities*, *relationships* and *attributes* (of both entities and relationships). A collection of similar entities is an *entity set*, and a collection of similar relationships is a *relationship set*. Additional constructs include *weak entities* (whose identity and existence depend on another entity), *class hierarchies* (which allow us to classify a collection of entities into a hierarchy of classes with varying degrees of similarity), and *aggregation* (which allows us to treat a relationship as an entity when it participates in another relationship).

We can also express a variety of integrity constraints in the ER model. We can define primary keys for entity sets and specify *key constraints* that influence the primary keys for relationship sets. We can specify *participation constraints* to describe the intended semantics of foreign key references. The semantics of ISA hierarchies can be refined using *overlap* and *covering* constraints. Some *foreign key* constraints are also implicit in the definition of a relationship set in terms of the participating entity sets.

Constraints play an important role in determining the best database design for an enterprise. The constraints in an ER diagram should be expressed in the SQL data definition statements used to create relations corresponding to entity sets and relationship sets whenever possible. Ideally, they should be expressed using primary key, foreign key and NULL constraints. If these constraints do not suffice, the use of table constraints, assertions, or even application-level code should be considered, balancing the importance of the constraint against the cost of enforcing it.

Although a rich set of constraints is expressible in the ER model, many other natural constraints *cannot* be expressed in the this model. This inability to express all constraints, in conjunction with the subjective nature of ER design, could lead to a database schema that contains potential redundancies or other problems. It is therefore important to further analyze and refine the relational schema obtained by translating an ER diagram. Functional dependencies are an important class of constraints that cannot (except for special cases such as primary key constraints) be expressed in the ER model, and *normalization* techniques, which are based on functional dependency information, are especially useful in this context.

Tools that allow a designer to draw ER diagrams and automatically produce SQL data definition statements for relations corresponding to entity sets and relationship sets can be very useful for large design tasks. The ER design, in addition to being a starting point for obtaining a collection of relation schemas, also serves as a high-level description of the information in the database and is a useful form of external documentation.

Our coverage of ER diagrams is far from exhaustive. Several extensions and variations have been proposed, although, unfortunately, there is no consensus or standard. Some important extensions include richer versions of cardinality constraints, weak entity sets with non binary identifying relationships, attributes that are structured or set-valued, and more elaborate class hierarachy mechanisms.

EXERCISES

Exercise 14.1 Explain the following terms briefly: *attribute, domain, entity, relationship, entity set, relationship set, one-to-many relationship, many-to-many relationship, participation constraint, overlap constraint, covering constraint, weak entity set, aggregation*, and *role indicator*.

Exercise 14.2 Explain why the addition of NOT NULL constraints to the SQL definition of the Manages relation (in Section 14.3.1) would not enforce the constraint that each department must have a manager. What, if anything, is achieved by requiring that the *ssn* field of Manages be non-null?

Exercise 14.3 Suppose that we have a ternary relationship R between entity sets A, B and C such that A has a key constraint and total participation and B has a key constraint; these are the only constraints. A has attributes $a1$ and $a2$, with $a1$ being the key; B and C are similar. R has no descriptive attributes. Write SQL statements that create tables corresponding to this information so as to capture as many of the constraints as possible. If you cannot capture some constraint, explain why.

Exercise 14.4 A university database contains information about professors (identified by social security number, or SSN) and courses (identified by courseid). Professors teach courses; each of the following situations concerns the Teaches relationship set. For each situation, draw an ER diagram that describes it (assuming that no further constraints hold). In addition, write SQL statements to create the corresponding relations, or explain why it is not possible to do so.

1. Professors can teach the same course in several semesters, and each offering must be recorded.

2. Professors can teach the same course in several semesters, and only the most recent such offering needs to be recorded. (Assume this condition applies in all subsequent questions.)

3. Every professor must teach some course.

4. Every professor teaches exactly one course (no more, no less).

5. Every professor teaches exactly one course (no more, no less), and every course must be taught by some professor.

6. Now suppose that certain courses can be taught by a team of professors jointly, but it is possible that no one professor in a team can teach the course. Model this situation, introducing additional entity sets and relationship sets if necessary.

Exercise 14.5 Consider the following information about a university database:

■ Professors have an SSN, a name, an age, a rank, and a research specialty.

■ Projects have a project number, a sponsor name (e.g., NSF), a starting date, an ending date, and a budget.

■ Graduate students have an SSN, a name, an age, and a degree program (e.g., M.S. or Ph.D.).

■ Each project is managed by one professor (known as the project's principal investigator).

■ Each project is worked on by one or more professors (known as the project's co-investigators).

■ Professors can manage and/or work on multiple projects.

■ Each project is worked on by one or more graduate students (known as the project's research assistants).

■ When graduate students work on a project, a professor must supervise their work on the project. Graduate students can work on multiple projects, in which case they will have a (potentially different) supervisor for each one.

■ Departments have a department number, a department name, and a main office.

■ Departments have a professor (known as the chairman) who runs the department.

■ Professors work in one or more departments, and for each department that they work in, a time percentage is associated with their job.

■ Graduate students have one major department in which they are working on their degree.

■ Each graduate student has another, more senior graduate student (known as a student advisor) who advises him or her on what courses to take.

1. Design and draw an ER diagram for the following collection of data. Use only the basic ER model here, that is, entities, relationships, and attributes. Be sure to indicate any key and participation constraints.

Exercise 14.6 A company database needs to store information about employees (identified by *ssn*, with *salary* and *phone* as attributes); departments (identified by *dno*, with *dname* and *budget* as attributes); and children of employees (with *name* and *age* as attributes). Employees *work* in departments; each department is *managed by* an employee; a child must be identified uniquely by *name* when the parent (who is an employee; assume that only one parent works for the company) is known. We are not interested in information about a child once the parent leaves the company.

1. Draw an ER diagram that captures this information.

2. Using SQL, create relations to hold the same information as the ER model.

Exercise 14.7 Notown Records has decided to store information on musicians who perform on their albums (as well as other company data) in a database. The company has wisely chosen to hire you as a database designer (at your usual consulting fee of $2500/day).

- Each musician that records at Notown has an SSN, a name, an address, and a phone number. Poorly paid musicians often share the same address, and no address has more than one phone.

- Each instrument that is used in songs recorded at Notown has a name (e.g., guitar, synthesizer, flute) and a musical key (e.g., C, B-flat, E-flat).

- Each album that is recorded on the Notown label has a title, a copyright date, a speed (e.g., 33 rpm or 45 rpm), and an album identifier.

- Each song recorded at Notown has a title and an author.

- Each musician may play several instruments, and a given instrument may be played by several musicians.

- Each album has a number of songs on it, but no song may appear on more than one album.

- Each song is performed by one or more musicians, and a musician may perform a number of songs.

- Each album has exactly one musician who acts as its producer. A musician may produce several albums, of course.

1. Design a conceptual schema for Notown and draw an ER diagram for your schema. The following information describes the situation that the Notown database must model. Be sure to indicate all key and cardinality constraints and any assumptions that you make. Identify any constraints that you are unable to capture in the ER diagram and briefly explain why you could not express them.

2. You have decided to recommend that Notown use a relational database system to store company data. Show the SQL statements for creating relations corresponding to the entity sets and relationship sets in your design. You decide not to use general **CHECK** constraints or assertions because they are expensive to check. Identify any constraints in the ER diagram that you are unable to capture in the SQL statements and briefly explain why you could not express them.

Exercise 14.8 Computer Sciences Department frequent fliers have been complaining to Dane County Airport officials about the poor organization at the airport. As a result, the officials have decided that all information related to the airport should be organized using a DBMS, and you've been hired to design the database. Your first task is to organize the information about all the airplanes that are stationed and maintained at the airport. The revelant information is as follows:

- Every airplane has a registration number, and each airplane is of a specific model.

- The airport accommodates a number of airplane models, and each model is identified by a model number (e.g., DC-10) and has a capacity and a weight.

- A number of technicians work at the airport. You need to store the name, SSN, address, phone number, and salary of each technician.

- Each technician is an expert on one or more plane model(s), and his or her expertise may overlap with that of other technicians. This information about technicians must also be recorded.

- Traffic controllers must have an annual medical examination. For each traffic controller, you must store the date of the most recent exam.

- All airport employees (including technicians) belong to a union. You must store the union membership number of each employee. You can assume that each employee is uniquely identified by the social security number.

- The airport has a number of tests that are used periodically to ensure that airplanes are still airworthy. Each test has an Federal Aviation Authority (FAA) test number, a name, and a maximum possible score.

- The FAA requires the airport to keep track of each time that a given airplane is tested by a given technician using a given test. For each testing event, the information needed is the date, the number of hours the technician spent doing the test, and the score that the airplane received on the test.

1. Draw an ER diagram for the airport database. Be sure to indicate the various attributes of each entity and relationship set; also specify the key and participation constraints for each relationship set. Specify any necessary overlap and covering constraints as well (in English).

2. Translate your ER diagram into a relational schema, and show the SQL statements needed to create the relations, using only key and null constraints. If your translation cannot capture any constraints in the ER diagram, explain why.

3. The FAA passes a regulation that tests on a plane must be conducted by a technician who is an expert on that model.

   (a) How would you express this constraint in the ER diagram? If you cannot express it, explain briefly.

   (b) Modify the SQL statements defining the relations obtained by mapping the ER diagram to check this constraint. If necessary, use general CHECK constraints or assertions.

Exercise 14.9 The Prescriptions-R-X chain of pharmacies has offered to give you a free lifetime supply of medicines if you design its database. Given the rising cost of health care, you agree. Here's the information that you gather:

■ Patients are identified by an SSN, and their names, addresses and ages must be recorded.

■ Doctors are identified by an SSN. For each doctor, the name, specialty and years of experience must be recorded.

■ Each pharmaceutical company is identified by name and has a phone number.

■ For each drug, the trade name and formula must be recorded. Each drug is sold by a given pharmaceutical company, and the trade name identifies a drug uniquely from among the products of that company. If a pharmaceutical company is deleted, you need not keep track of its products any longer.

■ Each pharmacy has a name, address and phone number.

■ Every patient has a primary physician. Every doctor has at least one patient.

■ Each pharmacy sells several drugs, and has a price for each. A drug could be sold at several pharmacies, and the price could vary from one pharmacy to another.

■ Doctors prescribe drugs for patients. A doctor could prescribe one or more drugs for several patients, and a patient could obtain prescriptions from several doctors. Each prescription has a date and a quantity associated with it. You can assume that if a doctor prescribes the same drug for the same patient more than once, only the last such prescription needs to be stored.

■ Pharmaceutical companies have long-term contracts with pharmacies. A pharmaceutical company can contract with several pharmacies, and a pharmacy can contract with several pharmaceutical companies. For each contract, you have to store a start date, an end date, and the text of the contract.

■ Pharmacies appoint a supervisor for each contract. There must always be a supervisor for each contract, but the contract supervisor can change over the lifetime of the contract.

1. Draw an ER diagram that captures the above information. Identify any constraints that are not captured by the ER diagram.

2. Define the relations corresponding to the entity sets and relationship sets in your design using SQL. Using general CHECK constraints if necessary, be sure to check each of the constraints given in the design specification.

3. How would your design change if each drug must be sold at a fixed price by all pharmacies?

4. How would your design change if the design requirements change as follows: If a doctor prescribes the same drug for the same patient more than once, several such prescriptions may have to be stored.

Exercise 14.10 Although you always wanted to be an artist, you ended up being an expert on databases because you love to cook data and you somehow confused 'data base' with 'data baste.' Your old love is still there, however, so you set up a database company, ArtBase, that builds a product for art galleries. The core of this product is a database with a schema that captures all the information that galleries need to maintain. Galleries keep information about artists, their names (which are unique), birthplaces, age, and style of art. For each piece of artwork, the artist, the year it was made, its unique title, its type of art (e.g., painting, lithograph, sculpture, photograph), and its price must be stored. Pieces of artwork are also classified into groups of various kinds, for example, portraits, still lifes, works by Picasso, or works of the 19th century; a given piece may belong to more than one group. Each group is identified by a name (like those above) that describes the group. Finally, galleries keep information about customers. For each customer, galleries keep their unique name, address, total amount of dollars they have spent in the gallery (very important!), and the artists and groups of art that each customer tends to like.

1. Draw the ER diagram for the database.

2. Write SQL statements to create the corresponding relations. Capture all the constraints in the specifications.

BIBLIOGRAPHIC NOTES

Several books provide a good treatment of conceptual design; these include [47] (which also contains a survey of commercial database design tools) and [538].

The ER model was proposed by Chen [125], and extensions have been proposed in a number of subsequent papers. Generalization and aggregation were introduced in [505]. [264] and [426] contain good surveys of semantic data models. Dynamic and temporal aspects of semantic data models are discussed in [552]. [539] discusses a design methodology based on developing an ER diagram and then translating to the relational model. Markowitz considers referential integrity in the context of ER to relational mapping, and discusses the support provided in some commercial systems (as of that date) in [368, 369]. The Entity-Relationship conference proceedings contain numerous papers on conceptual design, with an emphasis on the ER model, for example, [510].

View integration is discussed in several papers, including [75, 100, 132, 179, 382, 397, 396, 498, 509, 551]. [48] is a survey of several integration approaches.

15

SCHEMA REFINEMENT AND NORMAL FORMS

It is a melancholy truth that even great men have their poor relations.

—Charles Dickens

Conceptual database design gives us a set of relation schemas and integrity constraints (ICs) that can be regarded as a good starting point for the final database design. This initial design must be refined by taking the ICs into account more fully than is possible with just the ER model constructs, and also by considering performance criteria and typical workloads. In this chapter we discuss how ICs can be used to refine the conceptual schema produced by translating an ER model design into a collection of relations. Workload and performance considerations are discussed in Chapter 16.

We concentrate on an important class of constraints called *functional dependencies*. Other kinds of ICs, for example *multivalued dependencies* and *join dependencies*, also provide useful information. They can sometimes reveal redundancies that cannot be detected using functional dependencies alone. We discuss these other constraints briefly.

This chapter is organized as follows. Section 15.1 is an overview of the schema refinement approach discussed in this chapter. We introduce functional dependencies in Section 15.2. In Section 15.3 we present several examples that highlight the problems caused by redundancy and illustrate how relational schemas obtained by translating an ER model design can nonetheless suffer from these problems. Thus ER design is a good starting point, but we still need techniques to detect schemas with these problems and to refine such schemas to eliminate the problems. We lay the foundation for developing such schema refinement techniques in Section 15.4, where we show how to reason with functional dependency information to infer additional dependencies from a given set of dependencies.

We introduce normal forms for relations in Section 15.5; the normal form satisfied by a relation is a measure of the redundancy in the relation. A relation with redundancy can be refined by *decomposing it*, or replacing it with smaller relations that contain the same information, but without redundancy. We discuss decompositions and desirable properties of decompositions in Section 15.6. We show how relations can be decomposed into smaller relations that are in desirable normal forms in Section 15.7. Finally, we discuss the use of other kinds of dependencies for database design in Section 15.8.

15.1 INTRODUCTION TO SCHEMA REFINEMENT

We now present an overview of the problems that schema refinement is intended to address and a refinement approach based on decompositions. Redundant storage of information is the root cause of these problems. Although decomposition can eliminate redundancy, it can lead to problems of its own and should be used with caution.

15.1.1 Problems Caused by Redundancy

Storing the same information **redundantly**, that is, in more than one place within a database, can lead to several problems:

- **Redundant storage:** Some information is stored repeatedly.

- **Update anomalies:** If one copy of such repeated data is updated, an inconsistency is created unless all copies are similarly updated.

- **Insertion anomalies:** It may not be possible to store some information unless some other information is stored as well.

- **Deletion anomalies:** It may not be possible to delete some information without losing some other information as well.

Consider a relation obtained by translating a variant of the Hourly_Emps entity set from Chapter 14:

Hourly_Emps(*ssn, name, lot, rating, hourly_wages, hours_worked*)

In this chapter we will omit attribute type information for brevity, since our focus is on the grouping of attributes into relations. Indeed, we will often abbreviate an attribute name to a single letter and refer to a relation schema by a string of letters, one per attribute. For example, we will refer to the Hourly_Emps schema as *SNLRWH* (*W* denotes the *hourly_wages* attribute).

The key for Hourly_Emps is *ssn*. In addition, suppose that the *hourly_wages* attribute is determined by the *rating* attribute. That is, for a given *rating* value, there is only one permissible *hourly_wages* value. This IC is an example of a *functional dependency*. It leads to possible redundancy in the relation Hourly_Emps, as illustrated in Figure 15.1.

ssn	name	lot	rating	hourly_wages	hours_worked
123-22-3666	Attishoo	48	8	10	40
231-31-5368	Smiley	22	8	10	30
131-24-3650	Smethurst	35	5	7	30
434-26-3751	Guldu	35	5	7	32
612-67-4134	Madayan	35	8	10	40

Figure 15.1 An Instance of the Hourly_Emps Relation

If the same value appears in the *rating* column of two tuples, the IC tells us that the same value must appear in the *hourly_wages* column as well. This redundancy has several negative consequences:

- Some information is stored multiple times. For example, the rating value 8 corresponds to the hourly wage 10, and this association is repeated thrice. In addition to wasting space by storing the same information many times, redundancy leads to potential inconsistency. For example, the *hourly_wages* in the first tuple could be updated without making a similar change in the second tuple, which is an example of an *update anomaly*. Also, we cannot insert a tuple for an employee unless we know the hourly wage for the employee's rating value, which is an example of an *insertion anomaly*.

- If we delete all tuples with a given rating value (e.g., we delete the tuples for Smethurst and Guldu) we lose the association between that *rating* value and its *hourly_wage* value (a *deletion anomaly*).

Let us consider whether the use of *null* values can address some of these problems. Clearly, *null* values cannot help eliminate redundant storage or update anomalies. It appears that they can address insertion and deletion anomalies. For instance, to deal with the deletion anomaly example, we might consider storing a tuple with *null* values in all fields except *rating* and *hourly_wages* if the last tuple with a given *rating* would otherwise be deleted. However, this solution will not work because it requires the *ssn* value to be *null*, and primary key fields cannot be *null*. We will not discuss the use of *null* values further.

Ideally, we want schemas that do not permit redundancy, but at the very least we want to be able to identify schemas that do allow redundancy. Even if we choose to accept a schema with some of these drawbacks, perhaps owing to performance considerations, we want to make an informed decision.

15.1.2 Use of Decompositions

Intuitively, redundancy arises when a relational schema forces an association between attributes that is not natural. Functional dependencies (and, for that matter, other ICs) can be used to identify such situations and to suggest refinements to the schema. The essential idea is that many problems arising from redundancy can be addressed by replacing a relation with a collection of 'smaller' relations. Each of the smaller relations contains a (strict) subset of the attributes of the original relation. We refer to this process as *decomposition* of the larger relation into the smaller relations.

We can deal with the redundancy in Hourly_Emps by decomposing it into two relations:

Hourly_Emps2(*ssn*, *name*, *lot*, *rating*, *hours_worked*)
Wages(*rating*, *hourly_wages*)

The instances of these relations corresponding to the instance of Hourly_Emps relation in Figure 15.1 is shown in Figure 15.2.

ssn	name	lot	rating	hours_worked
123-22-3666	Attishoo	48	8	40
231-31-5368	Smiley	22	8	30
131-24-3650	Smethurst	35	5	30
434-26-3751	Guldu	35	5	32
612-67-4134	Madayan	35	8	40

rating	hourly_wages
8	10
5	7

Figure 15.2 Instances of Hourly_Emps2 and Wages

Note that we can easily record the hourly wage for any rating simply by adding a tuple to Wages, even if no employee with that rating appears in the current instance of Hourly_Emps. Changing the wage associated with a rating involves updating a single Wages tuple. This is more efficient than updating several tuples (as in the original design), and also eliminates the potential for inconsistency. Notice that the insertion and deletion anomalies have also been eliminated.

15.1.3 Problems Related to Decomposition

Unless we are careful, decomposing a relation schema can create more problems than it solves. Two important questions must be asked repeatedly:

1. Do we need to decompose a relation?

2. What problems (if any) does a given decomposition cause?

To help with the first question, several *normal forms* have been proposed for relations. If a relation schema is in one of these normal forms, we know that certain kinds of problems cannot arise. Considering the normal form of a given relation schema can thus help us to decide whether or not to decompose it further. If we decide that a relation schema must be decomposed further, we must choose a particular decomposition (i.e., a particular collection of smaller relations to replace the given relation).

With respect to the second question, two properties of decompositions are of particular interest. The *lossless-join* property enables us to recover any instance of the decomposed relation from corresponding instances of the smaller relations. The *dependency-preservation* property enables us to enforce any constraint on the original relation by simply enforcing some contraints on each of the smaller relations. That is, we need not perform joins of the smaller relations to check whether a constraint on the original relation is violated.

A serious drawback of decompositions is that queries over the original relation may require us to join the decomposed relations. If such queries are common, the performance penalty of decomposing the relation may not be acceptable. In this case we may choose to live with some of the problems of redundancy and not decompose the relation. It is important to be aware of the potential problems caused by such residual redundancy in the design, and to take steps to avoid them (e.g., by adding some checks to application code). We will not discuss the impact of decompositions on query performance in this chapter; this issue is covered in Section 16.8.

Our goal in this chapter is to explain some powerful concepts and design guidelines based on the theory of functional dependencies. A good database designer should have a firm grasp of normal forms and what problems they (do or do not) alleviate, the technique of decomposition, and potential problems with decompositions. For example, a designer will often ask questions such as these: Is a relation in a given normal form? Is a decomposition dependency-preserving? Our objective is to explain when to raise these questions, and the significance of the answers.

15.2   FUNCTIONAL DEPENDENCIES

A **functional dependency** (FD) is a kind of IC that generalizes the concept of a *key*. Let R be a relation schema and let X and Y be nonempty sets of attributes in R. We say that an instance r of R satisfies the FD $X \rightarrow Y$ [1] if the following holds for every pair of tuples t_1 and t_2 in r:

   If $t1.X = t2.X$, then $t1.Y = t2.Y$.

We use the notation $t1.X$ to refer to the projection of tuple t_1 onto the attributes in X, in a natural extension of our TRC notation $t.a$ for referring to attribute a of tuple t. An FD $X \rightarrow Y$ essentially says that if two tuples agree on the values in attributes X, they must also agree on the values in attributes Y.

Figure 15.3 illustrates the meaning of the FD $AB \rightarrow C$ by showing an instance that satisfies this dependency. The first two tuples show that an FD is not the same as a key constraint: although the FD is not violated, AB is clearly not a key for the relation. The third and fourth tuples illustrate that if two tuples differ in either the A field or the B field, they can differ in the C field without violating the FD. On the other hand, if we add a tuple $\langle a1, b1, c2, d1 \rangle$ to the instance shown in this figure, the resulting instance would violate the FD; to see this violation, compare the first tuple in the figure with the new tuple.

A	B	C	D
a1	b1	c1	d1
a1	b1	c1	d2
a1	b2	c2	d1
a2	b1	c3	d1

Figure 15.3   An Instance that Satisfies $AB \rightarrow C$

Recall that a *legal* instance of a relation must satisfy all specified ICs, including all specified FDs. As noted in Section 2.2, ICs must be identified and specified based on the semantics of the real-world enterprise being modeled. By looking at an instance of a relation, we might be able to tell that a certain FD does *not* hold. However, we can never deduce that an FD *does* hold by looking at one or more instances of the relation because an FD, like other ICs, is a statement about *all* possible legal instances of the relation.

---

[1] $X \rightarrow Y$ is read as X *functionally determines* Y, or simply as X *determines* Y.

A primary key constraint is a special case of an FD. The attributes in the key play the role of X, and the set of all attributes in the relation plays the role of Y. Note, however, that the definition of an FD does not require that the set X be minimal; this additional condition must be met for X to be a key. If $X \to Y$ holds, where Y is the set of all attributes, and there is some strict subset V of X such that $V \to Y$ holds, then X is a *superkey*, but not a key.

In the rest of this chapter, we will see several examples of FDs that are not key constraints.

15.3   EXAMPLES MOTIVATING SCHEMA REFINEMENT

It is natural to ask whether we need to decompose relations produced by translating an ER diagram. Shouldn't a good ER design lead to a collection of good relations? Unfortunately, ER design can indeed generate some schemas with redundancy problems, because it is a complex, subjective process, and certain constraints are not expressible in terms of ER diagrams. The examples in this section are intended to illustrate why decomposition of relations produced through ER design might well be necessary.

15.3.1   Constraints on an Entity Set

Consider the Hourly_Emps relation again. The constraint that attribute *ssn* is a key can be expressed as an FD:

$$\{ssn\} \to \{ssn, \ name, \ lot, \ rating, \ hourly\_wages, \ hours\_worked\}$$

For brevity, we will write this FD as $S \to SNLRWH$, using a single letter to denote each attribute and omitting the set braces, but the reader should remember that both sides of an FD contain sets of attributes. In addition, the constraint that the *hourly_wages* attribute is determined by the *rating* attribute is an FD: $R \to W$.

As we saw in Section 15.1.1, this FD led to redundant storage of rating–wage associations. *It cannot be expressed in terms of the ER model, which supports only the special case of key constraints.* Therefore, we could not detect it when we considered Hourly_Emps as an entity set during ER modeling.

We could argue that the problem with the original design was an artifact of a poor ER design, which could have been avoided by introducing an entity set called Wage_Table (with attributes *rating* and *hourly_wages*) and a relationship set Has_Wages associating Hourly_Emps and Wage_Table. The point, however, is that we could easily arrive at the original design given the subjective nature of ER modeling. Having formal techniques to identify the problem with this design, and to guide us to a better design, is very useful. The value of such techniques cannot be underestimated when designing large schemas—schemas with more than a hundred tables are not uncommon!

15.3.2   Constraints on a Relationship Set

The previous example illustrated how FDs can help to refine the subjective decisions made during ER design, but one could argue that the best possible ER diagram would have led to the same final set of relations. Our next example shows how FD information can lead to a set of relations that eliminate some redundancy problems and are unlikely to be arrived at solely through ER design.

We revisit an example from Chapter 14. Suppose that we have entity sets Parts, Suppliers, and Departments, as well as a relationship set Contracts that involves all of them. We refer to the schema for Contracts as $CQPSD$. A contract with contract id C specifies that a supplier S will supply some quantity Q of a part P to a department D. (We have added the contract id field C to the version of the Contracts relation that was discussed in Chapter 14.)

We might have a policy that a department purchases at most one part from any given supplier. Thus if there are several contracts between the same supplier and department, we know that the same part must be involved in all of them. This constraint is an FD, $DS \rightarrow P$.

Again we have redundancy and its associated problems. We can address this situation by decomposing Contracts into two relations with attributes $CQSD$ and SDP. Intuitively, the relation SDP records the part supplied to a department by a supplier, and the relation $CQSD$ records additional information about a contract. It is unlikely that we would arrive at such a design solely through ER modeling, since it is hard to formulate an entity or relationship that corresponds naturally to $CQSD$.

15.3.3   Identifying Attributes of Entities

This example illustrates how a careful examination of FDs can lead to a better understanding of the entities and relationships underlying the relational tables; in particular, it shows that attributes can easily be associated with the 'wrong' entity set during ER design. The ER diagram in Figure 15.4 shows a relationship set called Works_In that is similar to the Works_In relationship set of Chapter 14, but with an additional key constraint indicating that an employee can work in at most one department. (Observe the arrow connecting Employees to Works_In.)

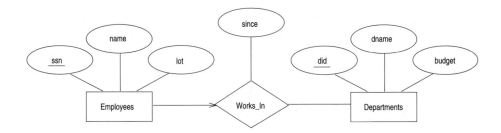

Figure 15.4 The Works_In Relationship Set

Using the key constraint, we can translate this ER diagram into two relations:

Workers(*ssn*, *name*, *lot*, *did*, *since*)
Departments(*did*, *dname*, *budget*)

The entity set Employees and the relationship set Works_In are mapped to a single relation, Workers. This translation is based on the second approach discussed in Section 14.3.1.

Now suppose that employees are assigned parking lots based on their department, and that all employees in a given department are assigned the same lot. This constraint is not expressible with respect to the ER diagram of Figure 15.4. It is another example of an FD: *did* → *lot*. The redundancy in this design can be eliminated by decomposing the Workers relation into two relations:

Workers2(*ssn*, *name*, *did*, *since*)
Dept_Lots(*did*, *lot*)

The new design has much to recommend it. We can change the lots associated with a department by updating a single tuple in the second relation (i.e., no update anomalies). We can associate a lot with a department even if it currently has no employees, without using *null* values (i.e., no deletion anomalies). We can add an employee to a department by inserting a tuple to the first relation even if there is no lot associated with the employee's department (i.e., no insertion anomalies).

Examining the two relations Departments and Dept_Lots, which have the same key, we realize that a Departments tuple and a Dept_Lots tuple with the same key value describe the same entity. This observation is reflected in the ER diagram shown in Figure 15.5.

Translating this diagram into the relational model would yield:

Workers2(*ssn*, *name*, *did*, *since*)

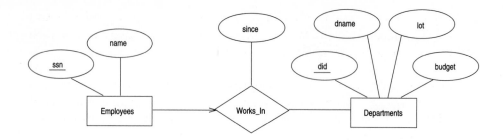

Figure 15.5   Refined Works_In Relationship Set

Departments(*did*, *dname*, *budget*, *lot*)

It seems intuitive to associate lots with employees; on the other hand, the ICs reveal that in this example lots are really associated with departments. The subjective process of ER modeling could miss this point. The rigorous process of normalization would not.

15.3.4   Identifying Entity Sets

As another example illustrating how FD information can be used to refine an ER design, This example also illustrates how FD information can be used to refine an ER design; in particular, it shows that FD information can help to decide whether a concept should be modeled as an entity or as an attribute.

Consider a variant of the Reserves schema used in earlier chapters. Let Reserves contain attributes S, B and D as before, indicating that sailor S has a reservation for boat B on day D. In addition, let there be an attribute C denoting the credit card to which the reservation is charged.

Suppose that every sailor uses a unique credit card for reservations. This constraint is expressed by the FD $S \rightarrow C$. This constraint indicates that in relation Reserves, we store the credit card number for a sailor as often as we have reservations for that sailor, and we have redundancy and potential update anomalies. A solution is to decompose Reserves into two relations with attributes SBD and SC. Intuitively, one holds information about reservations, and the other holds information about credit cards.

It is instructive to think about an ER design that would lead to these relations. One approach is to introduce an entity set called Credit_Cards, with the sole attribute *cardno*, and a relationship set Has_Card associating Sailors and Credit_Cards. By noting that each credit card belongs to a single sailor, we can map Has_Card and Credit_Cards to a single relation with attributes SC. We would probably not model credit card numbers as entities if our main interest in card numbers is to indicate how a reservation is to be paid for; it suffices to use an attribute to model card numbers in this situation.

A second approach is to make *cardno* an attribute of Sailors. But this approach is not very natural—a sailor may well have several cards, and we are not interested in all of them. Our interest is in the one card that is used to pay for reservations, which is best modeled as an attribute of the relationship Reserves.

A helpful way to think about the design problem in this example is that we first make *cardno* an attribute of Reserves, and then refine the resulting tables by taking into account the FD information. (Whether we refine the design by adding *cardno* to the table obtained from Sailors or by creating a new table with attributes SC is a separate issue.)

15.4 REASONING ABOUT FUNCTIONAL DEPENDENCIES

The discussion up to this point has highlighted the need for techniques that allow us to carefully examine and further refine relations obtained through ER design (or, for that matter, through other approaches to conceptual design). Before proceeding with the main task at hand, which is the discussion of such schema refinement techniques, we digress to examine FDs in more detail because they play such a central role in schema analysis and refinement.

Given a set of FDs over a relation schema R, there are typically several additional FDs that hold over R whenever all of the given FDs hold. As an example, consider:

Workers(*ssn, name, lot, did, since*)

We know that $ssn \rightarrow did$ holds, since *ssn* is the key, and FD $did \rightarrow lot$ is given to hold. Therefore, in any legal instance of Workers, if two tuples have the same *ssn* value, they must have the same *did* value (from the first FD), and because they have the same *did* value, they must also have the same *lot* value (from the second FD). Thus the FD $ssn \rightarrow lot$ also holds on Workers.

We say that an FD f **is implied by** a given set F of FDs if f holds on every relation instance that satisfies all dependencies in F, that is, f holds whenever all FDs in F hold. Note that it is not sufficient for f to hold on some instance that satisfies all dependencies in F; rather, f must hold on *every* instance that satisfies all dependencies in F.

15.4.1 Closure of a Set of FDs

The set of all FDs implied by a given set F of FDs is called the **closure of F** and is denoted as F^+. An important question is how we can **infer**, or compute, the closure of a given set F of FDs. It turns out that the answer is simple and elegant. The following three rules, called *Armstrong's Axioms*, can be applied repeatedly to infer all FDs implied by a set F of FDs. We use X, Y and Z to denote sets of attributes over a relation schema R:

- **Reflexivity:** If $X \supseteq Y$, then $X \rightarrow Y$.

- **Augmentation:** If $X \rightarrow Y$, then $XZ \rightarrow YZ$ for any Z.

- **Transitivity:** If $X \rightarrow Y$ and $Y \rightarrow Z$, then $X \rightarrow Z$.

Armstrong's Axioms are **sound** in that they generate only FDs in F^+ when applied to a set F of FDs. They are **complete** in that repeated application of these rules will generate all FDs in the closure F^+. (We will not prove these claims.) It is convenient to use some additional rules while reasoning about F^+:

- **Union:** If $X \rightarrow Y$ and $X \rightarrow Z$, then $X \rightarrow YZ$.

- **Decomposition:** If $X \rightarrow YZ$, then $X \rightarrow Y$ and $X \rightarrow Z$.

These additional rules are not essential; their soundness can be proved using Armstrong's Axioms.

To illustrate the use of these inference rules for FDs, consider a relation schema ABC with FDs $A \rightarrow B$ and $B \rightarrow C$. A **trivial FD** is one in which the right side contains only attributes that also appear on the left side; such dependencies always hold. Using reflexivity, we can generate all trivial dependencies, which are of the form:

$X \rightarrow Y$, where $Y \subseteq X$, $X \subseteq ABC$, and $Y \subseteq ABC$.

From transitivity we get $A \rightarrow C$. From augmentation we get the nontrivial dependencies:

$AC \rightarrow BC$, $AB \rightarrow AC$, $AB \rightarrow CB$.

As a second example, we use a more elaborate version of the Contracts relation:

Contracts(*cid, supplierid, projectid, deptid, partid, qty, value*)

We denote the schema for Contracts as $CSJDPQV$. The meaning of a tuple in this relation is that the contract with *cid* C is an agreement that supplier S (*supplierid*) will supply Q items of part P (*partid*) to project J (*projectid*) associated with department D (*deptid*); the value V of this contract is equal to *value*.

The following ICs are known to hold:

1. The contract id C is a key: $C \rightarrow CSJDPQV$.

2. A project purchases a given part using a single contract: $JP \rightarrow C$.

3. A department purchases at most one part from a supplier: $SD \rightarrow P$.

Several additional FDs hold in the closure of the set of given FDs:

From $JP \rightarrow C$, $C \rightarrow CSJDPQV$, and transitivity, we infer $JP \rightarrow CSJDPQV$.

From $SD \rightarrow P$ and augmentation, we infer $SDJ \rightarrow JP$.

From $SDJ \rightarrow JP$, $JP \rightarrow CSJDPQV$, and transitivity, we infer $SDJ \rightarrow CSJDPQV$. (Incidentally, while it may appear tempting to do so, we *cannot* conclude $SD \rightarrow CSDPQV$, 'canceling' J on both sides. FD inference is not like arithmetic multiplication!)

We can infer several additional FDs that are in the closure by using augmentation or decomposition. For example, from $C \rightarrow CSJDPQV$, using decomposition we can infer:

$$C \rightarrow C, \ C \rightarrow S, \ C \rightarrow J, \ C \rightarrow D, \text{ etc.}$$

Finally, we have a number of trivial FDs from the reflexivity rule.

15.4.2 Attribute Closure

If we just want to check whether a given dependency, say, $X \rightarrow Y$, is in the closure of a set F of FDs, we can do so efficiently without computing F^+. We first compute the **attribute closure** X^+ with respect to F, which is the set of attributes A such that $X \rightarrow A$ can be inferred using the Armstrong Axioms. The algorithm for computing the attribute closure of a set X of attributes is shown in Figure 15.6.

This polynomial-time algorithm can be modified to find keys by starting with set X containing a single attribute and stopping as soon as *closure* contains all attributes in the relation schema. By varying the starting attribute and the order in which the algorithm considers FDs, we could obtain several candidate keys.

$$closure = X;$$

repeat until there is no change: {

  if there is an FD $U \rightarrow V$ in F such that $U \subseteq closure$,

  then set $closure = closure \cup V$

}

Figure 15.6   Computing the Attribute Closure of Attribute Set X

15.5   NORMAL FORMS

Given a relation schema, we need to decide whether it is a good design or whether we need to decompose it into smaller relations. Such a decision must be guided by an understanding of what problems, if any, arise from the current schema. To provide such guidance, several **normal forms** have been proposed. If a relation schema is in one of these normal forms, we know that certain kinds of problems cannot arise.

The normal forms based on FDs are *first normal form (1NF)*, *second normal form (2NF)*, *third normal form (3NF)*, and *Boyce-Codd normal form (BCNF)*. These forms have increasingly restrictive requirements: Every relation in BCNF is also in 3NF, every relation in 3NF is also in 2NF, and every relation in 2NF is in 1NF. A relation is in **First Normal Form** if every field contains only atomic values, that is, not lists or sets. This requirement is implicit in our definition of the relational model. Although some of the newer database systems are relaxing this requirement, in this chapter we will assume that it always holds. 2NF is mainly of historical interest. 3NF and BCNF are important from a database design standpoint.

While studying normal forms, it is important to appreciate the role played by FDs. Consider a relation schema R with attributes ABC. In the absence of any ICs, any set of ternary tuples is a legal instance and there is no potential for redundancy. On the other hand, suppose that we have the FD $A \rightarrow B$. Now if several tuples have the same A value, they must also have same B value. This potential redundancy can be predicted using the FD information. If more detailed ICs are specified, we may be able to detect more subtle redundancies as well.

We will primarily discuss redundancy that is revealed by FD information. In Section 15.8, we discuss more sophisticated ICs called *multivalued dependencies* and *join dependencies* and normal forms based on them.

15.5.1 Boyce-Codd Normal Form

Let R be a relation schema, X be a subset of the attributes of R, and let A be an attribute of R. R is in **Boyce-Codd Normal Form** if for every FD $X \to A$ that holds over R, one of the following statements is true:

- $A \in X$; that is, it is a trivial FD, or

- X is a superkey.

Note that if we are given a set F of FDs, according to this definition, we must consider each dependency $X \to A$ in the closure F^+ to determine whether R is in BCNF. However, we can prove that it is sufficient to check whether the left side of each dependency in F is a superkey (by computing the attribute closure and seeing if it includes all attributes of R).

Intuitively, in a BCNF relation the only nontrivial dependencies are those in which a key determines some attribute(s). Thus each tuple can be thought of as an entity or relationship, identified by a key and described by the remaining attributes. Kent puts this colorfully, if a little loosely: "Each attribute must describe [an entity or relationship identified by] the key, the whole key, and nothing but the key." If we use ovals to denote attributes or sets of attributes and draw arcs to indicate FDs, a relation in BCNF has the structure illustrated in Figure 15.7, considering just one key for simplicity. (If there are several candidate keys, each candidate key can play the role of KEY in the figure, with the other attributes being the ones not in the chosen candidate key.)

Figure 15.7 FDs in a BCNF Relation

BCNF ensures that no redundancy can be detected using FD information alone. It is thus the most desirable normal form (from the point of view of redundancy) if we take into account only FD information. This point is illustrated in Figure 15.8.

This figure shows (two tuples in) an instance of a relation with three attributes X, Y and A. There are two tuples with the same value in the X column. Now suppose that we know that this instance satisfies an FD $X \to A$. We can see that one of the tuples has the value a in the A column. What can we infer about the value in the A column in the second tuple? Using the FD, we can conclude that the second tuple also has the value a in this column. (Note that this is really the

X	Y	A
x	y_1	a
x	y_2	?

Figure 15.8 Instance Illustrating BCNF

only kind of inferrence we can make about values in the fields of tuples by using FDs.)

But isn't this situation an example of redundancy? We indeed appear to have stored the value a twice. Can such a situation arise in a BCNF relation? No! If this relation is in BCNF, because A is distinct from X it follows that X must be a key. (Otherwise, the FD $X \rightarrow A$ would violate BCNF.) If X is a key, then $y_1 = y_2$, which means that the two tuples are identical. Since a relation is defined to be a *set* of tuples, we cannot have two copies of the same tuple and the situation shown in Figure 15.8 cannot arise.

Thus if a relation is in BCNF, every field of every tuple records a piece of information that cannot be inferred (using only FDs) from the values in all other fields in the relation instance.

15.5.2   Third Normal Form

Let R be a relation schema, X be a subset of the attributes of R, and A be an attribute of R. R is in **Third Normal Form** if for every FD $X \rightarrow A$ that holds over R, one of the following statements is true:

- $A \in X$; that is, it is a trivial FD, or

- X is a superkey, or

- A is part of some key for R.

The definition of 3NF is similar to that of BCNF, with the only difference being the third condition. Every BCNF relation is also in 3NF. To understand the third condition, recall that a key for a relation is a *minimal* set of attributes that uniquely determines all other attributes. A must be part of a key (any key, if there are several). It is not enough for A to be part of a superkey, because the latter condition is satisfied by each and every attribute! Finding all keys of a relation schema is known to be an NP-complete problem, and so is the problem of determining whether a relation schema is in 3NF.

Suppose that a dependency $X \to A$ causes a violation of 3NF. There are two cases:

- X *is a proper subset of some key* K. Such a dependency is sometimes called a **partial dependency**. In this case we store *(X, A)* pairs redundantly. As an example, consider the Reserves relation with attributes *SBDC* from Section 15.3.4. The only key is *SBD*, and we have the FD $S \to C$. We store the credit card number for a sailor as many times as there are reservations for that sailor.

- X *is not a proper subset of any key.* Such a dependency is sometimes called a **transitive dependency** because it means we have a chain of dependencies $K \to X \to A$.[2] The problem is that we cannot associate an X value with a K value unless we also associate an A value with an X value. As an example, consider the Hourly_Emps relation with attributes *SNLRWH* from Section 15.3.1. The only key is *S*, but there is an FD $R \to W$, which gives rise to the chain $S \to R \to W$. The consequence is that we cannot record the fact that employee S has rating R without knowing the hourly wage for that rating. This condition leads to insertion, deletion and update anomalies.

Partial dependencies are illustrated in Figure 15.9, and transitive dependencies are illustrated in Figure 15.10. Note that in Figure 15.10, the set X of attributes may or may not have some attributes in common with KEY; the diagram should be interpreted as indicating only that X is not a subset of KEY.

KEY   Attributes X   Attribute A   **Case 1: A not in KEY**

Figure 15.9   Partial Dependencies

The motivation for 3NF is really rather technical. By making an exception for certain dependencies involving key attributes, we can ensure that every relation schema can be decomposed into a collection of 3NF relations using only decompositions that have certain desirable properties (Section 15.6). Such a guarantee does not exist for BCNF relations; the 3NF definition weakens the BCNF requirements just enough to make this guarantee possible. We may therefore compromise by settling for a 3NF design. As we shall see in Chapter 16, we may sometimes accept this compromise (or even settle for a non-3NF schema) for other reasons as well.

---

[2] Incidentally, the definition of **Second Normal Form** is essentially that partial dependencies are not allowed. Thus if a relation is in 3NF (which precludes both partial and transitive dependencies), it is also in 2NF.

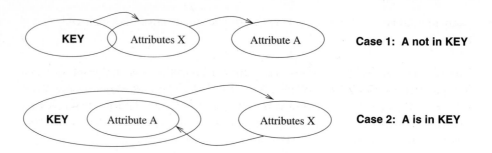

Figure 15.10   Transitive Dependencies

Unlike BCNF, however, some redundancy is possible with 3NF. The problems associated with partial and transitive dependencies persist if there is a nontrivial dependency $X \rightarrow A$ and X is not a superkey, even if the relation is in 3NF because A is part of a key. To understand this point, let us revisit the Reserves relation with attributes $SBDC$ and the FD $S \rightarrow C$, which states that a sailor uses a unique credit card to pay for reservations. S is not a key, and C is not part of a key. (In fact, the only key is SBD.) Thus this relation is not in 3NF; *(S, C)* pairs are stored redundantly. However, if we also know that credit cards uniquely identify the owner, we have the FD $C \rightarrow S$, which means that CBD is also a key for Reserves. Therefore, the dependency $S \rightarrow C$ does not violate 3NF, and Reserves is in 3NF. Nonetheless, in all tuples containing the same S value, the same *(S, C)* pair is redundantly recorded.

15.6 DECOMPOSITIONS

As we have seen, a relation in BCNF is free of redundancy (to be precise, redundancy that can be detected using FD information), and a relation schema in 3NF comes close. If a relation schema is not in one of these normal forms, the FDs that cause a violation can give us insight into the potential problems. The main technique for addressing such redundancy-related problems is decomposing a relation schema into relation schemas with fewer attributes.

A **decomposition of a relation schema** R consists of replacing the relation schema by two (or more) relation schemas that each contain a subset of the attributes of R and together include all attributes in R. Intuitively, we want to store the information in any given instance of R by storing projections of the instance. This section examines the use of decompositions through several examples.

We begin with the Hourly_Emps example from Section 15.3.1. This relation has attributes $SNLRWH$, and two FDs: $S \rightarrow SNLRWH$ and $R \rightarrow W$. Since R is not a key and W is not part of any key, the second dependency causes a violation of 3NF.

The alternative design consisted of replacing Hourly_Emps with two relations having attributes $SNLRH$ and RW. $S \rightarrow SNLRH$ holds over $SNLRH$, and S is a key. $R \rightarrow W$ holds over RW, and R is a key for RW. The only other dependencies that hold over these schemas are those obtained by augmentation. Thus both schemas are in BCNF.

Our decision to decompose $SNLRWH$ into $SNLRH$ and RW, rather than, say, $SNLR$ and $LRWH$, was not just a good guess. It was guided by the observation that the dependency $R \rightarrow W$ caused the violation of 3NF; the most natural way to deal with this violation is to remove the attribute W from this schema. To compensate for removing W from the main schema, we can add a relation RW, because each R value is associated with a unique W value according to the FD $R \rightarrow W$.

A very important question must be asked at this point: If we replace a legal instance r of relation schema $SNLRWH$ with its projections on $SNLRH$ (r_1) and RW (r_2), can we recover r from r_1 and r_2? The decision to decompose $SNLRWH$ into $SNLRH$ and RW is equivalent to saying that we will store instances r_1 and r_2 instead of r. However, it is the instance r that captures the intended entities or relationships. If we cannot compute r from r_1 and r_2, our attempt to deal with redundancy has effectively thrown out the baby with the bath water.

15.6.1 Lossless-Join Decomposition

Let R be a relation schema and let F be a set of FDs over R. A decomposition of R into two schemas with attribute sets X and Y is said to be a **lossless-join decomposition with respect to F** if for every instance r of R that satisfies the dependencies in F, $\pi_X(r) \bowtie \pi_Y(r) = r$.

This definition can easily be extended to cover a decomposition of R into more than two relations. It is easy to see that $r \subseteq \pi_X(r) \bowtie \pi_Y(r)$ always holds. In general, though, the other direction does not hold. If we take projections of a relation and recombine them using natural join, we typically obtain some tuples that were not in the original relation. This situation is illustrated in Figure 15.11.

By replacing the instance r shown in Figure 15.11 with the instances $\pi_{SP}(r)$ and $\pi_{PD}(r)$, we lose some information. In particular, suppose that the tuples in r denote relationships. We can no longer tell that the relationships (s_1, p_1, d_3) and (s_3, p_1, d_1) do not hold. The decomposition of schema SPD into SP and PD is therefore a 'lossy' decomposition if the instance r shown in the figure is legal,

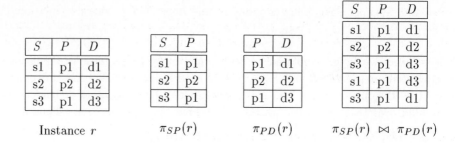

Figure 15.11 Instances Illustrating Lossy Decompositions

that is, if this instance could arise in the enterprise being modeled. (Observe the similarities between this example and the Contracts relationship set in Section 14.4.3.)

It is essential that all decompositions used to eliminate redundancy be lossless. The following simple test is very useful:

> Let R be a relation and F be a set of FDs that hold over R. The decomposition of R into relations with attribute sets R_1 and R_2 is lossless if and only if F^+ contains either the FD $R_1 \cap R_2 \rightarrow R_1$ or the FD $R_1 \cap R_2 \rightarrow R_2$.

In other words, the attributes common to R_1 and R_2 must contain a key for either R_1 or R_2. If a relation is decomposed into two relations, this test is a necessary and sufficient condition for the decomposition to be lossless-join. If a relation is decomposed into more than two relations, an efficient (time polynomial in the size of the dependency set) algorithm is available to test whether or not the decomposition is lossless, but we will not discuss it.

Consider the Hourly_Emps relation again. It has attributes $SNLRWH$, and the FD $R \rightarrow W$ causes a violation of 3NF. We dealt with this violation by decomposing the relation into $SNLRH$ and RW. Since R is common to both decomposed relations, and $R \rightarrow W$ holds, this decomposition is lossless-join.

This example illustrates a general observation:

> If an FD $X \rightarrow Y$ holds over a relation R and $X \cap Y$ is empty, the decomposition of R into $R - Y$ and XY is lossless.

X appears in both $R-Y$ (since $X \cap Y$ is empty) and XY, and it is a key for XY. Thus the above observation follows from the test for a lossless-join decomposition.

Another important observation has to do with repeated decompositions. Suppose that a relation R is decomposed into $R1$ and $R2$ through a lossless-join decomposition, and that $R1$ is decomposed into $R11$ and $R12$ through another lossless-join decomposition. Then the decomposition of R into $R11$, $R12$, and $R2$ is lossless-join; by joining $R11$ and $R12$ we can recover $R1$, and by then joining $R1$ and $R2$, we can recover R.

15.6.2 Dependency-Preserving Decomposition

Consider the Contracts relation with attributes $CSJDPQV$ from Section 15.4.1. The given FDs are $C \to CSJDPQV$, $JP \to C$, and $SD \to P$. Because SD is not a key the dependency $SD \to P$ causes a violation of BCNF.

We can decompose Contracts into two relations with schemas $CSJDQV$ and SDP to address this violation; the decomposition is lossless-join. There is one subtle problem, however. We can enforce the integrity constraint $JP \to C$ easily when a tuple is inserted into Contracts by ensuring that no existing tuple has the same JP values (as the inserted tuple) but different C values. Once we decompose Contracts into $CSJDQV$ and SDP, enforcing this constraint requires an expensive join of the two relations whenever a tuple is inserted into $CSJDQV$. We say that this decomposition is not dependency-preserving.

Intuitively, a *dependency-preserving decomposition* allows us to enforce all FDs by examining a single relation instance on each insertion or modification of a tuple. (Note that deletions cannot cause violation of FDs.) To define dependency-preserving decompositions precisely, we have to introduce the concept of a projection of FDs.

Let R be a relation schema that is decomposed into two schemas with attribute sets X and Y, and let F be a set of FDs over R. The **projection of F on X** is the set of FDs in the closure F^+ (not just F!) that involve only attributes in X. We will denote the projection of F on attributes X as F_X. Note that a dependency $U \to V$ in F^+ is in F_X only if *all* the attributes in U and V are in X.

The decomposition of relation schema R with FDs F into schemas with attribute sets X and Y is **dependency-preserving** if $(F_X \cup F_Y)^+ = F^+$. That is, if we take the dependencies in F_X and F_Y and compute the closure of their union, we get back all dependencies in the closure of F. Therefore, we need to enforce only the dependencies in F_X and F_Y; all FDs in F^+ are then sure to be satisfied. To enforce F_X, we need to examine only relation X (on inserts to that relation). To enforce F_Y, we need to examine only relation Y.

To appreciate the need to consider the closure F^+ while computing the projection of F, suppose that a relation R with attributes ABC is decomposed into relations with attributes AB and BC. The set F of FDs over R includes $A \rightarrow B$, $B \rightarrow C$, and $C \rightarrow A$. Of these, $A \rightarrow B$ is in F_{AB} and $B \rightarrow C$ is in F_{BC}. But is this decomposition dependency-preserving? What about $C \rightarrow A$? This dependency is not implied by the dependencies listed (thus far) for F_{AB} and F_{BC}.

The closure of F contains all dependencies in F plus $A \rightarrow C$, $B \rightarrow A$, and $C \rightarrow B$. Consequently, F_{AB} also contains $B \rightarrow A$, and F_{BC} contains $C \rightarrow B$. Thus $F_{AB} \cup F_{BC}$ contains $A \rightarrow B$, $B \rightarrow C$, $B \rightarrow A$, and $C \rightarrow B$. The closure of the dependencies in F_{AB} and F_{BC} now includes $C \rightarrow A$ (which follows from $C \rightarrow B$, $B \rightarrow A$, and transitivity). Thus the decomposition preserves the dependency $C \rightarrow A$.

A direct application of the definition gives us a straightforward algorithm for testing whether a decomposition is dependency-preserving. (This algorithm is exponential in the size of the dependency set; a polynomial algorithm is available, although we will not discuss it.)

We began this section with an example of a lossless-join decomposition that was not dependency-preserving. Other decompositions are dependency-preserving, but not lossless. A simple example consists of a relation ABC with FD $A \rightarrow B$ that is decomposed into AB and BC.

15.7   NORMALIZATION

Having covered the concepts needed to understand the role of normal forms and decompositions in database design, we now consider algorithms for converting relations to BCNF or 3NF. If a relation schema is not in BCNF, it is possible to obtain a lossless-join decomposition into a collection of BCNF relation schemas. Unfortunately, there may not be any dependency-preserving decomposition into a collection of BCNF relation schemas. However, there is always a dependency-preserving, lossless-join decomposition into a collection of 3NF relation schemas.

15.7.1   Decomposition into BCNF

We now present an algorithm for decomposing a relation schema R into a collection of BCNF relation schemas:

1. Suppose that R is not in BCNF. Let $X \subset R$, A be a single attribute in R, and $X \rightarrow A$ be an FD that causes a violation of BCNF. Decompose R into $R - A$ and XA.

2. If either $R - A$ or XA is not in BCNF, decompose them further by a recursive application of this algorithm.

$R - A$ denotes the set of attributes other than A in R, and XA denotes the union of attributes in X and A. Since $X \to A$ violates BCNF, it is not a trivial dependency; further, A is a single attribute. Therefore, A is not in X; that is, $X \cap A$ is empty. Thus each decomposition carried out in Step (1) is lossless-join.

The set of dependencies associated with $R - A$ and XA is the projection of F onto their attributes. If one of the new relations is not in BCNF, we decompose it further in Step (2). Since a decomposition results in relations with strictly fewer attributes, this process will terminate, leaving us with a collection of relation schemas that are all in BCNF. Further, joining instances of the (two or more) relations obtained through this algorithm will yield precisely the corresponding instance of the original relation (i.e., the decomposition into a collection of relations that are each in BCNF is a lossless-join decomposition).

Consider the Contracts relation with attributes $CSJDPQV$ and key C. We are given FDs $JP \to C$ and $SD \to P$. By using the dependency $SD \to P$ to guide the decomposition, we get the two schemas SDP and $CSJDQV$. SDP is in BCNF. Suppose that we also have the constraint that each project deals with a single supplier: $J \to S$. This means that the schema $CSJDQV$ is not in BCNF. So we decompose it further into JS and $CJDQV$. $C \to JDQV$ holds over $CJDQV$; the only other FDs that hold are those obtained from this FD by augmentation, and therefore all FDs contain a key in the left side. Thus each of the schemas SDP, JS and $CJDQV$ is in BCNF, and this collection of schemas also represents a lossless-join decomposition of $CSJDQV$.

The steps in this decomposition process can be visualized as a tree, as shown in Figure 15.12. The root is the original relation $CSJDPQV$, and the leaves are the BCNF relations that are the result of the decomposition algorithm, namely, SDP, JS and $CSDQV$. Intuitively, each internal node is replaced by its children through a single decomposition step that is guided by the FD shown just below the node.

Redundancy in BCNF Revisited

The decomposition of $CSJDQV$ into SDP, JS and $CJDQV$ is not dependency-preserving. Intuitively, dependency $JP \to C$ cannot be enforced without a join. One way to deal with this situation is to add a relation with attributes CJP. In effect, this solution amounts to storing some information redundantly in order to make the dependency enforcement cheaper.

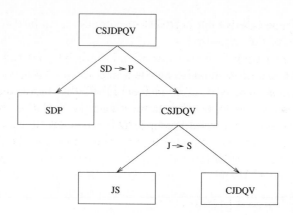

Figure 15.12   Decomposition of $CSJDQV$ into SDP, JS, and $CJDQV$

This is a subtle point: Each of the schemas CJP, SDP, JS and $CJDQV$ is in BCNF, yet there is some redundancy that can be predicted by FD information. In particular, if we join the relation instances for SDP and $CJDQV$ and project onto the attributes CJP, we must get exactly the instance stored in the relation with schema CJP. We saw in Section 15.5.1 that there is no such redundancy within a single BCNF relation. The current example shows that redundancy can still occur across relations.

Alternatives in Decomposing to BCNF

Suppose that several dependencies violate BCNF. Depending on which of these dependencies we choose to guide the next decomposition step, we may arrive at quite different collections of BCNF relations. Consider Contracts. We just decomposed it into SDP, JS and $CJDQV$. Suppose that we choose to decompose the original relation $CSJDPQV$ into JS and $CJDPQV$, based on the FD $J \rightarrow S$. The only dependencies that hold over $CJDPQV$ are $JP \rightarrow C$ and the key dependency $C \rightarrow CJDPQV$. Since JP is a key, $CJDPQV$ is in BCNF. Thus the schemas JS and $CJDPQV$ represent a lossless-join decomposition of Contracts into BCNF relations.

The lesson to be learned here is that the theory of dependencies can tell us when there is redundancy and give us clues about possible decompositions to address the problem, but it cannot really discriminate between decomposition alternatives. A designer has to consider the alternatives and choose one based on the semantics of the application.

BCNF and Dependency-Preservation

Sometimes, there simply is no decomposition into BCNF that is dependency preserving. As an example, consider the relation schema SBD, in which a tuple denotes that sailor S has reserved boat B on date D. If we have the FDs $SB \rightarrow D$ (a sailor can reserve a given boat for at most one day) and $D \rightarrow B$ (on any given day at most one boat can be reserved), SBD is not in BCNF because D is not a key. If we try to decompose it, however, we cannot preserve the dependency $SB \rightarrow D$.

15.7.2 Decomposition into 3NF *

Clearly, the approach that we outlined for lossless-join decomposition into BCNF will also give us a lossless-join decomposition into 3NF. (Typically, we can stop a little earlier if we are satisfied with a collection of 3NF relations.) But this approach does not ensure dependency-preservation.

A simple modification, however, yields a decomposition into 3NF relations that is lossless-join and dependency-preserving. Before we describe this modification, we need to introduce the concept of a minimal cover for a set of FDs.

Minimal Cover for a Set of FDs

A **minimal cover** for a set F of FDs is a set G of FDs such that:

1. Every dependency in G is of the form $X \rightarrow A$, where A is a single attribute.

2. The closure F^+ is equal to the closure G^+.

3. If we obtain a set H of dependencies from G by deleting one or more dependencies, or by deleting attributes from a dependency in G, then $F^+ \neq H^+$.

Intuitively, a minimal cover is an equivalent set of dependencies that is *minimal* in two respects: (1) Every dependency is as small as possible; that is, each attribute on the left side is necessary and the right side is a single attribute. (2) Every dependency in it is required in order for the closure to be equal to F^+.

As an example, let F be the set of dependencies:

$$A \rightarrow B, \ ABCD \rightarrow E, \ EF \rightarrow G, \ EF \rightarrow H, \text{ and } ACDF \rightarrow EG.$$

First, let us rewrite $ACDF \rightarrow EG$ so that every right side is a single attribute:

$$ACDF \rightarrow E \text{ and } ACDF \rightarrow G.$$

Next consider $ACDF \rightarrow G$. This dependency is implied by the following FDs:

$$A \rightarrow B, \; ABCD \rightarrow E, \text{ and } EF \rightarrow G.$$

Therefore, we can delete it. Similarly, we can delete $ACDF \rightarrow E$. Next consider $ABCD \rightarrow E$. Since $A \rightarrow B$ holds, we can replace it with $ACD \rightarrow E$. (At this point, the reader should verify that each remaining FD is minimal and required.) Thus a minimal cover for F is the set:

$$A \rightarrow B, \; ACD \rightarrow E, \; EF \rightarrow G, \text{ and } EF \rightarrow H.$$

The preceding example suggests a general algorithm for obtaining a minimal cover of a set F of FDs:

1. **Put the FDs in a standard form:** Obtain a collection G of equivalent FDs with a single attribute on the right side (using the decomposition axiom).

2. **Minimize the left side of each FD:** For each FD in G, check each attribute in the left side to see if it can be deleted while preserving equivalence to F^+.

3. **Delete redundant FDs:** Check each remaining FD in G to see if it can be deleted while preserving equivalence to F^+.

Note that the order in which we consider FDs while applying these steps could produce different minimal covers; there could be several minimal covers for a given set of FDs.

More important, it is necessary to minimize the left sides of FDs *before* checking for redundant FDs. If these two steps are reversed, the final set of FDs could still contain some redundant FDs (i.e., not be a minimal cover), as the following example illustrates. Let F be the set of dependencies, each of which is already in the standard form:

$$ABCD \rightarrow E, \; E \rightarrow D, \; A \rightarrow B, \text{ and } AC \rightarrow D.$$

Observe that none of these FDs is redundant; thus if we checked for redundant FDs first, we would get the same set of FDs F. The left side of $ABCD \rightarrow E$ can be replaced by AC while preserving equivalence to F^+, and we would stop here if we checked for redundant FDs in F before minimizing the left sides. However, the set of FDs we have is not a minimal cover:

$$AC \rightarrow E, \; E \rightarrow D, \; A \rightarrow B, \text{ and } AC \rightarrow D.$$

From transitivity, the first two FDs imply the last FD, which can therefore be deleted while preserving equivalence to F^+. The important point to note is that

$AC \rightarrow D$ becomes redundant only after we replace $ABCD \rightarrow E$ with $AC \rightarrow E$. If we minimize left sides of FDs first and then check for redundant FDs, we are left with the first three FDs in the preceding list, which is indeed a minimal cover for F.

Dependency-Preserving Decomposition into 3NF

Returning to the problem of obtaining a lossless-join, dependency-preserving decomposition into 3NF relations, let R be a relation with a set F of FDs that is a minimal cover, and let R_1, R_2, ... , R_n be a lossless-join decomposition of R. For $1 \leq i \leq n$, suppose that each R_i is in 3NF and let F_i denote the projection of F onto the attributes of R_i. Do the following:

- Identify the set N of dependencies in F that are not **preserved**, that is, not included in the closure of the union of F_is.

- For each FD $X \rightarrow A$ in N, create a relation schema XA and add it to the decomposition of R.

Obviously, every dependency in F is preserved if we replace R by the R_is plus the schemas of the form XA added in this step. The R_is are given to be in 3NF. We can show that each of the schemas XA is in 3NF as follows: Since $X \rightarrow A$ is in the minimal cover F, $Y \rightarrow A$ does not hold for any Y that is a strict subset of X. Therefore, X is a key for XA. Further, if any other dependencies hold over XA, the right side can involve only attributes in X because A is a single attribute (because $X \rightarrow A$ is an FD in a minimal cover). Since X is a key for XA, none of these additional dependencies causes a violation of 3NF (although they might cause a violation of BCNF).

As an optimization, if the set N contains several FDs with the same left side, say, $X \rightarrow A_1$, $X \rightarrow A_2$, ... , $X \rightarrow A_n$, we can replace them with a single equivalent FD $X \rightarrow A_1 \ldots A_n$. Therefore, we produce one relation schema $XA_1 \ldots A_n$, instead of several schemas $XA_1, \ldots, XA_n$, which is generally preferable.

Consider the Contracts relation with attributes $CSJDPQV$ and FDs $JP \rightarrow C$, $SD \rightarrow P$, and $J \rightarrow S$. If we decompose $CSJDPQV$ into SDP and $CSJDQV$, then SDP is in BCNF, but $CSJDQV$ is not even in 3NF. So we decompose it further into JS and $CJDQV$. The relation schemas SDP, JS and $CJDQV$ are in 3NF (in fact, in BCNF), and the decomposition is lossless-join. However, the dependency $JP \rightarrow C$ is not preserved. This problem can be addressed by adding a relation schema CJP to the decomposition.

3NF Synthesis

We have assumed that the design process starts with an ER diagram, and that our use of FDs is primarily to guide decisions about decomposition. The algorithm for obtaining a lossless-join, dependency-preserving decomposition was presented in the previous section from this perspective—a lossless-join decomposition into 3NF is straightforward, and the algorithm addresses dependency-preservation by adding extra relation schemas.

An alternative approach, called **synthesis**, is to take all the attributes over the original relation R and a minimal cover F for the FDs that hold over it, and to add a relation schema XA to the decomposition of R for each FD $X \to A$ in F.

The resulting collection of relation schemas is in 3NF and preserves all FDs. If it is not a lossless-join decomposition of R, we can make it so by adding a relation schema that contains just those attributes that appear in some key. This algorithm gives us a lossless-join, dependency-preserving decomposition into 3NF, and has polynomial complexity—polynomial algorithms are available for computing minimal covers, and a key can be found in polynomial time (even though finding all keys is known to be NP-complete). The existence of a polynomial algorithm for obtaining a lossless-join, dependency-preserving decomposition into 3NF is surprising when we consider that testing whether a given schema is in 3NF is NP-complete.

As an example, consider a relation ABC with FDs $F = \{A \to B, \ C \to B\}$. The first step yields the relation schemas AB and BC. This is not a lossless-join decomposition of ABC; $AB \cap BC$ is B, and neither $B \to A$ nor $B \to C$ is in F^+. If we add a schema AC, we have the lossless-join property as well. Although the collection of relations AB, BC, and AC is a dependency-preserving, lossless-join decomposition of ABC, we obtained it through a process of *synthesis*, rather than through a process of repeated decomposition. We note that the decomposition produced by the synthesis approach is heavily dependent on the minimal cover that is used.

As another example of the synthesis approach, consider the Contracts relation with attributes $CSJDPQV$ and the following FDs:

$$C \to CSJDPQV, \ JP \to C, \ SD \to P, \text{ and } J \to S.$$

This set of FDs is not a minimal cover, and so we must find one. We first replace $C \to CSJDPQV$ with the FDs:

$$C \to S, \ C \to J, \ C \to D, \ C \to P, \ C \to Q \text{ and } C \to V.$$

The FD $C \rightarrow P$ is implied by $C \rightarrow S$, $C \rightarrow D$, and $SD \rightarrow P$; so we can delete it. The FD $C \rightarrow S$ is implied by $C \rightarrow J$ and $J \rightarrow S$; so we can delete it. This leaves us with a minimal cover:

$$C \rightarrow J, C \rightarrow D, C \rightarrow Q, C \rightarrow V, JP \rightarrow C, SD \rightarrow P, \text{ and } J \rightarrow S.$$

Using the algorithm for ensuring dependency-preservation, we obtain the relational schema CJ, CD, CQ, CV, CJP, SDP, and JS. We can improve this schema by combining relations for which C is the key into $CDJPQV$. In addition, we have SDP and JS in our decomposition. Since one of these relations ($CDJPQV$) is a superkey, we are done.

Comparing this decomposition with the one that we obtained earlier in this section, we find that they are quite close, with the only difference being that one of them has $CDJPQV$ instead of CJP and $CJDQV$. In general, however, there could be significant differences.

Database designers typically use a conceptual design methodology (e.g., ER design) to arrive at an initial database design. Given this, the approach of repeated decompositions to rectify instances of redundancy is likely to be the most natural use of FDs and normalization techniques. However, a designer can also consider the alternative designs suggested by the synthesis approach.

15.8 OTHER KINDS OF DEPENDENCIES *

FDs are probably the most common and important kind of constraint from the point of view of database design. However, there are several other kinds of dependencies. In particular, there is a well developed theory for database design using *multivalued dependencies* and *join dependencies*. By taking such dependencies into account, we can identify potential redundancy problems that cannot be detected using FDs alone.

This section illustrates the kinds of redundancy that can be detected using multivalued dependencies. Our main observation, however, is that simple guidelines (which can be checked using only FD reasoning) can tell us whether we even need to worry about complex constraints such as multivalued and join dependencies. We also comment on the role of *inclusion dependencies* in database design.

15.8.1 Multivalued Dependencies

Suppose that we have a relation with attributes *course*, *teacher* and *book*, which we denote as CTB. The meaning of a tuple is that teacher T can teach course C, and book B is a recommended text for the course. There are no FDs; the key is *CTB*. However, the recommended texts for a course are independent of the instructor. The instance shown in Figure 15.13 illustrates this situation.

course	*teacher*	*book*
Physics101	Green	Mechanics
Physics101	Green	Optics
Physics101	Brown	Mechanics
Physics101	Brown	Optics
Math301	Green	Mechanics
Math301	Green	Vectors
Math301	Green	Geometry

Figure 15.13   BCNF Relation with Redundancy That Is Revealed by MVDs

There are three points to note here:

- The relation schema *CTB* is in BCNF; thus we would not consider decomposing it further if we looked only at the FDs that hold over *CTB*.

- There is redundancy. The fact that Green can teach Physics101 is recorded once per recommended text for the course. Similarly, the fact that Optics is a text for Physics101 is recorded once per potential teacher.

- The redundancy can be eliminated by decomposing *CTB* into *CT* and *CB*.

The redundancy in this example is due to the constraint that the texts for a course are independent of the instructors, which cannot be expressed in terms of FDs. This constraint is an example of a *multivalued dependency*, or MVD. Ideally, we should model this situation using two binary relationship sets, Instructors with attributes *CT* and Text with attributes *CB*. Because these are two essentially independent relationships, modeling them with a single ternary relationship set with attributes *CTB* is inappropriate. (See Section 14.4.3 for a further discussion of ternary versus binary relationships.)   Given the subjectivity of ER design, however, we might create a ternary relationship. A careful analysis of the MVD information would then reveal the problem.

Let R be a relation schema and let X and Y be subsets of the attributes of R. Intuitively, the **multivalued dependency** $X \rightarrow\rightarrow Y$ is said to hold over R if, in every legal instance r of R, each X value is associated with a set of Y values and this set is independent of the values in the other attributes.

Formally, if the MVD $X \rightarrow\rightarrow Y$ holds over R and $Z = R - XY$, the following must be true for every legal instance r of R:

If $t_1 \in r$, $t_2 \in r$ and $t_1.X = t_2.X$, then there must be some $t_3 \in r$ such that $t_1.XY = t_3.XY$ and $t_2.Z = t_3.Z$.

Figure 15.14 illustrates this definition. If we are given the first two tuples and told that the MVD $X \twoheadrightarrow Y$ holds over this relation, we can infer that the relation instance must also contain the third tuple. Indeed, by interchanging the roles of the first two tuples—treating the first tuple as t_2 and the second tuple as t_1—we can deduce that the tuple t_4 must also be in the relation instance.

X	Y	Z	
a	b_1	c_1	— tuple t_1
a	b_2	c_2	— tuple t_2
a	b_1	c_2	— tuple t_3
a	b_2	c_1	— tuple t_4

Figure 15.14 Illustration of MVD Definition

This table suggests another way to think about MVDs: If $X \twoheadrightarrow Y$ holds over R, then $\pi_{YZ}(\sigma_{X=x}(R)) = \pi_Y(\sigma_{X=x}(R)) \times \pi_Z(\sigma_{X=x}(R))$ in every legal instance of R, for any value x that appears in the X column of R. In other words, consider groups of tuples in R with the same X-value, for each X-value. In each such group consider the projection onto the attributes YZ. This projection must be equal to the cross-product of the projections onto Y and Z. That is, for a given X-value, the Y-values and Z-values are independent. (From this definition it is easy to see that $X \twoheadrightarrow Y$ must hold whenever $X \to Y$ holds. If the FD $X \to Y$ holds, there is exactly one Y-value for a given X-value, and the conditions in the MVD definition hold trivially. The converse does not hold, as Figure 15.14 illustrates.)

Returning to our *CTB* example, the constraint that course texts are independent of instructors can be expressed as $C \twoheadrightarrow T$. In terms of the definition of MVDs, this constraint can be read as follows:

"If (there is a tuple showing that) C is taught by teacher T,
and (there is a tuple showing that) C has book B as text,
then (there is a tuple showing that) C is taught by T and has text B.

Given a set of FDs and MVDs, in general we can infer that several additional FDs and MVDs hold. A sound and complete set of inference rules consists of the three Armstrong Axioms plus five additional rules. Three of the additional rules involve only MVDs:

- **MVD Complementation:** If $X \twoheadrightarrow Y$, then $X \twoheadrightarrow R - XY$.

- **MVD Augmentation:** If $X \rightarrow\rightarrow Y$ and $W \supseteq Z$, then $WX \rightarrow\rightarrow YZ$.

- **MVD Transitivity:** If $X \rightarrow\rightarrow Y$ and $Y \rightarrow\rightarrow Z$, then $X \rightarrow\rightarrow (Z - Y)$.

As an example of the use of these rules, since we have $C \rightarrow\rightarrow T$ over CTB, MVD complementation allows us to infer that $C \rightarrow\rightarrow CTB - CT$ as well, that is, $C \rightarrow\rightarrow B$. The remaining two rules relate FDs and MVDs:

- **Replication:** If $X \rightarrow Y$, then $X \rightarrow\rightarrow Y$.

- **Coalescence:** If $X \rightarrow\rightarrow Y$ and there is a W such that $W \cap Y$ is empty, $W \rightarrow Z$, and $Y \supseteq Z$, then $X \rightarrow Z$.

Observe that replication states that every FD is also an MVD.

15.8.2 4NF

Fourth normal form is a direct generalization of BCNF. Let R be a relation schema, X and Y be nonempty subsets of the attributes of R, and F be a set of dependencies that includes both FDs and MVDs. R is said to be in **Fourth Normal Form (4NF)** if for every MVD $X \rightarrow\rightarrow Y$ that holds over R, one of the following statements is true:

- $Y \subseteq X$ or $XY = R$, or

- X is a superkey.

In reading this definition, it is important to understand that the definition of a key has not changed—the key must uniquely determine all attributes through FDs alone. $X \rightarrow\rightarrow Y$ is a **trivial MVD** if $Y \subseteq X \subseteq R$ or $XY = R$; such MVDs always hold.

The relation CTB is not in 4NF because $C \rightarrow\rightarrow T$ is a nontrivial MVD and C is not a key. We can eliminate the resulting redundancy by decomposing CTB into CT and CB; each of these relations is then in 4NF.

To use MVD information fully, we must understand the theory of MVDs. However, the following result due to Date and Fagin identifies conditions—detected using only FD information!—under which we can safely ignore MVD information. That is, using MVD information in addition to the FD information will not reveal any redundancy. Therefore, if these conditions hold, we do not even need to identify all MVDs.

If a relation schema is in BCNF, and at least one of its keys consists of a single attribute, it is also in 4NF.

An important assumption is implicit in any application of the preceding result: *The set of FDs identified thus far is indeed the set of all FDs that hold over the relation.* This assumption is important because the result relies on the relation being in BCNF, which in turn depends on the set of FDs that hold over the relation.

We illustrate this point using an example. Consider a relation schema $ABCD$ and suppose that the FD $A \rightarrow BCD$ and the MVD $B \rightarrow\rightarrow C$ are given. Considering only these dependencies, this relation schema appears to be a counter-example to the result. The relation has a simple key, appears to be in BCNF, and yet is not in 4NF because $B \rightarrow\rightarrow C$ causes a violation of the 4NF conditions. But let's take a closer look.

Figure 15.15 shows three tuples from an instance of $ABCD$ that satisfies the given MVD $B \rightarrow\rightarrow C$. From the definition of an MVD, given tuples t_1 and t_2, it follows

B	C	A	D	
b	c_1	a_1	d_1	— tuple t_1
b	c_2	a_2	d_2	— tuple t_2
b	c_1	a_2	d_2	— tuple t_3

Figure 15.15 Three Tuples from a Legal Instance of $ABCD$

that tuple t_3 must also be included in the instance. Consider tuples t_2 and t_3. From the given FD $A \rightarrow BCD$ and the fact that these tuples have the same A-value, we can deduce that $c_1 = c_2$. Thus we see that the FD $B \rightarrow C$ must hold over $ABCD$ whenever the FD $A \rightarrow BCD$ and the MVD $B \rightarrow\rightarrow C$ hold. If $B \rightarrow C$ holds, the relation $ABCD$ is not in BCNF (unless additional FDs hold that make B a key)!

Thus the apparent counter-example is really not a counter-example—rather, it illustrates the importance of correctly identifying all FDs that hold over a relation. In this example $A \rightarrow BCD$ is not the only FD; the FD $B \rightarrow C$ also holds, but was not identified initially. Given a set of FDs and MVDs, the inference rules can be used to infer additional FDs (and MVDs); to apply the Date-Fagin result without first using the MVD inference rules, we must be certain that we have identified all the FDs.

In summary, the Date-Fagin result offers a convenient way to check that a relation is in 4NF (without reasoning about MVDs) if we are confident that we have identified all FDs. At this point the reader is invited to go over the examples we have discussed in this chapter and see if there is a relation that is not in 4NF.

15.8.3 Join Dependencies

A join dependency is a further generalization of MVDs. A **join dependency** (JD) $\bowtie \{R_1, \ldots, R_n\}$ is said to hold over a relation R if $R_1, \ldots, R_n$ is a lossless-join decomposition of R.

An MVD $X \twoheadrightarrow Y$ over a relation R can be expressed as the join dependency $\bowtie \{XY, X(R-Y)\}$. As an example, in the CTB relation, the MVD $C \twoheadrightarrow T$ can be expressed as the join dependency $\bowtie \{CT, CB\}$.

Unlike FDs and MVDs, there is no set of sound and complete inference rules for JDs.

15.8.4 5NF

A relation schema R is said to be in **Fifth Normal Form (5NF)** if for every JD $\bowtie \{R_1, \ldots, R_n\}$ that holds over R, one of the following statements is true:

- $R_i = R$ for some i, or

- The JD is implied by the set of those FDs over R in which the left side is a key for R.

The second condition deserves some explanation, since we have not presented inference rules for FDs and JDs taken together. Intuitively, we must be able to show that the decomposition of R into $\{R_1, \ldots, R_n\}$ is lossless-join whenever the **key dependencies** (FDs in which the left side is a key for R) hold. $\bowtie \{R_1, \ldots, R_n\}$ is a **trivial JD** if $R_i = R$ for some i; such a JD always holds.

The following result, also due to Date and Fagin, identifies conditions—again, detected using only FD information—under which we can safely ignore JD information.

> If a relation schema is in 3NF and each of its keys consists of a single attribute, it is also in 5NF.

The conditions identified in this result are sufficient for a relation to be in 5NF, but not necessary. The result can be very useful in practice because it allows us to conclude that a relation is in 5NF *without ever identifying the MVDs and JDs that may hold over the relation.*

15.8.5 Inclusion Dependencies

MVDs and JDs can be used to guide database design, as we have seen, although they are less common than FDs and harder to recognize and reason about. In contrast, inclusion dependencies are very intuitive and are quite common. However, they typically have little influence on database design (beyond the ER design stage).

Informally, an inclusion dependency is a statement of the form that some columns of a relation are contained other columns (usually of a second relation). A foreign key constraint is an example of an inclusion dependency; the referring column(s) in one relation must be contained in the primary key column(s) of the referenced relation. As another example, if R and S are two relations obtained by translating two entity sets such that every R entity is also an S entity, we would have an inclusion dependency; projecting R on its key attributes yields a relation that is contained in the relation obtained by projecting S on its key attributes.

The main point to bear in mind is that we should not split groups of attributes that participate in an inclusion dependency. For example, if we have an inclusion dependency $AB \subseteq CD$, while decomposing the relation schema containing AB, we should ensure that at least one of the schemas obtained in the decomposition contains both A and B. Otherwise, we cannot check the inclusion dependency $AB \subseteq CD$ without reconstructing the relation containing AB.

Most inclusion dependencies in practice are *key-based*, that is, involve only keys. Foreign key constraints are a good example of key-based inclusion dependencies. An ER diagram that involves ISA hierarchies also leads to key-based inclusion dependencies. If all inclusion dependencies are key-based, we rarely have to worry about splitting attribute groups that participate in inclusions, since decompositions usually do not split the primary key. Note however that going from 3NF to BCNF always involves splitting some key (hopefully not the primary key!), since the dependency guiding the split is of the form $X \rightarrow A$ where A is part of a key.

15.9 SUMMARY

ICs such as FDs provide valuable information about relations and can be used to rigorously check whether certain kinds of redundancy can arise. If a relation schema allows redundancy, the schema may have to be restructured; one common restructuring technique is to decompose the schema into a collection of smaller relations.

In decomposing a relation schema, we must ensure that it is always possible to compute the correct instance of the original relation from the corresponding instances of the relations that it is decomposed into. This is called the *lossless-join* property. Another useful property, called *dependency-preservation*, is that by checking integrity constraints with respect to each of the new relations, we can ensure that all ICs specified on the original relation are satisfied. That is, we do not need to consider two or more of the new relations (i.e., joins) to enforce all the ICs on the original relation.

Decomposition is not always a good idea because queries that involve attributes from several of the new relations will now require joins, which can be expensive; similarly, checking ICs can involve joins if the decomposition is not dependency-preserving. An alternative to decomposition is to accept the possibility of redundancy, possibly guarding against it in some other way, for example, in the logic of an application program used to control updates of the database.

The use of formal techniques in this area is two-fold. First, it can tell us whether a relation schema holds the potential for redundancy, and if so, what kinds of redundancy. Several *normal forms* have been identified, and if a relation is in one of these forms, it is free of certain kinds of redundancy. In particular, if a relation is in BCNF, it is free of any redundancy that can be detected using only FD information. Second, formal techniques can give us insight into the options available to us for dealing with redundancy. For example, there may be several ways of decomposing a relation schema such that the resulting relation schemas are all in a desired normal form.

Using formal techniques, especially with the help of good tools that automate tedious details of the various algorithms involved, we can significantly improve the quality of a database design. Although FDs, which generalize primary key constraints, are the most widely studied and used form of IC in database design, several other classes of constraints have also been studied, including multivalued and join dependencies. These dependencies can sometimes reveal redundancy that is not detectable using FD information alone.

EXERCISES

Exercise 15.1 Briefly answer the following questions.

1. Define the term *functional dependency*.

2. Give a set of FDs for the relation schema $R(A,B,C,D)$ with primary key AB under which R is in 1NF but not in 2NF.

3. Give a set of FDs for the relation schema $R(A,B,C,D)$ with primary key AB under which R is in 2NF but not in 3NF.

4. Consider the relation schema $R(A,B,C)$, which has the FD $B \rightarrow C$. If A is a candidate key for R, is it possible for R to be in BCNF? If so, under what conditions? If not, explain why not.

5. Suppose that we have a relation schema $R(A,B,C)$ representing a relationship between two entity sets with keys A and B, respectively, and suppose that R has (among others) the FDs $A \rightarrow B$ and $B \rightarrow A$. Explain what such a pair of dependencies means (i.e., what they imply about the relationship that the relation models).

Exercise 15.2 Consider a relation R with five attributes $ABCDE$. You are given the following dependencies: $A \rightarrow B$, $BC \rightarrow E$, and $ED \rightarrow A$.

1. List all keys for R.

2. Is R in 3NF?

3. Is R in BCNF?

Exercise 15.3 Consider the following collection of relations and dependencies. Assume that each relation is obtained through decomposition from a relation with attributes $ABCDEFGHI$ and that all the known dependencies over relation $ABCDEFGHI$ are listed for each question. (The questions are independent of each other, obviously, since the given dependencies over $ABCDEFGHI$ are different.) For each (sub) relation: (a) State the strongest normal form that the relation is in. (b) If it is not in BCNF, decompose it into a collection of BCNF relations.

1. $R1(A,C,B,D,E)$, $A \rightarrow B$, $C \rightarrow D$

2. $R2(A,B,F)$, $AC \rightarrow E$, $B \rightarrow F$

3. $R3(A,D)$, $D \rightarrow G$, $G \rightarrow H$

4. $R4(D,C,H,G)$, $A \rightarrow I$, $I \rightarrow A$

5. $R5(A,I,C,E)$

Exercise 15.4 Suppose that we have the following three tuples in a legal instance of a relation schema S with three attributes ABC (listed in order): (1,2,3), (4,2,3), and (5,3,3).

1. Which of the following dependencies can you infer does *not* hold over schema S?

   (a) $A \rightarrow B$ (b) $BC \rightarrow A$ (c) $B \rightarrow C$

2. Can you identify any dependencies that hold over S?

Exercise 15.5 Suppose you are given a relation R with four attributes, $ABCD$. For each of the following sets of FDs, assuming those are the only dependencies that hold for R, do the following: (a) Identify the candidate key(s) for R. (b) Identify the best normal form that R satisfies (1NF, 2NF, 3NF, or BCNF). (c) If R is not in BCNF, decompose it into a set of BCNF relations that preserve the dependencies.

1. $C \rightarrow D$, $C \rightarrow A$, $B \rightarrow C$

2. $B \rightarrow C$, $D \rightarrow A$

3. $ABC \rightarrow D$, $D \rightarrow A$

4. $A \rightarrow B$, $BC \rightarrow D$, $A \rightarrow C$

5. $AB \rightarrow C$, $AB \rightarrow D$, $C \rightarrow A$, $D \rightarrow B$

Exercise 15.6 Consider the attribute set $R = ABCDEGH$ and the FD set $F = \{AB \rightarrow C, AC \rightarrow B, AD \rightarrow E, B \rightarrow D, BC \rightarrow A, E \rightarrow G\}$.

1. For each of the following attribute sets, do the following: (i) Compute the set of dependencies that hold over the set and write down a minimal cover. (ii) Name the strongest normal form that is not violated by the relation containing these attributes. (iii) Decompose it into a collection of BCNF relations if it is not in BCNF.

   (a) ABC (b) $ABCD$ (c) $ABCEG$ (d) $DCEGH$ (e) $ACEH$

2. Which of the following decompositions of $R = ABCDEG$, with the same set of dependencies F, is (a) dependency-preserving? (b) lossless-join?

   (a) $\{AB, BC, ABDE, EG\}$
   (b) $\{ABC, ACDE, ADG\}$

Exercise 15.7 Let R be decomposed into R_1, R_2, ..., R_n. Let F be a set of FDs specified on R.

1. Define what it means for F to *be preserved* in the set of decomposed relations.

2. Describe a polynomial-time algorithm to test dependency-preservation.

3. Projecting the FDs stated over a set of attributes X onto a subset of attributes Y requires that we consider the closure of the FDs. Give an example where considering the closure is important in testing dependency-preservation; that is, considering just the given FDs gives incorrect results.

Exercise 15.8 Consider a relation R that has three attributes ABC. It is decomposed into relations R_1 with attributes AB and R_2 with attributes BC.

1. State the definition of a lossless-join decomposition with respect to this example. Answer this question concisely by writing a relational algebra equation involving R, R_1 and R_2.

2. If you are given the following instances of R_1 and R_2, what can you say about the instance of R from which these were obtained? Answer this question by listing tuples that are definitely in R and listing tuples that are possibly in R.

   Instance of $R_1 = \{(5,1), (6,1)\}$
   Instance of $R_2 = \{(1,8), (1,9)\}$

   Can you say that attribute B definitely *is* or *is not* a key for R?

Exercise 15.9 Suppose you are given a relation $R(A,B,C,D)$. For each of the following sets of FDs, assuming they are the only dependencies that hold for R, do the following: (a) Identify the candidate key(s) for R. (b) State whether or not the proposed decomposition of R into smaller relations is a good decomposition, and briefly explain why or why not.

1. $B \rightarrow C, D \rightarrow A$; decompose into BC and AD.

2. $AB \rightarrow C, C \rightarrow A, C \rightarrow D$; decompose into ACD and BC.

3. $A \rightarrow BC$, $C \rightarrow AD$; decompose into ABC and AD.

4. $A \rightarrow B$, $B \rightarrow C$, $C \rightarrow D$; decompose into AB and ACD.

5. $A \rightarrow B$, $B \rightarrow C$, $C \rightarrow D$; decompose into AB, AD and CD.

Exercise 15.10 Suppose that we have the following four tuples in a relation S with three attributes ABC (listed in order): (1,2,3), (4,2,3), (5,3,3), (5,3,4). Which of the following functional ($\rightarrow$) and multivalued ($\rightarrow\rightarrow$) dependencies can you infer does *not* hold over relation S?

1. $A \rightarrow B$

2. $A \rightarrow\rightarrow B$

3. $BC \rightarrow A$

4. $BC \rightarrow\rightarrow A$

5. $B \rightarrow C$

6. $B \rightarrow\rightarrow C$

Exercise 15.11 Consider a relation R with five attributes $ABCDE$.

1. For each of the following instances of R, state whether (a) it violates the FD $BC \rightarrow D$, and (b) it violates the MVD $BC \rightarrow\rightarrow D$:

   (a) { } (i.e., empty relation)

   (b) {(a,2,3,4,5), (2,a,3,5,5)}

   (c) {(a,2,3,4,5), (2,a,3,5,5), (a,2,3,4,6)}

   (d) {(a,2,3,4,5), (2,a,3,4,5), (a,2,3,6,5)}

   (e) {(a,2,3,4,5), (2,a,3,7,5), (a,2,3,4,6)}

   (f) {(a,2,3,4,5), (2,a,3,4,5), (a,2,3,6,5), (a,2,3,6,6)}

   (g) {(a,2,3,4,5), (a,2,3,6,5), (a,2,3,6,6), (a,2,3,4,6)}

2. Suppose that each instance for R listed above is legal. What can you say about the FD $A \rightarrow B$?

Exercise 15.12 JDs are motivated by the fact that sometimes a relation that cannot be decomposed into two smaller relations in a lossless-join manner can be so decomposed into three or more relations. An example is a relation with attributes *supplier*, *part* and *project*, denoted SPJ, with no FDs or MVDs. The JD $\bowtie \{SP, PJ, JS\}$ holds.

From the JD, the set of relation schemes SP, PJ and JS is a lossless-join decomposition of SPJ. Construct an instance of SPJ to illustrate that no two of these schemes suffice.

Exercise 15.13 Consider a relation R with attributes $ABCDE$. Let the following FDs be given: $A \rightarrow BC$, $BC \rightarrow E$, and $E \rightarrow DA$. Similarly, let S be a relation with attributes $ABCDE$ and let the following FDs be given: $A \rightarrow BC$, $B \rightarrow E$, and $E \rightarrow DA$. (Only the second dependency differs from those that hold over R.) You do not know whether or which other (join) dependencies hold.

1. Is R in BCNF?

2. Is R in 4 NF?

3. Is R in 5 NF?

4. Is S in BCNF?

5. Is S in 4 NF?

6. Is S in 5 NF?

Exercise 15.14 Let us say that an FD $X \to Y$ is *simple* if Y is a single attribute.

1. Replace the FD $AB \to CD$ by the smallest equivalent collection of simple FDs.

2. Prove that every FD $X \to Y$ in a set of FDs F can be replaced by a set of simple FDs such that F^+ is equal to the closure of the new set of FDs.

Exercise 15.15 Prove that Armstrong's Axioms are sound and complete for FD inference. That is, show that repeated application of these axioms on a set F of FDs produces exactly the dependencies in F^+.

Exercise 15.16 Describe a linear-time (in the size of the set of FDs, where the size of each FD is the number of attributes involved) algorithm for finding the attribute closure of a set of attributes with respect to a set of FDs.

Exercise 15.17 Consider a relation scheme R with FDs F that is decomposed into schemes with attributes X and Y. Show that this decomposition is dependency-preserving if $F \subseteq (F_X \cup F_Y)^+$.

Exercise 15.18 Let R be a relation schema with a set F of FDs. Prove that the decomposition of R into R_1 and R_2 is lossless-join if and only if F^+ contains $R_1 \cap R_2 \to R_1$ or $R_1 \cap R_2 \to R_2$.

Exercise 15.19 Prove that the optimization of the algorithm for lossless-join, dependency-preserving decomposition into 3NF relations (Section 15.7.2) is correct.

Exercise 15.20 Prove that the 3NF synthesis algorithm produces a lossless-join decomposition of the relation containing all the original attributes.

Exercise 15.21 Prove that an MVD $X \to\!\!\!\to Y$ over a relation R can be expressed as the join dependency $\bowtie \{XY, X(R-Y)\}$.

Exercise 15.22 Prove that if R has only one key, it is in BCNF if and only if it is in 3NF.

Exercise 15.23 Prove that if R is in 3NF and every key is simple, then R is in BCNF.

Exercise 15.24 Prove these statements:

1. If a relation scheme is in BCNF and at least one of its keys consists of a single attribute, it is also in 4NF.

2. If a relation scheme is in 3NF and each of its keys consists of a single attribute, it is also in 5NF.

Exercise 15.25 Give an algorithm for testing whether a relation scheme is in BCNF. The algorithm should be polynomial in the size of the set of given FDs. (The *size* is the sum over all FDs of the number of attributes that appear in the FD.) Is there a polynomial algorithm for testing whether a relation scheme is in 3NF?

PROJECT-BASED EXERCISES

Exercise 15.26 Minibase provides a tool called Designview for doing database design using FDs. It lets you check whether a relation is in a particular normal form, to test whether decompositions have nice properties, to compute attribute closures, to try several decomposition sequences and switch between them, to generate SQL statements to create the final database schema, and so on.

1. Use Designview to check your answers to exercises that call for computing closures, testing normal forms, decomposing into a desired normal form, and so on.

2. (*Note to instructors: This question should be made more specific by providing additional details. See Appendix A.*) Apply Designview to a large, real-world design problem.

BIBLIOGRAPHIC NOTES

Textbook presentations of dependency theory and its use in database design include [4, 35, 359, 366, 550]. Good survey articles on the topic include [556, 285].

FDs were introduced in [135], along with the concept of 3NF, and axioms for inferring FDs were presented in [29]. BCNF was introduced in [136]. The concept of a legal relation instance and dependency satisfaction are studied formally in [224]. FDs were generalized to semantic data models in [565].

Finding a key is shown to be NP-complete in [355]. Lossless-join decompositions were studied in [22, 360, 451]. Dependency-preserving decompositions were studied in [55]. [61] introduced minimal covers. Decomposition into 3NF is studied by [61, 76] and decomposition into BCNF is addressed in [546]. [283] shows that testing whether a relation is in 3NF is NP-complete. [185] introduced 4NF and discussed decomposition into 4NF. Fagin introduced other normal forms in [186] (Project-Join normal form) and [187] (Domain-Key normal form). In contrast to the extensive study of vertical decompositions, there has been relatively little formal investigation of horizontal decompositions. [152] investigates horizontal decompositions.

MVDs were discovered independently by Delobel [153], Fagin [185], and Zaniolo [577]. Axioms for FDs and MVDs were presented in [54]. [428] shows that there is no axiomatization for JDs, although [476] provides an axiomatization for a more general class of dependencies. The sufficient conditions for 4NF and 5NF in terms of FDs that were discussed in Section 15.8 are from [148]. An approach to database design that uses dependency information to construct sample relation instances is described in [365, 366].

PHYSICAL DATABASE DESIGN
AND TUNING

Advice to a client who complained about rain leaking through the roof onto the dining table: "Move the table."

—Architect Frank Lloyd Wright

The performance of a DBMS on commonly asked queries and typical update operations is the ultimate measure of a database design. A DBA can improve performance by adjusting some DBMS parameters (e.g., the size of the buffer pool or the frequency of checkpointing), and by identifying performance bottlenecks and adding hardware to eliminate such bottlenecks. The first step in achieving good performance, however, is to make good database design choices, which is the focus of this chapter.

After we have designed the *conceptual* and *external* schemas, that is, created a collection of relations and views along with a set of integrity constraints, we must address performance goals through **physical database design**, in which we design the *physical* schema. As user requirements evolve, it is usually necessary to **tune**, or adjust, all aspects of a database design for good performance.

This chapter is organized as follows. We give an overview of physical database design and tuning in Section 16.1. The most important physical design decisions concern the choice of indexes. We present guidelines for deciding which indexes to create in Section 16.2. These guidelines are illustrated through several examples and developed further in Sections 16.3, 16.4, 16.5, and 16.6. In Section 16.3 we present examples that highlight basic alternatives in index selection. In Section 16.4 we look closely at the important issue of clustering; we discuss how to choose clustered indexes, and whether to store tuples from different relations near each other (an option supported by some DBMSs). In Section 16.5 we consider the use of indexes with composite or multiple-attribute search keys. In Section 16.6 we emphasize how well-chosen indexes can enable some queries to be answered without ever looking at the actual data records.

In Section 16.7 we survey the main issues of database tuning. In addition to tuning indexes, we may have to tune the conceptual schema, as well as frequently used query and view definitions. We discuss how to refine the conceptual schema in Section 16.8 and how to refine queries and view definitions in Section 16.9.

We briefly discuss the performance impact of concurrent access in Section 16.10. We conclude the chapter with a short discussion of DBMS benchmarks in Section 16.11; benchmarks help evaluate the performance of alternative DBMS products.

16.1 INTRODUCTION TO PHYSICAL DATABASE DESIGN

Like all other aspects of database design, physical design must be guided by the nature of the data and its intended use. In particular, it is important to understand the typical **workload** that the database must support; the workload consists of a mix of queries and updates. Users also have certain requirements about how fast certain queries or updates must run, or how many transactions must be processed per second. The workload description and users' performance requirements are the basis on which a number of decisions have to be made during physical database design.

To create a good physical database design and to tune the system for performance in response to evolving user requirements, the designer needs to understand the workings of a DBMS, especially the indexing and query processing techniques supported by the DBMS. If the database is expected to be accessed concurrently by many users, or is a *distributed database*, the task becomes more complicated, and other features of a DBMS come into play; we consider this aspect of design only briefly.

16.1.1 Database Workloads

The key to good physical design is arriving at an accurate description of the expected workload. A **workload description** includes the following elements:

1. A list of queries and their frequencies, as a fraction of all queries and updates.

2. A list of updates and their frequencies.

3. Performance goals for each type of query and update.

For each query in the workload, we must identify:

- Which relations are accessed.

- Which attributes are retained (in the SELECT clause).

- Which attributes have selection or join conditions expressed on them (in the WHERE clause) and how selective these conditions are likely to be.

Similarly, for each update in the workload, we must identify:

- Which attributes have selection or join conditions expressed on them (in the `WHERE` clause) and how selective these conditions are likely to be.

- The type of update (`INSERT`, `DELETE` or `UPDATE`), and the updated relation.

- For `UPDATE` commands, the fields that are modified by the update.

Remember that queries and updates typically have parameters, for example, a debit or credit operation involves a particular account number. The values of these parameters determine selectivity of selection and join conditions.

Updates have a query component that is used to find the target tuples. This component can benefit from a good physical design and the presence of indexes. On the other hand, updates typically require additional work to maintain indexes on the attributes that they modify. Thus, while queries can only benefit from the presence of an index, an index may either speed up or slow down a given update. Designers should keep this trade-off in mind when creating indexes.

16.1.2 Physical Design and Tuning Decisions

Important decisions made during physical database design and database tuning include the following:

1. *Which indexes to create.*

   - Which relations to index and which field or combination of fields to choose as index search keys.

   - For each index, should it be clustered or unclustered? Should it be dense or sparse?

2. *Whether we should make changes to the conceptual schema in order to enhance performance.* For example, we have to consider:

   - *Alternative normalized schemas:* We usually have more than one way to decompose a schema into a desired normal form (BCNF or 3NF). A choice can be made on the basis of performance criteria.

   - *Denormalization:* We might want to reconsider schema decompositions carried out for normalization during the conceptual schema design process, to improve the performance of queries that involve attributes from several previously decomposed relations.

   - *Vertical partitioning:* Under certain circumstances we might want to further decompose relations to improve the performance of queries that involve only a few attributes.

- *Views:* We might want to add some views to mask the changes in the conceptual schema from users.

3. *Whether frequently executed queries and transactions should be rewritten to run faster.*

In parallel or distributed databases, which we discuss in Chapter 19, there are additional choices to consider, such as whether to partition a relation across different sites or whether to store copies of a relation at multiple sites.

16.1.3 Need for Database Tuning

Accurate, detailed workload information may be hard to come by while doing the initial design of the system. Consequently, tuning a database after it has been designed and deployed is important—we must refine the initial design in the light of actual usage patterns to obtain the best possible performance.

The distinction between database design and database tuning is somewhat arbitrary. We could consider the design process to be over once an initial conceptual schema is designed and a set of indexing and clustering decisions is made. Any subsequent changes to the conceptual schema or the indexes, say, would then be regarded as a tuning activity. Alternatively, we could consider some refinement of the conceptual schema (and physical design decisions affected by this refinement) to be part of the physical design process.

Where we draw the line between design and tuning is not very important, and we will simply discuss the issues of index selection and database tuning without regard to when the tuning activities are carried out.

16.2 GUIDELINES FOR INDEX SELECTION

In considering which indexes to create, we begin with the list of queries (including queries that appear as part of update operations). Obviously, only relations accessed by some query need to be considered as candidates for indexing, and the choice of attributes to index on is guided by the conditions that appear in the **WHERE** clauses of the queries in the workload. The presence of suitable indexes can significantly improve the evaluation plan for a query, as we saw in Chapter 13.

One approach to index selection is to consider the most important queries in turn, and for each to determine which plan the optimizer would choose given the indexes that are currently on our list of (to be created) indexes. Then we consider whether we can arrive at a substantially better plan by adding more indexes; if so, these additional indexes are candidates for inclusion in our list of indexes. In general, range retrievals will benefit from a B+ tree index, and exact-match retrievals will benefit from a hash index. Clustering will benefit range queries, and will benefit exact-match queries if several data entries contain the same key value.

Before adding an index to the list, however, we must consider the impact of having this index on the updates in our workload. As we noted earlier, although an index can speed up the query component of an update, all indexes on an updated attribute—on *any* attribute, in the case of inserts and deletes—must be updated whenever the value of the attribute is changed. Therefore, we must sometimes consider the trade-off of slowing some update operations in the workload in order to speed up some queries.

Clearly, choosing a good set of indexes for a given workload requires an understanding of the available indexing techniques, and of the workings of the query optimizer. The following guidelines for index selection summarize our discussion:

Guideline 1 (Whether to index): The obvious points are often the most important. Don't build an index unless some query—including the query components of updates—will benefit from it; and whenever possible, choose indexes that speed up more than one query.

Guideline 2 (Choice of search key): Attributes mentioned in a `WHERE` clause are candidates for indexing.

- An exact-match selection condition suggests that we should consider an index on the selected attributes, ideally, a hash index.

- A range selection condition suggests that we should consider a B+ tree (or ISAM) index on the selected attributes. A B+ tree index is usually preferable to an ISAM index. An ISAM index may be worth considering if the relation is infrequently updated, but we will assume that a B+ tree index is always chosen over an ISAM index, for simplicity.

Guideline 3 (Multiple-attribute search keys): Indexes with multiple-attribute search keys should be considered in the following two situations:

- A `WHERE` clause includes conditions on more than one attribute of a relation.

- They enable index-only evaluation strategies (i.e., accessing the relation can be avoided) for important queries. (This situation could lead to attributes being in the search key even if they do not appear in `WHERE` clauses.)

When creating indexes on search keys with multiple attributes, if range queries are expected, be careful to order the attributes in the search key to match the queries.

Guideline 4 (Whether to cluster): At most one index on a given relation can be clustered, and clustering affects performance greatly; so the choice of clustered index is important.

- As a rule of thumb, range queries are likely to benefit the most from clustering. If several range queries are posed on a relation, involving different sets of attributes, consider the selectivity of the queries and their relative frequency in the workload when deciding which index should be clustered.

- If an index enables an index-only evaluation strategy for the query it is intended to speed up, the index need not be clustered. (Clustering matters only when the index is used to retrieve tuples from the underlying index.)

Guideline 5 (Hash versus tree index): A B+ tree index is usually preferable because it supports range queries as well as equality queries. A hash index is better in the following situations:

- The index is intended to support index nested loops join; the indexed relation is the inner relation, and the search key includes the join columns. In this case, the slight improvement of a hash index over a B+ tree for equality selections is magnified, because an equality selection is generated for each tuple in the outer relation.

- There is a very important equality query, and there are no range queries, involving the search key attributes.

Guideline 6 (Balancing the cost of index maintenance): After drawing up a 'wish-list' of indexes to create, consider the impact of each index on the updates in the workload.

- If maintaining an index slows down important update operations, consider dropping the index.

- Keep in mind, however, that adding an index may well speed up a given update operation. For example, an index on employee ids could speed up the operation of increasing the salary of a given employee (specified by id).

16.3 BASIC EXAMPLES OF INDEX SELECTION

The following examples illustrate how to choose indexes during database design. The schemas used in the examples are not described in detail; in general they contain the attributes named in the queries. Additional information is presented when necessary.

Let us begin with a simple query:

> **SELECT** E.ename, D.mgr
> **FROM** Employees E, Departments D
> **WHERE** D.dname='Toy' **AND** E.dno=D.dno

The relations mentioned in the query are Employees and Departments, and both conditions in the **WHERE** clause involve equalities. Our guidelines suggest that we should build hash indexes on the attributes involved. It seems clear that we should build a hash index on the *dname* attribute of Departments. But consider the equality *E.dno=D.dno*. Should we build an index (hash, of course) on the *dno* attribute of Departments or of Employees (or both)? Intuitively, we want to retrieve Departments tuples using the index on *dname* because few tuples are likely to satisfy the equality selection *D.dname='Toy'*,[1] and for each qualifying Departments tuple find matching Employees tuples by using an index on the *dno* attribute of Employees. Thus we should build an index on the *dno* field of Employees. (Note that nothing is gained by building an additional index on the *dno* field of Departments because Departments tuples are retrieved using the *dname* index.)

Our choice of indexes was guided by a query evaluation plan that we wanted to utilize. This consideration of a potential evaluation plan is common while making physical design decisions; understanding query optimization is therefore very useful for physical design. We show the desired plan for this query in Figure 16.1.

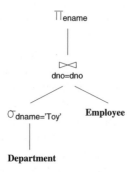

Figure 16.1 A Desirable Query Evaluation Plan

---

[1] This is only a heuristic. If *dname* is not the key, and we do not have statistics to verify this claim, it is certainly possible that several tuples satisfy this condition!

As a variant of this query, suppose that the WHERE clause is modified to be WHERE *D.dname='Toy'* AND *E.dno=D.dno* AND *E.age=25*. Let us consider alternative evaluation plans. One good plan is to retrieve Departments tuples that satisfy the selection on *dname*, and to retrieve matching Employees tuples by using an index on the *dno* field; the selection on *age* is then applied on-the-fly. However, unlike the previous variant of this query, we do not really need to have an index on the *dno* field of Employees if we have an index on *age*. In this case we can retrieve Departments tuples that satisfy the selection on *dname* (by using the index on *dname*, as before), retrieve Employees tuples that satisfy the selection on *age* by using the index on *age*, and join these sets of tuples. This plan is likely to be somewhat poorer than using an index on *dno*, but it is a reasonable alternative. Therefore, if we have an index on *age* already (prompted by some other query in the workload), this variant of the sample query does not justify creating an index on the *dno* field of Employees.

Our next query involves a range selection:

```
SELECT  E.ename, D.dname
FROM    Employees E, Departments D
WHERE   E.sal BETWEEN 10,000 AND 20,000
        AND E.hobby='Stamps' AND E.dno=D.dno
```

This query illustrates the use of the BETWEEN operator for expressing range selections. It is equivalent to the condition:

$$10,000 \leq \text{E.sal} \; \text{AND} \; \text{E.sal} \leq 20,000$$

The use of BETWEEN to express range conditions is recommended; it makes it easier for both the user and the optimizer to recognize both parts of the range selection.

Returning to the example query, both (non join) selections are on the Employees relation. Therefore, it is clear that a plan in which Employees is the outer relation and Departments is the inner relation is the best, as in the previous query, and we should build a hash index on the *dno* attribute of Departments. But which index should we build on Employees? A B+ tree index on the *sal* attribute would help with the range selection, especially if it is clustered. A hash index on the *hobby* attribute would help with the equality selection. If one of these indexes is available, we could retrieve Employees tuples using this index, retrieve matching Departments tuples using the index on *dno*, and apply all remaining selections and projections on-the-fly. If both indexes are available, the optimizer would choose the more selective access path for the given query; that is, it would consider which selection (the range condition or the equality on *hobby*) has fewer qualifying tuples. In general, which access path is more selective depends on the data. If there are very few people with salaries in the given range, and many people collect stamps, the B+ tree index is best. Otherwise, the hash index on *hobby* is best.

If the query constants are known (as in our example), the selectivities can be estimated if statistics on the data are available. Otherwise, as a rule of thumb, an equality selection is likely to be more selective, and a reasonable decision would be to create a hash index on *hobby*. Sometimes, the query constants are not known—we might obtain a query by expanding a query on a view at run-time, or we might have a query in dynamic SQL, which allows constants to be specified as *wild-card variables* (e.g., *%X*) and instantiated at run-time. In this case, if the query is very important, we might choose to create a B+ tree index on *sal* and a hash index on *hobby*, and leave the choice to be made by the optimizer at run-time.

16.4   CLUSTERING AND INDEXING *

Range queries are good candidates for improvement with a clustered index:

```
SELECT   E.dno
FROM     Employees E
WHERE    E.age > 40
```

If we have a B+ tree index on *age*, we can use it to retrieve only tuples that satisfy the selection *E.age*> 40. Whether such an index is worthwhile depends first of all on the selectivity of the condition. What fraction of the employees are older than 40? If virtually everyone is older than 40, we don't gain much by using an index on *age*; a sequential scan of the relation would do almost as well. However, suppose that only 10% of the employees are older than 40. Now, is an index useful? The answer depends on whether the index is clustered. If the index is unclustered, we could have one page I/O per qualifying employee, and this could be more expensive than a sequential scan even if only 10% of the employees qualify! On the other hand, a clustered B+ tree index on *age* requires only 10% of the I/Os for a sequential scan (ignoring the few I/Os needed to traverse from the root to the first retrieved leaf page).

As another example, consider the following refinement of the previous query:

```
SELECT   E.dno, COUNT(*)
FROM     Employees E
WHERE    E.age > 10
GROUP BY E.dno
```

If a B+ tree index is available on *age*, we could retrieve tuples using it, sort the retrieved tuples on *dno*, and so answer the query. However, this may not be a good plan if virtually all employees are more than 10 years old. This plan is especially bad if the index is not clustered.

Let us consider whether an index on *dno* might suit our purposes better. We could use the index to retrieve all tuples, grouped by *dno*, and for each *dno* count the number of tuples with *age* > 10. (This strategy can be used with both hash and B+ tree indexes; we only require the tuples to be *grouped*, not necessarily *sorted*, by *dno*.) Again, the efficiency depends crucially on whether the index is clustered. If it is, this plan is likely to be the best if the condition on *age* is not very selective. (Even if we have a clustered index on *age*, if the condition on *age* is not selective, the cost of sorting qualifying tuples on *dno* is likely to be high.) If the index is not clustered, we could perform one page I/O per tuple in Employees, and this plan would be terrible. Indeed, if the index is not clustered, the optimizer will choose the straightforward plan based on sorting on *dno*. Thus this query suggests that we build a clustered index on *dno* if the condition on *age* is not very selective. If the condition is very selective, we should consider building an index (not necessarily clustered) on *age* instead.

Clustering is also important for an index on a search key that does not include a candidate key, that is, an index in which several data entries can have the same key value. To illustrate this point, we present the following query:

> SELECT E.dno
> FROM   Employees E
> WHERE   E.hobby='Stamps'

If many people collect stamps, retrieving tuples through an unclustered index on *hobby* can be very inefficient. Indeed, it may be cheaper to simply scan the relation to retrieve all tuples and to apply the selection on-the-fly to the retrieved tuples. Therefore, if such a query is important, we should consider making the index on *hobby* a clustered index. On the other hand, if we assume that *eid* is a key for Employees, and replace the condition *E.hobby='Stamps'* by *E.eid=552*, we know that at most one Employees tuple will satisfy this selection condition. In this case, there is no advantage to making the index clustered.

Clustered indexes can be especially important while accessing the inner relation in an index nested loops join. To understand the relationship between clustered indexes and joins, let us revisit our first example.

> SELECT E.ename, D.mgr
> FROM   Employees E, Departments D
> WHERE   D.dname='Toy' AND E.dno=D.dno

We concluded that a good evaluation plan is to use an index on *dname* to retrieve Departments tuples satisfying the condition on *dname* and to find matching Employees tuples using an index on *dno*. Should these indexes be clustered? Given our assumption that the number of tuples satisfying *D.dname='Toy'* is likely to be small, we should build an unclustered index on *dname*. On the other hand, Employees is the inner relation in an index nested loops join, and *dno* is not a candidate key. This situation is a strong argument that the index on the *dno* field of Employees should be clustered. In fact, because the join consists of repeatedly posing equality selections on the *dno* field of the inner relation, this type of query is a stronger justification for making the index on *dno* be clustered than a simple selection query such as the previous selection on *hobby*. (Of course, factors such as selectivities and frequency of queries have to be taken into account as well.)

The following example, very similar to the previous one, illustrates how clustered indexes can be used for sort-merge joins.

> **SELECT** E.ename, D.mgr
> **FROM**   Employees E, Departments D
> **WHERE**   E.hobby='Stamps' **AND** E.dno=D.dno

This query differs from the previous query in that the condition *E.hobby='Stamps'* replaces *D.dname='Toy'*. Based on the assumption that there are few employees in the Toy department, we chose indexes that would facilitate an indexed nested loops join with Departments as the outer relation. Now let us suppose that many employees collect stamps. In this case, a block nested loops or sort-merge join might be more efficient. A sort-merge join can take advantage of a clustered B+ tree index on the *dno* attribute in Departments to retrieve tuples and thereby avoid sorting Departments. Note that an unclustered index is not useful—since all tuples are retrieved, performing one I/O per tuple is likely to be prohibitively expensive. If there is no index on the *dno* field of Employees, we could retrieve Employees tuples (possibly using an index on *hobby*, especially if the index is clustered), apply the selection *E.hobby='Stamps'* on-the-fly, and sort the qualifying tuples on *dno*.

As our discussion has indicated, when we retrieve tuples using an index, the impact of clustering depends on the number of retrieved tuples, that is, the number of tuples that satisfy the selection conditions that match the index. An unclustered index is just as good as a clustered index for a selection that retrieves a single tuple (e.g., an equality selection on a candidate key). As the number of retrieved tuples increases, the unclustered index quickly becomes more expensive than even a sequential scan of the entire relation. Although the sequential scan retrieves all tuples, it has the property that each page is retrieved exactly once, whereas a page may be retrieved as often as the number of tuples it contains if an unclustered index is used. If blocked I/O is performed (as is common), the relative advantage of sequential scan versus an unclustered index increases further. (Blocked I/O also speeds up access using a clustered index, of course.)

We illustrate the relationship between the number of retrieved tuples, viewed as a percentage of the total number of tuples in the relation, and the cost of various access methods in Figure 16.2. We assume that the query is a selection on a single relation, for simplicity. (Note that this figure reflects the cost of writing out the result; otherwise, the line for sequential scan would be flat.)

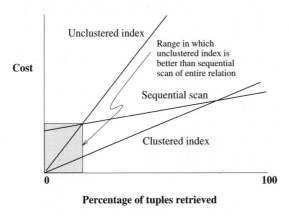

Figure 16.2   The Impact of Clustering

16.4.1   Co-clustering Two Relations

In our description of a typical database system architecture in Chapter 3, we explained how a relation is stored as a file of records. Although a file usually contains only the records of some one relation, some systems allow records from more than one relation to be stored in a single file. The database user can request that the records from two relations be interleaved physically in this manner. This data layout is sometimes referred to as **co-clustering** the two relations. We now discuss when co-clustering can be beneficial.

As an example, consider two relations with the following schemas:

> Parts(*pid:* `integer`, *pname:* `string`, *cost:* `integer`, *supplierid:* `integer`)
> Assembly(*partid:* `integer`, *componentid:* `integer`, *quantity:* `integer`)

In this schema the *componentid* field of Assembly is intended to be the *pid* of some part that is used as a component in assembling the part with *pid* equal to *partid*. Thus the Assembly table represents a 1:N relationship between parts and their subparts; a part can have many subparts, but each part is the subpart of at most one part. In the Parts table *pid* is the key. For composite parts (those assembled from other parts, as indicated by the contents of Assembly), the *cost* field is taken to be the cost of assembling the part from its subparts.

Suppose that a frequent query is to find the (immediate) subparts of all parts that are supplied by a given supplier:

        SELECT P.pid, A.componentid
        FROM   Parts P, Assembly A
        WHERE   P.pid = A.partid AND P.supplierid = 'Acme'

A good evaluation plan is to apply the selection condition on Parts and to then retrieve matching Assembly tuples through an index on the *partid* field. Ideally, the index on *partid* should be clustered. This plan is reasonably good. However, if such selections are common and we want to optimize them further, we can *co-cluster* the two tables. In this approach we store records of the two tables together, with each Parts record *P* followed by all the Assembly records *A* such that *P.pid = A.partid*. This approach improves on storing the two relations separately and having a clustered index on *partid* because it doesn't need an index lookup to find the Assembly records that match a given Parts record. Thus for each selection query, we save a few (typically two or three) index page I/Os.

If we are interested in finding the immediate subparts of *all* parts (i.e., the above query without the selection on *supplierid*), creating a clustered index on *partid* and doing an index nested loops join with Assembly as the inner relation offers good performance. An even better strategy is to create a clustered index on the *partid* field of Assembly and the *pid* field of Parts, and to then do a sort-merge join, using the indexes to retrieve tuples in sorted order. This strategy is comparable to doing the join using a co-clustered organization, which involves just one scan of the set of tuples (of Parts and Assembly, which are stored together in interleaved fashion).

The real benefit of co-clustering is illustrated by the following query:

        SELECT P.pid, A.componentid
        FROM   Parts P, Assembly A
        WHERE   P.pid = A.partid AND P.cost=10

Suppose that many parts have *cost* = 10. This query essentially amounts to a collection of queries in which we are given a Parts record and want to find matching Assembly records. If we have an index on the *cost* field of Parts, we can retrieve qualifying Parts tuples. For each such tuple we have to use the index on Assembly to locate records with the given *pid*. The index access for Assembly is avoided if we have a co-clustered organization. (Of course, we still require an index on the *cost* attribute of Parts tuples.)

Such an optimization is especially important if we want to traverse several levels of the part-subpart hierarchy. For example, a common query is to find the total cost of a part, which requires us to repeatedly carry out joins of Parts and Assembly. Incidentally, if we don't know the number of levels in the hierarchy in advance, the number of joins varies and the query cannot be expressed in SQL. The query can be answered by embedding an SQL statement for the join inside an iterative host language program. How to express the query is orthogonal to our main point here, which is that co-clustering is especially beneficial when the join in question is carried out very frequently (either because it arises repeatedly in an important query such as finding total cost, or because the join query is itself asked very frequently).

To summarize co-clustering:

- It can speed up joins, in particular key–foreign key joins corresponding to 1:N relationships.

- Sequential scans of one of the relations become slower. (In our example, since several Assembly tuples are stored in between consecutive Parts tuples, scans of Parts become slower.)

- Inserts, deletes and updates that alter record lengths all become slower, thanks to the overheads involved in maintaining the clustering. (We will not discuss the implementation issues involved in co-clustering.)

16.5   INDEXES ON MULTIPLE-ATTRIBUTE SEARCH KEYS *

It is sometimes best to build an index on a search key that contains more than one field. For example, if we want to retrieve Employees records with $age=30$ and $sal=4000$, an index with search key $\langle age, sal \rangle$ (or $\langle sal, age \rangle$) is superior to an index with search key age or an index with search key sal. (Of course, it does not make sense to build two indexes, one on age and one on sal, to answer this query!)

Issues such as whether to make the index clustered or unclustered, dense or sparse, and so on are orthogonal to the choice of the search key. We will call indexes on multiple-attribute search keys *composite indexes*. In addition to supporting equality queries on more than one attribute, composite indexes can be used to support multidimensional range queries.

Consider the following query, which returns all employees with $20 < age < 30$ and $3000 < sal < 5000$:

    SELECT E.eid

```
FROM    Employees E
WHERE   E.age BETWEEN 20 AND 30
        AND E.sal BETWEEN 3000 AND 5000
```

A composite index on $\langle age, sal \rangle$ could help if the conditions in the WHERE clause are fairly selective. Obviously, a hash index will not help; a B+ tree (or ISAM) index is required. It is also clear that a clustered index is likely to be superior to an unclustered index. For this query, in which the conditions on *age* and *sal* are equally selective, a composite, clustered B+ tree index on $\langle age, sal \rangle$ is as effective as a composite, clustered B+ tree index on $\langle sal, age \rangle$. However, the order of search key attributes can sometimes make a big difference, as the next query illustrates:

```
SELECT  E.eid
FROM    Employees E
WHERE   E.age = 25
        AND E.sal BETWEEN 3000 AND 5000
```

In this query a composite, clustered B+ tree index on $\langle age, sal \rangle$ will give good performance because records are sorted by *age* first and then (if two records have the same *age* value) by *sal*. Thus all records with $age = 25$ are clustered together. On the other hand, a composite, clustered B+ tree index on $\langle sal, age \rangle$ will not perform as well. In this case, records are sorted by *sal* first, and therefore two records with the same *age* value (in particular, with $age = 25$) may be quite far apart. In effect, this index allows us to use the range selection on *sal*, but not the equality selection on *age*, to retrieve tuples. (Good performance on both variants of the query can be achieved using a single *multidimensional* index; we discussed multidimensional indexes in Section 5.9. However, such index structures are not supported by most relational DBMSs.)

Some points about composite indexes are worth mentioning. Since data entries in the index contain more information about the data record (i.e., more fields than a single-attribute index), the opportunities for index-only evaluation strategies are increased (see Section 16.6). On the negative side, a composite index must be updated in response to any operation (insert, delete or update) that modifies *any* field in the search key. A composite index is likely to be larger than a single-attribute search key index because the size of entries is larger. For a composite B+ tree index, this also means a potential increase in the number of levels, although key compression can be used to alleviate this problem.

16.6   INDEXES THAT ENABLE INDEX-ONLY PLANS *

This section considers a number of queries for which we can find efficient plans that avoid retrieving tuples from one of the referenced relations; instead, these plans scan an associated index (which is likely to be much smaller). An index that is used (only) for index-only scans does *not* have to be clustered because tuples from the indexed relation are not retrieved! However, only dense indexes can be used for the index-only strategies discussed here.

This query retrieves the managers of departments with at least one employee:

```
SELECT  D.mgr
FROM    Departments D, Employees E
WHERE   D.dno=E.dno
```

Observe that no attributes of Employees are retained. If we have a dense index on the *dno* field of Employees, the optimization of doing an index nested loops join using an index-only scan for the inner relation is applicable; this optimization is discussed in Section 13.12. Note that it does not matter whether this index is clustered because we do not retrieve Employees tuples anyway. Given this variant of the query, the correct decision is to build an unclustered, dense index on the *dno* field of Employees, rather than a (dense or sparse) clustered index.

The next query takes this idea a step further:

```
SELECT  D.mgr, E.eid
FROM    Departments D, Employees E
WHERE   D.dno=E.dno
```

If we have an index on the *dno* field of Employees, we can use it to retrieve Employees tuples, but unless the index is clustered, this approach will not be efficient. On the other hand, suppose that we have a dense B+ tree index on $\langle dno, eid \rangle$. Now all the information we need about an Employees tuple is contained in the data entry for this tuple in the index. We can use the index to find the first data entry with a given *dno*; all data entries with the same *dno* are stored together in the index. (Note that a hash index on the composite key $\langle dno, eid \rangle$ cannot be used to locate an entry with just a given *dno*!) We can therefore evaluate this query using an index nested loops join with Departments as the outer relation and an index-only scan of the inner relation.

The next query shows how aggregate operations can influence the choice of indexes:

```
SELECT    E.dno, COUNT(*)
FROM      Employees E
GROUP BY  E.dno
```

A straightforward plan for this query is to sort Employees on *dno* in order to compute the count of employees for each *dno*. However, if an index—hash or B+

tree—is available, we can answer this query by scanning only the index. For each *dno* value, we simply count the number of data entries in the index with this value for the search key. Note that it does not matter whether the index is clustered because we never retrieve tuples of Employees.

Here is a variation of the previous example:

```
SELECT    E.dno, COUNT(*)
FROM      Employees E
WHERE     E.sal=10,000
GROUP BY  E.dno
```

An index on *dno* alone will not allow us to evaluate this query with an index-only scan, because we need to look at the *sal* field of each tuple to verify that $sal = 10,000$.

However, we can use an index-only plan if we have a composite B+ tree index on $\langle sal, dno \rangle$ or $\langle dno, sal \rangle$. In an index with key $\langle sal, dno \rangle$, all data entries with $sal = 10,000$ are arranged contiguously (whether or not the index is clustered). Further, these entries are sorted by *dno*, making it easy to obtain a count for each *dno* group. Note that we need to retrieve only data entries with $sal = 10,000$. It is worth observing that this strategy will not work if the WHERE clause is modified to use $sal > 10,000$. Although it suffices to retrieve only index data entries—that is, an index-only strategy still applies—these entries must now be sorted by *dno* to identify the groups (because, for example, two entries with the same *dno* but different *sal* values may not be contiguous).

In an index with key $\langle dno, sal \rangle$, data entries with a given *dno* value are stored together, and each such group of entries is itself sorted by *sal*. For each *dno* group, we can eliminate the entries with *sal* not equal to 10,000 and count the rest. This method is less efficient than an index-only scan with key $\langle sal, dno \rangle$ because we must read all data entries. We observe that this strategy works perfectly well even if the WHERE clause uses $sal > 10,000$.

As another example, suppose that we want to find the minimum *sal* for each *dno*:

```
SELECT    E.dno, MIN(E.sal)
FROM      Employees E
GROUP BY  E.dno
```

An index on *dno* alone will not allow us to evaluate this query with an index-only scan. However, we can use an index-only plan if we have a composite B+ tree index on $\langle dno, sal \rangle$. Notice that all data entries in the index with a given *dno* value are stored together (whether or not the index is clustered). Further, this group of entries is itself sorted by *sal*. An index on $\langle sal, dno \rangle$ would enable us to avoid retrieving data records, but the index data entries must be sorted on *dno*.

Finally consider the following query:

```
SELECT AVG (E.sal)
FROM   Employees E
WHERE  E.age = 25
       AND E.sal BETWEEN 3000 AND 5000
```

A dense, composite B+ tree index on $\langle age, sal \rangle$ allows us to answer the query with an index-only scan. A dense, composite B+ tree index on $\langle sal, age \rangle$ will also allow us to answer the query with an index-only scan, although more index entries are retrieved in this case than with an index on $\langle age, sal \rangle$.

16.7 OVERVIEW OF DATABASE TUNING

After the initial phase of database design, actual use of the database provides a valuable source of detailed information that can be used to refine the initial design. Many of the original assumptions about the expected workload can be replaced by observed usage patterns; in general, some of the initial workload specification will be validated, and some of it will turn out to be wrong. Initial guesses about the size of data can be replaced with actual statistics from the system catalogs (although, of course, this information will keep changing as the system evolves). Careful monitoring of queries can reveal unexpected problems; for example, the optimizer may not be using some indexes as intended to produce good plans.

Continued database tuning is therefore important to get the best possible performance. In this section, we introduce three kinds of tuning: *tuning indexes, tuning the conceptual schema,* and *tuning queries.* Our discussion of index selection also applies to index tuning decisions. Conceptual schema and query tuning are discussed further in Sections 16.8 and 16.9.

16.7.1 Tuning Indexes

The initial choice of indexes may be refined for one of several reasons. The simplest reason is that the observed workload reveals that some queries and updates considered important in the initial workload specification are not very frequent. The observed workload may also identify some new queries and updates that *are* important. The initial choice of indexes has to be reviewed in the light of this new information. Some of the original indexes may be dropped, and new ones added. The reasoning involved is similar to that used in the initial design.

It may also be discovered that the optimizer in a given system is not finding some of the plans that it was expected to. For example, consider the following query, which we discussed earlier:

```
SELECT  D.mgr
FROM    Employees E, Departments D
WHERE   D.dname='Toy' AND E.dno=D.dno
```

A good plan here would be to use an index on *dname* to retrieve Departments tuples with *dname='Toy'* and to use a dense index on the *dno* field of Employees as the inner relation, using an index-only scan. Anticipating that the optimizer would find such a plan, we might have created a dense, unclustered index on the *dno* field of Employees.

Now suppose that queries of this form take an unexpectedly long time to execute. We can ask to see the plan produced by the optimizer. (Most commercial systems provide a simple command to do this.) If the plan indicates that an index-only scan is not being used, but that Employees tuples are being retrieved, we have to rethink our initial choice of index, given this revelation about our system's (unfortunate) limitations. An alternative to consider here would be to drop the unclustered index on the *dno* field of Employees and to replace it with a clustered index.

Some other common limitations of optimizers are that they do not handle selections involving string expressions, arithmetic, or *null* values efficiently. We discuss these points further when we consider query tuning in Section 16.9.

In addition to re-examining our choice of indexes, it pays to periodically reorganize some indexes. For example, a static index such as an ISAM index may have developed long overflow chains. Dropping the index and rebuilding it—if feasible, given the interrupted access to the indexed relation—can substantially improve access times through this index. Even for a dynamic structure such as a B+ tree, if the implementation does not merge pages on deletes, space occupancy can decrease considerably in some situations. This in turn makes the size of the index (in pages) larger than necessary, and could increase the height and therefore the access time. Rebuilding the index should be considered. Extensive updates to a clustered index might also lead to overflow pages being allocated, thereby decreasing the degree of clustering. Again, rebuilding the index may be worthwhile.

Finally, note that the query optimizer relies on statistics maintained in the system catalogs. These statistics are updated only when a special utility program is run; be sure to run the utility frequently enough to keep the statistics reasonably current.

16.7.2   Tuning the Conceptual Schema

In the course of database design, we may realize that our current choice of relation schemas does not enable us meet our performance objectives for the given workload with any (feasible) set of physical design choices. If so, we may have to redesign our conceptual schema (and re-examine physical design decisions that are affected by the changes that we make).

We may realize that a redesign is necessary during the initial design process or later, after the system has been in use for a while. Once a database has been designed and populated with tuples, changing the conceptual schema requires a significant effort in terms of mapping the contents of relations that are affected. Nonetheless, it may sometimes be necessary to revise the conceptual schema in the light of experience with the system. (Such changes to the schema of an operational system are sometimes referred to as **schema evolution**.) We now consider the issues involved in conceptual schema (re)design from the point of view of performance.

The main point to understand is that *our choice of conceptual schema should be guided by a consideration of the queries and updates in our workload, in addition to the issues of redundancy that motivate normalization* (which we discussed in Chapter 15). Several options must be considered while tuning the conceptual schema:

- We may decide to settle for a 3NF design instead of a BCNF design.

- If there are two ways to decompose a given schema into 3NF or BCNF, our choice should be guided by the workload.

- Sometimes we might decide to further decompose a relation that is *already* in BCNF.

- In other situations we might *denormalize*. That is, we might choose to replace a collection of relations obtained by a decomposition from a larger relation with the original (larger) relation, even though it suffers from some redundancy problems. Alternatively, we might choose to add some fields to certain relations to speed up some important queries, even if this leads to a redundant storage of some information (and consequently, a schema that is in neither 3NF nor BCNF).

- This discussion of normalization has concentrated on the technique of *decomposition*, which amounts to vertical partitioning of a relation. Another technique to consider is *horizontal partitioning* of a relation, which would lead to our having two relations with identical schemas. Note that we are not talking about physically partitioning the tuples of a single relation; rather, we want to create two distinct relations (possibly with different constraints and indexes on each).

Incidentally, when we redesign the conceptual schema, especially if we are tuning an existing database schema, it is worth considering whether we should create views to mask these changes from users for whom the original schema is more natural. We will discuss the choices involved in tuning the conceptual schema in Section 16.8.

16.7.3   Tuning Queries and Views

If we notice that a query is running much slower than we expected, we have to examine the query carefully to find the problem. Some rewriting of the query, perhaps in conjunction with some index tuning, can often fix the problem. Similar tuning may be called for if queries on some view run slower than expected. We will not discuss view tuning separately; just think of queries on views as queries in their own right (after all, queries on views are indeed expanded to account for the view definition before being optimized) and consider how to tune them.

When tuning a query, the first thing to verify is that the system is indeed using the plan that you expect it to use. It may well be that the system is not finding the best plan for a variety of reasons. Some common situations that are not handled efficiently by many optimizers follow.

- A selection condition involving *null* values.

- Selection conditions involving arithmetic or string expressions or conditions using the **OR** connective. For example, if we have a condition $E.age = 2*D.age$ in the **WHERE** clause, the optimizer may correctly utilize an available index on $E.age$ but fail to utilize an available index on $D.age$. Replacing the condition by $E.age/2 = D.age$ would reverse the situation.

- Inability to recognize a sophisticated plan such as an index-only scan for an aggregation query involving a **GROUP BY** clause. Of course, virtually no optimizer will look for plans outside the plan space described in Chapters 12 and 13, such as non left-deep join trees. So a good understanding of what an optimizer typically does is important. In addition, the more aware you are of a given system's strengths and limitations, the better off you are.

If the optimizer is not smart enough to find the best plan (using access methods and evaluation strategies supported by the DBMS), some systems allow users to guide the choice of a plan by providing hints to the optimizer; for example, users might be able to force the use of a particular index or choose the join order and join method. A user who wishes to guide optimization in this manner should have a thorough understanding of both optimization and the capabilities of the given DBMS. We will discuss query tuning further in Section 16.9.

16.8   CHOICES IN TUNING THE CONCEPTUAL SCHEMA *

We now illustrate the choices involved in tuning the conceptual schema through several examples using the following schemas:

> Contracts(*cid:* `integer`, *supplierid:* `integer`, *projectid:* `integer`,
>   *deptid:* `integer`, *partid:* `integer`, *qty:* `integer`, *value:* `real`)
> Departments(*did:* `integer`, *budget:* `real`, *annualreport:* `varchar`)
> Parts(*pid:* `integer`, *cost:* `integer`)
> Projects(*jid:* `integer`, *mgr:* `char(20)`)
> Suppliers(*sid:* `integer`, *address:* `char(50)`)

For brevity, we will often use the common convention of denoting attributes by a single character and denoting relation schemas by a sequence of characters. Consider the schema for the relation Contracts, which we will denote as CSJDPQV, with each letter denoting an attribute. The meaning of a tuple in this relation is that the contract with *cid* C is an agreement that supplier S (with *sid* equal to *supplierid*) will supply Q items of part P (with *pid* equal to *partid*) to project J (with *jid* equal to *projectid*) associated with department D (with *deptid* equal to *did*), and that the value V of this contract is equal to *value*.[2]

There are two known integrity constraints with respect to Contracts. A project purchases a given part using a single contract; thus there will not be two distinct contracts in which the same project buys the same part. This constraint is represented using the FD $JP \rightarrow C$. Also, a department purchases at most one part from any given supplier. This constraint is represented using the FD $SD \rightarrow P$. In addition, of course, the contract id C is a key. The meaning of the other relations should be obvious, and we will not describe them further because our focus will be on the Contracts relation.

16.8.1   Settling for a Weaker Normal Form

Consider the Contracts relation. Should we decompose it into smaller relations? Let us see what normal form it is in. The candidate keys for this relation are C and JP. (C is given to be a key, and JP functionally determines C.) The only non key dependency is $SD \rightarrow P$, and P is a *prime* attribute because it is part of

---

[2] If this schema seems complicated, note that real-life situations often call for considerably more complex schemas!

candidate key JP. Thus the relation is not in BCNF—because there is a non key dependency—but it is in 3NF.

By using the dependency $SD \rightarrow P$ to guide the decomposition, we get the two schemas SDP and CSJDQV. This decomposition is lossless, but it is not dependency-preserving. However, by adding the relation scheme CJP, we obtain a lossless-join and dependency-preserving decomposition into BCNF. Using the guideline that a dependency-preserving, lossless-join decomposition into BCNF is good, we might decide to replace Contracts by three relations with schemas CJP, SDP and CSJDQV.

However, suppose that the following query is very frequently asked: Find the number of copies Q of part P ordered in contract C. This query requires a join of the decomposed relations CJP and CSJDQV (or of SDP and CSJDQV), whereas it can be answered directly using the relation Contracts. The added cost for this query could persuade us to settle for a 3NF design, and not decompose Contracts further.

16.8.2 Denormalization

The reasons motivating us to settle for a weaker normal form may in fact lead us to take an even more extreme step: deliberately introduce some redundancy. As an example, consider the Contracts relation, which is in 3NF. Now, suppose that a frequent query is to check that the value of a contract is less than the budget of the contracting department. We might decide to add a budget field B to Contracts. Since *did* is a key for Departments, we now have the dependency $D \rightarrow B$ in Contracts, which means Contracts is not in 3NF any more. Nonetheless, we might choose to stay with this design if the motivating query is sufficiently important. Such a decision is clearly subjective and comes at the cost of significant redundancy.

16.8.3 Choice of Decompositions

Consider the Contracts relation again. Several choices are possible for dealing with the redundancy in this relation:

- We can leave Contracts as it is and accept the redundancy associated with its being in 3NF rather than BCNF.

- We might decide that we want to avoid the anomalies resulting from this redundancy by decomposing Contracts into BCNF using one of the following methods:

- We have a lossless-join decomposition into PartInfo with attributes SDP and ContractInfo with attributes CSJDQV. As noted previously, this decomposition is not dependency-preserving, and to make it dependency-preserving would require us to add a third relation CJP, whose sole purpose is to allow us to check the dependency $JP \rightarrow C$.

- We could choose to replace Contracts by just PartInfo and ContractInfo even though this decomposition is not dependency-preserving.

Replacing Contracts by just PartInfo and ContractInfo does not prevent us from enforcing the constraint $JP \rightarrow C$; it only makes this more expensive. We could create an assertion in SQL-92 to check this constraint:

```
CREATE ASSERTION checkDep
CHECK      ( NOT EXISTS
           ( SELECT  *
           FROM      PartInfo PI, ContractInfo CI
           WHERE     PI.supplierid=CI.supplierid
                     AND PI.deptid=CI.deptid
           GROUP BY  CI.projectid, PI.partid
           HAVING    COUNT (cid) > 1 ) )
```

This assertion is expensive to evaluate because it involves a join followed by a sort (to do the grouping). In comparison, the system can check that JP is a primary key for table CJP by maintaining an index on JP. This difference in integrity-checking cost is the motivation for dependency-preservation. On the other hand, if updates are infrequent, this increased cost may be acceptable; therefore, we might choose not to maintain the table CJP (and quite likely, an index on it).

As another example illustrating decomposition choices, consider the Contracts relation again, and suppose that we also have the integrity constraint that a department uses a given supplier for at most one of its projects: $SPQ \rightarrow V$. Proceeding as before, we have a lossless-join decomposition of Contracts into SDP and CSJDQV. Alternatively, we could begin by using the dependency $SPQ \rightarrow V$ to guide our decomposition, and replace Contracts with SPQV and CSJDPQ. We can then decompose CSJDPQ, guided by $SD \rightarrow P$, to obtain SDP and CSJDQ.

Thus we now have two alternative lossless-join decompositions of Contracts into BCNF, neither of which is dependency-preserving. The first alternative is to replace Contracts with the relations SDP and CSJDQV. The second alternative is to replace it with SPQV, SDP and CSJDQ. The addition of CJP makes the second decomposition (but not the first!) dependency-preserving. Again, the cost of maintaining the three relations CJP, SPQV and CSJDQ (versus just CSJDQV) may lead us to choose the first alternative. In this case, enforcing the given FDs becomes more expensive. We might consider not enforcing them, but we then risk a violation of the integrity of our data.

16.8.4   Vertical Decomposition

Suppose that we have decided to decompose Contracts into SDP and CSJDQV. These schemas are in BCNF, and there is no reason to decompose them further from a normalization standpoint. However, suppose that the following queries are very frequent:

- Find the contracts held by supplier S.

- Find the contracts placed by department D.

These queries might lead us to decompose CSJDQV into CS, CD and CJQV. The decomposition is lossless, of course, and the two important queries can be answered by examining much smaller relations.

Whenever we decompose a relation, we have to consider which queries the decomposition might adversely affect, especially if the only motivation for the decomposition is improved performance. For example, if another important query is to find the total value of contracts held by a supplier, it would involve a join of the decomposed relations CS and CJQV. In this situation we might decide against the decomposition.

16.8.5   Horizontal Decomposition

Thus far, we have essentially considered how to replace a relation with a collection of vertical decompositions. Sometimes, it is worth considering whether to replace a relation with two relations that have the same attributes as the original relation, each containing a subset of the tuples in the original. Intuitively, this technique is useful when different subsets of tuples are queried in very distinct ways.

For example, different rules may govern large contracts, which are defined as contracts with values greater than 10,000. (Perhaps such contracts have to be awarded through a bidding process.) This constraint could lead to a number of queries in which Contracts tuples are selected using a condition of the form $value > 10,000$. One way to approach this situation is to build a clustered B+ tree index on the *value* field of Contracts. Alternatively, we could replace Contracts with two relations called LargeContracts and SmallContracts, with the obvious meaning. If this query is the only motivation for the index, horizontal decomposition offers all the benefits of the index without the overhead of index maintenance. This alternative is especially attractive if other important queries on Contracts also require clustered indexes (on fields other than *value*).

If we replace Contracts by two relations LargeContracts and SmallContracts, we could mask this change by defining a view called Contracts:

```
CREATE VIEW Contracts(cid, supplierid, projectid, deptid, partid, qty, value)
       AS ((SELECT *
            FROM    LargeContracts)
            UNION
            (SELECT  *
            FROM    SmallContracts))
```

However, any query that deals solely with LargeContracts should be expressed directly on LargeContracts, and not on the view. Expressing the query on the view Contracts with the selection condition *value* $> 10,000$ is equivalent to expressing the query on LargeContracts, but less efficient. This point is quite general: Although we can mask changes to the conceptual schema by adding view definitions, users concerned about performance have to be aware of the change.

As another example, if Contracts had an additional field *year* and queries typically dealt with the contracts in some one year, we might choose to partition Contracts by year. Of course, queries that involved contracts from more than one year might require us to pose queries against each of the decomposed relations.

16.9   CHOICES IN TUNING QUERIES AND VIEWS *

The first step in tuning a query is to understand the plan that is used by the DBMS to evaluate the query. Systems usually provide some facility for identifying the plan used to evaluate a query. Once we understand the plan selected by the system, we can consider how to improve performance. We can consider a different choice of indexes, or perhaps co-clustering two relations for join queries, guided by our understanding of the old plan and a better plan that we want the DBMS to use. The details are similar to the initial design process.

One point worth making is that before creating new indexes we should consider whether rewriting the query will achieve acceptable results with existing indexes. For example, consider the following query with an **OR** connective:

```
SELECT E.dno
FROM    Employees E
WHERE   E.hobby='Stamps' OR E.age=10
```

If we have indexes on both *hobby* and *age*, we can use these indexes to retrieve the necessary tuples, but an optimizer might fail to recognize this opportunity. The optimizer might view the conditions in the WHERE clause as a whole as not matching either index, do a sequential scan of Employees, and apply the selections on-the-fly. Suppose we rewrite the query as the union of two queries, one with the clause WHERE *E.hobby='Stamps'* and the other with the clause WHERE *E.age=10*. Now each of these queries will be answered efficiently with the aid of the indexes on *hobby* and *age*.

We should also consider rewriting the query to avoid some expensive operations. For example, including DISTINCT in the SELECT clause leads to duplicate elimination, which can be costly. Thus we should omit DISTINCT whenever possible. For example, for a query on a single relation, we can omit DISTINCT whenever either of the following conditions holds:

- We do not care about the presence of duplicates.

- The attributes mentioned in the SELECT clause include a candidate key for the relation.

Sometimes a query with GROUP BY and HAVING can be replaced by a query without these clauses, thereby eliminating a sort operation. For example, consider:

```
SELECT    MIN (E.age)
FROM      Employees E
GROUP BY  E.dno
HAVING    E.dno=102
```

This query is equivalent to

```
SELECT    MIN (E.age)
FROM      Employees E
WHERE     E.dno=102
```

Complex queries are often written in steps, using a temporary relation. We can usually rewrite such queries without the temporary relation to make them run faster. Consider the following query for computing the average salary of departments managed by Robinson:

```
SELECT    * INTO Temp
FROM      Employees E, Departments D
WHERE     E.dno=D.dno AND  D.mgrname='Robinson'
```

```
SELECT    T.dno, AVG (T.sal)
FROM      Temp T
GROUP BY  T.dno
```

This query can be rewritten as

```
SELECT    E.dno, AVG (E.sal)
FROM      Employees E, Departments D
WHERE     E.dno=D.dno AND D.mgrname='Robinson'
GROUP BY  E.dno
```

The rewritten query does not materialize the intermediate relation Temp and is therefore likely to be faster. In fact, the optimizer may even find a very efficient index-only plan that never retrieves Employees tuples if there is a dense, composite B+ tree index on $\langle dno, sal \rangle$. This example illustrates a general observation: By rewriting queries to avoid unnecessary temporaries, we not only avoid creating the temporary relations, we also open up more optimization possibilities for the optimizer to explore.

In some situations, however, if the optimizer is unable to find a good plan for a complex query (typically a nested query with correlation), it may be worthwhile to rewrite the query using temporary relations to guide the optimizer towards a good plan.

In fact, nested queries are a common source of inefficiency because many optimizers deal poorly with them, as discussed in Section 13.7. Whenever possible, it is better to rewrite a nested query without nesting and to rewrite a correlated query without correlation. As already noted, a good reformulation of the query may require us to introduce new, temporary relations, and techniques to do so systematically (ideally, to be done by the optimizer) have been widely studied. Often though, it is possible to rewrite nested queries without nesting or the use of temporary relations, as illustrated in Section 13.7.

16.10   IMPACT OF CONCURRENCY *

In a system with many concurrent users, several additional points must be considered. As we saw in Chapter 1, each user's program (*transaction*) obtains *locks* on the pages that it reads or writes. Other transactions cannot access locked pages until this transaction completes and releases the locks. This restriction can lead to *contention* for locks on heavily used pages.

■   The duration for which transactions hold locks can affect performance significantly. Tuning transactions by writing to local program variables and deferring changes to the database until close to the end of the transaction (and thereby delaying the acquisition of the corresponding locks) can greatly improve performance. On a related note, performance can be improved by replacing a transaction by several smaller transactions, each of which holds locks for a shorter time.

- At the physical level, a careful partitioning of the tuples in a relation and its associated indexes across a collection of disks can significantly improve concurrent access. For example, if we have the relation on one disk and an index on another, accesses to the index can proceed without interfering with accesses to the relation, at least at the level of disk reads.

- If a relation is updated frequently, B+ tree indexes in particular can become a concurrency control bottleneck because all accesses through the index must go through the root; thus the root and index pages just below it can become **hot-spots**, that is, pages for which there is heavy contention. If the DBMS uses specialized locking protocols for tree indexes, and in particular, sets fine-granularity locks, this problem is greatly alleviated. Many current systems use such techniques. Nonetheless, this consideration may lead us to choose an ISAM index in some situations. Because the index levels of an ISAM index are static, we do not need to obtain locks on these pages; only the leaf pages need to be locked. An ISAM index may be preferable to a B+ tree index, for example, if frequent updates occur but we expect the relative distribution of records and the number (and size) of records with a given range of search key values to stay approximately the same. In this case the ISAM index offers a lower locking overhead (and reduced contention for locks), and the distribution of records is such that few overflow pages will be created.

  Hashed indexes do not create such a concurrency bottleneck, unless the data distribution is very skewed and many data items are concentrated in a few buckets. In this case the directory entries for these buckets can become a hot-spot.

- The *pattern* of updates to a relation can also become significant. For example, if tuples are inserted into the Employees relation in *eid* order and we have a B+ tree index on *eid*, each insert will go to the last leaf page of the B+ tree. This leads to hot-spots along the path from the root to the right-most leaf page. Such considerations may lead us to choose a hash index over a B+ tree index, or to index on a different field. (Note that this pattern of access leads to poor performance for ISAM indexes as well, since the last leaf page becomes a hot spot.)

  Again, this is not a problem for hash indexes because the hashing process randomizes the bucket into which a record is inserted.

- SQL features for specifying transaction properties, which we discuss in Section 17.7, can be used for improving performance. If a transaction does not modify the database, we should specify that its *access mode* is **READ ONLY**. Sometimes it is acceptable for a transaction (e.g., one that computes statistical summaries) to see some anomalous data due to concurrent execution. For such transactions, more concurrency can be achieved by controlling a parameter called the *isolation level*.

16.11 DBMS BENCHMARKING *

Thus far, we have considered how to improve the design of a database to obtain better performance. As the database grows, however, the underlying DBMS may no longer be able to provide adequate performance even with the best possible design, and we have to consider upgrading our system, typically by buying faster hardware and additional memory. We may also consider migrating our database to a new DBMS.

When evaluating DBMS products, performance is an important consideration. A DBMS is a complex piece of software, and different vendors may target their systems towards different market segments by putting more effort into optimizing certain parts of the system, or by choosing different system designs. For example, some systems are designed to run complex queries efficiently, while others are designed to run many simple transactions per second. Within each category of systems, there are many competing products. In order to assist users in choosing a DBMS that is well suited to their needs, several **performance benchmarks** have been developed.

Benchmarks should be portable, easy to understand, and scale naturally to larger problem instances. They should measure *peak performance* (e.g., *transactions per second*, or *tps*) as well as *price/performance ratios* (e.g., $/tps) for typical workloads in a given application domain. The Transaction Processing Council (TPC) was created to define benchmarks for transaction processing and database systems. Other well-known benchmarks have been proposed by academic researchers and industry organizations. Benchmarks that are proprietary to a given vendor are not very useful for comparing different systems (although they may be useful in determining how well a given system would handle a particular workload).

16.11.1 Well-Known DBMS Benchmarks

On-line Transaction Processing Benchmarks: The TPC-A and TPC-B benchmarks constitute the standard definition of the *tps* and $/tps measures. TPC-A measures the performance and price of a computer network in addition to the DBMS, whereas the TPC-B benchmark considers the DBMS by itself. These benchmarks involve a simple transaction that updates three data records, from three different tables, and appends a record to fourth table. A number of details (e.g., transaction arrival distribution, interconnect method, system properties) are rigorously specified, ensuring that results for different systems can be meaningfully compared. The TPC-C benchmark is a more complex suite of transactional tasks than TPC-A and TPC-B. It models a warehouse that tracks items supplied to customers, and involves five types of transactions. Each TPC-C transaction is much more expensive than a TPC-A or TPC-B transaction, and TPC-C exercises a much wider range of system capabilities, such as use of secondary indexes and transaction aborts. It has more or less completely replaced TPC-A and TPC-B as the standard transaction processing benchmark.

Query Benchmarks: The Wisconsin benchmark is widely used for measuring the performance of simple relational queries. The Set Query benchmark measures the performance of a suite of more complex queries, and the AS^3AP benchmark measures the performance of a mixed workload of transactions, relational queries, and utility functions. The TPC-D benchmark is a suite of complex SQL queries, intended to be representative of the decision-support application domain. The OLAP Council has also developed a benchmark for complex decision-support queries, including some queries that cannot be expressed easily in SQL; this is intended to measure systems for *on-line analytic processing (OLAP)*, which we discuss in Chapter 22, rather than traditional SQL systems. The Sequoia 2000 benchmark is designed to compare DBMS support for geographic information systems.

Object-Database Benchmarks: The 001 and 007 benchmarks measure the performance of object-oriented database systems. The Bucky benchmark measures the performance of object-relational database systems. (We discuss object database systems in Chapter 21.)

16.11.2   Using a Benchmark

Benchmarks should be used with a good understanding of what they are designed to measure, and the application environment in which a DBMS is to be used. When you use benchmarks to guide your choice of a DBMS, keep the following guidelines in mind:

- **How meaningful is a given benchmark?** Benchmarks that try to distill performance into a single number can be overly simplistic. A DBMS is a complex piece of software used in a variety of applications. A good benchmark should have a suite of tasks that are carefully chosen to cover a particular application domain, and to test DBMS features that are important for that domain.

- **How well does a benchmark reflect your workload?** You should consider your expected workload and compare it with the benchmark. Give more weight to the performance of those benchmark tasks (i.e., queries and updates) that are similar to important tasks in your workload. Also consider how benchmark numbers are measured. For example, elapsed times for individual queries might be misleading if considered in a multiuser setting: a system may have higher elapsed times because of slower I/O, and on a multiuser workload, given sufficient disks for parallel I/O, might outperform a system with a lower elapsed time.

- **Create your own benchmark:** Vendors often tweak their systems in ad hoc ways to obtain good numbers on important benchmarks. To counter this, create your own benchmark by modifying standard benchmarks slightly or by replacing the tasks in a standard benchmark with similar tasks from your workload.

16.12 SUMMARY

To do a good job of physical database design, the designer must understand the following issues:

- The nature of the workload, including the relative frequency of various queries and updates and which operations are likely to execute concurrently.

- Properties of available index types and implementation techniques for various operations.

- The plans explored by the query optimizer for the given system.

After the initial design, the statistics must be updated regularly and the actual workload must be carefully monitored. Periodic reorganization of indexes and occasional tuning of the conceptual schema and query/view definitions play an important role in maintaining good performance.

Physical database design and tuning is an important task, and involves a good understanding of how a DBMS works. The alternative ways in which a query can be expressed, the alternatives for choosing indexes, the alternatives available in the DBMS for implementing various relational operations, how the query optimizer works, the implications of a particular logical design with respect to redundancy and with respect to the cost of important queries—each of these issues can significantly affect a database design, and the list goes on.

It is true that a relational DBMS allows casual users to pose queries and get answers without too much concern for efficiency issues. However, database designers, who develop queries and views used repeatedly by many users, and anyone who deals with very large datasets (and therefore expensive data manipulation operations!) must have a thorough understanding of all aspects of a DBMS.

Benchmarks are standardized suites of tasks that can be used to evaluate different DBMS products. They should be used with a good understanding of what they measure, and how closely they reflect a user's expected workload.

EXERCISES

Exercise 16.1 Consider the following relations:

> Emp(*eid:* integer, *ename:* varchar, *sal:* integer, *age:* integer, *did:* integer)
> Dept(*did:* integer, *budget:* integer, *floor:* integer, *mgr_eid:* integer)

Salaries range from $10,000 to $100,000, ages vary from 20 to 80, each department has about five employees on average, there are 10 floors, and budgets vary from $10,000 to $1,000,000. You can assume uniform distributions of values.

For each of the following queries, which of the listed index choices would you would choose in order to speed up the query? If your database system does not consider index-only plans (i.e., data records are always retrieved even if enough information is available in the index entry), how would your answer change? Explain briefly.

1. Query: *Print ename, age and sal for all employees.*

    (a) Clustered, dense hash index on ⟨*ename, age, sal*⟩ fields of Emp.

    (b) Unclustered hash index on ⟨*ename, age, sal*⟩ fields of Emp.

    (c) Clustered, sparse B+ tree index on ⟨*ename, age, sal*⟩ fields of Emp.

    (d) Unclustered hash index on ⟨*eid, did*⟩ fields of Emp.

    (e) No index.

2. Query: *Find the dids of departments that are on the 10th floor and that have a budget of less than $15,000.*

    (a) Clustered, dense hash index on the *floor* field of Dept.

    (b) Unclustered hash index on the *floor* field of Dept.

    (c) Clustered, dense B+ tree index on ⟨*floor, budget*⟩ fields of Dept.

    (d) Clustered, sparse B+ tree index on the *budget* field of Dept.

    (e) No index.

3. Query: *Find the names of employees who manage some department and have a salary greater than $12,000.*

    (a) Clustered, sparse B+ tree index on the *sal* field of Emp.

    (b) Clustered hash index on the *did* field of Dept.

    (c) Unclustered hash index on the *did* field of Dept.

    (d) Unclustered hash index on the *did* field of Emp.

    (e) Clustered B+ tree index on *sal* field of Emp and clustered hash index on the *did* field of Dept.

4. Query: *Print the average salary for each department.*

   (a) Clustered, sparse B+ tree index on the *did* field of Emp.

   (b) Clustered, dense B+ tree index on the *did* field of Emp.

   (c) Clustered, dense B+ tree index on ⟨*did, sal*⟩ fields of Emp.

   (d) Unclustered hash index on ⟨*did, sal*⟩ fields of Emp.

   (e) Clustered, dense B+ tree index on the *did* field of Dept.

Exercise 16.2 Consider the following relation:

Emp(*eid:* `integer`, *sal:* `integer`, *age:* `real`, *did:* `integer`)

There is a clustered index on *eid* and an unclustered index on *age*.

1. Which factors would you consider in deciding whether to make an index on a relation a clustered index? Would you always create at least one clustered index on every relation?

2. How would you use the indexes to enforce the constraint that *eid* is a key?

3. Give an example of an update that is *definitely speeded up* because of the available indexes. (English description is sufficient.)

4. Give an example of an update that is *definitely slowed down* because of the indexes. (English description is sufficient.)

5. Can you give an example of an update that is neither speeded up nor slowed down by the indexes?

Exercise 16.3 Consider the following BCNF schema for a portion of a simple corporate database (type information is not relevant to this question and is omitted):

Emp (*eid*, *ename*, *addr*, *sal*, *age*, *yrs*, *deptid*)
Dept (*did*, *dname*, *floor*, *budget*)

Suppose you know that the following queries are the six most common queries in the workload for this corporation and that all six are roughly equivalent in frequency and importance:

- List the id, name, and address of employees in a user-specified age range.

- List the id, name, and address of employees who work in the department with a user-specified department name.

- List the id and address of employees with a user-specified employee name.

- List the overall average salary for employees.

- List the average salary for employees of each age; that is, for each age in the database, list the age and the corresponding average salary.

- List all the department information, ordered by department floor numbers.

1. Given this information, and assuming that these queries are more important than any updates, design a physical schema for the corporate database that will give good performance for the expected workload. In particular, decide which attributes will be indexed and whether each index will be a clustered index or an unclustered index. Assume that B+ tree indexes are the only index type supported by the DBMS and that both single- and multiple-attribute keys are permitted. Specify your physical design by identifying the attributes that you recommend indexing on via clustered or unclustered B+ trees.

2. Redesign the physical schema assuming that the set of important queries is changed to be the following:

   - List the id and address of employees with a user-specified employee name.

   - List the overall maximum salary for employees.

   - List the average salary for employees by department; that is, for each *deptid* value, list the *deptid* value and the average salary of employees in that department.

   - List the sum of the budgets of all departments by floor; that is, for each floor, list the floor and the sum.

Exercise 16.4 Consider the following BCNF relational schema for a portion of a university database (type information is not relevant to this question and is omitted):

Prof(*ssno*, *pname*, *office*, *age*, *sex*, *specialty*, *dept_did*)
Dept(*did*, *dname*, *budget*, *num_majors*, *chair_ssno*)

Suppose you know that the following queries are the five most common queries in the workload for this university and that all five are roughly equivalent in frequency and importance:

- List the names, ages, and offices of professors of a user-specified sex (male or female) who have a user-specified research specialty (e.g., *recursive query processing*). Assume that the university has a diverse set of faculty members, making it very uncommon for more than a few professors to have the same research speciality.

- List all the department information for departments with professors in a user-specified age range.

- List the department id, department name, and chairperson name for departments with a user-specified number of majors.

- List the lowest budget for a department in the university.

- List all the information about professors who are department chairpersons.

These queries occur much more frequently than updates, so you should build whatever indexes you need to speed up these queries. However, you should not build any unnecessary indexes, as updates will indeed occur (and would of course be slowed down by unnecessary indexes). Given this information, design a physical schema for the university database that will give good performance for the expected workload. In particular, decide which attributes should be indexed and whether each index should be a clustered index or an unclustered index. Assume that both B+ trees and hashed indexes are supported by the DBMS and that both single- and multiple-attribute index search keys are permitted.

1. Specify your physical design by identifying the attributes that you recommend indexing on, indicating whether each index should be clustered or unclustered and whether it should be a B+ tree or a hashed index.

2. Redesign the physical schema assuming that the set of important queries is changed to be the following:

   ■ List the number of different specialties covered by professors in each department, by department.

   ■ Find the department with the fewest majors.

   ■ Find the youngest professor who is a department chairperson.

Exercise 16.5 Consider the following BCNF relational schema for a portion of a company database (type information is not relevant to this question and is omitted):

Project(*pno*, *proj_name*, *proj_base_dept*, *proj_mgr*, *topic*, *budget*)
Manager(*mid*, *mgr_name*, *mgr_dept*, *salary*, *age*, *sex*)

Note that each project is based in some department, each manager is employed in some department, and the manager of a project need not be employed in the same department (in which the project is based). Suppose you know that the following queries are the five most common queries in the workload for this university and that all five are roughly equivalent in frequency and importance:

■ List the names, ages, and salaries of managers of a user-specified sex (male or female) working in a given department. You can assume that while there are many departments, each department contains very few project managers.

■ List the names of all projects with managers whose ages are in a user-specified range (e.g., younger than 30).

■ List the names of all departments such that a manager in this department manages a project based in this department.

■ List the name of the project with the lowest budget.

■ List the names of all managers in the same department as a given project.

These queries occur much more frequently than updates, so you should build whatever indexes you need to speed up these queries. However, you should not build any unnecessary indexes, as updates will indeed occur (and would of course be slowed down by unnecessary indexes). Given this information, design a physical schema for the company database that will give good performance for the expected workload. In particular, decide which attributes should be indexed and whether each index should be a clustered index or an unclustered index. Assume that both B+ trees and hashed indexes are supported by the DBMS, and that both single- and multiple-attribute index keys are permitted.

1. Specify your physical design by identifying the attributes that you recommend indexing on, indicating whether each index should be clustered or unclustered and whether it should be a B+ tree or a hashed index.

2. Redesign the physical schema assuming that the set of important queries is changed to be the following:

   ■ Find the total of the budgets for projects managed by each manager; that is, list *proj_mgr* and the total of the budgets of projects managed by that manager, for all values of *proj_mgr*.

   ■ Find the total of the budgets for projects managed by each manager but only for managers who are in a user-specified age range.

   ■ Find the number of male managers.

   ■ Find the average age of managers.

Exercise 16.6 The Globetrotters Club is organized into chapters. The president of a chapter can never serve as the president of any other chapter, and each chapter gives its president some salary. Chapters keep moving to new locations, and a new president is elected when (and only when) a chapter moves. The above data is stored in a relation G(C,S,L,P), where the attributes are chapters (C), salaries (S), locations (L), and presidents (P). Queries of the following form are frequently asked, and you *must* be able to answer them without computing a join: "Who was the president of chapter X when it was in location Y?"

1. List the FDs that are given to hold over G.

2. What are the candidate keys for relation G?

3. What normal form is the schema G in?

4. Design a good database schema for the club. (Remember that your design *must* satisfy the query requirement stated above!)

5. What normal form is your good schema in? Give an example of a query that is likely to run slower on this schema than on the relation G.

6. Is there a lossless-join, dependency-preserving decomposition of G into BCNF?

7. Is there ever a good reason to accept something less than 3NF when designing a schema for a relational database? Use this example, if necessary adding further constraints, to illustrate your answer.

Exercise 16.7 Consider the following BCNF relation, which lists the ids, types (e.g., nuts or bolts), and costs of various parts, along with the number that are available or in stock:

Parts (*pid, pname, cost, num_avail*)

You are told that the following two queries are extremely important:

■ Find the total number available by part type, for all types. (That is, the sum of the *num_avail* value of all nuts, the sum of the *num_avail* value of all bolts, etc.)

■ List the *pid*s of parts with the highest cost.

1. Describe the physical design that you would choose for this relation. That is, what kind of a file structure would you choose for the set of Parts records, and what indexes would you create?

2. Suppose that your customers subsequently complain that performance is still not satisfactory (given the indexes and file organization that you chose for the Parts relation in response to the previous question). Since you cannot afford to buy new hardware or software, you have to consider a schema redesign. Explain how you would try to obtain better performance by describing the schema for the relation(s) that you would use and your choice of file organizations and indexes on these relations.

3. How would your answers to the above two questions change, if at all, if your system did not support indexes with multiple-attribute search keys?

Exercise 16.8 Consider the following BCNF relations, which describe employees and departments that they work in:

Emp (*eid, sal, did*)
Dept (*did, location, budget*)

You are told that the following queries are extremely important:

■ Find the location where a user-specified employee works.

■ Check whether the budget of a department is greater than the salary of each employee in that department.

1. Describe the physical design that you would choose for this relation. That is, what kind of a file structure would you choose for these relations, and what indexes would you create?

2. Suppose that your customers subsequently complain that performance is still not satisfactory (given the indexes and file organization that you chose for the relations in response to the previous question). Since you cannot afford to buy new hardware or software, you have to consider a schema redesign. Explain how you would try to obtain better performance by describing the schema for the relation(s) that you would use and your choice of file organizations and indexes on these relations.

3. Suppose that your database system has very inefficient implementations of index structures. What kind of a design would you try in this case?

Exercise 16.9 Consider the following BCNF relations, which describe departments in a company and employees:

Dept(*did, dname, location, managerid*)
Emp(*eid, sal*)

You are told that the following queries are extremely important:

■ List the names and ids of managers for each department in a user-specified location, in alphabetical order by department name.

■ Find the average salary of employees who manage departments in a user-specified location. You can assume that no one manages more than one department.

1. Describe the file structures and indexes that you would choose.

2. You subsequently realize that updates to these relations are frequent. Because indexes incur a high overhead, can you think of a way to improve performance on these queries without using indexes?

Exercise 16.10 For each of the following queries, identify one possible reason why an optimizer might not find a good plan. Rewrite the query so that a good plan is likely to be found. Any available indexes or known constraints are listed before each query; assume that the relation schemas are consistent with the attributes referred to in the query.

1. An index is available on the *age* attribute.

```
SELECT  E.dno
FROM    Employee E
WHERE   E.age=20 OR E.age=10
```

2. A B+ tree index is available on the *age* attribute.

```
SELECT  E.dno
FROM    Employee E
WHERE   E.age<20 AND E.age>10
```

3. An index is available on the *age* attribute.

```
SELECT  E.dno
FROM    Employee E
WHERE   2*E.age<20
```

4. No indexes are available.

```
SELECT DISTINCT *
FROM    Employee E
```

5. No indexes are available.

```
SELECT    AVG (E.sal)
FROM      Employee E
GROUP BY  E.dno
HAVING    E.dno=22
```

6. *sid* in Reserves is a foreign key that refers to Sailors.

```
SELECT  S.sid
FROM    Sailors S, Reserves R
WHERE   S.sid=R.sid
```

Exercise 16.11 Consider the following two ways of computing the names of employees who earn more than $100,000 and whose age is equal to their manager's age. First, a nested query:

```
SELECT  E1.ename
FROM    Emp E1
WHERE   E1.sal > 100 AND E1.age = ( SELECT  E2.age
                                    FROM    Emp E2, Dept D2
                                    WHERE   E1.dname = D2.dname
                                            AND D2.mgr = E2.ename )
```

Second, a query that uses a view definition:

```
SELECT    E1.ename
FROM      Emp E1, MgrAge A
WHERE     E1.dname = A.dname AND E1.sal > 100 AND E1.age = A.age

CREATE VIEW MgrAge (dname, age)
      AS SELECT D.dname, E.age
         FROM   Emp E, Dept D
         WHERE  D.mgr = E.ename
```

1. Describe a situation in which the first query is likely to outperform the second query.

2. Describe a situation in which the second query is likely to outperform the first query.

3. Can you construct an equivalent query that is likely to beat both these queries when every employee who earns more than $100,000 is either 35 or 40 years old? Explain briefly.

PROJECT-BASED EXERCISES

Exercise 16.12 Minibase's Designview tool does not provide any support for choosing indexes or, in general, physical database design. How do you see Designview being used, if at all, in the context of physical database design?

BIBLIOGRAPHIC NOTES

[473] is an early discussion of physical database design. [474] discusses the performance implications of normalization and observes that denormalization may improve performance for certain queries. The ideas underlying a physical design tool from IBM are described in [195]. A physical design tool from Microsoft is described in [119]. Other approaches to physical database design are described in [107, 461]. [493] considers *transaction tuning*, which we discussed only briefly. The issue is how an application should be structured into a collection of transactions to maximize performance.

The following books on database design cover physical design issues in detail; they are recommended for further reading. [197] is largely independent of specific products, although many examples are based on DB2 and Teradata systems. [573] deals primarily with DB2. [491] is a very readable treatment of performance tuning and is not specific to any one system.

[229] contains several papers on benchmarking database systems and has accompanying software. It includes articles on the AS^3AP, Set Query, TPC-A, TPC-B, Wisconsin, and 001 benchmarks written by the original developers. The Bucky benchmark is described in [96], the 007 benchmark is described in [95], and the TPC-D benchmark is described in [543]. The Sequoia 2000 benchmark is described in [528].

CONCURRENCY CONTROL

Pooh was sitting in his house one day, counting his pots of honey, when there came a knock on the door.

"Fourteen," said Pooh. "Come in. Fourteen. Or was it fifteen? Bother. That's muddled me."

"Hallo, Pooh," said Rabbit. "Hallo, Rabbit. Fourteen, wasn't it?"

"What was?" "My pots of honey what I was counting."

"Fourteen, that's right."

"Are you sure?"

"No," said Rabbit. "Does it matter?"

—A.A. Milne, *The House at Pooh Corner*

In this chapter we discuss just how a DBMS interleaves the actions of different user programs that are executed concurrently. A **transaction** is *any one execution* of a user program in a DBMS, and differs from an execution of a program outside the DBMS (e.g., a C program executing on Unix) in important ways. (Executing the same program several times will generate several transactions.) The transaction concept is central to the concurrency control and recovery facilities in a DBMS.

Section 17.1 reviews the transaction concept, which we discussed briefly in Chapter 1. Section 17.2 presents an abstract way of describing an interleaved execution of several transactions, called a *schedule*. Section 17.3 discusses various problems that can arise due to interleaved execution and identifies some desirable properties of schedules, in particular, serializability and recoverability.

Next, we take a more pragmatic turn and consider how a DBMS ensures that only schedules that do not suffer from these problems are permitted. The most widely used approach is based on *locking* objects to ensure mutual exclusion between transactions. Section 17.4 covers locking protocols that guarantee various notions of consistency, and Section 17.5 covers how locking protocols are implemented in a DBMS. Section 17.6 discusses three specialized locking protocols—for locking sets of objects identified by some predicate, for locking nodes in tree-structured indexes, and for locking collections of related objects. Section 17.7 presents the SQL-92 features related to transactions, and Section 17.8 examines some alternatives to the locking approach.

17.1   THE CONCEPT OF A TRANSACTION

A user writes data access/update programs in terms of the high-level query and update language supported by the DBMS. To understand how the DBMS handles such requests, with respect to concurrency control and recovery, it is convenient to regard an execution of a user program, or **transaction**, as a series of **reads** and **writes** of database objects:

- To read a database object, it is first brought into main memory (specifically, some frame in the buffer pool) from disk, and then its value is copied into a program variable.

- To write a database object, an in-memory copy of the object is first modified, and then written to disk.

Database 'objects' are the units in which programs read or write information. The units could be pages, records, and so on, but this is dependent on the DBMS and is not central to the principles underlying concurrency control or recovery.

There are three important properties of transactions that a DBMS must ensure to maintain data in the face of concurrent access and system failures:

1. Users should be able to understand a transaction without considering the effect of other concurrently executing transactions, even if the DBMS interleaves the actions of several transactions for performance reasons. This property is sometimes referred to as **isolation**: transactions are isolated, or protected, from the effects of concurrently scheduling other transactions.

2. Users should be able to regard the execution of each transaction as **atomic**: either all actions are carried out or none are. Users should not have to worry about the effect of incomplete transactions (say, when a system crash occurs).

3. Once the DBMS informs the user that a transaction has successfully completed, its effects should persist even if the system crashes before all its changes are reflected on disk. This property is called **durability**.

17.1.1   Concurrent Execution and Database Consistency

The first property of a transaction is ensured by guaranteeing that even though actions of several transactions might be interleaved, the net effect is identical to executing all transactions one after the other in some serial order. For example, if two transactions $T1$ and $T2$ are executed concurrently, the net effect is guaranteed to be equivalent to executing (all of) $T1$ followed by executing $T2$ or executing $T2$ followed by executing $T1$. (The DBMS provides no guarantees about which of these orders is effectively chosen.)

Users are responsible for ensuring that each transaction, when run to completion by itself against a 'consistent' database instance, leaves the database in a 'consistent' state. The notion of consistency referred to here is entirely user-dependent; the DBMS has no real understanding of the meaning of user actions. As we will see in later chapters, a DBMS provides mechanisms to enforce some **integrity constraints**; for example, all student *gpa* values must be less than 4. These mechanisms can be useful in avoiding inconsistent changes to the database, but users typically have consistency requirements that go beyond the integrity constraints enforced by the DBMS.

For example, the user may (naturally!) have the consistency criterion that fund transfers between bank accounts should not change the total amount of money in the accounts. To transfer money from one account to another, a transaction must debit one account, temporarily leaving the database inconsistent in a global sense, even though the new account balance may satisfy any integrity constraints with respect to the range of acceptable account balances. The user's notion of a consistent database is preserved when the second account is credited with the transferred amount. If a faulty transfer program always credits the second account with one dollar less than the amount debited from the first account, the DBMS cannot be expected to detect inconsistencies due to such errors in the user program's logic.

A DBMS interleaves the actions of different transactions conservatively, and ensures that the net effect on the database of the interleaved execution is equivalent to executing these transactions in some serial order. If each transaction maps a consistent database instance to another consistent database instance, executing several transactions one after the other (on a consistent initial database instance) will also result in a consistent final database instance. Database **consistency** is the property that every transaction sees a consistent database instance. Consistency follows from transaction atomicity, isolation, and the assumption that each completed transaction maps a consistent state of the database to another consistent state.[1]

17.1.2 Incomplete Transactions and Crash Recovery

Transactions can be incomplete for three kinds of reasons. First, a transaction can be **aborted**, or terminated unsuccessfully, by the DBMS because some anomaly arises during execution. If a transaction is aborted by the DBMS for some internal reason, it is automatically restarted and executed anew. Second, the system may crash (e.g., because the power supply is interrupted) while one or more

---

[1] The acronym ACID is sometimes used to refer to the four properties of transactions that we have presented here: Atomicity, Consistency, Isolation and Durability.

transactions are in progress. Third, a transaction may encounter an unexpected situation (for example, read an unexpected data value or be unable to access some disk) and decide to abort (i.e., terminate itself).

Of course, since users think of transactions as being atomic, a transaction that is interrupted in the middle may well leave the database in an inconsistent state. Thus a DBMS must find a way to remove the effects of partial transactions from the database, that is, it must ensure transaction atomicity: either all of a transaction's actions are carried out, or none are. A DBMS ensures transaction atomicity by *undoing* the actions of incomplete transactions. We discuss how incomplete transactions are undone in Chapter 18.

17.2 TRANSACTIONS AND SCHEDULES

In most of this chapter, we will consider a database to be a *fixed* collection of *independent* objects. When objects are added to or deleted from a database, or there are relationships between database objects that we want to exploit for performance, some additional issues arise; we discuss these issues in Section 17.6.

A transaction is seen by the DBMS as a series, or *list*, of **actions**. The actions that can be executed by a transaction include **reads** and **writes** of **database objects**. We note that a transaction can also be defined as a set of actions that are *partially* ordered. That is, the relative order of some of the actions may not be important. In order to concentrate on the main issues, we will treat transactions (and later, schedules) as a *list* of actions. Further, to keep our notation simple, we'll assume that an object O is always read into a program variable that is also named O. We can therefore denote the action of a transaction T reading an object O as $R_T(O)$; similarly, we can denote writing as $W_T(O)$. When the transaction T is clear from the context, we will omit the subscript.

In addition to reading and writing, each transaction *must* specify as its final action either **commit** (i.e., complete successfully) or **abort** (i.e., terminate and undo all the actions carried out thus far). $Abort_T$ denotes the action of T aborting, and $Commit_T$ denotes T committing.

A **schedule** is a list of actions (reading, writing, aborting or committing) from a set of transactions, and the order in which two actions of a transaction T appear in a schedule must be the same as the order in which they appear in T. Intuitively, a schedule represents an actual or potential execution sequence. For example, the schedule in Figure 17.1 shows an execution order for actions of two transactions $T1$ and $T2$. We move forward in time as we go down from one row to the next. We emphasize that a schedule describes the actions of transactions *as seen by the DBMS*. In addition to these actions, a transaction may carry out

$T1$	$T2$
$R(A)$	
$W(A)$	
	$R(B)$
	$W(B)$
$R(C)$	
$W(C)$	

Figure 17.1   A Schedule Involving Two Transactions

other actions, such as reading or writing from operating system files, evaluating arithmetic expressions, and so on. In particular, a transaction can modify the in-memory copy of a database object that it has read! The details of such a modification are encoded in the user's application code, which the DBMS has no way to understand.

Notice that the schedule in Figure 17.1 does not contain an abort or commit action for either transaction. A schedule that contains either an abort or a commit for each transaction whose actions are listed in it is called a **complete schedule**. A complete schedule must contain all the actions of every transaction that appears in it. If the actions of different transactions are not interleaved—that is, transactions are executed from start to finish, one by one—we call the schedule a **serial schedule**.

17.3   NOTIONS OF CONSISTENCY

Now that we've introduced the concept of a schedule, we have a convenient way to describe interleaved executions of transactions. The DBMS interleaves the actions of different transactions to improve performance, in terms of increased throughput or improved response times for short transactions, but not all interleavings should be allowed. In this section we consider what interleavings, or schedules, a DBMS should allow.

17.3.1   Serializability

To begin with, we assume that the database designer has defined some notion of a **consistent database state**. For example, we can define a consistency criterion for a university database to be that the sum of employee salaries in each department should be less than 80% of the budget for that department. We require that each transaction must **preserve** database consistency; it follows that any complete serial schedule will also preserve database consistency. That is, when a complete serial schedule is executed against a consistent database, the result is also a consistent database.

A **serializable schedule** over a set S of committed transactions is a schedule whose effect on any consistent database instance is guaranteed to be identical to that of some complete serial schedule over S. That is, the database instance that results from executing the given schedule is identical to the database instance that results from executing the transactions in *some* serial order. There are some important points to note in this definition:

- Executing the transactions serially in different orders may produce different results, but all are presumed to be acceptable; the DBMS makes no guarantees about which of them will be the outcome of an interleaved execution.

- The above definition of a serializable schedule does not cover the case of schedules containing aborted transactions. For simplicity, we begin by discussing interleaved execution of a set of complete, committed transactions, and consider the impact of aborted transactions in Section 17.3.3.

- If a transaction computes a value and prints it to the screen, this is an 'effect' that is not directly captured in the state of the database. We will assume that all such values are also written into the database, for simplicity.

17.3.2 Some Anomalies Associated with Interleaved Execution *

We now illustrate three main ways in which a schedule involving two consistency preserving, committed transactions could run against a consistent database and leave it in an inconsistent state. Two actions on the same data object **conflict** if at least one of them is a write. The three anomalous situations can be described in terms of when the actions of two transactions $T1$ and $T2$ conflict with each other: in a **Write-Read (WR) conflict** $T2$ reads a data object previously written by $T1$; we define **Read-Write (RW)** and **Write-Write (WW)** conflicts similarly.

Reading Uncommitted Data (WR Conflicts)

The first source of anomalies is that a transaction $T2$ could read a database object A that has been modified by another transaction $T1$, which has not yet committed. Such a read is called a **dirty read**. A simple example illustrates how such a schedule could lead to an inconsistent database state. Consider two transactions $T1$ and $T2$, each of which, run alone, preserves database consistency: $T1$ transfers $100 from A to B, and $T2$ increments both A and B by 6% (e.g., an annual interest is deposited into these two accounts). Suppose that their actions are interleaved so that (1) the account transfer program $T1$ deducts $100 from account A, then (2) the interest deposit program $T2$ reads the current values of accounts A and B and adds 6% interest to each, and then (3) the account transfer program credits \$100 to account B. The corresponding schedule, which is the view the DBMS has of this series of events, is illustrated in Figure 17.2. The result of

$T1$	$T2$
$R(A)$	
$W(A)$	
	$R(A)$
	$W(A)$
	$R(B)$
	$W(B)$
	Commit
$R(B)$	
$W(B)$	
Commit	

Figure 17.2   Reading Uncommitted Data

this schedule is different from any result that we would get by running one of the two transactions first and then the other. The problem can be traced to the fact that the value of A written by $T1$ is read by $T2$ before $T1$ has completed all its changes.

The general problem illustrated here is that $T1$ may write some value into A that makes the database inconsistent. As long as $T1$ overwrites this value with a 'correct' value of A before committing, no harm is done if $T1$ and $T2$ run in some serial order, because $T2$ would then not see the (temporary) inconsistency. On the other hand, interleaved execution can expose this inconsistency, and lead to an inconsistent final database state.

Note that although a transaction must leave a database in a consistent state *after* it completes, it is not required to keep the database consistent while it is still in progress. Indeed, such a requirement would be too restrictive: To transfer money from one account to another, a transaction *must* debit one account, temporarily leaving the database inconsistent, and then credit the second account, restoring consistency again.

Unrepeatable Reads (RW Conflicts)

The second way in which anomalous behavior could result is that a transaction $T2$ could change the value of an object A that has been read by a transaction $T1$, while $T1$ is still in progress. This situation causes two problems.

First, if $T1$ tries to read the value of A again, it will get a different result, even though it has not modified A in the meantime. This situation could not arise in a serial execution of two transactions; it is called an **unrepeatable read**.

Second, suppose that both $T1$ and $T2$ read the same value of A, say, 5, and then $T1$, which wants to increment A by 1, changes it to 6, and $T2$, which wants to decrement A by 1, decrements the value that it read (i.e., 5) and changes A to 4. Running these transactions in any serial order should leave A with a final value of 5; thus the interleaved execution leads to an inconsistent state. The underlying problem here is that although $T2$'s change is not directly read by $T1$, it invalidates $T1$'s assumption about the value of A, which is the basis for some of $T1$'s subsequent actions.

Overwriting Uncommitted Data (WW Conflicts)

The third source of anomalous behavior is that a transaction $T2$ could overwrite the value of an object A, which has already been modified by a transaction $T1$, while $T1$ is still in progress. Even if $T2$ does not read the value of A written by $T1$, a potential problem exists as the following example illustrates.

Suppose that Harry and Larry are two employees, and their salaries must be kept equal. Transaction $T1$ sets their salaries to $1,000 and transaction $T2$ sets their salaries to $2,000. If we execute these in the serial order $T1$ followed by $T2$, both receive the salary $2,000; the serial order $T2$ followed by $T1$ gives each the salary $1,000. Either of these is acceptable from a consistency standpoint (although Harry and Larry may prefer a higher salary!). Notice that neither transaction reads a salary value before writing it—such a write is called a **blind write**, for obvious reasons.

Now, consider the following interleaving of the actions of $T1$ and $T2$: $T1$ sets Harry's salary to $1,000, $T2$ sets Larry's salary to $2,000, $T1$ sets Larry's salary to $1,000, and finally $T2$ sets Harry's salary to $2,000. The result is not identical to the result of either of the two possible serial executions, and the interleaved schedule is therefore not serializable. Indeed, it violates the desired consistency criterion that the two salaries must be equal.

17.3.3 Schedules Involving Aborted Transactions

We now extend our definition of serializability to include aborted transactions.[2] Intuitively, all actions of aborted transactions are to be undone, and we can therefore imagine that they were never carried out to begin with. This observation leads to the following definition: A **serializable schedule** over a set S of transactions is a schedule whose effect on any consistent database instance is guaranteed to be identical to that of some complete serial schedule over the set of *committed* transactions in S.

This definition of serializability relies on the actions of aborted transactions being undone completely, which may be impossible in some situations. For example, suppose that (1) an account transfer program $T1$ deducts \$100 from account A, then (2) an interest deposit program $T2$ reads the current values of accounts A and B and adds 6% interest to each, then commits, and then (3) $T1$ is aborted. The corresponding schedule is shown in Figure 17.3. Now, $T2$ has read a value for

$T1$	$T2$
$R(A)$	
$W(A)$	
	$R(A)$
	$W(A)$
	$R(B)$
	$W(B)$
	Commit
Abort	

Figure 17.3   An Unrecoverable Schedule

A that should never have been there! (Recall that aborted transactions' effects are not supposed to be visible to other transactions.) If $T2$ had not yet committed, we could deal with the situation by *cascading* the abort of $T1$ and also aborting $T2$; this process would recursively abort any transaction that read data written by $T2$, and so on. But $T2$ has already committed, and so we cannot undo its actions! We say that such a schedule is *unrecoverable*. A **recoverable** schedule is one in which transactions commit only after (and if!) all transactions whose changes they read commit. If transactions read only the changes of committed transactions, not only is the schedule recoverable, aborting a transaction can be

---

[2]We must also consider incomplete transactions for a rigorous discussion of system failures, because transactions that are active when the system fails are neither aborted nor committed. However, system recovery usually begins by aborting all active transactions, and for our informal discussion, considering schedules involving committed and aborted transactions is sufficient.

accomplished without cascading the abort to other transactions. Such a schedule is said to **avoid cascading aborts**.

There is another potential problem in undoing the actions of a transaction. Suppose that a transaction $T2$ overwrites the value of an object A that has been modified by a transaction $T1$, while $T1$ is still in progress, and $T1$ subsequently aborts. All of $T1$'s changes to database objects are undone by restoring the value of any object that it modified to the value of the object before $T1$'s changes. (We will look at the details of how a transaction abort is handled in Chapter 18.) When $T1$ is aborted, and its changes are undone in this manner, $T2$'s changes are lost as well, even if $T2$ decides to commit. So, for example, if A originally had the value 5, then was changed by $T1$ to 6, and by $T2$ to 7, if $T1$ now aborts, the value of A becomes 5 again. Even if $T2$ commits, its change to A is inadvertently lost. A concurrency control technique called Strict 2PL can prevent this problem (Section 17.4.2).

17.4 LOCK-BASED CONCURRENCY CONTROL

A DBMS must be able to ensure that only serializable, recoverable schedules are allowed, and that no actions of committed transactions are 'lost' in the course of undoing aborted transactions. A DBMS typically uses a **locking protocol** to achieve this.

17.4.1 Strict Two-Phase Locking (Strict 2PL)

The most widely used locking protocol, called *Strict Two-Phase Locking*, or *Strict 2PL*, has two rules. The first rule is

(1) If a transaction T wants to *read* (respectively, *modify*) an object, it first requests a *shared* (respectively *exclusive*) lock on the object.

Of course, a transaction that has an exclusive lock can also read the object; an additional shared lock is not required. A transaction that requests a lock is suspended until the DBMS is able to grant it the requested lock. The DBMS keeps track of the locks it has granted, and ensures that if a transaction holds an exclusive lock on an object, no other transaction holds a shared or exclusive lock on the same object. The second rule in Strict 2PL is:

(2) All locks held by a transaction are released when the transaction is completed.

Requests to acquire and release locks can be automatically inserted into transactions by the DBMS; users need not worry about these details.

In effect the locking protocol allows only 'safe' interleavings of transactions. If two transactions access completely independent parts of the database, they will be able to concurrently obtain the locks that they need and proceed merrily on their ways. On the other hand, if two transactions access the same object, and one of them wants to modify it, their actions are effectively ordered serially—all actions of one of these transactions (the one that gets the lock on the common object first) are completed before (this lock is released and) the other transaction can proceed.

We denote the action of a transaction T requesting a shared (respectively, exclusive) lock on object O as $S_T(O)$ (respectively, $X_T(O)$), and omit the subscript denoting the transaction when it is clear from the context. As an example, consider the schedule shown in Figure 17.2. This interleaving could result in a state that cannot result from any serial execution of the three transactions. For instance, $T1$ could change A from 10 to 20, then $T2$ (which reads the value 20 for A) could change B from 100 to 200, and then $T1$ would read the value 200 for B. If run serially, either $T1$ or $T2$ would execute first, and read the values 10 for A and 100 for B: clearly, the interleaved execution is not equivalent to either serial execution.

If the Strict 2PL protocol is used, the above interleaving is disallowed. Let us see why. Assuming that the transactions proceed at the same relative speed as before, $T1$ would obtain an exclusive lock on A first, and then read and write A (Figure 17.4). Then, $T2$ would request a lock on A. However, this request cannot

$T1$	$T2$
$X(A)$	
$R(A)$	
$W(A)$	

Figure 17.4   Schedule Illustrating Strict 2PL

be granted until $T1$ releases its exclusive lock on A, and the DBMS therefore suspends $T2$. $T1$ now proceeds to obtain an exclusive lock on B, reads and writes B, then finally commits, at which time its locks are released. $T2$'s lock request is now granted, and it proceeds. In this example the locking protocol results in a serial execution of the two transactions, shown in Figure 17.5. In general, however, the actions of different transactions could be interleaved. As an example, consider the interleaving of $T1$ and $T2$ shown in Figure 17.6, which is permitted by the Strict 2PL protocol.

T1	T2
X(A)	
R(A)	
W(A)	
X(B)	
R(B)	
W(B)	
Commit	
	X(A)
	R(A)
	W(A)
	X(B)
	R(B)
	W(B)
	Commit

Figure 17.5   Schedule Illustrating Strict 2PL with Serial Execution

T1	T2
X(A)	
R(A)	
W(A)	
	X(B)
	R(B)
	W(B)
	Commit
X(C)	
R(C)	
W(C)	
Commit	

Figure 17.6   Schedule Following Strict 2PL with Interleaved Actions

17.4.2 2PL, Serializability, and Recoverability

Two schedules are said to be **conflict equivalent** if they involve the (same set of) actions of the same transactions, and they order every pair of conflicting actions of two committed transactions in the same way.

As we saw in Section 17.3.2, two actions conflict if they operate on the same data object and at least one of them is a write. The outcome of a schedule depends only on the order of conflicting operations; we can interchange any pair of non-conflicting operations without altering the effect of the schedule on the database. If two schedules are conflict equivalent, it is easy to see that they have the same effect on a database. Indeed, because they order all pairs of conflicting operations in the same way, we can obtain one of them from the other by repeatedly swapping pairs of nonconflicting actions, that is, by swapping pairs of actions whose relative order does not alter the outcome.

A schedule is **conflict serializable** if it is conflict equivalent to some serial schedule. Every conflict serializable schedule is serializable, if we assume that the set of items in the database does not grow or shrink; that is, values can be modified but items are not added or deleted. We will make this assumption for now, and consider its consequences in Section 17.6.1. However, some serializable schedules are not conflict serializable, as illustrated in Figure 17.7. This schedule is equiv-

$T1$	$T2$	$T3$
$R(A)$		
	$W(A)$	
	Commit	
$W(A)$		
Commit		
		$W(A)$
		Commit

Figure 17.7   Serializable Schedule That Is Not Conflict Serializable

alent to executing the transactions serially in the order $T1$, $T2$, $T3$, but it is not conflict equivalent to this serial schedule because the writes of $T1$ and $T2$ are ordered differently.

It is useful to capture all potential conflicts between the transactions in a schedule in a **precedence graph**, also called a **serializability graph**. The precedence graph for a schedule S contains:

■   A node for each committed transaction in S.

- An arc from Ti to Tj if an action of Ti precedes and conflicts with one of Tj's actions.

The precedence graphs for the schedules shown in Figures 17.5, 17.6 and 17.7 are shown in Figure 17.8 (parts (a), (b) and (c), respectively).

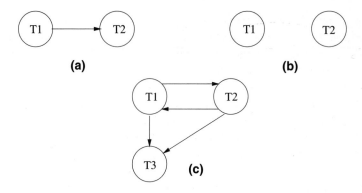

Figure 17.8   Examples of Precedence Graphs

The Strict 2PL protocol allows only serializable schedules, as is seen from the following two results:

1. A schedule S is conflict serializable if and only if its precedence graph is acyclic. (An equivalent serial schedule in this case is given by any topological sort over the precedence graph.)

2. Strict 2PL ensures that the precedence graph for any schedule that it allows is acyclic.

A widely studied variant of Strict 2PL, called **Two-Phase Locking (2PL)**, relaxes the second rule of Strict 2PL to allow transactions to release locks before the end, that is, before the commit or abort action. For 2PL, the second rule is replaced by the following rule:

   (2PL) (2) A transaction cannot request additional locks once it releases *any* lock.

Thus every transaction has a 'growing' phase in which it acquires locks, followed by a 'shrinking' phase in which it releases locks.

It can be shown that even (non strict) 2PL ensures acyclicity of the precedence graph, and therefore allows only serializable schedules. Intuitively, an equivalent serial order of transactions is given by the order in which transactions enter their shrinking phase: If $T2$ reads or writes an object written by $T1$, $T1$ must have released its lock on the object before $T2$ requested a lock on this object. Thus $T1$ will precede $T2$. (A similar argument shows that $T1$ precedes $T2$ if $T2$ writes an object previously read by $T1$. A formal proof of the claim would have to show that there is no cycle of transactions that 'precede' each other by this argument.)

A schedule is said to be **strict** if a value written by a transaction T is not read or overwritten by other transactions until T either aborts or commits. Strict schedules are recoverable, do not require cascading aborts, and actions of aborted transactions can be undone by restoring the original values of modified objects. (See the last example in Section 17.3.3.) Strict 2PL improves upon 2PL by guaranteeing that every allowed schedule is strict, in addition to being conflict serializable. The reason is that when a transaction T writes an object under Strict 2PL, it holds the (exclusive) lock until it commits or aborts. Thus no other transaction can see or modify this object until T is complete.

The reader is invited to revisit the examples in Section 17.3.2 to see how the corresponding schedules are disallowed by Strict 2PL and 2PL. Similarly, it would be instructive to work out how the schedules for the examples in Section 17.3.3 are disallowed by Strict 2PL but not by 2PL.

17.4.3   View Serializability *

Conflict serializability is sufficient but not necessary for serializability. A more general sufficient condition is view serializability. Two schedules $S1$ and $S2$ over the same set of transactions—any transaction that appears in either $S1$ or $S2$ must also appear in the other—are **view equivalent** under these conditions:

1. If Ti reads the initial value of object A in $S1$, it must also read the initial value of A in $S2$.

2. If Ti reads a value of A written by Tj in $S1$, it must also read the value of A written by Tj in $S2$.

3. For each data object A, the transaction (if any) that performs the final write on A in $S1$ must also perform the final write on A in $S2$.

A schedule is **view serializable** if it is view equivalent to some serial schedule. Every conflict serializable schedule is view serializable, although the converse is not true. For example, the schedule shown in Figure 17.7 is view serializable, although it is not conflict serializable. Incidentally, note that this example contains blind writes. This is not a coincidence; it can be shown that any view serializable schedule that is not conflict serializable contains a blind write.

As we saw in Section 17.4.2, efficient locking protocols allow us to ensure that only conflict serializable schedules are allowed. Enforcing or testing view serializability turns out to be much more expensive, and the concept therefore has little practical use, although it increases our understanding of serializability.

17.5 LOCK MANAGEMENT *

The part of the DBMS that keeps track of the locks issued to transactions is called the **lock manager**. The lock manager maintains a **lock table**, which is a hash table with the data object identifier as the key. The DBMS also maintains a descriptive entry for each transaction in a **transaction table**, and among other things, the entry contains a pointer to a list of locks held by the transaction.

A **lock table entry** for an object—which can be a page, a record, and so on, depending on the DBMS—contains the following information: the number of transactions currently holding a lock on the object (this can be more than one if the object is locked in shared mode), the nature of the lock (shared or exclusive), and a pointer to a queue of lock requests.

17.5.1 Implementing Lock and Unlock Requests

According to the Strict 2PL protocol, before a transaction T reads or writes a database object O, it must obtain a shared or exclusive lock on O, and must hold on to the lock until it commits or aborts. When a transaction needs a lock on an object, it issues a lock request to the lock manager:

1. If a shared lock is requested, the queue of requests is empty, and the object is not currently locked in exclusive mode, the lock manager grants the lock and updates the lock table entry for the object (indicating that the object is locked in shared mode, and incrementing the number of transactions holding a lock by one).

2. If an exclusive lock is requested, and no transaction currently holds a lock on the object (which also implies the queue of requests is empty), the lock manager grants the lock and updates the lock table entry.

3. Otherwise, the requested lock cannot be immediately granted, and the lock request is added to the queue of lock requests for this object. The transaction requesting the lock is suspended.

When a transaction aborts or commits, it releases all its locks. When a lock on an object is released, the lock manager updates the lock table entry for the object and examines the lock request at the head of the queue for this object. If this request can now be granted, the transaction that made the request is woken up and given the lock. Indeed, if there are several requests for a shared lock on the object at the front of the queue, all of these requests can now be granted together.

Note that if $T1$ has a shared lock on O, and $T2$ requests an exclusive lock, $T2$'s request is queued. Now, if $T3$ requests a shared lock, its request enters the queue behind that of $T2$, even though the requested lock is compatible with the lock held by $T1$. This rule ensures that $T2$ does not *starve*, that is, wait indefinitely while a stream of other transactions acquire shared locks and thereby prevent $T2$ from getting the exclusive lock that it is waiting for.

Atomicity of Locking and Unlocking

The implementation of *lock* and *unlock* commands must ensure that these are atomic operations. To ensure atomicity of these operations when several instances of the lock manager code can execute concurrently, access to the lock table has to be guarded by an operating system synchronization mechanism such as a semaphore.

To understand why, suppose that a transaction requests an exclusive lock. The lock manager checks and finds that no other transaction holds a lock on the object, and therefore decides to grant the request. But in the meantime, another transaction might have requested and *received* a conflicting lock! To prevent this, the entire sequence of actions in a lock request call (checking to see if the request can be granted, updating the lock table, etc.) must be implemented as an atomic operation.

Additional Issues: Lock Upgrades, Convoys, Latches

The DBMS maintains a transaction table, which contains (among other things) a list of the locks currently held by a transaction. This list can be checked before requesting a lock, to ensure that the same transaction does not request the same lock twice. However, a transaction may need to acquire an exclusive lock on an object for which it already holds a shared lock. Such a **lock upgrade** request is handled specially by granting the write lock immediately if no other transaction holds a shared lock on the object, and inserting the request at the front of the queue otherwise. The rationale for favoring the transaction thus is that it already holds a shared lock on the object, and queuing it behind another transaction that wants an exclusive lock on the same object causes both transactions to wait for each other and therefore be blocked forever; we discuss such situations in Section 17.5.2.

We have concentrated thus far on how the DBMS schedules transactions, based on their requests for locks. This interleaving interacts with the operating system's scheduling of processes' access to the CPU, and can lead to a situation called a **convoy**, where most of the CPU cycles are spent on process switching. The problem is that a transaction T holding a heavily used lock may be suspended by the operating system. Until T is resumed, every other transaction that needs this lock is queued. Such queues, called convoys, can quickly become very long; a convoy, once formed, tends to be stable. Convoys are one of the drawbacks of building a DBMS on top of a general-purpose operating system with preemptive scheduling.

In addition to locks, which are held over a long duration, a DBMS also supports short-duration **latches**. Setting a latch before reading or writing a page ensures that the physical read or write operation is atomic; otherwise, two read/write operations might conflict if the objects being locked do not correspond to disk pages (the units of I/O). Latches are unset immediately after the physical read or write operation is completed.

17.5.2 Deadlocks

Consider the following example: transaction $T1$ gets an exclusive lock on object A, $T2$ gets an exclusive lock on B, $T1$ requests an exclusive lock on B and is queued, and $T2$ requests an exclusive lock on A and is queued. Now, $T1$ is waiting for $T2$ to release its lock and $T2$ is waiting for $T1$ to release its lock! Such a cycle of transactions waiting for locks to be released is called a **deadlock**. Clearly, these two transactions will make no further progress. Worse, they hold locks that may be required by other transactions. The DBMS must either prevent or detect (and resolve) such deadlock situations.

Deadlock Prevention

We can prevent deadlocks by giving each transaction a priority and ensuring that lower priority transactions are not allowed to wait for higher priority transactions (or vice-versa). One way to assign priorities is to give each transaction a **timestamp** when it starts up. The lower the timestamp, the higher the transaction's priority, that is, the oldest transaction has the highest priority.

If a transaction Ti requests a lock and transaction Tj holds a conflicting lock, the lock manager can use one of the following two policies:

- **Wait-Die:** If Ti has higher priority, it is allowed to wait; else, it is aborted.

- **Wound-Wait:** If Ti has higher priority, abort Tj; else Ti waits.

In the Wait-Die scheme, lower priority transactions can never wait for higher priority transactions. In the Wound-Wait scheme, higher priority transactions never wait for lower priority transactions. In either case no deadlock cycle can develop.

A subtle point is that we must also ensure that no transaction is perennially aborted because it never has a sufficiently high priority. (Note that in both schemes, the higher priority transaction is never aborted.) When a transaction is aborted and restarted, it should be given the same timestamp that it had originally. Reissuing timestamps in this way ensures that each transaction will eventually become the oldest transaction, and thus the one with the highest priority, and will get all the locks that it requires.

The Wait-Die scheme is nonpreemptive; only a transaction requesting a lock can be aborted. As a transaction grows older (and its priority increases), it tends to wait for more and more younger transactions. A younger transaction that conflicts with an older transaction may be repeatedly aborted (a disadvantage with respect to Wound-Wait), but on the other hand, a transaction that has all the locks it needs will never be aborted for deadlock reasons (an advantage with respect to Wound-Wait, which is preemptive).

Deadlock Detection

Deadlocks tend to be rare and typically involve very few transactions. This observation suggests that rather than taking measures to prevent deadlocks, it may be better to detect and resolve deadlocks as they arise. In the detection approach, the DBMS must periodically check for deadlocks.

When a transaction Ti is suspended because a lock that it requests cannot be granted, it must wait until all transactions Tj that currently hold conflicting locks release them. The lock manager maintains a structure called a **waits-for graph** to detect deadlock cycles. The nodes correspond to active transactions, and there is an arc from Ti to Tj if (and only if) Ti is waiting for Tj to release a lock. The lock manager adds edges to this graph when it queues lock requests, and removes edges when it grants lock requests.

Consider the schedule shown in Figure 17.9. The last step, shown below the line, creates a cycle in the waits-for graph. Figure 17.10 shows the waits-for graph before and after this step.

Observe that the waits-for graph describes all active transactions, some of which will eventually abort. If there is an edge from Ti to Tj in the waits-for graph, and both Ti and Tj eventually commit, there will be an edge in the opposite

T1	T2	T3	T4
$S(A)$			
$R(A)$			
	$X(B)$		
	$W(B)$		
$S(B)$			
		$S(C)$	
		$R(C)$	
	$X(C)$		
			$X(B)$
		$X(A)$	

Figure 17.9 Schedule Illustrating Deadlock

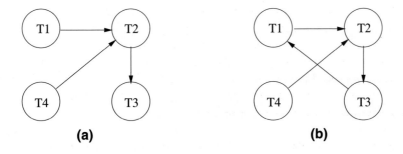

(a)   **(b)**

Figure 17.10 Waits-for Graph before and after Deadlock

direction (from Tj to Ti) in the precedence graph (which involves only committed transactions).

The waits-for graph is periodically checked for cycles, which indicate deadlock. A deadlock is resolved by aborting a transaction that is on a cycle and releasing its locks; this action allows some of the waiting transactions to proceed.

As an alternative to maintaining a waits-for graph, a simplistic way to identify deadlocks is to use a timeout mechanism: if a transaction has been waiting too long for a lock, we can assume (pessimistically) that it is in a deadlock cycle and abort it.

17.5.3   Performance of Lock-Based Concurrency Control

Designing a good lock-based concurrency control mechanism in a DBMS involves making a number of choices:

- Should we use deadlock-prevention or deadlock-detection?

- If we use deadlock-detection, how frequently should we check for deadlocks?

- If we use deadlock-detection and identify a deadlock, which transaction (on some cycle in the waits-for graph, of course) should we abort?

Lock-based schemes are designed to resolve conflicts between transactions, and use one of two mechanisms: *blocking* and *aborting* transactions. Both mechanisms involve a performance penalty; blocked transactions may hold locks that force other transactions to wait, and aborting and restarting a transaction obviously wastes the work done thus far by that transaction. A deadlock represents an extreme instance of blocking in which a set of transactions is forever blocked unless one of the deadlocked transactions is aborted by the DBMS.

Detection versus Prevention

In prevention-based schemes, the abort mechanism is used preemptively in order to avoid deadlocks. On the other hand, in detection-based schemes, the transactions in a deadlock cycle hold locks that prevent other transactions from making progress. System throughput is reduced because many transactions may be blocked, waiting to obtain locks currently held by deadlocked transactions.

This is the fundamental trade-off between these prevention and detection approaches to deadlocks: loss of work due to preemptive aborts versus loss of work due to blocked transactions in a deadlock cycle. We can increase the frequency with which we check for deadlock cycles, and thereby reduce the amount of work lost due to blocked transactions, but this entails a corresponding increase in the cost of the deadlock detection mechanism.

A variant of 2PL called **Conservative 2PL** can also prevent deadlocks. Under Conservative 2PL, a transaction obtains all the locks that it will ever need when it begins, or blocks waiting for these locks to become available. This scheme ensures that there will not be any deadlocks, and, perhaps more importantly, ensures that a transaction that already holds some locks will not block waiting for other locks. The trade-off is that a transaction acquires locks earlier. If lock contention is low, locks are held longer under Conservative 2PL. If lock contention is heavy, on the other hand, Conservative 2PL can reduce the time that locks are held on average, because transactions that hold locks are never blocked.

Frequency of Deadlock Detection

Empirical results indicate that deadlocks are relatively infrequent, and detection-based schemes work well in practice. However, if there is a high level of contention for locks, and therefore an increased likelihood of deadlocks, prevention-based schemes could perform better.

Choice of Deadlock Victim

When a deadlock is detected, the choice of which transaction to abort can be made using several criteria: the one with the fewest locks, the one that has done the least work, the one that is farthest from completion, and so on. Further, a transaction might have been repeatedly restarted and then chosen as the victim in a deadlock cycle. Such transactions should eventually be favored during deadlock detection and allowed to complete.

The issues involved in designing a good concurrency control mechanism are complex, and we have only outlined them briefly. For the interested reader, there is a rich literature on the topic, and some of this work is mentioned in the bibliography.

17.6 SPECIALIZED LOCKING TECHNIQUES *

Thus far, we have treated a database as a *fixed* collection of *independent* data objects in our presentation of locking protocols. We now relax each of these restrictions and discuss the consequences.

If the collection of database objects is not fixed, but can grow and shrink through the insertion and deletion of objects, we must deal with a subtle complication known as the **phantom problem**. We discuss this problem in Section 17.6.1.

Although treating a database as an independent collection of objects is perfectly adequate for a discussion of serializability and recoverability, much better performance can sometimes be obtained using protocols that recognize and exploit the relationships between objects. We discuss two such cases, namely, locking in tree-structured indexes (Section 17.6.2) and locking a collection of objects with containment relationships between them (Section 17.6.3).

17.6.1 Dynamic Databases and the Phantom Problem

Consider the following example: Transaction $T1$ scans the Sailors relation to find the oldest sailor for each of the *rating* levels 1 and 2. First, $T1$ identifies and locks all pages (assuming that page-level locks are set) containing sailors with rating 1 and then finds the age of the oldest sailor, which is, say, 71. Next, transaction $T2$ inserts a new sailor with rating 1 and age 96. Observe that this new Sailors record can be inserted onto a page that does not contain other sailors with rating 1; thus an exclusive lock on this page does not conflict with any of the locks held by $T1$. $T2$ also locks the page containing the oldest sailor with rating 2, and deletes this sailor (whose age is, say, 80). $T2$ then commits and releases its locks. Finally, transaction $T1$ identifies and locks pages containing (all remaining) sailors with rating 2, and finds the age of the oldest such sailor, which is, say, 63.

The result of the interleaved execution is that ages 71 and 63 are printed in response to the query. If $T1$ had run first, then $T2$, we would have gotten the ages 71 and 80; if $T2$ had run first, then $T1$, we would have gotten the ages 96 and 63. Thus the result of the interleaved execution is not identical to any serial exection of $T1$ and $T2$, even though both transactions follow Strict 2PL and commit! The problem is that $T1$ assumes that the pages it has locked include *all* pages containing Sailors records with rating 1, and this assumption is violated when $T2$ inserts a new such sailor on a different page.

The flaw is not in the Strict 2PL protocol. Rather, it is in $T1$'s implicit assumption that it has locked the set of all Sailors records with *rating* value 1. $T1$'s semantics requires it to identify all such records, but locking pages that contain such records *at a given time* does not prevent new "phantom" records from being added on other pages. $T1$ has therefore *not* locked the set of desired Sailors records.

Strict 2PL guarantees conflict serializability; indeed, there are no cycles in the precedence graph for this example because conflicts are defined with respect to objects (in this example, pages) read/written by the transactions. However, because the set of objects that *should* have been locked by $T1$ was altered by the actions of $T2$, the outcome of the schedule differed from the outcome of any serial execution. This example brings out an important point about conflict serializability: If new items are added to the database, conflict serializability does not guarantee serializability!

A closer look at how a transaction identifies pages containing Sailors records with *rating* 1 suggests how the problem can be handled:

■ If there is no index, and all pages in the file must be scanned, $T1$ must somehow ensure that no new pages are added to the file, in addition to locking all existing pages.

■ If there is a dense index[3] on the *rating* field, $T1$ can obtain a lock on the index page—again, assuming that physical locking is done at the page level—that contains a data entry with *rating=1*. If there are no such data entries, that is, no records with this *rating* value, the page that *would* contain a data entry for *rating=1* is locked, in order to prevent such a record from being inserted. Any transaction that tries to insert a record with *rating=1* into the Sailors relation must insert a data entry pointing to the new record into this index page, and is blocked until $T1$ releases its locks. This technique is called **index locking**.

Both techniques effectively give $T1$ a lock on the set of Sailors records with *rating=1*: each existing record with *rating=1* is protected from changes by other transactions, and additionally, new records with *rating=1* cannot be inserted.

An independent issue is how transaction $T1$ can efficiently identify and lock the index page containing *rating=1*. We discuss this issue for the case of tree-structured indexes in Section 17.6.2.

We note that index locking is a special case of a more general concept called **predicate locking**. In our example, the lock on the index page implicitly locked all Sailors records that satisfy the logical predicate *rating=1*. More generally, we can support implicit locking of all records that match an arbitrary predicate. General predicate locking is expensive to implement, and is therefore not commonly used.

17.6.2   Concurrency Control in Tree Indexes

A straightforward approach to concurrency control for tree-structured indexes is to ignore the index structure, treat each page as a data object, and to use some version of 2PL. This simplistic locking strategy would lead to very high

---

[3]This idea can be adapted to work with sparse indexes as well.

lock contention in the higher levels of the tree because every tree search begins at the root and proceeds along some path to a leaf node. Fortunately, much more efficient locking protocols that exploit the hierarchical structure of a tree index are known to reduce the locking overhead while ensuring serializability and recoverability. We discuss some of these approaches briefly, concentrating on the search and insert operations.

Two observations provide the necessary insight:

1. The higher levels of the tree only serve to direct searches, and all the 'real' data is in the leaf levels (in the format of one of the three alternatives for data entries).

2. For inserts, a node must be locked (in exclusive mode, of course) only if a split can propagate up to it from the modified leaf.

Searches should obtain shared locks on nodes, starting at the root and proceeding along a path to the desired leaf. The first observation suggests that a lock on a node can be released as soon as a lock on a child node is obtained, because searches never go back up.

A conservative locking strategy for inserts would be to obtain exclusive locks on all nodes as we go down from the root to the leaf node to be modified, because splits can propagate all the way from a leaf to the root. However, once we lock the child of a node, the lock on the node is required only in the event that a split propagates back up to it. In particular, if the child of this node (on the path to the modified leaf) is not full when it is locked, any split that propagates up to the child can be resolved at the child, and will not propagate further to the current node. Thus when we lock a child node, we can release the lock on the parent if the child is not full. The locks held thus by an insert force any other transaction following the same path to wait at the earliest point (i.e., the node nearest the root) that might be affected by the insert.

We illustrate B+ tree locking using the tree shown in Figure 17.11. To search for the data entry 38*, a transaction Ti must obtain an S lock on node A, read the contents and determine that it needs to examine node B, obtain an S lock on node B and release the lock on A, then obtain an S lock on node C and release the lock on B, then obtain an S lock on node D and release the lock on C.

Ti always maintains a lock on one node in the path, in order to force new transactions that want to read or modify nodes on the same path to wait until the current transaction is done. If transaction Tj wants to delete 38*, for example, it must also traverse the path from the root to node D, and is forced to wait until Ti is done. Of course, if some transaction Tk holds a lock on, say, node C before Ti reaches this node, Ti is similarly forced to wait for Tk to complete.

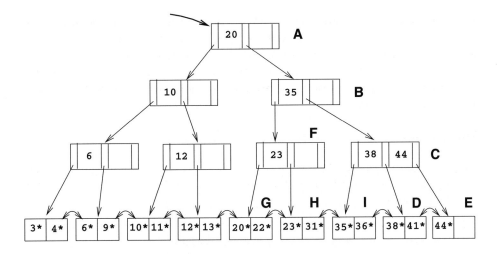

Figure 17.11   B+ Tree Locking Example

To insert data entry 45*, a transaction must obtain an S lock on node A, obtain an S lock on node B and release the lock on A, then obtain an S lock on node C and release the lock on B, then obtain an X lock on node E and release the lock on C. Because node E has space for the new entry, the insert is accomplished by modifying this node.

In contrast, consider the insertion of data entry 25*. Proceeding as for the insert of 45*, we obtain an X lock on node H. Unfortunately, this node is full and must be split. Splitting H requires that we also modify the parent, node F, but the transaction has only an S lock on F. Thus it must request an upgrade of this lock to an X lock. If no other transaction holds an S lock on F, the upgrade is granted, and since F has space, the split will not propagate further, and the insertion of 45* can proceed (by splitting H and locking G to modify the sibling pointer in I to point to the newly created node). However, if another transaction holds an S lock on node F, the first transaction is suspended until this transaction releases its S lock.

Observe that if another transaction holds an S lock on F, and also wants to access node H, we have a deadlock because the first transaction has an X lock on H! The above example also illustrates an interesting point about sibling pointers: When we split leaf node H, the new node *must* be added to the *left* of H, since otherwise the node whose sibling pointer is to be changed would be node I, which has a different parent. In order to modify a sibling pointer on I, we would have to lock its parent, node C (and possibly ancestors of C, in order to lock C).

We note that except for the locks on intermediate nodes that we indicated could be released early, some variant of 2PL must be used to govern when locks can be released, in order to ensure serializability and recoverability.

This approach improves considerably upon the naive use of 2PL, but several exclusive locks are still set unnecessarily, and although they are quickly released, affect performance substantially. One way to improve performance is for inserts to obtain shared locks instead of exclusive locks, except for the leaf, which is locked in exclusive mode. In the vast majority of cases, a split is not required, and this approach works very well. If the leaf is full, however, we must upgrade from shared locks to exclusive locks for all nodes to which the split propagates. Note that such lock upgrade requests can also lead to deadlocks.

The tree locking ideas that we have described illustrate the potential for efficient locking protocols in this very important special case, but are by no means the current state of the art. The interested reader should pursue the leads in the bibliography.

17.6.3   Multiple-Granularity Locking

Another specialized locking strategy is called **multiple-granularity locking**, and it allows us to efficiently set locks on objects that contain other objects.

For instance, a database contains several files, a file is a collection of pages, and a page is a collection of records. A transaction that expects to access most of the pages in a file should probably set a lock on the entire file, rather than locking individual pages (or records!) as and when it needs them. Doing so reduces the locking overhead considerably. On the other hand, other transactions that require access to parts of the file—even parts that are not needed by this transaction—are blocked. If a transaction accesses relatively few pages of the file, it is therefore better to lock only those pages. Similarly, if a transaction accesses several records on a page, it should lock the entire page, and if it accesses just a few records, it should lock just those records.

The question to be addressed is how a lock manager can efficiently ensure that a page, for example, is not locked by a transaction while another transaction holds a conflicting lock on the file containing the page (and therefore, implicitly, on the page).

The idea is to exploit the hierarchical nature of the 'contains' relationship. A database contains a set of files, each file contains a set of pages, and each page contains a set of records. This containment hierarchy can be thought of as a tree of objects, where each node contains all its children. (The approach can easily be extended to cover hierarchies that are not trees, but we will not discuss this extension.) A lock on a node locks that node and, implicitly, all its descendants. (Note that this interpretation of a lock is very different from B+ tree locking, where locking a node does *not* lock any descendants implicitly!)

In addition to shared (S) and exclusive (X) locks, multiple-granularity locking protocols also use two new kinds of locks, called **intention shared** (IS) and **intention exclusive** (IX) locks. IS locks conflict only with X locks. IX locks conflict with S and X locks. To lock a node in S (respectively X) mode, a transaction must first lock all its ancestors in IS (respectively IX) mode. Thus if a transaction locks a node in S mode, no other transaction can have locked any ancestor in X mode; similarly, if a transaction locks a node in X mode, no other transaction can have locked any ancestor in S or X mode. This ensures that no other transaction holds a lock on an ancestor that conflicts with the requested S or X lock on the node.

A common situation is that a transaction needs to read an entire file and modify a few of the records in it; that is, it needs an S lock on the file and an IX lock so that it can subsequently lock some of the contained objects in X mode. It is useful to define a new kind of lock called an SIX lock that is logically equivalent to holding an S lock and an IX lock. A transaction can obtain a single SIX lock (which conflicts with any lock that conflicts with either S or IX) instead of an S lock and an IX lock.

A subtle point is that locks must be released in leaf-to-root order for this protocol to work correctly. To see this, consider what happens when a transaction Ti locks all nodes on a path from the root (corresponding to the entire database) to the node corresponding to some page p in IS mode, locks p in S mode, and then releases the lock on the root node. Another transaction Tj could now obtain an X lock on the root. This lock implicitly gives Tj an X lock on page p, which conflicts with the S lock currently held by Ti.

Multiple-granularity locking must be used with 2PL in order to ensure serializability. 2PL dictates when locks can be released. At that time, locks obtained using multiple-granularity locking can be released, and further, must be released in leaf-to-root order.

Finally, there is the question of how to decide what granularity of locking is appropriate for a given transaction. One approach is to begin by obtaining fine granularity locks (e.g., at the record level) and after the transaction requests a certain number of locks at that granularity, to start obtaining locks at the next higher granularity (e.g., at the page level). This procedure is called **lock escalation**.

17.7   TRANSACTION SUPPORT IN SQL-92 *

We have thus far studied transactions and transaction management using an abstract model of a transaction as a sequence of read, write and abort/commit actions. We now consider what support SQL provides for users to specify transaction-level behavior.

A transaction is automatically started when a user executes a statement that modifies either the database or the catalogs, such as a `SELECT` query, an `UPDATE` command, or a `CREATE TABLE` statement.[4] Once a transaction is started, other statements can be executed as part of this transaction until the transaction is terminated by either a `COMMIT` command or a `ROLLBACK` (the SQL keyword for abort) command.

17.7.1   Transaction Characteristics

Every transaction has three characteristics: **access-mode**, **diagnostics-size** and **isolation-level**. The **diagnostics-size** determines the number of error conditions that can be recorded; we will not discuss this feature further.

If the **access-mode** is `READ ONLY`, the transaction is not allowed to modify the database. Thus `INSERT`, `DELETE`, `UPDATE` and `CREATE` commands cannot be executed. If we have to execute one of these commands, the access-mode should be set to `READ WRITE`. For transactions with `READ ONLY` access-mode, only shared locks need to be obtained, thereby increasing concurrency.

The **isolation-level** controls the extent to which a given transaction is exposed to the actions of other transactions executing concurrently. By choosing one of four possible isolation-level settings, a user can obtain greater concurrency at the cost of increasing the transaction's exposure to other transactions' uncommitted changes.

The isolation-level choices are `READ UNCOMMITTED`, `READ COMMITTED`, `REPEATABLE READ` and `SERIALIZABLE`. The effect of these levels is summarized in Figure 17.12. In this context, *dirty read* and *unrepeatable read* are defined as usual. **Phantom** is defined to be the possibility that a transaction retrieves a collection of objects (in SQL terms, a collection of tuples) twice and sees different results, even though it does not modify any of these tuples itself. The highest degree of isolation from the effects of other transactions is achieved by setting isolation-level for a transaction T to `SERIALIZABLE`. This isolation-level ensures that T reads only the changes made by committed transactions, that no value read or written by T is changed

---

[4]There are some SQL statements that do not require the creation of a transaction.

Level	Dirty Read	Unrepeatable Read	Phantom
READ UNCOMMITTED	Maybe	Maybe	Maybe
READ COMMITTED	No	Maybe	Maybe
REPEATABLE READ	No	No	Maybe
SERIALIZABLE	No	No	No

Figure 17.12   Transaction Isolation Levels in SQL-92

by any other transaction until T is complete, and that if T reads a set of values based on some search condition, this set is not changed by other transactions until T is complete (i.e., T avoids the phantom phenomenon).

In terms of a lock-based implementation, a **SERIALIZABLE** transaction obtains locks before reading or writing objects, including locks on sets of objects that it requires to be unchanged (see Section 17.6.1), and holds them until the end, according to Strict 2PL.

REPEATABLE READ ensures that T reads only the changes made by committed transactions, and that no value read or written by T is changed by any other transaction until T is complete. However, T could experience the phantom phenomenon, for example, while T examines all Sailors records with *rating=1*, another transaction might add a new such Sailors record, which is missed by T.

A **REPEATABLE READ** transaction uses the same locking protocol as a **SERIALIZABLE** transaction, except that it does not do index locking, that is, it locks only individual objects, not sets of objects.

READ COMMITTED ensures that T reads only the changes made by committed transactions, and that no value written by T is changed by any other transaction until T is complete. However, a value read by T may well be modified by another transaction while T is still in progress, and T is, of course, exposed to the phantom problem.

A **READ COMMITTED** transaction obtains exclusive locks before writing objects and holds these locks until the end. It also obtains shared locks before reading objects, but these locks are released immediately; their only effect is to guarantee that the transaction that last modified the object is complete. (This guarantee relies on the fact that *every* SQL transaction obtains exclusive locks before writing objects and holds exclusive locks until the end.)

A READ UNCOMMITTED transaction T can read changes made to an object by an ongoing transaction; obviously, the object can be changed further while T is in progress, and T is clearly vulnerable to the phantom problem.

Such a transaction obtains exclusive locks before writing objects, and holds these locks until the end, but does not obtain shared locks before reading objects. This mode represents the greatest exposure to uncommitted changes of other transactions; so much so that SQL prohibits such a transaction from making any changes itself—a READ UNCOMMITTED transaction is required to have an access mode of READ ONLY.

The SERIALIZABLE isolation-level is generally the safest, and is recommended for most transactions. Some transactions, however, can run with a lower isolation-level, and the smaller number of locks requested can contribute to improved system performance. For example, a statistical query that finds the average sailor age can be run at the READ COMMITTED level, or even the READ UNCOMMITTED level, because a few incorrect or missing values will not significantly affect the result if the number of sailors is large.

The isolation-level and access-mode can be set using the SET TRANSACTION command. For example, the following command declares the current transaction to be SERIALIZABLE and READ ONLY:

```
SET TRANSACTION ISOLATION LEVEL SERIALIZABLE READ ONLY
```

When a transaction is started, the default is SERIALIZABLE and READ WRITE.

17.7.2   Transactions and Constraints

SQL constructs for defining integrity constraints were presented in Chapter 2. As noted there, an integrity constraint represents a condition that must be satisfied by the database state. An important question that arises is when to check integrity constraints.

By default, a constraint is checked at the end of every SQL statement that could lead to a violation, and if there is indeed a violation, the statement is rejected. Sometimes this approach is too inflexible. Consider the following variants of the Sailors and Boats relations; every sailor is assigned to a boat, and every boat is required to have a captain.

```
CREATE TABLE Sailors ( sid     INTEGER,
                       sname   CHAR(10),
                       rating  INTEGER,
```

```
                         age       REAL,
                         assigned  INTEGER NOT NULL
                         PRIMARY KEY (sid) )
                         FOREIGN KEY (assigned) REFERENCES Boats (bid)

CREATE TABLE Boats (     bid       INTEGER,
                         bname     CHAR(10),
                         color     CHAR(10),
                         captain   INTEGER NOT NULL
                         PRIMARY KEY (bid)
                         FOREIGN KEY (captain) REFERENCES Sailors (sid) )
```

Whenever a Boats tuple is inserted, there is a check to see if the captain is in the Sailors relation, and whenever a Sailors tuple is inserted, there is a check to see that the assigned boat is in the Boats relation. How are we to insert the very first boat or sailor tuple? One cannot be inserted without the other. The only way to accomplish this insertion is to **defer** the constraint checking that would normally be carried out at the end of an **INSERT** statement.

SQL allows a constraint to be in **DEFERRED** or **IMMEDIATE** mode.

```
    SET CONSTRAINT ConstraintFoo DEFERRED
```

A constraint that is in deferred mode is checked at commit time. In our example, the foreign key constraints on Boats and Sailors can both be declared to be in deferred mode. We can then insert a boat with a nonexistent sailor as the captain (temporarily making the database inconsistent), insert the sailor (restoring consistency), then commit and check that both constraints are satisfied.

17.8 CONCURRENCY CONTROL WITHOUT LOCKING *

Locking is the most widely used approach to concurrency control in a DBMS, but it is not the only one. We now consider some alternative approaches.

17.8.1 Optimistic Concurrency Control

Locking protocols take a pessimistic approach to conflicts between transactions, and use either transaction abort or blocking to resolve conflicts. In a system with relatively light contention for data objects, the overhead of obtaining locks and following a locking protocol must nonetheless be paid.

In optimistic concurrency control, the basic premise is that most transactions will not conflict with other transactions, and the idea is to be as permissive as possible in allowing transactions to execute. Transactions proceed in three phases:

1. **Read:** The transaction executes, reading values from the database and writing to a private workspace.

2. **Validation:** If the transaction decides that it wants to commit, the DBMS checks whether the transaction could possibly have conflicted with any other concurrently executing transaction. If there is a possible conflict, the transaction is aborted; its private workspace is cleared and it is restarted.

3. **Write:** If validation determines that there are no possible conflicts, the changes to data objects made by the transaction in its private workspace are copied into the database.

If, indeed, there are few conflicts, and validation can be done efficiently, this approach should lead to better performance than locking does. If there are many conflicts, the cost of repeatedly restarting transactions (thereby wasting the work they've done) will hurt performance significantly.

Each transaction Ti is assigned a timestamp $TS(Ti)$ at the beginning of its validation phase, and the validation criterion checks whether the timestamp-ordering of transactions is an equivalent serial order. For every pair of transactions Ti and Tj such that $TS(Ti) < TS(Tj)$, one of the following conditions must hold:

1. Ti completes (all three phases) before Tj begins; or

2. Ti completes before Tj starts its Write phase, and Ti does not write any database object that is read by Tj; or

3. Ti completes its Read phase before Tj completes its Read phase, and Ti does not write any database object that is either read or written by Tj.

To validate Tj, we must check to see that one of these conditions holds with respect to each committed transaction Ti such that $TS(Ti) < TS(Tj)$. Each of these conditions ensures that Tj's modifications are not visible to Ti.

Further, the first condition allows Tj to see some of Ti's changes, but clearly, they execute completely in serial order with respect to each other. The second condition allows Tj to read objects while Ti is still modifying objects, but there is no conflict because Tj does not read any object modified by Ti. Although Tj might overwrite some objects written by Ti, all of Ti's writes precede all of Tj's writes. The third condition allows Ti and Tj to write objects at the same time, and thus have even more overlap in time than the second condition, but the sets of objects written by the two transactions cannot overlap. Thus no RW, WR or WW conflicts are possible if any of these three conditions is met.

Checking these validation criteria requires us to maintain lists of objects read and written by each transaction. Further, while one transaction is being validated, no other transaction can be allowed to commit; otherwise, the validation of the first transaction might miss conflicts with respect to the newly committed transaction.

Clearly, it is not the case that optimistic concurrency control has no concurrency control overhead; rather, the locking overheads of lock-based approaches are replaced with the overheads of recording read-lists and write-lists for transactions, checking for conflicts, and copying changes from the private workspace. Similarly, the implicit cost of blocking in a lock-based approach is replaced by the implicit cost of the work wasted by restarted transactions.

17.8.2 Timestamp-Based Concurrency Control

In lock-based concurrency control, conflicting actions of different transactions are ordered by the order in which locks are obtained, and the lock protocol extends this ordering on actions to transactions, thereby ensuring serializability. In optimistic concurrency control, a timestamp ordering is imposed on transactions, and validation checks that all conflicting actions occurred in the same order.

Timestamps can also be used in another way: each transaction can be assigned a timestamp at startup, and we can ensure, at execution time, that if action ai of transaction Ti conflicts with action aj of transaction Tj, ai occurs before aj if $TS(Ti) < TS(Tj)$. If an action violates this ordering, the transaction is aborted and restarted.

To implement this concurrency control scheme, every database object O is given a **read timestamp** $RTS(O)$ and a **write timestamp** $WTS(O)$. If transaction T wants to read object O, and $TS(T) < WTS(O)$, the order of this read with respect to the most recent write on O would violate the timestamp order between this transaction and the writer. Therefore, T is aborted and restarted *with a new, larger timestamp*. If $TS(T) > WTS(O)$, T reads O, and $RTS(O)$ is set to the larger of $RTS(O)$ and $TS(T)$. (Note that there is a physical change—the change to $RTS(O)$—to be written to disk, and to be recorded in the log for recovery purposes, even on reads. This write operation is a significant overhead.)

Observe that if T is restarted with the same timestamp, it is guaranteed to be aborted again, due to the same conflict. Contrast this behavior with the use of timestamps in 2PL for deadlock prevention: there, transactions were restarted with the *same* timestamp as before in order to avoid repeated restarts. This shows that the two uses of timestamps are quite different, and should not be confused.

Next, let us consider what happens when transaction T wants to write object O:

1. If $TS(T) < RTS(O)$, the write action conflicts with the most recent read action of O, and T is therefore aborted and restarted.

2. If $TS(T) < WTS(O)$, a naive approach would be to abort T because its write action conflicts with the most recent write of O, and is out of timestamp order. It turns out that we can safely ignore such writes and continue. Ignoring outdated writes is called the **Thomas Write Rule**.

3. Otherwise, T writes O and $WTS(O)$ is set to $TS(T)$.

The Thomas Write Rule

We now consider the justification for the Thomas Write Rule. If $TS(T) < WTS(O)$, the current write action has, in effect, been made obsolete by the most recent write of O, which *follows* the current write according to the timestamp ordering on transactions. We can think of T's write action as if it had occurred immediately *before* the most recent write of O, and was never read by anyone.

If the Thomas Write Rule is not used, that is, T is aborted in case (2) above, the timestamp protocol, like 2PL, allows only conflict serializable schedules. (Both 2PL and this timestamp protocol allow schedules that the other does not.) If the Thomas Write Rule is used, some serializable schedules are permitted that are not conflict serializable, as illustrated by the schedule in Figure 17.13. Because $T2$'s

$T1$	$T2$
$R(A)$	
	$W(A)$
	Commit
$W(A)$	
Commit	

Figure 17.13   A Serializable Schedule That Is Not Conflict Serializable

write follows $T1$'s read and precedes $T1$'s write of the same object, this schedule is not conflict serializable. The Thomas Write Rule relies on the observation that $T2$'s write is never seen by any transaction and the schedule in Figure 17.13 is therefore equivalent to the serializable schedule obtained by deleting this write action, which is shown in Figure 17.14.

T1	T2
R(A)	
	Commit
W(A)	
Commit	

Figure 17.14   A Conflict Serializable Schedule

Recoverability

Unfortunately, the timestamp protocol presented above permits schedules that are not recoverable, as illustrated by the schedule in Figure 17.15. If $TS(T1) = 1$

T1	T2
W(A)	
	R(A)
	W(B)
	Commit

Figure 17.15   An Unrecoverable Schedule

and $TS(T2) = 2$, this schedule is permitted by the timestamp protocol (with or without the Thomas Write Rule). The timestamp protocol can be modified to disallow such schedules by **buffering** all write actions until the transaction commits. In the example, when $T1$ wants to write A, $WTS(A)$ is updated to reflect this action, but the change to A is not carried out immediately; instead, it is recorded in a private workspace, or buffer. When $T2$ wants to read A subsequently, its timestamp is compared with $WTS(A)$, and the read is seen to be permissible. However, $T2$ is blocked until $T1$ completes. If $T1$ commits, its change to A is copied from the buffer; otherwise, the changes in the buffer are discarded. $T2$ is then allowed to read A.

This blocking of $T2$ is similar to the effect of $T1$ obtaining an exclusive lock on A! Nonetheless, even with this modification the timestamp protocol permits some schedules that are not permitted by 2PL; the two protocols are not quite the same.

Because recoverability is essential, such a modification must be used for the timestamp protocol to be practical. Given the added overheads this entails, on top of the (considerable) cost of maintaining read and write timestamps, timestamp concurrency control is unlikely to beat lock-based protocols in centralized systems.

Indeed, it has mainly been studied in the context of distributed database systems (Chapter 19).

17.8.3   Multiversion Concurrency Control

This protocol represents yet another way of using timestamps, assigned at startup time, to achieve serializability. The goal is to ensure that a transaction never has to wait to read a database object, and the idea is to maintain several versions of each database object, each with a write timestamp, and to let transaction Ti read the most recent version whose timestamp precedes $TS(Ti)$.

If transaction Ti wants to write an object, we must ensure that the object has not already been read by some other transaction Tj such that $TS(Ti) < TS(Tj)$. If we allow Ti to write such an object, its change should be seen by Tj for serializability, but obviously Tj, which read the object at some time in the past, will not see Ti's change.

To check this condition, every object also has an associated read timestamp, and whenever a transaction reads the object, the read timestamp is set to the maximum of the current read timestamp and the reader's timestamp. If Ti wants to write an object O and $TS(Ti) < RTS(O)$, Ti is aborted and restarted with a new, larger timestamp. Otherwise, Ti creates a new version of O, and sets the read and write timestamps of the new version to $TS(Ti)$.

The drawbacks of this scheme are similar to those of timestamp concurrency control, and in addition there is the cost of maintaining versions. On the other hand, reads are never blocked, which can be important for workloads dominated by transactions that only read values from the database.

17.9   SUMMARY

Concurrency control is one of the most important aspects of a DBMS. The functionality provided is essential in a wide range of applications, and is often an important factor in the adoption of a DBMS. Users are able to think of their programs, called transactions, as atomic 'all-or-nothing' actions that execute serially. In reality, the actions of transactions are interleaved for greater concurrency, and therefore better performance.

Transactions can complete successfully and commit, or terminate unsuccessfully and abort. The concurrency control mechanism ensures that the interleaved execution has the same effect as some serial execution of all committed transactions; this property is called serializability. The concurrency control mechanism also ensures that the actions of all transactions that execute partially but do not commit can be completely erased and have no effect on committed transactions; this property is called recoverability. (The actual task of erasing the actions of aborted transactions is given to the recovery manager, which we cover in Chapter 18.)

The implementation of the concurrency control mechanism has a substantial impact on system performance. Most systems today, and virtually all centralized systems, use some form of locking to ensure serializability and recoverability; Strict 2PL is widely used. One of the drawbacks of locking is the possibility of deadlock, which is a cycle of transactions that are all waiting for another transaction in the cycle to release a lock. Deadlock prevention or detection schemes are used to resolve deadlocks. Specialized locking techniques can be used to improve performance for index structures and for collections of objects related by containment.

Several concurrency control schemes based on different uses of timestamps, rather than locking, have also been proposed.

EXERCISES

Exercise 17.1 Give brief answers to the following questions:

1. What is a transaction? In what ways is it different from an ordinary program (in a language such as C)?

2. Define these terms: *blind write, dirty read, unrepeatable read, serializable schedule, conflict-serializable schedule, recoverable schedule, avoids-cascading-aborts schedule, view-serializable schedule.*

3. Describe each of the following locking protocols: *2PL, Strict 2PL, Conservative 2PL.*

4. What is the phantom problem? Can it occur in a database where the set of database objects is fixed and only the values of objects can be changed?

5. Why must lock and unlock be atomic operations?

6. Identify one difference in the timestamps assigned to restarted transactions when timestamps are used for deadlock prevention versus when timestamps are used for concurrency control.

7. State and justify the Thomas Write Rule.

Exercise 17.2 Consider the following (incomplete) schedule S:

T1:R(X), T1:R(Y), T1:W(X), T2:R(Y), T3:W(Y), T1:W(X), T2:R(Y)

1. Can you determine the serializability graph for this schedule? Assuming that all three transactions eventually commit, show the serializability graph.

2. For each of the following, modify S to create a complete schedule that satisfies the stated condition. If a modification is not possible, explain briefly. If it is possible, use the smallest possible number of actions (read, write, commit, or abort). You are free to add new actions anywhere in the schedule S, including in the middle.

   (a) Resulting schedule avoids cascading aborts but is not recoverable.

   (b) Resulting schedule is recoverable.

   (c) Resulting schedule is conflict-serializable.

Exercise 17.3 Consider the following classes of schedules: *serializable, conflict-serializable, view-serializable, recoverable, avoids-cascading-aborts,* and *strict.* For each of the following schedules, state which of the above classes it belongs to. If you cannot decide whether a schedule belongs in a certain class based on the listed actions, explain briefly.

The actions are listed in the order they are scheduled, and prefixed with the transaction name. If a commit or abort is not shown, the schedule is incomplete; assume that abort/commit must follow all the listed actions.

   1. T1:R(X), T2:R(X), T1:W(X), T2:W(X)

   2. T1:W(X), T2:R(Y), T1:R(Y), T2:R(X)

   3. T1:R(X), T2:R(Y), T3:W(X), T2:R(X), T1:R(Y)

   4. T1:R(X), T1:R(Y), T1:W(X), T2:R(Y), T3:W(Y), T1:W(X), T2:R(Y)

   5. T1:R(X), T2:W(X), T1:W(X), T2:Abort, T1:Commit

   6. T1:R(X), T2:W(X), T1:W(X), T2:Commit, T1:Commit

   7. T1:W(X), T2:R(X), T1:W(X), T2:Abort, T1:Commit

   8. T1:W(X), T2:R(X), T1:W(X), T2:Commit, T1:Commit

   9. T1:W(X), T2:R(X), T1:W(X), T2:Commit, T1:Abort

   10. T2: R(X), T3:W(X), T3:Commit, T1:W(Y), T1:Commit, T2:R(Y), T2:W(Z), T2:Commit

   11. T1:R(X), T2:W(X), T2:Commit, T1:W(X), T1:Commit, T3:R(X), T3:Commit

   12. T1:R(X), T2:W(X), T1:W(X), T3:R(X), T1:Commit, T2:Commit, T3:Commit

Exercise 17.4 Consider the following concurrency control protocols: 2PL, Strict 2PL, Conservative 2PL, Optimistic, Timestamp without the Thomas Write Rule, Timestamp with the Thomas Write Rule, and Multiversion. For each of the schedules in Exercise 17.3, state which of these protocols allows it, that is, allows the actions to occur in exactly the order shown.

For the timestamp-based protocols, assume that the timestamp for transaction Ti is i and that a version of the protocol that ensures recoverability is used. Further, if the Thomas Write Rule is used, show the equivalent serial schedule.

Exercise 17.5 Consider the following sequences of actions, listed in the order they are submitted to the DBMS:

- **Sequence S1:** T1:R(X), T2:W(X), T2:W(Y), T3:W(Y), T1:W(Y), T1:Commit, T2:Commit, T3:Commit

- **Sequence S2:** T1:R(X), T2:W(Y), T2:W(X), T3:W(Y), T1:W(Y), T1:Commit, T2:Commit, T3:Commit

For each sequence and for each of the following concurrency control mechanisms, describe how the concurrency control mechanism handles the sequence.

Assume that the timestamp of transaction Ti is i. For lock-based concurrency control mechanisms, add lock and unlock requests to the above sequence of actions as per the locking protocol. The DBMS processes actions in the order shown. If a transaction is blocked, assume that all of its actions are queued until it is resumed; the DBMS continues with the next action (according to the listed sequence) of an unblocked transaction.

1. Strict 2PL with timestamps used for deadlock prevention.

2. Strict 2PL with deadlock detection. (Show the waits-for graph if a deadlock cycle develops.)

3. Conservative (and strict, i.e., with locks held until end-of-transaction) 2PL.

4. Optimistic concurrency control.

5. Timestamp concurrency control with buffering of reads and writes (to ensure recoverability) and the Thomas Write Rule.

6. Multiversion concurrency control.

Exercise 17.6 For each of the following locking protocols, assuming that every transaction follows that locking protocol, state which of these desirable properties are ensured: serializability, conflict-serializability, recoverability, avoid cascading aborts.

1. Always obtain an exclusive lock before writing; hold exclusive locks until end-of-transaction. No shared locks are ever obtained.

2. In addition to (1), obtain a shared lock before reading; shared locks can be released at any time.

3. As in (2), and in addition, locking is two-phase.

4. As in (2), and in addition, all locks held until end-of-transaction.

Exercise 17.7 The Venn diagram (from [69]) in Figure 17.16 shows the inclusions between several classes of schedules. Give one example schedule for each of the regions S1 through S12 in the diagram.

Exercise 17.8 Briefly answer the following questions:

1. Draw a Venn diagram that shows the inclusions between the classes of schedules permitted by the following concurrency control protocols: *2PL, Strict 2PL, Conservative 2PL, Optimistic, Timestamp without the Thomas Write Rule, Timestamp with the Thomas Write Rule,* and *Multiversion*.

2. Give one example schedule for each region in the diagram.

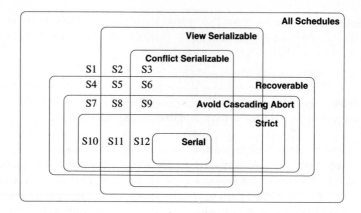

Figure 17.16   Venn Diagram for Classes of Schedules

3. Extend the Venn diagram to include the class of serializable and conflict-serializable schedules.

Exercise 17.9 Answer each of the following questions briefly. The questions are based on the following relational schema:

Emp(*eid:* integer, *ename:* string, *age:* integer, *salary:* real, *did:* integer)
Dept(*did:* integer, *dname:* string, *floor:* integer)

and on the following update command:

replace (salary = 1.1 * EMP.salary) where EMP.ename = 'Santa'

1. Give an example of a query that would conflict with this command (in a concurrency control sense) if both were run at the same time. Explain what could go wrong, and how locking tuples would solve the problem.

2. Give an example of a query or a command that would conflict with this command, such that the conflict could not be resolved by just locking individual tuples or pages, but requires index locking.

3. Explain what index locking is and how it resolves the preceding conflict.

Exercise 17.10 SQL-92 supports four isolation-levels and two access-modes, for a total of eight combinations of isolation-level and access-mode. Each combination implicitly defines a class of transactions; the following questions refer to these eight classes.

1. For each of the eight classes, describe a locking protocol that allows only transactions in this class. Does the locking protocol for a given class make any assumptions about the locking protocols used for other classes? Explain briefly.

2. Consider a schedule generated by the execution of several SQL transactions. Is it guaranteed to be conflict-serializable? to be serializable? to be recoverable?

3. Consider a schedule generated by the execution of several SQL transactions, each of which has **READ ONLY** access-mode. Is it guaranteed to be conflict-serializable? to be serializable? to be recoverable?

4. Consider a schedule generated by the execution of several SQL transactions, each of which has **SERIALIZABLE** isolation-level. Is it guaranteed to be conflict-serializable? to be serializable? to be recoverable?

5. Can you think of a timestamp-based concurrency control scheme that can support the eight classes of SQL transactions?

Exercise 17.11 Suppose that a DBMS recognizes *increment*, which increments an integer-valued object by 1, and *decrement* as actions, in addition to reads and writes. A transaction that increments an object need not know the value of the object; increment and decrement are versions of blind writes. In addition to shared and exclusive locks, two special locks are supported: An object must be locked in I mode before incrementing it and locked in D mode before decrementing it. An I lock is compatible with another I or D lock on the same object, but not with S and X locks.

1. Illustrate how the use of I and D locks can increase concurrency. (Show a schedule allowed by Strict 2PL that only uses S and X locks. Explain how the use of I and D locks can allow more actions to be interleaved, while continuing to follow Strict 2PL.)

2. Informally explain how Strict 2PL guarantees serializability even in the presence of I and D locks. (Identify which pairs of actions 'conflict,' in the sense that their relative order can affect the result, and show that the use of S, X, I and D locks according to Strict 2PL orders all conflicting pairs of actions to be the same as the order in some serial schedule.)

Exercise 17.12 Consider the tree shown in Figure 17.11. Describe the steps involved in executing each of the following operations according to the tree-index concurrency control algorithm discussed in Section 17.6.2, in terms of the order in which nodes are locked, unlocked, read and written. Be specific about the kind of lock obtained and answer each part independently of the others, always starting with the tree shown in Figure 17.11.

1. Search for data entry 40*.

2. Search for all data entries $k*$ with $k \leq 40$.

3. Insert data entry 62*.

4. Insert data entry 40*.

5. Insert data entries 62* and 75*.

Exercise 17.13 Consider a database that is organized in terms of the following hierarachy of objects: The database itself is an object (D), and it contains two files ($F1$ and $F2$), each of which contains 1000 pages ($P1 \ldots P1000$ and $P1001 \ldots P2000$, respectively). Each page contains 100 records, and records are identified as $p : i$, where p is the page identifier and i is the slot of the record on that page.

Multiple-granularity locking is used, with S, X, IS, IX and SIX locks, and database-level, file-level, page-level and record-level locking. For each of the following operations, indicate the sequence of lock requests that must be generated by a transaction that wants to carry out (just) these operations:

1. Read record $P1200 : 5$.

2. Read records $P1200 : 98$ through $P1205 : 2$.

3. Read all (records on all) pages in file $F1$.

4. Read pages $P500$ through $P520$.

5. Read pages $P10$ through $P980$.

6. Read all pages in $F1$ and modify about 10 pages, which can be identified only after reading $F1$.

7. Delete record $P1200 : 98$. (This is a blind write.)

8. Delete the first record from each page. (Again, these are blind writes.)

9. Delete all records.

BIBLIOGRAPHIC NOTES

Two-phase locking is introduced in [184], a fundamental paper that also discusses the concepts of transactions, phantoms and predicate locks. Formal treatments of serial-izability appear in [72, 420]. The transaction concept and some of its limitations are discussed in [227]. A formal transaction model that generalizes several earlier transac-tion models is proposed in [131]. Multiple-granularity locking is introduced in [231] and studied further in [92, 315].

Concurrent access to B trees is considered in several papers, including [52, 320, 333, 363, 492]. A concurrency control method that works with the ARIES recovery method is presented in [390]. Another paper that considers concurrency control issues in the context of recovery is [350]. Algorithms for building indexes without stopping the DBMS are presented in [393] and [6]. The performance of B tree concurrency control algorithms is studied in [512]. Concurrency control techniques for Linear Hashing are presented in [175] and [388].

Timestamp-based multiversion concurrency control is studied in [446]. Multiversion concurrency control algorithms are studied formally in [67]. Lock-based multiversion techniques are considered in [324]. Optimistic concurrency control is introduced in [321]. Transaction management issues for real-time database systems are discussed in [2, 11, 250, 256, 260, 314]. Performance of various concurrency control algorithms is discussed in [12, 537]. [319] is a comprehensive collection of papers on this topic. There is a large body of theoretical results on database concurrency control. [421, 69] offer thorough textbook presentations of this material.

18

CRASH RECOVERY

Humpty Dumpty sat on a wall.
Humpty Dumpty had a great fall.
All the King's horses and all the King's men
Could not put Humpty together again.

—Old nursery rhyme.

The **recovery manager** of a DBMS is responsible for ensuring two important properties of transactions: *atomicity* and *durability*. It ensures atomicity by undoing the actions of transactions that do not commit, and durability by making sure that all actions of committed transactions survive **system crashes**, (e.g., a core dump caused by a bus error) and **media failures** (e.g., a disk is corrupted).

The recovery manager is one of the hardest components of a DBMS to design and implement. It must deal with a wide variety of database states because it is called on during system failures. We present the **ARIES** recovery algorithm, which is conceptually simple, works well with a wide range of concurrency control mechanisms, and is being used in an increasing number of database sytems.

We begin with an introduction to crash recovery in Section 18.1 and an overview of ARIES in Section 18.2. We discuss recovery from a crash in Section 18.3. Aborting (or rolling back) a single transaction is a special case of Undo, and is discussed in Section 18.3.3. We concentrate on recovery from system crashes in most of the chapter, and discuss media failures in Section 18.4. We consider recovery only in a centralized DBMS; recovery in a distributed DBMS is discussed in Chapter 19.

18.1 INTRODUCTION TO CRASH RECOVERY

When a DBMS is restarted after crashes, the recovery manager is given control and must bring the database to a consistent state. The recovery manager is also responsible for undoing the actions of an aborted transaction. To see what it takes to implement a recovery manager, it is necessary to understand what happens during normal execution.

A transaction consists of a series of *reads* and *writes* of database objects, followed by either a *commit* or an *abort*.

- To **read** a database object, it is first brought into a buffer pool page in main memory from disk, and then its value is copied into a program variable.

- To **write** a database object, an in-memory copy of the object (in some buffer pool page) is first modified, and then written to disk.

The **transaction manager** of a DBMS controls the execution of transactions. Before reading and writing objects during normal execution, locks must be acquired (and released at some later time) according to a chosen locking protocol.[1] For simplicity of exposition, we make the following assumption:

Atomic Writes: Writing a page to disk is an atomic action.

This implies that the system does not crash while a write is in progress and is unrealistic. In practice, disk writes do not have this property, and steps must be taken during restart after a crash (Section 18.3) to verify that the most recent write to a given page was completed successfully, and to deal with the consequences if not.

18.1.1 Stealing Frames and Forcing Pages

With respect to writing objects, two additional questions arise:

1. Can the changes made to an object O in the buffer pool by a transaction T be written to disk before T commits? Such writes are executed when another transaction wants to bring in a page and the buffer manager chooses to replace the page containing O; of course, this page must have been unpinned by T. If such writes are allowed, we say that a **steal** approach is used. (Informally, the second transaction 'steals' a frame from T.)

2. When a transaction commits, must we ensure that all the changes it has made to objects in the buffer pool are immediately forced to disk? If so, we say that a **force** approach is used.

From the standpoint of implementing a recovery manager, it is simplest to use a buffer manager with a no-steal, force approach. If no-steal is used, we don't have to undo the changes of an aborted transaction (because these changes have not been written to disk), and if force is used, we don't have to redo the changes of a committed transaction if there is a subsequent crash (because all these changes are guaranteed to have been written to disk at commit time).

---

[1] A non locking concurrency control technique could be used instead, but we will assume that locking is used.

However, these policies have important drawbacks. The no-steal approach assumes that all pages modified by ongoing transactions can be accommodated in the buffer pool, and in the presence of large transactions (typically run in batch mode, e.g., payroll processing), this assumption is unrealistic. The force approach results in excessive page I/O costs. If a highly used page is updated in succession by twenty transactions, it would be written to disk twenty times. With a no-force approach, on the other hand, the in-memory copy of the page would be successively modified and written to disk just once, reflecting the effects of all twenty updates, when the page is eventually replaced in the buffer pool (in accordance with the buffer manager's page replacement policy).

For these reasons, most systems use a steal, no-force approach. Thus if a frame is dirty and chosen for replacement, the page it contains is written to disk even if the modifying transaction is still active (*steal*); in addition, pages in the buffer pool that are modified by a transaction are not forced to disk when the transaction commits (*no-force*).

18.1.2 Recovery-Related Steps during Normal Execution

The recovery manager of a DBMS maintains some information during normal execution of transactions in order to enable it to perform its task in the event of a failure. In particular, a **log** of all modifications to the database is saved on **stable storage**, which is guaranteed (with very high probability) to survive crashes and media failures. Stable storage is implemented by maintaining multiple copies of information (perhaps in different locations) on nonvolatile storage devices such as disks or tapes. It is important to ensure that the log entries describing a change to the database are written to stable storage *before* the change is made; otherwise, the system might crash just after the change, leaving us without a record of the change.

The log enables the recovery manager to undo the actions of aborted and incomplete transactions and to redo the actions of committed transactions. For example, a transaction that committed before the crash may have made updates to a copy (of a database object) in the buffer pool, and this change may not have been written to disk before the crash, because of a no-force approach. Such changes must be identified using the log, and must be written to disk. Further, changes of transactions that did not commit prior to the crash might have been written to disk because of a steal approach. Such changes must be identified using the log, and then undone.

18.2   OVERVIEW OF ARIES

ARIES is a recovery algorithm that is designed to work with a steal, no-force approach. When the recovery manager is invoked after a crash, restart proceeds in three phases:

1. **Analysis:** Identifies dirty pages in the buffer pool (i.e., changes that have not been written to disk) and active transactions at the time of the crash.

2. **Redo:** Repeats all actions, starting from an appropriate point in the log, and restores the database state to what it was at the time of the crash.

3. **Undo:** Undoes the actions of transactions that did not commit, so that the database reflects only the actions of committed transactions.

Consider the simple execution history illustrated in Figure 18.1. When the system

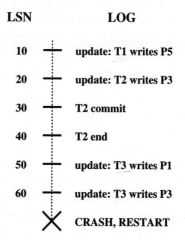

LSN		LOG
10		update: T1 writes P5
20		update: T2 writes P3
30		T2 commit
40		T2 end
50		update: T3 writes P1
60		update: T3 writes P3
		CRASH, RESTART

Figure 18.1   Execution History with a Crash

is restarted, the Analysis phase identifies $T1$ and $T3$ as transactions that were active at the time of the crash, and therefore to be undone; $T2$ as a committed transaction, and all its actions, therefore, to be written to disk; and $P1$, $P3$ and $P5$ as potentially dirty pages. All the updates (including those of $T1$ and $T3$) are reapplied in the order shown during the Redo phase. Finally, the actions of $T1$ and $T3$ are undone in reverse order during the Undo phase; that is, $T3$'s write of $P3$ is undone, $T3$'s write of $P1$ is undone, and then $T1$'s write of $P5$ is undone.

There are three main principles behind the ARIES recovery algorithm:

■ **Write-Ahead Logging:** Any change to a database object is first recorded in the log; the record in the log must be written to stable storage before the change to the database object is written to disk.

■ **Repeating History during Redo:** Upon restart following a crash, ARIES retraces all actions of the DBMS prior to the crash and brings the system back to the exact state that it was in at the time of the crash. Then, it undoes the actions of transactions that were still active at the time of the crash (effectively aborting them).

■ **Logging Changes during Undo:** Changes made to the database while undoing a transaction are logged in order to ensure that such an action is not repeated in the event of repeated (failures causing) restarts.

The second point distinguishes ARIES from other recovery algorithms and is the basis for much of its simplicity and flexibility. In particular, ARIES can support concurrency control protocols that involve locks of finer granularity than a page (e.g., record-level locks). The second and third points are also important in dealing with operations such that redoing and undoing the operation are not exact inverses of each other. We discuss the interaction between concurrency control and crash recovery in Section 18.5, where we also discuss other approaches to recovery briefly.

18.2.1   The Log

The log, sometimes called the **trail** or **journal**, is a history of actions executed by the DBMS. Physically, the log is a file of records stored in stable storage, which is assumed to survive crashes; this durability can be achieved by maintaining two or more copies of the log on different disks (perhaps in different locations), so that the chance of all copies of the log being simultaneously lost is negligibly small.

The most recent portion of the log, called the **log tail**, is kept in main memory and is periodically forced to stable storage. This way, log records and data records are written to disk at the same granularity (pages or sets of pages).

Every **log record** is given a unique *id* called the **log sequence number (LSN)**. As with any record id, we can fetch a log record with one disk access given the LSN. Further, LSNs should be assigned in monotonically increasing order; this property is required for the ARIES recovery algorithm. If the log is a sequential file, in principle growing indefinitely, the LSN can simply be the address of the first byte of the log record.[2]

---

[2] In practice, various techniques are used to identify portions of the log that are 'too old' to ever be needed again, in order to bound the amount of stable storage used for the log. Given

For recovery purposes, every page in the database contains the LSN of the most recent log record that describes a change to this page. This LSN is called the **pageLSN**.

A log record is written for each of the following actions:

- **Updating a Page**: After modifying the page, an *update* type record (described later in this section) is appended to the log tail. The pageLSN of the page is then set to the LSN of the update log record. (The page must be pinned in the buffer pool while these actions are carried out.)

- **Commit**: When a transaction decides to commit, it **force-writes** a *commit* type log record containing the transaction id. That is, the log record is appended to the log, and the log tail is written to stable storage, up to and including the commit record.[3] The transaction is considered to have committed at the instant that its commit log record is written to stable storage. (Some additional steps must be taken, e.g., removing the transaction's entry in the transaction table; these follow the writing of the commit log record.)

- **Abort**: When a transaction is aborted, an *abort* type log record containing the transaction id is appended to the log, and Undo is initiated for this transaction (Section 18.3.3).

- **End**: As noted above, when a transaction is aborted or committed, some additional actions must be taken beyond writing the abort or commit log record. After all these additional steps are completed, an *end* type log record containing the transaction id is appended to the log.

- **Undoing an Update:** When a transaction is rolled back (because the transaction is aborted, or during recovery from a crash), its updates are undone. When the action described by an update log record is undone, a *compensation log record*, or CLR, is written.

Every log record has certain fields: **prevLSN**, **transID**, and **type**. The set of all log records for a given transaction is maintained as a linked list going back in time, using the **prevLSN** field; this list must be updated whenever a log record is added. The transID field is the id of the transaction generating the log record, and the type field obviously indicates the type of the log record.

Additional fields depend on the type of the log record. We have already mentioned the additional contents of the various log record types, with the exception of the update and compensation log record types, which we describe next.

---

such a bound, the log may be implemented as a 'circular' file, in which case the LSN may be the log record id plus a *wrap-count*.

[3]Note that this step requires the buffer manager to be able to selectively *force* pages to stable storage.

Update Log Records

The fields in an **update** log record are illustrated in Figure 18.2. The **pageID**

| prevLSN | transID | type | pageID | length | offset | before-image | after-image |

Fields common to all log records   Additional fields for update log records

Figure 18.2   Contents of an Update Log Record

field is the page id of the modified page; the length in bytes and the offset of the change are also included. The **before-image** is the value of the changed bytes before the change; the **after-image** is the value after the change. An update log record that contains both before- and after-images can be used to redo the change and to undo it. In certain contexts, which we will not discuss further, we can recognize that the change will never be undone (or, perhaps, redone). A **redo-only update** log record will contain just the after-image; similarly a **undo-only update** record will contain just the before-image.

Compensation Log Records

A **compensation log record (CLR)** is written just before the change recorded in an update log record U is undone. (Such an undo can happen during normal system execution when a transaction is aborted, or during recovery from a crash.) A compensation log record C describes the action taken to undo the actions recorded in the corresponding update log record, and is appended to the log tail just like any other log record. The compensation log record C also contains a field called **undoNextLSN**, which is the LSN of the next log record that is to be undone for the transaction that wrote update record U; this field in C is set to the value of prevLSN in U.

As an example, consider the fourth update log record shown in Figure 18.3. If this update is undone, a CLR would be written, and the information in it would include the transID, pageID, length, offset, and before-image fields from the update record. Notice that the CLR records the (undo) action of changing the affected bytes back to the before-image value; thus this value and the location of the affected bytes constitute the redo information for the action described by the CLR. The undoNextLSN field is set to the LSN of the first log record in Figure 18.3.

Unlike an update log record, a CLR describes an action that will never be *undone*, that is, we never undo an undo action. The reason is simple: an update log record describes a change made by a transaction during normal execution and the transaction may subsequently be aborted, whereas a CLR describes an action taken to rollback a transaction for which the decision to abort has already been made. Thus the transaction *must* be rolled back, and the undo action described by the CLR is definitely required. This observation is very useful because it bounds the amount of space needed for the log during restart from a crash: the number of CLRs that can be written during Undo is no more than the number of update log records for active transactions at the time of the crash.

It may well happen that a CLR is written to stable storage (following WAL, of course) but that the undo action that it describes is not yet written to disk when the system crashes again. In this case the undo action described in the CLR is reapplied during the Redo phase, just like the action described in update log records.

For these reasons, a CLR contains the information needed to reapply, or redo, the change described, but not to reverse it.

18.2.2 Other Recovery-Related Data Structures

In addition to the log, the following two tables contain important recovery-related information:

- **Transaction Table:** This table contains one entry for each active transaction. The entry contains (among other things) the transaction id, the status, and a field called **lastLSN**, which is the LSN of the most recent log record for this transaction. The **status** of a transaction can be that it is in progress, is committed, or is aborted. (In the latter two cases, the transaction will be removed from the table once certain 'clean up' steps are completed.)

- **Dirty Page Table:** This table contains one entry for each dirty page in the buffer pool, that is, each page with changes that are not yet reflected on disk. The entry contains a field **recLSN**, which is the LSN of the first log record that caused the page to become dirty. Note that this LSN identifies the earliest log record that might have to be redone for this page during restart from a crash.

During normal operation, these are maintained by the transaction manager and the buffer manager, respectively, and during restart after a crash, these tables are reconstructed in the Analysis phase of restart.

Consider the following simple example. Transaction $T1000$ changes the value of bytes 21 to 23 on page $P500$ from 'ABC' to 'DEF', transaction $T2000$ changes 'HIJ' to 'KLM' on page $P600$, transaction $T2000$ changes bytes 20 through 22 from 'GDE' to 'QRS' on page $P500$, then transaction $T1000$ changes 'TUV' to

'WXY' on page $P505$. The dirty page table, the transaction table[4] and the log at this instant are shown in Figure 18.3. Observe that the log is shown growing

pageID	recLSN		prevLSN	transID	type	pageID	length	offset	before-image	after-image
P500				T1000	update	P500	3	21	ABC	DEF
P600				T2000	update	P600	3	41	HIJ	KLM
P505				T2000	update	P500	3	20	GDE	QRS
				T1000	update	P505	3	21	TUV	WXY

DIRTY PAGE TABLE

transID	lastLSN
T1000	
T2000	

TRANSACTION TABLE

LOG

Figure 18.3 Instance of Log and Transaction Table

from top to bottom; older records are at the top. Although the records for each transaction are linked together using the prevLSN field, the log as a whole also has a sequential order that is important—for example, $T2000$'s change to page $P500$ follows $T1000$'s change to page $P500$, and in the event of a crash, these changes must be redone in the same order.

18.2.3 The Write-Ahead Log Protocol

Before writing a page to disk, every update log record that describes a change to this page must be forced to stable storage. This is accomplished by forcing all log records up to and including the one with LSN equal to the pageLSN to stable storage before writing the page to disk.

The importance of the WAL protocol cannot be overemphasized—WAL is the fundamental rule that ensures that a record of every change to the database is available while attempting to recover from a crash. If a transaction made a change and committed, the no-force approach means that some of these changes may not have been written to disk at the time of a subsequent crash. Without a record of these changes, there would be no way to ensure that the changes of a committed transaction survive crashes. Note that the definition of a *committed transaction* is effectively "a transaction whose log records, including a commit record, have all been written to stable storage"!

Observe that when a transaction is committed, the log tail is forced to stable storage, even if a no-force approach is being used. It is worth contrasting this

---

[4] The status field is not shown in the figure for space reasons; all transactions are in progress.

operation with the actions taken under a force approach: If a force approach is used, all the pages modified by the transaction, rather than a portion of the log that includes all its records, must be forced to disk when the transaction commits. The set of all changed pages is typically much larger than the log tail because the size of an update log record is close to (twice) the size of the changed bytes, which is likely to be much smaller than the page size. Further, the log is maintained as a sequential file, and thus all writes to the log are sequential writes. Consequently, the cost of forcing the log tail is much smaller than the cost of writing all changed pages to disk.

18.2.4   Checkpointing

A **checkpoint** is like a snapshot of the DBMS state, and by taking checkpoints periodically, as we will see, the DBMS can reduce the amount of work to be done during restart in the event of a subsequent crash.

Checkpointing in ARIES has three steps. First, a **begin_checkpoint** record is written to indicate when the checkpoint starts. Second, an **end_checkpoint** record is constructed, including in it the current contents of the transaction table and the dirty page table, and appended to the log. The third step is carried out after the **end_checkpoint** record is written to stable storage: a special **master** record containing the LSN of the *begin_checkpoint* log record is written to a known place on stable storage. While the end_checkpoint record is being constructed, the DBMS continues executing transactions and writing other log records; the only guarantee we have is that the transaction table and dirty page table are accurate *as of the time of the begin_checkpoint record.*

This kind of checkpoint is called a **fuzzy checkpoint**, and is inexpensive because it does not require quiescing the system or writing out pages in the buffer pool (unlike some other forms of checkpointing). On the other hand, the effectiveness of this checkpointing technique is limited by the earliest recLSN of pages in the dirty pages table, because during restart we must redo changes starting from the log record whose LSN is equal to this recLSN. Having a background process that periodically writes dirty pages to disk helps to limit this problem.

When the system comes back up after a crash, the restart process begins by locating the most recent checkpoint record. For uniformity, the system always begins normal execution by taking a checkpoint, in which the transaction table and dirty page table are both empty.

18.3 RECOVERING FROM A SYSTEM CRASH *

When the system is restarted after a crash, the recovery manager proceeds in three phases, as shown in Figure 18.4.

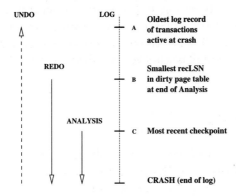

Figure 18.4 Three Phases of Restart in ARIES

The Analysis phase begins by examining the most recent begin_checkpoint record, whose LSN is denoted as C in Figure 18.4, and proceeds forward in the log until the last log record. The Redo phase follows Analysis, and redoes all changes to any page that might have been dirty at the time of the crash; this set of pages and the starting point for Redo (the smallest recLSN of any dirty page) are determined during Analysis. The Undo phase follows Redo, and undoes the changes of all transactions that were active at the time of the crash; again, this set of transactions is identified during the Analysis phase. Notice that Redo reapplies changes in the order in which they were originally carried out; Undo reverses changes in the opposite order, reversing the most recent change first.

Observe that the relative order of the three points A, B and C in the log may differ from that shown in Figure 18.4. The three phases of restart are described in more detail in the following sections.

18.3.1 Analysis Phase

The **Analysis** phase performs three tasks:

1. It determines the point in the log at which to start the Redo pass.

2. It determines (a conservative superset of the) pages in the buffer pool that were dirty at the time of the crash.

3. It identifies transactions that were active at the time of the crash, and must therefore be undone.

Analysis begins by examining the most recent begin_checkpoint log record and initializing the dirty page table and transaction table to the copies of those structures in the next end_checkpoint record. Thus these tables are initialized to the set of dirty pages and active transactions at the time of the checkpoint. (If there are additional log records between the begin_checkpoint and end_checkpoint records, the tables must be adjusted to reflect the information in these records, but we omit the details of this step. See Exercise 18.9.) Analysis then scans the log in the forward direction until it reaches the end of the log:

- If an end log record for a transaction T is encountered, T is removed from the transaction table because it is no longer active.

- If a log record other than an end record for a transaction T is encountered, an entry for T is added to the transaction table if it is not already there. Further, the entry for T is modified:

  1. The lastLSN field is set to the LSN of this log record.
  2. If the log record is a commit record, the status is set to C, otherwise it is set to U (indicating that it is to be undone).

- If a redoable log record affecting page P is encountered, and P is not in the dirty page table, an entry is inserted into this table with page id P and recLSN equal to the LSN of this redoable log record. This LSN identifies the oldest change affecting page P that may not have been written to disk.

At the end of the Analysis phase, the transaction table contains an accurate list of all transactions that were active at the time of the crash—this is the set of transactions with status U. The dirty page table includes all pages that were dirty at the time of the crash, but may also contain some pages that were written to disk. If an *end_write* log record were written at the completion of each write operation, the dirty page table constructed during Analysis could be made more accurate, but in ARIES, the additional cost of writing end_write log records is not considered to be worth the gain.

As an example, consider the execution illustrated in Figure 18.3. Let us extend this execution by assuming that $T2000$ commits, then $T1000$ modifies another page, say, $P700$, and appends an update record to the log tail, and then the system crashes (before this update log record is written to stable storage).

The dirty page table and the transaction table, held in memory, are lost in the crash. The most recent checkpoint is the one that was taken at the beginning of the execution, with an empty transaction table and dirty page table; it is not shown in Figure 18.3. After examining this log record, which we assume is just before the first log record shown in the figure, Analysis initializes the two tables to be empty. Scanning forward in the log, $T1000$ is added to the transaction table;

in addition, $P500$ is added to the dirty page table with recLSN equal to the LSN of the first shown log record. Similarly, $T2000$ is added to the transaction table and $P600$ is added to the dirty page table. There is no change based on the third log record, and the fourth record results in the addition of $P505$ to the dirty page table. The commit record for $T2000$ (not in the figure) is now encountered, and $T2000$ is therefore removed from the transaction table.

The Analysis phase is now complete, and it is recognized that the only active transaction at the time of the crash is $T1000$, with lastLSN equal to the LSN of the fourth record in Figure 18.3. The dirty page table reconstructed in the Analysis phase is identical to that shown in the figure. The update log record for the change to $P700$ is lost in the crash, and is not seen during the Analysis pass. Thanks to the WAL protocol, however, all is well—the corresponding change to page $P700$ cannot have been written to disk either!

Observe that some of the updates may indeed have been written to disk; for concreteness, let us assume that the change to $P600$ (and only this update) was written to disk before the crash. Thus $P600$ is not dirty, yet it is included in the dirty page table. The pageLSN on page $P600$, however, reflects the write because it is now equal to the LSN of the third update log record shown in Figure 18.3.

18.3.2 Redo Phase

During the **Redo** phase, ARIES reapplies the updates of *all* transactions, committed or otherwise. Further, if a transaction was aborted before the crash and its updates were undone, as indicated by CLRs, the actions described in the CLRs are also reapplied. This **repeating history** paradigm distinguishes ARIES from other proposed WAL-based recovery algorithms and causes the database to be brought to the same state that it was in at the time of the crash.

The Redo phase begins with the log record that has the smallest recLSN of all pages in the dirty page table constructed by the Analysis pass, because this log record identifies the oldest update that may not have been written to disk prior to the crash. Starting from this log record, Redo scans forward until the end of the log. For each redoable log record (update or CLR) encountered, Redo checks whether the logged action must be redone. The action must be redone unless one of the following conditions holds:

- The affected page is not in the dirty page table, or

- The affected page is in the dirty page table, but the recLSN for the entry is *greater than* the LSN of the log record being checked, or

- The pageLSN (stored on the page, which must be retrieved to check this condition) is *greater than or equal* to the LSN of the log record being checked.

The first condition obviously means that all changes to this page have been written to disk. Because the recLSN is the first update to this page that may not have been written to disk, the second condition means that the update being checked was indeed propagated to disk. The third condition, which is checked last because it requires us to retrieve the page, also ensures that the update being checked was written to disk, because either this update or a later update to the page was written. (Recall our assumption that a write to a page is atomic; this assumption is important here!)

If the logged action must be redone:

1. The logged action is reapplied.

2. The pageLSN on the page is set to the LSN of the redone log record. No additional log record is written at this time.

Let us continue with the example discussed in Section 18.3.1. From the dirty page table, the smallest recLSN is seen to be the LSN of the first log record shown in Figure 18.3. Clearly the changes recorded by earlier log records (there happen to be none in this example) have all been written to disk. Now, Redo fetches the affected page, $P500$, and compares the LSN of this log record with the pageLSN on the page, and, because we assumed that this page was not written to disk before the crash, finds that the pageLSN is less. The update is therefore reapplied; bytes 21 through 23 are changed to 'DEF', and the pageLSN is set to the LSN of this update log record.

Redo then examines the second log record. Again, the affected page, $P600$, is fetched and the pageLSN is compared to the LSN of the update log record. In this case, because we assumed that $P600$ was written to disk before the crash, they are equal, and the update does not have to be redone.

The remaining log records are processed similarly, bringing the system back to the exact state it was at the time of the crash. Notice that the first two conditions indicating that a redo is unnecessary never hold in this example. Intuitively, they come into play when the dirty page table contains a very old recLSN, going back to before the most recent checkpoint. In this case, as Redo scans forward from the log record with this LSN, it will encounter log records for pages that were written to disk prior to the checkpoint, and were therefore not in the dirty page table in the checkpoint. Some of these pages may be dirtied again after the checkpoint; nonetheless, the updates to these pages prior to the checkpoint need not be redone. Although the third condition alone is sufficient to recognize that these updates need not be redone, it requires us to fetch the affected page. The first two conditions allow us to recognize this situation without fetching the page. (The reader is encouraged to construct examples that illustrate the use of each of these conditions; see Exercise 18.8.)

At the end of the Redo phase, end type records are written for all transactions with status C, which are removed from the transaction table.

18.3.3 Undo Phase

The Undo phase, unlike the other two phases, scans backward from the end of the log. The goal of this phase is to undo the actions of all transactions there were active at the time of the crash, that is, to effectively abort them. This set of transactions is identified in the transaction table constructed by the Analysis phase.

The Undo Algorithm

Undo begins with the transaction table constructed by the Analysis phase, which identifies all transactions that were active at the time of the crash, and includes the LSN of the most recent log record (the lastLSN field) for each such transaction. Such transactions are called **loser transactions**. All actions of losers must be undone, and further, these actions must be undone in the reverse of the order in which they appear in the log.

Consider the set of lastLSN values for all loser transactions. Let us call this set **ToUndo**. Undo repeatedly chooses the largest (i.e., most recent) LSN value in this set and processes it, until ToUndo is empty. To process a log record:

1. If it is a CLR, and the undoNextLSN value is not *null*, the undoNextLSN value is added to the set ToUndo; if the undoNextLSN is *null*, an end record is written for the transaction because it is completely undone, and the CLR is discarded.

2. If it is an update record, a CLR is written and the corresponding action is undone, as described in Section 18.2.1, and the prevLSN value in the update log record is added to the set ToUndo.

When the set ToUndo is empty, the Undo phase is complete. Restart is now complete, and the system can proceed with normal operations.

Let us continue with the scenario discussed in Sections 18.3.1 and 18.3.2. The only active transaction at the time of the crash was determined to be $T1000$.

From the transaction table, we get the LSN of its most recent log record, which is the fourth update log record in Figure 18.3. The update is undone, and a CLR is written with undoNextLSN equal to the LSN of the first log record in the figure. The next record to be undone for transaction $T1000$ is the first log record in the figure. After this is undone, a CLR and an end log record for $T1000$ are written, and the Undo phase is complete.

Observe that in this example, undoing the action recorded in the first log record causes the action of the third log record, which is due to a committed transaction, to be overwritten and thereby lost! This situation arises because $T2000$ overwrote a data item written by $T1000$ while $T1000$ was still active; if Strict 2PL were followed, $T2000$ would not have been allowed to overwrite this data item.

Aborting a Transaction

Aborting a transaction is just a special case of the Undo phase of Restart in which a single transaction, rather than a set of transactions, is undone. The example in Figure 18.5, discussed next, illustrates this point.

Crashes during Restart

It is important to understand how the Undo algorithm presented in Section 18.3.3 handles repeated system crashes. Because the details of precisely how the action described in an update log record is undone are straightforward, we will discuss Undo in the presence of system crashes using an execution history, shown in Figure 18.5, that abstracts away unnecessary detail. This example illustrates how aborting a transaction is a special case of Undo, and how the use of CLRs ensures that the Undo action for an update log record is not applied twice.

The log shows the order in which the DBMS executed various actions; notice that the LSNs are in ascending order, and that each log record for a transaction has a prevLSN field that points to the previous log record for that transaction. We have not shown *null* prevLSNs, that is, some special value used in the prevLSN field of the first log record for a transaction to indicate that there is no previous log record. We have also compacted the figure by occasionally displaying two log records on a single line.

Log record (with LSN) 30 indicates that $T1$ aborts. All actions of this transaction should be undone in reverse order, and the only action of $T1$, described by the update log record 10, is indeed undone as indicated by CLR 40.

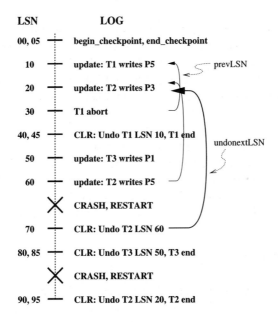

LSN	LOG
00, 05	begin_checkpoint, end_checkpoint
10	update: T1 writes P5
20	update: T2 writes P3
30	T1 abort
40, 45	CLR: Undo T1 LSN 10, T1 end
50	update: T3 writes P1
60	update: T2 writes P5
	CRASH, RESTART
70	CLR: Undo T2 LSN 60
80, 85	CLR: Undo T3 LSN 50, T3 end
	CRASH, RESTART
90, 95	CLR: Undo T2 LSN 20, T2 end

prevLSN

undonextLSN

Figure 18.5 Example of Undo with Repeated Crashes

After the first crash, Analysis identifies $P1$ (with recLSN 50), $P3$ (with recLSN 20) and $P5$ (with recLSN 10) as dirty pages. Log record 45 shows that $T1$ is a completed transaction; thus the transaction table identifies $T2$ (with lastLSN 60) and $T3$ (with lastLSN 50) as active at the time of the crash. The Redo phase begins with log record 10, which is the minimum recLSN in the dirty page table, and reapplies all actions (for the update and CLR records), as per the Redo algorithm presented in Section 18.3.2.

The ToUndo set consists of LSNs 60, for $T2$, and 50, for $T3$. The Undo phase now begins by processing the log record with LSN 60 because 60 is the largest LSN in the ToUndo set. The update is undone, and a CLR (with LSN 70) is written to the log. This CLR has undoNextLSN equal to 20, which is the prevLSN value in log record 60; 20 is the next action to be undone for $T2$. Now the largest remaining LSN in the ToUndo set is 50. The write corresponding to log record 50 is now undone, and a CLR describing the change is written. This CLR has LSN 80, and its undoNextLSN field is *null* because 50 is the only log record for transaction $T3$. Thus $T3$ is completely undone, and an end record is written. Log records 70, 80 and 85 are written to stable storage before the system crashes a second time; however, the changes described by these records may not have been written to disk.

When the system is restarted after the second crash, Analysis determines that the only active transaction at the time of the crash was $T2$; in addition, the dirty page table is identical to what it was during the previous restart. Log records 10 through 85 are processed again during Redo. (If some of the changes made during the previous Redo were written to disk, the pageLSNs on the affected pages are used to detect this situation and avoid writing these pages again.) The Undo phase considers the only LSN in the ToUndo set, 70, and processes it by adding the undoNextLSN value (20) to the ToUndo set. Next, log record 20 is processed by undoing $T2$'s write of page $P3$, and a CLR is written (LSN 90). Because 20 is the first of $T2$'s log records—and therefore, the last of its records to be undone—the undoNextLSN field in this CLR is *null*, an end record is written for $T2$, and the ToUndo set is now empty.

Recovery is now complete, and normal execution can resume with the writing of a checkpoint record.

This example illustrated repeated crashes during the Undo phase. For completeness, let us consider what happens if the system crashes while Restart is in the Analysis or Redo phases. If a crash occurs during the Analysis phase, all the work done in this phase is lost, and on restart the Analysis phase starts afresh with the same information as before. If a crash occurs during the Redo phase, the only effect that survives the crash is that some of the changes made during Redo may have been written to disk prior to the crash. Restart starts again with the Analysis phase and then the Redo phase, and some update log records that were redone the first time around will not be redone a second time because the pageLSN will now be equal to the update record's LSN (although the pages will have to fetched again to detect this).

We can take checkpoints during Restart to minimize repeated work in the event of a crash, but we will not discuss this point.

18.4 MEDIA RECOVERY *

Media recovery is based on periodically making a copy of the database. Because copying a large database object such as a file can take a long time, and the DBMS must be allowed to continue with its operations in the meantime, creating a copy is handled in a manner similar to taking a fuzzy checkpoint.

When a database object such as a file or a page is corrupted, the copy of that object is brought up-to-date by using the log to identify and reapply the changes of committed transactions and undo the changes of uncommitted transactions (as of the time of the media recovery operation).

To minimize the work in reapplying changes of committed transactions, the begin_checkpoint LSN of the most recent complete checkpoint is recorded along with the copy of the database object. Let us compare the smallest recLSN of a dirty page in the corresponding end_checkpoint record with the LSN of the begin_checkpoint record and call the smaller of these two LSNs I. We observe that the actions recorded in all log records with LSNs less than I must be reflected in the copy. Thus only log records with LSNs greater than I need to be reapplied to the copy.

Finally, the updates of transactions that are incomplete at the time of media recovery or that were aborted after the fuzzy copy was completed need to be undone to ensure that the page reflects only the actions of committed transactions. The set of such transactions can be identified as in the Analysis pass, and we omit the details.

18.5 OTHER ALGORITHMS AND INTERACTION WITH CONCURRENCY CONTROL *

ARIES is a fairly recent algorithm, and there are other recovery algorithms that we have not discussed. Like ARIES, the most popular alternatives also maintain a log of database actions according to WAL protocol. A major distinction between ARIES and these variants is that the Redo phase in ARIES *repeats history*, that is, redoes the actions of *all* transactions, not just the non losers. Other algorithms redo only the non losers, and the Redo phase follows the Undo phase, in which the actions of losers are rolled back.

Thanks to the repeating history paradigm and the use of CLRs, ARIES is able to support fine-granularity locks (record-level locks) and logging of logical operations, rather than just byte-level modifications. For example, consider a transaction T that inserts a data entry 15* into a B+ tree index. Between the time this insert is done and the time that T is eventually aborted, other transactions may also insert and delete entries from the tree. If record-level locks are set, rather than page-level locks, it is possible that the entry 15* is on a different physical page when T aborts from the one that T inserted it into. In this case the undo operation for the insert of 15* must be recorded in logical terms because the physical (byte-level) actions involved in undoing this operation are not the inverse of the physical actions involved in inserting the entry.

Logging logical operations yields considerably higher concurrency, although the use of fine-granularity locks can lead to increased locking activity (because more locks must be set). Thus there is a trade-off between different WAL-based recovery schemes, although we have chosen to cover ARIES because it has several attractive properties.

One of the earliest recovery algorithms, used in the System R prototype at IBM, takes a very different approach. There is no logging and, of course, no WAL protocol. Instead, the database is treated as a collection of pages and accessed through a **page table**, which maps page ids to disk addresses. When a transaction makes changes to a data page, it actually makes a copy of the page, called the **shadow** of the page, and changes the shadow page. The transaction copies the appropriate part of the page table and changes the entry for the changed page to point to the shadow, so that it can see the changes; however, other transactions continue to see the original page table, and therefore the original page, until this transaction commits. Aborting a transaction is simple: just discard its shadow versions of the page table and the data pages. Committing a transaction involves making its version of the page table public and discarding the original data pages that are superseded by shadow pages.

This scheme suffers from a number of problems. First, data becomes highly fragmented due to the replacement of pages by shadow versions, which may be located far from the original page. This phenomenon reduces data clustering, and makes good garbage-collection imperative. Second, the scheme does not yield a sufficiently high degree of concurrency. Third, there is a substantial storage overhead due to the use of shadow pages. Fourth, the process aborting a transaction can itself run into deadlocks, and this situation must be specially handled because the semantics of aborting an abort transaction gets murky.

For these reasons, even in System R, shadow paging was eventually superseded by WAL-based recovery techniques.

18.6 SUMMARY

The recovery manager has the difficult job of restarting the system after a crash, rolling back the actions of incomplete transactions (to ensure transaction atomicity), and restoring the actions of committed transactions (to ensure transaction durability).

Current systems use recovery algorithms based on maintaining a log of database activity in accordance with the WAL protocol, which requires that each change to the database be logged to stable storage before the change itself is written to disk. We have studied ARIES, a WAL-based recovery algorithm, in detail, and seen how it successfully achieves the goals of recovery even in the presence of repeated crashes.

The recovery algorithm can limit the locking techniques available to the concurrency control mechanism. In particular, locks of finer granularity than a page can cause problems with a page-oriented recovery manager; one of the nice properties of ARIES is that it does indeed support such locks.

We have concentrated on recovery in a centralized DBMS. Additional issues must be addressed in the context of a distributed DBMS.

EXERCISES

Exercise 18.1 Briefly answer the following questions:

1. How does the recovery manager ensure atomicity of transactions? How does it ensure durability?

2. What is the difference between stable storage and disk?

3. What is the difference between a system crash and a media failure?

4. Explain the WAL protocol.

5. Describe the steal and no-force policies.

Exercise 18.2 Briefly answer the following questions:

1. What are the properties required of LSNs?

2. What are the fields in an update log record? Explain the use of each field.

3. What are redoable log records?

4. What are the differences between update log records and CLRs?

Exercise 18.3 Briefly answer the following questions:

1. What is the role of the Analysis, Redo and Undo phases in ARIES?

2. Consider the execution shown in Figure 18.6.

   (a) What is done during Analysis? (Be precise about the points at which Analysis begins and ends and describe the contents of any tables constructed in this phase.)

   (b) What is done during Redo? (Be precise about the points at which Redo begins and ends.)

   (c) What is done during Undo? (Be precise about the points at which Undo begins and ends.)

Exercise 18.4 Consider the execution shown in Figure 18.7.

1. Extend the figure to show prevLSN and undonextLSN values.

2. Describe the actions taken to rollback transaction $T2$.

3. Show the log after $T2$ is rolled back, including all prevLSN and undonextLSN values in log records.

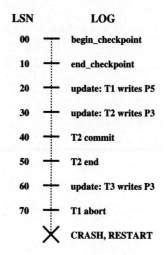

LSN	LOG
00	begin_checkpoint
10	end_checkpoint
20	update: T1 writes P5
30	update: T2 writes P3
40	T2 commit
50	T2 end
60	update: T3 writes P3
70	T1 abort
	CRASH, RESTART

Figure 18.6   Execution with a Crash

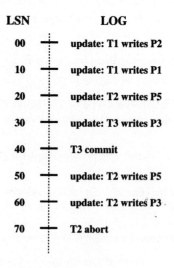

LSN	LOG
00	update: T1 writes P2
10	update: T1 writes P1
20	update: T2 writes P5
30	update: T3 writes P3
40	T3 commit
50	update: T2 writes P5
60	update: T2 writes P3
70	T2 abort

Figure 18.7   Aborting a Transaction

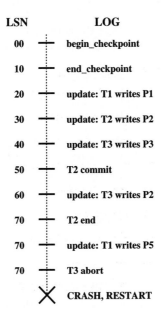

LSN	LOG
00	begin_checkpoint
10	end_checkpoint
20	update: T1 writes P1
30	update: T2 writes P2
40	update: T3 writes P3
50	T2 commit
60	update: T3 writes P2
70	T2 end
70	update: T1 writes P5
70	T3 abort
	CRASH, RESTART

Figure 18.8 Execution with Multiple Crashes

Exercise 18.5 Consider the execution shown in Figure 18.8. In addition, the system crashes during recovery after writing two log records to stable storage and again after writing another two log records.

1. What is the value of the LSN stored in the master log record?
2. What is done during Analysis?
3. What is done during Redo?
4. What is done during Undo?
5. Show the log when recovery is complete, including all non-null prevLSN and undonextLSN values in log records.

Exercise 18.6 Briefly answer the following questions:

1. How is checkpointing done in ARIES?
2. Checkpointing can also be done as follows: Quiesce the system so that only checkpointing activity can be in progress, write out copies of all dirty pages, and include the dirty page table and transaction table in the checkpoint record. What are the pros and cons of this approach versus the checkpointing approach of ARIES?
3. What happens if a second begin_checkpoint record is encountered during the Analysis phase?
4. Can a second end_checkpoint record be encountered during the Analysis phase?
5. Why is the use of CLRs important for the use of undo actions that are not the physical inverse of the original update?

6. Give an example that illustrates how the paradigm of repeating history and the use of CLRs allow ARIES to support locks of finer granularity than a page.

Exercise 18.7 Briefly answer the following questions:

1. If the system fails repeatedly during recovery, what is the maximum number of log records that can be written (as a function of the number of update and other log records written before the crash) before restart completes successfully?

2. What is the oldest log record that we need to retain?

3. If a bounded amount of stable storage is used for the log, how can we ensure that there is always enough stable storage to hold all log records written during restart?

Exercise 18.8 Consider the three conditions under which a redo is unnecessary (Section 18.3.2).

1. Why is it cheaper to test the first two conditions?

2. Describe an execution that illustrates the use of the first condition.

3. Describe an execution that illustrates the use of the second condition.

Exercise 18.9 The description in Section 18.3.1 of the Analysis phase made the simplifying assumption that no log records appeared between the begin_checkpoint and end_checkpoint records for the most recent complete checkpoint. The following questions explore how such records should be handled.

1. Explain the reason why log records could be written between the begin_checkpoint and end_checkpoint records.

2. Describe how the Analysis phase could be modified to handle such records.

3. Consider the execution shown in Figure 18.9. Show the contents of the end_checkpoint record.

4. Illustrate your modified Analysis phase on the execution shown in Figure 18.9.

Exercise 18.10 Answer the following questions briefly:

1. Explain how media recovery is handled in ARIES.

2. What are the pros and cons of using fuzzy dumps for media recovery?

3. What are the similarities and differences between checkpoints and fuzzy dumps?

4. Contrast ARIES with other WAL-based recovery schemes.

5. Contrast ARIES with shadow-page based recovery.

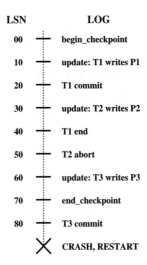

LSN	LOG
00	begin_checkpoint
10	update: T1 writes P1
20	T1 commit
30	update: T2 writes P2
40	T1 end
50	T2 abort
60	update: T3 writes P3
70	end_checkpoint
80	T3 commit
	CRASH, RESTART

Figure 18.9 Log Records between Checkpoint Records

BIBLIOGRAPHIC NOTES

Our discussion of the ARIES recovery algorithm is based on [389]. [199] is a survey article that contains a very readable, short description of ARIES. [386, 390] also discuss ARIES. Fine-granularity locking increases concurrency but at the cost of more locking activity; [387] suggests a technique based on LSNs for alleviating this problem. [322] presents a formal verification of ARIES.

[242] is an excellent survey that provides a broader treatment of recovery algorithms than our coverage, in which we have chosen to concentrate on one particular algorithm. [13] considers performance of concurrency control and recovery algorithms, taking into account their interactions. The impact of recovery on concurrency control is also discussed in [566]. [449] contains a performance analysis of various recovery techniques. [172] compares recovery techniques for main memory database systems, which are optimized for the case that most of the active data set fits in main memory. [233]Reuter A. provides an encyclopedic treatment of transaction processing.

[337] presents a description of a recovery algorithm based on write-ahead logging in which 'loser' transactions are first undone and then (only) transactions that committed before the crash are redone. Shadow paging is described in [351, 232]. A scheme that uses a combination of shadow paging and in-place updating is described in [448].

PARALLEL AND DISTRIBUTED DATABASES

> No man is an island, entire of itself; every man is a piece of the continent, a part of the main.

> —John Donne

We have thus far considered centralized database management systems, in which all the data is maintained at a single site, and assumed that the processing of individual transactions is essentially sequential. One of the most important trends in databases is the increased use of parallel evaluation techniques and data distribution. There are four distinct motivations:

- **Performance:** Using several resources (e.g., CPUs and disks) in parallel can significantly improve performance.

- **Increased availability:** If a site containing a relation goes down, the relation continues to be available if a copy is maintained at another site.

- **Distributed access to data:** An organization may have branches in several cities. Although analysts may need to access data corresponding to different sites, we usually find locality in the access patterns (e.g., a bank manager is likely to look up the accounts of customers at the local branch), and this locality can be exploited by distributing the data accordingly.

- **Analysis of distributed data:** Organizations increasingly want to examine all the data available to them, even when it is stored across multiple sites and on multiple database systems. Support for such integrated access involves many issues; even enabling access to widely distributed data can be a challenge.

A **parallel database system** is one that seeks to improve performance through parallel implementation of various operations such as loading data, building indexes and evaluating queries. Although data may be stored in a distributed fashion in such a system, the distribution is governed solely by performance considerations.

In a **distributed database system**, data is physically stored across several sites, and each site is typically managed by a DBMS that is capable of running independently of the other sites. The location of data items and the degree of autonomy of individual sites have a significant impact on all aspects of the system, including query optimization and processing, concurrency control, and recovery. In contrast to parallel databases, the distribution of data is governed by factors such as local ownership and increased availability, in addition to performance issues.

In this chapter we look at the issues of parallelism and data distribution in a DBMS. In Section 19.1 we discuss alternative hardware configurations for a parallel DBMS. In Section 19.2 we introduce the concept of data partitioning and consider its influence on parallel query evaluation. In Section 19.3 we show how data partitioning can be used to parallelize several relational operations. In Section 19.4 we conclude our treatment of parallel query processing with a discussion of parallel query optimization. The rest of the chapter is devoted to distributed databases. We begin by discussing some alternative architectures for a distributed DBMS in Section 19.6. We present an overview of distributed databases in Section 19.5 and describe options for distributing data in Section 19.7. In Section 19.9 we discuss query optimization and evaluation for distributed databases, in Section 19.10 we discuss updating distributed data, and finally, in Sections 19.12 and 19.13 we discuss distributed transaction management.

19.1 ARCHITECTURES FOR PARALLEL DATABASES

The basic idea behind parallel databases is to carry out evaluation steps in parallel whenever possible, in order to improve performance. There are many opportunities for parallelism in a DBMS; indeed, databases represent one of the most successful instances of parallel computing.

Three main architectures have been proposed for building parallel DBMSs. In a **shared-memory** system, multiple CPUs are attached to an interconnection network, and can access a common region of main memory. In a **shared-disk** system, each CPU has a private memory and direct access to all disks through an interconnection network. In a **shared-nothing** system, each CPU has local main memory and disk space, but no two CPUs can access the same storage area; all communication between CPUs is through a network connection. The three architectures are illustrated in Figure 19.1.

The shared memory architecture is closer to a conventional machine, and many commercial database systems have been ported to shared memory platforms with relative ease. Communication overheads are low, because main memory can be used for this purpose, and operating system services can be leveraged to utilize the additional CPUs. Although this approach is attractive for achieving moderate parallelism—a few tens of CPUs can be exploited in this fashion—memory con-

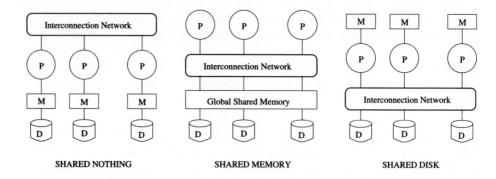

Figure 19.1   Physical Architectures for Parallel Database Systems

tention becomes a bottleneck as the number of CPUs increases. The shared-disk architecture faces a similar problem because large amounts of data are shipped through the interconnection network.

The basic problem with the shared-memory and shared-disk architectures is **interference**: As more CPUs are added, existing CPUs are slowed down because of the increased contention for memory accesses and network bandwidth. It has been noted that even an average 1% slow-down per additional CPU means that the maximum speedup is a factor of 37, and adding additional CPUs actually slows down the system; a system with 1000 CPUs is only 4% as effective as a *single CPU* system! This observation has motivated the development of the shared-nothing architecture, which is now widely considered to be the best architecture for large parallel database systems.

The shared-nothing architecture requires more extensive reorganization of the DBMS code, but it has been shown to provide linear **speed-up**, in that the time taken for operations decreases in proportion to the increase in the number of CPUs and disks, and linear **scale-up**, in that performance is sustained if the number of CPUs and disks are increased in proportion to the amount of data. Consequently, ever-more powerful parallel database systems can be built by taking advantage of rapidly improving performance for single CPU systems and connecting as many CPUs as desired.

Speed-up and scale-up are illustrated in Figure 19.2. The speed-up curves show how, for a fixed database size, more transactions can be executed per second by adding CPUs. The scale-up curves show how adding more resources (in the form of CPUs) enables us to process larger problems. The first scale-up graph measures the number of transactions executed per second as the database size is increased and the number of CPUs is correspondingly increased. An alternative way to measure scale-up is to consider the time taken per transaction as more CPUs are added to process an increasing number of transactions per second; the goal here is to sustain the response time per transaction.

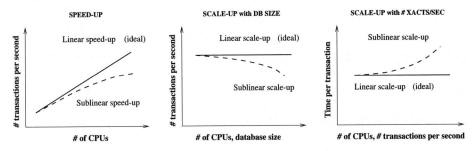

Figure 19.2 Speed-up and Scale-up

19.2 PARALLEL QUERY EVALUATION

In this section we discuss parallel evaluation of relational queries in a DBMS with a shared-nothing architecture. A relational query execution plan is a graph of relational algebra operators and the operators in a graph can be executed in parallel. If an operator consumes the output of a second operator, we have **pipelined parallelism** (the output of the second operator is worked on by the first operator as soon as it is generated); if not, the two operators can proceed essentially independently. Pipelined parallelism is limited by the presence of operators (e.g., sorting or aggregation) that *block*, or produce no output until they have consumed all their inputs.

In addition to evaluating different operators in parallel, we can evaluate each individual operator in a query plan in a parallel fashion. The key to evaluating an operator in parallel is to *partition* the input data; we can then work on each partition in parallel, and combine the results. This approach is called **data-partitioned parallel evaluation**. By exercising some care, existing code for sequentially evaluating relational operators can be ported easily for data-partitioned parallel evaluation.

An important observation, which explains why shared-nothing parallel database systems have been very successful, is that database query evaluation is very amenable to data-partitioned parallel evaluation. The goal is to minimize data shipping by partitioning the data and by structuring the algorithms to do most of the processing at individual processors. (We use *processor* to refer to a CPU together with its local disk.)

We now consider data partitioning and parallelization of existing operator evaluation code in more detail.

19.2.1   Data Partitioning

Partitioning a large dataset across several disks enables us to exploit the I/O bandwidth of the disks by reading and writing them in parallel. There are several ways to horizontally partition a relation. We can assign tuples to processors in a round-robin fashion, we can use hashing, or we can assign tuples to processors by ranges of field values. If there are n processors, the ith tuple is assigned to processor $i \bmod n$ in **round-robin partitioning**. In **hash partitioning**, a hash function is applied to (selected fields of) a tuple to determine its processor. In **range partitioning**, tuples are sorted (conceptually), and n ranges are chosen for the sort key values so that each range contains roughly the same number of tuples; tuples in range i are assigned to processor i.

Round-robin partitioning is suitable for efficiently evaluating queries that access the entire relation. If only a subset of the tuples (e.g., those that satisfy the selection condition $age = 20$) is required, hash partitioning and range partitioning are better than round-robin partitioning because they enable us to access only those disks that contain matching tuples. (Of course, this statement assumes that the tuples are partitioned on the attributes in the selection condition; if $age = 20$ is specified, the tuples must be partitioned on age.) If range selections such as $15 < age < 25$ are specified, range partitioning is superior to hash partitioning because qualifying tuples are likely to be clustered together on a few processors. On the other hand, range partitioning can lead to **data skew**; that is, partitions with widely varying numbers of tuples across partitions or disks. Skew causes processors dealing with large partitions to become performance bottlenecks. Hash partitioning has the additional virtue that it keeps data evenly distributed even if the data grows and shrinks over time.

To reduce skew in range partitioning, the main question is how to choose the ranges by which tuples are distributed. One effective approach is to take samples from each processor, collect and sort all samples, and divide the sorted set of samples into equally sized subsets. If tuples are to be partitioned on age, the age ranges of the sampled subsets of tuples can be used as the basis for redistributing the entire relation.

19.2.2   Parallelizing Sequential Operator Evaluation Code

An elegant software architecture for parallel DBMSs enables us to readily parallelize existing code for sequentially evaluating a relational operator. The basic idea is to use parallel data streams. Streams (from different disks or the output of other operators) are *merged* as needed to provide the inputs for a relational operator, and the output of an operator is *split* as needed to parallelize subsequent processing.

A parallel evaluation plan consists of a dataflow network of relational, merge, and split operators. The merge and split operators should be able to buffer some data, and should be able to halt the operators producing their input data. They can then regulate the speed of the execution according to the execution speed of the operator that consumes their output.

As we will see, obtaining good parallel versions of algorithms for sequential operator evaluation requires careful consideration; there is no magic formula for taking sequential code and producing a parallel version. Good use of split and merge in a dataflow software architecture, however, can greatly reduce the effort of implementing parallel query evaluation algorithms, as we illustrate in Section 19.3.3.

19.3 PARALLELIZING INDIVIDUAL OPERATIONS

This section shows how various operations can be implemented in parallel in a shared-nothing architecture. We assume that each relation is horizontally partitioned across several disks, although this partitioning may or may not be appropriate for a given query. The evaluation of a query must take the initial partitioning criteria into account, and repartition if necessary.

19.3.1 Bulk Loading and Scanning

We begin with two simple operations: *scanning* a relation and *loading* a relation. Pages can be read in parallel while scanning a relation, and the retrieved tuples can then be merged, if the relation is partitioned across several disks. More generally, the idea also applies when retrieving all tuples that meet a selection condition. If hashing or range partitioning is used, selection queries can be answered by going to just those processors that contain relevant tuples.

A similar observation holds for bulk loading. Indeed, bulk loading a relation that has associated indexes can benefit even more from parallelism because any sorting of data entries required for building the indexes can also be done in parallel (see below).

19.3.2 Sorting

A simple idea is to let each CPU sort the part of the relation that is on its local disk, and to then merge these sorted sets of tuples. The degree of parallelism is likely to be limited by the merging phase.

A better idea is to first redistribute all tuples in the relation using range partitioning. For example, if we want to sort a collection of employee tuples by salary, salary values range from 10 to 210, and we have 20 processors, we could send all tuples with salary values in the range 10 to 20 to the first processor, all in the range 21 to 30 to the second processor, and so on. (Prior to the redistribution, while tuples are distributed across the processors, we cannot assume that they are distributed according to salary ranges.)

Each processor then sorts the tuples assigned to it, using some sequential sorting algorithm. For example, a processor can collect tuples until its memory is full, then sort these tuples and write out a run, until all incoming tuples have been written to such sorted runs on the local disk. These runs can then be merged to create the sorted vesion of the set of tuples assigned to this processor. The entire sorted relation can be retrieved by visiting the processors in an order corresponding to the ranges assigned to them and simply scanning the tuples.

The basic challenge in parallel sorting is to do the range partitioning so that each processor receives roughly the same number of tuples; otherwise, a processor that receives a disproportionately large number of tuples to sort becomes a bottleneck, and limits the scalability of the parallel sort. One good approach to range partitioning is to obtain a sample of the entire relation by taking samples at each processor that initially contains part of the relation. The (relatively small) sample is sorted and used to identify ranges with equal numbers of tuples. This set of range values, called a **splitting vector**, is then distributed to all processors and used to range partition the entire relation.

A particularly important application of parallel sorting is sorting the data entries in tree-structured indexes. Sorting data entries can significantly speed up the process of bulk-loading an index.

19.3.3 Joins

In this section we consider how the join operation can be parallelized. We present the basic idea behind the parallelization, and also illustrate the use of the merge and split operators described in Section 19.2.2. We focus on parallel hash join, which is widely used, and briefly outline how sort-merge join can be similarly parallelized. Other join algorithms can be parallelized as well, although not as effectively as these two algorithms.

Suppose that we want to join two relations, say, A and B, on the *age* attribute. We assume that they are initially distributed across several disks in some way that is not useful for the join operation, that is, the initial partitioning is not based on the join attribute. The basic idea for joining A and B in parallel is to decompose the join into a collection of k smaller joins. We can decompose the join by partitioning both A and B into a collection of k logical buckets or partitions. By using the same partitioning function for both A and B, we ensure that the union of the k smaller joins computes the join of A and B; this idea is similar to intuition behind the partitioning phase of sequential hash join, described in Section 12.5.3. Because A and B are initially distributed across several processors, the partitioning step can itself be done in parallel at these processors. At each processor, all local tuples are retrieved and hashed into one of k partitions, with the same hash function used at all sites, of course.

Alternatively, we can partition A and B by dividing the range of the join attribute *age* into k disjoint subranges, and placing A and B tuples into partitions according to the subrange to which their *age* values belong. For example, suppose that we have ten processors, the join attribute is *age*, with values from 0 to 100. Assuming uniform distribution, A and B tuples with $0 \leq age < 10$ go to processor 1, $10 \leq age < 20$ go to processor 2, and so on. This approach is likely to be more susceptible than hash partitioning to data skew (i.e., the number of tuples to be joined can vary widely across partitions), unless the subranges are carefully determined; we will not discuss how good subrange boundaries can be identified.

Having decided on a partitioning strategy, we can assign each partition to a processor and carry out a local join, using any join algorithm we want to locally. In this case the number of partitions k is chosen to be equal to the number of processors n that are available for carrying out the join, and during partitioning, each processor sends tuples in the ith partition to processor i. After partitioning, each processor joins the A and B tuples assigned to it. Each join process executes sequential join code, and receives input A and B tuples from several processors; a merge operator merges all incoming A tuples, and another merge operator merges all incoming B tuples. Depending on how we want to distribute the result of the join of A and B, the output of the join process may be split into several data streams. The network of operators for parallel join is shown in Figure 19.3; to simplify the figure, we assume that the processors doing the join are distinct from the processors that initially contain tuples of A and B.

If range partitioning is used, the algorithm outlined above leads to a parallel version of sort-merge join, with the advantage that the output is available in sorted order. If hash partitioning is used, we obtain a parallel version of hash join.

Improved Parallel Hash Join

A hash-based refinement of the approach offers improved performance. The main observation is that if A and B are very large, and the number of partitions k is

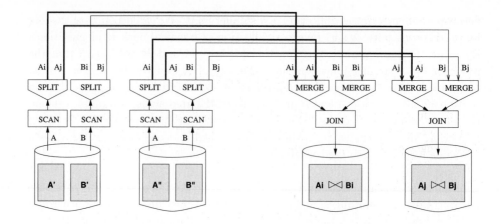

Figure 19.3   Dataflow Network of Operators for Parallel Join

chosen to be equal to the number of processors n, the size of each partition may still be large, leading to a high cost for each local join at the n processors.

An alternative is to execute the smaller joins $A_i \bowtie B_i$, for $i = 1 \dots k$, one after the other; but with each join executed in parallel using all processors. This approach allows us to utilize the total available main memory at all n processors in each join $A_i \bowtie B_i$, and is described in more detail as follows:

1. At each site, apply a hash function $h1$ to partition the A and B tuples at this site into partitions $i = 1 \dots k$. Let A be the smaller relation. The number of partitions k is chosen such that each partition of A fits into the *aggregate* or combined memory of all n processors.

2. For $i = 1 \dots k$, process the join of the ith partitions of A and B. To compute $A_i \bowtie B_i$, do the following at every site:
    (a) Apply a second hash function $h2$ to all A_i tuples to determine where they should be joined, and send tuple t to site $h2(t)$.
    (b) As A_i tuples arrive to be joined, add them to an in-memory hash table.
    (c) After all A_i tuples have been distributed, apply $h2$ to B_i tuples to determine where they should be joined, and send tuple t to site $h2(t)$.
    (d) As B_i tuples arrive to be joined, probe the in-memory table of A_i tuples and output result tuples.

The use of the second hash function $h2$ ensures that tuples are (more or less) uniformly distributed across all n processors participating in the join. This approach greatly reduces the cost for each of the smaller joins, and therefore reduces the overall join cost. Observe that all available processors are fully utilized, even though the smaller joins are carried out one after the other.

The reader is invited to adapt the network of operators shown in Figure 19.3 to reflect the improved parallel join algorithm.

19.4 PARALLEL QUERY OPTIMIZATION

In addition to parallelizing individual operations, we can obviously execute different operations in a query in parallel and execute multiple queries in parallel. Optimizing a single query for parallel execution has received more attention; systems typically optimize queries without regard to other queries that might be executing at the same time.

Two kinds of interoperation parallelism can be exploited within a query:

- The result of one operator can be pipelined into another. For example, consider a left-deep plan in which all the joins use index nested loops. The result of the first (i.e., the bottom-most) join is the outer relation tuples for the next join node. As tuples are produced by the first join, they can be used to probe the inner relation in the second join. The result of the second join can similarly be pipelined into the next join, and so on.

- Multiple independent operations can be executed concurrently. For example, consider a (non left-deep) plan in which relations A and B are joined, relations C and D are joined, and the results of these two joins are finally joined. Clearly, the join of A and B can be executed concurrently with the join of C and D.

An optimizer that seeks to parallelize query evaluation has to consider several issues, and we will only outline the main points. The cost of executing individual operations in parallel (e.g., parallel sorting) obviously differs from executing them sequentially, and the optimizer should estimate operation costs accordingly.

Next, the plan that returns answers quickest may not be the plan with the least cost. For example, the cost of $A \bowtie B$ plus the cost of $C \bowtie D$ plus the cost of joining their results may be more than the cost of the cheapest left-deep plan. However, the time taken is the time for the more expensive of $A \bowtie B$ and $C \bowtie D$, plus the time to join their results. This time may well be less than the time taken by the cheapest left-deep plan. This observation suggests that a parallelizing optimizer should not restrict itself to only left-deep trees, and should also consider *bushy* trees, which significantly enlarge the space of plans to be considered.

Finally, there are a number of parameters such as available buffer space and the number of free processors that will be known only at run-time. This comment holds in a multiuser environment even if only sequential plans are considered; a multiuser environment is a simple instance of interquery parallelism.

19.5   INTRODUCTION TO DISTRIBUTED DATABASES

As we observed earlier, data in a distributed database system is stored across several sites, and each site is typically managed by a DBMS that can run independently of the other sites. The classical view of a distributed database system is that the system should make the impact of data distribution **transparent**. In particular, the following properties are considered desirable:

- **Distributed Data Independence:** Users should be able to ask queries without specifying where the referenced relations, or copies or fragments of the relations, are located. This principle is a natural extension of physical and logical data independence; we discuss it in Section 19.7. Further, queries that span multiple sites should be optimized systematically in a cost-based manner, taking into account communication costs and differences in local computation costs. We discuss distributed query optimization in Section 19.9.

- **Distributed Transaction Atomicity:** Users should be able to write transactions that access and update data at several sites just as they would write transactions over purely local data. In particular, the effects of a transaction across sites should continue to be atomic; that is, all changes persist if the transaction commits, and none persist if it aborts. We discuss this distributed transaction processing in Sections 19.10, 19.12 and 19.13.

Although most people would agree that the above properties are in general desirable, it is recognized that in certain situations, for example, when sites are connected by a slow long-distance network, these properties are not efficiently achievable. Indeed, it has been argued that when sites are globally distributed, these properties are not even desirable. The argument essentially is that the administrative overhead of supporting a system with distributed data independence and transaction atomicity—in effect, coordinating all activities across all sites in order to support the view of the whole as a unified collection of data—is prohibitive, over and above DBMS performance considerations.

Keep these remarks about distributed databases in mind as we cover the topic in more detail in the rest of this chapter. There is no real consensus on what the design objectives of distributed databases should be, and the field is evolving in response to users' needs.

19.5.1   Types of Distributed Databases

If data is distributed but all servers run the same DBMS software, we have a **homogeneous distributed database system**. If different sites run under the control of different DBMSs, essentially autonomously, and are connected together somehow to enable access to data from multiple sites, we have a **heterogeneous distributed database system**, also referred to as a **multidatabase system**.

The key to building heterogeneous systems is to have well-accepted standards for **gateways**. A gateway can be thought of as a piece of software that accepts requests (in some subset of SQL), submits them to the local DBMS, and then returns the answers to the requestor (in some standard format). By accessing database servers through gateways, their differences (in capabilities, data formats, etc.) are masked, and the differences between the different servers in a distributed system are bridged to a large degree.

Gateways are not a panacea, however. They add a layer of processing that can be expensive, and they do not completely mask the differences between servers. For example, a server may not be capable of providing the services required for distributed transaction management (see Sections 19.12 and 19.13), and even if it is capable, standardizing gateway protocols all the way down to this level of interaction poses challenges that have not yet been resolved satisfactorily.

Distributed data management, in the final analysis, comes at a significant cost in terms of performance, software complexity, and administration difficulty. This observation is especially true of heterogeneous systems.

19.6 DISTRIBUTED DBMS ARCHITECTURES

There are two alternative approaches to separating functionality across different DBMS-related processes; these alternative distributed DBMS architectures are called *Client-Server* and *Collaborating Servers*.

19.6.1 Client-Server Systems

A **Client-Server** system, has one or more client processes and one or more server processes, and a client process can send a query to any one server process. Clients are responsible for user-interface issues, and servers manage data and execute transactions. Thus a client process could run on a personal computer, and send queries to a server running on a mainframe.

This architecture has become very popular for several reasons. First, it is relatively simple to implement due to its clean separation of functionality, and the fact that the server is centralized. Second, an expensive server machine is fully utilized because dealing with mundane user-interactions is relegated to inexpensive client machines. Third, users can run a graphical user-interface that they are familiar with, rather than the (possibly unfamiliar and unfriendly) user-interface on the server.

While writing Client-Server applications, it is important to remember the boundary between the client and the server, and to keep the communication between them as set-oriented as possible. In particular, opening a cursor and fetching tuples one at a time generates many messages, and should be avoided. (Even if we fetch several tuples and cache them at the client, messages must be exchanged when the cursor is advanced to ensure that the current row is locked.) Indeed, techniques to exploit client-side caching to reduce communication overhead have been extensively studied, although we will not discuss them further.

19.6.2   Collaborating Server Systems

The Client-Server architecture does not allow a single query to span multiple servers because the client process would have to be capable of breaking such a query into appropriate subqueries to be executed at different sites and then piecing together the answers to the subqueries. The client process would thus be quite complex, and its capabilities would begin to overlap with the server; distinguishing between clients and servers becomes harder. Indeed, eliminating this distinction altogether leads us to an alternative to the Client-Server architecture: We can have a collection of database servers, each capable of running transactions against local data, which cooperatively execute transactions spanning multiple servers.

When a server receives a query that requires access to data at other servers, it generates appropriate subqueries to be executed by other servers, and puts the results together to compute answers to the original query. Ideally, the decomposition of the query should be done using cost-based optimization, taking into account the costs of network communication as well as local processing costs.

19.7   STORING DATA IN A DISTRIBUTED DBMS

In a distributed DBMS, relations are stored across several sites. Accessing a relation that is stored at a remote site incurs message-passing costs, and to reduce this overhead, a single relation may be **partitioned** or **fragmented** across several sites, with fragments stored at the sites where they are most often accessed; or **replicated** at each site where the relation is in high demand.

19.7.1   Fragmentation

Fragmentation consists of breaking a relation into smaller relations or fragments, and storing the fragments (instead of the relation itself), possibly at different sites. In **horizontal fragmentation**, each fragment consists of a subset of *rows* of the original relation. In **vertical fragmentation**, each fragment consists of a subset of *columns* of the original relation. Horizontal and vertical fragments are illustrated in Figure 19.4.

TID	eid	name	city	age	sal
t1	53666	Jones	Madras	18	35
t2	53688	Smith	Chicago	18	32
t3	53650	Smith	Chicago	19	48
t4	53831	Madayan	Bombay	11	20
t5	53832	Guldu	Bombay	12	20

       Vertical Fragment　　　　　　　　　　　　**Horizontal Fragment**

Figure 19.4　Horizontal and Vertical Fragmentation

Typically, the tuples that belong to a given horizontal fragment are identified by a selection query; for example, employee tuples might be organized into fragments by city, with all students in a given city assigned to the same fragment. The horizontal fragment shown in Figure 19.4 corresponds to Chicago. By storing fragments in the (database site at the) corresponding city, we achieve locality of reference—Chicago data is most likely to be updated and queried from Chicago, and storing this data in Chicago makes it local (and reduces communication costs) for most queries. Similarly, the tuples in a given vertical fragment are identified by a projection query. The vertical fragment in the figure results from projection on the first two columns of the employees relation.

When a relation is fragmented, we must be able to recover the original relation from the fragments:

- **Horizontal Fragmentation:** The union of the horizontal fragments must be equal to the original relation. Fragments are usually also required to be disjoint.

- **Vertical Fragmentation:** The collection of vertical fragments should be a lossless-join decomposition, as per the definition in Chapter 15.

To ensure that a vertical fragmentation is lossless-join, systems often assign a unique tuple id to each tuple in the original relation, as shown in Figure 19.4, and attach this id to the projection of the tuple in each fragment. If we think of the original relation as containing an additional tuple-id field that is a key, this field is added to each vertical fragment. Such a decomposition is guaranteed to be lossless.

In general a relation can be (horizontally or vertically) fragmented, and each resulting fragment can be further fragmented. For simplicity of exposition, in the rest of this chapter we will assume that fragments are not recursively fragmented in this manner.

19.7.2 Replication

Replication means that we store copies of a relation or relation fragment. An entire relation can be replicated at one or more sites. Similarly, one or more fragments of a relation can be replicated at other sites. For example, if a relation R is fragmented into $R1$, $R2$ and $R3$, there might be just one copy of $R1$, whereas $R2$ is replicated at two other sites and $R3$ is replicated at all sites.

The motivation for replication is twofold:

- **Increased Availability of Data:** If a site that contains a replica goes down, we can find the same data at other sites. Similarly, if local copies of remote relations are available, we are less vulnerable to failure of communication links.

- **Faster Query Evaluation:** Queries can execute faster by using a local copy of a relation instead of going to a remote site.

There are two kinds of replication, called *synchronous* and *asynchronous* replication, which differ primarily in how replicas are kept current when the relation is modified. (See Section 19.10.)

19.8 DISTRIBUTED CATALOG MANAGEMENT

Keeping track of data that is distributed across several sites can get complicated. We must keep track of how relations are fragmented and replicated, that is distributed across several sites and where (copies of) fragments are stored, in addition to the usual schema, authorization and statistical information.

19.8.1 Naming Objects

If a relation is fragmented and replicated, we must be able to uniquely identify each replica of each fragment. Generating such unique names requires some care. If we use a global name-server to assign globally unique names, local autonomy is compromised; we want (users at) each site to be able to assign names to local objects without reference to names system-wide.

The usual solution to the naming problem is to use names consisting of several fields. For example, we could have:

- A *local-name* field, which is the name assigned locally at the site where the relation is created. Two objects at different sites could possibly have the same local name, but two objects at a given site cannot have the same local name.

- A *birth-site* field, which identifies the site where the relation was created, and where information is maintained about all fragments and replicas of the relation.

These two fields identify a relation uniquely; we call the combination a **global relation name**. To identify a replica (of a relation or a relation fragment), we take the global relation name and add a *replica-id* field; we call the combination a **global replica name**.

19.8.2 Catalog Structure

A centralized system catalog can be used, but is vulnerable to failure of the site containing the catalog. An alternative is to maintain a copy of a global system catalog, which describes all the data, at every site. Although this approach is not vulnerable to a single-site failure, it compromises site autonomy, just like the first solution, because every change to a local catalog must now be broadcast to all sites.

A better approach, which preserves local autonomy and is not vulnerable to a single-site failure, was developed in the R* distributed database project, which was a successor to the System R project at IBM. Each site maintains a local catalog that describes all copies of data stored at that site. In addition, the catalog at the birth-site for a relation is responsible for keeping track of where replicas of the relation (in general, of fragments of the relation) are stored. In particular, a precise description of each replica's contents—a list of columns for a vertical fragment or a selection condition for a horizontal fragment—is stored in the birth-site catalog. Whenever a new replica is created, or a replica is moved across sites, the information in the birth-site catalog for the relation must be updated.

In order to locate a relation, the catalog at its birth-site must be looked up. This catalog information can be cached at other sites for quicker access, but the cached information may become out-of-date if, for example, a fragment is moved. We will discover that the locally cached information is out-of-date when we use it to access the relation, and at that point, we must update the cache by looking up the catalog at the birth-site of the relation. (The birth-site of a relation is recorded in each local cache that describes the relation, and the birth-site never changes, even if the relation is moved.)

19.8.3 Distributed Data Independence

Distributed data independence means that users should be able to write queries without regard to how a relation is fragmented or replicated; it is the responsibility of the DBMS to compute the relation as needed (by locating suitable copies of fragments, joining the vertical fragments and taking the union of horizontal fragments).

In particular, this property implies that users should not have to specify the full name for the data objects accessed while evaluating a query. Let us see how users can be enabled to access relations without considering how the relations are distributed. The *local-name* of a relation in the system catalog (Section 19.8.1) is really a combination of a *user-name* and a user-defined *relation-name*. Users can give whatever names they wish to their relations, without regard to the relations created by other users. When a user writes a program or SQL statement that refers to a relation, he or she simply uses the relation-name. The DBMS adds the user-name to the relation-name to get a local-name, then adds the user's site-id as the (default) birth-site to obtain a global relation name. By looking up the global relation name—in the local catalog if it is cached there, or in the catalog at the birth-site—the DBMS can locate replicas of the relation.

A user may want to create objects at several sites, or to refer to relations created by other users. To do this, a user can create a **synonym** for a global relation name, using an SQL-style command (although such a command is not currently part of the SQL-92 standard), and can subsequently refer to the relation using the synonym. For each user known at a site, the DBMS maintains a table of synonyms as part of the system catalog at that site, and uses this table to find the global relation name. Note that a user's program will run unchanged even if replicas of the relation are moved, because the global relation name is never changed until the relation itself is destroyed.

Users may want to run queries against specific replicas, especially if asynchronous replication is used. To support this, the synonym mechanism can be adapted to also allow users to create synonyms for global replica names.

19.9 DISTRIBUTED QUERY PROCESSING

We first discuss the issues involved in evaluating relational algebra operations in a distributed database through examples and then outline distributed query optimization. Consider the following two relations:

Sailors(*sid:* `integer`, *sname:* `string`, *rating:* `integer`, *age:* `real`)
Reserves(*sid:* `integer`, *bid:* `integer`, *day:* `date`, *rname:* `string`)

As in Chapter 12, assume that each tuple of Reserves is 40 bytes long, that a page can hold 100 Reserves tuples, and that we have 1000 pages of such tuples. Similarly, assume that each tuple of Sailors is 50 bytes long, that a page can hold 80 Sailors tuples, and that we have 500 pages of such tuples.

To estimate the cost of an evaluation strategy, in addition to counting the number of page I/Os, we must count the number of pages that are shipped—no pun intended—from one site to another because communication costs are a significant component of overall cost in a distributed database. We must also change our cost model to count the cost of shipping the result tuples to the site where the query is posed from the site where the result is assembled! In this chapter we will denote the time taken to read one page from disk (or to write one page to disk) as t_d, and the time taken to ship one page (from anywhere to anywhere) as t_s.

19.9.1 Nonjoin Queries in a Distributed DBMS

Even simple operations such as scanning a relation, selection, and projection are affected by fragmentation and replication. Consider the following query:

```
SELECT  S.age
FROM    Sailors S
WHERE   S.rating > 3 AND S.rating < 7
```

Suppose that the Sailors relation is horizontally fragmented, with all tuples having a rating less than 5 at Shanghai, and all tuples having a rating greater than 5 at Tokyo.

The DBMS must answer this query by evaluating it at both sites and taking the union of the answers. If the **SELECT** clause contained **AVG** *(S.age)*, combining the answers cannot be done by simply taking the union—the DBMS must compute the sum and count of *age* values at the two sites, and use this information to compute the average age of all sailors.

If the WHERE clause contained just the condition $S.rating > 6$, on the other hand, the DBMS should recognize that this query can be answered by just executing it at Tokyo.

As another example, suppose that the Sailors relation is vertically fragmented, with the *sid* and *rating* fields at Shanghai, and the *sname* and *age* fields at Tokyo. Observe that no field is stored at both sites. This vertical fragmentation would therefore be a lossy decomposition, except for the fact that a field containing the id of the corresponding Sailors tuple is included by the DBMS in both fragments! Now, the DBMS has to reconstruct the Sailors relation by joining the two fragments on the common tuple-id field, and execute the query over this reconstructed relation.

Finally, suppose that the entire Sailors relation is stored at both Shanghai and Tokyo. We can answer any of the queries mentioned above by executing it at either Shanghai or Tokyo. Where should the query be executed? This depends on the cost of shipping the answer to the query site (which may be Shanghai, Tokyo, or some other site), as well as the cost of executing the query at Shanghai and at Tokyo—the local processing costs may differ depending on what indexes are available on Sailors at the two sites, for example.

19.9.2   Joins in a Distributed DBMS

Joins of relations at different sites can be very expensive, and we now consider the evaluation options that must be considered in a distributed environment. Suppose that the Sailors relation is stored at London, and that the Reserves relation is stored at Paris. We will consider the cost of various strategies for computing $Sailors \bowtie Reserves$.

Fetch As Needed

We could do page-oriented nested loops join in London with Sailors as the outer, and for each Sailors page, fetch all Reserves pages from Paris. If we cache the fetched Reserves pages in London until the join is complete, pages are fetched only once, but let's assume that Reserves pages are not cached, just to see how bad things can get. (The situation can get much worse if we use a tuple-oriented nested loops join!)

The cost is $500t_d$ to scan Sailors plus, for each Sailors page, the cost of scanning and shipping all of Reserves, which is $1000(t_d + t_s)$. The total cost is therefore $500t_d + 500,000(t_d + t_s)$.

In addition, if the query was not submitted at the London site, we must add the cost of shipping the result to the query site; this cost depends on the size of the result. Because *sid* is a key for Sailors, the number of tuples in the result is 100,000 (the number of tuples in Reserves) and each tuple is $40 + 50 = 90$ bytes long; thus $4000/90 = 44$ result tuples fit on a page, and the result size is $100,000/44 = 2273$ pages. The cost of shipping the answer to another site, if necessary, is $2273t_s$. In the rest of this section we will assume that the query is posed at the site where the result is computed; if not, the cost of shipping the result to the query site must be added to the cost.

In this example observe that if the query site is not London or Paris, the cost of shipping the result is greater than the cost of shipping both Sailors and Reserves to the query site! Thus it would be cheaper to ship both relations to the query site and compute the join there.

Alternatively, we could do an index nested loops join in London, fetching all matching Reserves tuples for each Sailors tuple. Suppose that we have an unclustered hash index on the *sid* column of Reserves. Because there are 100,000 Reserves tuples and 40,000 Sailors tuples, on average each sailor has 2.5 reservations. The cost of finding the 2.5 Reservations tuples that match a given Sailors tuple is $(1.2 + 2.5)t_d$, assuming 1.2 I/Os to locate the appropriate bucket in the index. The total cost is the cost of scanning Sailors plus the cost of finding and fetching matching Reserves tuples for each Sailors tuple, and is $500t_d + 40,000(3.7t_d + 2.5t_s)$.

Both algorithms fetch required Reserves tuples from a remote site as needed. Clearly, this is not a good idea; the cost of shipping tuples dominates the total cost even for a fast network.

Ship to One Site

We can ship Sailors from London to Paris and carry out the join there, ship Reserves to London and carry out the join there, or ship both to the site where the query was posed and compute the join there. Note that the query could have been posed in London, Paris, or perhaps a third site, say, Timbuktu!

The cost of shipping Sailors and doing the join at Paris is $500t_s + 4500t_d$, assuming that the version of the sort-merge join described in Section 12.10 is used, and that we have an adequate number of buffer pages. In the rest of this section we will assume that sort-merge join is the join method used when both relations are at the same site.

The cost of shipping Reserves and doing the join at London is $1000t_s + 4500t_d$.

Semijoins and Bloomjoins

Consider the strategy of shipping Reserves to London and computing the join at London. Some tuples in (the current instance of) Reserves do not join with any tuple in (the current instance of) Sailors. If we could somehow identify Reserves tuples that are guaranteed not to join with any Sailors tuples, we could avoid shipping them.

Two techniques have been proposed for reducing the number of Reserves tuples to be shipped. The first technique is called **Semijoin**. The idea is to proceed in three steps:

1. At London, compute the projection of Sailors onto the join columns (in this case just the *sid* field), and ship this projection to Paris.

2. At Paris, compute the natural join of the projection received from the first site with the Reserves relation; the result of this join is called the **reduction** of Reserves with respect to Sailors. Clearly, only those Reserves tuples in the reduction will join with tuples in the Sailors relation. Therefore, ship the reduction of Reserves to London, rather than the entire Reserves relation.

3. At London, compute the join of the reduction of Reserves with Sailors.

Let us compute the cost of using this technique for our example join query. Suppose that we have a straightforward implementation of projection based on first scanning Sailors and creating a temporary relation with tuples that have only an *sid* field, then sorting the temporary and scanning the sorted temporary to eliminate duplicates. If we assume that the size of the *sid* field is 10 bytes, the cost of projection is $500t_d$ for scanning Sailors, plus $100t_d$ for creating the temporary, plus $400t_d$ for sorting it (in two passes), plus $100t_d$ for the final scan, plus $100t_d$ for writing the result into another temporary relation; a total of $1200t_d$. (Because *sid* is a key, there are no duplicates to be eliminated; if the optimizer is good enough to recognize this, the cost of projection is just $(500 + 100)t_d$!)

The cost of computing the projection and shipping it to Paris is therefore $1200t_d + 100t_s$. The cost of computing the reduction of Reserves is $3*(100+1000) = 3300t_d$, assuming that sort-merge join is used. (The cost does not reflect the fact that the projection of Sailors is already sorted; the cost would decrease slightly if the refined sort-merge join exploits this.)

What is the size of the reduction? If every sailor holds at least one reservation, the reduction includes every tuple of Reserves! The effort invested in shipping the projection and reducing Reserves is a total waste. Indeed, because of this observation, we note that Semijoin is especially useful in conjunction with a selection on one of the relations. For example, if we want to compute the join of

Sailors tuples with a *rating* greater than 8 with the Reserves relation, the size of the projection on *sid* for tuples that satisfy the selection would be just 20% of the original projection, that is, 20 pages.

Let us now continue the example join, with the assumption that we have the additional selection on *rating*. (The cost of computing the projection of Sailors goes down a bit, the cost of shipping it goes down to $20t_s$, and the cost of the reduction of Reserves also goes down a little, but we will ignore these reductions for simplicity.) We will assume that only 20% of the Reserves tuples are included in the reduction, thanks to the selection. Thus the reduction contains 200 pages, and the cost of shipping it is $200t_s$.

Finally, at London, the reduction of Reserves is joined with Sailors, at a cost of $3 * (200 + 500) = 2100t_d$. Observe that there are over 6500 page I/Os versus about 200 pages shipped, using this join technique. In contrast, to ship Reserves to London and do the join there costs $1000t_s$ plus $4500t_d$. With a high-speed network, the cost of Semijoin may well be more than the cost of shipping Reserves in its entirety, even though the shipping cost itself is much less ($200t_s$ versus $1000t_s$).

The second technique, called **Bloomjoin**, is actually quite similar. The main difference is that a bit-vector is shipped in the first step, instead of the projection of Sailors. A bit-vector of (some chosen) size k is computed by hashing each tuple of Sailors into the range 0 to $k - 1$, and setting bit i to 1 if some tuple hashes to i, and 0 otherwise. In the second step, the reduction of Reserves is computed by hashing each tuple of Reserves into the range 0 to $k - 1$, using the same hash function used to construct the bit-vector, and discarding tuples whose hash value i corresponds to a 0 bit. Because no Sailors tuples hash to such an i, no Sailors tuple can join with any Reserves tuple that is not in the reduction.

The costs of shipping a bit-vector and reducing Reserves using the vector are less than the corresponding costs in Semijoin. On the other hand, the size of the reduction of Reserves is likely to be larger than in Semijoin; thus the costs of shipping the reduction and joining it with Sailors are likely to be higher.

Let us estimate the cost of this approach. The cost of computing the bit-vector is essentially the cost of scanning Sailors, which is $500t_d$. The cost of sending the bit-vector depends on the size we choose for the the bit-vector, which is certainly smaller than the size of the projection; we will take this cost to be $20t_s$, for concreteness. The cost of reducing Reserves is just the cost of scanning Reserves; it is $1000t_d$. The size of the reduction of Reserves is likely to be about the same as or a little larger than the size of the reduction in the Semijoin approach; instead of 200, we will take this size to be 220 pages. (We assume that the selection on Sailors is included, in order to permit a direct comparison with the cost of

Semijoin.) The cost of shipping the reduction is therefore $220t_s$. The cost of the final join at London is $3 * (500 + 220) = 2160t_d$.

Thus in comparison to Semijoin, the shipping cost of this approach is about the same, although it could be higher if the bit-vector is not as selective as the projection of Sailors in terms of reducing Reserves. Typically, though, the reduction of Reserves is no more than 10% to 20% larger than the size of the reduction in Semijoin. In exchange for this slightly higher shipping cost, Bloomjoin achieves a significantly lower processing cost; less than $3700t_d$ versus more than $6500t_d$ for Semijoin. Indeed, Bloomjoin has a lower I/O cost and a lower shipping cost than the strategy of shipping all of Reserves to London! These numbers indicate why Bloomjoin is an attractive distributed join method; but the sensitivity of the method to the effectiveness of bit-vector hashing (in reducing Reserves) should be kept in mind.

19.9.3   Cost-Based Query Optimization

We have seen how data distribution can affect the implementation of individual operations such as selection, projection, aggregation and join. In general, of course, a query involves several operations, and optimizing queries in a distributed database poses the following additional challenges:

- Communication costs must be considered. If we have several copies of a relation, we must also make a decision about which copy to use.

- If individual sites are run under the control of different DBMSs, the autonomy of each site must be respected while doing global query planning.

Query optimization proceeds essentially as in a centralized DBMS, as described in Chapter 13, with information about relations at remote sites obtained from the system catalogs. Of course, there are more alternative methods to consider for each operation (e.g., consider the new options for distributed joins), and the cost metric must account for communication costs as well, but the overall planning process is essentially unchanged if we take the cost metric to be the total cost of all operations. (If we consider response time, the fact that certain subqueries can be carried out in parallel at different sites would require us to change the optimizer as per the discussion in Section 19.4.)

In the overall plan, local manipulation of relations at the site where they are stored (in order to compute an intermediate relation that is to be shipped elsewhere) is encapsulated into a *suggested* local plan. The overall plan includes several such local plans, which we can think of as subqueries executing at different sites. While generating the global plan, the suggested local plans provide realistic cost estimates for the computation of the intermediate relations; the suggested local plans are constructed by the optimizer mainly to provide these local cost estimates. A site is free to ignore the local plan suggested to it if it is able to find a cheaper plan by using more current information in the local catalogs. Thus site autonomy is respected in the optimization and evaluation of distributed queries.

19.10 UPDATING DISTRIBUTED DATA

The classical view of a distributed DBMS is that it should behave just like a centralized DBMS from the point of view of a user; issues arising from distribution of data should be transparent to the user, although, of course, they must be addressed at the implementation level.

With respect to queries, this view of a distributed DBMS means that users should be able to ask queries without worrying about how and where relations are stored; we have already seen the implications of this requirement on query evaluation.

With respect to updates, this view means that transactions should continue to be atomic actions, regardless of data fragmentation and replication. In particular, all copies of a modified relation must be updated before the modifying transaction commits. We will refer to replication with this semantics as **synchronous replication**; before an update transaction commits, it synchronizes all copies of modified data.

An alternative approach to replication, called **asynchronous replication**, has come to be widely used in commercial distributed DBMSs. Copies of a modified relation are updated only periodically in this approach, and a transaction that reads different copies of the same relation may see different values. Thus asynchronous replication compromises distributed data independence, but it is more efficiently implementable than synchronous replication.

19.10.1 Synchronous Replication

There are two basic techniques for ensuring that transactions see the same value regardless of which copy of an object they access. In the first technique, called **voting**, a transaction must write a majority of copies in order to modify an object, and read at least enough copies to make sure that one of the copies is current. For example, if there are 10 copies, and 7 copies are written by update transactions, then at least 4 copies must be read. Each copy has a version number, and the copy with the highest version number is current. This technique is not attractive in most situations because reading an object requires reading multiple copies; in most applications, objects are read much more frequently than they are updated, and efficient performance on reads is very important.

In the second technique, called **read-any write-all**, to read an object, a transaction can read any one copy, but to write an object, it must write all copies. Reads are fast, especially if we have a local copy, but writes are slower, relative to the first technique. This technique is attractive when reads are much more frequent than writes, and it is usually adopted for implementing synchronous replication.

19.10.2   Asynchronous Replication

Synchronous replication comes at a significant cost. Before an update transaction can commit, it must obtain exclusive locks on all copies—assuming that the read-any write-all technique is used—of modified data. The transaction may have to send lock requests to remote sites, and wait for the locks to be granted, and during this potentially long period, it continues to hold all its other locks. If sites or communication links fail, the transaction cannot commit until all sites at which it has modified data recover and are reachable. Finally, even if locks are obtained readily and there are no failures, committing a transaction requires several additional messages to be sent as part of a *commit protocol* (Section 19.13.1).

For these reasons, synchronous replication is undesirable or even unachievable in many situations. Asynchronous replication is therefore gaining in popularity, even though it allows different copies of the same object to have different values for short periods of time. This situation violates the principle of distributed data independence; users must be aware of which copy they are accessing, recognize that copies are brought up-to-date only periodically, and live with this reduced level of data consistency. Nonetheless, this seems to be a practical compromise that is indeed acceptable in many situations.

Primary Site versus Peer-to-Peer Replication

Asynchronous replication comes in two flavors. In **primary site** asynchronous replication, one copy of a relation is designated as the **primary** or **master** copy. Replicas of the entire relation or of fragments of the relation can be created at other sites; these are **secondary** copies, and, unlike the primary copy, they cannot be updated. A common mechanism for setting up primary and secondary copies is that users first **register** or **publish** the relation at the primary site, and subsequently **subscribe** to a fragment of a registered relation from another (secondary) site.

In **peer-to-peer** asynchronous replication, more than one copy (although perhaps not all) can be designated as being updatable, that is, a master copy. In addition to propagating changes, a *conflict resolution* strategy must be used to deal with conflicting changes made at different sites. For example, Joe's age may be changed to 35 at one site and to 38 at another. Which value is 'correct'? Many more subtle kinds of conflicts can arise in peer-to-peer replication, and in general peer-to-peer replication leads to ad hoc conflict resolution. Some special situations in which peer-to-peer replication does not lead to conflicts arise quite often, and it is in such situations that peer-to-peer replication is best utilized. For example:

- Each master is allowed to update only a fragment (typically a horizontal fragment) of the relation, and any two fragments updatable by different masters are disjoint. For example, it may be that salaries of British employees are updated only in London, and salaries of Indian employees are updated only in Madras, even though the entire relation is stored at both London and Madras.

- Updating rights are held by only one master at a time. For example, one site is designated as a *backup* to another site. Changes at the master site are propagated to other sites and updates are not allowed at other sites (including the backup). But if the master site fails, the backup site takes over and updates are now permitted at (only) the backup site.

We will not discuss peer-to-peer replication further.

Implementing Primary Site Asynchronous Replication

The main issue in implementing primary site replication is determining how changes to the primary copy are propagated to the secondary copies. Changes are usually propagated in two steps called **Capture** and **Apply**; changes made by committed transactions to the primary copy are somehow identified during the Capture step, and subsequently propagated to secondary copies during the Apply step.

In contrast to synchronous replication, a transaction that modifies a replicated relation directly locks and changes only the primary copy. It is typically committed long before the Apply step is carried out. Systems vary considerably in their implementation of these steps. We present an overview of some of the alternatives.

Capture

The Capture step is implemented using one of two approaches. In **log-based** Capture, the log maintained for recovery purposes is used to generate a record of updates. Basically, when the log tail is written to stable storage, all log records that affect replicated relations are also written to a separate **change data table (CDT)**. Since the transaction that generated the update log record may still be active when the record is written to the CDT, it may subsequently abort. Update log records written by transactions that subsequently abort must therefore be removed from the CDT to obtain a stream of updates due (only) to committed transactions. This stream can be obtained as part of the Capture step or subsequently in the Apply step if commit log records are added to the CDT; for concreteness, we will assume that the committed update stream is obtained as part of the Capture step, and that the CDT sent to the Apply step contains only update log records of committed transactions.

In **procedural** Capture, a procedure that is automatically invoked by the DBMS or an application program initiates the Capture process, which consists typically of taking a **snapshot** of the primary copy. A snapshot is just a copy of the relation as it existed at some instant in time. A procedure that is automatically invoked by the DBMS is called a *trigger*. We will discuss triggers in Chapter 20.

Log-based Capture has a smaller overhead than procedural Capture and, because it is driven by changes to the data, results in a smaller delay between the time the primary copy is changed and the time that the change is propagated to the secondary copies. (Of course, this delay is also dependent on how the Apply step is implemented.) In particular, only changes are propagated, and related changes (e.g., updates to two tables with a referential integrity constraint between them) are propagated together. The disadvantage is that implementing log-based Capture requires a detailed understanding of the structure of the log, which is quite system specific. Therefore a vendor cannot easily implement a log-based Capture mechanism that will capture changes made to data in another vendor's DBMS.

Apply

The Apply step takes the changes collected by the Capture step, which are in the CDT table or a snapshot, and propagates them to the secondary copies. This can be done by having the primary site continuously send the CDT, or by periodically requesting (the latest portion of) the CDT or a snapshot from the primary site. Typically, each secondary site runs a copy of the Apply process and 'pulls' the changes in the CDT from the primary site using periodic requests. The interval between such requests can be controlled by a timer or by a user's application program. Once the changes are available at the secondary site, they can be directly applied to the replica.

In some systems, the replica need not be just a fragment of the original relation— it can be a view defined using SQL, and the replication mechanism is sufficiently sophisticated to maintain such a view at a remote site incrementally (by re-evaluating only the part of the view affected by changes recorded in the CDT).

Log-based Capture in conjunction with continuous Apply minimizes the delay in propagating changes. It is the best combination in situations where the primary and secondary copies are both used as part of an operational DBMS and replicas must be as closely synchronized with the primary copy as possible. Log-based Capture with continuous Apply is essentially a less expensive substitute for synchronous replication. Procedural Capture and application-driven Apply offer the most flexibility in processing source data and changes before altering the replica; this flexibility is often useful in data warehousing applications where the ability to 'clean' and filter the retrieved data is more important than the currency of the replica.

Data Warehousing: An Example of Replication

Complex decision support queries that look at data from multiple sites are becoming very important. The paradigm of executing queries that span multiple sites is simply inadequate for performance reasons. One way to provide such complex query support over data from multiple sources is to create a copy of all the data at some one location, and to use the copy rather than going to the individual sources. Such a copied collection of data is called a **data warehouse**. Specialized systems for building, maintaining and querying data warehouses have become important tools in the marketplace.

Data warehouses can be seen as one instance of asynchronous replication, in which copies are updated relatively infrequently. When we talk of replication, we typically mean copies maintained under the control of a single DBMS, whereas with data warehousing, the original data may be on different software platforms (including database systems and OS filesystems), and even belong to different organizations. This distinction, however, is likely to become blurred as vendors adopt more 'open' strategies to replication. For example, some products already support the maintenance of replicas of relations stored in one vendor's DBMS in another vendor's DBMS.

We note that data warehousing involves more than just replication. We discuss other aspects of data warehousing in Chapter 22.

19.11 INTRODUCTION TO DISTRIBUTED TRANSACTION MANAGEMENT

In a distributed DBMS, a given transaction is submitted at some one site, but it can access data at other sites as well. In this chapter we will refer to the activity of a transaction at a given site as a **subtransaction**. When a transaction is submitted at some site, the transaction manager at that site breaks it up into a collection of one or more subtransactions that execute at different sites, submits them to transaction managers at the other sites, and coordinates their activity.

We now consider aspects of concurrency control and recovery that require additional attention because of data distribution. As we saw in Chapter 17, there are many concurrency control protocols; in this chapter, for concreteness we will assume that Strict 2PL with deadlock detection is used. We discuss the following issues in subsequent sections:

- **Distributed Concurrency Control:** How can locks for objects stored across several sites be managed? How can deadlocks be detected in a distributed database?

- **Distributed Recovery:** Transaction atomicity must be ensured—when a transaction commits, all its actions, across all the sites that it executes at, must persist. Similarly, when a transaction aborts, none of its actions must be allowed to persist.

19.12   DISTRIBUTED CONCURRENCY CONTROL

In Section 19.10.1, we described two techniques for implementing synchronous replication, and in Section 19.10.2, we discussed various techniques for implementing asynchronous replication. The choice of technique determines *which* objects are to be locked. *When* locks are obtained and released is determined by the concurrency control protocol. We now consider how lock and unlock requests are implemented in a distributed environment.

Lock management can be distributed across sites in many ways:

- **Centralized:** A single site is in charge of handling lock and unlock requests for all objects.

- **Primary Copy:** One copy of each object is designated as the primary copy. All requests to lock or unlock a copy of this object are handled by the lock manager at the site where the primary copy is stored, regardless of where the copy itself is stored.

- **Fully Distributed:** Requests to lock or unlock a copy of an object stored at a site are handled by the lock manager at the site where the copy is stored.

The centralized scheme is vulnerable to failure of the single site that controls locking. The primary copy scheme avoids this problem, but in general, reading an object requires communication with two sites: the site where the primary copy resides and the site where the copy to be read resides. This problem is avoided in the fully distributed scheme because locking is done at the site where the copy to be read resides. However, while writing, locks must be set at all sites where copies are modified in the fully distributed scheme, whereas locks need only be set at some one site in the other two schemes.

Clearly, the fully distributed locking scheme is the most attractive scheme if reads are much more frequent than writes, as is usually the case.

19.12.1 Distributed Deadlock

One issue that requires special attention when using either primary copy or fully distributed locking is deadlock detection. (Of course, a deadlock prevention scheme can be used instead, but we will focus on deadlock detection, which is widely used.) As in a centralized DBMS, deadlocks must be detected and resolved (by aborting some deadlocked transaction).

Each site maintains a local waits-for graph, and of course, a cycle in a local graph indicates a deadlock. However, there can be a deadlock even if no local graph contains a cycle. For example, suppose that two sites, A and B, both contain copies of objects $O1$ and $O2$, and that the read-any write-all technique is used. $T1$, which wants to read $O1$ and write $O2$, obtains an S lock on $O1$ and an X lock on $O2$ at Site A, then requests an X lock on $O2$ at Site B. $T2$, which wants to read $O2$ and write $O1$, meantime obtains an S lock on $O2$ and an X lock on $O1$ at Site B, then requests an X lock on $O1$ at Site A. As Figure 19.5 illustrates, $T2$ is waiting for $T1$ at Site A and $T1$ is waiting for $T2$ at Site B; thus we have a deadlock, which neither site can detect based solely on its local waits-for graph.

Figure 19.5 Distributed Deadlock

To detect such deadlocks, a **distributed deadlock detection** algorithm must be used. We describe three such algorithms.

The first algorithm, which is centralized, consists of periodically sending all local waits-for graphs to some one site that is responsible for global deadlock detection. At this site, the global waits-for graph is generated by combining all the local graphs; the set of nodes is the union of nodes in the local graphs, and there is an edge from one node to another if there is such an edge in any of the local graphs.

The second algorithm, which is hierarchical, groups sites into a hierarchy. For instance, sites might be grouped by state, then by country, and finally into a single group that contains all sites. Every node in this hierarchy constructs a waits-for graph that reveals deadlocks involving only sites contained in (the subtree rooted at) this node. Thus all sites periodically (e.g., every 10 seconds) send their local waits-for graph to the site responsible for constructing the waits-for graph for their state. The sites constructing waits-for graphs at the state level periodically (e.g., every minute) send the state waits-for graph to the site constructing the waits-for graph for their country. The sites constructing waits-for graphs at the country level periodically (e.g., every 10 minutes) send the country waits-for graph to the site constructing the global waits-for graph. This scheme is based on the observation that more deadlocks are likely across closely related sites than across unrelated sites, and puts more effort into detecting deadlocks across related sites. All deadlocks will eventually be detected, but a deadlock involving two different countries may take a while to detect.

The third algorithm is simple: If a transaction waits longer than some chosen time-out interval, it is aborted. Although this algorithm may cause many unnecessary restarts, the overhead of deadlock detection is (obviously!) low, and in a heterogeneous distributed database, if the participating sites cannot cooperate to the extent of sharing their waits-for graphs, it may be the only option.

A subtle point to note with respect to distributed deadlock detection is that delays in propagating local information might cause the deadlock detection algorithm to identify 'deadlocks' that do not really exist. Such situations are called **phantom deadlocks**, and lead to unnecessary aborts. For concreteness, we discuss the centralized algorithm, although the hierarchical algorithm suffers from the same problem.

Consider a modification of the previous example. As before, the two transactions wait on each other, generating the local waits-for graphs shown in Figure 19.5, and the local waits-for graphs are sent to the global deadlock-detection site. However, $T2$ is now aborted for reasons other than deadlock. (For example, $T2$ may also be executing at a third site, where it reads an unexpected data value and decides to abort.) At this point, the local waits-for graphs have changed so that there is no cycle in the 'true' global waits-for graph. However, the constructed global waits-for graph will contain a cycle, and $T1$ may well be picked as the victim!

19.13 DISTRIBUTED RECOVERY

Recovery in a distributed DBMS is more complicated than in a centralized DBMS for the following reasons:

- New kinds of failure can arise, namely, failure of communication links and failure of a remote site at which a subtransaction is executing.

- Either all subtransactions of a given transaction must commit, or none must commit, and this property must be guaranteed despite any combination of site and link failures. This guarantee is achieved using a **commit protocol**.

As in a centralized DBMS, certain actions are carried out as part of normal execution in order to provide the necessary information to recover from failures. A log is maintained at each site, and in addition to the kinds of information maintained in a centralized DBMS, actions taken as part of the commit protocol are also logged. The most widely used commit protocol is called *Two-Phase Commit (2PC)*; in fact, a variant called *2PC with presumed abort* has been adopted as an industry standard.

In this section we first describe the steps taken during normal execution, concentrating on the commit protocol, and then discuss recovery from failures.

19.13.1 Normal Execution and Commit Protocols

During normal execution, each site maintains a log, and the actions of a subtransaction are logged at the site where it executes. The logging activity described in Chapter 18 is carried out, of course, and we will not discuss it further. In addition, a commit protocol is followed to ensure that all subtransactions of a given transaction either commit or abort uniformly. The transaction manager at the site where the transaction originated is called the **coordinator** for the transaction; transaction managers at sites where its subtransactions execute are called **subordinates** (with respect to the coordination of this transaction).

We now describe the **two-phase commit (2PC)** protocol, in terms of the messages exchanged and the log records written. When the user decides to commit a transaction, the commit command is sent to the coordinator for the transaction. This initiates the 2PC protocol:

1. The coordinator sends a *prepare* message to each subordinate.

2. When a subordinate receives a *prepare* message, it decides whether to abort or commit its subtransaction. It force-writes an abort or **prepare** log record, and *then* sends a *no* or *yes* message to the coordinator. Notice that a prepare

log record is not used in a centralized DBMS; it is unique to the commit protocol.

3. If the coordinator receives *yes* messages from all subordinates, it force-writes a commit log record, and then sends a *commit* message to all subordinates. If it receives even one *no* message, or does not receive any response from some subordinate for a specified time-out interval, it force-writes an abort log record, and then sends an *abort* message to all subordinates.[1]

4. When a subordinate receives an *abort* message, it force-writes an abort log record, sends an *ack* message to the coordinator, and aborts the subtransaction. When a subordinate receives a *commit* message, it force-writes a commit log record, sends an *ack* message to the coordinator, and commits the subtransaction.

5. When the coordinator receives *ack* messages from all subordinates, it writes an end log record for the transaction.

The name *two-phase commit* reflects the fact that two rounds of messages are exchanged: first a voting phase, then a termination phase, both initiated by the coordinator. The basic principle is that any of the transaction managers involved (including the coordinator) can unilaterally abort a transaction, whereas there must be unanimity to commit a transaction. When a message is sent in 2PC, it signals a decision by the sender. In order to ensure that this decision survives a crash at the sender's site, the log record describing the decision is always forced to stable storage *before* the message is sent.

A transaction is officially committed at the time the coordinator's commit log record reaches stable storage. Subsequent failures cannot affect the outcome of the transaction; it is irrevocably committed. Log records written to record the commit protocol actions contain the type of the record, the transaction id, and the identity of the coordinator. A coordinator's commit or abort log record also contains the identities of the subordinates.

19.13.2 Restart after a Failure

When a site comes back up after a crash, we invoke a recovery process that reads the log and processes all transactions that were executing the commit protocol at the time of the crash. The transaction manager at this site could have been the coordinator for some of these transactions, and a subordinate for others. We do the following in the recovery process:

---

[1]As an optimization, the coordinator need not send *abort* messages to subordinates who voted *no*.

- If we have a commit or abort log record for transaction T, its status is clear; we redo or undo T, respectively. If this site is the coordinator, which can be determined from the commit or abort log record, we must periodically resend—because there may well be other link or site failures in the system— a *commit* or *abort* message to each subordinate until we receive an *ack*; once we receive an *ack*, we write an end log record for T.

- If we have a prepare log record for T, but no commit or abort log record, this site is a subordinate, and the coordinator can be determined from the prepare record. We must repeatedly contact the coordinator site to determine the status of T. Once the coordinator responds with either commit or abort, we write a corresponding log record, redo or undo the transaction, and then write an end log record for T.

- If we have no prepare, commit or abort log record for transaction T, T certainly could not have voted to commit before the crash; so we can unilaterally abort and undo T, and write an end log record. In this case we have no way to determine whether the current site is the coordinator or a subordinate for T. However, if this site is the coordinator, it might have sent a *prepare* message prior to the crash, and if so, other sites may have voted *yes*. If such a subordinate site contacts the recovery process at the current site, we now know that the current site is the coordinator for T, and given that there is no commit or abort log record, the response to the subordinate should be to abort T.

Observe that if the coordinator site for a transaction T fails, subordinates who have voted *yes* cannot decide whether to commit or abort T until the coordinator site recovers; we say that T is **blocked**. In principle, the active subordinate sites could communicate among themselves, and if at least one of them contains an abort or commit log record for T, its status becomes globally known. In order to communicate among themselves, all subordinates must be told the identity of the other subordinates at the time they are sent the *prepare* message. However, 2PC is still vulnerable to coordinator failure during recovery because even if all subordinates have voted *yes*, the coordinator (who also has a vote!) may have decided to abort T, and this decision cannot be determined until the coordinator site recovers.

We have covered how a site recovers from a crash, but what should a site that is involved in the commit protocol do if a site that it is communicating with fails? If the current site is the coordinator, it should simply abort the transaction. If the current site is a subordinate, and it has not yet responded to the coordinator's *prepare* message, it can (and should) abort the transaction. If it is a subordinate and has voted *yes*, then it cannot unilaterally abort the transaction, and it cannot commit either; it is therefore blocked. It must periodically contact the coordinator until it receives a reply.

Failures of communication links are seen by active sites as failure of other sites that they are communicating with, and therefore the solutions just outlined apply to this case as well.

19.13.3   Two-Phase Commit Revisited

Now that we have examined how a site recovers from a failure, and seen the interaction between the 2PC protocol and the recovery process, it is instructive to consider how 2PC can be refined further. In doing so, we will arrive at a more efficient version of 2PC, but equally important perhaps, we will understand the role of the various steps of 2PC more clearly. There are three basic observations:

1. The *ack* messages in 2PC are used to determine when a coordinator (or the recovery process at a coordinator site following a crash) can 'forget' about a transaction T. Until the coordinator knows that all subordinates are aware of the commit/abort decision for T, it must keep information about T in the transaction table.

2. If the coordinator site fails after sending out *prepare* messages, but before writing a commit or abort log record, when it comes back up it has no information about the transaction's commit status prior to the crash. However, it is still free to abort the transaction unilaterally (because it has not written a commit record, it can still cast a *no* vote itself). If another site inquires about the status of the transaction, the recovery process, as we have seen, therefore responds with an *abort* message. Thus in the absence of information, a transaction is *presumed to have aborted*.

3. If a subtransaction does no updates, it has no changes to either redo or undo; in other words, its commit or abort status is irrelevant.

The first two observations suggest several refinements:

- When a coordinator aborts a transaction T, it can undo T and remove it from the transaction table immediately. After all, removing T from the table results in a 'no information' state with respect to T, and the default response (to an enquiry about T) in this state, which is *abort*, is indeed the correct response for an aborted transaction.

- By the same token, if a subordinate receives an *abort* message, it need not send an *ack* message. The coordinator is not waiting to hear from subordinates after sending an *abort* message! If, for some reason, a subordinate that receives a *prepare* message (and voted *yes*) does not receive an *abort* or *commit* message for a specified time-out interval, it will contact the coordinator again. In the event that the coordinator decided to abort, there may no longer be an entry in the transaction table for this transaction, but the subordinate will receive the default *abort* message, which is the correct response.

■ Because the coordinator is not waiting to hear from subordinates after deciding to abort a transaction, the names of subordinates need not be recorded in the abort log record for the coordinator.

■ All abort log records (for the coordinator as well as subordinates) can simply be appended to the log tail, instead of doing a force-write. After all, if they are not written to stable storage before a crash, the default decision is to abort the transaction.

The third basic observation suggests some additional refinements:

■ If a subtransaction does no updates (which can be easily detected by keeping a count of update log records), the subordinate can respond to a *prepare* message from the coordinator with a *reader* message, instead of *yes* or *no*. The subordinate writes no log records whatsoever in this case.

■ When a coordinator receives a *reader* message, it treats the message as a *yes* vote, but with the optimization that it does not send any more messages to the subordinate, because the subordinate's commit or abort status is irrelevant.

■ If all the subtransactions, including the subtransaction at the coordinator site, send a *reader* message, we don't need the second phase of the commit protocol. Indeed, we can simply remove the transaction from the transaction table, without writing any log records at any site for this transaction.

The 2PC commit protocol with the refinements discussed in this section is called **two-Phase commit with presumed abort**.

19.13.4 Three-Phase Commit

A commit protocol called **three-phase commit (3PC)** can avoid blocking even if the coordinator site fails during recovery. The basic idea is that when the coordinator sends out *prepare* messages and receives *yes* votes from all subordinates, it sends all sites a *precommit* message, rather than a *commit* message. When a sufficient number—more than the maximum number of failures that must be handled—of *acks* have been received, the coordinator force-writes a *commit* log record and sends a *commit* message to all subordinates. In 3PC the coordinator effectively postpones the decision to commit until it is sure that enough sites know about the decision to commit; if the coordinator subsequently fails, these sites can communicate with each other and detect that the transaction must be committed—conversely, aborted, if none of them has received a *precommit* message—without waiting for the coordinator to recover.

The 3PC protocol imposes a significant additional cost during normal execution, and requires that communication link failures do not lead to a network partition (wherein some sites cannot reach some other sites through any path) in order to ensure freedom from blocking. For these reasons, it is not used in practice.

19.14   SUMMARY

Parallel database management systems seek to achieve high performance by utilizing several CPUs and disks. The objective of a parallel DBMS is to store data across multiple disks and to parallelize query evaluation across multiple processors in such a manner as to achieve linear speed-up and scale-up. That is, as more processors are added, execution must be speeded up proportionally, and for a given performance level, the amount of data that can be processed must increase proportionally. Beyond improved performance, however, a parallel DBMS should appear just like a centralized DBMS to a user. All data is administered in a centralized fashion, and is typically in one geographical location.

In a distributed DBMS, on the other hand, data is typically stored across several sites, often geographically separated and independently administered. Users must be able to access and modify both local and remote data, in as uniform a manner as possible. Distributed data indepence requires that users be able to view the data just as in a centralized system, without regard to how and where it is actually stored. This principle is difficult to achieve due to performance and administrative reasons, and indeed may sometimes be inappropriate for these reasons, but is nonetheless a useful ideal that is often desirable.

The differences between centralized and distributed database systems can be summarized along the following dimensions: where data is stored and who manages it, how it is queried, how it is updated, and how concurrency control and recovery mechanisms are implemented. In terms of data storage, data is stored across several sites; fragments (a subset of rows and columns) of a relation can reside at different sites, and a given fragment or relation can be replicated at several sites. If a fragment is replicated at several sites, and a transaction changes one copy, all the other copies must be updated as well before the transaction commits. Such a policy, called synchronous replication, is necessary for distributed data independence, but is expensive. In many situations, it is acceptable for copies to be updated only periodically; this policy, called asynchronous replication, is gaining in popularity.

Data distribution has a profound effect on queries, updates, and transaction management, as is to be expected. When users ask queries over data spanning multiple sites, the optimizer must find a good plan taking into account data distribution, differing local execution costs, and communication costs. If a transaction updates data at several sites, locks must be obtained and released across all sites so as to ensure serializability, and the recovery algorithm must ensure transaction atomicity. In particular, a commit protocol is used to guarantee that either all the changes due to a transaction are committed at all sites where the transaction executed, or none of the changes are committed.

EXERCISES

Exercise 19.1 Give brief answers to the following questions:

1. What are the similarities and differences between parallel and distributed database management systems?

2. Would you expect to see a parallel database built using a wide-area network? Would you expect to see a distributed database built using a wide-area network? Explain.

3. Define the terms *scale-up* and *speed-up*.

4. Why is a shared-nothing architecture attractive for parallel database systems?

5. The idea of building specialized hardware to run parallel database applications received considerable attention but has fallen out of favor. Comment on this trend.

6. What are the advantages of a distributed database management system over a centralized DBMS?

7. Briefly describe and compare the Client-Server and Collaborating Servers architectures.

8. In the Collaborating Servers architecture, when a transaction is submitted to the DBMS, briefly describe how its activities at various sites are coordinated. In particular, describe the role of transaction managers at the different sites, the concept of *subtransactions*, and the concept of *distributed transaction atomicity*.

Exercise 19.2 Give brief answers to the following questions:

1. Define the terms *fragmentation* and *replication*, in terms of where data is stored.

2. What is the difference between *synchronous* and *asynchronous* replication?

3. Define the term *distributed data independence*. Specifically, what does this mean with respect to querying and with respect to updating data in the presence of data fragmentation and replication?

4. Consider the *voting* and *read-one write-all* techniques for implementing synchronous replication. What are their respective pros and cons?

5. Give an overview of how asynchronous replication can be implemented. In particular, explain the terms *capture* and *apply*.

6. What is the difference between log-based and procedural approaches to implementing capture?

7. Why is giving database objects unique names more complicated in a distributed DBMS?

8. Describe a catalog organization that permits any replica (of an entire relation or a fragment) to be given a unique name, and that provides the naming infrastructure required for ensuring distributed data independence.

9. If information from remote catalogs is cached at other sites, what happens if the cached information becomes outdated? How can this condition be detected and resolved?

Exercise 19.3 Consider a parallel DBMS in which each relation is stored by horizontally partitioning its tuples across all disks.

Employees(*eid:* `integer`, *did:* `integer`, *sal:* `real`)
Departments(*did:* `integer`, *mgrid:* `integer`, *budget:* `integer`)

The *mgrid* field of Departments is the *eid* of the manager. Each relation contains 20-byte tuples, and the *sal* and *budget* fields both contain uniformly distributed values in the range 0 to 1,000,000. The Employees relation contains 100,000 pages, the Departments relation contains 5000 pages, and each processor has 100 buffer pages of 4000 bytes each. The cost of one page I/O is t_d, and the cost of shipping one page is t_s; tuples are shipped in units of one page by waiting for a page to be filled before sending a message from processor i to processor j. There are no indexes, and all joins that are local to a processor are carried out using Sort-Merge Join. Assume that the relations are initially partitioned using a round-robin algorithm and that there are 10 processors.

For each of the following queries, describe the evaluation plan briefly and give its cost in terms of t_d and t_s. You should compute the total cost across all sites as well as the 'elapsed time' cost (i.e., if several operations are carried out concurrently, the time taken is the maximum over these operations).

1. Find the highest paid employee.

2. Find the highest paid employee in the department with *did* 55.

3. Find the highest paid employee over all departments with *budget* less than 100,000.

4. Find the highest paid employee over all departments with *budget* less than 300,000.

5. Find the average salary over all departments with *budget* less than 300,000.

6. Find the salaries of all managers.

7. Find the salaries of all managers who manage a department with a budget less than 300,000 and earn more than 100,000.

8. Print the *eid*s of all employees, ordered by increasing salaries. Each processor is connected to a separate printer, and the answer can appear as several sorted lists, each printed by a different processor, as long as we can obtain a fully sorted list by concatenating the printed lists (in some order).

Exercise 19.4 Consider the same scenario as in Exercise 19.3, except that the relations are originally partitioned using range partitioning on the *sal* and *budget* fields.

Exercise 19.5 Repeat Exercises 19.3 and 19.4 with the number of processors equal to (i) 1, and (ii) 100.

Exercise 19.6 Consider the Employees and Departments relations described in Exercise 19.3. They are now stored in a distributed DBMS with all of Employees stored at Naples and all of Departments stored at Berlin. There are no indexes on these relations. The cost of various operations is as described in Exercise 19.3. Consider the query:

```
SELECT *
FROM    Employees E, Departments D
WHERE   E.eid = D.mgrid
```

The query is posed at Delhi, and you are told that only 1% of employees are managers. Find the cost of answering this query using each of the following plans:

1. Compute the query at Naples by shipping Departments to Naples; then ship the result to Delhi.

2. Compute the query at Berlin by shipping Employees to Berlin; then ship the result to Delhi.

3. Compute the query at Delhi by shipping both relations to Delhi.

4. Compute the query at Naples using Bloomjoin; then ship the result to Delhi.

5. Compute the query at Berlin using Bloomjoin; then ship the result to Delhi.

6. Compute the query at Naples using Semijoin; then ship the result to Delhi.

7. Compute the query at Berlin using Semijoin; then ship the result to Delhi.

Exercise 19.7 Consider your answers in Exercise 19.6. Which plan minimizes shipping costs? Is it necessarily the cheapest plan? Which do you expect to be the cheapest?

Exercise 19.8 Consider the Employees and Departments relations described in Exercise 19.3. They are now stored in a distributed DBMS with 10 sites. The Departments tuples are horizontally partitioned across the 10 sites by *did*, with the same number of tuples assigned to each site and with no particular order to how tuples are assigned to sites. The Employees tuples are similarly partitioned, by *sal* ranges, with $sal \leq 100,000$ assigned to the first site, $100,000 < sal \leq 200,00$ assigned to the second site, and so on. In addition, the partition $sal \leq 100,000$ is frequently accessed and infrequently updated, and it is therefore replicated at every site. No other Employees partition is replicated.

1. Describe the best plan (unless a plan is specified) and give its cost:

   (a) Compute the natural join of Employees and Departments using the strategy of shipping all fragments of the smaller relation to every site containing tuples of the larger relation.

   (b) Find the highest paid employee.

   (c) Find the highest paid employee with salary less than $100,000$.

   (d) Find the highest paid employee with salary greater than $400,000$ and less than $500,000$.

   (e) Find the highest paid employee with salary greater than $450,000$ and less than $550,000$.

   (f) Find the highest paid manager for those departments stored at the query site.

   (g) Find the highest paid manager.

2. Assuming the same data distribution, describe the sites visited and the locks obtained for the following update transactions, assuming that *synchronous* replication is used for the replication of Employees tuples with $sal \leq 100,000$:

   (a) Give employees with salary less than $100,000$ a 10% raise, with a maximum salary of $100,000$ (i.e., the raise cannot increase the salary to more than $100,000$).

   (b) Give all employees a 10% raise. The conditions of the original partitioning of Employees must still be satisfied after the update.

3. Assuming the same data distribution, describe the sites visited and the locks obtained for the following update transactions, assuming that *asynchronous* replication is used for the replication of Employees tuples with $sal \leq 100,000$.

   (a) For all employees with salary less than $100,000$ give them a 10% raise, with a maximum salary of $100,000$.

   (b) Give all employees a 10% raise. After the update is completed, the conditions of the original partitioning of Employees must still be satisfied.

Exercise 19.9 Consider the Employees and Departments relations from Exercise 19.3. You are a DBA dealing with a distributed DBMS, and you need to decide how to distribute these two relations across two sites, Manila and Nairobi. Your DBMS supports only unclustered B+ tree indexes. You have a choice between synchronous and asynchronous replication. For each of the following scenarios, describe how you would distribute them and what indexes you would build at each site. If you feel that you have insufficient information to make a decision, explain briefly.

1. Half the departments are located in Manila, and the other half are in Nairobi. Department information, including that for employees in the department, is changed only at the site where the department is located, but such changes are quite frequent. (Although the location of a department is not included in the Departments schema, this information can be obtained from another table.)

2. Half the departments are located in Manila, and the other half are in Nairobi. Department information, including that for employees in the department, is changed only at the site where the department is located, but such changes are infrequent. Finding the average salary for each department is a frequently asked query.

3. Half the departments are located in Manila, and the other half are in Nairobi. Employees tuples are frequently changed (only) at the site where the corresponding department is located, but the Departments relation is almost never changed. Finding a given employee's manager is a frequently asked query.

4. Half the employees work in Manila, and the other half work in Nairobi. Employees tuples are frequently changed (only) at the site where they work.

Exercise 19.10 Suppose that the Employees relation is stored in Madison and the tuples with $sal \leq 100,000$ are replicated at New York. Consider the following three options for lock management: all locks managed at a *single site*, say, Milwaukee; *primary copy* with Madison being the primary for Employees; and *fully distributed*. For each of the lock management options, explain what locks are set (and at which site) for the following queries. Also state which site the page is read from.

1. A query submitted at Austin wants to read a page containing Employees tuples with $sal \leq 50,000$.

2. A query submitted at Madison wants to read a page containing Employees tuples with $sal \leq 50,000$.

3. A query submitted at New York wants to read a page containing Employees tuples with $sal \leq 50,000$.

Exercise 19.11 Briefly answer the following questions:

1. Compare the relative merits of centralized and hierarchical deadlock detection in a distributed DBMS.

2. What is a *phantom deadlock*? Give an example.

3. Give an example of a distributed DBMS with three sites such that no two local waits-for graphs reveal a deadlock, yet there is a global deadlock.

4. Consider the following modification to a local waits-for graph: Add a new node T_{ext}, and for every transaction T_i that is waiting for a lock at another site, add the edge $T_i \rightarrow T_{ext}$. Also add an edge $T_{ext} \rightarrow T_i$ if a transaction executing at another site is waiting for T_i to release a lock at this site.

   (a) If there is a cycle in the modified local waits-for graph that does not involve T_{ext}, what can you conclude? If every cycle involves T_{ext}, what can you conclude?

   (b) Suppose that every site is assigned a unique integer *site-id*. Whenever the local waits-for graph suggests that there might be a global deadlock, send the local waits-for graph to the site with the next higher site-id. At that site, combine the received graph with the local waits-for graph. If this combined graph does not indicate a deadlock, ship it on to the next site, and so on, until either a deadlock is detected or we are back at the site that originated this round of deadlock detection. Is this scheme guaranteed to find a global deadlock if one exists?

Exercise 19.12 Timestamp-based concurrency control schemes can be used in a distributed DBMS, but we must be able to generate globally unique, monotonically increasing timestamps without a bias in favor of any one site. One approach is to assign timestamps at a single site. Another is to use the local clock time and to append the site-id. A third scheme is to use a counter at each site. Compare these three approaches.

Exercise 19.13 Consider the Multiple-Granularity locking protocol described in Chapter 17. In a distributed DBMS the site containing the root object in the hierarchy can become a bottleneck. You hire a database consultant who tells you to modify your protocol to allow only intention locks on the root, and to implicitly grant all possible intention locks to every transaction.

1. Explain why this modification works correctly, in that transactions continue to be able to set locks on desired parts of the hierarchy.

2. Explain how it reduces the demand upon the root.

3. Why isn't this idea included as part of the standard Multiple-Granularity locking protocol for a centralized DBMS?

Exercise 19.14 Briefly answer the following questions:

1. Explain the need for a commit protocol in a distributed DBMS.

2. Describe 2PC. Be sure to explain the need for force-writes.

3. Why are *ack* messages required in 2PC?

4. What are the differences between 2PC and 2PC with presumed abort?

5. Give an example execution sequence such that 2PC and 2PC with presumed abort generate an identical sequence of actions.

6. Give an example execution sequence such that 2PC and 2PC with presumed abort generate different sequences of actions.

7. What is the intuition behind 3PC? What are its pros and cons relative to 2PC?

8. Suppose that a site does not get any response from another site for a long time. Can the first site tell whether the connecting link has failed or the other site has failed? How is such a failure handled?

9. Suppose that the coordinator includes a list of all subordinates in the *prepare* message. If the coordinator fails after sending out either an *abort* or *commit* message, can you suggest a way for active sites to terminate this transaction without waiting for the coordinator to recover? Assume that some but not all of the *abort/commit* messages from the coordinator are lost.

10. Suppose that 2PC with presumed abort is used as the commit protocol. Explain how the system recovers from failure and deals with a particular transaction T in each of the following cases:

    (a) A subordinate site for T fails before receiving a *prepare* message.

    (b) A subordinate site for T fails after receiving a *prepare* message but before making a decision.

    (c) A subordinate site for T fails after receiving a *prepare* message and force-writing an abort log record but before responding to the *prepare* message.

    (d) A subordinate site for T fails after receiving a *prepare* message and force-writing a prepare log record but before responding to the *prepare* message.

    (e) A subordinate site for T fails after receiving a *prepare* message, force-writing an abort log record, and sending a *no* vote.

(f) The coordinator site for T fails before sending a *prepare* message.

(g) The coordinator site for T fails after sending a *prepare* message but before collecting all votes.

(h) The coordinator site for T fails after writing an *abort* log record but before sending any further messages to its subordinates.

(i) The coordinator site for T fails after writing a *commit* log record but before sending any further messages to its subordinates.

(j) The coordinator site for T fails after writing an *end* log record. Is it possible for the recovery process to get an inquiry about the status of T from a subordinate?

Exercise 19.15 Consider a heterogeneous distributed DBMS.

1. Define the terms *multidatabase system* and *gateway*.

2. Describe how queries that span multiple sites are executed in a multidatabase system. Explain the role of the gateway with respect to catalog interfaces, query optimization, and query execution.

3. Describe how transactions that update data at multiple sites are executed in a multidatabase system. Explain the role of the gateway with respect to lock management, distributed deadlock detection, two-phase commit, and recovery.

4. Schemas at different sites in a multidatabase system are probably designed independently. This situation can lead to *semantic heterogeneity*; that is, units of measure may differ across sites (e.g., inches versus centimeters), relations containing essentially the same kind of information (e.g., employee salaries and ages) may have slightly different schemas, and so on. What impact does this heterogeneity have on the end-user? In particular, comment on the concept of distributed data independence in such a system.

BIBLIOGRAPHIC NOTES

Work on parallel algorithms for sorting and various relational operations is discussed in the bibliographies for Chapters 7 and 12. Our discussion of parallel joins follows [160], and our discussion of parallel sorting follows [163]. [161] makes the case that for future high performance database systems, parallelism will be the key. Scheduling in parallel database systems is discussed in [374]. [354] contains a good collection of papers on query processing in parallel database systems.

Textbook discussions of distributed databases include [59, 105, 419]. Good survey articles include [65], which focuses on concurrency control; [459], which is about distributed databases in general; and [576], which concentrates on distributed query processing. Two major projects in the area were SDD-1 [458] and R* [571].

Fragmentation in distributed databases is considered in [116, 150]. Replication is considered in [8, 10, 98, 174, 173, 262, 259, 230, 398, 433]. For good overviews of current trends in asynchronous replication, see [170, 517, 567]. Papers on view maintenance mentioned in the bibliography of Chapter 10 are also relevant in this context.

Query processing in the SDD-1 distributed database is described in [68]. One of the notable aspects of SDD-1 query processing was the extensive use of semijoins. Theoretical studies of semijoins are presented in [63, 66, 284]. Query processing in R* is described in [482]. The R* query optimizer is validated in [358]; much of our discussion of distributed query processing is drawn from the results reported in this paper. Query processing in Distributed Ingres is described in [182]. Optimization of queries for parallel execution is discussed in [212, 220, 257]. [201] discusses the trade-offs between *query-shipping*, the more traditional approach in relational databases, and *data-shipping*, which consists of shipping data to the client for processing and is widely used in object-oriented systems.

Concurrency control in the SDD-1 distributed database is described in [71]. Transaction management in R* is described in [392]. Concurrency control in Distributed Ingres is described in [522]. [544] provides an introduction to distributed transaction management and various notions of distributed data independence. Optimizations for read-only transactions are discussed in [216]. Multiversion concurrency control algorithms based on timestamps were proposed in [446]. Timestamp-based concurrency control algorithms are discussed in [64, 243]. Concurrency control algorithms based on voting are discussed in [214, 219, 280, 316, 540]. The rotating primary copy scheme is described in [384]. Optimistic concurrency control in distributed databases is discussed in [475]. Adaptive concurrency control in distributed databases is discussed in [346].

Two-phase commit was introduced in [328, 226]. The presumed abort version of 2PC is described in [391], together with another version called *2PC with presumed commit*. A variation of presumed commit is proposed in [327]. The three-phase commit protocol was described in [504]. The deadlock detection algorithms in R* are described in [410]. Many papers discuss deadlocks, for example, [115, 178, 376, 454]. [308] is a survey of several algorithms in this area. Distributed clock synchronization is discussed by [326]. [228] argues that distributed data independence is not always a good idea, due to processing and administrative overheads. The ARIES algorithm is applicable for distributed recovery, but the details of how messages should be handled are not discussed in [389]. The approach taken to recovery in SDD-1 is described in [33]. [85] also addresses distributed recovery. [311] is a survey article that discusses concurrency control and recovery in distributed systems. [73] contains several articles that address these topics.

Multidatabase systems are discussed in several papers, including [7, 84, 167, 168, 177, 335, 343, 373, 372, 432, 462, 564, 584]. [83, 344, 497] are surveys of multidatabase transaction management and interoperability.

20

DEDUCTIVE AND ACTIVE DATABASES

For 'Is' and 'Is-Not' though with Rule and Line,
And 'Up-and-Down' by Logic I define,
Of all that one should care to fathom, I
Was never deep in anything but—Wine.

—Rubaiyat of Omar Khayyam, Translated by Edward Fitzgerald

Relational database management systems have been enormously successful for administrative data processing. In recent years, however, as people have tried to use database systems in increasingly complex applications, some important limitations of these systems have been exposed. For some applications, the query language and constraint definition capabilities have been found to be inadequate. As an example, some companies maintain a huge parts inventory database, and frequently want to ask questions such as "Are we running low on any parts needed to build a ZX600 sports car?" or "What is the total component and assembly cost to build a ZX600 at today's part prices?" These queries cannot be expressed in SQL-92.

Applications that require support for complex data types expose a different kind of limitation. For example, a multimedia company that has a large number of images, maps, and audio and video recordings may want to use a DBMS to manage its assets. Unfortunately, the only support provided for this in a relational DBMS is the ability to store such objects as **binary large objects (blobs)**, or large byte-strings. The DBMS can store and retrieve a blob, but understands nothing about its contents.

These limitations have motivated considerable work on how to extend the relational model. This chapter considers two important extensions that enhance the query language and constraint enforcement capabilities of a relational DBMS, while retaining the basic tabular structure of relations. We will discuss how complex data types can be supported in a DBMS in Chapter 21.

We begin this chapter by discussing some queries that cannot be expressed in relational algebra or SQL, and present a more powerful relational language called *Datalog*. Queries and views in SQL can be understood as **if–then** rules: "If some tuples exist in tables mentioned in the FROM clause that satisfy the conditions listed in the WHERE clause, **then** the tuple described in the SELECT clause is included in the answer." Datalog definitions retain this **if–then** reading, with the significant new feature that definitions can be *recursive*, that is, a table can be defined in terms of itself.

Evaluating Datalog queries poses some additional challenges, beyond those encountered in evaluating relational algebra queries, and we discuss some important implementation and optimization techniques that were developed to address these challenges. Interestingly, some of these techniques have been found to improve performance of even nonrecursive SQL queries, and have therefore been implemented in several current relational DBMS products. Some systems, notably IBM's DB2 DBMS, support recursive queries and the current draft of the SQL standard to follow SQL-92, called SQL3, requires support for recursive queries.

The second extension of the relational model that we discuss in this chapter is the concept of an *active database*. An **active database** has a collection of **triggers**, which are specified by the DBA. A trigger describes actions to be taken when certain situations arise. The DBMS monitors the database, detects these situations, and invokes the trigger. Several current relational DBMS products support some form of triggers, and the current draft of the SQL3 standard requires support for triggers.

We concentrate on the main ideas behind recursive queries and active databases, and outline some of the challenges that they pose to DBMS implementors and database designers. We will not present the SQL3 features that cover these ideas in detail because SQL3 is currently only a draft, and likely to undergo changes before becoming a standard.

20.1   INTRODUCTION TO RECURSIVE QUERIES

We begin with a simple example that illustrates the limits of SQL-92 queries and the power of recursive definitions. Let Assembly be a relation with three fields *part, subpart* and *qty*. An example instance of Assembly is shown in Figure 20.1. Each tuple in Assembly indicates how many copies of a particular subpart are contained in a given part. The first tuple indicates, for example, that a trike contains three wheels. The Assembly relation can be visualized as a tree, as shown in Figure 20.2. A tuple is shown as an edge going from the part to the subpart, with the *qty* value as the edge label.

A natural question to ask is "What are the components of a trike?" Rather surprisingly, this query is impossible to write in SQL-92. Of course, if we look at a given instance of the Assembly relation, we can write a 'query' that takes the union of the parts that are used in a trike. But such a query is not interesting—we

part	subpart	qty
trike	wheel	3
trike	frame	1
frame	seat	1
frame	pedal	1
wheel	spoke	2
wheel	tire	1
tire	rim	1
tire	tube	1

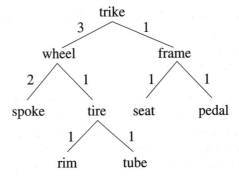

Figure 20.1   An Instance of Assembly   **Figure 20.2**   Assembly Instance Seen as a Tree

want a query that identifies all components of a trike for *any* instance of Assembly, and such a query cannot be written in relational algebra or in SQL-92. Intuitively, the problem is that we are forced to join the Assembly relation with itself in order to recognize that *trike* contains *spoke* and *tire*, that is, to go one level down the Assembly tree. For each additional level, we need an additional join; two joins are needed to recognize that *trike* contains *rim*, which is a subpart of *tire*. Thus the number of joins needed to identify all subparts of *trike* depends on the height of the Assembly tree, that is, on the given instance of the Assembly relation. There is no relational algebra query that works for all instances; given any query, we can construct an instance whose height is greater than the number of joins in the query.

20.1.1   Datalog

We now define a relation called Components that identifies the components of every part. Consider the following **program**, or collection of **rules**:

```
Components(Part, Subpart) :-  Assembly(Part, Subpart, Qty).
Components(Part, Subpart) :-  Assembly(Part, Part2, Qty),
                             Components(Part2, Subpart).
```

These are rules in **Datalog**, a relational query language inspired by Prolog; indeed, the notation follows Prolog. The first rule should be read as follows:

For all values of Part, Subpart and Qty,
if there is a tuple ⟨Part, Subpart, Qty⟩ in Assembly,
then there must be a tuple ⟨Part, Subpart⟩ in Components.

The second rule should be read as follows:

For all values of Part, Part2, Subpart and Qty,

> **if** there is a tuple ⟨Part, Part2, Qty⟩ in Assembly **and**
>   a tuple ⟨Part2, Subpart⟩ in Components,
> **then** there must be a tuple ⟨Part, Subpart⟩ in Components.

The part to the right of the ':-' symbol is called the **body** of the rule, and the part to the left is called the **head** of the rule. The symbol ':-' denotes logical implication; if the tuples mentioned in the body exist in the database, it is implied that the tuple mentioned in the head of the rule must also be in the database. Therefore, if we are given a set of Assembly and Components tuples, each rule can be used to **infer**, or **deduce**, some new tuples that belong in Components. This is why database systems that support Datalog rules are often called **deductive database systems**.

Each rule is really a *template* for making inferences: by assigning constants to the variables that appear in a rule, we can infer specific Components facts. For example, by setting Part=*trike*, Subpart=*wheel* and Qty=*3*, we can infer that ⟨*trike, wheel*⟩ is in Components. By considering each tuple in Assembly in turn, the first rule allows us to infer that the set of tuples obtained by taking the projection of Assembly onto its first two fields is in Components.

The second rule then allows us to combine previously discovered Components tuples with Assembly tuples to infer new Components tuples. We can apply the second rule by considering the cross-product of Assembly and (the current instance of) Components, and assigning values to the variables in the rule for each row of the cross-product, one row at a time. Observe how the repeated use of the variable Part2 prevents certain rows of the cross-product from contributing any new tuples; in effect, it specifies an equality join condition on Assembly and Components. The tuples obtained by one application of this rule are shown in Figure 20.3. (In addition, Components contains the tuples obtained by applying the first rule; these are not shown.)

part	subpart
trike	spoke
trike	tire
trike	seat
trike	pedal
wheel	rim
wheel	tube

part	subpart
trike	spoke
trike	tire
trike	seat
trike	pedal
wheel	rim
wheel	tube
trike	rim
trike	tube

Figure 20.3 Components Tuples Obtained by Applying Rule 2 Once

Figure 20.4 Components Tuples Obtained by Applying Rule 2 Twice

The tuples obtained by a second application of this rule are shown in Figure 20.4. Note that each tuple shown in Figure 20.3 is reinferred. Only the last two tuples are new.

Applying the second rule a third time does not generate any additional tuples. The set of Components tuples shown in Figure 20.4 includes all the tuples that can be inferred using the two Datalog rules defining Components and the given instance of Assembly. The components of a trike can now be obtained by selecting all Components tuples with the value *trike* in the first field.

Each rule application can be understood in terms of relational algebra. The first rule simply applies projection to the Assembly relation, and adds the tuples to the Components relation, which is initially empty. The second rule joins Assembly with Components and then does a projection. The result of each rule application is combined with the existing set of Components tuples using union. The only operation that goes beyond relational algebra is the *repeated* application of the rules defining Components until no new tuples are generated. This repeated application of a set of rules is called the *fixpoint* operation, and we develop this idea further in the next section.

We conclude this section by rewriting the Datalog definition of Components in terms of extended SQL, using the syntax proposed in the SQL3 draft and currently supported in IBM's DB2 Version 2 DBMS:

```
WITH RECURSIVE Components(Part, Subpart) AS
          (SELECT A1.Part, A1.Subpart FROM Assembly A1)
          UNION
          (SELECT A2.Part, C1.Subpart
          FROM    Assembly A2, Components C1
          WHERE   A2.Subpart = C1.Part)

SELECT    * FROM Components C2
```

The WITH clause introduces a relation that is part of a query definition; this relation is similar to a view, but the scope of a relation introduced using WITH is local to the query definition. The RECURSIVE keyword signals that the table (in our example, Components) is recursively defined. The structure of the definition closely parallels the Datalog rules. Incidentally, if we wanted to find the components of a particular part, for example, *trike*, we can simply replace the last line with the following:

```
SELECT * FROM Components C2
WHERE   C2.Part = 'trike'
```

20.1.2   The Fixpoint Operator

A **fixpoint** of a function f is a value v such that the function applied to the value returns the same value, that is, $f(v) = v$. Consider a function that is applied to a set of values and also returns a set of values. For example, we can define *double* to be a function that multiplies every element of the input set by two, and *double+* to be *double* $\cup$ *identity*. Thus *double*({1,2,5}) = {2,4,10}, and *double+*({1,2,5}) = {1,2,4,5,10}. The set of all even integers—which happens to be an infinite set!—is a fixpoint of the function *double+*. Another fixpoint of the function *double+* is the set of all integers. The first fixpoint (the set of all even integers) is *smaller* than the second fixpoint (the set of all integers) because it is contained in the latter.

The **least fixpoint** of a function is a fixpoint that is smaller than every other fixpoint of that function. In general it is not guaranteed that a function has a least fixpoint. For example, there may be two fixpoints, neither of which is smaller than the other. (Does *double* have a least fixpoint? What is it?)

Now let us turn to functions over sets of tuples, in particular functions defined using relational algebra expressions. The Components relation can be defined by an equation of the form:

$$Components = \pi_{1,5}(Assembly \bowtie_{2=1} Components) \cup \pi_{1,2}(Assembly)$$

This equation has the form

$$Components = f(Components)$$

where the function f is defined using a relational algebra expression.

The least fixpoint of f is an instance of Components that satisfies the above equation. Clearly the projection of the first two fields of the tuples in Assembly must be included in this instance of Components. In addition, any tuple obtained by joining (this instance of) Components with Assembly and projecting the appropriate fields must also be in (this instance of) Components. This description of the least fixpoint of f is very similar to the reading of the Datalog definition of Components.

A little thought shows that the instance of Components that is the least fixpoint of f can be computed using repeated applications of the Datalog rules shown in the previous section. Indeed, applying the two Datalog rules is identical to evaluating the relational expression used in defining Components. If an application generates Components tuples that are not in the current instance of the Components relation, the current instance cannot be the fixpoint. Therefore, we add the new tuples to Components and evaluate the relational expression (equivalently, the two Datalog rules) again. This process is repeated until every tuple generated is already in the current instance of Components; at this point, we have reached a fixpoint. If Components is initialized to the empty set of tuples, intuitively we infer only tuples that are necessary by the definition of a fixpoint, and the fixpoint computed is the least fixpoint.

As we noted earlier in this section, not every function has a least fixpoint. Fortunately, every function defined in terms of relational algebra expressions that do not contain set-difference is guaranteed to have a least fixpoint, and the least fixpoint can be computed by repeatedly evaluating the function. (We will not discuss the proof of this claim.) Unfortunately, this claim is not true once set-difference is allowed. We consider this point further in the next section.

20.2 RECURSIVE QUERIES WITH NEGATION

Consider the following rules:

```
Big(Part) :-    Assembly(Part, Subpart, Qty), Qty > 2,
                not Small(Part).
Small(Part) :-  Assembly(Part, Subpart, Qty), not Big(Part).
```

These two rules can be thought of as an attempt to divide parts (those that are mentioned in the first column of the Assembly table) into two classes, Big and Small. The first rule defines Big to be the set of parts that use at least three copies of some subpart and that are not classified as small parts. The second rule defines Small as the set of parts that are not classified as big parts.

If we apply these rules to the instance of Assembly shown in Figure 20.1, *trike* is the only part that uses at least three copies of some subpart. Should the tuple $\langle trike \rangle$ be in Big or Small? If we apply the first rule and then the second rule, this tuple is in Big. To apply the first rule, we consider the tuples in Assembly, choose those with Qty > 2 (which is just $\langle trike \rangle$), discard those that are in the current instance of Small (both Big and Small are initially empty), and add the tuples that are left to Big. Therefore, an application of the first rule adds $\langle trike \rangle$ to Big. Proceeding similarly, we can see that if the second rule is applied before the first, $\langle trike \rangle$ is added to Small instead of Big!

This program has two fixpoints, neither of which is smaller than the other, as shown in Figure 20.5. The first fixpoint has a Big tuple that does not appear in the second fixpoint; therefore, it is not smaller than the second fixpoint. The second fixpoint has a Small tuple that does not appear in the first fixpoint; therefore, it is not smaller than the first fixpoint. The order in which we apply the rules determines which fixpoint is computed, and this situation is very unsatisfactory.

We want users to be able to understand their queries without thinking about exactly how the evaluation proceeds.

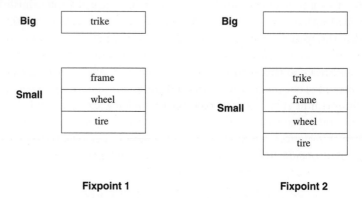

Figure 20.5 Two Fixpoints for the Big/Small Program

The root of the problem is the use of **not**. When we apply the first rule, some inferences are disallowed because of the presence of tuples in Small. Parts that satisfy the other conditions in the body of the rule are candidates for addition to Big, and we remove the parts in Small from this set of candidates. Thus some inferences that are possible if Small is empty (as it is before the second rule is applied) are disallowed if Small contains tuples (generated by applying the second rule before the first rule). Here is the difficulty: If **not** is used, the addition of tuples to a relation can *disallow* the inference of other tuples. Without **not**, this situation can never arise; the addition of tuples to a relation can *never* disallow the inference of other tuples.

20.2.1 Stratification

A widely used solution to the problem caused by negation, or the use of **not**, is to impose certain syntactic restrictions on programs. These restrictions can be easily checked, and for programs that satisfy them, there is a natural meaning.

We say that a table T **depends on** a table S if some rule with T in the head contains S, or (recursively) contains a predicate that depends on S, in the body. A recursively defined predicate always depends on itself. For example, Big depends on Small (and on itself). Indeed, the tables Big and Small are **mutually recursive**, that is, the definition of Big depends on Small and vice versa. We say that a table T **depends negatively on** a table S if some rule with T in the head contains **not** S, or (recursively) contains a predicate that depends negatively on S, in the body.

Suppose that we classify the tables in a program into **strata** or **layers** as follows. The tables that do not depend on any other tables are in stratum 0. In our Big/Small example, Assembly is the only table in stratum 0. Next, we identify tables in stratum 1; these are tables that depend only on tables in stratum 0 or stratum 1, and depend negatively only on tables in stratum 0. Higher strata are similarly defined: the tables in stratum i are those that do not appear in lower strata, depend only on tables in stratum i or lower strata, and depend negatively only on tables in lower strata. A **stratified program** is a program whose tables can be classified into strata according to the above algorithm.

The Big/Small program is not stratified. Since Big and Small depend on each other, they must be in the same stratum. However, they depend negatively on each other, violating the requirement that a table can depend negatively only on tables in lower strata. Consider the following variant of the Big/Small program, in which the first rule has been modified:

```
Big2(Part) :- Assembly(Part, Subpart, Qty), Qty > 2.
Small2(Part) :- Assembly(Part, Subpart, Qty), not Big2(Part).
```

This program is stratified. Small2 depends on Big2 but Big2 does not depend on Small2. Assembly is in stratum 0, Big is in stratum 1, and Small2 is in stratum 2.

A stratified program is evaluated stratum-by-stratum, starting with stratum 0. To evaluate a stratum, we compute the fixpoint of all rules defining tables that belong to this stratum. When evaluating a stratum, any occurrence of **not** involves a table from a lower stratum, which has therefore been completely evaluated by now. The tuples in the negated table will still disallow some inferences, but the effect is completely deterministic, given the stratum-by-stratum evaluation. In the example, Big2 is computed before Small2 because it is in a lower stratum than Small2; $\langle trike \rangle$ is added to Big2. Next, when we compute Small2, we recognize that $\langle trike \rangle$ is not in Small2 because it is already in Big2.

Incidentally, observe that the stratified Big/Small program is not even recursive! If we replaced Assembly by Components, we would obtain a recursive, stratified program: Assembly would be in stratum 0, Components would be in stratum 1, Big2 would also be in stratum 1, and Small2 would be in stratum 2.

Intuition behind Stratification

The requirement that programs be stratified gives us a natural order for evaluating rules. When the rules are evaluated in this order, the result is a unique fixpoint that is one of the minimal fixpoints of the program. The fixpoint computed by the stratified fixpoint evaluation usually corresponds well to our intuitive reading of a stratified program, even if the program has more than one minimal fixpoint.

Consider the stratified version of the Big/Small program. The rule defining Big2 forces us to add ⟨*trike*⟩ to Big2, and it is natural to assume that ⟨*trike*⟩ is the only tuple in Big2, because we have no supporting evidence for any other tuple being in Big2. The minimal fixpoint computed by stratified fixpoint evaluation is consistent with this intuition. However, there is another minimal fixpoint: We can place every part in Big2, and make Small2 be empty. While this assignment of tuples to relations seems unintuitive, it is nonetheless a minimal fixpoint!

Relational Algebra and Stratified Datalog

We observe that every relational algebra query can be written as a stratified Datalog program. (Of course, not all Datalog programs can be expressed in relational algebra; for example, the Components program.) We sketch the translation from algebra to stratified Datalog by writing a Datalog program for each of the basic algebra operations, in terms of two example tables R and S, each with two fields:

Selection: Result(Y) :- R(X,Y), X=c.
Projection: Result(Y) :- R(X,Y).
Cross-product: Result(X,Y,U,V) :- R(X,Y), S(U,V).
Set-difference: Result(X,Y) :- R(X,Y), **not** S(U,V).
Union: Result(X,Y) :- R(X,Y).
                    Result(X,Y) :- S(X,Y).

We conclude our discussion of stratification by noting that the SQL3 draft requires programs to be stratified. The stratified Big/Small program is shown below in SQL3 notation, with a final additional selection on Big2:

```
WITH
Big2(Part) AS
            (SELECT    A1.Part FROM  Assembly A1 WHERE  Qty > 2)
Small2(Part) AS
            ((SELECT   A2.Part FROM  Assembly A2)
            EXCEPT
            (SELECT    B1.Part from Big2 B1))

SELECT     * FROM  Big2 B2
```

20.2.2 Aggregate Operations

Datalog can be extended with SQL-style grouping and aggregation operations. Consider the following program:

```
NumParts(Part, SUM(⟨Qty⟩)) :- Assembly(Part, Subpart, Qty).
```

This program is equivalent to the SQL query:

```
SELECT      A.Part, SUM (A.Qty)
FROM        Assembly A
GROUP BY    A.Part
```

The angular brackets ⟨...⟩ notation was introduced in the LDL deductive system. We use it to denote **multiset-generation**, or the creation of multiset-values. In principle, the rule defining NumParts is evaluated by first creating the temporary relation shown in Figure 20.6. We create the temporary relation by sorting on the *part* attribute (which appears in the left side of the rule, along with the ⟨...⟩ term) and collecting the multiset of *qty* values for each *part* value. We then apply the SUM aggregate to each multiset-value in the second column to obtain the answer, which is shown in Figure 20.7.

part	⟨qty⟩
trike	{3,1}
frame	{1,1}
wheel	{2,1}
tire	{1,1}

part	SUM(⟨qty⟩)
trike	4
frame	2
wheel	3
tire	2

Figure 20.6 Temporary Relation   **Figure 20.7** The Tuples in NumParts

The temporary relation shown in Figure 20.6 need not be materialized in order to compute NumParts—for example, SUM can be applied on-the-fly, or Assembly can simply be sorted and aggregated as described in Section 12.7. However, we observe that several deductive database systems (e.g., LDL, Coral) in fact allowed the materialization of this temporary relation; the following program would do so:

```
TempReln(Part,⟨Qty⟩) :- Assembly(Part, Subpart, Qty).
```

The tuples in this relation are not in first-normal form, and there is no way to create this relation using SQL. (We will return to this point when we discuss extensions to the data types supported in relational systems in Chapter 21.)

The use of aggregate operations leads to problems similar to those caused by **not**, and the idea of stratification can restrict the use of aggregate operations as well. Consider the following program:

```
NumComps(Part, COUNT(⟨Subpart⟩) ) :- Components(Part, Subpart).
Components(Part, Subpart) :-  Assembly(Part, Subpart, Qty).
Components(Part, Subpart) :-  Assembly(Part, Part2, Qty),
                             Components(Part2, Subpart).
```

The idea is to count the number of subparts for each part; by aggregating over Components rather than Assembly, we can count subparts at any level in the hierarchy instead of just immediate subparts. The important point to note in this example is that we must wait until Components has been completely evaluated before we apply the NumComps rule. Otherwise, we obtain incomplete counts. This situation is analogous to the problem we faced with negation; we have to evaluate the negated relation completely before applying a rule that involves the use of **not**. If a program is stratified with respect to uses of ⟨...⟩ as well as **not**, stratified fixpoint evaluation gives us meaningful results.

20.3   EFFICIENT EVALUATION OF RECURSIVE QUERIES

The evaluation of recursive queries has been widely studied. While all the problems of evaluating nonrecursive queries continue to be present, the newly introduced fixpoint operation creates additional difficulties. A straightforward approach to evaluating recursive queries is to compute the fixpoint by repeatedly applying the rules as illustrated in Section 20.1.1. This approach has two main disadvantages:

- **Repeated inferences:** As Figures 20.3 and 20.4 illustrate, inferences are repeated across iterations. That is, the same fact is inferred repeatedly in *the same way*, that is, using the same rule and the same facts for tables in the body of the rule.

- **Unnecessary inferences:** Suppose that we only want to find the components of a *wheel*. Computing the entire Components table is wasteful, and does not take advantage of information in the query.

In this section we discuss how each of these difficulties can be overcome. We will consider only Datalog programs without negation.

20.3.1   Fixpoint Evaluation without Repeated Inferences

Computing the fixpoint by repeatedly applying all rules is called **Naive fixpoint evaluation**. Naive evaluation is guaranteed to compute the least fixpoint, but every application of a rule repeats all inferences made by earlier applications of this rule. We illustrate this point using the following rule:

```
Components(Part, Subpart) :-   Assembly(Part, Part2, Qty),
                               Components(Part2, Subpart).
```

When this rule is applied for the first time, after applying the first rule defining Components, the Components table contains the projection of Assembly on the first two fields. Using these Components tuples in the body of the rule, we generate the tuples shown in Figure 20.3. For example, the tuple ⟨*wheel, rim*⟩ is generated through the following inference:

```
Components(wheel, rim) :-   Assembly(wheel, tire, 1),
                           Components(tire, rim).
```

When this rule is applied a second time, the Components table contains the tuples shown in Figure 20.3, in addition to the tuples that it contained before the first application. Using the Components tuples shown in Figure 20.3 leads to new inferences, for example:

```
Components(trike, rim) :-   Assembly(trike, wheel, 3),
                           Components(wheel, rim).
```

However, every inference carried out in the first application of this rule is also repeated in the second application of the rule, since all the Assembly and Components tuples used in the first rule application are considered again. For example, the inference of ⟨*wheel, rim*⟩ shown above is repeated in the second application of this rule.

The solution to this repetition of inferences consists of remembering which inferences were carried out in earlier rule applications, and not carrying them out again. It turns out that we can 'remember' previously executed inferences efficiently by simply keeping track of which Components tuples were generated for the first time in the most recent application of the recursive rule. Suppose that we keep track by introducing a new relation called *delta*_Components and storing just the newly generated Components tuples in it. Now, we can use only the tuples in *delta*_Components in the next application of the recursive rule; any inference using other Components tuples should have been carried out in earlier rule applications.

This refinement of fixpoint evaluation is called **Seminaive fixpoint evaluation**. Let us trace Seminaive fixpoint evaluation on our example program. The first application of the recursive rule produces the Components tuples shown in Figure 20.3, just like Naive fixpoint evaluation, and these tuples are placed in *delta*_Components. In the second application, however, only *delta*_Components tuples are considered, which means that only the following inferences are carried out in the second application of the recursive rule:

```
Components(trike, rim)  :-     Assembly(trike, wheel, 3),
                               delta_Components(wheel, rim).
Components(trike, tube) :-     Assembly(trike, wheel, 3),
                               delta_Components(wheel, tube).
```

Next, the book keeping relation *delta*_Components is updated to contain just these two Components tuples. In the third application of the recursive rule, only these two *delta*_Components tuples are considered, and thus no additional inferences can be made. The fixpoint of Components has been reached.

To implement Seminaive fixpoint evaluation for general Datalog programs, we apply all the recursive rules in a program together in an **iteration**. Iterative application of all recursive rules is repeated until no new tuples are generated in some iteration. To summarize how Seminaive fixpoint evaluation is carried out, there are two important differences with respect to Naive fixpoint evaluation:

■ We maintain a *delta* version of every recursive predicate to keep track of the tuples generated for this predicate in the most recent iteration; for example, *delta*_Components for Components. The *delta* versions are updated at the end of each iteration.

■ The original program rules are rewritten to ensure that every inference uses at least one *delta* tuple, that is, one tuple that was not known before the previous iteration. This property guarantees that the inference could not have been carried out in earlier iterations.

We will not discuss the details of Seminaive fixpoint evaluation, such as how program rules are rewritten to ensure the use of a *delta* tuple.

20.3.2 Pushing Selections to Avoid Irrelevant Inferences

Consider a nonrecursive view definition. If we want only those tuples in the view that satisfy an additional selection condition, the selection can be added to the plan as a final selection operation, and the relational algebra transformations for commuting selections with other relational operators allow us to 'push' the selection ahead of more expensive operations such as cross-products and joins. In effect, we are able to restrict the computation by utilizing selections in the query specification. The problem is more complicated for recursively defined views.

We will use the following program as an example in this section:

```
SameLevel(S1, S2) :-  Assembly(P1, S1, Q1), Assembly(P2, S2, Q2).
SameLevel(S1, S2) :-  Assembly(P1, S1, Q1),
                      SameLevel(P1, P2), Assembly(P2, S2, Q2).
```

Consider the tree representation of Assembly tuples illustrated in Figure 20.2. There is a tuple ⟨S1, S2⟩ in SameLevel if there is a path from S1 to S2 that goes up a certain number of edges in the tree and then comes down the same number of edges.

Suppose that we want to find all SameLevel tuples with the first field equal to *spoke*. Since SameLevel tuples can be used to compute other SameLevel tuples, we cannot just compute those tuples with *spoke* in the first field. For example, the tuple ⟨*wheel, frame*⟩ in SameLevel allows us to infer a SameLevel tuple with *spoke* in the first field:

```
SameLevel(spoke, seat) :-  Assembly(wheel, spoke, 2),
                           SameLevel(wheel, frame),
                           Assembly(frame, seat, 1).
```

Intuitively, we have to compute all SameLevel tuples whose first field contains a value that is on the path from *spoke* to the root in Figure 20.2. Each such tuple has the potential to contribute to answers for the given query. On the other hand, computing the entire SameLevel table is wasteful; for example, the SameLevel tuple ⟨*tire, seat*⟩ cannot be used to infer any answer to the given query (or indeed, to infer any fact that can in turn be used to infer an answer fact). We can define a new table, which we will call Magic, such that each tuple in this table identifies a value m for which we have to compute all SameLevel tuples with m in the first column, in order to answer the given query:

```
Magic(P1) :-    Magic(S1), Assembly(P1, S1, Q1).
Magic(spoke) :- .
```

Consider the tuples in Magic. Obviously we have ⟨*spoke*⟩. Using this Magic tuple, and the Assembly tuple ⟨*wheel, spoke, 2*⟩, we can infer that the tuple ⟨*wheel*⟩ is in Magic. Using this tuple and the Assembly tuple ⟨*trike, wheel, 3*⟩, we can infer that the tuple ⟨*trike*⟩ is in Magic. Thus Magic contains each node that is on the path from *spoke* to the root in Figure 20.2. The Magic table can be used as a filter to restrict the computation:

```
SameLevel(S1, S2) :-  Magic(S1),
                      Assembly(P1, S1, Q1), Assembly(P2, S2, Q2).
SameLevel(S1, S2) :-  Magic(S1), Assembly(P1, S1, Q1),
                      SameLevel(P1, P2), Assembly(P2, S2, Q2).
```

These rules together with the rules defining Magic give us a program for computing all SameLevel facts with *spoke* in the first column. Notice that the new program depends on the query constant *spoke* only in the second rule defining Magic. Thus the program for computing all SameLevel tuples with *seat* in the first column, for instance, is identical except that the second Magic rule is:

```
Magic(seat) :- .
```

The number of inferences made using the 'Magic' program can be far fewer than the number of inferences made using the original program, depending on just how much the selection in the query restricts the computation.

We will not describe the algorithm for obtaining the Magic version of a program, given a query. We remark, however, that this rewriting technique, called **Magic Sets**, has turned out to be quite effective for computing correlated nested SQL queries, even if there is no recursion, and is used for this purpose in many commercial DBMSs even though these systems do not currently support recursive queries.

20.4   INTRODUCTION TO ACTIVE DATABASES

As noted earlier, a *trigger* is a procedure that is automatically invoked by the DBMS in response to specified changes to the database, and an *active database* has a set of associated triggers, typically specified by the DBA. A trigger description contains three parts:

- **Event**: A change to the database that **activates** the trigger.

- **Condition**: A query or test that is run when the trigger is activated.

- **Action**: A procedure that is executed when the trigger is activated and its condition is true.

A trigger can be thought of as a 'daemon' that monitors a database, and is executed when the database is modified in a way that matches the *event* specification. An insert, delete or update statement could activate a trigger, regardless of which user or application invoked the activating statement; users may not even be aware that a trigger was executed as a side effect of their program.

A *condition* in a trigger can be a true/false statement (e.g., all employee salaries are less than $100,000) or a query. A query is interpreted as *true* if the answer set is nonempty, and *false* if the query has no answers. If the condition part evaluates to true, the action associated with the trigger is executed.

A trigger *action* can examine the answers to the query in the condition part of the trigger, refer to old and new values of tuples modified by the statement activating the trigger, execute new queries, and make changes to the database. In fact, an action can even execute a series of data-definition commands (e.g., create new tables, change authorizations) and transaction-oriented commands (e.g., commit), or call host-language procedures.

An important issue is when the action part of a trigger executes in relation to the statement that activated the trigger. For example, a statement that inserts records into the Students table may activate a trigger that is used to maintain statistics on how many students younger than 18 are inserted at a time by a typical insert statement. Depending on exactly what the trigger does, we may want its action to execute *before* changes are made to the Students table, or *after*: a trigger that initializes a variable used to count the number of qualifying insertions should be executed before, and a trigger that executes once per qualifying inserted record and increments the variable should be executed after each record is inserted (because we may want to examine the values in the new record to determine the action).

20.4.1 Examples of Triggers in SQL

The examples shown in Figure 20.8, written using Oracle 7 Server syntax for defining triggers, illustrate the basic concepts behind triggers. (The SQL3 syntax for these triggers is similar; we will see an example using SQL3 syntax shortly.) The trigger called *init_count* initializes a counter variable before every execution of an **INSERT** statement that adds tuples to the Students relation. The trigger called *incr_count* increments the counter for each inserted tuple that satisfies the condition $age < 18$.

One of the example triggers in Figure 20.8 executes before the activating statement, and the other example executes after. A trigger can also be scheduled to execute *instead of* the activating statement, or in *deferred* fashion, at the end of the transaction containing the activating statement, or in *asynchronous* fashion, as part of a separate transaction.

The example in Figure 20.8 illustrates another point about trigger execution: A user must be able to specify whether a trigger is to be executed once per modified record or once per activating statement. If the action depends on individual changed records, for example, we have to examine the *age* field of the inserted Students record to decide whether to increment the count, the triggering event should be defined to occur for each modified record; the **FOR EACH ROW** clause is used to do this. Such a trigger is called a **row-level trigger**. On the other hand, the *init_count* trigger is executed just once per **INSERT** statement, regardless of the

```
CREATE TRIGGER init_count BEFORE INSERT ON Students        /* Event */
    DECLARE
        count INTEGER;
    BEGIN                                                  /* Action */
        count := 0;
    END


CREATE TRIGGER incr_count AFTER INSERT ON Students         /* Event */
    WHEN (new.age < 18)        /* Condition; 'new' is just-inserted tuple */
    FOR EACH ROW
    BEGIN              /* Action; a procedure in Oracle's PL/SQL syntax */
        count := count + 1;
    END
```

Figure 20.8   Examples Illustrating Triggers

number of records inserted, because we have omitted the **FOR EACH ROW** phrase. Such a trigger is called a **statement-level trigger**.

In Figure 20.8, the keyword **new** refers to the newly inserted tuple. If an existing tuple were modified, the keywords **old** and **new** could be used to refer to the values before and after the modification. The SQL3 draft also allows the action part of a trigger to refer to the *set* of changed records, rather than just one changed record at a time. For example, it would be useful to be able to refer to the set of inserted Students records in a trigger that executes once after the **INSERT** statement; we could count the number of inserted records with *age* < 18 through an SQL query over this set. Such a trigger is shown in Figure 20.9 and is an alternative to the triggers shown in Figure 20.8.

The definition in Figure 20.9 uses the syntax of the SQL3 draft, in order to illustrate the similarities and differences with respect to the syntax used in a typical current DBMS. The keyword clause **NEW TABLE** enables us to give a table name (InsertedTuples) to the set of newly inserted tuples. The **FOR EACH STATEMENT** clause specifies a statement-level trigger and can be omitted because it is the default. This definition does not have a **WHEN** clause; if such a clause is included, it follows the **FOR EACH STATEMENT** clause, just before the action specification.

The trigger is evaluated once for each SQL statement that inserts tuples into Students, and inserts a single tuple into a table that contains statistics on modifications to database tables. The first two fields of the tuple contain constants (identifying the modified table, Students, and the kind of modifying statement, an **INSERT**), and the third field is the number of inserted Students tuples with *age*

< 18. (The triggers in Figure 20.8 only compute the count; an additional trigger is required to insert the appropriate tuple into the statistics table.)

```
CREATE TRIGGER set_count AFTER INSERT ON Students        /* Event */
REFERENCING NEW TABLE AS InsertedTuples
FOR EACH STATEMENT
    INSERT                                                /* Action */
        INTO StatisticsTable(ModifiedTable, ModificationType, Count)
        SELECT 'Students', 'Insert', COUNT *
        FROM InsertedTuples I
        WHERE I.age < 18
```

Figure 20.9   Set-Oriented Trigger

20.5   DESIGNING ACTIVE DATABASES

Triggers offer a powerful mechanism for dealing with changes to a database, but they must be used with caution. The effect of a collection of triggers can be very complex, and maintaining an active database can become very difficult. Often, a judicious use of integrity constraints can replace the use of triggers.

20.5.1   Why Triggers Can Be Hard to Understand

In an active database system, when the DBMS is about to execute a statement that modifies the database, it checks whether some trigger is activated by the statement. If so, the DBMS processes the trigger by evaluating its condition part, and then (if the condition evaluates to true) executing its action part.

If a statement activates more than one trigger, the DBMS typically processes all of them, in some arbitrary order. An important point is that the execution of the action part of a trigger could in turn activate another trigger. In particular, the execution of the action part of a trigger could again activate the same trigger; such triggers are called **recursive triggers**. The potential for such *chain* activations, and the unpredictable order in which a DBMS processes activated triggers, can make it difficult to understand the effect of a collection of triggers.

20.5.2   Constraints versus Triggers

A common use of triggers is to maintain database consistency, and in such cases, we should always consider whether using an integrity constraint (e.g., a foreign key constraint) will achieve the same goals. The meaning of a constraint is not defined operationally, unlike the effect of a trigger. This property makes a constraint easier to understand, and also gives the DBMS more opportunities to optimize execution. A constraint also prevents the data from being made inconsistent by *any* kind of statement, whereas a trigger is activated by a specific kind of statement (e.g., an insert or delete statement). Again, this restriction makes a constraint easier to understand.

On the other hand, triggers allow us to maintain database integrity in more flexible ways, as the following examples illustrate.

- Suppose that we have a table called Orders with fields *itemid, quantity, customerid* and *unitprice*. When a customer places an order, the first three field values are filled in by the user (in this example, a sales clerk). The fourth field's value can be obtained from a table called Items, but it is important to include it in the Orders table to have a complete record of the order, in case the price of the item is subsequently changed. We can define a trigger to look up this value and include it in the fourth field of a newly inserted record. In addition to reducing the number of fields that the clerk has to type in, this trigger eliminates the possibility of an entry error leading to an inconsistent price in the Orders table.

- Continuing with the above example, we may want to perform some additional actions when an order is received. For example, if the purchase is being charged to a credit line issued by the company, we may want to check whether the total cost of the purchase is within the current credit limit. We can use a trigger to do the check; indeed, we can even use a CHECK constraint. Using a trigger, however, allows us to implement more sophisticated policies for dealing with purchases that exceed a credit limit. For instance, we may allow purchases that exceed the limit by no more than 10% if the customer has dealt with the company for at least a year, and add the customer to a table of candidates for credit limit increases.

20.5.3 Other Uses of Triggers

Many potential uses of triggers go beyond integrity maintenance. Triggers can also alert users to unusual events (as reflected in updates to the database). For example, we may want to check whether a customer placing an order has made enough purchases in the past month to qualify for an additional discount; if so, the sales clerk must be informed so that he can tell the customer, and possibly generate additional sales! We can relay this information by using a trigger that checks recent purchases and prints a message if the customer qualifies for the discount.

Triggers can generate a log of events and to support auditing and security checks. For example, each time a customer places an order, we can create a record with the customer's id and current credit limit, and insert this record in a customer history table. Subsequent analysis of this table might suggest candidates for an increased credit limit (e.g., customers who've never failed to pay a bill on time and who've come within 10% of their credit limit at least three times in the last month).

As the examples in Section 20.4 illustrate, we can use triggers to gather statistics on table accesses and modifications. Some database systems even use triggers internally as the basis for managing replicas of relations (Section 19.10.1). Our list of potential uses of triggers is not exhaustive; for example, triggers have also been considered for workflow management and enforcing business rules.

20.6 SUMMARY

In this chapter we discussed extensions to the query language and constraint specification components of a relational DBMS.

The first extension enhances SQL by allowing recursive definitions. There are a number of queries that cannot be expressed in SQL-92 without such an extension. Recursive definitions are like ordinary SQL queries except that the **FROM** clause can include the table being defined. A DBMS that supports recursive definitions is often called a deductive database system.

The meaning of a recursive table definition is given in terms of fixpoints. A recursively defined table is evaluated by repeatedly computing the defining relational expression. If negation (set-difference) is used in the defining relational expression, the meaning of the definition becomes ambiguous. Recursive definitions must therefore be *stratified*; in essence, a table cannot depend negatively on itself. Stratified definitions have a clear meaning, and every relational algebra expression can be written as a stratified table definition.

The evaluation of recursively defined tables consists of repeatedly inferring tuples for the defined relation by evaluating the defining expression. It poses two major challenges: avoiding repetition of inferences, and avoiding irrelevant inferences (inferences of tuples that are not required for computing answers to a given query). Seminaive fixpoint evaluation and magic sets program rewriting are optimization techniques that address these problems.

The second extension considered in this chapter is the use of active rules or triggers. A trigger is executed by the DBMS when an associated event (typically, a change to some database table) occurs. When the trigger is executed, an associated condition is evaluated first. If this condition evaluates to *true*, an associated action is executed. The action can refer to the result of the condition evaluation and to the old and new values of the modified tuples. It can consist of any SQL statements or even external procedures.

Important parameters of a trigger definition include when the trigger is to be executed relative to the activating statement (the statement that changed the database and caused the trigger to be executed), and whether the trigger is to execute once per modified tuple or once per modifying statement.

Triggers significantly enhance a DBMS's ability to respond to changes to the data. However, the procedural nature of triggers can make the effect of a collection of triggers hard to understand and lead to unexpected results. Triggers should therefore be used with caution.

EXERCISES

Exercise 20.1 Consider the Flights relation:

> Flights(*flno:* integer, *from:* string, *to:* string, *distance:* integer,
> *departs:* time, *arrives:* time)

Write the following queries in Datalog and SQL3 syntax:

1. Find the *flno* of all flights that depart from Madison.
2. Find the *flno* of all flights that leave Chicago after Flight 101 arrives in Chicago and no later than one hour after.
3. Find the *flno* of all flights that do not depart from Madison.
4. Find all cities reachable from Madison through a series of one or more connecting flights.
5. Find all cities reachable from Madison through a chain of one or more connecting flights, with no more than one hour spent on any connection. (That is, every connecting flight must depart within an hour of the arrival of the previous flight in the chain.)
6. Find the shortest time to fly from Madison to Madras, using a chain of one or more connecting flights.
7. Find the *flno* of all flights that do not depart from Madison or a city that is reachable from Madison through a chain of flights.

Exercise 20.2 Consider the definition of Components in Section 20.1.1. Suppose that the second rule is replaced by

```
Components(Part, Subpart) :-  Components(Part, Part2, Qty),
                             Components(Part2, Subpart).
```

1. If the modified program is evaluated on the Assembly relation in Figure 20.1, how many iterations does Naive fixpoint evaluation take, and what Components facts are generated in each iteration?

2. Extend the given instance of Assembly so that Naive fixpoint iteration takes two more iterations.

3. Write this program in SQL3 syntax, using the WITH clause.

4. Write a program in Datalog syntax to find the part with the most distinct subparts; if several parts have the same maximum number of subparts, your query should return all of these parts.

5. How would your answer to the previous part be changed if you also wanted to list the number of subparts for the part with the most distinct subparts?

6. Rewrite your answers to the previous two parts in SQL3 syntax.

7. Suppose that you want to find the part with the most subparts, taking into account the quantity of each subpart used in a part, how would you modify the Components program? (*Hint:* To write such a query you reason about the number of inferences of a fact. For this, you have to rely on SQL's maintaining as many copies of each fact as the number of inferences of that fact, and take into account the properties of Seminaive evaluation.)

Exercise 20.3 Consider the definition of Components in Exercise 20.2. Suppose that the recursive rule is rewritten as follows for Seminaive fixpoint evaluation:

```
Components(Part, Subpart) :-   delta_Components(Part, Part2, Qty),
                               delta_Components(Part2, Subpart).
```

1. At the end of an iteration, what steps must be taken to update *delta*_Components to contain just the new tuples generated in this iteration? Can you suggest an index on Components that might help to make this faster?

2. Even if the *delta* relation is correctly updated, fixpoint evaluation using the preceding rule will not always produce all answers. Show an instance of Assembly that illustrates the problem.

3. Can you suggest a way to rewrite the recursive rule in terms of *delta*_Components so that Seminaive fixpoint evaluation always produces all answers and no inferences are repeated across iterations?

4. Show how your version of the rewritten program performs on the example instance of Assembly that you used to illustrate the problem with the given rewriting of the recursive rule.

Exercise 20.4 Consider the definition of SameLevel in Section 20.3.2 and the Assembly instance shown in Figure 20.1.

1. Rewrite the recursive rule for Seminaive fixpoint evaluation, and show how Seminaive evaluation proceeds.

2. Consider the rules defining the relation Magic, with *spoke* as the query constant. For Seminaive evaluation of the 'Magic' version of the SameLevel program, all tuples in Magic are computed first. Show how Seminaive evaluation of the Magic relation proceeds.

3. After the Magic relation is computed, it can be treated as a fixed database relation, just like Assembly, in the Seminaive fixpoint evaluation of the rules defining SameLevel in the 'Magic' version of the program. Rewrite the recursive rule for Seminaive evaluation and show how Seminaive evaluation of these rules proceeds.

Exercise 20.5 Discuss the strengths and weaknesses of the trigger mechanism. Contrast triggers with other integrity constraints supported by SQL.

Exercise 20.6 Consider the following relational schema. An employee can work in more than one department; the *pct_time* field of the Works relation shows the percentage of time that a given employee works in a given department.

Emp(*eid:* integer, *ename:* string, *age:* integer, *salary:* real)
Works(*eid:* integer, *did:* integer, *pct_time:* integer)
Dept(*did:* integer, *budget:* real, *managerid:* integer)

Write SQL-92 integrity constraints (domain, key, foreign key, or CHECK constraints; or assertions) or SQL3 triggers to ensure each of the following requirements, considered independently.

1. Employees must make a minimum salary of $1000.

2. Every manager must be also be an employee.

3. The total percentage of all appointments for an employee must be under 100%.

4. A manager must always have a higher salary than any employee that he or she manages.

5. Whenever an employee is given a raise, the manager's salary must be increased to be at least as much.

6. Whenever an employee is given a raise, the manager's salary must be increased to be at least as much. Further, whenever an employee is given a raise, the department's budget must be increased to be greater than the sum of salaries of all employees in the department.

BIBLIOGRAPHIC NOTES

The use of logic as a query language is discussed in several papers in [211, 383], which arose out of influential workshops. Good textbook discussions of deductive databases can be found in [550, 4, 104, 582, 361]. [442] is a recent survey article that provides an overview and covers the major prototypes in the area, including LDL [127], Glue-Nail! [395] and [156], EKS-V1 [559], Aditi [443], Coral [441], LOLA [589], and XSB [465].

The fixpoint semantics of logic programs (and deductive databases as a special case) is presented in [553], which also shows equivalence of the fixpoint semantics to a *least-model* semantics. The use of stratification to give a natural semantics to programs with negation was developed independently in [113, 28, 405, 554].

Efficient evaluation of deductive database queries has been widely studied, and [43] is a survey and comparison of several early techniques; [440] is a more recent survey. Seminaive fixpoint evaluation was independently proposed several times; a good treatment appears in [39]. The Magic Sets technique was proposed in [42] and was generalized to cover all deductive database queries without negation in [58]. The Alexander method [453] was independently developed and is equivalent to a variant of Magic Sets called *Supplementary Magic Sets* in [58]. [399] showed how Magic Sets offers significant performance benefits even for nonrecursive SQL queries. [488] describes a version of Magic Sets designed for SQL queries with correlation, and its implementation in the Starburst system (which led to its implementation in IBM's DB2 DBMS). [485] discusses how Magic Sets can be incorporated into a System R style cost-based optimization framework. The Magic Sets technique is extended to programs with stratified negation in [57, 38]. [88] compares Magic Sets with top-down evaluation strategies derived from Prolog.

[463] develops a program rewriting technique related to Magic Sets called *Magic Counting*. Other related methods that are not based on program rewriting but rather on run-time control strategies for evaluation include [296, 557, 558, 166]. The ideas in [166] have been developed further to design an *abstract machine* for logic program evaluation using tabling in [535] and [439]; this is the basis for the XSB system [465].

[568] contains a collection of papers that cover the active database field. [582] includes a good in-depth introduction to active rules, covering semantics, applications and design issues. [183] discusses SQL extensions for specifying integrity constraint checks through triggers. [90] also discusses a procedural mechanism, called an *alerter*, for monitoring a database. [133] is a recent paper that suggests how triggers might be incorporated into SQL extensions. Influential active database prototypes include Ariel [248], HiPAC [370], ODE [14], Postgres [529], RDL [503], and Sentinel [27]. [108] compares various architectures for active database systems.

[26] considers conditions under which a collection of active rules has the same behavior, independent of evaluation order. Semantics of active databases is also studied in [202] and [580]. Designing and managing complex rule systems is discussed in [45, 165]. [103] discusses rule management using Chimera, a data model and language for active database systems.

Drafts of the SQL3 and SQL4 standards are available at the following URL:

```
ftp://jerry.ece.umassd.edu/isowg3/
```

21

OBJECT-DATABASE SYSTEMS

with Joseph M. Hellerstein
U. C. Berkeley

You know my methods, Watson. Apply them.

—Arthur Conan Doyle, *The Memoirs of Sherlock Holmes*

Relational database systems support a small, fixed collection of data types (e.g., integers, dates, strings), which has proven adequate for traditional application domains such as administrative data processing. In many application domains, however, much more complex kinds of data must be handled. Typically this complex data has been stored in OS file systems or specialized data structures, rather than in a DBMS. Examples of domains with complex data include computer-aided design and modeling (CAD/CAM), multimedia repositories, and document management.

As the amount of data grows, the many features offered by a DBMS for data management—for example, reduced application development time, concurrency control and recovery, indexing support, and query capabilities—become increasingly attractive, and ultimately, necessary. In order to support such applications, a DBMS must support complex data types. Object-oriented concepts have strongly influenced efforts to enhance database support for complex data, and have led to the development of object-database systems, which we discuss in this chapter.

Object-database systems have developed along two distinct paths:

■ **Object-oriented database systems:** Object-oriented database systems are proposed as an alternative to relational systems, and are aimed at application domains where complex objects play a central role. The approach is heavily influenced by object-oriented programming languages, and can be understood as an attempt to add DBMS functionality to a programming language environment.

■ **Object-relational database systems:** Object-relational database systems can be thought of as an attempt to extend relational database systems with the functionality necessary to support a broader class of applications, and in many ways, provide a bridge between the relational and object-oriented paradigms.]

We will use acronyms for relational database management systems (**RDBMS**), object-oriented database management systems (**OODBMS**) and object-relational database management systems (**ORDBMS**). In this chapter we focus on OR-DBMSs, and emphasize how they can be viewed as a development of RDBMSs, rather than as an entirely different paradigm. Except for Section 21.8, where we discuss OODBMSs and their relationship to ORDBMSs, our presentation is aimed at describing ORDBMSs. Although many of the concepts discussed are common to both ORDBMSs and OODBMSs, the reader should keep in mind that not all our remarks apply to OODBMSs.

The draft version of the SQL3 standard includes support for many of the complex data type features discussed in this chapter, although some features are likely to be deferred to a later version of the standard, SQL4. The SQL3 standard is based on the ORDBMS model, rather than the OODBMS model. (We briefly discuss the ODL/OQL standard proposed for OODBMSs in Section 21.8.) We have concentrated on developing the fundamental concepts, rather than an accurate treatment of the current SQL3 draft; some of the features that we discuss are not included in SQL3. We have tried to be consistent with the current SQL3 draft for notation, although we have occasionally diverged slightly for clarity.

It seems clear from current trends in the marketplace that most RDBMS vendors will soon support ORDBMS functionality (to varying degrees) in their products, and it is important to recognize how the existing body of knowledge about the design and implementation of relational databases can be leveraged to deal with the ORDBMS extensions. It is also important to understand the challenges and opportunities that these extensions present to database users, designers and implementors.

This chapter is organized as follows. We begin by presenting an example in Section 21.1 that illustrates why extensions to the relational model are needed to cope with some new application domains. This is used as a running example throughout the chapter. We discuss how abstract data types can be defined and manipulated in Section 21.2, and how types can be composed into constructed types in Section 21.3. We then consider objects and object identity in Section 21.4, and inheritance and type hierarchies in Section 21.5.

Having described the additional functionality offered by ORDBMSs, we turn to the question of ORDBMS database design in Section 21.6. In Section 21.7, we discuss some of the new implementation challenges posed by object-relational systems, and then present a brief comparison of ORDBMSs and OODBMSs in Section 21.8.

21.1 MOTIVATING EXAMPLE

As a specific example of the need for object-relational systems, we focus on a new business data processing problem that is both harder and (in our view) more entertaining than the dollars and cents book-keeping of previous decades. Today, companies in industries like entertainment are in the business of selling *bits*; their basic corporate assets are not tangible products, but rather software artifacts like video and audio.

We consider the fictional Dinky Entertainment Company, a large Hollywood conglomerate whose main assets are a collection of cartoon characters, especially the cuddly and internationally beloved Herbert the Worm. Dinky has a number of Herbert the Worm films, many of which are being shown in theaters around the world at any given time. Dinky also makes a good deal of money licensing Herbert's image, voice, and video footage for various purposes: action figures, video games, product endorsements and so on. Dinky's database is used to manage the sales and leasing records for the various Herbert-related products, as well as the video and audio data that make up Herbert's many films.

21.1.1 New Data Types

A basic problem confronting Dinky's database designers is that they need support for considerably richer data types than is available in a relational DBMS:

- **User-defined abstract data types (ADTs):** Dinky's assets include Herbert's image, voice and video footage, and these must be stored in the database. Further, we need special functions to manipulate these objects. For example, we may want to write functions that produce a compressed version of an image, or a lower-resolution image. (See Section 21.2.)

- **Constructed types:** In this application, as indeed in many traditional business data processing applications, we need new types built up from atomic types using constructors for creating sets, tuples, arrays, sequences, and so on. (See Section 21.3.)

- **Inheritance:** As the number of data types grows, it is important to recognize the commonality between different types and to take advantage of it. For example, compressed images and lower-resolution images are both, at some level, just images. It is therefore desirable to *inherit* some features of image objects while defining (and later, manipulating) compressed image objects and lower-resolution image objects. (See Section 21.5.)

How might we address these issues in an RDBMS? We could store images, videos and so on as *blobs* in current relational systems. Recall that a blob is just a long stream of bytes, and the DBMS's support consists of storing and retrieving blobs in such a manner that a user does not have to worry about the size of the blob; a blob can span several pages, unlike a traditional attribute. All further processing of the blob has to be done by the user's application program, in the host language in which the SQL code is embedded. This solution is not efficient because we are forced to retrieve all blobs in a collection even if most of them could be filtered out of the answer by applying user-defined functions (within the DBMS). It is not satisfactory from a data consistency standpoint either because the semantics of the data is now heavily dependent on the host-language application code and cannot be enforced by the DBMS.

As for constructed types and inheritance, there is simply no support in the relational model. We are forced to map data with such complex structure into a collection of flat tables. (We saw examples of such mappings when we discussed the translation from ER diagrams with inheritance to relations in Chapter 14.)

This application clearly requires features that are not available in the relational model. As an illustration of these features, Figure 21.1 presents SQL3 DDL statements for a portion of Dinky's ORDBMS schema that will be used in subsequent examples. Although the DDL is very similar to that of a traditional relational system, it has some important distinctions that highlight the new data modeling capabilities of an ORDBMS. A quick glance at the DDL statements is sufficient for now; we will study them in detail in the next section, after presenting some of the basic concepts that our sample application suggests are needed in a next-generation DBMS.

21.1.2 Manipulating the New Kinds of Data

Thus far, we have described the new kinds of data that must be stored in the Dinky database. We have not yet said anything about how to *use* these new types in queries, so let's study two queries that Dinky's database needs to support. The syntax of the queries is not critical; it is sufficient to understand what they express. We will return to the specifics of the queries' syntax as we proceed.

Our first challenge comes from the Clog breakfast cereal company. They produce a cereal called Delirios, and they want to lease an image of Herbert the Worm in front of a sunrise, to incorporate in the Delirios box design. A query to present a collection of possible images and their lease prices can be expressed in SQL-like syntax as in Figure 21.2. Dinky has a number of methods written in an imperative language like C and registered with the database system. These methods can be used in queries in the same way as built-in methods such as $=, +, -, <, >$, are used

1. CREATE TABLE Frames
     (*frameno* integer, *image* jpeg_image, *category* integer);
2. CREATE TABLE Categories
     (*cid* integer, *name* text, *lease_price* float, *comments* text);
3. CREATE ROW TYPE theater_t
     (*tno* integer, *name* text, *address* text, *phone* text);
4. CREATE TABLE Theaters OF TYPE theater_t WITH IDENTITY;
5. CREATE TABLE Nowshowing
     (*film* integer, *theater* ref(theater_t), *start* date, *end* date);
6. CREATE TABLE Films
     (*filmno* integer, *title* text, *stars* setof(text),
     director text, *budget* float);
7. CREATE TABLE Countries
     (*name* text, *boundary* polygon, *population* integer, *language* text);

Figure 21.1   DDL Statements for Dinky Schema

in a relational language like SQL. The *thumbnail* method in the Select clause produces a small version of its full-size input image. The *is_sunrise* method is a boolean function that analyzes an image and returns *true* if the image contains a sunrise; the *is_herbert* method returns *true* if the image contains a picture of Herbert. The query produces the frame code number, image thumbnail and price for all frames that contain Herbert and a sunrise.

```
SELECT  F.frameno, thumbnail(F.image), C.lease_price
FROM    Frames F, Categories C
WHERE   F.category = C.cid AND is_sunrise(F.image) AND is_herbert(F.image)
```

Figure 21.2   Extended SQL to Find Pictures of Herbert at Sunrise

The second challenge comes from Dinky's executives. They know that Delirios is exceedingly popular in the tiny country of Andorra, so they want to make sure that a number of Herbert films are playing at theaters near Andorra when the cereal hits the shelves. To check on the current state of affairs, the executives want to find the names of all theaters showing Herbert films within 100 kilometers of Andorra. Figure 21.3 shows this query in an SQL-like syntax.

The *theater* attribute of the Nowshowing table is a reference to an object in another table, which has attributes *name*, *address* and *location*. This object-referencing allows for the notation *N.theater->name* and *N.theater->address*, each of which refers to attributes of the theater_t object referenced in the Nowshowing row N. The *stars* attribute of the *films* table is a set of names of each film's stars. The *radius* method returns a circle centered at its first argument

```
SELECT  N.theater->name, N.theater->address, F.title
FROM    Nowshowing N, Films F, Countries C
WHERE   N.film = F.filmno AND
        overlaps(C.boundary, radius(N.theater->address, 100)) AND
        C.name = 'Andorra' AND 'Herbert the Worm' ∈ F.stars
```

Figure 21.3   Extended SQL to Find Herbert Films Playing Near Andorra

with radius equal to its second argument. The **overlaps** method tests for spatial overlap. Thus Nowshowing and Films are joined by the equijoin clause, while Nowshowing and Countries are joined by the spatial overlap clause. The selections to 'Andorra' and films containing 'Herbert the Worm' complete the query.

These two object-relational queries are similar to SQL-92 queries, but have some unusual features:

- **Operators for constructed types:** Along with the constructed types available in the data model, ORDBMSs provide the natural methods for those types. For example, the **setof** types have the standard set methods $\in, \ni, \subset, \subseteq, =, \supseteq, \supset, \cup, \cap$, and $-$ (Section 21.3.1).

- **Operators for reference types:** Reference types are *derefenced* via an arrow (–>) notation (Section 21.4.2).

- **User-defined methods:** User-defined abstract types are manipulated via their methods, for example, *is_herbert* (Section 21.2).

To summarize the points highlighted by our motivating example, traditional relational systems offer limited flexibility in the data types available. Data is stored in tables, and the type of each field value is limited to be a simple atomic type (e.g., integer or string), with a small, fixed set of such types to choose from. This limited type system can be extended in three main ways: *user-defined abstract data types, constructed types,* and *reference types.* Collectively, we refer to these new types as **complex types**. In the rest of this chapter we consider how a DBMS can be extended to provide support for defining new complex types and manipulating objects of these new types.

21.2 USER-DEFINED ABSTRACT DATA TYPES

Consider the Frames table of Figure 21.1. It has a column *image* of type **jpeg_image**, which stores a compressed image representing a single frame of a film. The **jpeg_image** type is not one of the DBMS's built-in types, and was defined by a user for the Dinky application, to store image data compressed using the JPEG standard. As another example, Line 7 of Figure 21.1 defines a column *boundary* of type `polygon`, which contains representations of the shapes of countries' outlines on a world map.

Allowing users to define arbitrary new data types is a key feature of ORDBMSs. The DBMS allows users to store and retrieve objects of type `jpeg_image`, just like an object of any other type, such as `integer`. New atomic data types usually need to have type-specific operations defined by the user who creates them. For example, one might define operations on an image data type such as `compress`, `rotate`, `shrink`, and `crop`. The combination of an atomic data type and its associated methods is called an **abstract data type**, or **ADT**. Traditional SQL comes with built-in ADTs, such as integers (with the associated arithmetic methods), or strings (with the equality, comparison and `LIKE` methods). Object-relational systems include these ADTs, and also allow users to define their own ADTs.

The label 'abstract' is applied to these data types because the database system does not need to know how an ADT's data is stored, nor how the ADT's methods work. It merely needs to know what methods are available, and the input and output types for the methods. Hiding of ADT internals is called **encapsulation**.[1] Note that even in a relational system, atomic types such as integers have associated methods that are encapsulated into ADTs. In the case of integers, the standard methods for the ADT are the usual arithmetic operators and comparators. To evaluate the addition operator on integers, the database system need not understand the laws of addition—it merely needs to know how to invoke the addition operator's code, and what type of data to expect in return.

In an object-relational system, the simplification due to encapsulation is critical because it hides any substantive distinctions between data types, and allows an ORDBMS to be implemented without anticipating the types and methods that users might want to add. For example, adding integers and overlaying images can be treated uniformly by the system, with the only significant distinctions being that different code is invoked for the two operations, and differently typed objects are expected to be returned from that code.

21.2.1   Defining Methods of an ADT

At a minimum, for each new atomic type a user must define methods that enable the DBMS to read in and to output objects of this type and to compute the

---

[1]Some ORDBMSs actually refer to ADTs as **opaque types** because they are encapsulated and hence one cannot see their details.

amount of storage needed to hold the object. The user who creates a new atomic type must **register** the following methods with the DBMS:

- **size**: Returns the number of bytes of storage required for items of the type, or the special value *variable*, if items vary in size.

- **import**: Creates new items of this type from textual inputs (e.g., INSERT statements).

- **export**: Maps items of this type to a form suitable for printing, or for use in an application program (e.g., an ASCII string or a file handle).

In order to register a new method for an atomic type, users must write the code for the method, and then inform the database system about the method. The code to be written depends on the languages supported by the DBMS and operating system in question. For example, the ORDBMS may handle C code for the Linux operating system. In this case the method code must be written in C and compiled into an object file stored in a Linux file system. Then an SQL-style method registration command is given to the ORDBMS so that it recognizes the new method:

```
CREATE FUNCTION is_sunrise(jpeg_image) RETURNS boolean
     AS EXTERNAL NAME '/a/b/c/dinky.o';
```

This statement defines the salient aspects of the method: the type of the associated ADT, the return type, and the location of the code. Once the method is registered, the DBMS uses the operating system's dynamic linking facility to link the method code into the database system so that it can be invoked. Figure 21.4 presents a number of method registration commands for our Dinky database.

```
1. CREATE FUNCTION thumbnail(jpeg_image) RETURNS jpeg_image
       AS EXTERNAL NAME '/a/b/c/dinky.o';
2. CREATE FUNCTION is_sunrise(jpeg_image) RETURNS boolean
       AS EXTERNAL NAME '/a/b/c/dinky.o';
3. CREATE FUNCTION is_herbert(jpeg_image) RETURNS boolean
       AS EXTERNAL NAME '/a/b/c/dinky.o';
4. CREATE FUNCTION radius(polygon, float) RETURNS polygon
       AS EXTERNAL NAME '/a/b/c/dinky.o';
5. CREATE FUNCTION overlaps(polygon, polygon) RETURNS boolean
       AS EXTERNAL NAME '/a/b/c/dinky.o';
```

Figure 21.4 Method Registration Commands for the Dinky Database

Type definition statements for the user-defined atomic data types in the Dinky schema are given in Figure 21.5.

1. CREATE ABSTRACT DATA TYPE jpeg_image
   (*internallength* = **VARIABLE**, *input* = jpeg_in, *output* = jpeg_out);
2. CREATE ABSTRACT DATA TYPE polygon
   (*internallength* = **VARIABLE**, *input* = poly_in, *output* = poly_out);

Figure 21.5   Atomic Type Declaration Commands for Dinky Database

21.3   CONSTRUCTED TYPES

Atomic types and user-defined types can be combined to describe more complex structures using **type constructors**. For example, Line 6 of Figure 21.1 defines a column *stars* of type **setof(text)**; each entry in that column is a set of text strings, representing the stars in a film. The **setof** syntax is an example of a type constructor. Other common type constructors include:

■   **row**(n_1 t_1, ..., n_n t_n): A type representing a row, or tuple, of n fields with fields $n_1, ..., n_n$ of types $t_1, ..., t_n$ respectively.

■   **listof**(base): A type representing a sequence of **base**-type items.

■   **arrayof**(base): A type representing an array of **base**-type items.

■   **setof**(base): A type representing a *set* of **base**-type items. Sets cannot contain duplicate elements.

■   **bagof**(base): A type representing a *bag* or *multiset* of **base**-type items. A **bag** is an unordered collection of elements, like a set, but there can be several copies of each element in the bag, and the number of copies is important. For example, {a, b, b} and {b, a, b} denote the same bag, and differ from the bag {a, a, b}.

To fully appreciate the power of type constructors, observe that they can be composed; for example, **setof(arrayof(integer))**. Types defined using type constructors are called **constructed types**. Those using listof, arrayof, bagof or **setof** as the outermost type constructor are sometimes referred to as **collection types, or bulk data types**.

In SQL3 the **row** type has a special role because every table is a collection of rows. A table can be a multiset or set of rows, as in SQL-92, or even a list of rows with an ordering over the rows. Values of other types can appear only in columns of some table. (Indeed, the type constructors to be supported in SQL3 are still under discussion.)

We observe that the introduction of constructed types changes a fundamental characteristic of relational databases, that all fields contain atomic values. A relation that contains a constructed type object is not in first normal form! We discuss this point further in Section 21.6.

21.3.1 Manipulating Data of Constructed Types

The DBMS provides built-in methods for the types supported through type constructors. These methods are analogous to built-in operations such as addition and multiplication for atomic types such as integers. In this section we present the methods for various type constructors and illustrate how SQL queries can create and manipulate values with constructed types.

Built-in Operators for Constructed Types

We now consider built-in operators for each of the constructed types that we presented in Section 21.3.

Rows: Given an item i of type `row(`$n_1\ t_1, ..., n_n\ t_n$`)`, the field extraction method allows us to access an an individual field n_k using the traditional dot notation $i.n_k$. If row constructors are nested in a type definition, dots may be nested to access the fields of the nested row; for example $i.n_k.m_l$. If we have a collection of rows, the dot notation gives us a collection as a result. For example, if i is a list of rows, $i.n_k$ gives us a list of items of type t_n; if i is a set of rows, $i.n_k$ gives us a set of items of type t_n.

This nested-dot notation is often called a **path expression** because it describes a path through the nested structure.

Sets and multisets: Set objects can be compared using the traditional set methods $\subset, \subseteq, =, \supseteq, \supset$. An item of type `setof(foo)` can be compared with an item of type `foo` using the $\in$ method, as illustrated in Figure 21.3, which contains the comparison '*Herbert the Worm*' $\in$ *F.stars*. Two set objects (having elements of the same type) can be combined to form a new object using the $\cup, \cap$ and $-$ operators.

Each of the methods for sets can be defined for multisets, taking the number of copies of elements into account. The $\cup$ operation simply adds up the number of copies of an element, the $\cap$ operation counts the number of times a given element appears in each of the two input multisets, and $-$ subtracts the number of times a given element appears in the second multiset from the number of times it appears in the first multiset. For example $\cup(\{1,2,2,2\}, \{2,2,3\}) = \{1,2,2,2,2,2,3\}$; $\cap(\{1,2,2,2\}, \{2,2,3\}) = \{2,2\}$; and $-(\{1,2,2,2\}, \{2,2,3\}) = \{1,2\}$.

Lists: Traditional list operations include *head*, which returns the first element; *tail*, which returns the list obtained by removing the first element; *cons*, which takes an element and inserts it as the first element in a list; and *append*, which appends one list to another.

Arrays: Array types support an 'array index' method to allow users to access array items at a particular offset. A postfix 'square bracket' syntax is usually used; for example, `foo_array[5]`.

Other: The operators listed above are just a sample. We also have the aggregate operators *count, sum, avg, max* and *min*, which can (in principle) be applied to any object of a collection type. Operators for type conversions are also common. For example, we can provide operators to convert a multiset object to a set object by eliminating duplicates.

We note that while collection types are included in drafts of the SQL3 standard, full support for them will probably be deferred to a subsequent standard, SQL4.

Examples of Queries Involving Nested Collections

We now present some examples to illustrate how relations that contain nested collections can be queried, using SQL syntax. Note that the examples here may or may not eventually be included in the SQL3 standard; our use of SQL notation is only illustrative.

Consider the Films relation. Each tuple describes a film, uniquely identified by *filmno*, and contains a set (of stars in the film) as a field value. Our first example illustrates how we can apply an aggregate operator to such a nested set. It identifies films with more than two stars by counting the number of stars; the *count* operator is applied once per Films tuple.[2]

```
SELECT  F.filmno
FROM    Films F
WHERE   count(F.stars) > 2
```

Our second query illustrates an operation called **unnesting**. Consider the instance of Films shown in Figure 21.6. A flat version of the same information is shown in Figure 21.7; for each film and star in the film, we have a tuple in Films_flat.

---

[2]The SQL3 draft limits the use of aggregate operators on nested collections; to emphasize this restriction, we have used *count* rather than COUNT, which we reserve for legal uses of the operator in SQL.

filmno	title	stars
98	Casablanca	{Bogart, Bergman}
54	Earth Worms Are Juicy	{Herbert, Wanda}

Figure 21.6 A Nested Relation, Films

filmno	title	star
98	Casablanca	Bogart
98	Casablanca	Bergman
54	Earth Worms Are Juicy	Herbert
54	Earth Worms Are Juicy	Wanda

Figure 21.7 A Flat Version, Films_flat

The following query generates the instance of Films_flat from Films:

```
SELECT  F.filmno, F.title, S AS star
FROM    Films F, F.stars AS S
```

The variable F is successively bound to tuples in Films, and for each value of F, the variable S is successively bound to the set in the *stars* field of F. Conversely, we may want to generate the instance of Films from Films_flat. We can generate the Films instance using a generalized form of SQL's **GROUP BY** construct, as the following query illustrates:

```
SELECT   F.filmno, F.title, set_gen(F.star)
FROM     Films_flat F
GROUP BY F.filmno
```

The operator *set_gen*, to be used with **GROUP BY**, requires some explanation. The **GROUP BY** clause partitions the Films_flat table by sorting on the *filmno* attribute; all tuples in a given partition have the same *filmno* (and therefore the same *title*). Consider the set of values in the *star* column of a given partition. This set cannot be returned in the result of an SQL-92 query, and we have to summarize it by applying an aggregate operator such as **COUNT**. Now that we allow relations to contain sets as field values, however, we would like to return the set of *star* values as a field value in a single answer tuple; the answer tuple also contains the *filmno* of the corresponding partition. The *set_gen* operator collects the set of *star* values in a partition and creates a set-valued object. This operation is called **nesting**. We can imagine similar generator functions for creating multisets, lists, and so on. However, such generators are not included in the current SQL3 draft.

21.4   OBJECTS, OBJECT IDENTITY, AND REFERENCE TYPES

In object-database systems, data objects can be given an **object identifier (oid)**, which is some value that is unique in the database across time. The DBMS is responsible for generating oids and ensuring that an oid identifies an object uniquely over its entire lifetime. In SQL3, for example, every tuple in a table can be given an oid by adding the phrase **WITH IDENTITY** to the table definition, as in Line 4 of Figure 21.1. In some systems, all tuples stored in any table are objects, and are automatically assigned unique oids. Often, there are also facilities for generating oids for larger structures (e.g., tables) as well as smaller structures (e.g., instances of data values such as a copy of the integer 5, or a JPEG image).

An object's oid can be used to refer (or 'point') to it from elsewhere in the data. Such a reference has a type (similar to the type of a pointer in a programming language), with a corresponding type constructor:

> **ref**(base): a type representing a reference to an object of type base.

For example, Line 5 of Figure 21.1 defines a column *theater* of type **ref**(theater_t). Items in this column are references to objects of type **theater_t**, such as the rows in the Theaters table, which is defined in Line 4.

The **ref** type constructor can be interleaved with the type constructors for constructed types; for example, **setof**(**ref**(**arrayof**(**integer**))).

21.4.1   Notions of Equality

The distinction between reference types and reference-free constructed types raises another issue: the definition of equality. Two objects having the same type are defined to be **deep equal** if and only if:

- The objects are of atomic type and have the same value, or

- The objects are of reference type, and the *deep equals* operator is true for the two referenced objects, or

- The objects are of constructed type, and the *deep equals* operator is true for all the corresponding subparts of the two objects.

Two objects that have the same reference type are defined to be **shallow equal** if and only if they both refer to the same object (i.e., both references use the same oid). The definition of shallow equality can be extended to objects of arbitrary type by taking the definition of deep equality and replacing *deep equals* by *shallow equals* in parts (2) and (3).

As an example, consider the complex objects **row**(538, **t89**, 6-3-97,8-7-97) and **row**(538, **t33**, 6-3-97,8-7-97), whose type is the type of rows in the table Nowshowing (Figure 21.1). These two objects are not shallow equal because they differ in the second attribute value. Nonetheless, they might be deep equal, if, for instance, the oids **t89** and **t33** refer to objects of type **theater_t** that have the same value; for example, **tuple**(54, 'Majestic', '115 King', '2556698').

While two deep equal objects may not be shallow equal, as the example illustrates, two shallow equal objects are always deep equal, of course. The default choice of deep versus shallow equality for reference types is different across systems, although typically we are given syntax to specify either semantics.

21.4.2 Dereferencing Reference Types

An item of reference type **ref(foo)** is not the same as the **foo** item to which it points. In order to access the referenced **foo** item, a built-in **deref()** method is provided along with the **ref** type constructor. For example, given a tuple from the Nowshowing table, one can access the *name* field of the referenced **theater_t** object with the syntax Nowshowing.**deref***(theater).name*. Since references to tuple types are common, some systems provide a C-style arrow operator, which combines a postfix version of the dereference operator with a tuple-type dot operator. Using the arrow notation, the name of the referenced theater can be accessed with the equivalent syntax Nowshowing.*theater–>name*, as in Figure 21.3.

At this point we have covered all the basic type extensions used in the Dinky schema. The reader is invited to revisit the schema and to examine the structure and content of each table, and how the new features are used in the various sample queries.

21.5 INHERITANCE

We considered the concept of inheritance in the context of the ER model in Chapter 14, and discussed how ER diagrams with inheritance were translated into tables. In object-database systems, unlike relational systems, inheritance is supported directly, and allows type definitions to be reused and refined very easily. It can be very helpful when modeling similar but slightly different classes of objects. In object-database systems, inheritance can be used in two ways: for reusing and refining types, and for creating hierarchies of collections of similar but not identical objects.

21.5.1 Defining Types with Inheritance

In the Dinky database, we model movie theaters with the type `theater_t`. Dinky also wants their database to represent a new marketing technique in the theater business: the *theater-cafe*, which serves pizza and other meals while screening movies. Theater-cafes require additional information to be represented in the database. In particular, a theater-cafe is just like a theater, but has an additional attribute representing the theater's menu. Inheritance allows us to capture this 'specialization' explicitly in the database design with the following DDL statement:

```
CREATE TYPE theatercafe_t UNDER theater_t (menu text);
```

This statement creates a new type, `theatercafe_t`, which has the same attributes and methods as `theater_t`, along with one additional attribute *menu* of type `text`. Methods defined on `theater_t` apply to objects of type `theatercafe_t`, but not vice versa. We say that `theatercafe_t` **inherits** the attributes and methods of `theater_t`.

Note that the inheritance mechanism is not merely a 'macro' to shorten **CREATE** statements. It creates an explicit relationship in the database between the **subtype** (`theatercafe_t`) and the **supertype** (`theater_t`): An object of the subtype *is also considered to be an object of the supertype*. This treatment means that any operations that apply to the supertype (methods as well as query operators such as projection or join) also apply to the subtype. This is generally expressed in the following principle:

The Substitution Principle: Given a supertype A, and a subtype B, it is always possible to substitute an object of type B into a legal expression written for objects of type A, without producing type errors.

This principle enables easy code reuse because queries and methods written for the supertype can be applied to the subtype without modification.

Note that inheritance can also be used for atomic types, in addition to row types. Given a supertype `image_t` with methods *title()*, *number_of_colors()*, and *display()*, we can define a subtype `thumbnail_image_t` for small images that inherits the methods of `image_t`.

21.5.2 Binding of Methods

In defining a subtype, it is sometimes useful to replace a method for the supertype with a new version that operates differently on the subtype. Consider the `image_t` type, and the subtype **jpeg_image_t** from the Dinky database. Unfortunately, the *display()* method for standard images does not work for JPEG images, which are specially compressed. Thus in creating type **jpeg_image_t**, we write a special *display()* method for JPEG images, and register it with the database system using the **CREATE FUNCTION** command:

```
CREATE FUNCTION display(jpeg_image) RETURNS jpeg_image
        AS EXTERNAL NAME '/a/b/c/jpeg.o';
```

Registering a new method with the same name as an old method is called **overloading** the method name.

Because of overloading, the system must understand which method is intended in a particular expression. For example, when the system needs to invoke the *display()* method on an object of type **jpeg_image_t**, it uses the specialized *display* method. When it needs to invoke *display* on an object of type **image_t** that is not otherwise subtyped, it invokes the standard *display* method. The process of deciding which method to invoke is called **binding** the method to the object. In certain situations, this binding can be done when an expression is parsed (**early binding**), but in other cases the most specific type of an object cannot be known until runtime, so the method cannot be bound until then (**late binding**).

21.5.3   Collection Hierarchies, Type Extents, and Queries

Type inheritance was invented for object-oriented programming languages, and our discussion of inheritance up to this point differs little from the discussion one might find in a book on an object-oriented language such as C++ or Java.

However, because database systems provide query languages over tabular datasets, the mechanisms from programming languages are enhanced in object databases to deal with tables and queries as well. In particular, in object-relational systems we can define a table containing objects of a particular type, like the Theaters table in the Dinky schema. Given a new subtype such as **theater_cafe**, we would like to create another table Theater_cafes to store the information about theater cafes. But when writing a query over the Theaters table, it is sometimes desirable to ask the same query over the Theater_cafes table; after all, if we project out the additional columns, an instance of the Theater_cafes table can be regarded as an instance of the Theaters table.

Rather than requiring the user to specify a separate query for each such table, we can inform the system that a new table of the subtype is to be treated as part of a table of the supertype, with respect to queries over the latter table. In our example, we can say:

```
CREATE TABLE Theater_cafes OF TYPE theater_cafe_t UNDER Theaters;
```

This statement tells the system that queries over the **theaters** table should actually be run over the union of the **theaters** and **Theater_cafes** tables. In such cases, if the subtype definition involves method overloading, late-binding is used to ensure that the appropriate methods are called for each tuple.

In general, the **UNDER** clause can be used to generate an arbitrary tree of tables, called a **collection hierarchy**. Queries over a particular table T in the hierarchy are run over the union of T and all its descendants. Sometimes, a user may want the query to run only on T, and not on the descendants; additional syntax, for example, the keyword **ONLY**, can be used in the query's **FROM** clause.

Some systems automatically create special tables for each type, which contain references to every instance of the type that exists in the database. These tables are called **type extents** and allow queries over all objects of a given type, regardless of where the objects actually reside in the database. Type extents naturally form a collection hierarchy that parallels the type hierarchy.

21.6   DATABASE DESIGN FOR AN ORDBMS

The rich variety of data types in an ORDBMS offers a database designer many opportunities for a more natural or more efficient design. In this section we illustrate the differences between RDBMS and ORDBMS database design through several examples.

21.6.1   Constructed Types and ADTs

Our first example involves several space probes, each of which continuously records a video. A single video stream is associated with each probe, and while this stream was collected over a certain time period, we assume that it is now a complete object associated with the probe. During the time period over which the video was collected, the probe's location was periodically recorded (such information can easily be 'piggy-backed' onto the header portion of a video stream conforming to the MPEG standard). Thus the information associated with a probe has three parts: (1) a *probe id* that identifies a probe uniquely, (2) a *video stream*, (3) a *location sequence* of ⟨*time, location*⟩ pairs. What kind of a database schema should we use to store this information?

An RDBMS Database Design

In an RDBMS, we must store each video stream as a blob, and each location sequence as tuples in a table. A possible RDBMS database design is illustrated below:

Probes(*pid:* `integer`, *time:* `timestamp`, *lat:* `real`, *long:* `real`,
      camera: `string`, *video:* `blob`)

There is a single table called Probes, and it has several rows for each probe. Each of these rows has the same *pid*, *camera* and *video* values, but different *time*, *lat*, and *long* values. (We have used latitude and longitude to denote location.) The key for this table can be represented as a functional dependency: $PTLN \rightarrow CV$, where N stands for longitude. There is another dependency: $P \rightarrow CV$. This relation is therefore not in BCNF; indeed, it is not even in 3NF. We can decompose Probes to obtain a BCNF schema:

Probes_Loc(*pid:* `integer`, *time:* `timestamp`, *lat:* `real`, *long:* `real`)
Probes_Video(*pid:* `integer`, *camera:* `string`, *video:* `blob`)

This design is about the best we can achieve in an RDBMS. However, it suffers from several drawbacks.

First, representing videos as blobs means that we have to write application code in an external language to manipulate a video object in the database. Consider this query: "For probe 10, display the video recorded between 1:10 p.m. and 1:15 p.m. on May 10 1996." We have to retrieve the entire video object associated with probe 10, recorded over several hours, in order to display a segment recorded over 5 minutes.

Next, the fact that each probe has an associated sequence of location readings is obscured, and the sequence information associated with a probe is dispersed across several tuples. A third drawback is that we are forced to separate the video information from the sequence information for a probe. These limitations are exposed by queries that require us to consider all the information associated with each probe; for example, "For each probe, print the earliest time at which it recorded, and the camera type." This query now involves a join of Probes_Loc and Probes_Video on the *pid* field.

An ORDBMS Database Design

An ORDBMS supports a much better solution. First, we can store the video as an ADT object, and write methods that capture any special manipulation that we wish to perform. Second, because we are allowed to store constructed types such as lists, we can store the location sequence for a probe in a single tuple, along with the video information! This layout eliminates the need for joins in queries that involve both the sequence and video information. An ORDBMS design for our example consists of a single relation called Probes_AllInfo:

> Probes_AllInfo(*pid:* **integer**, *locseq:* **location_seq**, *camera:* **string**,
> *video:* **mpeg_stream**)

This definition involves two new types, **location_seq** and **mpeg_stream**. The **mpeg_stream** type is defined as an ADT, with a method *display()* that takes a start time and an end time and displays the portion of the video recorded during that interval. This method can be implemented efficiently by looking at the total recording duration and the total length of the video, and interpolating to extract the segment recorded during the interval specified in the query.

Our first query is shown below in extended SQL syntax; using this *display* method: we now retrieve only the required segment of the video, rather than the entire video.

```
SELECT  display(P.video, 1:10 p.m. May 10 1996, 1:15 p.m. May 10 1996)
FROM    Probes_AllInfo P
WHERE   P.pid = 10
```

Now consider the **location_seq** type. We could define it as a **list** type, containing a list of **row** type objects:

```
CREATE TYPE location_seq listof
        (row (time: timestamp, lat: real, long: real ))
```

Consider the *locseq* field in a row for a given probe. This field contains a list of rows, each of which has three fields. If the ORDBMS implements collection types in their full generality, we should be able to extract the *time* column from this list to obtain a list of **timestamp** values, and to apply the **MIN** aggregate operator to this list to find the earliest time at which the given probe recorded. Such support for collection types would enable us to express our second query as shown below:

```
SELECT  P.pid, MIN ( P.locseq.time)
FROM    Probes_AllInfo P
```

It is worth emphasizing at this point that current ORDBMSs are not as general and clean as this example query suggests. For instance, the system may not recognize that projecting the *time* column from a list of rows gives us a list of timestamp values; or the system may only allow us to apply an aggregate operator to a table, and not to a nested list value.

Continuing with our example, we may want to do specialized operations on our location sequences that go beyond the standard aggregate operators. For instance, we may want to define a method that takes a time interval and computes the distance traveled by the probe during this interval. The code for this method must understand details of a probe's trajectory and geospatial coordinate systems. For these reasons, we might choose to define `location_seq` as an ADT.

Clearly, an (ideal) ORDBMS gives us many useful design options that are not available in an RDBMS.

21.6.2 Object Identity

We now discuss some of the consequences of using reference types or oids. The use of oids is especially significant when the size of the object is large, either because it is a constructed data type or because it is a big object such as an image.

Although reference types and constructed types seem similar, they are actually quite different. For example, consider a constructed type `my_theater tuple(`*tno* `integer,` *name* `text,` *address* `text,` *phone* `text)`, and the reference type `theater ref(theater_t)` of Figure 21.1. There are important differences in the way that database updates affect these two types:

- **Deletion:** Objects with references can be affected by the deletion of objects that they reference, while reference-free constructed objects are not affected by deletion of other objects. For example, if the Theaters table were dropped from the database, an object of type `theater` might change value to *null*, because the `theater_t` object that it refers to has been deleted, while a similar object of type `my_theater` would not change value.

- **Update:** Objects of reference types will change value if the referenced object is updated. Objects of reference-free constructed types change value only if updated directly.

- **Sharing versus Copying:** An identified object can be referenced by multiple reference-type items, so that each update to the object is reflected in many places. To get a similar affect in reference-free types requires updating all 'copies' of an object.

There are also important storage distinctions between reference types and non reference types, which might affect performance:

- **Storage Overhead:** Storing copies of a large value in multiple constructed type objects may use much more space than storing the value once and referring to it elsewhere through reference type objects. This additional storage requirement can affect both disk usage and buffer management (if many copies are accessed at once).

- **Clustering:** The subparts of a constructed object are typically stored together on disk. Objects with references may point to other objects that are far away on the disk, and the disk arm may require significant movement to assemble the object and its references together. Constructed objects can thus be more efficient than reference types if they are typically accessed in their entirety.

Many of these issues also arise in traditional programming languages such as C or Pascal, which distinguish between the notions of referring to objects *by value* and *by reference*. In database design, the choice between using a constructed type or a reference type will typically include consideration of the storage costs, clustering issues, and the effect of updates.

Object Identity versus Foreign Keys

Using an oid to refer to an object is similar to using a foreign key to refer to a tuple in another relation, but not quite the same: An oid can point to an object of `theater_t` that is stored *anywhere* in the database, whereas a foreign key reference is constrained to point to an object in a particular referenced relation. This restriction makes it possible for the DBMS to provide much greater support for referential integrity than for arbitrary oid pointers. In general, if an object is deleted while there are still oid-pointers to it, the best the DBMS can do is to recognize the situation by maintaining a reference count. (Even this limited support becomes impossible if oids can be copied freely.) Thus the responsibility for avoiding dangling references rests largely with the user if oids are used to refer to objects. This burdensome responsibility suggests that we should use oids with great caution, and use foreign keys instead whenever possible.

21.6.3 Extending the ER Model

The ER model as we described it in Chapter 14 is not adequate for ORDBMS design. We have to use an extended ER model that supports constructed attributes (i.e., sets, lists, arrays as attribute values), distinguishes whether entities have object ids, and allows us to model entities whose attributes include methods. We illustrate these comments using an extended ER diagram to describe the space probe data in Figure 21.8; our notational conventions are ad hoc, and only for illustrative purposes.

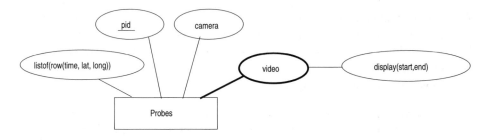

Figure 21.8 The Space Probe Entity Set

The definition of Probes in Figure 21.8 has two new aspects. First, it has a constructed-type attribute `listof(row(`*time, lat, long*`))`; each value assigned to this attribute in a Probes entity is a list of tuples with three fields. Second, Probes has an attribute called videos that is an abstract data type object, which is indicated by a dark oval for this attribute with a dark line connecting it to Probes. Further, this attribute has an 'attribute' of its own, which is a method of the ADT.

Alternatively, we could model each video as an entity by using an entity set called Videos. The association between Probes entities and Videos entities could then be captured by defining a relationship set that links them. Since each video is collected by precisely one probe, and every video is collected by some probe, this relationship can be maintained by simply storing a reference to a probe object with each Videos entity; this technique is essentially the second translation approach from ER diagrams to tables discussed in Section 14.3.1.

If we also make Videos a weak entity set in this alternative design, we can add a referential integrity constraint that causes a Videos entity to be deleted when the corresponding Probes entity is deleted. More generally, this alternative design illustrates a strong similarity between storing references to objects and foreign keys; the foreign key mechanism achieves the same effect as storing oids, but in a controlled manner. If oids are used, the user must ensure that there are no dangling references when an object is deleted, with very little support from the DBMS.

Finally, we note that a significant extension to the ER model is required to support the design of nested collections. For example, if a location sequence is modeled as an entity, and we want to define an attribute of Probes that contains a set of such entities, there is no way to do this without extending the ER model. We will not discuss this point further at the level of ER diagrams, but consider an example below that illustrates when to use a nested collection.

21.6.4   Using Nested Collections

Nested collections offer great modeling power, but also raise difficult design decisions. Consider the following way to model location sequences (other information about probes is omitted here to simplify the discussion):

Probes1(*pid:* `integer`, *locseq:* `location_seq`)

This is a good choice if the important queries in the workload require us to look at the location sequence for a particular probe, as in the query "For each probe, print the earliest time at which it recorded, and the camera type." On the other hand, consider a query that requires us to look at all location sequences: "Find the earliest time at which a recording exists for *lat=5, long=90.*" This query can be answered more efficiently if the following schema is used:

Probes2(*pid:* `integer`, *time:* `timestamp`, *lat:* `real`, *long:* `real`)

The choice of schema must therefore be guided by the expected workload (as always!). As another example, consider the following schema:

Can_Teach1(*cid:* `integer`, *teachers:* `setof`(*ssn:* `string`), *sal:* `integer`)

If tuples in this table are to be interpreted as "Course *cid* can be taught by any of the teachers in the *teachers* field, at a cost *sal*" then we have the option of using the following schema instead:

Can_Teach2(*cid:* `integer`, *teacher_ssn:* `string`, *sal:* `integer`)

A choice between these two alternatives can be made based on how we expect to query this table. On the other hand, suppose that tuples in Can_Teach1 are to be interpreted as "Course *cid* can be taught by the team *teachers*, at a combined cost of *sal*." Can_Teach2 is no longer a viable alternative. If we wanted to flatten Can_Teach1, we would have to use a separate table to encode teams:

Can_Teach2(*cid:* `integer`, *team_id:* `oid`, *sal:* `integer`)
    Teams(*tid:* `oid`, *ssn:* `string`)

As these examples illustrate, nested collections are appropriate in certain situations, but this feature can easily be misused; nested collections should therefore be used with care.

21.7   NEW CHALLENGES IN IMPLEMENTING AN ORDBMS

The enhanced functionality of ORDBMSs raises several implementation challenges. Some of these are well understood and solutions have been implemented in products; others are subjects of current research. In this section we examine a few of the key challenges that arise in implementing an efficient, fully functional ORDBMS. Many more issues are involved than those discussed here; the interested reader is encouraged to revisit the previous chapters in this book and consider whether the implementation techniques described there apply naturally to ORDBMSs or not.

21.7.1 Storage and Access Methods

Since object-relational databases store new types of data, ORDBMS implementors need to revisit some of the storage and indexing issues discussed in earlier chapters. In particular, the system must efficiently store ADT objects and constructed objects, and provide efficient indexed access to both.

Storing Large ADT and Constructed Type Objects

Large ADT objects and constructed objects complicate the layout of data on disk. This problem is well understood, and has been solved in essentially all ORDBMSs and OODBMSs. We present some of the main issues here.

User-defined ADTs can be quite large. In particular, they can be bigger than a single disk page. Large ADTs, like blobs, require special storage, typically in a different location on disk from the tuples that contain them. Disk-based pointers are maintained from the tuples to the objects they contain.

Constructed objects can also be large, but unlike ADT objects they often vary in size during the lifetime of a database. For example, consider the *stars* attribute of the *films* table in Figure 21.1. As the years pass, some of the 'bit actors' in an old movie may become famous.[3] When a bit actor becomes famous, Dinky might want to advertise their presence in the earlier films. This involves an insertion into the *stars* attribute of an individual tuple in *films*. Because these bulk attributes can grow arbitrarily, flexible disk layout mechanisms are required.

An additional complication arises with array types. Traditionally, array elements are stored sequentially on disk in a row-by-row fashion; for example

$$A_{11}, \ldots A_{1n}, A_{21}, \ldots, A_{2n}, \ldots A_{m1}, \ldots, A_{mn}$$

However, queries may often request subarrays that are not stored contiguously on disk (e.g., $A_{11}, A_{21}, \ldots, A_{m1}$). Such requests can result in a very high I/O cost for retrieving the subarray. In order to reduce the number of I/Os required in

---

[3] A well-known example is Marilyn Monroe, who had a bit part in the Bette Davis classic *All About Eve*.

general, arrays are often broken into contiguous *chunks*, which are then stored in some order on disk. Although each chunk is some contiguous region of the array, chunks need not be row-by-row or column-by-column. For example, a chunk of size 4 might be $A_{11}, A_{12}, A_{21}, A_{22}$, which is a square region if we think of the array as being arranged row-by-row in two dimensions.

Indexing New Types

One important reason for users to place their data in a database is to allow for efficient access via indexes. Unfortunately, the standard RDBMS index structures support only equality conditions (B+ trees and hash indexes) and range conditions (B+ trees). An important issue for ORDBMSs is to provide efficient indexes for ADT methods and operators on constructed objects.

Many specialized index structures have been proposed by researchers for particular applications such as cartography, genome research, multimedia repositories, Web search, and so on. An ORDBMS company cannot possibly implement every index that has been invented. Instead, the set of index structures in an ORDBMS should be user-extendible. Extensibility would allow an expert in cartography, for example, to not only register an ADT for points on a map (i.e., latitude/longitude pairs), but also implement an index structure that supports natural map queries (e.g., the R-tree, which matches conditions such as "Find me all theaters within 100 miles of Andorra").

One way to make the set of index structures extendible is to publish an *access method interface* that lets users implement an index structure *outside* of the DBMS. The index and data can be stored in a file system, and the DBMS simply issues the *open*, *next* and *close* iterator requests to the user's external index code. Such functionality makes it possible for a user to connect a DBMS to a Web search engine, for example. A main drawback of this approach is that data in an external index is not protected by the DBMS's support for concurrency and recovery. An alternative is for the ORDBMS to provide a generic 'template' index structure that is sufficiently general to encompass most index structures that users might invent. Because such a structure is implemented within the DBMS, it can support high concurrency and recovery. The *Generalized Search Tree* (GiST) is such a structure. It is a template index structure based on B+ trees, which allows most of the tree index structures invented so far to be implemented with only a few lines of user-defined ADT code.

21.7.2   Query Processing

ADTs and constructed types call for new functionality in processing queries in ORDBMSs. They also change a number of assumptions which affect the efficiency of queries. In this section we look at two functionality issues (user-defined aggregates and security) and two efficiency issues (method caching and pointer swizzling).

User-Defined Aggregation Functions

Since users are allowed to define new methods for their ADTs, it is not unreasonable to expect them to want to define new aggregation functions for their ADTs as well. For example, the usual SQL aggregates—`COUNT, SUM, MIN, MAX, AVG`— are not particularly appropriate for the `image` type in the Dinky schema.

Most ORDBMSs allow users to register new aggregation functions with the system. To register an aggregation function, a user must implement three methods, which we will call *initialize, iterate,* and *terminate.* The *initialize* method initializes the internal state for the aggregation. The *iterate* method updates that state for every tuple seen, while the *terminate* method computes the aggregation result based on the final state, and then cleans up. As an example, consider an aggregation function to compute the second-highest value in a field. The *initialize* call would allocate storage for the top two values, the *iterate* call would compare the current tuple's value with the top two and update the top two as necessary, and the *terminate* call would delete the storage for the top two values, returning a copy of the second-highest value.

Method Security

ADTs give users the power to add code to the DBMS; this power can be abused. A buggy or malicious ADT method can bring down the database server or even corrupt the database. The DBMS must have mechanisms to prevent buggy or malicious user code from causing problems. It may make sense to override these mechanisms for efficiency in production environments with vendor-supplied methods. However it is important for the mechanisms to exist, if only to support debugging of ADT methods; otherwise method writers would have to write bug-free code before registering their methods with the DBMS—not a very forgiving programming environment!

One mechanism to prevent problems is to have the user methods be *interpreted* rather than *compiled.* The DBMS can check that the method is well behaved either by restricting the power of the interpreted language, or by ensuring that each step taken by a method is safe before executing it. Typical interpreted languages for this purpose include Java and the procedural portions of SQL3.

An alternative mechanism is to allow user methods to be compiled from a general-purpose programming language such as C++, but to run those methods in a different address space than the DBMS. In this case the DBMS sends explicit interprocess communications (IPCs) to the user method, which sends IPCs back in return. This approach prevents bugs in the user methods (e.g., stray pointers) from corrupting the state of the DBMS or database, and prevents malicious methods from reading or modifying the DBMS state or database as well. Note that the user writing the method need not know that the DBMS is running their method in a separate process: the user code can be linked with a 'wrapper' that turns method invocations and return values into IPCs.

Method Caching

User-defined ADT methods can be very expensive to execute, and in fact can account for the bulk of the time spent in processing a query. During query processing it may make sense to cache the results of methods, in case they are invoked multiple times with the same argument. Within the scope of a single query, one can avoid calling a method twice on duplicate values in a column by either sorting the table on that column or using a hash-based scheme much like that used for aggregation (see Section 12.7). An alternative is to maintain a *cache* of method inputs and matching outputs as a table in the database. Then to find the value of a method on particular inputs, you essentially join the input tuples with the cache table. These two approaches can also be combined.

Pointer Swizzling

In some applications, objects are retrieved into memory and accessed frequently through their oids; dereferencing must be implemented very efficiently. Some systems maintain a table of oids of objects that are (currently) in memory. When an object O is brought into memory, they check each oid contained in O, and replace oids of in-memory objects by in-memory pointers to those objects. This technique is called **pointer swizzling**, and makes references to in-memory objects very fast. The downside is that when an object is paged out, in-memory references to it must somehow be invalidated and replaced with its oid.

21.7.3   Query Optimization

New indexes and query processing techniques widen the choices available to a query optimizer. In order to handle the new query processing functionality, an optimizer must know about the new functionality and use it appropriately. In this section we discuss two issues in exposing information to the optimizer (new indexes and ADT method estimation), and an issue in query planning that was ignored in relational systems (expensive selection optimization).

Registering Indexes with the Optimizer

As new index structures are added to a system—either via external interfaces or built-in template structures like GiSTs—the optimizer must be informed of their existence, and their costs of access. In particular, for a given index structure the optimizer must know (a) what WHERE-clause conditions are matched by that index, and (b) what the cost of fetching a tuple is for that index. Given this information, the optimizer can use any index structure in constructing a query plan. Different ORDBMSs vary in the syntax for registering new index structures. Most systems require users to state a number representing the cost of access, but an alternative is for the DBMS to measure the structure as it is used, and keep running statistics on cost.

Reduction Factor and Cost Estimation for ADT Methods

In Section 13.4.2 we discussed how to estimate the reduction factor of various selection and join conditions including $=$, $<$, and so on. For user-defined conditions such as *is_herbert()*, the optimizer also needs to be able to estimate reduction factors. Estimating reduction factors for user-defined conditions is a difficult problem and is being actively studied. The currently popular approach is to leave it up to the user—a user who registers a method can also register an auxiliary function to estimate the method's reduction factor. If such a function is not registered, the optimizer uses an arbitrary value such as $\frac{1}{10}$.

ADT methods can be quite expensive and it is important for the optimizer to know just how much these methods cost to execute. Again, estimating method costs is open research. In current systems users who register a method are able to specify the method's cost as a number, typically in units of the cost of an I/O in the system. Such estimation is hard for users to do accurately. An attractive alternative is for the ORDBMS to run the method on objects of various sizes and attempt to estimate the method's cost automatically, but this approach has not been investigated in detail, and is not implemented in commercial ORDBMSs.

Expensive Selection Optimization

In relational systems, selection is expected to be a zero-time operation. For example, it requires no I/Os and few CPU cycles to test if *emp.salary < 10*. However, conditions such as *is_herbert(Frames.image)* can be quite expensive because they may fetch large objects off the disk, and process them in memory in complicated ways.

ORDBMS optimizers must consider carefully how to order selection conditions. For example, consider a selection query that tests tuples in the Frames table with two conditions: *Frames.frameno < 100 ∧ is_herbert(Frame.image)*. It is probably preferable to check the *frameno* condition before testing *is_herbert*. The first condition is quick and may often return false, saving the trouble of checking the second condition. In general, the best ordering among selections is a function of their costs and reduction factors. It can be shown that selections should be ordered by increasing *rank*, where rank = (reduction factor − 1)/cost. If a selection with very high rank appears in a multitable query, it may even make sense to postpone the selection until after performing joins. Note that this approach is the opposite of the heuristic for pushing selections presented in Section 13.5! The details of optimally placing expensive selections among joins are somewhat complicated, adding to the complexity of optimization in ORDBMSs.

21.8   COMPARING RDBMS WITH OODBMS AND ORDBMS

Now that we have covered the main object-oriented DBMS extensions, it is time to consider the two main variants of object-databases, OODBMSs and ORDBMSs, and to compare them with RDBMSs. Although we have presented the concepts underlying object-databases, we still need to define the terms OODBMS and ORDBMS.

An **ORDBMS** is a relational DBMS with the extensions discussed in this chapter. (Not all ORDBMS systems support all the extensions in the general form that we have discussed them, but our concern in this section is the paradigm itself rather than specific systems.) An **OODBMS** is a programming language with a type system that supports the features discussed in this chapter, and allows any data object to be **persistent**, that is, to survive across different program executions. Many current systems conform to neither definition entirely, but are much closer to one or the other, and can be classified accordingly.

21.8.1   OODBMS: ODL and OQL

Although we defined an OODBMS as a programming language with support for persistent objects, the fact that OODBMSs support *collection types* makes it possible to provide a query language over collections. Indeed, a standard has been developed by the Object Database Management Group (ODMG), and is called **Object Query Language**, or **OQL**. OQL is similar to SQL, with a **SELECT–**

FROM–WHERE–style syntax (even *GROUP BY, HAVING,* and *ORDER BY* are supported) and many of the proposed SQL3 extensions. Notably, OQL supports constructed types, including sets, bags, arrays, and lists. The OQL treatment of collections is more uniform in that it does not give special treatment to collections of rows; for example, OQL allows the aggregate operation COUNT to be applied to a list to compute the length of the list. OQL also supports reference types, path expressions, ADTs and inheritance, type extents, and SQL-style nested queries. There is also a standard data definition language for OODBMSs (**Object Data Language**, or **ODL**) that is similar to the DDL subset of SQL, but supports the additional features found in OODBMSs, such as ADT definitions.

21.8.2 RDBMS versus ORDBMS

Comparing an RDBMS with an ORDBMS is straightforward. An RDBMS does not support the extensions discussed in this chapter. The resulting simplicity of the data model makes it easier to optimize queries for efficient execution, for example. A relational system is also easier to use because there are fewer features to master. On the other hand, it is less versatile than an ORDBMS.

21.8.3 OODBMS versus ORDBMS: Similarities

OODBMSs and ORDBMSs both support user-defined ADTs, constructed types, object identity and reference types, and inheritance. Both support a query language for manipulating collection types. ORDBMSs support an extended form of SQL, and OODBMSs support ODL/OQL. The similarities are by no means accidental: ORDBMSs consciously try to add OODBMS features to an RDBMS, and OODBMSs in turn have developed query languages based on relational query languages. Both OODBMSs and ORDBMSs provide DBMS functionality such as concurrency control and recovery.

21.8.4 OODBMS versus ORDBMS: Differences

The fundamental difference is really a philosophy that is carried all the way through: OODBMSs try to add DBMS functionality to a programming language, whereas ORDBMSs try to add richer data types to a relational DBMS. Although the two kinds of object-databases are converging in terms of functionality, this difference in their underlying philosophies (and for most systems, their implementation approach) has important consequences in terms of the issues emphasized in the design of these DBMSs, and the efficiency with which various features are supported, as the following comparison indicates:

■   OODBMSs aim to achieve seamless integration with a programming language such as C++ or Smalltalk. Such integration is not an important goal for an ORDBMS. SQL3, like SQL-92, allows us to embed SQL commands in a host language, but the interface is very evident to the SQL programer. (SQL3 also provides extended programming language constructs of its own, incidentally.)

■   An OODBMS is aimed at applications where an object-centric viewpoint is appropriate, that is, typical user sessions consist of retrieving a few objects and working on them for long periods, with related objects (e.g., objects referenced by the original objects) fetched occasionally. Objects may be extremely large, and may have to be fetched in pieces; thus attention must be paid to buffering parts of objects. It is expected that most applications will be able to cache the objects they require in memory, once the objects are retrieved from disk. Thus considerable attention is paid to making references to in-memory objects efficient. Transactions are likely to be of very long duration and holding locks until the end of a transaction may lead to poor performance; thus alternatives to Two Phase locking must be used.

An ORDBMS is optimized for applications where large data collections are the focus, even though objects may have rich structure and be fairly large. It is expected that applications will retrieve data from disk extensively, and that optimizing disk accesses is still the main concern for efficient execution. Transactions are assumed to be relatively short, and traditional RDBMS techniques are typically used for concurrency control and recovery.

■   The query facilities of OQL are not supported efficiently in most OODBMSs, whereas the query facilities are the centerpiece of an ORDBMS. To some extent, this situation is the result of different concentrations of effort in the development of these systems. To a significant extent, it is also a consequence of the systems' being optimized for very different kinds of applications.

21.9 SUMMARY

Object-database systems significantly enhance the type facilities found in relational database systems. Object-Relational DBMSs do this by starting with SQL and relations, and adding new features: ADTs, type constructors, object identity and inheritance. Object-Oriented DBMSs do this by starting with an object-oriented language such as C++, and adding DBMS facilities such as persistent data, indexes, concurrency and recovery.

An object-relational database system provides all the functionality of a relational system plus new object modeling features. These new features remove some of the constraints of relational database design. In particular, tables in an ORDBMS need not even be in 1NF, and users can define new data types. The new features change the rules for database design and many new design choices must be considered.

An important advantage of object-database systems is that they can store code as well as data. ADT methods are collected in the database, and the set of methods for a given type can be found by querying the database catalogs. Methods can be composed in ad hoc ways in query expressions. Viewed thus, an ORDBMS is like a software repository, with built-in query support for identifying software modules and flexibly combining methods to generate new applications. In contrast, Web browsers and applets provide only a crude type system, no support for querying the available applets, and no simple way for applets to interact with each other.

There is also a performance advantage to storing code in the database: ADTs bring the *code to the data* rather than the *data to the code*. For example, if a large object appears in the database, a ADT method that compresses it can be applied at the database server rather than at the client, preventing expensive network overheads in shipping the data to the client. Similarly, customized methods can be used in selections to prevent shipping tuples from the server to the client when it is not necessary to do so. This capability is a significant advantage over traditional RDBMSs. It also contrasts with Web browsers, which bring both code and data to the client.

Finally, there are logical advantages to keeping the code in the DBMS. In order to preserve data consistency, the DBMS provides automatic management of constraints. In an ORDBMS, these constraints can include user-defined methods. The alternative in an RDBMS is for complex logic to remain in client applications, which prevents the data semantics from being enforced by the DBMS.

It is reasonable to expect that all RDBMSs on the market today will have OR-DBMS functionality within the next few years. Unfortunately, the remaining challenges in implementation are unlikely to be completely solved as quickly. We should expect that the newer features in an ORDBMS will not be as efficient as traditional relational processing, at least for a while. Similarly, the database design issues for ORDBMSs are just beginning to be studied, and we should expect the complexities of database design to become even greater with the advent of ORDBMSs. Thus object-databases, like all new technology, provide a rich mix of enhanced features and challenges.

EXERCISES

Exercise 21.1 Briefly answer the following questions.

1. What are the two kinds of new data types supported in object-database systems? Give an example of each, and discuss how the example situation would be handled if only an RDBMS was available.

2. What must a user do to define a new ADT data type?

3. Allowing users to define methods can lead to efficiency gains. Give an example.

4. What is dynamic binding of methods? Give an example of inheritance that illustrates the need for dynamic binding.

5. What are collection hierarchies? Give an example that illustrates how collection hierarchies facilitate querying.

6. Discuss how a DBMS exploits encapsulation in implementing support for ADTs.

7. Give an example illustrating the nesting and unnesting operations.

8. Describe two objects that are deep equal but not shallow equal, or explain why this is not possible.

9. Describe two objects that are shallow equal but not deep equal, or explain why this is not possible.

10. Compare RDBMSs with ORDBMSs. Describe an application scenario for which you would choose an RDBMS, and explain why. Similarly, describe an application scenario for which you would choose an ORDBMS, and explain why.

Exercise 21.2 Consider the Dinky schema shown in Figure 21.1, and all related methods defined in the chapter. Write the following queries in extended SQL:

1. How many films were shown at theater $tno = 5$ between January 1 and February 1 of 1997?

2. What is the lowest budget for a film with at least two stars?

3. Consider theaters at which a film directed by Steven Spielberg started showing on January 1, 1997. For each such theater, print the names of all countries within a 100 mile radius. (You can use the *overlap* and *radius* methods illustrated in Figure 21.2.)

Exercise 21.3 In a company database, you need to store information about employees, departments, and children of employees. For each employee, identified by *ssn*, you must record *years* (the number of years that the employee has worked for the company), *phone* and *photo* information. There are two subclasses of employees: contract and regular. Salary is computed by invoking a method that takes *years* as a parameter; this method has a different implementation for each subclass. Further, for each regular employee, you must record the name and age of every child. The most common queries involving children are similar to "Find the average age of Bob's children" and "Print the names of all of Bob's children."

A photo is a large image object and can be stored in one of several image formats (e.g., gif, jpeg). You want to define a *display* method for image objects; display must be defined differently for each image format. For each department, identified by *dno*, you must record *dname*, *budget* and *workers* information. *Workers* is the set of employees who work in a given department. Typical queries involving workers include "Find the average salary of all workers (across all departments)."

1. Using extended SQL, design an ORDBMS schema for the company database. Show all type definitions, including method definitions.

2. If you have to store this information in an RDBMS, what is the best possible design?

3. Compare the ORDBMS and RDBMS designs.

4. If you are told that a common request is to display the images of all employees in a given department, how would you use this information for physical database design?

5. If you are told that an employee's image must be displayed whenever any information about the employee is retrieved, would this affect your schema design?

6. If you are told that a common query is to find all employees who look similar to a given image, and given code that lets you create an index over all images to support retrieval of similar images, what would you do to utilize this code in an ORDBMS?

Exercise 21.4 ORDBMSs need to support efficient access over collection hierarchies. Consider the collection hierarchy of Theaters and Theater_cafes presented in the Dinky example. You must evaluate three storage alternatives for these tuples:

■ All tuples for all kinds of theaters are stored together on disk in an arbitrary order.

■ All tuples for all kinds of theaters are stored together on disk, with the tuples that are from Theater_cafes stored directly after the last of the non cafe tuples.

■ Tuples from Theater_cafes are stored separately from the rest of the (non cafe) theater tuples.

1. For each storage option, describe a mechanism for distinguishing plain theater tuples from Theater_cafe tuples.

2. For each storage option, describe how to handle the insertion of a new non cafe tuple.

3. Which storage option is most efficient for queries over all theaters? Over just Theater_cafes? In terms of the number of I/Os, how much more efficient is the best technique for each type of query compared to the other two techniques?

Exercise 21.5 Different ORDBMSs use different techniques for building indexes to evaluate queries over collection hierarchies. For our Dinky example, to index theaters by name there are two common options:

■ Build one B+ tree index over Theaters.*name* and another B+ tree index over Theater_cafes.*name*.

■ Build one B+ tree index over the union of Theaters.*name* and Theater_cafes.*name*.

1. Describe how to efficiently evaluate the following query using each indexing option (this query is over all kinds of theater tuples):

    SELECT * FROM Theaters T WHERE T.name = 'Majestic'

Give an estimate of the number of I/Os required in the two different scenarios, assuming there are 1,000,000 standard theaters, and 1,000 theater-cafes. Which option is more efficient?

2. Perform the same analysis over the following query:

   SELECT * FROM Theater_cafes T WHERE T.name = 'Majestic'

3. For clustered indexes, does the choice of indexing technique interact with the choice of storage options? For unclustered indexes?

Exercise 21.6 Consider the following query:

   SELECT thumbnail(I.image)
   FROM   Images I

Given that the *I.image* column may contain duplicate values, describe how to use hashing to avoid computing the *thumbnail* function more than once per distinct value in processing this query.

Exercise 21.7 You are given a two-dimensional, $n \times n$ array of objects. Assume that you can fit 100 objects on a disk page. Describe a way to lay out (chunk) the array onto pages so that retrievals of square $m \times m$ subregions of the array are efficient. (Different queries will request subregions of different sizes, i.e., different m values, and your arrangement of the array onto pages should provide good performance, on average, for all such queries.)

Exercise 21.8 An ORDBMS optimizer is given a single-table query with n expensive selection conditions, $\sigma_n(...(\sigma_1(T)))$. For each condition σ_i, the optimizer can estimate the cost c_i of evaluating the condition on a tuple and the reduction factor of the condition r_i. Assume that there are t tuples in T.

1. How many tuples appear in the output of this query?

2. Assuming that the query is evaluated as shown (without reordering selections), what is the total cost of the query? Be sure to include the cost of scanning the table and applying the selections.

3. In Section 21.7.2 it was asserted that the optimizer should reorder selections so that they are applied to the table in order of increasing rank, where $\text{rank}_i = (r_i - 1)/c_i$. Prove that this assertion is optimal. That is, show that no other ordering could result in a query of lower cost. (Hint: It may be easiest to consider the special case where $n = 2$ first and generalize from there.)

BIBLIOGRAPHIC NOTES

A number of the object-oriented features described here are based in part on fairly old ideas in the programming languages community. [32] provides a good overview of these ideas in a database context. Stonebraker coined the term *object-relational*, and his book [527] describes the vision of ORDBMSs embodied by his company's early product, Illustra (now a product of Informix). Current commercial DBMSs with object-relational support include Informix Universal Server, IBM DB/2 CS V2, and UniSQL. An new version of Oracle is scheduled to include ORDBMS features as well.

Many of the ideas in current object-relational systems came out of a few prototypes built in the 1980s, especially POSTGRES [530], Starburst [239], and O2 [158].

The idea of an object-oriented database was first articulated in [143], which described the GemStone prototype system. Other prototypes include DASDBS [472], EXODUS [94], IRIS [196], ObjectStore [325], ODE, [14] ORION [299], SHORE [93] and THOR [340]. O2 is actually an early example of a system that was beginning to merge the themes of ORDBMSs and OODBMSs—it could fit in this list as well. [31] lists a collection of features that are generally considered to belong in an OODBMS. Current commercially available OODBMSs include GemStone, Itasca, O2, Objectivity, ObjectStore, Ontos, Poet, and Versant. [298] compares OODBMSs and RDBMSs.

Database support for ADTs was first explored in the INGRES and POSTGRES projects at U.C. Berkeley. The basic ideas are described in [524], including mechanisms for query processing and optimization with ADTs as well as extensible indexing. Support for ADTs was also investigated in the Darmstadt database system, [338]. Using the POST-GRES index extensibility correctly required intimate knowledge of DBMS-internal transaction mechanisms. Generalized search trees were proposed to solve this problem; they are described in [254], with concurrency and ARIES-based recovery details presented in [313]. [487] proposes that users must be allowed to define operators over ADT objects and properties of these operators that can be utilized for query optimization, rather than just a collection of methods.

Array chunking is described in [470]. Techniques for method caching and optimizing queries with expensive methods are presented in [253, 121]. Client-side data caching in a client-server OODBMS is studied in [200]. Clustering of objects on disk is studied in [545]. Work on nested relations was an early precursor of recent research on complex objects in OODBMSs and ORDBMSs. One of the first nested relation proposals is [362]. MVDs play an important role in reasoning about redundancy in nested relations; see, for example, [418]. Storage structures for nested relations were studied in [157].

Formal models and query languages for object-oriented databases have been widely studied; papers include [5, 41, 56, 91, 266, 265, 295, 417, 532]. [294] proposes SQL extensions for querying object-oriented databases. An early and elegant extension of SQL with path expressions and inheritance was developed in GEM [579]. There has been much interest in combining deductive and object-oriented features. Papers in this area include [34, 205, 353, 402, 514, 581]. See [4] for a thorough textbook discussion of formal aspects of object-orientation and query languages.

[300, 302, 531, 583] include papers on DBMSs that would now be termed object-relational and/or object-oriented. [582] contains a detailed overview of schema and database evolution in object-oriented database systems. Drafts of the SQL3 and SQL4 standards are available electronically at URL `ftp://jerry.ece.umassd.edu/isowg3/`. OQL is described in [102]. It is based to a large extent on the O2 query language, which is described, together with other aspects of O2, in the collection of papers [40].

22

DECISION SUPPORT SYSTEMS

> Nothing is more difficult, and therefore more precious, than to be able to decide.
>
> —Napoleon Bonaparte

Database management systems are widely used by organizations for maintaining data that documents their everyday operations. In applications that update such *operational data*, transactions typically make small changes (for example, adding a reservation or depositing a check) and a large number of transactions must be reliably and efficiently processed. Such **On-Line Transaction Processing (OLTP)**, applications have driven the growth of the DBMS industry in the past three decades, and will doubtless continue to be important. DBMSs have traditionally been optimized extensively to perform well in such applications.

Recently, however, organizations have increasingly emphasized applications in which current and historical data are comprehensively analyzed and explored, identifying useful trends and creating summaries of the data, in order to support high-level decision making. Such applications are referred to as **decision support**. Decision support has rapidly grown into a multibillion dollar industry, and further growth is expected. There are a number of vendors offering database systems and tools to facilitate decision support. Industry organizations are emerging to set standards and create consensus on issues like language and architecture design. In this chapter our goal is to provide an introduction to the major new issues, and to place decision support systems in the broader context of database management systems.

22.1 INTRODUCTION TO DECISION SUPPORT

Organizational decision making requires a comprehensive view of all aspects of an enterprise, and many organizations have therefore created consolidated **data warehouses** that contain data drawn from several databases maintained by different business units, together with historical and summary information.

The trend towards data warehousing is complemented by an increased emphasis on powerful analysis tools. Three broad classes of analysis tools are emerging.

First, there are DBMSs that support traditional SQL-style queries, but designed to support complex queries efficiently. Such systems can be regarded as relational DBMSs optimized for decision support applications.

Second, there are systems that support a class of stylized queries that typically involve group-by and aggregation operators. Applications dominated by such queries are called **On-Line Analytic Processing**, or **OLAP**. These systems support a querying style in which the data is best thought of as a multidimensional array, and are influenced by end-user tools such as spreadsheets, in addition to database query languages.

Third, there are tools for **exploratory data analysis** or **data mining**, in which a user looks for interesting patterns in the data. For example, an analyst looking at credit-card usage histories may want to detect unusual activity indicating misuse of a lost or stolen card. A catalog merchant may want to look at customer records to identify promising customers for a new promotion; this identification would depend on income levels, buying patterns, demonstrated interest areas, and so on. In situations such as these, although an analyst can recognize an 'interesting pattern' when shown such a pattern, it is very difficult to formulate a query that captures the essence of an interesting pattern, and the amount of data is too large to permit manual analysis or even traditional statistical analysis.

Clearly, evaluating OLAP or data mining queries over globally distributed data is likely to be excruciatingly slow. Further, for such complex analysis, often statistical in nature, it is not essential that the most current version of the data be used. The natural solution is to create a centralized repository of all the data, that is, a data warehouse. Thus the availability of a warehouse facilitates the application of OLAP and data mining tools, and conversely, the desire to apply such analysis tools is a strong motivation for building a data warehouse.

In the rest of this chapter we discuss warehousing, OLAP and mining in more detail. We cover data warehousing in Section 22.2. We present on-line analytic processing, or OLAP, in Section 22.3 and discuss implementation techniques to support OLAP in Section 22.4. We then discuss data mining in Section 22.5.

22.2 DATA WAREHOUSING

Data warehouses contain consolidated data from many sources, spanning long time periods, and augmented with summary information. Warehouses are much larger than other kinds of databases; sizes ranging from several gigabytes to terabytes are common. Typical workloads involve ad hoc, fairly complex queries, and fast response times are important. These characteristics differentiate warehouse applications from OLTP applications, and different DBMS design and implementation techniques must be used to achieve satisfactory results. A distributed DBMS with good scalability and high availability (achieved by storing tables redundantly at more than one site) is required for very large warehouses.

A typical data warehousing architecture is illustrated in Figure 22.1.

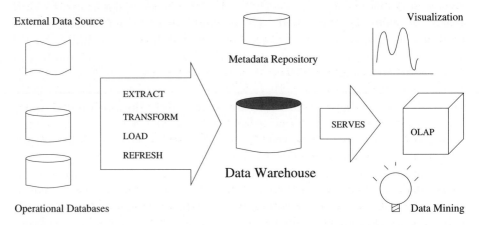

Figure 22.1   A Typical Data Warehousing Architecture

An organization's daily operations access and modify **operational databases**. Data from these operational databases and other external sources (e.g., customer profiles supplied by external consultants) are **extracted** by using **gateways**, or standard external interfaces supported by the underlying DBMSs. Standards such as *Open Database Connectivity (ODBC)* from Microsoft are emerging for gateways; ODBC is an application program interface that allows client programs to generate SQL statements to be executed at a server.

22.2.1   Creating and Maintaining a Warehouse

There are many challenges in creating and maintaining a large data warehouse. A good database schema must be designed to hold an integrated collection of data copied from diverse sources. For example, a company warehouse might include the Inventory and Personnel departments' databases, together with Sales databases maintained by offices in different countries. Since the source databases are often created and maintained by different groups, there are a number of semantic mismatches across these databases, such as different currency units, different names for the same attribute, and differences in how tables are normalized or structured; these differences must be reconciled when data is brought into the warehouse. After the warehouse schema is designed, the warehouse must be populated, and over time, it must be kept consistent with the primary data sources.

Data extracted from operational databases and external sources is first **cleaned** to minimize errors and fill in missing information when possible, and **transformed** to reconcile semantic mismatches. Transforming data is typically accomplished by defining a relational view over the tables in the data sources (the operational databases and other external sources). Loading data consists of materializing such views and storing them in the warehouse. Unlike a standard view in a relational DBMS, therefore, the view is stored in a database (the warehouse) that is different from the database(s) containing the tables it is defined over.

The cleaned and transformed data is finally **loaded** into the warehouse. Additional preprocessing such as sorting and generation of summary information is carried out at this stage. Data is partitioned and indexes are built for efficiency. The large volume of data to be loaded means that loading is a slow process; loading a terabyte of data sequentially can take weeks. Parallelism is therefore important for loading warehouses.

After data is loaded into a warehouse, additional measures must be taken to ensure that the data in the warehouse is periodically **refreshed** to reflect updates to the data sources, and to periodically **purge** data that is too old from the warehouse (perhaps onto archival media). Observe the connection between the problem of refreshing warehouse tables and asynchronously maintaining replicas of tables in a distributed DBMS. Maintaining replicas of source relations is an essential part of warehousing, and this application domain is an important factor in the popularity of asynchronous replication (Section 19.10.2), despite the fact that asynchronous replication violates the principle of distributed data independence. The problem of refreshing warehouse tables (which are materialized views over tables in the source databases) has also renewed interest in incremental maintenance of materialized views.

An important task in maintaining a warehouse is keeping track of the data currently stored in it; this book keeping is done by storing information about the warehouse data in the system catalogs. The system catalogs associated with a warehouse are very large, and are often stored and managed in a separate database called a **metadata repository**. The size and complexity of the catalogs is in part due to the size and complexity of the warehouse itself, and in part because a lot of administrative information must be maintained. For example, we must keep track of the source of each warehouse table, and when it was last refreshed, in addition to describing its fields.

The value of a warehouse is ultimately in the analysis that it enables. The data in a warehouse is typically accessed and analyzed using a variety of tools, including OLAP query engines, data mining algorithms, information visualization tools, statistical packages and report generators.

22.3   OLAP

OLAP applications are dominated by ad hoc, complex queries. In SQL terms, these are queries that involve group-by and aggregation operators. The natural way to think about typical OLAP queries, however, is in terms of a multidimensional model of data. We begin this section by presenting the multidimensional data model and comparing it with a relational representation of data. We describe OLAP queries in terms of this model, and then consider some new implementation techniques designed to support such queries. Finally, we briefly contrast database design for OLAP applications with more traditional relational database design.

22.3.1   Multidimensional Data Model

In the multidimensional model, the focus is on a collection of numeric **measures**. Each measure depends on a set of **dimensions**. We will use a running example based on sales data. The measure in our example is *sales*. The dimensions are Product, Location and Time. Given a product, a location, and a time, we have at most associated one sales value. If we identify a product by a unique identifier *pid*, and similarly identify location by *locid* and time by *timeid*, we can think of sales information as being arranged in a three-dimensional array Sales. This array is shown in Figure 22.2; for clarity, we show only the values for a single *locid* value, *locid*= 1, which can be thought of as a slice parallel to the *locid* axis.

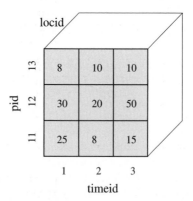

Figure 22.2   Sales: A Multidimensional Dataset

This view of data as a multidimensional array is readily generalized to more than three dimensions. In OLAP applications, the bulk of the data can be represented in such a multidimensional array. Indeed, some OLAP systems, for example, Essbase from Arbor Software, actually store data in a multidimensional array (of course, implemented without the usual programming language assumption that the entire array fits in memory). OLAP systems that use arrays to store multidimensional datasets are called **Multidimensional OLAP (MOLAP)** systems.

The data in a multidimensional array can also be represented as a relation, as illustrated in Figure 22.3, which shows the same data as in Figure 22.2; additional rows corresponding to the 'slice' *locid*= 2 are shown in addition to the data visible in Figure 22.3. This relation, which relates the dimensions to the measure of interest, is called the **fact table**.

pid	timeid	locid	sales
11	1	1	25
11	2	1	8
11	3	1	15
12	1	1	30
12	2	1	20
12	3	1	50
13	1	1	8
13	2	1	10
13	3	1	10
11	1	2	35
11	2	2	22
11	3	2	10
12	1	2	26
12	2	2	45
12	3	2	20
13	1	2	20
13	2	2	40
13	3	2	5

Figure 22.3 Sales Represented as a Relation

Now let us turn to dimensions. Each dimension can have a set of associated attributes. For example, the Location dimension is identified by the *locid* attribute, which we used to identify a location in the Sales table. We will assume that it also has attributes *country*, *state* and *city*. We will also assume that the Product dimension has attributes *pname*, *category* and *price*, in addition to the identifier *pid*. The *category* of a product indicates its general nature; for example, a product *pant* could have category value *apparel*. We will assume that the Time dimension has attributes *date*, *week*, *month*, *quarter*, *year* and *holiday_flag*, in addition to the identifier *timeid*.

For each dimension, the set of associated values can be structured as a hierarchy. For example, cities belong to states, and states belong to countries. Dates belong to weeks and to months, both weeks and months are contained in quarters, and quarters are contained in years. (Note that a week could span a month; thus weeks are not contained in months.) Some of the attributes of a dimension describe the position of a dimension value with respect to this underlying hierarchy of dimension values. The hierarchies for the Product, Location and Time hierarchies in our example are shown at the attribute level in Figure 22.4.

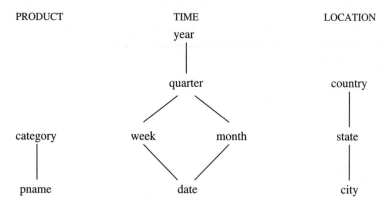

Figure 22.4   Dimension Hierarchies

Information about dimensions can also be represented as a collection of relations:

Locations(*locid:* **integer**, *city:* **string**, *state:* **string**, *country:* **string**)
Products(*pid:* **integer**, *pname:* **string**, *category:* **string**, *price:* **real**)
Times(*timeid:* **integer**, *date:* **string**, *week:* **integer**, *month:* **integer**,
      quarter: **integer**, *year:* **integer**, *holiday_flag:* **boolean**)

These relations are much smaller than the fact table in a typical OLAP application; they are called the **dimension tables**. OLAP systems that store all information, including fact tables, as relations are called **Relational OLAP (ROLAP)** systems.

The Times table illustrates the attention paid to the Time dimension in typical OLAP applications. SQL's date and timestamp data types are not adequate; in order to support summarizations that reflect business operations, information such as fiscal quarters, holiday status, and so on is maintained for each time value.

22.3.2   OLAP Queries

Now that we've seen the multidimensional model of data, let's consider how such data can be queried and manipulated. The operations supported by this model are strongly influenced by end-user tools such as spreadsheets. The goal is to give end-users who are not SQL experts an intuitive and powerful interface for common business-oriented analysis tasks. Users are expected to pose ad hoc queries directly, without relying on database application programmers. In this section we assume that the user is working with a multidimensional dataset, and that each operation returns either a different presentation or summarization of this underlying dataset; the underlying dataset is always available for the user to manipulate, regardless of the level of detail at which it is currently viewed.

A very common operation is aggregating a measure over one or more dimensions. The following queries are typical:

- Find the total sales.

- Find total sales for each city.

- Find total sales for each state.

- Find the top five products ranked by total sales.

The first three queries can be expressed as SQL queries over the fact and dimension tables, but the last query cannot be expressed in SQL (although we can approximate it if we return answers in sorted order by total sales, using ORDER BY).

When we aggregate a measure on one or more dimensions, the aggregated measure depends on fewer dimensions than the original measure. For example, when we compute the total sales by city, the aggregated measure is *total sales* and it depends only on the Location dimension, whereas the original *sales* measure depended on Location, Time and Product dimensions. Aggregating on a dimension is often referred to as **dimensionality reduction** in the OLAP literature.

Another use of aggregation is to summarize at different levels of a dimension hierarchy. If we are given total sales per city, we can aggregate on the Location dimension to obtain sales per state. This operation is called **roll-up** in the OLAP literature. The inverse of roll-up is **drill-down**: given total sales by state, we can ask for a more detailed presentation by drilling down on Location. We can ask for sales by city, or just sales by city for a selected state (with sales presented on a per-state basis for the remaining states, as before). We can also drill down on a dimension other than Location. For example, we can ask for total sales for each product for each state, drilling down on the Product dimension.

Another common operation is **pivoting**. Consider a tabular presentation of the Sales table. If we pivot it on the Location and Time dimensions, we obtain a table of total sales for each location for each time value. This information can be presented as a two-dimensional chart in which the axes are labeled with location and time values, and the entries in the chart correspond to the total sales for that location and time. Thus values that appear in columns of the original presentation become labels of axes in the result presentation. Of course, pivoting can be combined with aggregation; we can pivot to obtain yearly sales by state. The result of pivoting is called a **cross-tabulation**, and is illustrated in Figure 22.5. Observe that in spreadsheet style, in addition to the total sales by year and state (taken together), we also have additional summaries of sales by year and sales by state.

	WI	CA	Total
1995	63	81	144
1996	38	107	145
1997	75	35	110
Total	176	223	399

Figure 22.5   Cross-Tabulation of *sales* by *year* and *state*

Pivoting can also be used to change the dimensions of the cross-tabulation; from a presentation of sales by year and state, we can obtain a presentation of sales by product and year.

The Time dimension is very important in OLAP. Typical queries include:

- Find total sales by month.

- Find total sales by month for each city.

- Find the percentage change in the total monthly sales for each product.

- Find the trailing n day moving average of sales. (For each day, we must compute the average daily sales over the preceding n days.)

The first two queries can be expressed as SQL queries over the fact and dimension tables. The third query can be expressed too, but is quite complicated in SQL. The last query cannot be expressed in SQL if n is to be a parameter of the query.

Clearly, the OLAP framework makes it convenient to pose a broad class of queries. We remark that it also gives catchy names to some familiar operations: **slicing** a dataset amounts to an equality selection on one or more dimensions, possibly also with some dimensions projected out. **Dicing** a dataset amounts to a range selection. These terms come from visualizing the effect of these operations on a cube or cross-tabulated representation of the data.

Comparison with SQL Queries

Some OLAP queries cannot be expressed, or cannot be easily expressed, in SQL, as we saw in the above discussion. Notably, queries that rank results and queries that involve time-oriented operations fall into this category.

A large number of OLAP queries, however, can be expressed in SQL. Typically, they involve grouping and aggregation, and a single OLAP operation leads to several closely related SQL queries. For example, consider the cross-tabulation shown in Figure 22.5, which was obtained by pivoting the Sales table. To obtain the same information, we would issue the following queries:

```
SELECT    SUM (S.sales)
FROM      Sales S, Times T, Locations L
WHERE     S.timeid=T.timeid AND S.timeid=L.timeid
GROUP BY  T.year, L.state
```

This query generates the entries in the body of the chart (outlined by the dark lines). The summary row at the bottom is generated by the query:

```
SELECT    SUM (S.sales)
FROM      Sales S, Times T
WHERE     S.timeid=T.timeid
GROUP BY  T.year
```

The summary column on the right is generated by the query:

```
SELECT    SUM (S.sales)
FROM      Sales S, Locations L
WHERE     S.timeid=L.timeid
GROUP BY  L.state
```

The example cross-tabulation can be thought of as roll-up on the Location dimension, on the Time dimension, and on the Location and Time dimensions together. Each roll-up corresponds to a single SQL query with grouping. In general, given a measure with k associated dimensions, we can roll up on any subset of these k dimensions, and so we have a total of 2^k possible such SQL queries.

Through high-level operations such as pivoting, users can generate many of these 2^k SQL queries. Recognizing the commonalities between these queries enables more efficient, coordinated computation of the set of queries. A proposed extension to SQL called the **CUBE** is equivalent to a collection of **GROUP BY** statements, with one **GROUP BY** statement for each subset of the k dimensions. We illustrate it using the Sales relation. Consider the following query:

CUBE pid, locid, timeid **BY SUM** Sales

This query will roll up the table Sales on all eight subsets of the set {pid, locid, timeid} (including the empty subset). It is equivalent to eight queries of the form:

```
SELECT    SUM (S.sales)
FROM      Sales S
GROUP BY  grouping-list
```

The queries differ only in the *grouping-list*, which is some subset of the set {pid, locid, timeid}.

We conclude our discussion of the relationship of SQL and OLAP queries by noting that they complement each other, and both are important for decision support. The goal of OLAP is to enable end-users to ask a broad class of business-oriented queries easily and with interactive response times over very large datasets. SQL, on the other hand, can be used to write complex queries that combine information from several relations. The data need not be in star schemas, and the OLAP querying idioms are not always applicable. Such complex queries are written by application programmers, compiled, and made available to end-users as 'canned' programs, often through a menu-driven graphical interface. The importance of such SQL applications is reflected in the increased attention being paid to optimizing complex SQL queries, and the emergence of decision support oriented SQL benchmarks, such as TPC-D.

A Note on Statistical Databases

Many OLAP concepts are present in earlier work on **Statistical Databases (SDBs)**, which are database systems designed to support statistical applications, although this connection has not been sufficiently recognized because of differences in application domains and terminology. The multidimensional data model, with the notions of a measure associated with dimensions, and classification hierarchies for dimension values, is also used in SDBs. OLAP operations such as roll-up and drill-down have counterparts in SDBs. Indeed, some implementation techniques developed for OLAP have also been applied to SDBs.

Nonetheless, there are some differences arising from the different domains that OLAP and SDBs were developed to support. SDBs are used in socioeconomic applications, for example, whereas OLAP has been developed for business-oriented applications. Classification hierarchies in SDBs are more complex than in OLAP, and have received more attention, along with issues such as potential breaches of privacy. (The privacy issue concerns whether a user with access to summarized data can reconstruct the original, unsummarized data.) In OLAP, efficient handling of very large datasets has received more attention.

22.3.3 Database Design for OLAP

Figure 22.6 shows the tables in our running sales example.

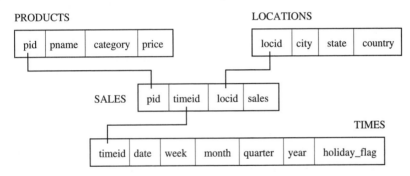

Figure 22.6 An Example of a Star Schema

It suggests a star, centered at the fact table Sales; such a combination of a fact table and dimension tables is called a **star schema**. This schema pattern is very common in databases designed for OLAP. The bulk of the data is typically in the fact table, which has no redundancy; it is usually in BCNF. In fact, to minimize the size of the fact table, dimension identifiers (such as *pid* and *timeid*) are system-generated identifiers.

Information about dimension values is maintained in the dimension tables. Dimension tables are usually not normalized. The rationale is that a database used for OLAP is static, and update, insertion and deletion anomalies are not important. Further, because the size of the database is dominated by the fact table, the space saved by normalizing dimension tables is negligible. Therefore, minimizing the computation time for combining facts in the fact table with dimension information is the main design criterion, which suggests that we avoid breaking a dimension table into smaller tables (which might lead to additional joins).

Interactive response times are important in OLAP, and most systems support the materialization of summary tables (typically generated through queries using grouping). Ad hoc queries posed by users are answered using the original tables along with precomputed summaries. A very important design issue is which summary tables should be materialized to achieve the best use of available memory and to answer commonly asked ad hoc queries with interactive response times. In current OLAP systems, deciding which summary tables to materialize may well be the most important design decision.

Finally, new storage structures and indexing techniques have been developed to support OLAP, and they present the database designer with additional physical design choices. We cover some of these implementation techniques briefly in the next section.

22.4   IMPLEMENTATION TECHNIQUES FOR OLAP

In this section we survey some implementation techniques motivated by the OLAP environment. The goal is to provide a feel for how OLAP systems differ from more traditional SQL systems; our discussion is far from comprehensive.

22.4.1   Indexing Methods

The mostly-read environment of OLAP systems makes the CPU overhead of maintaining indexes negligible, and the requirement of interactive response times for queries over very large datasets makes the availability of suitable indexes very important. This combination of factors has led to the development of new indexing techniques; we briefly discuss two of them.

Bit Map Indexes

Consider a table that describes customers:

Customers(*custid:* **integer**, *name:* **string**, *sex:* **boolean**, *rating:* **integer**)

The *rating* value is an integer in the range 1 to 5, and only two values are recorded for *sex*. Columns with few possible values are called **sparse**. We can exploit sparsity to construct a new kind of index that greatly speeds up queries on these columns.

The idea is to record values for sparse columns as a sequence of bits, one for each possible value. For example, a *sex* value is either 10 or 01; a 1 in the first position denotes male, and 1 in the second position denotes female. Similarly, 10000 denotes the *rating* value 1, and 00001 denotes the *rating* value 5.

If we consider the *sex* values for all rows in the Customers table, we can treat this as a collection of two **bit vectors**, one of which has the associated value 'Male' and the other the associated value 'Female'. Each bit vector has one bit per row, indicating whether the value in the that row is the value associated with the bit vector. The collection of bit vectors for a column is called a **bit map index** for that column.

An example instance of the Customers table, together with the bit map indexes for *sex* and *rating*, is shown in Figure 22.7.

sex
10
10
01
10

custid	name	sex	rating
112	Joe	M	3
115	Ram	M	5
119	Sue	F	5
112	Woo	M	4

rating
00100
00001
00001
00010

Figure 22.7   Bit Map Indexes on Customers Relation

Bit map indexes offer two important advantages over conventional hash and tree indexes. First, they allow the use of efficient bit operations to answer queries. For example, consider the query "How many male customers have a rating of 5?" We can take the first bit vector for *sex* and do a bit-wise **AND** with the fifth bit vector for *rating* to obtain a bit vector that has 1 for every male customer with rating 5. We can then count the number of 1s in this bit vector to answer the query. Second, bit map indexes can be much more compact than a traditional B+ tree index, and are very amenable to the use of compression techniques.

Bit vectors correspond closely to the rid-lists used to represent data entries in Alternative (3) for a traditional B+ tree index (see Section 4.3.1). In fact, we can think of a bit vector for a given *age* value, say, as an alternative representation of the rid-list for that value. This leads to a possible way to combine bit vectors (and their advantages of bit-wise processing) with B+ tree indexes on columns that are not sparse; we can use Alternative (3) for data entries, using a bit vector representation of rid-lists. A caveat is that if an rid-list is very small, the bit vector representation may be much larger than a list of rid values, even if the bit vector is compressed. Further, the use of compression leads to decompression costs, offsetting some of the computational advantages of the bit vector representation.

Join Indexes

Computing joins of very large relations with interactive response times is extremely hard. One approach to this problem is to create an index that is designed to speed up specific join queries. Suppose that the Customers table is to be joined with a table called Purchases (recording purchases made by customers) on the *custid* field. We can create a collection of $\langle c, p \rangle$ pairs, where p is the rid of a Purchases record that joins with a Customers record with *custid c*.

This idea can be generalized to support joins over more than two relations; a common example is a star schema, in which the fact table is likely to be joined with several dimension tables.

22.4.2 File Organizations

Since many OLAP queries involve just a few columns of a large relation, vertical partitioning becomes attractive. However, storing a relation column-wise can degrade performance for queries that involve several columns. An alternative in a mostly-read environment is to store the relation row-wise, but to also store each column separately.

A more radical file organization is to regard the fact table as a large multidimensional array, and to store it and index it as such. Since the array is much larger than available main memory, it is broken up into contiguous chunks, as discussed in Section 21.7. In addition, traditional B+ tree indexes are created to enable quick retrieval of chunks that contain tuples with values in a given range for one or more dimensions. This approach is taken in MOLAP systems.

22.4.3 Additional OLAP Implementation Issues

Our discussion of OLAP implementation techniques is far from complete. A number of other implementation issues must be considered for efficient OLAP query evaluation.

First, the use of compression is becoming widespread in database systems aimed at OLAP. The amount of information is so large that compression is obviously attractive. Further, the use of structures like bit map indexes, which are highly amenable to compression techniques, makes compression even more attractive.

Second, deciding which views to precompute and store in order to facilitate evaluation of ad hoc queries is a challenging problem. Especially for aggregate queries, the rich structure of operators such as CUBE offers many opportunities for a clever choice of views to precompute and store. Although the choice of views to precompute is made by the database designer in current systems, ongoing research is aimed at automating this choice.

Third, many OLAP systems are enhancing query language and optimization features in novel ways. As an example of query language enhancement, the Redbrick version of SQL allows users to define new aggregation operators by writing code for *initialization, iteration,* and *termination.* For example, if tuples with fields *department, employee* and *salary* are retrieved in sorted order by *department,* we can compute the standard deviation of salaries for each department; the initialization function would initialize the variables used to compute standard deviation, the iteration function would update the variables as each tuple is retrieved and processed, and the termination function would output the standard deviation for a department as soon as the first tuple for the next department is encountered. (Several ORDBMSs also support user-defined aggregate functions, and it is likely that this feature will be included in future versions of the SQL standard.) As an example of novel optimization features, some OLAP systems try to combine multiple scans, possibly part of different transactions, over a table. This seemingly simple optimization can be challenging: If the scans begin at different times, for example, we must keep track of the records seen by each scan to make sure that each scan sees every tuple exactly once; we must also deal with differences in the speeds at which the scan operations process tuples.

Finally, the emphasis on query processing and decision support applications in OLAP systems is being complemented by a greater emphasis on evaluating complex SQL queries in traditional SQL systems. Eventually, we may see traditional SQL systems evolving to support OLAP-style queries more efficiently; conversely, OLAP systems could evolve to support a broader class of traditional SQL queries efficiently, in addition to the class of queries motivated by the multidimensional view of data.

22.5 DATA MINING

Data mining consists of finding interesting trends or patterns in large datasets, in order to guide decisions about future activities. There is a general expectation that data mining tools should be able to identify interesting patterns in the data with minimal user input. The patterns identified by such tools can give a data analyst useful and unexpected insights that can be more carefully investigated subsequently, perhaps using other decision support tools.

Data mining is related to the subarea of statistics called *exploratory data analysis,* which has similar goals and relies on statistical measures. It is also closely related to the subareas of artificial intelligence called *knowledge discovery* and *machine learning.* The important distinguishing characteristic of data mining is that the volume of data is assumed to be very large; although ideas from these related areas of study are applicable to data mining problems, scalability with respect to data size is an important new criterion. Old algorithms must be adapted or new algorithms must be developed to ensure scalability.

Finding useful trends in datasets is a rather loose definition of data mining: In a certain sense, all database queries can be thought of as doing just this. Indeed, we have a continuum of analysis and exploration tools with SQL queries at one end, OLAP queries in the middle, and data mining techniques at the other end. SQL queries are constructed using relational algebra (with some extensions); OLAP provides higher-level querying idioms based on the multidimensional data model; and data mining provides the most abstract analysis operations. We can think of different data mining tasks as complex 'queries' specified at a high level, with a few parameters that are user-definable, and for which specialized algorithms are implemented.

In this section, we discuss several widely studied data mining tasks. There are commercial tools available for each of these tasks from major vendors, and the area is rapidly growing in importance as these tools gain acceptance from the user community.

It is important to recognize that in the real world, data mining is much more than simply applying one of these algorithms. Data is often noisy or incomplete, and unless this is understood and corrected for, it is likely that many interesting patterns will be missed and the reliability of detected patterns will be low. Further, the analyst must decide what kinds of mining algorithms are called for, apply them to a well-chosen subset of data samples and variables (i.e., tuples and attributes), digest the results, apply other decision support and mining tools, and iterate the process. In this section however, we will limit ourselves to looking at algorithms for a few specific data mining tasks; these are typical of the algorithms that the mining process is built around.

22.5.1   Introduction to Mining for Rules

Many algorithms have been proposed for discovering various forms of rules that succintly describe the data. We look at some widely discussed forms of rules and algorithms for discovering them. We begin by considering *association rules*, which are motivated by problems such as market basket analysis. A **market basket** is a collection of items purchased by a customer in a single **customer transaction**, that is, a single visit to a store or a single order through a mail-order catalog. (We will often abbreviate *customer transaction* to *transaction* when there is no confusion with the usual meaning of *transaction* in a DBMS context, which is an execution of a user program.) Retailers want to identify sets of items that are purchased together; this information can be used to improve the layout of goods in a store or the layout of catalog pages.

We will use the Purchases table shown in Figure 22.8 to illustrate association rules.

transid	custid	date	item	price	qty
111	201	3/12/91	pen	$35	2
111	201	3/12/91	ink	$2	1
111	201	3/12/91	diary	$5	3
111	201	3/12/91	soap	$1	6
112	105	6/2/96	pen	$35	1
112	105	6/2/96	ink	$2	1
112	105	6/2/96	diary	$5	1
113	106	6/2/96	pen	$35	1
113	106	6/2/96	diary	$5	1
114	201	8/3/96	pen	$35	2
114	201	8/3/96	ink	$2	2
114	201	8/3/96	soap	$1	4

Figure 22.8 The Purchases Relation for Market Basket Analysis

The tuples are shown sorted into groups by transaction. All tuples in a group have the same *transid*, and together they describe a customer transaction, which involves purchases of one or more items. A transaction occurs on a given date, and the name and price of each purchased item is recorded, along with the purchased quantity.

By examining the set of transaction groups in Purchases, we can identify rules of the form:

$$\{pen\} \Rightarrow \{ink\}$$

This rule should be read as follows: "If a pen is purchased in a transaction, it is likely that ink will also be purchased in that transaction." It is a statement that describes the transactions in the database; extrapolation to future transactions should be done with caution, as discussed in Section 22.5.2. More generally, an **association rule** has the form $LHS \Rightarrow RHS$, where both LHS and RHS are sets of items; if every item in LHS is purchased in a transaction, then it is likely that the items in RHS will also be purchased.

There are two important measures for an association rule:

- **Support:** The support for a set of items is the percentage of transactions that contain all of these items. The support for a rule $LHS \Rightarrow RHS$ is support for the set of items $LHS \cup RHS$. If support for a rule is low, the rule may have arisen purely by chance. For example, if support for the rule {diary} ⇒ {soap} is low, only a small percentage of the transactions involve both diaries and soap, which means that we don't have enough evidence to draw conclusions about the correlation between diary and soap purchases.

- **Confidence:** Consider transactions that contain all items in *LHS*. The confidence for a rule *LHS* ⇒ *RHS* is the percentage of such transactions that also contain all items in *RHS*; it indicates the degree of correlation (in the database) between purchases of these sets of items. For example, if the rule {diary} ⇒ {soap} has a low confidence, then the purchase of a diary is not highly correlated with the purchase of soap in the given database.

22.5.2 The Use of Association Rules for Prediction

Association rules are widely used for prediction, but it is important to recognize that such predictive use is not justified without additional analysis or domain knowledge; association rules describe existing data accurately, but can be misleading when used naively for prediction. For example, consider the rule

$$\{pen\} \Rightarrow \{ink\}$$

The confidence associated with this rule is the conditional probability of an ink purchase given a pen purchase *over the given database*; that is, it is a *descriptive* measure. We might use this rule to guide future sales promotions. For example, we might offer a discount on pens in order to increase the sales of pens and, therefore, also increase sales of ink.

However, such a promotion assumes that pen purchases are good indicators of ink purchases in *future* customer transactions (in addition to transactions in the current database). This assumption is justified if there is a *causal link* between pen purchases and ink purchases; that is, if buying pens causes the buyer to also buy ink. However, we can infer association rules with high support and confidence in some situations where there is no causal link between *LHS* and *RHS*! For example, suppose that pens are always purchased together with pencils, perhaps because of customers' tendency to order writing instruments together. We would then infer the rule

$$\{pencil\} \Rightarrow \{ink\}$$

with the same support and confidence as the rule

$$\{pen\} \Rightarrow \{ink\}$$

However, there is no causal link between pencils and ink; there is no reason to buy more ink because we have bought more pencils. A sales promotion that discounted pencils in order to increase the sales of ink would fail.

In practice, one would expect that by examining a large database of past transactions (collected over a long time and a variety of circumstances) and restricting attention to rules that occur often (i.e., that have high support), we minimize inferring misleading rules. However, we should bear in mind that misleading, noncausal rules could well be generated, and treat the generated rules as possibly, rather than conclusively, identifying causal relationships. Although association rules do not indicate causal relationships between the *LHS* and *RHS*, we emphasize that they provide a useful starting point for identifying such relationships, using either further analysis or a domain expert's judgment; this is the reason for their popularity.

The comments in this section about predictive use of association rules also apply to the other forms of rules discussed in this chapter.

22.5.3 An Algorithm for Finding Association Rules

A user can ask for all association rules that have a specified minimum support (*minsup*) and minimum confidence (*minconf*), and various algorithms have been developed for finding such rules efficiently. These algorithms first find **frequent itemsets**, or sets of items that have support greater than *minsup*. Next, they generate candidate rules by partitioning each frequent itemset into two sets, *LHS* and *RHS*. For each candidate rule, the algorithms compute the confidence for the rule, and retain rules with confidence greater than *minconf*.

Once frequent itemsets are identified, the generation of all candidate rules by partitioning each itemset into an *LHS* and *RHS* is straightforward. To compute confidence values, we can maintain two counters per candidate rule, *lhscount* and *rhscount*, and scan the set of all transactions once. If a transaction contains all items in *LHS* for a candidate rule, the *lhscount* for that rule is incremented; and if it additionally contains all items in *RHS* for a candidate rule, the *rhscount* for that rule is incremented. The ratio *rhscount/lhscount* for a candidate rule is its confidence value.

The expensive step is the identification of frequent itemsets, and this is where algorithms for finding association rules mostly differ. We show an algorithm for identifying frequent itemsets in Figure 22.9. This algorithm relies upon a simple yet fundamental property of frequent itemsets:

> **The A Priori Property**: Every subset of a frequent itemset must also be a frequent itemset.

The algorithm proceeds iteratively, first identifying frequent itemsets with just one item. In each subsequent iteration, frequent itemsets identified in the previous iteration are extended with another item to generate larger candidate itemsets. By considering only itemsets obtained by enlarging frequent itemsets, we greatly reduce the number of candidate frequent itemsets; this optimization is crucial for efficient execution. The a priori property guarantees that this optimization is correct, that is, we don't miss any frequent itemsets. A single scan of all transactions (the Purchases table in our example) suffices to determine which candidate itemsets generated in an iteration are frequent itemsets. The algorithm terminates when no new frequent itemsets are identified in an iteration.

```
foreach item,                                          // Level 1
      check if it is a frequent itemset      // appears in > minsup transactions
   repeat                    // Iterative, level-wise identification of frequent itemsets
         foreach new frequent itemset I_k with k items              // Level k + 1
            generate all itemsets I_{k+1} with k + 1 items, I_k ⊂ I_{k+1}
         Scan all transactions once and check if
         the generated k + 1-itemsets are frequent
   until no new frequent itemsets are identified
```

Figure 22.9   An Algorithm for Finding Frequent Itemsets

We illustrate the algorithm on the Purchases table in Figure 22.8, with $minsup=$ 70%. In the first iteration (Level 1), we scan Purchases and determine that each of these one-item sets is a frequent itemset: $\{pen\}$ (appears in all four transactions), $\{ink\}$ (appears in three out of four transactions), and $\{diary\}$ (appears in three out of four transactions).

In the second iteration (Level 2), we extend each frequent itemset with an additional item, and generate the following candidate itemsets: $\{pen, ink\}$, $\{pen, diary\}$, $\{pen, soap\}$, $\{ink, diary\}$, $\{ink, soap\}$, and $\{diary, soap\}$. By scanning Purchases again, we determine that the following are frequent itemsets: $\{pen, ink\}$ (appears in three out of four transactions), and $\{pen, diary\}$ (appears in three out of four transactions).

In the third iteration (Level 3), we extend these itemsets with an additional item, and generate the following candidate itemsets: $\{pen, ink, diary\}$, $\{pen, ink, soap\}$, and $\{pen, diary, soap\}$. (Observe that $\{ink, diary, soap\}$ is not generated.) A third scan of Purchases allows us to determine that none of these is a frequent itemset.

Returning to the problem of identifying association rules, the frequent itemset $\{pen, ink\}$ suggests two candidate rules with 70% minimum support:

$$\{pen\} \Rightarrow \{ink\}$$

$$\{ink\} \Rightarrow \{pen\}$$

Suppose that the user wants rules with *minconf*=80%. Since *pen* appears in all four transactions and *ink* appears in only three, the first rule only has confidence 75%, and does not qualify. Since *pen* appears in every transaction in which *ink* appears, the second rule has confidence 100%, and qualifies. It is the only association rule that holds over the Purchases table with minimum support of 70% and minimum confidence of 80%.

The simple algorithm presented here for finding frequent itemsets illustrates many of the features of a good algorithm, such as the iterative generation and testing of candidate itemsets. Some important refinements to this algorithm follow:

- The idea of generating candidate itemsets by adding an item to a known frequent itemset is an attempt to limit the number of candidate itemsets using the a apriori property. More generally, this property can be used to prune the set of candidate itemsets further by checking whether every subset of a candidate itemset is a frequent itemset.

- Instead of looking for association rules over the entire Purchases relation, we can look for rules in a randomly chosen 'representative' subset of the relation that fits in main memory. This will find most of the association rules that hold over Purchases, but not all of them. However, we can refine this approach to ensure that all association rules over Purchases are found by using additional scans over the entire Purchases relation; we will not discuss the refinement. If a good sample of Purchases is used initially, this approach works well.

22.5.4   Generalized Association Rules

Although association rules have been most widely studied in the context of market basket analysis, or analysis of customer transactions, the concept is more general. Consider the Purchases table as shown in Figure 22.10, grouped by *custid*.

By examining the set of customer groups, we can identify association rules, as before:

$$\{pen\} \Rightarrow \{ink\}$$

This rule should now be read as follows: "If a pen is purchased by a customer, it is likely that ink will also be purchased by that customer." Similarly, we can group tuples by date, and identify association rules that indicate likelihood of items being purchased on the same date.

Thus one important parameter in identifying association rules in a table like Purchases is the attribute that is used to group tuples. Fundamentally, association

transid	custid	date	item	price	qty
112	105	6/2/96	pen	$35	1
112	105	6/2/96	ink	$2	1
112	105	6/2/96	diary	$5	1
113	106	6/2/96	pen	$35	1
113	106	6/2/96	diary	$5	1
114	201	8/3/96	pen	$35	2
114	201	8/3/96	ink	$2	2
114	201	8/3/96	soap	$1	4
111	201	3/12/91	pen	$35	2
111	201	3/12/91	ink	$2	1
111	201	3/12/91	diary	$5	3
111	201	3/12/91	soap	$1	6

Figure 22.10   The Purchases Relation Sorted on Customer Id

rules are statements about *groups of tuples*, of the form "if some things are true about a group, some other things are true as well."

It has also been proposed that we should allow more general specifications of the conditions that must be true within a group for a rule to hold with respect to that group. For example, consider Figure 22.10. We might want to say that all items in the *LHS* must cost more than $5 and be purchased on the same date *d1*, all items in the *RHS* must cost more than $5 and be purchased on the same date *d2*, and *d2* > *d1*.

Another way to specify complex conditions is based on a hierarchy over the set of items. Thus we might want to identify association rules of the form

$$\{apparel\} \Rightarrow \{stationery\}$$

where *apparel* is a generalization of *pant* and *shirt*, and *stationery* is a generalization of *pen*, *ink* and *diary*. A group of tuples supports this rule if it contains both an *apparel* item and a *stationery* item; for example, both a *pant* and a *pen*.

Using different choices for the grouping attribute and sophisticated conditions as in the above examples, we can identify rules that are more complex than the basic association rules discussed earlier. These more complex rules, nonetheless, retain the essential structure of an association rule as a condition over a group of tuples, with support and confidence measures defined as usual.

22.5.5   Sequential Patterns

Consider the Purchases relation shown in Figure 22.10. Each group of tuples, having the same *custid* value, can be thought of as a *sequence* of transactions, ordered by *date*. This allows us to identify frequently arising buying patterns over time.

We begin by introducing the concept of a sequence of itemsets. Each transaction is represented by a set of tuples, and by looking at the values in the *item* column, we get a set of items purchased in that transaction. Thus the sequence of transactions associated with a customer corresponds naturally to a sequence of itemsets purchased by the customer. For example, the sequence of purchases for customer 201 is {pen,ink,soap}, {pen,ink,diary,soap}.

A **subsequence** of a sequence of itemsets is obtained by deleting one or more itemsets, and is another sequence of itemsets. We say that a sequence $\{a_1, \ldots a_m\}$ is **contained** in another sequence S if S has a subsequence $\{b_1, \ldots b_m\}$ such that $a_i \subseteq b_i$, for $1 \leq i < m$. Thus the sequence {pen}, {ink,diary}, {pen,soap} is contained in {pen,ink}, {shirt}, {milk,ink,diary}, {soap,pen,diary}. Note that the order of items within each itemset does not matter. However, the order of itemsets does matter: the sequence {pen}, {ink,diary}, {pen,soap} is not contained in {pen,ink}, {shirt}, {soap,pen,diary}, {milk,ink,diary}.

The **support** for a sequence S of itemsets is the percentage of customer sequences of which S is a subsequence. The problem of identifying sequential patterns is to find all sequences that have a user-specified minimum support. A sequence $s_1, s_2, s_3, \ldots, s_n$ with minimum support tells us that a customer who buys the items in set s_1 in a transaction is likely to buy the items in set s_2 in a subsequent transaction, then the items in set s_3 in a later transaction, and so on.

Like association rules, sequential patterns are statements about groups of tuples in the current database. Computationally, algorithms for finding sequential patterns resemble algorithms for finding frequent itemsets. Longer and longer sequences with the required minimum support are identified iteratively in a manner that is very similar to the iterative identification of frequent itemsets.

A variation on sequential patterns is to look for patterns of *events* in a time-series. For example, over a sequence of daily closing stock prices, we might define an event to be three consective days of increasing prices followed by two days of falling prices. Finding all such events over one or more given sequences is an interesting problem for which efficient algorithms have been proposed.

22.5.6   Classification Rules

Consider a table of credit information maintained by a bank:

BankInfo(*custid:* `integer`, *balance:* `real`, *age:* `integer`, *default:* `boolean`)

Every customer's age and balance are recorded, as well as a flag indicating whether the customer has defaulted on a loan. The bank would like to use this information to identify rules of the form "If *age* is in a certain range and *balance* is in a certain range, then the customer is likely to default on a loan." Once such rules are learned from existing data, they can be used to predict whether a customer who applies for credit (and for whom we don't have a *default* value yet) is a good credit risk.

We call such rules **classification rules**. The general form is:

$$(l1 \leq X1 < h1) \land \ldots \land (lk \leq Xk < hk) \Rightarrow Y = c$$

The attributes $X1 \ldots Xk$ are used to predict, or classify, the value of attribute Y. Both sides of a classification rule can be interpreted as conditions on attributes of a tuple of some relation, which is BankInfo in our example.

These rules differ from association rules by considering continuous, numeric attributes, rather than attributes that take on discrete values, and identifying such rules efficiently presents a new set of problems, which we will not discuss. We can define support and confidence for classification rules, as for association rules:

- **Support:** The support for a condition C is the percentage of tuples that satisfy C. The support for a rule $C1 \Rightarrow C2$ is the support for the condition $C1 \land C2$.

- **Confidence:** Consider those tuples that satisfy condition $C1$. The confidence for a rule $C1 \Rightarrow C2$ is the percentage of such tuples that also satisfy condition $C2$.

In contrast to association rules, classification rules are statements about individual tuples, rather than about groups of tuples.[1] Classification rules are sometimes called **quantitative association rules**.

Consider the right side of a classification rule: $Y = c$. There is a small set of possible values for c, and each rule predicts the value of Y for a given tuple based

---

[1] If we think of Purchases as a table with one attribute *per item*, we can express association rules as statements about individual tuples, but this is rather artificial.

on $X1 \ldots Xk$. A generalization of classification rules aims to predict more general functions:

$$(l1 \leq X1 < h1) \wedge \ldots \wedge (lk \leq Xk < hk) \Rightarrow Y = f(X1 \ldots Xk)$$

where f is some function. Such rules are called **regression rules**. Example applications of regression rules include financial forecasting, where the price of coffee futures could be some function of the rainfall in Colombia a month ago; direct mail prospecting, where the likelihood of a given customer's responding to a promotion is a function of his or her income level and age; and medical prognosis, where the likelihood of a tumor's being cancerous is a function of measured attributes of the tumor.

22.5.7   Additional Data Mining Tasks

We have concentrated on the problem of association rules and related rule-oriented knowledge discovery tasks. There are several other equally important data mining tasks, some of which we discuss briefly below. The bibliographic references at the end of the chapter provide many pointers for further study.

Bayesian Networks: Finding causal relationships is a challenging task, as we saw in Section 22.5.2. In general, if certain events are highly correlated, there are many possible explanations. For example, suppose that pens, pencils and ink are purchased together frequently. It might be the case that the purchase of one of these items (e.g., ink) depends causally upon the purchase of another item (e.g., pen). Or it might be the case that the purchase of one of these items (e.g., pen) is strongly correlated with the purchase of another (e.g., pencil) because there is some underlying phenomenon (e.g., users' tendency to think about writing instruments together) that causally influences both purchases. How can we identify the true causal relationships that hold between these events in the real world?

One approach is to consider each possible combination of causal relationships among the variables or events of interest to us, and to evaluate the likelihood of each combination on the basis of the data available to us. If we think of each combination of causal relationships as a *model* of the real world underlying the collected data, we can assign a score to each model by considering how consistent it is (in terms of probabilities, with some simplifying assumptions) with the observed data. Bayesian Networks are graphs that can be used to describe a class of such models, with one node per variable or event, and arcs between nodes to indicate causality. For example, a good model for our running example of pens, pencils and ink is shown in Figure 22.11. In general, the number of possible models is exponential in the number of variables, and considering all models is expensive, so some subset of all possible models is evaluated.

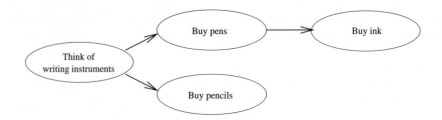

Figure 22.11   Bayesian Network Showing Causality

Clustering: This problem is closely related to classification because the goal is again to put each data tuple into a class. We map each data tuple to a point in a multidimensional space and identify clusters in this space based on spatial proximity; the data tuples that are mapped to a cluster form a class. By mapping data tuples to points in a well-chosen multidimensional space (a step that typically requires a good understanding of the domain described by the data) we can obtain clusters that classify the data in a meaningful way.

For example, if we photograph a scene at several bandwidths, each photograph gives us a measurement (at the corresponding bandwidth) for each pixel in the scene image. For example, if we photograph a scene at three bandwidths (e.g., visual, near infrared, far infrared), for each pixel (identified by an X-Y pair) in the image we obtain a vector with three fields. Each vector can be regarded as a point in a three-dimensional space and the set of vectors can be partitioned into clusters based on proximity in this space; by clustering the vectors we also classify the corresponding image pixels. By choosing the coordinate space for clustering carefully (e.g., assigning suitable weights to each bandwidth), the classes of image pixels can be made to correspond to meaningful subregions. This approach has been used to classify imagery of vegetation into regions corresponding to leaves, branches, sky, and so on. Regions can be hierarchically clustered to obtain more detail; for example, we can partition (the set of pixels corresponding to) leaves into (pixels corresponding to) leaves in shadow and sunlit leaves.

Clustering has been widely studied in statistics, with an emphasis on finding good clusters for a wide variety of data distributions, but the algorithms typically break down on datasets with more than a few thousand points. Finding scalable approaches to clustering large datasets has received attention recently.

Decision Trees: Another approach to classification is to build a *decision tree*, in which the leaves correspond to classes and the rest of the tree determines the leaf to which a data point is assigned. A decision tree can be used to classify a tuple by starting at the root of the tree and comparing field values in the tuple with edge labels to move the tuple down to a particular leaf; each leaf represents a class. This approach has been widely studied in machine learning, and algorithms that scale to large datasets have been proposed recently.

Sampling: One way to explore a large dataset is to obtain one or more *samples* and to analyze the samples. The advantage of sampling is that we can carry out detailed analysis on a sample that would be infeasible on the entire dataset, for very large datasets. The disadvantage of sampling is that obtaining a representative sample for a given task is difficult; we might miss important trends or patterns because they are not reflected in the sample. Current database systems also provide poor support for efficiently obtaining samples. Improving database support for obtaining samples with various desirable statistical properties is relatively straightforward, and is likely to be available in future DBMSs. Applying sampling for data mining is an area for further research.

Sequence Similarity: In a number of domains, time-series or observation traces of various kinds are collected. Finding patterns in these sequence databases is an important kind of data mining activity; a common way to describe a pattern is to give an example and to ask for 'similar' patterns, with similarity defined in many ways. For example, we could define *similar* to mean identical; or identical up to shifting and scaling within certain limits; or changing over time in a certain way (e.g., a stock that goes up by at least 10% for three consecutive days, followed by a drop of at least 25%), and so on.

Visualization: Visualization techniques can significantly assist in understanding complex datasets and detecting interesting patterns, and the importance of visualization in data mining is widely recognized.

22.6 SUMMARY

A data warehouse is a consolidated repository that contains data from several databases. It is intended to support complex analysis for decision support, and is designed for very fast query execution over very large datasets. The data in a warehouse is updated periodically to keep it current with the operational databases from which the data is drawn, but it is not modified routinely by users; thus efficient execution of update transactions is not important. Warehouses facilitate the use of OLAP and data mining tools for detailed analysis; conversely, the desire to use these tools is an important motivation for creating and maintaining a data warehouse.

OLAP systems support a class of business-oriented queries inspired by spreadsheets and other end-user tools, in addition to conventional database query languages. Grouping and aggregate operations are central to OLAP queries, and their efficient processing has been the subject of much current research.

Data mining complements OLAP by supporting more exploratory analysis. Specialized algorithms have been developed for finding various kinds of patterns in large datasets, with user-specified thresholds determining which patterns are returned. Association rules, sequential patterns, classification, clustering, and other data mining tasks are closely related to problems studied widely in statistics and machine learning. The main difference is that the size of datasets is expected to be much larger; this difference leads to a qualitative difference in the algorithms used to find patterns.

EXERCISES

Exercise 22.1 Briefly answer the following questions.

1. How do warehousing, OLAP and data mining complement each other?

2. What is the relationship between data warehousing and data replication? Which form of replication (synchronous or asynchronous) is better suited for data warehousing? Why?

3. What is the role of the metadata repository in a data warehouse? How does it differ from a catalog in a relational DBMS?

4. What are the considerations in designing a data warehouse?

5. Once a warehouse is designed and loaded, how it is kept current with respect to changes to the source databases?

6. One of the advantages of a warehouse is that we can use it to track how the contents of a relation change over time; in contrast, we have only the current snapshot of a relation in a regular DBMS. Discuss how you would maintain the history of a relation R, taking into account that 'old' information must somehow be purged to make space for new information.

7. Describe dimensions and measures in the multidimensional data model.

8. What is a fact table, and why is it so important from a performance standpoint?

9. What is the fundamental difference between MOLAP and ROLAP systems?

10. What is a star schema? Is it typically in BCNF? Why or why not?

11. How is data mining different from OLAP?

12. Define *support* and *confidence* for an association rule.

13. Explain why association rules cannot be used directly for prediction, without further analysis or domain knowledge.

14. Distinguish between *association rules, classification rules* (also called *quantitative association rules*), and *regression rules*.

15. Distinguish between *classification* and *clustering*.

16. What is the role of information visualization in data mining?

17. Give examples of queries over a database of stock price quotes, stored as sequences, one per stock, that cannot be expressed in SQL.

Exercise 22.2 Consider the instance of the Sales relation shown in Figure 22.3.

1. Show the result of pivoting the relation on *pid* and *timeid*.

2. Write a collection of SQL queries to obtain the same result as in the previous part.

3. Show the result of pivoting the relation on *pid* and *locid*.

Exercise 22.3 Consider the cross-tabulation of the Sales relation shown in Figure 22.5.

1. Show the result of roll-up on *locid* (i.e., state).

2. Write a collection of SQL queries to obtain the same result as in the previous part.

3. Show the result of roll-up on *locid* followed by drill-down on *pid*.

4. Write a collection of SQL queries to obtain the same result as in the previous part, starting with the cross-tabulation shown in Figure 22.5.

Exercise 22.4 Consider the Customers relation and the bit map indexes shown in Figure 22.7.

1. For the same data, if the underlying set of rating values is assumed to range from 1 to 10, show how the bit map indexes would change.

2. How would you use the bit map indexes to answer the following queries? If the bit map indexes are not useful, explain why.

   (a) How many customers with a rating less than 3 are male?

   (b) What percentage of customers are male?

   (c) How many customers are there?

   (d) How many customers are named Woo?

   (e) Find the rating value with the greatest number of customers and also find the number of customers with that rating value; if several rating values have the maximum number of customers, list the requested information for all of them. (Assume that very few rating values have the same number of customers.)

Exercise 22.5 In addition to the Customers table of Figure 22.7, assume that you have a table called Products, with fields *rating* and *prodid*. This table is used to identify products that might be of interest to customers, bsed on their rating.

1. Suppose that you also have a bit map index on the *rating* field of Products. Discuss whether or not the bit map indexes would help in computing the join of Customers and Products on *custid*.

2. Describe the use of a join index to support the join of these two relations on *custid*.

Exercise 22.6 Consider the Purchases table shown in Figure 22.8.

1. Simulate the algorithm for finding frequent itemsets on this table with *minsup*=90%, and then find association rules with *minconf*=90%.

2. Can you modify the table so that the same frequent itemsets are obtained with *minsup*=90% as with *minsup*=70% on the table shown in Figure 22.8?

3. Simulate the algorithm for finding frequent itemsets on the table in Figure 22.8 with *minsup*=10%, and then find association rules with *minconf*=90%.

4. Can you modify the table so that the same frequent itemsets are obtained with *minsup*=10% as with *minsup*=70% on the table shown in Figure 22.8?

Exercise 22.7 Consider the Purchases table shown in Figure 22.8. Modify the table so that there is a difference in the performance of the basic algorithm for finding frequent itemsets and the algorithm with the first optimization described in Section 22.5.1.

Exercise 22.8 Consider the Purchases table shown in Figure 22.8. Find all (generalized) association rules that indicate likelihood of items being purchased on the same date by the same customer, with *minsup*=10% and *minconf*=70%.

Exercise 22.9 Consider the Purchases table shown in Figure 22.8. Find all sequential patterns with *minsup*= 60%. (The text only sketches the algorithm for discovering sequential patterns, so you'll have to use brute force or look up one of the references for a complete algorithm.)

BIBLIOGRAPHIC NOTES

A good survey of data warehousing and OLAP is presented in [118], which is the source of Figure 22.1. [499] provides an overview of OLAP and statistical database research, showing the strong parallels between concepts and research in these two areas. The book by Kimball [303], one of the pioneers in warehousing, and the collection of papers [46] offer a good practical introduction to the area. The term OLAP was popularized by Codd's paper [139]. For a recent discussion of the performance of algorithms utilizing bit map and other nontraditional index structures, see [414].

[230] introduced the *cube* operator, and optimization of cube queries and efficient maintenance of the result of a cube query have been addressed in several papers, including [9, 249, 255, 460, 456, 500]. Related algorithms for processing queries with aggregates and grouping are presented in [117, 120]. [445] addresses the implementation of queries involving generalized quantifiers such as *a majority of*. [516] describes an access method to support processing of aggregate queries. Also see the bibliographic notes for Chapter 10 for references to work on maintaining materialized views.

Discovering useful knowledge from a large database is more than just applying a collection of data mining algorithms, and the point of view that it is an iterative process guided by an analyst is stressed in [192] and [481]. Work on exploratory data analysis in statistics, for example, [548], and on machine learning and knowledge discovery in artificial intelligence was a precursor to the current focus on data mining; the added emphasis on large volumes of data is the important new element. Good recent surveys of data mining algorithms include [269, 194, 364]. [193] contains additional surveys and articles on many aspects of data mining and knowledge discovery, including a tutorial on Bayesian Networks [252].

The first association rules algorithm for large data sets was presented in [15]. An efficient algorithm is described in [16]. A fast algorithm that exploits sampling techniques is proposed in [542]. Parallel algorithms are described in [18] and [471]. [207] presents an algorithm for discovering association rules over a continuous numeric attribute; association rules over numeric attributes are also discussed in [574]. The general form of association rules in which attributes other than the transaction id are grouped on is developed in [378]. Association rules over items in a hierarchy are discussed in [511, 246]. A further generalization of association rules is proposed in [86]. The problem of mining sequential patterns is discussed in [19].

Sequence queries have received a lot of attention recently. Extending relational systems, which deal with sets of records, to deal with sequences of records is investigated in [480, 334, 486]. Finding similar sequences from a large database of sequences is discussed in [191, 17, 494, 436].

For a good overview of classification algorithms, which have been widely studied in the Machine Learning literature, see [435]. Algorithms that scale well with increasing database size are presented in [489, 394]. A linear-time algorithm for clustering large multidimensional datasets is presented in [585]. See [279, 478] for a detailed discussion of clustering algorithms and density estimation. References for visualization are included in the bibliography for Chapter 23.

23

ADDITIONAL TOPICS

> This is not the end. It is not even the beginning of the end. But it is, perhaps, the end of the beginning.

> —Winston Churchill

In this book we have concentrated on relational database systems and discussed several fundamental issues in detail. However, our coverage of the database area, and indeed even the relational database area, is far from exhaustive. In this chapter we look briefly at several topics that we did not cover, with the goal of giving the reader some perspective, and indicating directions for further study.

We begin with a discussion of advanced transaction processing concepts in Section 23.1. We discuss the growing influence of computer networks on database systems in Section 23.2, and consider the impact of another technology trend, namely, increasingly larger main memory sizes, in Section 23.3. We discuss information visualization in Section 23.4. Finally, in Section 23.5 we consider a number of important application domains that are pushing the limits of currently available database technology, and are motivating the development of new techniques.

23.1 ADVANCED TRANSACTION PROCESSING

The concept of a transaction has wide applicability for a variety of distributed computing tasks, such as airline reservations, inventory management, and electronic commerce.

23.1.1 Transaction Processing Monitors

Complex applications are often built on top of several **resource managers**, such as database management systems, operating systems, user interfaces, and messaging software. A **transaction processing monitor** glues together the services of several resource managers and provides application programmers with a uniform interface for developing transactions with the ACID properties. In addition to providing a uniform interface to the services of different resource managers, a TP monitor also routes transactions to the appropriate resource managers. Finally, a

TP monitor ensures that an application behaves as a transaction by implementing concurrency control, logging, and recovery functions, and by exploiting the transaction processing capabilities of the underlying resource managers.

TP monitors are used in environments where applications require advanced features such as access to multiple resource managers; sophisticated request routing (also called **workflow management**); assigning priorities to transactions and doing priority-based load-balancing across servers; and so on. A DBMS provides many of the functions supported by a TP monitor in addition to processing queries and database updates efficiently. A DBMS is appropriate for environments where the wealth of transaction management capabilities provided by a TP monitor is not necessary, and in particular, where very high scalability (with respect to transaction processing activity) and interoperability are not essential.

The transaction processing capabilities of database systems are improving continually. For example, many vendors offer distributed DBMS products today in which a transaction can execute across several resource managers, each of which is a DBMS. Currently, all the DBMSs must be from the same vendor; however, as transaction-oriented services from different vendors become more standardized, distributed, heterogeneous DBMSs should become available. Eventually, perhaps, the functions of current TP monitors will also be available in many DBMSs; for now, TP monitors provide essential infrastructure for high-end transaction processing environments.

23.1.2   New Transaction Models

Consider an application such as computer-aided design, in which users retrieve large design objects from a database and interactively analyze and modify them. Each transaction takes a long time—minutes or even hours, whereas the TPC benchmark transactions take under a millisecond—and holding locks this long affects performance. Further, if a crash occurs, undoing an active transaction completely is unsatisfactory, since considerable user effort may be lost. Ideally we want to be able to restore most of the actions of an active transaction and resume execution. Finally, if several users are concurrently developing a design, they may want to see changes being made by others without waiting until the end of the transaction that changes the data.

To address the needs of long-duration activities, several refinements of the transaction concept have been proposed. The basic idea is to treat each transaction as a collection of related **subtransactions**. Subtransactions can acquire locks, and the changes made by a subtransaction become visible to other transactions after the subtransaction ends (and before the main transaction of which it is a part commits). In **multilevel transactions**, locks held by a subtransaction are released when the subtransaction ends. In **nested transactions**, locks held by a subtransaction are assigned to the parent (sub)transaction when the subtransaction ends. These refinements to the transaction concept have a significant effect on concurrency control and recovery algorithms.

23.1.3   Real-Time DBMSs

Some transactions must be executed within a user-specified **deadline**. A **hard deadline** means the value of the transaction is zero after the deadline. For example, in a DBMS designed to record bets on horse races, a transaction placing a bet is worthless once the race begins. Such a transaction should not be executed; the bet should not be placed. A **soft deadline** means the value of the transaction decreases after the deadline, eventually going to zero. For example, in a DBMS designed to monitor some activity (e.g., a complex reactor), a transaction that looks up the current reading of a sensor must be executed within a short time, say, one second. The longer it takes to execute the transaction, the less useful the reading becomes. In a real-time DBMS, the goal is to maximize the value of executed transactions, and the DBMS must prioritize transactions, taking their deadlines into account.

23.2   NETWORKED DATABASES

The proliferation of computer networks has enabled users to access a large number of data sources. This increased access to databases is likely to have a great practical impact; data and services can now be offered directly to customers in ways that were impossible until recently. This unprecedented access will lead to increased and novel demands upon DBMS technology.

23.2.1   World Wide Web

The Web makes it possible to access a file anywhere on the Internet. A file is identified by a **Universal Resource Locator (URL)**:

```
http://www.informatik.uni-trier.de/~ley/db/index.html
```

This URL identifies a file called `index.html`, stored in the directory `~ley/db/` on machine `www.informatik.uni-trier.de`. This file is a document formatted using **HyperText Markup Language (HTML)** and contains several **links** to other files (identified through their URLs). The formatting commands are interpreted by a browsing tool such as Netscape Navigator to display the document in an attractive manner, and the user can then navigate to other related documents by choosing links. A collection of such documents on a given machine is called a

Web site, and most organizations today maintain a Web site. (Incidentally, the URL shown above is the entry point to Michael Ley's Web site, which contains information on database and logic programming research publications. It is an invaluable resource for students and researchers in these areas.)

Audio, video, and even programs (written in Java, a highly portable language, and typically performing complex animations) can be included in HTML documents. When a user retrieves such a document using a suitable browser, images in the document are displayed, audio and video clips are played, and embedded programs are executed at the user's machine; the result is a rich multimedia presentation. The ease with which HTML documents can be created—there are now visual editors that automatically generate HTML—and accessed using Internet browsers has fueled the explosive growth of the Web.

Web Servers and Databases

The Web is widely expected to be the cornerstone of electronic commerce; many organizations already offer products through their Web sites, and customers can place orders by visiting a Web site. For such applications a URL must identify more than just a file, however rich the contents of the file; a URL must provide an entry point to services based on information in a database. To understand how such an entry point can be supported, and the connection between the Web and database systems, it is necessary to consider how Web sites are administered.

A **Web server** is a program that waits for URL requests at a given site. If the requested URL is a file name, the server returns a copy of the file. If the requested URL identifies a program to be executed at the server's site, the Web server creates a process to execute the program, and communicates with this process using the **common gateway interface (CGI)** protocol. If an HTML document is a *form*, the form is returned to the requestor (a user running an Internet browser). After the requestor fills in the form, the form is returned to the Web server, and the information filled in by the user can be used as parameters to a program executing at the server side. The results of the program can be used to create a customized HTML document that is returned to the requestor.

The ability to use a URL to invoke a program at the server leads us to the database connection: The program invoked by the Web server can generate a request to a database system or to a TP monitor. This capability allows us to easily place a database on a network, and make services that rely upon database access available over the Web. Applications that access a database through the Web are likely to become very common. The CGI protocol, which creates one process per request, is inefficient and cannot scale to deal with a large number of requests. Alternative protocols, in which the program invoked by a request is executed within the Web server process, have been proposed by Microsoft (*Internet Server API (ISAPI)*) and by Netscape (*Netscape Server API (NSAPI)*), and bring Web server architectures closer to TP monitor architectures. Indeed, the TPC-C benchmark has been executed, with good results, by sending requests from 1500 PC clients to a Web server, and through it to an SQL database server.

23.2.2   Integrated Access to Multiple Data Sources

As databases proliferate, users want to access data from more than one source. For example, if several travel agents market their travel packages through the Web, customers would like to look at packages from different agents and compare them. A more traditional example is that large organizations typically have several databases, created (and maintained) by different divisions such as Sales, Production, and Purchasing. While these databases contain much common information, determining the exact relationship between tables in different databases can be a complicated problem. For example, prices in one database might be in dollars per dozen items, while prices in another database might be in dollars per item. Such *semantic mismatches* can be resolved and hidden from users by defining relational views over the tables from the two databases. Defining a collection of views to give a group of users a uniform presentation of relevant data from multiple databases is called **semantic integration**. Creating views that mask semantic mismatches in a natural manner is a difficult task and has been widely studied. In practice, the task is made harder by the fact that the schemas of existing databases are often poorly documented; thus it is difficult to even understand the meaning of rows in existing tables, let alone define unifying views across several tables from different databases.

If the underlying databases are managed using different DBMSs, as is often the case, some kind of 'middleware' must be used to evaluate queries over the integrating views, retrieving data at query execution time by using gateways such as ODBC. Alternatively, the integrating views can be materialized and stored in a data warehouse, as discussed in Chapter 22. Queries can then be executed over the warehoused data without accessing the source DBMSs at run-time.

23.2.3   Mobility and Databases

The availability of portable computers and wireless communications has created a new breed of nomadic database users. At one level these users are simply accessing a database through a network. At another level the network now has several novel properties: users' locations are constantly changing, communication costs are measured differently (e.g., connection time and battery usage versus bytes transferred) and change constantly depending on location, and the likelihood of losing connections is much greater than in a traditional network. These changes affect basic assumptions in many components of a DBMS, including the query optimizer and recovery manager.

23.3 MAIN MEMORY DATABASES

The price of main memory is now low enough that we can buy enough main memory to hold the entire database for many applications; with 64-bit addressing, modern CPUs also have very large address spaces. Some commercial systems now have several *gigabytes* of main memory. This shift prompts a re-examination of some basic DBMS design decisions, since disk accesses no longer dominate processing time for a memory-resident database.

- Main memory does not survive system crashes, and so we still have to implement logging and recovery to ensure transaction atomicity and durability. Log records must be written to stable storage at commit time, and this process could become a bottleneck. To minimize this problem, rather than commit each transaction as it completes, we can collect completed transactions and commit them in batches; this is called **group commit**.

- The implementation of in-memory operations has to be optimized carefully since disk accesses are no longer the limiting factor for performance.

23.4 INFORMATION VISUALIZATION

As computers become faster and main memory becomes cheaper, it becomes increasingly feasible to create visual presentations of data, rather than just text-based reports. Data visualization makes it easier for users to understand the information in large complex datasets. The challenge here is to make it easy for users to develop visual presentation of their data and to interactively query such presentations. Although a number of data visualization tools are available, efficient visualization of large datasets presents many challenges.

The need for visualization is especially important in the context of decision support; when confronted with large quantities of high-dimensional data and various kinds of data summaries produced by using analysis tools such as SQL, OLAP, and data mining algorithms, the information can be overwhelming. Visualizing the data, together with the generated summaries, can be a powerful way to sift through this information and spot interesting trends or patterns. The human eye, after all, is very good at finding patterns. A good framework for data mining must combine analytic tools to process data, and bring out latent anomalies or trends, with a visualization environment in which a user can notice these patterns and interactively drill down to the original data for further analysis.

CHAPTER 23

23.5 DOMAIN-SPECIFIC DBMS ISSUES

This section considers some important application domains with special requirements. DBMSs that are targeted at these domains have to address new challenges that stretch currently available technology.

23.5.1 Geographic Information Systems

Geographic Information Systems (GIS) contain spatial information about cities, states, countries, streets, highways, lakes, rivers, and so on. Such information is most naturally thought of as being overlaid on maps. Typical queries include "What cities lie on I-94 between Madison and Chicago?" and "What is the shortest route from Madison to St. Louis?" An emerging application is in-vehicle navigation aids. With Global Positioning Systems (GPS) technology, a car's location can be pinpointed, and by accessing a database of local maps, a driver can receive directions from his or her current location to a desired destination; this application also involves mobile database access!

A DBMS that holds geographic information must be able to answer spatial queries, such as the preceding examples, which requires the use of new indexing and query processing techniques. For example, to find all cities near Chicago, it is desirable to cluster city information by geographic proximity. To do such clustering we need a multidimensional index, such as an R tree. (We discussed multidimensional indexes briefly in Section 5.9.)

23.5.2 Temporal and Sequence Databases

Currently available DBMSs provide little support for queries over ordered collections of records, or *sequences*, and over temporal data. Typical sequence queries include "Find the weekly moving average of the Dow Jones Industrial Average," and "Find the first five consecutively increasing temperature readings" (from a trace of temperature observations). Such queries can be easily expressed and often efficiently executed by systems that support query languages designed for sequences. Some commercial SQL systems now support such SQL extensions.

The first example is also a temporal query. However, temporal queries involve more than just record ordering. For example, consider the following query: "Find the longest interval in which the same person managed two different departments." If the period during which a given person managed a department is indicated by two fields *from* and *to*, we have to reason about a collection of intervals, rather than a sequence of records. Further, temporal queries require the DBMS to be aware of the anomalies associated with calendars (such as leap years). Temporal extensions are likely to be incorporated in future versions of the SQL standard.

23.5.3 Image and Video Databases

In an object-relational DBMS, users can define ADTs with appropriate methods, which is an improvement over an RDBMS. Nonetheless, supporting just ADTs falls short of what is required to deal with very large collections of images and videos. We outline some problems in this area:

- **Content-Based Image Retrieval:** Users must be able to specify selection conditions based on the contents of a desired image. Example queries include: "Find all images that are similar to this image" and "Find all images that contain at least three airplanes." As images are inserted into the database, the DBMS must analyze them and automatically *extract features* that will help answer such content-based queries. This information can then be used to search for images that satisfy a given query.

- **Distributed Multimedia Databases:** Relational DBMSs concentrate on tables that contain a large number of tuples, each of which is relatively small. Once multimedia objects like images, sound clips and videos are stored in a database, individual objects of very large size have to be handled efficiently. As an example, distributed DBMSs must develop techniques to efficiently retrieve such objects. Retrieval of multimedia objects in a distributed system has been addressed in limited contexts, such as client-server systems, but in general remains a difficult problem.

- **Video-on-Demand:** Many companies want to provide video-on-demand services that enable users to dial into a server and request a particular video. The video must then be delivered to the user's computer in real time, reliably and inexpensively. Ideally, users must be able to perform familiar VCR functions such as fast-forward and reverse. From a database perspective, the server has to contend with specialized real-time constraints; video delivery rates must be synchronized at the server and at the client, taking into account the characteristics of the communication network.

23.5.4 Information Retrieval and Text Databases

The field of information retrieval is closely related to database management and shares the goal of enabling users to query a large volume of data; updates, concurrency control and recovery have not been traditionally addressed in information retrieval systems because the data in typical applications is largely static. The focus has been on large collections of unstructured documents.

An important class of queries, based on **keyword search**, enables us to ask for all documents containing a given keyword. Some systems maintain a list of synonyms for important words, and return documents that contain a desired keyword or one of its synonyms; for example, a query asking for documents containing *car* will also retrieve documents containing *automobile*. A more complex query is "Find all documents that have *keyword1* `AND` *keyword2*." For such composite queries, constructed with `AND`, `OR`, and `NOT`, we can *rank* retrieved documents by the proximity of the query keywords in the document.

The criteria used to evaluate information retrieval systems include **precision**, which is the percentage of retrieved documents that are relevant to the query, and **recall**, which is the percentage of relevant documents in the database that are retrieved in response to a query.

The advent of the Web has given fresh impetus to information retrieval because millions of documents are now available to users and searching for desired information is a fundamental operation; without good search mechanisms, users would be overwhelmed. Numerous search engines are available on the Web. An index for an information retrieval system essentially contains ⟨*keyword, documentid*⟩ pairs; a Web search engine creates such an index for documents stored at several sites.

A novel aspect of documents on the Web is that they contain *links* to other documents. This feature imposes some structure on HTML documents, and they have been called **semistructured**. Another example of semistructured data is a bibliography file; some structure is imparted by fields such as *author* and *title* to an otherwise unstructured text file. Efficient and natural techniques for querying large collections of semi-structured data are the subject of ongoing research.

23.6   SUMMARY

The database area continues to grow vigorously, both in terms of technology and in terms of applications. The fundamental reason for this growth is that the amount of information stored and processed using computers is growing rapidly. Regardless of the nature of the data and its intended applications, users need database management systems and their services (concurrent access, crash recovery, easy and efficient querying, etc.) as the volume of data increases. As the range of applications is broadened, however, some shortcomings of current DBMSs become serious limitations. These problems are being actively studied in the database research community.

The coverage in this book provides a good introduction, but is not intended to cover all aspects of database systems. Ample material is available for further study, as this chapter illustrates, and we hope that the reader is motivated to pursue the leads in the bibliography. Bon voyage!

BIBLIOGRAPHIC NOTES

[233] contains a comprehensive treatment of all aspects of transaction processing. An introductory textbook treatment can be found in [70]. See [176] for several papers that describe new transaction models for nontraditional applications such as CAD/CAM. [1, 561, 416, 508, 519] are some of the many papers on real-time databases.

Determining which entities are the same across different databases is a difficult problem; it is an example of a semantic mismatch. Resolving such mismatches has been addressed in many papers, including [291, 335, 462, 477]. [263] is an overview of theoretical work in this area. Also see the bibliographic notes for Chapter 19 for references to related work on multidatabases, and see the notes for Chapter 14 for references to work on view integration.

[215] is an early paper on main memory databases. [278, 80] describe the Dali main memory storage manager. [288] surveys visualization idioms designed for large databases, and [236] discusses visualization for data mining. Visualization systems for databases include DataSpace [427], DEVise [347], IVEE [21], the MineSet suite from SGI, Tioga [25], and VisDB [287]. In addition, a number of general tools are available for data visualization.

Querying text repositories has been studied extensively in information retrieval; see [450] for a recent survey. This topic has generated considerable interest in the database community recently because of the widespread use of the Web, which contains many text sources. In particular, HTML documents have some structure if we interpret links as edges in a graph. Such documents are examples of semistructured data; see [3] for a good overview. Recent papers on queries over the Web include [3, 312, 377, 407].

See [415] for a survey of multimedia issues in database management. There has been much recent interest in database issues in a mobile computing environment, for example, [261, 270]. See [267] for a collection of articles on this subject. [536] contains several articles that cover all aspects of temporal databases. The use of constraints in databases has been actively investigated in recent years; [286] is a good overview. Geographic Information Systems have also been studied extensively; [423], describes the Paradise system, which is notable for its scalability.

The book [582] contains detailed discussions of temporal databases (including the TSQL2 language, which is influencing the SQL standard), spatial and multimedia databases, and uncertainty in databases.

A

THE MINIBASE SOFTWARE

Practice is the best of all instructors.

—Publius Syrus, 42 B.C.

Minibase is a small relational DBMS, together with a suite of visualization tools, that has been developed for use with this book. While the book makes no direct reference to the software and can be used independently, Minibase offers instructors an opportunity to design a variety of hands-on assignments, with or without programming. To see an on-line description of the software, visit this URL:

> http://www.cs.wisc.edu/~dbbook/minibase.html

The software is available freely through ftp. By registering themselves as users at the URL for the book, instructors can receive prompt notification of any major bug reports and fixes. Sample project assignments, which elaborate upon some of the briefly sketched ideas in the *project-based exercises* at the end of chapters, can be seen at

> http://www.cs.wisc.edu/~dbbook/minihwk.html

Instructors should consider making small modifications to each assignment to discourage undesirable 'code reuse' by students; assignment handouts formatted using Latex are available by ftp. Instructors can also obtain solutions to these assignments by contacting the author (raghu@cs.wisc.edu).

A.1 WHAT'S AVAILABLE

Minibase is intended to supplement the use of a commercial DBMS such as Oracle or Sybase in course projects, not to replace them. While a commercial DBMS is ideal for SQL assignments, it does not allow students to understand how the DBMS works. Minibase is intended to address the latter issue; the subset of SQL that it supports is intentionally kept small, and students should also be asked to use a comercial DBMS for writing SQL queries and programs. Minibase is provided on an as-is basis with no warranties or restrictions for educational or personal use. It includes the following:

- Code for a small single-user relational DBMS, including a parser and query optimizer for a subset of SQL, and components designed to be (re)written by students as project assignments: *heap files, buffer manager, B+ trees, sorting,* and *joins.*

- Graphical visualization tools to aid in students' exploration and understanding of the behavior of the *buffer management, B+ tree,* and *query optimization* components of the system. There is also a graphical tool to refine a relational database design using *normalization.*

A.2 OVERVIEW OF MINIBASE ASSIGNMENTS

Several assignments involving the use of Minibase are described below. Each of these has been tested in a course already, but the details of how Minibase is set up might vary at your school, so you may have to modify the assignments accordingly. If you plan to use these assignments, you are advised to download and try them at your site well in advance of handing them to students. We have done our best to test and document these assignments and the Minibase software, but bugs undoubtedly persist. Please report bugs at this URL:

    http://www.cs.wisc.edu/~dbbook/minibase.comments.html

I hope that users will contribute bug fixes, additional project assignments and extensions to Minibase. These will be made publicly available through the Minibase site, together with pointers to the authors.

A.2.1 Overview of Programming Projects

In several assignments, students are asked to rewrite a component of Minibase. The book provides the necessary background for all of these assignments, and the assignment handout provides additional system-level details. The on-line HTML documentation provides an overview of the software, in particular the component interfaces, and can be downloaded and installed at each school that uses Minibase. The projects listed below should be assigned after covering the relevant material from the indicated chapter.

- **Buffer Manager (Chapter 3):** Students are given code for the layer that manages space on disk and supports the concept of pages with page ids. They are asked to implement a buffer manager that brings requested pages into memory if they are not already there. One variation of this assignment could use different replacement policies. Students are asked to assume a single-user environment, with no concurrency control or recovery management.

- **HF Page (Chapter 3):** Students must write code that manages records on a page using a slot-directory page format to keep track of records on a page. Possible variants include fixed-length versus variable-length records and other ways to keep track of records on a page.

- **Heap Files (Chapter 3):** Using the HF Page and buffer manager code, students are asked to implement a layer that supports the abstraction of files of unordered pages, that is, heap files.

- **B+ trees (Chapter 5):** This is one of the more complex assignments. Students have to implement a page class that maintains records in sorted order within a page and implement the B+ tree index structure to impose a sort order across several leaf-level pages. Indexes store ⟨*key, record-pointer*⟩ pairs in leaf pages, and data records are stored separately (in heap files). Similar assignments can easily be created for Linear Hashing or Extendible Hashing index structures.

- **External Sorting (Chapter 7):** Building upon the buffer manager and heap file layers, students are asked to implement external merge-sort. The emphasis is on minimizing I/O, rather than on the in-memory sort used to create sorted runs.

- **Sort-Merge Join (Chapter 12):** Building upon the code for external sorting, students are asked to implement the sort-merge join algorithm. This assignment can be easily modified to create assignments that involve other join algorithms.

- **Index Nested-Loop Join (Chapter 12):** This assignment is similar to the sort-merge join assignment, but relies on B+ tree (or other indexing) code, instead of sorting code.

A.2.2 Overview of Nonprogramming Assignments

Four assignments that do not require students to write any code (other than SQL, in one assignment) are also available.

- **Optimizer Exercises (Chapter 13):** The Minibase optimizer visualizer offers a flexible tool to explore how a typical relational query optimizer works. It accepts single-block SQL queries (including some queries that cannot be executed in Minibase, such as queries involving grouping and aggregate operators). Students can inspect and modify synthetic catalogs, add and drop indexes, enable or disable different join algorithms, enable or disable index-only evaluation strategies, and see the effect of such changes on the plan produced for a given query. All (sub)plans generated by an iterative System R style optimizer can be viewed, ordered by the iteration in which they are generated, and details on a given plan can be obtained readily. All interaction with the optimizer visualizer is through a GUI and requires no programming.

The assignment introduces students to this tool and then requires them to answer questions involving specific catalogs, queries, and plans generated by controlling various parameters.

- **Buffer Manager Viewer (Chapter 12):** This viewer lets students visualize how pages are moved in and out of the buffer pool, their status (e.g., dirty bit, pin count) while in the pool, and some statistics (e.g., number of hits). The assignment requires students to generate traces by modifying some trace-generation code (provided) and to answer questions about these traces by using the visualizer to look at them. While this assignment can be used after covering Chapter 3, deferring it until after Chapter 12 enables students to examine traces that are representative of different relational operations.

- **B+ Tree Viewer (Chapter 5):** This viewer lets students see a B+ tree as it is modified through insert and delete statements. The assignment requires students to work with trace files, answer questions about them, and generate operation traces (i.e., a sequence of inserts and deletes) that create specified kinds of trees.

- **Normalization Tool (Chapter 15):** The normalization viewer is a tool for normalizing relational tables. It supports the concept of a *refinement session*, in which a schema is decomposed repeatedly and the resulting decomposition tree is then saved. For a given schema, a user might consider several alternative decompositions (more precisely, decomposition trees), and each of these can be saved as a refinement session. Refinement sessions are a very flexible and convenient mechanism for trying out several alternative decomposition strategies. The normalization assignment introduces students to this tool and asks design-oriented questions involving the use of the tool.

Assignments that require students to evaluate various components can also be developed. For example, students can be asked to compare different join methods, different index methods, and different buffer management policies.

A.3   ACKNOWLEDGMENTS

The Minibase software was inpired by Minirel, a small relational DBMS developed by David DeWitt for instructional use. Minibase was developed by a large number of dedicated students over a long time, and the design was guided by Mike Carey and the author. See the on-line documentation for more on Minibase's history.

REFERENCES

[1] R. Abbott and H. Garcia-Molina. Scheduling real-time transactions with disk resident data. In *Proc. of the Conf. on Very Large Databases*, 1989.

[2] R. Abbott and H. Garcia-Molina. Scheduling real-time transactions: a performance evaluation. *ACM Transactions on Database Systems*, 17(3), 1992.

[3] S. Abiteboul. Querying semi-structured data. In *Intl. Conf. on Database Theory*, 1997.

[4] S. Abiteboul, R. Hull, and V. Vianu. *Foundations of Databases*. Addison-Wesley, 1995.

[5] S. Abiteboul and P. Kanellakis. Object identity as a query language primitive. In *ACM SIGMOD Conf. on the Management of Data*, 1989.

[6] K. Achyutuni, E. Omiecinski, and S. Navathe. Two techniques for on-line index modification in shared nothing parallel databases. In *ACM SIGMOD Conf. on the Management of Data*, 1996.

[7] S. Adali, K. Candan, Y. Papakonstantinou, and V. Subrahmanian. Query caching and optimization in distributed mediator systems. In *ACM SIGMOD Conf. on the Management of Data*, 1996.

[8] M. E. Adiba. Derived relations: A unified mechanism for views, snapshots and distributed data. In *Proc. of the Conf. on Very Large Databases*, 1981.

[9] S. Agarwal, R. Agrawal, P. Deshpande, A. Gupta, J. Naughton, R. Ramakrishnan, and S. Sarawagi. On the computation of multidimensional aggregates. In *Proc. of the Conf. on Very Large Databases*, 1996.

[10] D. Agrawal and A. El Abbadi. The generalized tree quorum protocol: an efficient approach for managing replicated data. *ACM Transactions on Database Systems*, 17(4), 1992.

[11] D. Agrawal, A. El Abbadi, and R. Jeffers. Using delayed commitment in locking protocols for real-time databases. In *ACM SIGMOD Conf. on the Management of Data*, 1992.

[12] R. Agrawal, M. Carey, and M. Livny. Concurrency control performance-modeling: Alternatives and implications. In *ACM SIGMOD Conf. on the Management of Data*, 1985.

[13] R. Agrawal and D. DeWitt. Integrated concurrency control and recovery mechanisms: Design and performance evaluation. *ACM Transactions on Database Systems*, 10(4):529–564, 1985.

[14] R. Agrawal and N. Gehani. ODE (Object Database and Environment): The language and the data model. In *ACM SIGMOD Conf. on the Management of Data*, 1989.

[15] R. Agrawal, T. Imielinski, and A. Swami. Mining association rules between sets of items in large databases. In *ACM SIGMOD Conf. on the Management of Data*, 1993.

[16] R. Agrawal, H. Mannila, R. Srikant, H. Toivonen, and A. Verkamo. Fast discovery of association rules. In *Advances in Knowledge Discovery and Data Mining, U.M. Fayyad, G. Piatetsky-Shapiro, P. Smyth and R. Uthurusamy (eds.), MIT Press,* 1996.

[17] R. Agrawal, G. Psaila, E. Wimmers, and M. Zaot. Querying shapes of histories. In *Proc. of the Conf. on Very Large Databases,* 1995.

[18] R. Agrawal and J. Shafer. Parallel mining of association rules. *IEEE Transactions on Knowledge and Data Engineering,* 8(6):962–969, 1996.

[19] R. Agrawal and R. Srikant. Mining sequential patterns. In *Proc. IEEE CS Intl. Conf. on Data Engineering,* 1995.

[20] R. Ahad, K. BapaRao, and D. McLeod. On estimating the cardinality of the projection of a database relation. *ACM Transactions on Database Systems,* 14(1):28–40, 1989.

[21] C. Ahlberg and E. Wistrand. IVEE: an information visualization exploration environment. In *Intl. Symp. on Information Visualization,* 1995.

[22] A. Aho, C. Beeri, and J. Ullman. The theory of joins in relational databases. *ACM Transactions on Database Systems,* 4(3):297–314, 1979.

[23] A. Aho, J. Hopcroft, and J. Ullman. *The Design and Analysis of Computer Algorithms.* Addison-Wesley, 1983.

[24] A. Aho, Y. Sagiv, and J. Ullman. Equivalences among relational expressions. *SIAM Journal of Computing,* 8(2):218–246, 1979.

[25] A. Aiken, J. Chen, M. Stonebraker, and A. Woodruff. Tioga-2: A direct manipulation database visualization environment. In *Proc. IEEE CS Intl. Conf. on Data Engineering,* 1996.

[26] A. Aiken, J. Widom, and J. Hellerstein. Static analysis techniques for predicting the behavior of active database rules. *ACM Transactions on Database Systems,* 20(1):3–41, 1995.

[27] E. Anwar, L. Maugis, and U. Chakravarthy. A new perspective on rule support for object-oriented databases. In *ACM SIGMOD Conf. on the Management of Data,* 1993.

[28] K. Apt, H. Blair, and A. Walker. Towards a theory of declarative knowledge. In *Foundations of Deductive Databases and Logic Programming, J. Minker (ed.), Morgan Kaufmann,* 1988.

[29] W. Armstrong. Dependency structures of database relationships. In *Proc. IFIP Congress,* 1974.

[30] M. Astrahan, M. Blasgen, D. Chamberlin, K. Eswaran, J. Gray, P. Griffiths, W. King, R. Lorie, P. McJones, J. Mehl, G. Putzolu, I. Traiger, B. Wade, and V. Watson. System R: A relational approach to database management. *ACM Transactions on Database Systems,* 1(2):97–137, 1976.

[31] M. Atkinson, P. Bailey, K. Chisholm, P. Cockshott, and R. Morrison. An approach to persistent programming. In *Readings in Object-Oriented Databases, S.B. Zdonik and D. Maier (eds.), Morgan Kaufmann,* 1990.

[32] M. Atkinson and O. Buneman. Types and persistence in database programming languages. *ACM Computing Surveys,* 19(2):105–190, 1987.

[33] R. Attar, P. Bernstein, and N. Goodman. Site initialization, recovery, and back-up in a distributed database system. *IEEE Transactions on Software Engineering,* 10(6):645–650, 1983.

[34] P. Atzeni, L. Cabibbo, and G. Mecca. Isalog: a declarative language for complex objects with hierarchies. In *Proc. IEEE CS Intl. Conf. on Data Engineering*, 1993.

[35] P. Atzeni and V. De Antonellis. *RelationalDatabase Theory*. Benjamin-Cummings, 1993.

[36] D. Badal and G. Popek. Cost and performance analysis of semantic integrity validation methods. In *ACM SIGMOD Conf. on the Management of Data*, 1979.

[37] A. Badia, D. Van Gucht, and M. Gyssens. Querying with generalized quantifiers. In *Applications of Logic Databases, ed. R. Ramakrishnan, Kluwer Academic*, 1995.

[38] I. Balbin, G. Port, K. Ramamohanarao, and K. Meenakshi. Efficient bottom-up computation of queries on stratified databases. *Journal of Logic Programming*, 11(3):295–344, 1991.

[39] I. Balbin and K. Ramamohanarao. A generalization of the differential approach to recursive query evaluation. *Journal of Logic Programming*, 4(3):259–262, 1987.

[40] F. Bancilhon, C. Delobel, and P. Kanellakis. *Building an Object-Oriented Database System*. Morgan Kaufmann, 1991.

[41] F. Bancilhon and S. Khoshafian. A calculus for complex objects. *Journal of Computer and System Sciences*, 38(2):326–340, 1989.

[42] F. Bancilhon, D. Maier, Y. Sagiv, and J. Ullman. Magic sets and other strange ways to implement logic programs. In *ACM SIGACT-SIGMOD Symp. on Principles of Database Systems , Cambridge MA*, 1986.

[43] F. Bancilhon and R. Ramakrishnan. An amateur's introduction to recursive query processing strategies. In *ACM SIGMOD Conf. on the Management of Data*, 1986.

[44] F. Bancilhon and N. Spyratos. Update semantics of relational views. *ACM Transactions on Database Systems*, 6(4):557–575, 1981.

[45] E. Baralis, S. Ceri, and S. Paraboschi. Modularization techniques for active rules design. *ACM Transactions on Database Systems*, 21(1):1–29, 1996.

[46] R. Barquin and H. Edelstein. *Planning and Designing the Data Warehouse*. Prentice-Hall, 1997.

[47] C. Batini, S. Ceri, and S. Navathe. *Database Design: An Entity Relationship Approach*. Benjamin/Cummings Publishers, 1992.

[48] C. Batini, M. Lenzerini, and S. Navathe. A comparative analysis of methodologies for database schema integration. *ACM Computing Surveys*, 18(4):323–364, 1986.

[49] D. Batory, J. Barnett, J. Garza, K. Smith, K. Tsukuda, B. Twichell, and T. Wise. GENESIS: an extensible database management system. In *Readings in Object-Oriented Databases, eds. S.B. Zdonik and D. Maier, Morgan Kaufmann*, 1990.

[50] B. Baugsto and J. Greipsland. Parallel sorting methods for large data volumes on a hypercube database computer. In *Proc. Intl. Workshop on Database Machines*, 1989.

[51] R. Bayer and E. McCreight. Organization and maintenance of large ordered indexes. *Acta Informatica*, 1(3):173–189, 1972.

[52] R. Bayer and M. Schkolnick. Concurrency of operations on B-trees. *Acta Informatica*, 9(1):1–21, 1977.

[53] M. Beck, D. Bitton, and W. Wilkinson. Sorting large files on a backend multiprocessor. *IEEE Transactions on Computers*, 37(7):769–778, 1988.

[54] C. Beeri, R. Fagin, and J. Howard. A complete axiomatization of functional and multivalued dependencies in database relations. In *ACM SIGMOD Conf. on the Management of Data*, 1977.

[55] C. Beeri and P. Honeyman. Preserving functional dependencies. *SIAM Journal of Computing*, 10(3):647–656, 1982.

[56] C. Beeri and T. Milo. A model for active object-oriented database. In *Proc. of the Conf. on Very Large Databases*, 1991.

[57] C. Beeri, S. Naqvi, R. Ramakrishnan, O. Shmueli, and S. Tsur. Sets and negation in a logic database language (LDL1). In *ACM SIGACT-SIGMOD Symp. on Principles of Database Systems*, 1987.

[58] C. Beeri and R. Ramakrishnan. On the power of magic. In *ACM SIGACT-SIGMOD Symp. on Principles of Database Systems*, 1987.

[59] D. Bell and J. Grimson. *Distributed Database Systems*. Addison-Wesley, 1992.

[60] J. Bentley and J. Friedman. Data structures for range searching. *ACM Computing Surveys*, 13(3):397–409, 1979.

[61] P. Bernstein. Synthesizing third normal form relations from functional dependencies. *ACM Transactions on Database Systems*, 1(4):277–298, 1976.

[62] P. Bernstein, B. Blaustein, and E. Clarke. Fast maintenance of semantic integrity assertions using redundant aggregate data. In *Proc. of the Conf. on Very Large Databases*, 1980.

[63] P. Bernstein and D. Chiu. Using semi-joins to solve relational queries. *Journal of the ACM*, 28(1):25–40, 1981.

[64] P. Bernstein and N. Goodman. Timestamp-based algorithms for concurrency control in distributed database systems. In *Proc. of the Conf. on Very Large Databases*, 1980.

[65] P. Bernstein and N. Goodman. Concurrency control in distributed database systems. *ACM Computing Surveys*, 13(2):185–222, 1981.

[66] P. Bernstein and N. Goodman. Power of natural semijoins. *SIAM Journal of Computing*, 10(4):751–771, 1981.

[67] P. Bernstein and N. Goodman. Multiversion concurrency control—theory and algorithms. *ACM Transactions on Database Systems*, 8(4):465–483, 1983.

[68] P. Bernstein, N. Goodman, E. Wong, C. Reeve, and J. Rothnie. Query processing in a system for distributed databases (SDD-1). *ACM Transactions on Database Systems*, 6(4):602–625, 1981.

[69] P. Bernstein, V. Hadzilacos, and N. Goodman. *Concurrency Control and Recovery in Database Systems*. Addison-Wesley, 1987.

[70] P. Bernstein and E. Newcomer. *Principles of Transaction Processing*. Morgan Kaufmann, 1997.

[71] P. Bernstein, D. Shipman, and J. Rothnie. Concurrency control in a system for distributed databases (SDD-1). *ACM Transactions on Database Systems*, 5(1):18–51, 1980.

[72] P. Bernstein, D. Shipman, and W. Wong. Formal aspects of serializability in database concurrency control. *IEEE Transactions on Software Engineering*, 5(3):203–216, 1979.

[73] B. Bhargava (ed.). *Concurrency Control and Reliability in Distributed Systems*. Van Nostrand Reinhold, 1987.

[74] A. Biliris. The performance of three database storage structures for managing large objects. In *ACM SIGMOD Conf. on the Management of Data*, 1992.

[75] J. Biskup and B. Convent. A formal view integration method. In *ACM SIGMOD Conf. on the Management of Data*, 1986.

[76] J. Biskup, U. Dayal, and P. Bernstein. Synthesizing independent database schemas. In *ACM SIGMOD Conf. on the Management of Data*, 1979.

[77] D. Bitton and D. DeWitt. Duplicate record elimination in large data files. *ACM Transactions on Database Systems*, 8(2):255–265, 1983.

[78] J. Blakeley, P.-A. Larson, and F. Tompa. Efficiently updating materialized views. In *ACM SIGMOD Conf. on the Management of Data*, 1986.

[79] M. Blasgen and K. Eswaran. On the evaluation of queries in a database system. Technical report, IBM FJ (RJ1745), San Jose, 1975.

[80] P. Bohannon, D. Leinbaugh, R. Rastogi, S. Seshadri, A. Silberschatz, and S. Sudarshan. Logical and physical versioning in main memory databases. In *Proc. of the Conf. on Very Large Databases*, 1997.

[81] R. Boyce and D. Chamberlin. SEQUEL: a structured English query language. In *ACM SIGMOD Conf. on the Management of Data*, 1974.

[82] K. Bratbergsengen. Hashing methods and relational algebra operations. In *Proc. of the Conf. on Very Large Databases*, 1984.

[83] Y. Breitbart, H. Garcia-Molina, and A. Silberschatz. Overview of multidatabase transaction management. In *Proc. of the Conf. on Very Large Databases*, 1992.

[84] Y. Breitbart, A. Silberschatz, and G. Thompson. Reliable transaction management in a multidatabase system. In *ACM SIGMOD Conf. on the Management of Data*, 1990.

[85] Y. Breitbart, A. Silberschatz, and G. Thompson. An approach to recovery management in a multidatabase system. In *Proc. of the Conf. on Very Large Databases*, 1992.

[86] S. Brin, R. Motwani, and C. Silverstein. Beyond market baskets: Generalizing association rules to correlations. In *ACM SIGMOD Conf. on the Management of Data*, 1997.

[87] K. Brown, M. Carey, and M. Livny. Goal-oriented buffer management revisited. In *ACM SIGMOD Conf. on the Management of Data*, 1996.

[88] F. Bry. Towards an efficient evaluation of general queries: Quantifier and disjunction processing revisited. In *ACM SIGMOD Conf. on the Management of Data*, 1989.

[89] F. Bry and R. Manthey. Checking consistency of database constraints: a logical basis. In *Proc. of the Conf. on Very Large Databases*, 1986.

[90] O. Buneman and E. Clemons. Efficiently monitoring relational databases. *ACM Transactions on Database Systems*, 4(3), 1979.

[91] O. Buneman, S. Naqvi, V. Tannen, and L. Wong. Principles of programming with complex objects and collection types. *Theoretical Computer Science*, 149(1):3–48, 1995.

[92] M. Carey. Granularity hierarchies in concurrency control. In *ACM SIGACT-SIGMOD Symp. on Principles of Database Systems*, 1983.

[93] M. Carey, D. DeWitt, M. Franklin, N. Hall, M. McAuliffe, J. Naughton, D. Schuh, M. Solomon, C. Tan, O. Tsatalos, S. White, and M. Zwilling. Shoring up persistent applications. In *ACM SIGMOD Conf. on the Management of Data*, 1994.

[94] M. Carey, D. DeWitt, G. Graefe, D. Haight, J. Richardson, D. Schuh, E. Shekita, and S. Vandenberg. The EXODUS Extensible DBMS project: An overview. In *Readings in Object-Oriented Databases, S.B. Zdonik and D. Maier (eds.), Morgan Kaufmann*, 1990.

[95] M. Carey, D. DeWitt, and J. Naughton. The dec 007 benchmark. In *ACM SIGMOD Conf. on the Management of Data*, 1993.

[96] M. Carey, D. DeWitt, J. Naughton, M. Asgarian, J. Gehrke, and D. Shah. The BUCKY object-relational benchmark. In *ACM SIGMOD Conf. on the Management of Data*, 1997.

[97] M. Carey, D. DeWitt, J. Richardson, and E. Shekita. Object and file management in the Exodus extensible database system. In *Proc. of the Conf. on Very Large Databases*, 1986.

[98] M. Carey and M. Livny. Conflict detection tradeoffs for replicated data. *ACM Transactions on Database Systems*, 16(4), 1991.

[99] M. Casanova, L. Tucherman, and A. Furtado. Enforcing inclusion dependencies and referential integrity. In *Proc. of the Conf. on Very Large Databases*, 1988.

[100] M. Casanova and M. Vidal. Towards a sound view integration methodology. In *ACM SIGACT-SIGMOD Symp. on Principles of Database Systems*, 1983.

[101] S. Castano, M. Fugini, G. Martella, and P. Samarati. *Database Security*. Addison-Wesley, 1995.

[102] R. Cattell. *The Object Database Standard: ODMG-93 (Release 1.1)*. Morgan Kaufmann, 1994.

[103] S. Ceri, P. Fraternali, S. Paraboschi, and L. Tanca. Active rule management in Chimera. In *Active Database Systems, J. Widom and S. Ceri (eds.), Morgan Kaufmann*, 1996.

[104] S. Ceri, G. Gottlob, and L. Tanca. *Logic Programming and Databases*. Springer Verlag, 1990.

[105] S. Ceri and G. Pelagatti. *Distributed Database Design: Principles and Systems*. McGraw-Hill, 1984.

[106] S. Ceri and J. Widom. Deriving production rules for constraint maintenance. In *Proc. of the Conf. on Very Large Databases*, 1990.

[107] F. Cesarini, M. Missikoff, and G. Soda. An expert system approach for database application tuning. *Data and Knowledge Engineering*, 8:35–55, 1992.

[108] U. Chakravarthy. Architectures and monitoring techniques for active databases: An evaluation. *Data and Knowledge Engineering*, 16(1):1–26, 1995.

[109] U. Chakravarthy, J. Grant, and J. Minker. Logic-based approach to semantic query optimization. *ACM Transactions on Database Systems*, 15(2):162–207, 1990.

[110] D. Chamberlin. *Using the New DB2*. Morgan Kaufmann, 1996.

[111] D. Chamberlin, M. Astrahan, M. Blasgen, J. Gray, W. King, B. Lindsay, R. Lorie, J. Mehl, T. Price, P. Selinger, M. Schkolnick, D. Slutz, I. Traiger, B. Wade, and R. Yost. A history and evaluation of System R. *Communications of the ACM*, 24(10):632–646, 1981.

[112] D. Chamberlin, M. Astrahan, K. Eswaran, P. Griffiths, R. Lorie, J. Mehl, P. Reisner, and B. Wade. Sequel 2: A unified approach to data definition, manipulation, and control. *IBM Journal of Research and Development*, 20(6):560–575, 1976.

[113] A. Chandra and D. Harel. Structure and complexity of relational queries. *J. Computer and System Sciences*, 25:99–128, 1982.

[114] A. Chandra and P. Merlin. Optimal implementation of conjunctive queries in relational databases. In *Annual ACM SIGACT Symposium on Theory of Computing*, 1977.

[115] M. Chandy, L. Haas, and J. Misra. Distributed deadlock detection. *ACM Transactions on Computer Systems*, 1(3):144–156, 1983.

[116] C. Chang and D. Leu. Multi-key sorting as a file organization scheme when queries are not equally likely. In *Proc. of the Intl. Symp. on Database Systems for Advanced Applications*, 1989.

[117] D. Chatziantoniou and K. Ross. Groupwise processing of relational queries. In *Proc. of the Conf. on Very Large Databases*, 1997.

[118] S. Chaudhuri and U. Dayal. An overview of data warehousing and OLAP technology. *SIGMOD Record*, 26(1):65–74, 1997.

[119] S. Chaudhuri and V. Narasayya. An efficient cost-driven index selection tool for Microsoft SQL Server. In *Proc. of the Conf. on Very Large Databases*, 1997.

[120] S. Chaudhuri and K. Shim. Optimization queries with aggregate views. In *Intl. Conf. on Extending Database Technology*, 1996.

[121] S. Chaudhuri and K. Shim. Optimization of queries with user-defined predicates. In *Proc. of the Conf. on Very Large Databases*, 1996.

[122] J. Cheiney, P. Faudemay, R. Michel, and J. Thevenin. A reliable parallel backend using multiattribute clustering and select-join operator. In *Proc. of the Conf. on Very Large Databases*, 1986.

[123] C. Chen and N. Roussopoulos. Adaptive database buffer management using query feedback. In *Proc. of the Conf. on Very Large Databases*, 1993.

[124] C. Chen and N. Roussopoulos. Adaptive selectivity estimation using query feedback. In *ACM SIGMOD Conf. on the Management of Data*, 1994.

[125] P. P. Chen. The entity-relationship model—toward a unified view of data. *ACM Transactions on Database Systems*, 1(1):9–36, 1976.

[126] D. Childs. Feasibility of a set theoretical data structure—a general structure based on a reconstructed definition of relation. *Proc. of the Tri-annual IFIP Conference*, 1968.

[127] D. Chimenti, R. Gamboa, R. Krishnamurthy, S. Naqvi, S. Tsur, and C. Zaniolo. The ldl system prototype. *IEEE Transactions on Knowledge and Data Engineering*, 2(1):76–90, 1990.

[128] F. Chin and G. Ozsoyoglu. Statistical database design. *ACM Transactions on Database Systems*, 6(1):113–139, 1981.

[129] J. Chomicki. Real-time integrity constraints. In *ACM SIGACT-SIGMOD Symp. on Principles of Database Systems*, 1992.

[130] H.-T. Chou and D. DeWitt. An evaluation of buffer management strategies for relational database systems. In *Proc. of the Conf. on Very Large Databases*, 1985.

[131] P. Chrysanthis and K. Ramamritham. Acta: a framework for specifying and reasoning about transaction structure and behavior. In *ACM SIGMOD Conf. on the Management of Data*, 1990.

[132] F. Civelek, A. Dogac, and S. Spaccapietra. An expert system approach to view definition and integration. In *Proc. of the Entity-Relationship conference*, 1988.

[133] R. Cochrane, H. Pirahesh, and N. Mattos. Integrating triggers and declarative constraints in SQL database systems. In *Proc. of the Conf. on Very Large Databases*, 1996.

[134] D. CODASYL. *Report of the CODASYL Data Base Task Group*. ACM, 1971.

[135] E. Codd. A relational model of data for large shared data banks. *Communications of the ACM*, 13(6):377–387, 1970.

[136] E. Codd. Further normalization of the data base relational model. In *Data Base Systems, R. Rustin (ed.), Prentice-Hall*, 1972.

[137] E. Codd. Relational completeness of data base sub-languages. In *Data Base Systems, R. Rustin (ed.), Prentice-Hall*, 1972.

[138] E. Codd. Extending the database relational model to capture more meaning. *ACM Transactions on Database Systems*, 4(4):397–434, 1979.

[139] E. Codd. Twelve rules for on-line analytic processing. *Computerworld*, April 13 1995.

[140] L. Colby, T. Griffin, L. Libkin, I. Mumick, and H. Trickey. Algorithms for deferred view maintenance. In *ACM SIGMOD Conf. on the Management of Data*, 1996.

[141] L. Colby, A. Kawaguchi, D. Lieuwen, I. Mumick, and K. Ross. Supporting multiple view maintenance policies: Concepts, algorithms, and performance analysis. In *ACM SIGMOD Conf. on the Management of Data*, 1997.

[142] D. Comer. The ubiquitous B-tree. *ACM C. Surveys*, 11(2):121–137, 1979.

[143] D. Copeland and D. Maier. Making SMALLTALK a database system. In *ACM SIGMOD Conf. on the Management of Data*, 1984.

[144] C. Date. A critique of the SQL database language. *ACM SIGMOD Record*, 14(3):8–54, 1984.

[145] C. Date. *Relational Database: Selected Writings*. Addison-Wesley, 1986.

[146] C. Date. *An Introduction to Database Systems (6th ed.)*. Addison-Wesley, 1995.

[147] C. Date and H. Darwen. *A Guide to the SQL Standard (3rd ed.)*. Addison-Wesley, 1993.

[148] C. Date and R. Fagin. Simple conditions for guaranteeing higher normal forms in relational databases. *ACM Transactions on Database Systems*, 17(3), 1992.

[149] C. Date and D. McGoveran. *A Guide to Sybase and SQL Server*. Addison-Wesley, 1993.

[150] U. Dayal and P. Bernstein. On the updatability of relational views. In *Proc. of the Conf. on Very Large Databases*, 1978.

[151] U. Dayal and P. Bernstein. On the correct translation of update operations on relational views. *ACM Transactions on Database Systems*, 7(3), 1982.

[152] P. DeBra and J. Paredaens. Horizontal decompositions for handling exceptions to FDs. In *Advances in Database Theory, H. Gallaire, J. Minker and J-M. Nicolas (eds.), Plenum Press*, 1984.

[153] C. Delobel. Normalization and hierarchial dependencies in the relational data model. *ACM Transactions on Database Systems*, 3(3):201–222, 1978.

[154] D. Denning. Secure statistical databases with random sample queries. *ACM Transactions on Database Systems*, 5(3):291–315, 1980.

[155] D. E. Denning. *Cryptography and Data Security*. Addison-Wesley, 1982.

[156] M. Derr, S. Morishita, and G. Phipps. The glue-nail deductive database system: Design, implementation, and evaluation. *VLDB Journal*, 3(2):123–160, 1994.

[157] A. Deshpande. An implementation for nested relational databases. Technical report, PhD thesis, Indiana University, 1989.

[158] O. e. a. Deux. The story of O2. *IEEE Transactions on Knowledge and Data Engineering*, 2(1), 1990.

[159] D. DeWitt, H.-T. Chou, R. Katz, and A. Klug. Design and implementation of the Wisconsin Storage System. *Software Practice and Experience*, 15(10):943–962, 1985.

[160] D. DeWitt, R. Gerber, G. Graefe, M. Heytens, K. Kumar, and M. Muralikrishna. Gamma—a high performance dataflow database machine. In *Proc. of the Conf. on Very Large Databases*, 1986.

[161] D. DeWitt and J. Gray. Parallel database systems: The future of high-performance database systems. *Communications of the ACM*, 35(6):85–98, 1992.

[162] D. DeWitt, R. Katz, F. Olken, L. Shapiro, M. Stonebraker, and D. Wood. Implementation techniques for main memory databases. In *ACM SIGMOD Conf. on the Management of Data*, 1984.

[163] D. DeWitt, J. Naughton, and D. Schneider. Parallel sorting on a shared-nothing architecture using probabilistic splitting. In *Proc. of the Conf. on Parallel and Distributed Information Systems*, 1991.

[164] D. DeWitt, J. Naughton, D. Schneider, and S. Seshadri. Practical skew handling in parallel joins. In *Proc. of the Conf. on Very Large Databases*, 1992.

[165] O. Diaz, N. Paton, and P. Gray. Rule management in object-oriented databases: A uniform approach. In *Proc. of the Conf. on Very Large Databases*, 1991.

[166] S. Dietrich. Extension tables: Memo relations in logic programming. In *Proc. Intl. Symposium on Logic Programming*, 1987.

[167] W. Du and A. Elmagarmid. Quasi-serializability: a correctness criterion for global concurrency control in interbase. In *Proc. of the Conf. on Very Large Databases*, 1989.

[168] W. Du, R. Krishnamurthy, and M.-C. Shan. Query optimization in a heterogeneous DBMS. In *Proc. of the Conf. on Very Large Databases*, 1992.

[169] N. Duppel. Parallel SQL on TANDEM's NonStop SQL. *IEEE COMPCON*, 1989.

[170] H. Edelstein. The challenge of replication, Parts 1 and 2. *DBMS: Database and Client-Server Solutions*, 1995.

[171] W. Effelsberg and T. Haerder. Principles of database buffer management. *ACM Transactions on Database Systems*, 9(4):560–595, 1984.

[172] M. H. Eich. A classification and comparison of main memory database recovery techniques. In *Proc. IEEE CS Intl. Conf. on Data Engineering*, 1987.

[173] A. El Abbadi. Adaptive protocols for managing replicated distributed databases. In *IEEE Symp. on Parallel and Distributed Processing*, 1991.

[174] A. El Abbadi, D. Skeen, and F. Cristian. An efficient, fault-tolerant protocol for replicated data management. In *ACM SIGACT-SIGMOD Symp. on Principles of Database Systems*, 1985.

[175] C. Ellis. Concurrency in Linear Hashing. *ACM Transactions on Database Systems*, 12(2):195–217, 1987.

[176] A. Elmagarmid. *Database Transaction Models for Advanced Applications*. Morgan Kaufmann, 1992.

[177] A. Elmagarmid, J. Jing, W. Kim, O. Bukhres, and A. Zhang. Global committability in multidatabase systems. *IEEE Transactions on Knowledge and Data Engineering*, 8(5):816–824, 1996.

[178] A. Elmagarmid, A. Sheth, and M. Liu. Deadlock detection algorithms in distributed database systems. In *Proc. IEEE CS Intl. Conf. on Data Engineering*, 1986.

[179] R. Elmasri and S. Navathe. Object integration in database design. In *Proc. IEEE CS Intl. Conf. on Data Engineering*, 1984.

[180] R. Elmasri and S. Navathe. *Fundamentals of Database Systems (2nd ed.)*. Benjamin-Cummings, 1994.

[181] R. Epstein. Techniques for processing of aggregates in relational database systems. Technical report, UC-Berkeley, Electronics Research Laboratory, M798, 1979.

[182] R. Epstein, M. Stonebraker, and E. Wong. Distributed query processing in a relational data base system. In *ACM SIGMOD Conf. on the Management of Data*, 1978.

[183] K. Eswaran and D. Chamberlin. Functional specification of a subsystem for data base integrity. In *Proc. of the Conf. on Very Large Databases*, 1975.

[184] K. Eswaran, J. Gray, R. Lorie, and I. Traiger. The notions of consistency and predicate locks in a data base system. *Communications of the ACM*, 19(11):624–633, 1976.

[185] R. Fagin. Multivalued dependencies and a new normal form for relational databases. *ACM Transactions on Database Systems*, 2(3):262–278, 1977.

[186] R. Fagin. Normal forms and relational database operators. In *ACM SIGMOD Conf. on the Management of Data*, 1979.

[187] R. Fagin. A normal form for relational databases that is based on domains and keys. *ACM Transactions on Database Systems*, 6(3):387–415, 1981.

[188] R. Fagin, J. Nievergelt, N. Pippenger, and H. Strong. Extendible Hashing—a fast access method for dynamic files. *ACM Transactions on Database Systems*, 4(3), 1979.

[189] C. Faloutsos and H. Jagadish. On B-Tree indices for skewed distributions. In *Proc. of the Conf. on Very Large Databases*, 1992.

[190] C. Faloutsos, R. Ng, and T. Sellis. Predictive load control for flexible buffer allocation. In *Proc. of the Conf. on Very Large Databases*, 1991.

[191] C. Faloutsos, M. Ranganathan, and Y. Manolopoulos. Fast subsequence matching in time-series databases. In *ACM SIGMOD Conf. on the Management of Data*, 1994.

[192] U. Fayyad, G. Piatetsky-Shapiro, and P. Smyth. The kdd process for extracting useful knowledge from volumes of data. *Communications of the ACM*, 39(11):27–34, 1996.

[193] U. Fayyad, G. Piatetsky-Shapiro, P. Smyth, and R. Uthurusamy. *Advances in Knowledge Discovery and Data Mining*. MIT Press, 1996.

[194] U. Fayyad and E. Simoudis. Data mining and knowledge discovery: Tutorial notes. In *Intl. Joint Conf. on Artificial Intelligence*, 1997.

[195] S. Finkelstein, M. Schkolnick, and P. Tiberio. Physical database design for relational databases. *IBM Research Review RJ5034*, 1986.

[196] D. Fishman, D. Beech, H. Cate, E. Chow, T. Connors, J. Davis, N. Derrett, C. Hoch, W. Kent, P. Lyngbaek, B. Mahbod, M.-A. Neimat, T. Ryan, and M.-C. Shan. Iris: An object-oriented database management system. *ACM Transactions on Office Information Systems*, 5(1):48–69, 1987.

[197] C. Fleming and B. von Halle. *Handbook of Relational Database Design*. Addison-Wesley, 1989.

[198] F. Fotouhi and S. Pramanik. Optimal secondary storage access sequence for performing relational join. *IEEE Transactions on Knowledge and Data Engineering*, 1(3):318–328, 1989.

[199] M. Franklin. Concurrency control and recovery. In *Handbook of Computer Science, A.B. Tucker (ed.), CRC Press*, 1996.

[200] M. Franklin, M. Carey, and M. Livny. Local disk caching for client-server database systems. In *Proc. of the Conf. on Very Large Databases*, 1993.

[201] M. Franklin, B. Jonsson, and D. Kossman. Performance tradeoffs for client-server query processing. In *ACM SIGMOD Conf. on the Management of Data*, 1996.

[202] P. Fraternali and L. Tanca. A structured approach for the definition of the semantics of active databases. *ACM Transactions on Database Systems*, 20(4):414–471, 1995.

[203] M. W. Freeston. The BANG file: A new kind of Grid File. In *ACM SIGMOD Conf. on the Management of Data*, 1987.

[204] J. Freytag. A rule-based view of query optimization. In *ACM SIGMOD Conf. on the Management of Data*, 1987.

[205] O. Friesen, A. Lefebvre, and L. Vieille. VALIDITY: Applications of a DOOD system. In *Intl. Conf. on Extending Database Technology*, 1996.

[206] J. Fry and E. Sibley. Evolution of data-base management systems. *ACM Computing Surveys*, 8(1):7–42, 1976.

[207] T. Fukuda, Y. Morimoto, S. Morishita, and T. Tokuyama. Mining optimized association rules for numeric attributes. In *ACM SIGACT-SIGMOD Symp. on Principles of Database Systems*, 1996.

[208] A. Furtado and M. Casanova. Updating relational views. In *Query Processing in Database Systems, W. Kim, D.S. Reiner and D.S. Batory (eds.), Springer-Verlag*, 1984.

[209] S. Fushimi, M. Kitsuregawa, and H. Tanaka. An overview of the systems software of a parallel relational database machine: Grace. In *Proc. of the Conf. on Very Large Databases*, 1986.

[210] H. Gallaire, J. Minker, and J.-M. Nicolas (eds.). *Advances in Database Theory, Vols. 1 and 2*. Plenum Press, 1984.

[211] H. Gallaire and J. Minker (eds.). *Logic and Data Bases*. Plenum Press, 1978.

[212] S. Ganguly, W. Hasan, and R. Krishnamurthy. Query optimization for parallel execution. In *ACM SIGMOD Conf. on the Management of Data*, 1992.

[213] R. Ganski and H. Wong. Optimization of nested SQL queries revisited. In *ACM SIGMOD Conf. on the Management of Data*, 1987.

[214] H. Garcia-Molina and D. Barbara. How to assign votes in a distributed system. *Journal of the ACM*, 32(4), 1985.

[215] H. Garcia-Molina, R. Lipton, and J. Valdes. A massive memory system machine. *IEEE Transactions on Computers*, C33(4):391–399, 1984.

[216] H. Garcia-Molina and G. Wiederhold. Read-only transactions in a distributed database. *ACM Transactions on Database Systems*, 7(2):209–234, 1982.

[217] A. Garg and C. Gotlieb. Order preserving key transformations. *ACM Transactions on Database Systems*, 11(2):213–234, 1986.

[218] S. P. Ghosh. *Data Base Organization for Data Management (2nd ed.)*. Academic Press, 1986.

[219] D. Gifford. Weighted voting for replicated data. In *ACM Symposium on Operating Systems Principles*, 1979.

[220] G. Graefe. Encapsulation of parallelism in the Volcano query processing system. In *ACM SIGMOD Conf. on the Management of Data, Atlantic City*, 1990.

[221] G. Graefe. Query evaluation techniques for large databases. *ACM Computing Surveys*, 25(2), 1993.

[222] G. Graefe and D. DeWitt. The Exodus optimizer generator. In *ACM SIGMOD Conf. on the Management of Data*, 1987.

[223] G. Graefe and K. Ward. Dynamic query optimization plans. In *ACM SIGMOD Conf. on the Management of Data*, 1989.

[224] M. Graham, A. Mendelzon, and M. Vardi. Notions of dependency satisfaction. *Journal of the ACM*, 33(1):105–129, 1986.

[225] G. Grahne. *The Problem of Incomplete Information in Relational Databases*. Springer-Verlag, 1991.

[226] J. Gray. Notes on data base operating systems. In *Operating Systems: An Advanced Course, Bayer, Graham and Seegmuller (eds.)*. Springer-Verlag, 1978.

[227] J. Gray. The transaction concept: Virtues and limitations. In *Proc. of the Conf. on Very Large Databases*, 1981.

[228] J. Gray. Transparency in its place—the case against transparent access to geographically distributed data. *Tandem Computers, TR-89-1*, 1989.

[229] J. Gray. *The Benchmark Handbook: for Database and Transaction Processing Systems*. Morgan Kaufmann, 1991.

[230] J. Gray, A. Bosworth, A. Layman, and H. Pirahesh. Data cube: A relational aggregation operator generalizing group-by, cross-tab and sub-totals. In *Proc. IEEE CS Intl. Conf. on Data Engineering*, 1996.

[231] J. Gray, R. Lorie, G. Putzolu, and I. Traiger. Granularity of locks and degrees of consistency in a shared data base. In *Proc. of IFIP Working Conf. on Modelling of Data Base Management Systems*, 1977.

[232] J. Gray, P. McJones, M. Blasgen, B. Lindsay, R. Lorie, G. Putzolu, T. Price, and I. Traiger. The recovery manager of the System R database manager. *ACM Computing Surveys*, 13(2):223–242, 1981.

[233] J. Gray and A. Reuter. *Transaction Processing: Concepts and Techniques*. Morgan Kaufmann, 1992.

[234] P. Gray. *Logic, Algebra, and Databases*. John Wiley, 1984.

[235] P. Griffiths and B. Wade. An authorization mechanism for a relational database system. *ACM Transactions on Database Systems*, 1(3):242–255, 1976.

[236] G. Grinstein. Visualization and data mining. In *Intl. Conf. on Knowledge Discovery in Databases*, 1996.

[237] A. Gupta, I. Mumick, and V. Subrahmanian. Maintaining views incrementally. In *ACM SIGMOD Conf. on the Management of Data 93, Washington,DC*, 1993.

[238] A. Guttman. R-trees: a dynamic index structure for spatial searching. In *ACM SIGMOD Conf. on the Management of Data*, 1984.

[239] L. Haas, W. Chang, G. Lohman, J. McPherson, P. Wilms, G. Lapis, B. Lindsay, H. Pirahesh, M. Carey, and E. Shekita. Starburst mid-flight: As the dust clears. *IEEE Transactions on Knowledge and Data Engineering*, 2(1), 1990.

[240] P. Haas, J. Naughton, S. Seshadri, and L. Stokes. Sampling-based estimation of the number of distinct values of an attribute. In *Proc. of the Conf. on Very Large Databases*, 1995.

[241] P. Haas and A. Swami. Sampling-based selectivity estimation for joins using augmented frequent value statistics. In *Proc. IEEE CS Intl. Conf. on Data Engineering*, 1995.

[242] T. Haerder and A. Reuter. Principles of transaction oriented database recovery—a taxonomy. *ACM Computing Surveys*, 15(4), 1982.

[243] U. Halici and A. Dogac. Concurrency control in distributed databases through time intervals and short-term locks. *IEEE Transactions on Software Engineering*, 15(8):994–1003, 1989.

[244] P. Hall. Optimization of a simple expression in a relational data base system. *IBM Journal of Research and Development*, 20(3):244–257, 1976.

[245] M. Hammer and D. McLeod. Semantic integrity in a relational data base system. In *Proc. of the Conf. on Very Large Databases*, 1975.

[246] J. Han and Y. Fu. Discovery of multiple-level association rules from large databases. In *Proc. of the Conf. on Very Large Databases*, 1995.

[247] E. Hanson. A performance analysis of view materialization strategies. In *ACM SIGMOD Conf. on the Management of Data*, 1987.

[248] E. Hanson. Rule condition testing and action execution in Ariel. In *ACM SIGMOD Conf. on the Management of Data*, 1992.

[249] V. Harinarayan, A. Rajaraman, and J. Ullman. Implementing data cubes efficiently. In *ACM SIGMOD Conf. on the Management of Data*, 1996.

[250] J. Haritsa, M. Carey, and M. Livny. On being optimistic about real-time constraints. In *ACM SIGACT-SIGMOD Symp. on Principles of Database Systems*, 1990.

[251] J. Harrison and S. Dietrich. Maintenance of materialized views in deductive databases: An update propagation approach. In *Proc. of the Workshop on Deductive Databases, Washington, DC*, 1992.

[252] D. Heckerman. Bayesian networks for knowledge discovery. In *Advances in Knowledge Discovery and Data Mining, U.M. Fayyad, G. Piatetsky-Shapiro, P. Smyth and R. Uthurusamy (eds.), MIT Press*, 1996.

[253] J. Hellerstein. Optimization and execution techniques for queries with expensive methods. *Ph.D. thesis, University of Wisconsin-Madison*, 1995.

[254] J. Hellerstein, J. Naughton, and A. Pfeffer. Generalized search trees for database systems. In *Proc. of the Conf. on Very Large Databases*, 1995.

[255] C.-T. Ho, R. Agrawal, N. Megiddo, and R. Srikant. Range queries in OLAP data cubes. In *ACM SIGMOD Conf. on the Management of Data*, 1997.

[256] D. Hong, T. Johnson, and U. Chakravarthy. Real-time transaction scheduling: A cost conscious approach. In *ACM SIGMOD Conf. on the Management of Data*, 1993.

[257] W. Hong and M. Stonebraker. Optimization of parallel query execution plans in XPRS. In *Proc. Intl. Conf. on Parallel and Distributed Information Systems*, 1991.

[258] W.-C. Hou and G. Ozsoyoglu. Statistical estimators for aggregate relational algebra queries. *ACM Transactions on Database Systems*, 16(4), 1991.

[259] H. Hsiao and D. DeWitt. A performance study of three high availability data replication strategies. In *Proc. of the Intl. Conf. on Parallel and Distributed Information Systems*, 1991.

[260] J. Huang, J. Stankovic, K. Ramamritham, and D. Towsley. Experimental evaluation of real-time optimistic concurrency control schemes. In *Proc. of the Conf. on Very Large Databases*, 1991.

[261] Y. Huang, A. Sistla, and O. Wolfson. Data replication for mobile computers. In *ACM SIGMOD Conf. on the Management of Data*, 1994.

[262] Y. Huang and O. Wolfson. A competitive dynamic data replication algorithm. In *Proc. IEEE CS Intl. Conf. on Data Engineering*, 1993.

[263] R. Hull. Managing semantic heterogeneity in databases: A theoretical perspective. In *ACM SIGACT-SIGMOD Symp. on Principles of Database Systems*, 1997.

[264] R. Hull and R. King. Semantic database modeling: Survey, applications, and research issues. *ACM Computing Surveys*, 19(19):201–260, 1987.

[265] R. Hull and J. Su. Algebraic and calculus query languages for recursively typed complex objects. *Journal of Computer and System Sciences*, 47(1):121–156, 1993.

[266] R. Hull and M. Yoshikawa. ILOG: declarative creation and manipulation of object-identifiers. In *Proc. of the Conf. on Very Large Databases*, 1990.

[267] T. Imielinski and H. Korth (eds.). *Mobile Computing*. Kluwer Academic, 1996.

[268] T. Imielinski and W. Lipski. Incomplete information in relational databases. *Journal of the ACM*, 31(4):761–791, 1984.

[269] T. Imielinski and H. Mannila. A database perspective on knowledge discovery. *Communications of the ACM*, 38(11):58–64, 1996.

[270] T. Imielinski, S. Viswanathan, and B. Badrinath. Energy efficient indexing on air. In *ACM SIGMOD Conf. on the Management of Data*, 1994.

[271] Y. Ioannidis. Query optimization. In *Handbook of Computer Science, A.B. Tucker (ed.), CRC Press*, 1996.

[272] Y. Ioannidis and S. Christodoulakis. Optimal histograms for limiting worst-case error propagation in the size of join results. *ACM Transactions on Database Systems*, 1993.

[273] Y. Ioannidis and Y. Kang. Randomized algorithms for optimizing large join queries. In *ACM SIGMOD Conf. on the Management of Data, Atlantic City*, 1990.

[274] Y. Ioannidis and Y. Kang. Left-deep vs. bushy trees: An analysis of strategy spaces and its implications for query optimization. In *ACM SIGMOD Conf. on the Management of Data*, 1991.

[275] Y. Ioannidis, R. Ng, K. Shim, and T. Sellis. Parametric query processing. In *Proc. of the Conf. on Very Large Databases*, 1992.

[276] Y. Ioannidis and R. Ramakrishnan. Containment of conjunctive queries: Beyond relations as sets. *ACM Transactions on Database Systems*, 20(3):288–324, 1995.

[277] Y. E. Ioannidis. Universality of serial histograms. In *Proc. of the Conf. on Very Large Databases*, 1993.

[278] H. Jagadish, D. Lieuwen, R. Rastogi, A. Silberschatz, and S. Sudarshan. Dali: a high performance main-memory storage manager. In *Proc. of the Conf. on Very Large Databases*, 1994.

[279] A. Jain and R. Dubes. *Algorithms for Clustering Data*. Prentice-Hall, 1988.

[280] S. Jajodia and D. Mutchler. Dynamic voting algorithms for maintaining the consistency of a replicated database. *ACM Transactions on Database Systems*, 15(2):230–280, 1990.

[281] S. Jajodia and R. Sandhu. Polyinstantiation integrity in multilevel relations. In *Proc. IEEE Symposium on Security and Privacy*, 1990.

[282] M. Jarke and J. Koch. Query optimization in database systems. *ACM Computing Surveys*, 16(2):111–152, 1984.

[283] J. Jou and P. Fischer. The complexity of recognizing 3nf schemes. *Information Processing Letters*, 14(4):187–190, 1983.

[284] Y. Kambayashi, M. Yoshikawa, and S. Yajima. Query processing for distributed databases using generalized semi-joins. In *ACM SIGMOD Conf. on the Management of Data*, 1982.

[285] P. Kanellakis. Elements of relational database theory. In *Handbook of Theoretical Computer Science, J. Van Leeuwen (ed.), Elsevier*, 1991.

[286] P. Kanellakis. Constraint programming and database languages: A tutorial. In *ACM SIGACT-SIGMOD Symp. on Principles of Database Systems*, 1995.

[287] D. Keim and H.-P. Kriegel. VisDB: a system for visualizing large databases. In *ACM SIGMOD Conf. on the Management of Data*, 1995.

[288] D. Keim and H.-P. Kriegel. Visualization techniques for mining large databases: A comparison. *IEEE Transactions on Knowledge and Data Engineering*, 8(6):923–938, 1996.

[289] A. Keller. Algorithms for translating view updates to database updates for views involving selections, projections, and joins. *ACM SIGACT-SIGMOD Symp. on Principles of Database Systems*, 1985.

[290] W. Kent. *Data and Reality, Basic Assumptions in Data Processing Reconsidered*. North-Holland, 1978.

[291] W. Kent, R. Ahmed, J. Albert, M. Ketabchi, and M.-C. Shan. Object identification in multi-database systems. In *IFIP Intl. Conf. on Data Semantics*, 1992.

[292] L. Kerschberg, A. Klug, and D. Tsichritzis. A taxonomy of data models. In *Systems for Large Data Bases, P.C. Lockemann and E.J. Neuhold (eds.), North-Holland*, 1977.

[293] W. Kiessling. On semantic reefs and efficient processing of correlation queries with aggregates. In *Proc. of the Conf. on Very Large Databases*, 1985.

[294] M. Kifer, W. Kim, and Y. Sagiv. Querying object-oriented databases. In *ACM SIGMOD Conf. on the Management of Data*, 1992.

[295] M. Kifer, G. Lausen, and J. Wu. Logical foundations of object-oriented and frame-based languages. *Journal of the ACM*, 42(4):741–843, 1995.

[296] M. Kifer and E. Lozinskii. Sygraf: implementing logic programs in a database style. *IEEE Transactions on Software Engineering*, 14(7):922–935, 1988.

[297] W. Kim. On optimizing an SQL-like nested query. *ACM Transactions on Database Systems*, 7(3), 1982.

[298] W. Kim. Object-oriented database systems: Promise, reality, and future. In *Proc. of the Conf. on Very Large Databases*, 1993.

[299] W. Kim, J. Garza, N. Ballou, and D. Woelk. Architecture of the ORION next-generation database system. *IEEE Transactions on Knowledge and Data Engineering*, 2(1):109–124, 1990.

[300] W. Kim and F. Lochovsky (eds.). *Object-Oriented Concepts, Databases, and Applications*. Addison-Wesley, 1989.

[301] W. Kim, D. Reiner, and D. Batory (eds.). *Query Processing in Database Systems*. Springer Verlag, 1984.

[302] W. Kim (ed.). *Modern Database Systems*. ACM Press and Addison-Wesley, 1995.

[303] R. Kimball. *The Data Warehouse Toolkit*. John Wiley and Sons, 1996.

[304] J. King. Quist: a system for semantic query optimization in relational databases. In *Proc. of the Conf. on Very Large Databases*, 1981.

[305] A. Klug. Access paths in the ABE statistical query facility. In *ACM SIGMOD Conf. on the Management of Data*, 1982.

[306] A. Klug. Equivalence of relational algebra and relational calculus query languages having aggregate functions. *Journal of the ACM*, 29(3):699–717, 1982.

[307] A. Klug. On conjunctive queries containing inequalities. *Journal of the ACM*, 35(1):146–160, 1988.

[308] E. Knapp. Deadlock detection in distributed databases. *ACM Computing Surveys*, 19(4):303–328, 1987.

[309] D. Knuth. *The Art of Computer Programming, Vol.3—Sorting and Searching*. Addison-Wesley, 1973.

[310] G. Koch and K. Loney. *Oracle: The Complete Reference*. Oracle Press, Osborne-McGraw Hill, 1995.

[311] W. Kohler. A survey of techniques for synchronization and recovery in decentralized computer systems. *ACM Computing Surveys*, 13(2):149–184, 1981.

[312] D. Konopnicki and O. Shmueli. W3QS: a system for WWW querying. In *Proc. IEEE CS Intl. Conf. on Data Engineering*, 1997.

[313] M. Kornacker, C. Mohan, and J. Hellerstein. Concurrency and recovery in generalized search trees. In *ACM SIGMOD Conf. on the Management of Data*, 1997.

[314] H. Korth, N. Soparkar, and A. Silberschatz. Triggered real-time databases with consistency constraints. In *Proc. of the Conf. on Very Large Databases*, 1990.

[315] H. F. Korth. Deadlock freedom using edge locks. *ACM Transactions on Database Systems*, 7(4):632–652, 1982.

[316] N. Krishnakumar and A. Bernstein. High throughput escrow algorithms for replicated databases. In *Proc. of the Conf. on Very Large Databases*, 1992.

[317] R. Krishnamurthy, H. Boral, and C. Zaniolo. Optimization of nonrecursive queries. In *Proc. of the Conf. on Very Large Databases*, 1986.

[318] J. Kuhns. Logical aspects of question answering by computer. Technical report, Rand Corporation, RM-5428-Pr., 1967.

[319] V. Kumar. *Performance of Concurrency Control Mechanisms in Centralized Database Systems.* Prentice-Hall, 1996.

[320] H. Kung and P. Lehman. Concurrent manipulation of binary search trees. *ACM Transactions on Database Systems*, 5(3):354–382, 1980.

[321] H. Kung and J. Robinson. On optimistic methods for concurrency control. *Proc. of the Conf. on Very Large Databases*, 1979.

[322] D. Kuo. Model and verification of a data manager based on ARIES. In *Intl. Conf. on Database Theory*, 1992.

[323] M. LaCroix and A. Pirotte. Domain oriented relational languages. In *Proc. of the Conf. on Very Large Databases*, 1977.

[324] M.-Y. Lai and W. Wilkinson. Distributed transaction management in jasmin. In *Proc. of the Conf. on Very Large Databases*, 1984.

[325] C. Lam, G. Landis, J. Orenstein, and D. Weinreb. The Objectstore database system. *Communications of the ACM*, 34(10), 1991.

[326] L. Lamport. Time, clocks and the ordering of events in a distributed system. *Communications of the ACM*, 21(7):558–565, 1978.

[327] B. Lampson and D. Lomet. A new presumed commit optimization for two phase commit. In *Proc. of the Conf. on Very Large Databases*, 1993.

[328] B. Lampson and H. Sturgis. Crash recovery in a distributed data storage system. Technical report, Xerox PARC, 1976.

[329] C. Landwehr. Formal models of computer security. *ACM Computing Surveys*, 13(3):247–278, 1981.

[330] R. Langerak. View updates in relational databases with an independent scheme. *ACM Transactions on Database Systems*, 15(1):40–66, 1990.

[331] P.-A. Larson. Linear hashing with overflow-handling by linear probing. *ACM Transactions on Database Systems*, 10(1):75–89, 1985.

[332] P.-A. Larson. Linear hashing with separators—a dynamic hashing scheme achieving one-access retrieval. *ACM Transactions on Database Systems*, 13(3):366–388, 1988.

[333] P. Lehman and S. Yao. Efficient locking for concurrent operations on b trees. *ACM Transactions on Database Systems*, 6(4):650–670, 1981.

[334] T. Leung and R. Muntz. Temporal query processing and optimization in multiprocessor database machines. In *Proc. of the Conf. on Very Large Databases*, 1992.

[335] E.-P. Lim and J. Srivastava. Query optimization and processing in federated database systems. In *Proc. Intl. Conf. on Intelligent Knowledge Management*, 1993.

[336] B. Lindsay, J. McPherson, and H. Pirahesh. A data management extension architecture. In *ACM SIGMOD Conf. on the Management of Data*, 1987.

[337] B. Lindsay, P. Selinger, C. Galtieri, J. Gray, R. Lorie, G. Putzolu, I. Traiger, and B. Wade. Notes on distributed databases. Technical report, RJ2571, San Jose, 1979.

[338] V. Linnemann, K. Kuspert, P. Dadam, P. Pistor, R. Erbe, A. Kemper, N. Sud-kamp, G. Walch, and M. Wallrath. Design and implementation of an extensible database management system supporting user defined data types and functions. In *Proc. of the Conf. on Very Large Databases*, 1988.

[339] R. Lipton, J. Naughton, and D. Schneider. Practical selectivity estimation through adaptive sampling. In *ACM SIGMOD Conf. on the Management of Data*, 1990.

[340] B. Liskov, A. Adya, M. Castro, M. Day, S. Ghemawat, R. Gruber, U. Maheshwari, A. Myers, and L. Shrira. Safe and efficient sharing of persistent objects in Thor. In *ACM SIGMOD Conf. on the Management of Data*, 1996.

[341] W. Litwin. Linear Hashing: A new tool for file and table addressing. In *Proc. of the Conf. on Very Large Databases*, 1980.

[342] W. Litwin. Trie Hashing. In *ACM SIGMOD Conf. on the Management of Data*, 1981.

[343] W. Litwin and A. Abdellatif. Multidatabase interoperability. *IEEE Computer*, 12(19):10–18, 1986.

[344] W. Litwin, L. Mark, and N. Roussopoulos. Interoperability of multiple autonomous databases. *ACM Computing Surveys*, 22(3), 1990.

[345] W. Litwin, M.-A. Neimat, and D. Schneider. LH*—a scalable, distributed data structure. *ACM Transactions on Database Systems*, 21(4):480–525, 1996.

[346] M. Liu, A. Sheth, and A. Singhal. An adaptive concurrency control strategy for distributed database system. In *Proc. IEEE CS Intl. Conf. on Data Engineering*, 1984.

[347] M. Livny, R. Ramakrishnan, K. Beyer, G. Chen, D. Donjerkovic, S. Lawande, J. Myllymaki, and K. Wenger. DEVise: Integrated querying and visual exploration of large datasets. In *ACM SIGMOD Conf. on the Management of Data*, 1997.

[348] G. Lohman. Grammar-like functional rules for representing query optimization alternatives. In *ACM SIGMOD Conf. on the Management of Data*, 1988.

[349] D. Lomet and B. Salzberg. The hB-Tree: A multiattribute indexing method with good guaranteed performance. *ACM Transactions on Database Systems*, 15(4), 1990.

[350] D. Lomet and B. Salzberg. Access method concurrency with recovery. In *ACM SIGMOD Conf. on the Management of Data*, 1992.

[351] R. Lorie. Physical integrity in a large segmented database. *ACM Transactions on Database Systems*, 2(1):91–104, 1977.

[352] R. Lorie and H. Young. A low communication sort algorithm for a parallel database machine. In *Proc. of the Conf. on Very Large Databases*, 1989.

[353] Y. Lou and Z. Ozsoyoglu. LLO: an object-oriented deductive language with methods and method inheritance. In *ACM SIGMOD Conf. on the Management of Data*, 1991.

[354] H. Lu, B.-C. Ooi, and K.-L. Tan (eds.). *Query Processing in Parallel Relational Database Systems*. IEEE Computer Society Press, 1994.

[355] C. Lucchesi and S. Osborn. Candidate keys for relations. *J. Computer and System Sciences*, 17(2):270–279, 1978.

[356] V. Lum. Multi-attribute retrieval with combined indexes. *Communications of the ACM*, 1(11):660–665, 1970.

[357] T. Lunt, D. Denning, R. Schell, M. Heckman, and W. Shockley. The seaview security model. *IEEE Transactions on Software Engineering*, 16(6):593–607, 1990.

[358] L. Mackert and G. Lohman. R* optimizer validation and performance evaluation for local queries. Technical report, IBM RJ-4989, San Jose, CA, 1986.

[359] D. Maier. *The Theory of Relational Databases*. Computer Science Press, 1983.

[360] D. Maier, A. Mendelzon, and Y. Sagiv. Testing implication of data dependencies. *ACM Transactions on Database Systems*, 4(4), 1979.

[361] D. Maier and D. Warren. *Computing with Logic: Logic Programming with Prolog*. Benjamin/Cummings Publishers, 1988.

[362] A. Makinouchi. A consideration on normal form of not-necessarily-normalized relation in the relational data model. In *Proc. of the Conf. on Very Large Databases*, 1977.

[363] U. Manber and R. Ladner. Concurrency control in a dynamic search structure. *ACM Transactions on Database Systems*, 9(3):439–455, 1984.

[364] H. Mannila. Methods and problems in data mining. In *Intl. Conf. on Database Theory*, 1997.

[365] H. Mannila and K.-J. Raiha. Design by Example: An application of Armstrong relations. *Journal of Computer and System Sciences*, 33(2):126–141, 1986.

[366] H. Mannila and K.-J. Raiha. *The Design of Relational Databases*. Addison-Wesley, 1992.

[367] M. Mannino, P. Chu, and T. Sager. Statistical profile estimation in database systems. *ACM Computing Surveys*, 20(3):191–221, 1988.

[368] V. Markowitz. Representing processes in the extended entity-relationship model. In *Proc. IEEE CS Intl. Conf. on Data Engineering*, 1990.

[369] V. Markowitz. Safe referential integrity structures in relational databases. In *Proc. of the Conf. on Very Large Databases*, 1991.

[370] D. McCarthy and U. Dayal. The architecture of an active data base management system. In *ACM SIGMOD Conf. on the Management of Data*, 1989.

[371] W. McCune and L. Henschen. Maintaining state constraints in relational databases: A proof theoretic basis. *Journal of the ACM*, 36(1):46–68, 1989.

[372] S. Mehrotra, R. Rastogi, Y. Breitbart, H. Korth, and A. Silberschatz. Ensuring transaction atomicity in multidatabase systems. In *ACM SIGACT-SIGMOD Symp. on Principles of Database Systems*, 1992.

[373] S. Mehrotra, R. Rastogi, H. Korth, and A. Silberschatz. The concurrency control problem in multidatabases: Characteristics and solutions. In *ACM SIGMOD Conf. on the Management of Data*, 1992.

[374] M. Mehta, V. Soloviev, and D. DeWitt. Batch scheduling in parallel database systems. In *Proc. IEEE CS Intl. Conf. on Data Engineering*, 1993.

[375] J. Melton and A. Simon. *Understanding the New SQL: A Complete Guide*. Morgan Kaufmann, 1993.

[376] D. Menasce and R. Muntz. Locking and deadlock detection in distributed data bases. *IEEE Transactions on Software Engineering*, 5(3):195–222, 1979.

[377] A. Mendelzon and T. Milo. Formal models of web queries. In *ACM SIGACT-SIGMOD Symp. on Principles of Database Systems*, 1997.

[378] R. Meo, G. Psaila, and S. Ceri. A new SQL-like operator for mining association rules. In *Proc. of the Conf. on Very Large Databases*, 1996.

[379] T. Merrett. The extended relational algebra, a basis for query languages. In *Databases, Shneiderman (ed.), Academic Press*, 1978.

[380] T. Merrett. *Relational Information Systems*. Reston Publishing Company, 1983.

[381] K. Mikkilineni and S. Su. An evaluation of relational join algorithms in a pipelined query processing environment. *IEEE Transactions on Software Engineering*, 14(6):838–848, 1988.

[382] R. Miller, Y. Ioannidis, and R. Ramakrishnan. The use of information capacity in schema integration and translation. In *Proc. of the Conf. on Very Large Databases*, 1993.

[383] J. Minker (ed.). *Foundations of Deductive Databases and Logic Programming*. Morgan Kaufmann, 1988.

[384] T. Minoura and G. Wiederhold. Resilient extended true-copy token scheme for a distributed database. *IEEE Transactions in Software Engineering*, 8(3):173–189, 1982.

[385] G. Mitchell, U. Dayal, and S. Zdonik. Control of an extensible query optimizer: A planning-based approach. In *Proc. of the Conf. on Very Large Databases*, 1993.

[386] C. Mohan. ARIES/NT: a recovery method based on write-ahead logging for nested. In *Proc. of the Conf. on Very Large Databases*, 1989.

[387] C. Mohan. Commit LSN: A novel and simple method for reducing locking and latching in transaction processing systems. In *Proc. of the Conf. on Very Large Databases*, 1990.

[388] C. Mohan. ARIES/LHS: a concurrency control and recovery method using write-ahead logging for linear hashing with separators. In *Proc. IEEE CS Intl. Conf. on Data Engineering*, 1993.

[389] C. Mohan, D. Haderle, B. Lindsay, H. Pirahesh, and P. Schwarz. ARIES: a transaction recovery method supporting fine-granularity locking and partial rollbacks using write-ahead logging. *ACM Transactions on Database Systems*, 17(1):94–162, 1992.

[390] C. Mohan and F. Levine. ARIES/IM an efficient and high concurrency index management method using write-ahead logging. In *ACM SIGMOD Conf. on the Management of Data*, 1992.

[391] C. Mohan and B. Lindsay. Efficient commit protocols for the tree of processes model of distributed transactions. In *ACM SIGACT-SIGOPS Symp. on Principles of Distributed Computing*, 1983.

[392] C. Mohan, B. Lindsay, and R. Obermarck. Transaction management in the R* distributed database management system. *ACM Transactions on Database Systems*, 11(4):378–396, 1986.

[393] C. Mohan and I. Narang. Algorithms for creating indexes for very large tables without quiescing updates. In *ACM SIGMOD Conf. on the Management of Data*, 1992.

[394] Y. Morimoto, H. Ishii, and S. Morishita. Efficient construction of regression trees with range and region splitting. In *Proc. of the Conf. on Very Large Databases*, 1997.

[395] K. Morris, J. Naughton, Y. Saraiya, J. Ullman, and A. Van Gelder. YAWN! (Yet Another Window on NAIL!). *Database Engineering*, 6:211–226, 1987.

[396] A. Motro. Superviews: Virtual integration of multiple databases. *IEEE Transactions on Software Engineering*, 13(7):785–798, 1987.

[397] A. Motro and O. Buneman. Constructing superviews. In *ACM SIGMOD Conf. on the Management of Data*, 1981.

[398] R. Mukkamala. Measuring the effect of data distribution and replication models on performance evaluation of distributed database systems. In *Proc. IEEE CS Intl. Conf. on Data Engineering*, 1989.

[399] I. Mumick, S. Finkelstein, H. Pirahesh, and R. Ramakrishnan. Magic is relevant. In *ACM SIGMOD Conf. on the Management of Data*, 1990.

[400] I. Mumick, S. Finkelstein, H. Pirahesh, and R. Ramakrishnan. Magic conditions. *ACM Transactions on Database Systems*, 21(1):107–155, 1996.

[401] I. Mumick, H. Pirahesh, and R. Ramakrishnan. Duplicates and aggregates in deductive databases. In *Proc. of the Conf. on Very Large Databases*, 1990.

[402] I. Mumick and K. Ross. Noodle: a language for declarative querying in an object-oriented database. In *Intl. Conf. on Deductive and Object-Oriented Databases*, 1993.

[403] M. Muralikrishna. Improved unnesting algorithms for join aggregate SQL queries. In *Proc. of the Conf. on Very Large Databases*, 1992.

[404] M. Muralikrishna and D. DeWitt. Equi-depth histograms for estimating selectivity factors for multi-dimensional queries. In *ACM SIGMOD Conf. on the Management of Data*, 1988.

[405] S. Naqvi. Negation as failure for first-order queries. In *ACM SIGACT-SIGMOD Symp. on Principles of Database Systems*, 1986.

[406] M. Negri, G. Pelagatti, and L. Sbattella. Formal semantics of SQL queries. *ACM Transactions on Database Systems*, 16(3), 1991.

[407] T. Nguyen and V. Srinivasan. Accessing relational databases from the world wide web. In *ACM SIGMOD Conf. on the Management of Data*, 1996.

[408] J. Nievergelt, H. Hinterberger, and K. Sevcik. The Grid File: An adaptable symmetric multikey file structure. *ACM Transactions on Database Systems*, 9(1):38–71, 1984.

[409] C. Nyberg, T. Barclay, Z. Cvetanovic, J. Gray, and D. Lomet. Alphasort: a cache-sensitive parallel external sort. *VLDB Journal*, 4(4):603–627, 1995.

[410] R. Obermarck. Global deadlock detection algorithm. *ACM Transactions on Database Systems*, 7(2):187–208, 1981.

[411] F. Olken and D. Rotem. Simple random sampling from relational databases. In *Proc. of the Conf. on Very Large Databases*, 1986.

[412] F. Olken and D. Rotem. Maintenance of materialized views of sampling queries. In *Proc. IEEE CS Intl. Conf. on Data Engineering*, 1992.

[413] P. O'Neil. *Database Principles, Programming and Practice*. Morgan Kaufmann, 1994.

[414] P. O'Neil and D. Quass. Improved query performance with variant indexes. In *ACM SIGMOD Conf. on the Management of Data*, 1997.

[415] B. Ozden, R. Rastogi, and A. Silberschatz. Multimedia support for databases. In *ACM SIGACT-SIGMOD Symp. on Principles of Database Systems*, 1997.

[416] G. Ozsoyoglu, K. Du, S. Guruswamy, and W.-C. Hou. Processing real-time, non-aggregate queries with time-constraints in case-db. In *Proc. IEEE CS Intl. Conf. on Data Engineering*, 1992.

[417] G. Ozsoyoglu, Z. Ozsoyoglu, and V. Matos. Extending relational algebra and relational calculus with set-valued attributes and aggregate functions. *ACM Transactions on Database Systems*, 12(4):566–592, 1987.

[418] Z. Ozsoyoglu and L.-Y. Yuan. A new normal form for nested relations. *ACM Transactions on Database Systems*, 12(1):111–136, 1987.

[419] M. Ozsu and P. Valduriez. *Principles of Distributed Database Systems*. Prentice-Hall, 1991.

[420] C. Papadimitriou. The serializability of concurrent database updates. *Journal of the ACM*, 26(4):631–653, 1979.

[421] C. Papadimitriou. *The Theory of Database Concurrency Control*. Computer Science Press, 1986.

[422] J. Park and A. Segev. Using common subexpressions to optimize multiple queries. In *Proc. IEEE CS Intl. Conf. on Data Engineering*, 1988.

[423] J. Patel, Y. J-B., K. Tufte, B. Nag, J. Burger, N. Hall, K. Ramasamy, R. Lueder, C. Ellman, J. Kupsch, S. Guo, D. DeWitt, and J. Naughton. Building a scaleable geo-spatial DBMS: Technology, implementation, and evaluation. In *ACM SIGMOD Conf. on the Management of Data*, 1997.

[424] D. Patterson, G. Gibson, and R. Katz. RAID: redundant arrays of inexpensive disks. In *ACM SIGMOD Conf. on the Management of Data*, 1988.

[425] H.-B. Paul, H.-J. Schek, M. Scholl, G. Weikum, and U. Deppisch. Architecture and implementation of the Darmstadt database kernel system. In *ACM SIGMOD Conf. on the Management of Data*, 1987.

[426] J. Peckham and F. Maryanski. Semantic data models. *ACM Computing Surveys*, 20(3):153–189, 1988.

[427] E. Petajan, Y. Jean, D. Lieuwen, and V. Anupam. DataSpace: An automated visualization system for large databases. In *Proc. of SPIE, Visual Data Exploration and Analysis*, 1997.

[428] S. Petrov. Finite axiomatization of languages for representation of system properties. *Information Sciences*, 47:339–372, 1989.

[429] G. Piatetsky-Shapiro and C. Cornell. Accurate estimation of the number of tuples satisfying a condition. In *ACM SIGMOD Conf. on the Management of Data*, 1984.

[430] H. Pirahesh and J. Hellerstein. Extensible/rule-based query rewrite optimization in starburst. In *ACM SIGMOD Conf. on the Management of Data*, 1992.

[431] V. Poosala, Y. Ioannidis, P. Haas, and E. Shekita. Improved histograms for selectivity estimation of range predicates. In *ACM SIGMOD Conf. on the Management of Data*, 1996.

[432] C. Pu. Superdatabases for composition of heterogeneous databases. In *Proc. IEEE CS Intl. Conf. on Data Engineering*, 1988.

[433] C. Pu and A. Leff. Replica control in distributed systems: An asynchronous approach. In *ACM SIGMOD Conf. on the Management of Data*, 1991.

[434] X.-L. Qian and G. Wiederhold. Incremental recomputation of active relational expressions. *IEEE Transactions on Knowledge and Data Engineering*, 3(3):337–341, 1990.

[435] J. Quinlan. Learning decision tree classifiers. In *Handbook of Computer Science, A.B. Tucker (ed.), CRC Press*, 1996.

[436] D. Rafiei and A. Mendelzon. Similarity-based queries for time series data. In *ACM SIGMOD Conf. on the Management of Data*, 1997.

[437] M. Ramakrishna. An exact probability model for finite hash tables. In *Proc. IEEE CS Intl. Conf. on Data Engineering*, 1988.

[438] M. Ramakrishna and P.-A. Larson. File organization using composite perfect hashing. *ACM Transactions on Database Systems*, 14(2):231–263, 1989.

[439] I. Ramakrishnan, P. Rao, K. Sagonas, T. Swift, and D. Warren. Efficient tabling mechanisms for logic programs. In *Intl. Conf. on Logic Programming*, 1995.

[440] R. Ramakrishnan, D. Srivastava, and S. Sudarshan. Efficient bottom-up evaluation of logic programs. In *The State of the Art in Computer Systems and Software Engineering, J. Vandewalle (ed.), Kluwer Academic*, 1992.

[441] R. Ramakrishnan, D. Srivastava, S. Sudarshan, and P. Seshadri. The CORAL: deductive system. *VLDB Journal*, 3(2):161–210, 1994.

[442] R. Ramakrishnan and J. Ullman. A survey of deductive database systems. *Journal of Logic Programming*, 23(2):125–149, 1995.

[443] K. Ramamohanarao. Design overview of the Aditi deductive database system. In *Proc. IEEE CS Intl. Conf. on Data Engineering*, 1991.

[444] K. Ramamohanarao, J. Shepherd, and R. Sacks-Davis. Partial-match retrieval for dynamic files using linear hashing with partial expansions. In *Intl. Conf. on Foundations of Data Organization and Algorithms*, 1989.

[445] S. Rao, A. Badia, and D. Van Gucht. Providing better support for a class of decision support queries. In *ACM SIGMOD Conf. on the Management of Data*, 1996.

[446] D. Reed. Implementing atomic actions on decentralized data. *ACM Transactions on Database Systems*, 1(1):3–23, 1983.

[447] R. Reiter. A sound and sometimes complete query evaluation algorithm for relational databases with null values. *Journal of the ACM*, 33(2):349–370, 1986.

[448] A. Reuter. A fast transaction-oriented logging scheme for undo recovery. *IEEE Transactions on Software Engineering*, 6(4):348–356, 1980.

[449] A. Reuter. Performance analysis of recovery techniques. *ACM Transactions on Database Systems*, 9(4):526–559, 1984.

[450] E. Riloff and L. Hollaar. Text databases and information retrieval. In *Handbook of Computer Science, A.B. Tucker (ed.), CRC Press*, 1996.

[451] J. Rissanen. Independent components of relations. *ACM Transactions on Database Systems*, 2(4):317–325, 1977.

[452] R. Rivest. Partial match retrieval algorithms. *SIAM J. on Computing*, 5(1):19–50, 1976.

[453] J. Rohmer, F. Lescoeur, and J. Kerisit. The alexander method, a technique for the processing of recursive. *New Generation Computing*, 4(3):273–285, 1986.

[454] D. Rosenkrantz, R. Stearns, and P. Lewis. System level concurrency control for distributed database systems. *ACM Transactions on Database Systems*, 3(2), 1978.

[455] A. Rosenthal and U. Chakravarthy. Anatomy of a modular multiple query optimizer. In *Proc. of the Conf. on Very Large Databases*, 1988.

[456] K. Ross and D. Srivastava. Fast computation of sparse datacubes. In *Proc. of the Conf. on Very Large Databases*, 1997.

[457] K. Ross, D. Srivastava, and S. Sudarshan. Materialized view maintenance and integrity constraint checking: Trading space for time. In *ACM SIGMOD Conf. on the Management of Data*, 1996.

[458] J. Rothnie, P. Bernstein, S. Fox, N. Goodman, M. Hammer, T. Landers, C. Reeve, D. Shipman, and E. Wong. Introduction to a system for distributed databases (SDD-1). *ACM Transactions on Database Systems*, 5(1), 1980.

[459] J. Rothnie and N. Goodman. An overview of the preliminary design of SDD-1: A system for distributed data bases. In *Proc. of the Berkeley Workshop on Distributed Data Management and Computer Networks*, 1977.

[460] N. Roussopoulos, Y. Kotidis, and M. Roussopoulos. Cubetree: organization of and bulk updates on the data cube. In *ACM SIGMOD Conf. on the Management of Data*, 1997.

[461] S. Rozen and D. Shasha. Using feature set compromise to automate physical database design. In *Proc. of the Conf. on Very Large Databases*, 1991.

[462] M. Rusinkiewicz, A. Sheth, and G. Karabatis. Specifying interdatabase dependencies in a multidatabase environment. *IEEE Computer*, 24(12), 1991.

[463] D. Sacca and C. Zaniolo. Magic counting methods. In *ACM SIGMOD Conf. on the Management of Data*, 1987.

[464] Y. Sagiv and M. Yannakakis. Equivalence among expressions with the union and difference operators. *Journal of the ACM*, 27(4):633–655, 1980.

[465] K. Sagonas, T. Swift, and D. Warren. XSB as an efficient deductive database engine. In *ACM SIGMOD Conf. on the Management of Data*, 1994.

[466] B. Salzberg, A. Tsukerman, J. Gray, M. Stewart, S. Uren, and B. Vaughan. Fastsort: a distributed single-input single-output external sort. In *ACM SIGMOD Conf. on the Management of Data*, 1990.

[467] B. J. Salzberg. *File Structures*. Prentice-Hall, 1988.

[468] H. Samet. The Quad Tree and related hierarchical data structures. *ACM Computing Surveys*, 16(2), 1984.

[469] H. Samet. *The Design and Analysis of Spatial Data Structures*. Addison-Wesley, 1990.

[470] S. Sarawagi and M. Stonebraker. Efficient organization of large multidimensional arrays. In *Proc. IEEE CS Intl. Conf. on Data Engineering*, 1994.

[471] A. Savasere, E. Omiecinski, and S. Navathe. An efficient algorithm for mining association rules in large databases. In *Proc. of the Conf. on Very Large Databases*, 1995.

[472] H.-J. Schek, H.-B. Paul, M. Scholl, and G. Weikum. TheDASDBS project: Objects, experiences, and future projects. *IEEE Transactions on Knowledge and Data Engineering*, 2(1), 1990.

[473] M. Schkolnick. Physical database design techniques. In *NYU Symposium on Database Design*, 1978.

[474] M. Schkolnick and P. Sorenson. Theeffects of denormalization on database performance. Technical report, IBM RJ3082, San Jose, CA, 1981.

[475] G. Schlageter. Optimistic methods for concurrency control in distributed database systems. In *Proc. of the Conf. on Very Large Databases*, 1981.

[476] E. Sciore. A complete axiomatization of full join dependencies. *Journal of the ACM*, 29(2):373–393, 1982.

[477] E. Sciore, M. Siegel, and A. Rosenthal. Using semantic values to facilitate interoperability among heterogeneous information systems. *ACM Transactions on Database Systems*, 19(2):254–290, 1994.

[478] D. Scott. *Multivariate Density Estimation: Theory, Practice, and Visualization*. John Wiley, 1992.

[479] A. Segev and J. Park. Maintaining materialized views in distributed databases. In *Proc. IEEE CS Intl. Conf. on Data Engineering*, 1989.

[480] A. Segev and A. Shoshani. Logical modeling of temporal data. *ACM SIGMOD Conf. on the Management of Data*, 1987.

[481] P. Selfridge, D. Srivastava, and L. Wilson. IDEA: interactive data exploration and analysis. In *ACM SIGMOD Conf. on the Management of Data*, 1996.

[482] P. Selinger and M. Adiba. Access path selections in distributed data base management systems. In *Proc. Intl. Conf. on Databases, British Computer Society*, 1980.

[483] P. Selinger, M. Astrahan, D. Chamberlin, R. Lorie, and T. Price. Access path selection in a relational database management system. In *ACM SIGMOD Conf. on the Management of Data, Boston*, 1979.

[484] T. K. Sellis. Multiple query optimization. *ACM Transactions on Database Systems*, 13(1):23–52, 1988.

[485] P. Seshadri, J. Hellerstein, H. Pirahesh, T. Leung, R. Ramakrishnan, D. Srivastava, P. Stuckey, and S. Sudarshan. Cost-based optimization for Magic: Algebra and implementation. In *ACM SIGMOD Conf. on the Management of Data*, 1996.

[486] P. Seshadri, M. Livny, and R. Ramakrishnan. The design and implementation of a sequence database system. In *Proc. of the Conf. on Very Large Databases*, 1996.

[487] P. Seshadri, M. Livny, and R. Ramakrishnan. The case for enhanced abstract data types. In *Proc. of the Conf. on Very Large Databases*, 1997.

[488] P. Seshadri, H. Pirahesh, and T. Leung. Complex query decorrelation. In *Proc. IEEE CS Intl. Conf. on Data Engineering*, 1996.

[489] J. Shafer and R. Agrawal. SPRINT: a scalable parallel classifier for data mining. In *Proc. of the Conf. on Very Large Databases*, 1996.

[490] L. Shapiro. Join processing in database systems with large main memories. *ACM Transactions on Database Systems*, 11(3):239–264, 1986.

[491] D. Shasha. *Database Tuning: A Principled Approach*. Prentice-Hall, 1992.

[492] D. Shasha and N. Goodman. Concurrent search structure algorithms. *ACM Transactions on Database Systems*, 13:53–90, 1988.

[493] D. Shasha, E. Simon, and P. Valduriez. Simple rational guidance for chopping up transactions. In *ACM SIGMOD Conf. on the Management of Data*, 1992.

[494] H. Shatkay and S. Zdonik. Approximate queries and representations for large data sequences. In *Proc. IEEE CS Intl. Conf. on Data Engineering*, 1996.

[495] T. Sheard and D. Stemple. Automatic verification of database transaction safety. *ACM Transactions on Database Systems*, 1989.

[496] S. Shenoy and Z. Ozsoyoglu. Design and implementation of a semantic query optimizer. *IEEE Transactions on Knowledge and Data Engineering*, 1(3):344–361, 1989.

[497] A. Sheth and J. Larson. Federated database systems for managing distributed, heterogeneous, and autonomous databases. *Computing Surveys*, 22(3):183–236, 1990.

[498] A. Sheth, J. Larson, A. Cornelio, and S. Navathe. A tool for integrating conceptual schemas and user views. In *Proc. IEEE CS Intl. Conf. on Data Engineering*, 1988.

[499] A. Shoshani. OLAP and statistical databases: Similarities and differences. In *ACM SIGACT-SIGMOD Symp. on Principles of Database Systems*, 1997.

[500] A. Shukla, P. Deshpande, J. Naughton, and K. Ramasamy. Storage estimation for multidimensional aggregates in the presence of hierarchies. In *Proc. of the Conf. on Very Large Databases*, 1996.

[501] M. Siegel, E. Sciore, and S. Salveter. A method for automatic rule derivation to support semantic query optimization. *ACM Transactions on Database Systems*, 17(4), 1992.

[502] A. Silberschatz, H. Korth, and S. Sudarshan. *Database System Concepts (3rd ed.)*. McGraw-Hill, 1991.

[503] E. Simon, J. Kiernan, and C. de Maindreville. Implementing high-level active rules on top of relational databases. In *Proc. of the Conf. on Very Large Databases*, 1992.

[504] D. Skeen. Nonblocking commit protocols. In *ACM SIGMOD Conf. on the Management of Data*, 1981.

[505] J. Smith and D. Smith. Database abstractions: Aggregation and generalization. *ACM Transactions on Database Systems*, 1(1):105–133, 1977.

[506] K. Smith and M. Winslett. Entity modeling in the MLS relational model. In *Proc. of the Conf. on Very Large Databases*, 1992.

[507] P. Smith and M. Barnes. *Files and Databases: An Introduction*. Addison-Wesley, Reading MA., 1990.

[508] N. Soparkar, H. Korth, and A. Silberschatz. Databases with deadline and contingency constraints. *IEEE Transactions on Knowledge and Data Engineering*, 7(4):552–565, 1995.

[509] S. Spaccapietra, C. Parent, and Y. Dupont. Model independent assertions for integration of heterogeneous schemas. In *Proc. of the Conf. on Very Large Databases*, 1992.

[510] S. Spaccapietra (ed.). *Entity-Relationship Approach: Ten Years of Experience in Information Modeling, Proc. of the Entity-Relationship Conf.* North-Holland, 1987.

[511] R. Srikant and R. Agrawal. Mining generalized association rules. In *Proc. of the Conf. on Very Large Databases*, 1995.

[512] V. Srinivasan and M. Carey. Performance of B-Tree concurrency control algorithms. In *ACM SIGMOD Conf. on the Management of Data*, 1991.

[513] D. Srivastava, S. Dar, H. Jagadish, and A. Levy. Answering queries with aggregation using views. In *Proc. of the Conf. on Very Large Databases*, 1996.

[514] D. Srivastava, R. Ramakrishnan, P. Seshadri, and S. Sudarshan. Coral++: Adding object-orientation to a logic database language. In *Proc. of the Conf. on Very Large Databases*, 1993.

[515] J. Srivastava and D. Rotem. Analytical modeling of materialized view maintenance. In *ACM SIGACT-SIGMOD Symp. on Principles of Database Systems*, 1988.

[516] J. Srivastava, J. Tan, and V. Lum. Tbsam: an access method for efficient processing of statistical queries. *IEEE Transactions on Knowledge and Data Engineering*, 1(4):414–423, 1989.

[517] D. Stacey. Replication: DB2, Oracle or Sybase? *Database Programming and Design*, pages 42–50, December 1994.

[518] P. Stachour and B. Thuraisingham. Design of LDV: A multilevel secure relational database management system. *IEEE Transactions on Knowledge and Data Engineering*, 2(2), 1990.

[519] J. Stankovic and W. Zhao. On real-time transactions. In *ACM SIGMOD Conf. on the Management of Data Record*, 1988.

[520] T. Steel. Interim report of the ANSI-SPARC study group. In *ACM SIGMOD Conf. on the Management of Data*, 1975.

[521] M. Stonebraker. Implementation of integrity constraints and views by query modification. In *ACM SIGMOD Conf. on the Management of Data*, 1975.

[522] M. Stonebraker. Concurrency control and consistency of multiple copies of data in distributed ingres. *IEEE Transactions on Software Engineering*, 5(3), 1979.

[523] M. Stonebraker. Operating system support for database management. *Communications of the ACM*, 14(7):412–418, 1981.

[524] M. Stonebraker. Inclusion of new types in relational database systems. In *Proc. IEEE CS Intl. Conf. on Data Engineering*, 1986.

[525] M. Stonebraker. *The INGRES papers: Anatomy of a Relational Database System*. Addison-Wesley, 1986.

[526] M. Stonebraker. The design of the postgres storage system. In *Proc. of the Conf. on Very Large Databases*, 1987.

[527] M. Stonebraker. *Object-relational DBMSs—The Next Great Wave*. Morgan Kaufmann, 1996.

[528] M. Stonebraker, J. Frew, K. Gardels, and J. Meredith. The sequoia 2000 storage benchmark. In *ACM SIGMOD Conf. on the Management of Data 93, Washington,DC*, 1993.

[529] M. Stonebraker, A. Jhingran, J. Goh, and S. Potamianos. On rules, procedures, caching and views in data base systems. In *UCBERL M9036*, 1990.

[530] M. Stonebraker and G. Kemnitz. The POSTGRES next-generation database management system. *Communications of the ACM*, 34(10):78–92, 1991.

[531] M. Stonebraker (ed.). *Readings in Database Systems (2nd ed.)*. Morgan Kaufmann, 1994.

[532] B. Subramanian, T. Leung, S. Vandenberg, and S. Zdonik. The AQUA approach to querying lists and trees in object-oriented databases. In *Proc. IEEE CS Intl. Conf. on Data Engineering*, 1995.

[533] W. Sun, Y. Ling, N. Rishe, and Y. Deng. An instant and accurate size estimation method for joins and selections in a retrieval-intensive environment. In *ACM SIGMOD Conf. on the Management of Data*, 1993.

[534] A. Swami and A. Gupta. Optimization of large join queries: Combining heuristics and combinatorial techniques. In *ACM SIGMOD Conf. on the Management of Data*, 1989.

[535] T. Swift and D. Warren. An abstract machine for SLG resolution: Definite programs. In *Intl. Logic Programming Symposium*, 1994.

[536] A. Tansel, J. Clifford, S. Gadia, S. Jajodia, A. Segev, and R. Snodgrass. *Temporal Databases: Theory, Design and Implementation*. Benjamin-Cummings, 1993.

[537] Y. Tay, N. Goodman, and R. Suri. Locking performance in centralized databases. *ACM Transactions on Database Systems*, 10(4):415–462, 1985.

[538] T. Teorey. *Database Modeling and Design: The E-R Approach*. Morgan Kaufmann, 1990.

[539] T. Teorey, D.-Q. Yang, and J. Fry. A logical database design methodology for relational databases using the extended entity-relationship model. *ACM Computing Surveys*, 18(2):197–222, 1986.

[540] R. Thomas. A majority consensus approach to concurrency control for multiple copy databases. *ACM Transactions on Database Systems*, 4(2):180–209, 1979.

[541] S. Todd. The peterlee relational test vehicle. *IBM Systems Journal*, 15(4):285–307, 1976.

[542] H. Toivonen. Sampling large databases for association rules. In *Proc. of the Conf. on Very Large Databases*, 1996.

[543] TP Performance Council. TPC Benchmark D: Standard specification, rev. 1.2. Technical report, http://www.tpc.org/dspec.html, 1996.

[544] I. Traiger, J. Gray, C. Galtieri, and B. Lindsay. Transactions and consistency in distributed database systems. *ACM Transactions on Database Systems*, 25(9), 1982.

[545] M. Tsangaris and J. Naughton. On the performance of object clustering techniques. In *ACM SIGMOD Conf. on the Management of Data*, 1992.

[546] D.-M. Tsou and P. Fischer. Decomposition of a relation scheme into Boyce-Codd normal form. *SIGACT News*, 14(3):23–29, 1982.

[547] A. Tucker (ed.). *Computer Science and Engineering Handbook*. CRC Press, 1996.

[548] J. W. Tukey. *Exploratory Data Analysis*. Addison-Wesley, 1977.

[549] J. Ullman. The U.R. strikes back. In *ACM SIGACT-SIGMOD Symp. on Principles of Database Systems*, 1982.

[550] J. Ullman. *Principles of Database and Knowledgebase Systems, Vols. 1 and 2*. Computer Science Press, 1989.

[551] J. Ullman. Information integration using logical views. In *Intl. Conf. on Database Theory*, 1997.

[552] S. Urban and L. Delcambre. An analysis of the structural, dynamic, and temporal aspects of semantic data models. In *Proc. IEEE CS Intl. Conf. on Data Engineering*, 1986.

[553] M. Van Emden and R. Kowalski. The semantics of predicate logic as a programming language. *Journal of the ACM*, 23(4):733–742, 1976.

[554] A. Van Gelder. Negation as failure using tight derivations for general logic programs. In *Foundations of Deductive Databases and Logic Programming, J. Minker (ed.), Morgan Kaufmann*, 1988.

[555] M. Vardi. Incomplete information and default reasoning. In *ACM SIGACT-SIGMOD Symp. on Principles of Database Systems*, 1986.

[556] M. Vardi. Fundamentals of dependency theory. In *Trends in Theoretical Computer Science, E. Borger (ed.), Computer Science Press*, 1987.

[557] L. Vieille. Recursive axioms in deductive databases: The query-subquery approach. In *Intl. Conf. on Expert Database Systems*, 1986.

[558] L. Vieille. From QSQ towards QoSaQ: global optimization of recursive queries. In *Intl. Conf. on Expert Database Systems*, 1988.

[559] L. Vieille, P. Bayer, V. Kuchenhoff, and A. Lefebvre. EKS-V1, a short overview. In *AAAI-90 Workshop on Knowledge Base Management Systems*, 1990.

[560] G. von Bultzingsloewen. Translating and optimizing SQL queries having aggregates. In *Proc. of the Conf. on Very Large Databases*, 1987.

[561] G. von Bultzingsloewen, K. Dittrich, C. Iochpe, R.-P. Liedtke, P. Lockemann, and M. Schryro. Kardamom—a dataflow database machine for real-time applications. In *ACM SIGMOD Conf. on the Management of Data*, 1988.

[562] G. Vossen. *Date Models, Database Languages and Database Management Systems*. Addison-Wesley, 1991.

[563] R. Wagner. Indexing design considerations. *IBM Systems Journal*, 12(4):351–367, 1973.

[564] X. Wang, S. Jajodia, and V. Subrahmanian. Temporal modules: An approach toward federated temporal databases. In *ACM SIGMOD Conf. on the Management of Data*, 1993.

[565] G. Weddell. Reasoning about functional dependencies generalized for semantic data models. *ACM Transactions on Database Systems*, 17(1), 1992.

[566] W. Weihl. The impact of recovery on concurrency control. In *ACM SIGACT-SIGMOD Symp. on Principles of Database Systems*, 1989.

[567] C. White. Let the replication battle begin. In *Database Programming and Design*, pages 21–24, May 1994.

[568] J. Widom and S. Ceri. *Active Database Systems*. Morgan Kaufmann, 1996.

[569] G. Wiederhold. *Database Design (2nd ed.)*. McGraw-Hill, 1983.

[570] G. Wiederhold, S. Kaplan, and D. Sagalowicz. Physical database design research at Stanford. *IEEE Database Engineering*, 1:117–119, 1983.

[571] R. Williams, D. Daniels, L. Haas, G. Lapis, B. Lindsay, P. Ng, R. Obermarck, P. Selinger, A. Walker, P. Wilms, and R. Yost. R*: An overview of the architecture. Technical report, IBM RJ3325, San Jose, CA, 1981.

[572] M. S. Winslett. A model-based approach to updating databases with incomplete information. *ACM Transactions on Database Systems*, 13(2):167–196, 1988.

[573] G. Wiorkowski and D. Kull. *DB2: Design and Development Guide (3rd ed.)*. Addison-Wesley, 1992.

[574] Y. Yang and R. Miller. Association rules over interval data. In *ACM SIGMOD Conf. on the Management of Data*, 1997.

[575] K. Youssefi and E. Wong. Query processing in a relational database management system. In *Proc. of the Conf. on Very Large Databases*, 1979.

[576] C. Yu and C. Chang. Distributed query processing. *ACM Computing Surveys*, 16(4):399–433, 1984.

[577] C. Zaniolo. Analysis and design of relational schemata. Technical report, Ph.D. Thesis, UCLA, TR UCLA-ENG-7669, 1976.

[578] C. Zaniolo. Database relations with null values. *Journal of Computer and System Sciences*, 28(1):142–166, 1984.

[579] C. Zaniolo. The database language GEM. In *Readings in Object-Oriented Databases, S.B. Zdonik and D. Maier (eds.), Morgan Kaufmann*, 1990.

[580] C. Zaniolo. Active database rules with transaction-conscious stable-model semantics. In *Intl. Conf. on Deductive and Object-Oriented Databases*, 1996.

[581] C. Zaniolo, N. Arni, and K. Ong. Negation and aggregates in recursive rules: the LDL++ approach. In *Intl. Conf. on Deductive and Object-Oriented Databases*, 1993.

[582] C. Zaniolo, S. Ceri, C. Faloutsos, R. Snodgrass, V. Subrahmanian, and R. Zicari. *Advanced Database Systems*. Morgan Kaufmann, 1997.

[583] S. Zdonik and D. Maier (eds.). *Readings in Object-Oriented Databases*. Morgan Kaufmann, 1990.

[584] A. Zhang, M. Nodine, B. Bhargava, and O. Bukhres. Ensuring relaxed atomicity for flexible transactions in multidatabase systems. In *ACM SIGMOD Conf. on the Management of Data*, 1994.

[585] T. Zhang, R. Ramakrishnan, and M. Livny. BIRCH: a new data clustering algorithm and its applications. *Journal of Data Mining and Knowledge Discovery*, 1(2), 1997.

[586] Y. Zhuge, H. Garcia-Molina, J. Hammer, and J. Widom. View maintenance in a warehousing environment. In *ACM SIGMOD Conf. on the Management of Data*, 1995.

[587] M. Zloof. Office-by-example: a business language that unifies data and word processing and electronic mail. *IBM Systems Journal*, 21(3):272–304, 1982.

[588] M. M. Zloof. Query-by-example: a database language. *IBM Systems Journal*, 16(4):324–343, 1977.

[589] U. Zukowski and B. Freitag. The deductive database system LOLA. In *Proc. Intl. Conf. on Logic Programming and Non-Monotonic Reasoning*, 1997.

INDEX

2PC, 575
  with presumed abort, 579
3PC, 579
Abbott, R., 518, 691, 697
Abdellatif, A., 588, 714
Abiteboul, S., 20, 36, 435, 612, 649, 691, 697
Abstract data types, 619–620
Access control, 15, 226, 232
Access methods, 58
Access path, 272
  most selective, 273
Achyutuni, K.J., 518, 697
ACID transactions, 478
Ackaouy, E., xxv
Active databases, xxii, 590
Adali, S., 588, 697
Adiba, M.E., 587–588, 697, 721
ADT, 619–620
  encapsulation, 620
  registering methods, 620
Adya, A., 649, 714
Agarwal, S., 680, 697
Agrawal, D., 518, 587, 697
Agrawal, R., 543, 613, 649, 680–681, 697–698, 710, 721–722
Ahad, R., 356, 698
Ahlberg, C., 691, 698
Ahmed, R., 691, 711
Aho, A.V., 83, 356, 435, 698
Aiken, A., 613, 691, 698
Albert, J., 691, 711
Anupam, V., 691, 718
Anwar, E., 613, 698
Apt, K.R., 612, 698
Architecture of a DBMS, 14
ARIES recovery algorithm, 519
Armstrong, W.W., 435, 698
Arni, N., 649, 726
Array chunks, 638, 664
Arrays, 624
Asgarian, M., 475, 702
Association rules, 667, 671
  quantitative, 674

use for prediction, 668
Astrahan, M.M., 36, 224, 356, 698, 702, 721
Asynchronous replication
  Capture and Apply, 569
  change data table (CDT), 569
  peer-to-peer, 568
  primary site, 568
Atkinson, M.P., 648–649, 698
Attar, R., 588, 698
Atzeni, P., 20, 36, 435, 649, 699
Authorization, 15
B+ tree, 90
  bulk-loading, 104
  deletion, 97
  height, 91
  insertion, 93
  key compression, 103
  locking, 499
  order, 91
  search, 92
  sequence set, 90
Badal, D.Z., 37, 699
Badia, A., 180, 680, 699, 719
Badrinath, B.R., 691, 710
Bags, 622–623
Bailey, P., 698
Balbin, I., 613, 699
Ballou, N., 649, 712
Bancilhon, F., 254, 613, 649, 699
BapaRao, K.V., 356, 698
Baralis, E., 613, 699
Barbara, D., 588, 707
Barclay, T., 153, 717
Barnes, M.G., 83, 722
Barnett, J.R., 66, 699
Barquin, R., 680, 699
Batini, C., 394, 699
Batory, D.S., 356, 699, 712
Baugsto, B.A.W., 153, 699
Bayer, P., 612, 725
Bayer, R., 115, 699
Beck, M., 153, 699
Beech, D., 649, 707

Beeri, C., 435, 613, 649, 698, 700
Bektas, H., xxv
Bell, D., 587, 700
Benchmarks, 465, 475
Bentley, J.L., 115, 700
Bernstein, A.J., 588, 712
Bernstein, P.A., 37, 254, 435, 515, 518,
    587–588, 691, 698, 700–701, 704,
    720
Beyer, K., 691, 714
Bhargava, B.K., 588, 700
Biliris, A., 66, 701
Binding
  early vs. late, 629
Biskup, J., 394, 435, 701
Bit map indexes, 662
Bitton, D., 153, 309, 699, 701
Blair, H., 612, 698
Blakeley, J.A., 254, 701
Blanchard, L., xxv
Blasgen, M.W., 36, 309, 543, 698,
    701–702, 708
Blaustein, B.T., 37, 700
Blobs, 589, 617, 637
Blocked I/O, 145
Bloomjoin, 565
Bohannon, P., 691, 701
Boral, H., 309, 356, 712
Bosworth, A., 680, 708
Boyce, R.F., 224, 701
Bratbergsengen, K., 309, 701
Breitbart, Y., 588, 701, 715
Brin, S., 681, 701
Brown, K.P., 66, 701
Bry, F., 37, 613, 701
Buffer frame, 44
Buffer management
  DBMS vs. OS, 48
  force approach, 520
  replacement policy, 46
  sequential flooding, 47
  steal approach, 520
Buffer manager, 14, 38, 44
  forcing a page, 49
  page replacement, 45
  pinning, 45
  prefetching, 48
Buffer pool, 44
Bukhres, O.A., 588, 706
Bulk data types, 622
Buneman, O.P., 394, 613, 648–649, 698,
    701, 717

Burger, J., 691, 718
Bushy trees, 337
Cabibbo, L., 649, 699
Candan, K.S., 588, 697
Carey, M.J., xxiv–xxv, 66, 475, 518,
    587, 649, 695, 697, 701–702, 707,
    709, 722
Casanova, M.A., 37, 254, 394, 702, 707
Cascading operators, 328
Castano, S., 254, 702
Castro, M., 649, 714
Catalogs, 59, 317, 325
Cate, H.P., 649, 707
Cattell, R.G.G., 649, 702
Ceri, S., 37, 394, 587, 612–613, 649, 681,
    691, 699, 702, 716, 725
Cesarini, F., 475, 702
Chakravarthy, U.S., 356, 518, 613, 698,
    702, 710, 719
Chamberlin, D.D., 36–37, 224, 356, 613,
    698, 701–702, 706, 721
Chandra, A.K., 356, 612, 703
Chandy, M.K., 588, 703
Chang, C.C., 587, 703, 725
Chang, S.K., 587
Chang, W., 649, 709
Chan, M.C., 588
Chatziantoniou, D., 680, 703
Chaudhuri, S., 475, 649, 680, 703
Checkpoint, 528
  fuzzy, 528
Cheiney, J.P., 309, 703
Cheng, W.H., 587
Chen, C.M., 66, 356, 703
Chen, G., 691, 714
Chen, J., 691, 698
Chen, P.P.S., 703
Childs, D.L., 36, 703
Chimenti, D., 612, 703
Chin, F.Y., 254, 703
Chisholm, K., 698
Chiu, D.W., 588, 700
Chomicki, J., 37, 703
Chou, H., 66, 649, 703, 705
Chow, E.C., 649, 707
Christodoulakis, S., 356, 710
Chrysanthis, P.K., 518, 703
Chunking, 638, 664
Chu, P., 356, 715
Civelek, F.N., 394, 703
Clarke, E.M., 37, 700
Classification rules, 674

Clemons, E.K., 613, 701
Clifford, J., 691, 724
Cochrane, R.J., 613, 704
Cockshott, P., 698
CODASYL, D.B.T.G., 704
Codd, E.F., 36, 180, 435, 680, 704
Colby, L.S., 254, 704
Collection types, 622
Comer, D., 115, 704
Commit protocols, 575
  2PC, 575
  3PC, 579
Complex types, 619, 633
  vs. reference types, 633
Conceptual design, 357
  tuning, 455
  using the ER model, 376
Conceptual schema, 7
Concurrency control
  multiversion, 512
  optimistic, 507
  timestamp, 509
Concurrency, 16
Connell, C., 356
Connors, T., 649, 707
Constructed types, 621–622
Convent, B., 394, 701
Convoy phenomenon, 493
Copeland, D., 649, 704
Cornelio, A., 722, 394
Cornell, C., 718
Correlated queries, 344
Cosmadakis, S.S., 254
Cost model, 273
Cristian, F., 587, 705
CS564 at Wisconsin, xxiv
Cvetanovic, Z., 153, 717
Dadam, P., 66, 649, 714
Daniels, D., 587, 725
Darwen, H., 704
Dar, S., 254, 722
Data definition language, 7
Data dictionary, 59
Data independence, 15
  distributed, 554
  logical, 10, 227, 554
  physical, 10, 554
Data manipulation language, 11
Data mining, xxii, 651, 665
Data model, 5
  multidimensional, 654
  semantic, 5

Data partitioning, 548
Data skew, 548
Data warehouse, xxii, 571, 650–651
Database architecture
  Client-Server vs. peer servers, 555
  shared-memory vs. shared-nothing,
    545
Database design
  conceptual design, 357
  for an ORDBMS, 632
  for OLAP, 661
  impact of concurrent access, 463
  physical design, 358, 436
  requirements analysis phase, 357
  role of expected workload, 437
  role of inclusion dependencies, 429
  schema refinement, 358, 395
  tuning, 358, 436, 453, 456
Database management system, 1
Database, 1
Datalog, 589, 591
Date, C.J., 20, 36–37, 224, 426, 435, 704
Davis, J.W., 649, 707
Dayal, U., 254, 356, 435, 587, 613, 680,
    701, 703–704, 715–716
Day, M, 649, 714
DBMS architecture, 14
DBMS vs. OS, 48
DDL, 7
De Antonellis, V., 20, 36, 435, 699
De Maindreville, C., 613, 722
Deadlock
  detection, 494
  distributed, 573
  phantom, 574
  prevention, 493
DeBra, P., 435, 704
Decision support, xxii, 650
Decompositions, 412
  dependency-preservation, 415
  horizontal, 460
  in the absence of redundancy, 460
  into 3NF, 419
  into BCNF, 416
  lossless-join, 413
Deductive databases, xxii, 592
Delcambre, L.M.L., 394, 724
Delobel, C., 435, 649, 699, 704
Deng, Y., 356, 723
Denning, D.E., 254, 704, 715
Deppisch, U., 66, 718
Derrett, N., 649, 707

Derr, M., 612, 705
Deshpande, A., 649, 705
Deshpande, P., 680, 697, 722
Deux, O., 649, 705
DeWitt, D.J., xxiv, 66, 153, 309, 356,
    475, 543, 587, 649, 691, 695, 697,
    701–703, 705, 708, 710, 715,
    717–718
Diaz, O., 613, 705
Dietrich, S.W., 254, 613, 705, 709
Directory
  of pages, 57
  of slots, 53
Dirty read, 481
Disk space manager, 14, 38, 42
Disks, 39
  access times, 41
  blocks, 40
  cylinders, tracks, sectors, 40
  physical structure, 40
Distributed databases, 544
  commit protocols, 575
  global object names, 559
  heterogeneous, 555
  query processing, 561
  transparency, 554
Dittrich, K.R., 649, 691, 725
DML, 11
Dogac, A., 394, 588, 703, 709
Domain, 22
Donjerkovic, D., xxv, 691, 714
Double buffering, 147
Dubes, R.C., 681, 711
Dupont, Y., 394, 722
Duppel, N., 309, 705
Du, K., 691, 718
Du, W., 588, 705
Dynamic linking, 621
Edelstein, H., 588, 680, 699, 705
Effelsberg, W., 66, 705
Eich, M.H., 543, 705
El Abbadi, A., 518, 587, 697, 705
Ellis, C.S., 518, 705
Ellman, C., 691, 718
Elmagarmid, A.K., 588, 691, 705–706
Elmasri, R., 20, 394, 706
Epstein, R., 309, 588, 706
Equality
  deep vs. shallow, 626
ER model, 358
  aggregation, 374
  attribute domains, 359

attributes, 359
class hierarchies, 372
constraints that cannot be expressed,
    384
entities and entity sets, 359
ER diagram, 358
key constraints, 364
keys, 359
need for further design, 386
overlap and covering, 373
participation constraints, 367
relationships
  and relationship sets, 360
  one-to-many, 364
roles, 362
weak entities, 370
Erbe, R., 66, 649, 714
Eswaran, K.P., 36, 224, 309, 518, 613,
    698, 701–702, 706
Exploratory data analysis, 651
Expressive power
  algebra vs. calculus, 175
Extendible hashing, 118
  directory doubling, 121
  global depth, 121
  local depth, 122
External schema, 9
Fagin, R., xxiv, 136, 435, 700, 704, 706
Fagin, Ronald, 426
Failure
  media, 519
  system crash, 519
Faloutsos, C., 66, 115, 612–613, 649,
    681, 691, 706
Faudemay, P., 309, 703
Fayyad, U., 680
Fayyad, U.M., 680, 706
File of records, 55
File organization, 67
  hashed, 72
  random, 69
  sorted, 70
Finkelstein, S.J., 356, 475, 613, 707, 717
Fischer, C.N., xxvi
Fischer, P.C., 435, 711, 724
Fishman, D.H., 649, 707
Fixpoint, 594
  Seminaive evaluation, 601
Fleming, C.C., 475, 707
Flisakowski, S., xxv
Force-write, 524, 575
Fotouhi, F., 309, 707

Fox, S., 587, 720
Fragmentation, 557
Franklin, M.J., 588, 649, 701, 707
Fraternali, P., 613, 702, 707
Freeston, M.W., 115, 707
Freitag, B., 612
Frequent itemsets, 669
  a priori property, 669
Frew, J., 475, 723
Freytag, J.C., 356, 707
Friedman, J.H., 115, 700
Friesen, O., 649, 707
Fry, J.P., 20, 394, 707, 724
Fugini, M.G., 254, 702
Fukuda, T., 681, 707
Functional dependencies, 400
  Armstrong's Axioms, 406
  attribute closure, 407
  closure, 406
  projection, 415
Furtado, A.L., 37, 254, 702, 707
Fushimi, S., 309, 707
Fu, Y., 681, 709
Gadia, S., 691, 724
Gallaire, H., 36–37, 435, 612, 707
Galtieri, C.A., 543, 588, 713, 724
Gamboa, R., 612, 703
Ganguly, S., 588, 707
Ganski, R.A., 356, 707
Garcia-Molina, H., 254, 518, 588, 691,
    697, 701, 707–708
Gardels, K., 475, 723
Garg, A.K., 136, 708
Garza, J.F., 66, 649, 699, 712
Gateways, 555, 652
Gehani, N.H., 613, 649, 697
Gehrke, J., 475, 702
Gerber, R.H., 309, 587, 705
Ghemawat, S., 649, 714
Ghosh, S.P., 83, 708
Gibson, G.A., 66, 718
Gifford, D.K., 588, 708
GiST, 638
Goh, J., 613, 723
Goldweber, M., xxiv
Goodman, N., 515, 518, 587–588, 698,
    700, 720–721, 724
Gotlieb, C.C., 136, 708
Gottlob, G., 612, 702
Graefe, G., 309, 356, 587–588, 649, 702,
    705, 708
Graham, M.H., 435, 708

Grahne, G., 36, 708
Grant, J., 356, 702
Gray, J.N., 36, 153, 475, 518, 543,
    587–588, 680, 691, 698, 702,
    705–706, 708, 713, 717, 720, 724
Gray, P.M.D., 20, 613, 705, 708
Greipsland, J.F., 153, 699
Griffin, T., 254, 704
Griffiths, P.P., 36, 224, 254, 543, 698,
    702, 708
Grimson, J., 587, 700
Grinstein, G., 691, 709
Group commit, 687
Gruber, R., 649, 714
Guo, S., 691, 718
Gupta, A., 254, 356, 680, 697, 709, 723
Guruswamy, S., 691, 718
Guttman, A., 115, 709
Gyssens, M., 180, 699
Haas, L.M., 587–588, 649, 703, 709, 725
Haas, P.J., 356, 709, 718
Haber, E., xxv
Haderle, D., 543, 588, 716
Hadzilacos, V., 515, 518, 700
Haerder, T., 66, 543, 705, 709
Haight, D.M., 649, 702
Haines, M., xxiv
Halici, U., 588, 709
Hall, N.E., 649, 691, 701, 718
Hall, P.A.V., 309, 709
Hammer, J., 254
Hammer, M., 36, 587, 709, 720
Hanson, E.N., 254, 613, 709
Han, J., 681, 709
Harel, D., 612, 703
Harinarayan, V., 680, 709
Haritsa, J., 518, 709
Harrington, J., xxvi
Harrison, J., 254, 709
Harris, S., xxv
Hasan, W., 588, 707
Hash function, 72
Hash join, 296
Hash partitioning, 548
Hashed files, 72
Heap files, 55
Heckerman, D., 680, 709
Heckman, M., 254, 715
Helland, P., 587
Hellerstein, J.M., xxiv, 115, 356, 613,
    649, 698, 709, 712, 718, 721
Henschen, L.J., 37, 715

Heterogeneous databases, 555
  gateways, 555
Heytens, M.L., 309, 587, 705
Hinterberger, H., 115, 717
Hoch, C.G., 649, 707
Hollaar, L.A., 691, 719
Honeyman, P., 435, 700
Hong, D., 518, 710
Hong, W., 588, 710
Hopcroft, J.E., 83, 698
Hou, W-C., 356, 691, 710, 718
Howard, J.H., 435, 700
Ho, C-T., 680, 710
Hsiao, H., 587, 710
HTML links, 684
Huang, J., 518, 710
Huang, W., xxv
Huang, Y., 587, 691, 710
Hull, R., 20, 36, 394, 435, 612, 649, 691,
  697, 710
Imielinski, T., 36, 680–681, 691, 697, 710
Inclusion dependencies, 386
Index locking, 499
Index, 67, 74
  duplicate data entries, 80
  alternatives for data entries, 75
  B+ tree, 90
  bit map, 662
  clustered vs. unclustered, 78
  composite key, 80
  concatenated key, 80
  data entry, 74
  dense vs. sparse, 78
  dynamic, 90, 118, 124
  equality query, 80
  extendible hashing, 118
  hash, 117
    buckets, 117
    hash function, 117
    primary and overflow pages, 117
  in SQL, 81
  ISAM, 85
  linear hashing, 124
  matching a selection, 278
  multidimensional, 108
  primary vs. secondary, 79
  range query, 81
  search key, 58
  spatial, 108
  static hashing, 117
  static, 85
  unique, 80

Index-only scan, 285, 304, 335
Inheritance, 628
Integrity constraints, 15, 26
  domain, 23, 33
  foreign key, 29
  key, 26, 28
Internet, 249, 684, 686
Inverted file, 79
Ioannidis, Y., 716
Ioannidis, Y.E., xxiv, 356, 394, 710–711,
  718
Iochpe, C., 691, 725
Ishii, H., 681, 716
Iterator interface, 315
Jagadish, H.V., 66, 115, 254, 691, 706,
  711, 722
Jain, A.K., 681, 711
Jajodia, S., 254, 588, 691, 711, 724–725
Jarke, M., 356, 711
Jean, Y., 691, 718
Jeffers, R., 518, 697
Jhingran, A., 613, 723
Jing, J., 588, 706
Johnson, T., 518, 710
Join dependencies (JDs), 428
Joins
  Bloomjoin, 565
  definition, 160
  implementation, 286–287, 289, 291,
    295
  outer, 207
  Semijoin, 564
Jonsson, B.T., 588, 707
Jou, J.H., 435, 711
Kabra, N., 691, 718
Kambayashi, Y., 588, 711
Kanellakis, P.C., 36, 435, 649, 691, 697,
  699, 711
Kang, Y.C., 356, 710
Kaplan, S.J., 725
Karabatis, G., 588, 691, 720
Katz, R.H., 66, 309, 705, 718
Kawaguchi, A., 254, 704
Keim, D.A., 691, 711
Keller, A.M., 254, 711
Kemnitz, G., 649, 723
Kemper, A.A., 66, 649, 714
Kent, W., 20, 409, 649, 691, 707, 711
Kerisit, J.M., 613, 719
Kerschberg, L., 20, 711
Ketabchi, M.A., 691, 711
Key

candidate vs. search, 72
candidate, 28, 362
composite search, 80
foreign key, 29
foreign, 362
Khoshafian, S., 649, 699
Kiernan, J., 613, 722
Kiessling, W., 356, 711
Kifer, M., xxiv, 613, 649, 711–712
Kimball, R., 680, 712
Kimmel, W., xxv
Kim, W., 356, 588, 649, 706, 711–712
King, J.J., 356, 712
King, R., 394, 710
King, W.F., 36, 698, 702
Kitsuregawa, M., 309, 707
Klug, A.C., 20, 66, 180, 270, 356, 705,
   711–712
Knapp, E., 712
Knuth, D.E., 83, 153, 712
Koch, G., 37, 712
Koch, J., 356, 711
Kohler, W.H., 712
Konopnicki, D., 691, 712
Kornacker, M., 649, 712
Korth, H.F., 20, 518, 588, 691, 710, 712,
   715, 722
Kossman, D., 588, 707
Kotidis, Y., 680, 720
Kowalski, R.A., 612, 724
Kriegel, H-P., 691, 711
Krishnakumar, N., 588, 712
Krishnamurthy, R., 356, 588, 612, 703,
   705, 707, 712
Kuchenhoff, V., 612, 725
Kuhns, J.L., 36, 180, 713
Kulkarni, K., xxiv
Kull, D., 475, 725
Kumar, K.B., 309, 587, 705
Kumar, V., 518, 713
Kunchithapadam, K., xxv
Kung, H.T., 518, 713
Kuo, D., 713
Kupsch, J., 691, 718
Kuspert, K., 66, 649, 714
LaCroix, M., 180, 713
Ladner, R.E., 518, 715
Lai, M., 518, 713
Lamport, L., 588, 713
Lampson, B.W., 588, 713
Lam, C., 649, 713
Landers, T.A., 587, 720

Landis, G., 649, 713
Landwehr, C.L., 254
Langerak, R., 254, 713
Lapis, G., 587, 649, 709, 725
Larson, J.A., 394, 588, 722
Larson, P., 136, 254, 701, 713, 719
Latch, 493
Lausen, G., 649, 712
Lawande, S., 691, 714
Layman, A., 680, 708
Lee, M., xxv
Lefebvre, A., 612, 649, 707, 725
Leff, A., 587, 718
Left-deep trees, 337
Lehman, P.L., 518, 713
Leinbaugh, P., 691, 701
Lenzerini, M., 394, 699
Lescoeur, F., 613, 719
Leung, T.W., 649, 723
Leung, T.Y.C., 356, 613, 681, 713, 721
Leu, D.F., 703
Levine, F., 518, 543, 716
Levy, A.Y., 254, 722
Lewis, P., 588, 719
Ley, M., xxv, 685
Libkin, L., 254, 704
Liedtke, R., 691, 725
Lieuwen, D.F., 66, 254, 691, 704, 711,
   718
Lim, E-P., 588, 691, 713
Lindsay, B.G., 36, 66, 543, 587–588, 649,
   702, 708–709, 713, 716, 724–725
Linear hashing, 124
  family of hash functions, 124
  level counter, 124
Ling, Y., 356, 723
Linnemann, V., 66, 649, 714
Lipski, W., 36, 710
Lipton, R.J., 708, 356, 691, 714
Liskov, B., 649, 714
Litwin, W., 136, 588, 714
Liu, M.T., 588, 706, 714
Livny, M., 66, 518, 587, 649, 681, 691,
   697, 701–702, 707, 709, 714, 721
Lochovsky, F., 649, 712
Lockemann, P.C., 691, 725
Locking protocol, 13, 485
Locking
  B+ trees, 499
  Conservative 2PL, 497
  exclusive locks, 485
  lock escalation, 503

lock upgrade, 492
multiple-granularity, 502
performance implications, 463
performance, 496
Strict 2PL, 485
Locks, 13
shared, 485
Log, 13, 521, 523
force-write, 524
lastLSN, 526
pageLSN, 524
prevLSN, 524
sequence number (LSN), 523
tail, 523
update record format, 525
WAL, 13
Logical schema, 7
Lohman, G.M., 356, 588, 649, 709, 714–715
Lomet, D.B., 115, 153, 518, 588, 713–714, 717
Loney, K., 37, 712
Lorie, R.A., 36, 153, 224, 356, 518, 543, 698, 702, 706, 708, 713–714, 721
Lou, Y., 649, 714
Lozinskii, E.L., 613, 712
Lucchesi, C.L., 435, 714
Lueder, R., 691, 718
Lum, V.Y., 115, 680, 714, 723
Lunt, T., 254, 715
Lu, H., 587, 714
Lyngbaek, P., 649, 707
Mackert, L.F., 588, 715
Magic sets, 604
Mahbod, B., 649, 707
Maheshwari, U., 649, 714
Maier, D., 20, 36, 435, 612–613, 649, 699, 704, 715
Makinouchi, A., 649, 715
Manber, U., 518, 715
Mandatory access control, 232
Mannila, H., 435, 680–681, 698, 710, 715
Mannino, M.V., 356, 715
Manolopoulos, Y., 681, 706
Manthey, R., 37, 701
Market basket, 666
Markowitz, V.M., 394, 715
Mark, L., 588, 714
Martella, G., 254, 702
Maryanski, F., 394, 718
Matos, V., 180, 649, 718
Mattos, N., 613, 704

Maugis, L., 613, 698
McAuliffe, M.L., 649, 701
McCarthy, D.R., 613, 715
McCreight, E.M., 115, 699
McCune, W.W., 37, 715
McGoveran, D., 37, 704
McJones, P.R., 36, 543, 698, 708
McLeod, D., 36, 356, 698, 709
McPherson, J., 66, 649, 709, 713
Mecca, G., 649, 699
Meenakshi, K., 613, 699
Megiddo, N., 680, 710
Mehl, J.W., 36, 224, 698, 702
Mehrotra, S., 588, 715
Mehta, M., 587, 681, 715, 721
Melton, J., xxiv, 224, 715
Menasce, D.A., 588, 715
Mendelzon, A.O., 435, 681, 691, 708, 715, 719
Meo, R., 681, 716
Meredith, J., 475, 723
Merlin, P.M., 356, 703
Merrett, T.H., 83, 180, 716
Methods
interpreted vs. compiled, 639
Michel, R., 309, 703
Mikkilineni, K.P., 309, 716
Miller, R.J., 394, 681, 716, 725
Milo, T., 649, 691, 700, 715
Minibase software, 692
Minker, J., 36–37, 356, 435, 612, 702, 707, 716
Minoura, T., 588, 716
Misra, J., 588, 703
Missikoff, M., 475, 702
Mitchell, G., 356, 716
Mohan, C., xxiv, 518, 543, 588, 649, 712, 716
MOLAP, 655
Morimoto, Y., 681, 707, 716
Morishita, S., 612, 681, 705, 707, 716
Morrison, R., 698
Morris, K.A., 612, 716
Motro, A., 394, 717
Motwani, R., 681, 701
Mukkamala, R., 587, 717
Multidatabase system, 555
Multidimensional data model, 654
Multiset, 622
Multivalued dependencies, 423
Multiversion concurrency control, 512

Mumick, I.S., 254, 356, 613, 649, 704, 709, 717
Muntz, R.R., 588, 681, 713, 715
Muralikrishna, M., 309, 356, 587, 705, 717
Mutchler, D., 588, 711
Myers, A.C., 649, 714
Myllymaki, J., 691, 714
Nag, B., 691, 718
Naqvi, S.A., 612–613, 649, 700–701, 703, 717
Narang, I., 518, 716
Narasayya, V., 475, 703
Naughton, J.F., xxv, 115, 153, 309, 356, 475, 587, 612, 649, 680, 691, 697, 701–702, 705, 709, 714, 716, 718, 722, 724
Navathe, S.B., 20, 394, 518, 681, 697, 699, 706, 720, 722
Negri, M., 225, 717
Neimat, M-A., 136, 649, 707, 714
Nested relations
 nesting, 625
 unnesting, 624
Newcomer, E., 691, 700
Nguyen, T., 691, 717
Ng, P., 587, 725
Ng, R.T., 66, 706, 711
Nicolas, J-M., 37, 435, 707
Nievergelt, J., 115, 136, 706, 717
Nodine, M.H., 588
Normal forms, 408
 1NF, 408
 2NF, 411
 3NF, 410
  Synthesis, 422
 4NF, 426
 5NF, 428
 BCNF, 409
 normalization, 416
 tuning, 455
Null values
 implementation, 50
 in SQL, 32, 205
Nyberg, C., 153, 717
O'Neil, P., 20, 587, 680, 717
Obermarck, R., 587–588, 716–717, 725
Object identifiers, 626
Object-oriented DBMS, xxii, 642
Object-relational DBMS, xxii, 642
ODBC, 652
ODL and OQL, 642

Oids, 626
OLAP, xxii, 466, 651
 cross-tabulation, 658
 database design, 661
 pivoting, 658
 roll-up and drill-down, 657
Olken, F., 254, 309, 356, 705, 717
OLTP, 650
Omiecinski, E., 518, 681, 697, 720
On-Line Analytic Processing (OLAP), xxii, 651
On-Line Transaction Processing (OLTP), 650
On-the-fly evaluation, 314
Ong, K., 649
Ooi, B-C., 587, 714
Opaque types, 620
Optimistic concurrency control validation, 508
Orenstein, J., 649, 713
Osborn, S.L., 435, 714
Outer joins, 207
Overloading, 629
Ozden, B., 691, 717
Ozsoyoglu, G., 180, 254, 356, 649, 691, 703, 710, 718
Ozsoyoglu, Z.M., 180, 356, 649, 714, 718, 721
Ozsu, M.T., 587, 718
Page abstraction, 38, 42
Page formats, 51
 fixed-length records, 52
 variable-length records, 53
Papadimitriou, C.H., 254, 518, 718
Papakonstantinou, Y., 588, 697
Paraboschi, S., 613, 699, 702
Parallel databases, 544
Parallelism
 data partitioning, 547
 pipelined, 547
Paredaens, J., 435, 704
Parent, C., 394, 722
Park, J., 254, 356, 718, 721
Patel, J.M., 691, 718
Paton, N., 613, 705
Patterson, D.A., 66, 718
Paul, H., 66, 649, 718, 720
Peckham, J., 394, 718
Pelagatti, G., 225, 587, 702, 717
Petajan, E., 691, 718
Petrov, S.V., 435, 718
Pfeffer, A., 115, 649, 709

Phantoms, 498
  SQL, 504
Phipps, G., 612, 705
Physical design
  choices to make, 438
  clustered indexes, 444
  co-clustering, 447
  index selection, 439
  index-only plans, 450
  multiple-attribute indexes, 449
  tuning the choice of indexes, 453
Physical schema, 8
Piatetsky-Shapiro, G., 356, 680, 706,
    718
Pipelined evaluation, 313, 336, 338
Pippenger, N., 136, 706
Pirahesh, H., 66, 356, 543, 588, 613,
    649, 680, 704, 708–709, 713,
    716–718, 721
Pirotte, A., 180, 713
Pistor, P., 66, 649, 714
Polyinstantiation, 244
Poosala, V., 356, 718
Popek, G.J., 37, 699
Port, G.S., 613, 699
Potamianos, S., 613, 723
Pramanik, S., 309, 707
Precedence graph, 488
Predicate locking, 499
Prefetching, 48
Price, T.G., 36, 356, 543, 702, 708, 721
Primary term in a selection, 279
Prock, A., xxv
Projections
  definition, 157
  implementation, 280
Pruyne, J., xxv
Psaila, G., 681, 698, 716
Putzolu, G.R., 36, 518, 543, 698, 708,
    713
Pu, C., 587–588, 718
QBE
  aggregate operations, 260
  conditions box, 261
  domain variables, 256
  duplicates, 257
  example tables, 256
  join queries, 258
  ordering answers, 257
  relational completeness, 267
  unnamed fields, 263
  updates, 264

Qian, X., 254, 718
Quass, D., 680, 717
Query block, 316
Query evaluation plan, 312
Query language, 11, 32
  QBE, 255
  relational completeness, 176
  SQL, 181
Query optimization, 310
  bushy trees, 337
  enumeration of alternative plans, 332
  left-deep trees, 337
  overview, 310
  pushing selections, 320
  reduction factors, 326–327
  relational algebra equivalences, 327
  rule-based, 346
  SQL query block, 316
  statistics, 325
Query, 11
Quinlan, J.R., 681, 719
R Trees, 109
Rafiei, D., 681, 719
Raiha, K-J., 715
Raiha, K., 435
Rajaraman, A., 680, 709
Ramakrishnan, I.V., 613, 719
Ramakrishnan, R., 356, 394, 612–613,
    649, 680–681, 691, 695, 697,
    699–700, 711, 714, 716–717, 719,
    721–722
Ramakrishna, M.V., 136, 719
Ramamohanarao, K., 136, 612–613, 699,
    719
Ramamritham, K., 518, 703, 710
Ramamurty, R., xxv
Ramasamy, K., 680, 691, 718, 722
Ranganathan, M., 681, 706
Range partitioning, 548
Rao, P., 613, 719
Rao, S.G., 680, 719
Rastogi, R., 66, 588, 691, 701, 711, 715,
    717
Reames, M., xxvi
Record formats, 49
  fixed-length records, 49
  variable-length records, 50
Record, 22
Recovery manager, 519
Recovery, 16
  Analysis phase, 529
  ARIES, 519

checkpointing, 528
compensation log record, 525
fuzzy checkpoint, 528
log, 13
loser transactions, 533
Redo phase, 531
three phases of restart, 529
update log record, 525
Recursive rules, 589
Redundancy and anomalies, 397
Reed, D.P., 518, 588, 719
Reeve, C.L., 587–588, 700, 720
Reference types, 633
Regression, 675
Reiner, D.S., 356, 712
Reisner, P., 224, 702
Reiter, R., 36, 719
Relation, 5, 22
  cardinality, 24
  degree, 24
  instance, 22
  legal instance, 26
  schema, 22
Relational algebra, 156
  division, 162
  equivalences, 327
  expression, 156
  expressive power, 175
  join, 160
  projection, 157
  renaming operation, 160
  renaming, 159
  selection, 156
  set-operations, 157, 301
Relational calculus
  domain, 172
  expressive power, 175
  safety, 175
  tuple, 168
Relational database
  instance, 24
  schema, 24
Relational model, 5, 21
Replication
  asynchronous, 558, 567–568, 653
  synchronous, 558, 567
Reuter, A., 543, 691, 708–709, 719
Richardson, J.E., 649, 66, 702
Riloff, E., 691, 719
Rishe, N., 356, 723
Rissanen, J., 435, 719
Rivest, R.J., 136

Rivest, R.L., 719
Robinson, J.T., 518, 713
Rohmer, J., 613, 719
ROLAP, 656
Rosenkrantz, D.J., 588, 719
Rosenthal, A., 356, 691, 719, 721
Ross, K.A., 254, 649, 680, 703–704, 717,
  720
Rotem, D., 254, 356, 717, 722
Rothnie, J.B., 587–588, 700, 720
Round-robin partitioning, 548
Roussopoulos, M., 680, 720
Roussopoulos, N., 66, 356, 588, 680,
  703, 714, 720
Rozen, S., 475, 720
Rules in databases, xxii
Rusinkiewicz, M., 588, 691, 720
Ryan, T.A., 649, 707
Sacca, D., 613, 720
Sacks-Davis, R., 136, 719
Sagalowicz, D., 725
Sager, T., 356, 715
Sagiv, Y., 356, 435, 613, 649, 698–699,
  711, 715, 720
Sagonas, K.F., 612–613, 719–720
Salveter, S., 356, 722
Salzberg, B.J., 66, 83, 115, 153, 518,
  714, 720
Samarati, P., 254, 702
Samet, H., 115, 720
Sandhu, R., 254, 711
Saraiya, Y., 612, 716
Sarawagi, S., 649, 680, 697, 720
Savasere, A., 681, 720
Sbattella, L., 225, 717
Schedule, 479
  avoid cascading abort, 485
  conflict serializable, 488
  recoverable, 484
  serializable, 481, 484
  strict, 490
  view serializable, 490
Schek, H., 66, 649, 718, 720
Schell, R., 254, 715
Schema evolution, 455
Schema refinement, 395
  denormalization, 458
Schkolnick, M.M., 36, 475, 518, 699,
  702, 707, 720
Schlageter, G., 588, 720
Schneider, D.A., 136, 153, 309, 356, 587,
  705, 714

Scholl, M.H., 66, 649, 718, 720
Schryro, M., 691, 725
Schuh, D.T., 649, 701–702
Schumacher, L., xxv
Schwarz, P., 543, 588, 716
Sciore, E., 356, 435, 691, 721–722
Scott, D.W., 681, 721
Search key, 72
Security, 232
  discretionary access control, 232
  encryption, 248
  privileges, 232
  statistical database, 246
Segev, A., 254, 356, 681, 691, 718, 721,
  724
Selection condition
  conjunctive normal form, 277
  term, 277
Selections
  definition, 156
Selfridge, P.G., 680, 721
Selinger, P.G., 36, 224, 254, 356, 543,
  588, 702, 713, 721, 725
Sellis, T.K., 66, 356, 706, 711, 721
Semantic integration, 686
Semijoin reduction, 564
Semijoin, 564
Semistructured data, 690
Sequential patterns, 673
Serializability, 481, 484, 488
Seshadri, P., xxv, 356, 612–613, 649,
  681, 719, 721–722
Seshadri, S., 309, 356, 691, 701, 705, 709
Sevcik, K.C., 115, 717
Shafer, J.C., 681, 698, 721
Shaft, U., xxv
Shah, D., 475, 702
Shan, M-C., 649, 691, 705, 707, 711
Shapiro, L.D., xxiv, 309, 705, 721
Shasha, D., xxiv, 475, 518, 587, 720–721
Shatkay, H., 681, 721
Sheard, T., 37, 721
Shekita, E.J., 66, 356, 649, 702, 709, 718
Shenoy, S.T., 356, 721
Shepherd, J., 136, 719
Sheth, A.P., 394, 588, 691, 706, 714,
  720, 722, 588
Shim, K., 649, 680, 703, 711
Shipman, D.W., 518, 587–588, 700, 720
Shmueli, O., 613, 691, 700, 712
Shockley, W., 254, 715
Shoshani, A., 680–681, 721–722

Shrira, L., 649, 714
Shukla, A., xxv, 680, 722
Sibley, E.H., 20, 707
Siegel, M., 356, 691, 721–722
Silberschatz, A., 20, xxvi, 66, 518, 588,
  691, 701, 711–712, 715, 717, 722
Silverstein, C., 681, 701
Simon, A.R., 224, 715
Simon, E., 475, 613, 721–722
Simoudis, E., 680, 706
Singhal, A., 588, 714
Sistla, A.P., 691, 710
Skeen, D., 587–588, 705, 722
Slutz, D.R., 36, 702
Smith, D.C.P., 394, 722
Smith, J.M., 394, 722
Smith, K.P., 66, 254, 699, 722
Smith, P.D., 83, 722
Smyth, P., 680, 706
Snodgrass, R.T., 612–613, 649, 691, 724
Soda, G., 475, 702
Solomon, M.H., 649, 701
Soloviev, V., 587, 715
Soparkar, N., 518, 691, 712, 722
Sorenson, P., 475, 720
Sorting
  applications, 137
  blocked I/O, 145
  double buffering, 147
  external merge sort algorithm, 139
  using B+ trees, 148
So, B., xxv
Spaccapietra, S., 394, 703, 722
Speed-up vs. scale-up, 546
Spyratos, N., 254, 699
SQL
  access-mode, 504
  aggregate operations, 207
    definition, 197
    implementation, 302
  ALL, 194, 199
  ALTER TABLE, 228
  ANY, 194, 199
  AS, 187
  authorization id, 233
  BETWEEN, 443
  CASCADE, 236
  collations, 188
  correlated queries, 193
  CREATE DOMAIN, 216
  CREATE TABLE, 24
  creating views, 228

cursors, 211
  ordering rows, 214
  sensitivity, 214
  updatability, 213
DATE values, 187
DELETE, 31
DISTINCT, 183
DROP TABLE, 228
dynamic, 215
embedded language programming, 208
EXCEPT, 188, 195
EXISTS, 189, 206
expressions, 187, 206
giving names to constraints, 28
grant option, 233
GROUP BY, 199
HAVING, 199
IN, 189
indexing, 81
INSERT, 25, 31
integrity constraints
  assertions, 31, 217
  CHECK, 216
  deferred checking, 507
  domain constraints, 217
  effect on modifications, 31
  PRIMARY KEY, 28
  table constraints, 31, 216
  UNIQUE, 28
INTERSECT, 188, 195
IS NULL, 206
isolation-level, 504
nested subqueries
  definition, 192
  implementation, 344
NOT, 184
null values, 205
ORDER BY, 214
outer joins, 207
phantoms, 504
privileges, 232
query block, 316
referential integrity
  enforcement, 31
REVOKE, 236
security, 233
SELECT-FROM-WHERE, 183
SOME, 194
strings, 187
transaction support, 504
transactions and constraints, 506
UNION, 188

UNIQUE, 206
UPDATE, 25, 31
view updates, 231
Srikant, R., 680–681, 698, 710, 722
Srinivasan, V., 518, 691, 717, 722
Srivastava, D., 254, 356, 612–613, 649, 680, 719–722
Srivastava, J., 254, 588, 680, 691, 713, 722–723
Stable storage, 521, 523
Stacey, D., 588, 723
Stachour, P., 254, 723
Stankovic, J.A., 518, 691, 710, 723
Static hashing, 117
Statistical databases, 660
Stavropoulos, H., xxv
Stearns, R., 588, 719
Steel, T.B., 723
Stemple, D., 37, 721
Stewart, M., 153, 720
Stokes, L., 356, 709
Stonebraker, M., 20, 36–37, 66, 254, 309, 475, 588, 613, 648–649, 691, 698, 705–706, 710, 720, 723
Storage
  nonvolatile, 39
  primary, secondary and tertiary, 39
  stable, 521
Strong, H.R., 136, 706
Stuckey, P.J., 356, 613, 721
Sturgis, H.E., 588, 713
Subrahmanian, V.S., 254, 588, 612–613, 649, 691, 697, 709, 725
Subramanian, B., 649, 723
Sudarshan, S., 719, 20, xxv, 66, 254, 356, 612–613, 649, 691, 711, 719–722
Sudkamp, N., 66, 649, 714
Sun, W., 356, 723
Superkey, 27
Suri, R., 518, 724
Su, J., 649, 710
Su, S.Y.W., 309, 716
Swami, A., 356, 681, 697, 709, 723
Swift, T., 612–613, 719–720, 723
Synchronous replication
  read-any write-all technique, 568
  voting technique, 567
System catalogs, 7, 49, 59, 325
Table, 22
Tanaka, H., 309, 707
Tanca, L., 612–613, 702, 707

Tang, N., xxvi
Tannen, V.B., 649, 701
Tansel, A.U., 691, 724
Tan, C.K., 649, 701
Tan, J.S., 680, 723
Tan, K-L., 587, 714
Tay, Y.C., 518, 724
Teorey, T.J., 394, 724
Therber, A., xxv
Thevenin, J.M., 309, 703
Thomas Write Rule, 510
Thomas, R.H., 588, 724
Thompson, G.R., 588, 701
Three-phase commit, 579
Thuraisingham, B., 254, 723
Tiberio, P., 475, 707
Timestamp
  concurrency control, 510
  deadlock prevention in 2PL, 493
Todd, S.J.P., 36, 724
Toivonen, H., 681, 698, 724
Tokuyama, T., 681, 707
Tompa, F.W., 254, 701
Towsley, D., 518, 710
TP monitor, 682
Traiger, I.L., 36, 518, 543, 588, 698, 702,
    706, 708, 713, 724
Trail, 523
Transaction, 476–477
  abort, 479
  blind write, 483
  commit, 479
  conflicting actions, 481
  distributed, 554
  locks and performance, 463
  management in a distributed DBMS,
    571
  manager, 520
  multilevel and nested, 683
  properties, 12, 478
  read, 479
  schedule, 479
  table, 491
  write, 479
Transparency, 554
Trickey, H., 254, 704
Triggers, 590, 604
  activation, 604
  row vs. statement level, 606
  use in replication, 570
Trivial FD, 406
Tsangaris, M., 649, 724

Tsatalos, O.G., 649, 701
Tsichritzis, D.C., 20, 711
Tsou, D., 435, 724
Tsukerman, A., 153, 720
Tsukuda, K., 66, 699
Tsur, S., 612–613, 700, 703
Tucherman, L., 37, 702
Tucker, A.B., 20, 724
Tufte, K., 691, 718
Tukey, J.W., 724
Tuple, 22
Twichell, B.C., 66, 699
Two-phase commit, 575
  blocking, 577
Types
  complex vs. reference, 633
  constructors, 621
  extents, 630
  object equality, 626
Ullman, J.D., 20, xxvi, 36, 83, 136, 356,
    394, 435, 612–613, 680, 698–699,
    709, 716, 719, 724
Union compatibility, 158
Unrepeatable read, 483
Urban, S.D., 394, 724
Uren, S., 153, 720
URL, 684
User-defined types, 619
Uthurusamy, R., 680, 706
Valdes, J., 691, 708
Valduriez, P., 475, 587, 718, 721
Van Emden, M., 612, 724
Van Gelder, A., 612, 716, 724
Van Gucht, D., xxiv, 180, 649, 680, 699,
    719
Vandenberg, S.L., 649, 702, 723
Vardi, M.Y., 36, 435, 708, 724
Vaughan, B., 153, 720
Verkamo, A.I., 681, 698
Vianu, V., 20, 36, 435, 612, 649, 691,
    697
Vidal, M., 394, 702
Vieille, L., 612–613, 649, 707, 725
Views, 226
  query modification, 229
  updates on, 230
Viswanathan, S., 691, 710
Von Bultzingsloewen, G., 356, 691, 725
Von Halle, B., 475, 707
Vossen, G., 20, 725
Wade, B.W., 36, 224, 254, 543, 698, 702,
    708, 713

Wagner, R.E., 115, 725
Walch, G., 66, 649, 714
Walker, A., 587, 612, 698, 725
Wallrath, M., 66, 649, 714
Wang, X.S., 588, 725
Ward, K., 356, 708
Warehouse, 571, 651
Warren, D.S., 612–613, 715, 719–720, 723
Watson, V., 36, 698
Weddell, G.E., 435, 725
Weihl, W., 543, 725
Weikum, G., 66, 649, 718, 720
Weinreb, D., 649, 713
Wenger, K., 691, 714
White, C., 588, 725
White, S.J., 649, 701
Widom, J., 37, 254, 613, 698, 702, 725
Wiederhold, G., 20, xxv, 66, 83, 254, 588, 708, 716, 718, 725
Wilkinson, W.K., 153, 309, 518, 699, 713
Williams, R., 587, 725
Wilms, P.F., 587, 649, 709, 725
Wilson, L.O., 680, 721
Wimmers, E.L., 681, 698
Winslett, M.S., 254, 722, 725
Wiorkowski, G., 475, 725
Wise, T.E., 66, 699
Wistrand, E., 691, 698
Woelk, D., 649, 712
Wolfson, O., 587, 691, 710
Wong, E., 356, 587–588, 700, 706, 720, 725
Wong, H.K.T., 356, 707
Wong, L., 649, 701
Wong, W., 518, 700
Woodruff, A., 691, 698
Wood, D., 309, 705
Workflow management, 683
Wu, J., 649, 712
WWW, 249, 684, 686
Yajima, S., 588, 711
Yang, D., 394, 724
Yang, Y., 681, 725
Yannakakis, M., 356, 720
Yao, S.B., 518, 713
Yoshikawa, M., 588, 649, 710–711
Yost, R.A., 36, 587, 702, 725
Young, H.C., 153, 714
Youssefi, K., 356, 725
Yuan, L., 649, 718

Yu, C.T., 587, 725
Yu, J-B., 691, 718
Zaniolo, C., 36, 356, 435, 612–613, 649, 691, 703, 712, 720, 725
Zaot, M., 681, 698
Zdonik, S.B., xxv, 356, 649, 681, 716, 721, 723
Zhang, A., 588, 706
Zhang, T., 681
Zhao, W., 691, 723
Zhuge, Y., 254
Zicari, R., 612–613, 649, 691
Zloof, M.M., xxiv, 36, 270
Zukowski, U., 612
Zwilling, M.J., 649, 701Ω